Published in the United Kingdom by
Air-Britain (Historians) Ltd.

Sales Dept:
41 Penshurst Road, Leigh,
Tonbridge, Kent TN11 8HL

Correspondence regarding this publication to:
Colin N Dodds, 21 Tudor Close,
Grayshott, Surrey GU26 6HP

ISBN 0 85130 363 3

Printed in the United Kingdom by:
The Cromwell Press Ltd,
Aintree Avenue,
White Horse Business Park,
Trowbridge, Wiltshire BA14 0XB

Origination by Howard Marks,
Nigel Fellows, Ruth Feeny-Brown,
Dave Partington

Front cover photograph:
A nostalgic view of three surviving representatives of the Dragon family; the DH 84 Dragon EI-ABI (c/n 6105), the DH 90 Dragonfly G-AEDU (c/n 7526) and the DH 89B Dragon Rapide G-AGSH (c/n 6884). [Gordon Bain]

Rear cover, top to bottom:
Dragon Rapide G-ACZE c/n W1001 [Gordon Bain]; Dragon VH-AQU c/n 2048 [DHMC]; Dragon Rapide ZK-AKU/NZ528 c/n 6662 [Richard Waugh]; Dragonfly G-AEDT c/n 7508 [Gordon Bain]; and Dragon G-ECAN c/n 2048 [DHMC].

CONTENTS

Dragon VH-AQU in RAAF colours in 1986, before transfer to England, where she is still airworthy as G-ECAN. *[de Havilland Moth Club (DHMC)]*

FOREWORD

Here is the story of the first family of airliners ever to be built by the great de Havilland enterprise, together with their derivative the first DH "Executive twin".

Colin Dodds fascinatingly traces the conception and birth of the father of them all - the DH84 Dragon. Simple, sturdy and reliable of design, with its DH Moth parentage clearly recognisable from its outboard wings, the pugnacious Dragon airframe together with its dependable and robust DH Gypsy Major engines, was the ideal vehicle to pioneer short-haul airline routes - initially in the UK - and then world-wide.

With the subsequent requirement for a larger, faster and longer-range aircraft to pioneer the Empire routes of Imperial Airways and QANTAS, Geoffrey de Havilland's solution was a major scaling up of the DH84 to produce the DH86. The opportunity was taken to streamline the fuselage shape and also, for the first time, the characteristic elegantly-tapered high aspect ratio de Havilland wings were seen. Faced with the difficulty of finding suitable engines of sufficient power to enable the aircraft to perform as a twin, DH came up with the brave, but somewhat radical, solution of opting for four engines on what was still a comparatively small airliner. A solution the company was to repeat, many years later, when scaling up the Dove to produce the Heron, and was to adopt yet again, and for the last time, in the design of the HS146 - later to become the BAe 146.

With the continued success of the original DH84 the opportunity for a slightly larger and faster Dragon became clear. A more modest scaling-up of the DH84 was therefore next launched adopting the Gypsy Queens and tapered wing planform of the larger DH86. The resultant DH89 was to become the most successful of the whole Dragon family.

Finally Geoffrey de Havilland saw the opportunity to produce a comfortable five-seat "family aircraft" derivative of the now established Dragon dynasty - the DH90 Dragonfly. The most radical feature of the DH90 was that the fabric covered tubular fuselage frames of its forerunners were abandoned in favour of an all-wood monocoque construction using formed plywood skin. In this respect the DH90 pioneered the form of construction subsequently used with such spectacular success on the Mosquito.

Never before has the story of this complete, and highly regarded, family of characterful aircraft been told under one cover. Nor before have all the facts and figures been so faithfully, completely and interestingly described. Much of the information in this book is being published for the very first time, including many absorbing reflections and anecdotes from an array of distinguished aviation personalities. These include the great Richard Clarkson, responsible for the aerodynamics and flowing lines of some of the most beautiful aircraft to grace the skies, including the Comet Racer, Albatross, Mosquito, Comet Airliner and DH110; Geoffrey de Havilland Jr - one of the most gifted of all Test Pilots, Cyclops Brown and Lettice Curtis of wartime fame, Eric Franklin - the outstanding Chief Test Pilot of Armstrong Whitworth in the days of the Apollo and Argosy, the much missed Bill Bedford of Hunter and Harrier fame and Lord Trefgarne with whom I share many unforgettable memories of flying a DH90 from Australia to England and then on to the US. Nor will I forget the first time I ever flew a DH89. It was at a Hatfield employee family day when, no sooner had I been briefed on the controls than, much to my surprise, a full load of employee joyriders climbed aboard all blissfully unaware of the fact that their pilot had never set foot in a Rapide before - let alone flown one. Fortunately for them, and for me, the DH89 unquestionably exhibits the sweetest, most stable and most docile handling characteristics of all the Dragon family.

If would be hard to imagine anyone more appropriate, or better qualified, to tell the Dragon family story than Colin Dodds. We first met nearly 40 years ago at the Halfpenny Green Air Show. I was displaying a P-51D Mustang and Colin, very aptly, the RAF version of the 125 executive jet, the Dominie - the very last in the long line of DH twins which, during its design phase, had been named by Sir Geoffrey de Havilland himself "the Jet Dragon". Colin, like me, went on to fly both Vulcans and Nimrods but, it was at the early age of 17 that his love affair with DH aircraft began when he learnt to fly on Tiger Moths at the Newcastle Aero Club. Since that time hardly a DH type has escaped his log book. Indeed the range of different DH variants he has flown must be almost unique, spanning as it does, Tiger Moth, Gipsy Moth, Fox Moth, Leopard Moth, Moth Minor, Dove, Heron, Comet, 125, 146 and, of course, the Dragon, Rapide and Dragonfly.

With this background, with his love and sympathy for the subject and with his clarity of style Colin Dodds leads the reader on a wonderful journey of discovery. Not only will you find this book both interesting and enjoyable but also a most important historical reference.

Sir Charles Masefield
March 2005

Section 1: Introduction

DH 66 airliner G-AUJP, when with Western Australian Airways, 1929. *[M. Stroud]*

Section 1 – Chapter 1: The Commercial Aviation Scene

COMMERCIAL AVIATION IN 1932

The political environment of the Europe of 1932 consisted of the posturing and dancing of politicians around a flagpole of Disarmament. While members of the League of Nations nominally joined this Disarmament Dance, many others, notably Russia, France and Germany, whilst professing a desire to disarm, were actually increasing their war-like air assets at an exponential rate. Despite the continuing and deep world economic recession, civil aviation in these countries also began to increase at a steady rate, and in countries such as Germany and the United States, airlines were beginning to benefit from new technology and new designs, finally shaking free from the First World War ideas and methods of design and production.

Aircraft engine and propeller design, particularly in the USA, began to develop in line with a perceived need for greater speed and payload, and traditional construction materials were being replaced. Many new designs were now being constructed in metal, with metal coverings to flying surfaces, seen to be stronger than wood. Engines were getting more powerful, with radial engines replacing the simpler in-line types and equipment such as variable-speed propellers and high-lift devices such as flaps were making their presence felt in the desire for greater speed and longer range.

Whilst, in 1932, single-engined light transports were still the norm, the safety factor of multi-engined aircraft was being actively discussed. European aircraft in particular were still generally underpowered; most multi-engined aircraft could not maintain height after the loss of an engine, so there was little practical difference between the safety factors of single or twin-engined aircraft. Some airlines still held to the anomalous logic that more engines meant more chance of engines failing, so it was safer to have only one! The government-backed, subsidised Imperial Airways, formed in 1924, had first branched out in 1926 to use multi-engined transports, by buying five DH 66 Hercules, for use on routes to the Middle East. But, even using three 425 hp Bristol Jupiter engines to carry only twelve passengers, its bulk and slow speed made it rather uncompetitive, and only eleven were made.

Most of the smaller un-subsidised airlines were still using light, single-engined aircraft to cope with passenger traffic on short routes, in an attempt to gain a small profit for their efforts.

NAVIGATION AIDS

By 1932, there were only a few radio direction-finding stations in the UK to assist aircraft navigation in poor weather. The main ones were at Croydon and Heston Airports and at Lympne on the south coast of England. 1935 was the planned date for an expansion of facilities by the Air Ministry with new stations expected at Jersey, Pulham and a more comprehensive one to be operated "on the aural principle" due for completion at Croydon. This situation meant that "blind flying" in cloud or bad visibility by the very sparsely-equipped commercial aircraft was quite hazardous, causing many accidents when aircraft lost their way or inadvertently descended into the ground.

NEW COMMERCIAL AIRCRAFT TESTING PROCEDURES

The Air Ministry still tested all new aircraft made for commercial purposes. With the Royal Air Force already having a mature testing

TWA DC-2 in the mid-'30s. *[M. Stroud]*

The Gatwick 'beehive' passenger terminal, under construction, May 1936. *[Aeroplane]*

process for military aircraft, the government contracted all civilian testing to the same team at Royal Air Force Martlesham Heath - the Aircraft & Armament Experimental Establishment's landplane base. The final part of the civilian certification process for a new type was to have the A & AEE pilots and engineers take the aircraft through practical tests to confirm its safety and performance, following which the A & AEE staff would submit a report on the new type to the Air Ministry and to the makers, covering handling, performance and technical aspects, and recommend any modifications they considered necessary for safe operation of the aircraft. The final section of this report would recommend that the Air Ministry issue or refuse the grant of a Certificate of Airworthiness, which would then permit the aircraft to be used for civilian flying.

This testing process, even for more complex multi-engined types, was fairly elementary, particularly when compared to the exhaustive testing to which modern aircraft are subjected. Manufacturers of civilian aircraft, without the complications of armaments and weapons, could expect the Martlesham ground and flight tests to be completed within two or three days, so that, if all went well, they could expect to be granted a type C of A, albeit with slight modification provisos, within a few days of the end of the tests. This in no way implies criticism of the standards of the Martlesham staff, but merely reflects the methods considered universally acceptable at that stage in the development of aircraft manufacturing.

An example of the basic approach to testing was the method of testing for stability. Longitudinal stability was simply tested by trimming the aircraft at the selected cruising speed, checked by using a specially-installed sensitive Air Speed Indicator, then allowing the speed to stabilise for about a minute, after which elevators were used to disturb the aircraft in pitch until the speed had changed by 10 mph, either climbing or descending, at which point the elevator control was released. The aircraft's behaviour was then watched and noted. If it returned to its original speed and attitude, maintained its new speed, or deviated further, this indicated the positive, neutral or divergent stability of the aircraft. Three trimmed speed settings were used, variously in level flight, climbs and descents. The behaviour in the directional and lateral senses was less easily tested and defined, as the rudders and ailerons were separately used to disturb the aircraft in yaw or roll, then released, and the behaviour noted. The secondary effects of the roll or yaw tended to disguise the behaviour of the primary control, making the judgement of directional and lateral stability less straightforward, and more open to individual interpretation.

In contrast, performance testing was meticulously prepared and very carefully carried out, usually at the maker's declared maximum weight, and handling was tested at intermediate, forward, and aft CGs, in that order, quite sensibly beginning with the safest case, then progressing to the potentially more critical cases. All Public Transport aircraft were required to reach a minimum height of 66 feet after a take-off distance of 546 yards (adjusted where necessary to assume a 5 mph headwind), as well as achieving a height of 1,378 feet in three minutes. These seemingly arbitrary figures were those then considered by the Air Ministry to be the minima for safe operations from civil airfields.

These procedures changed little until 1939, when handling trials became the responsibility of the Royal Aircraft Establishments at Boscombe Down and Farnborough.

SEPTEMBER 12, 1934 Advertisements 11 THE AEROPLANE

SMITH'S

Blind Flying Made Easy!

1. Type Av.549 Airspeed Indicator.
2. Type Av.(P.3) Air Log.
3. Type Av.733 Fore-and-Aft Level, new slot-illuminated type, with adjustable Zero.
4. Type Av.882 Turn and Bank Indicator.
5. Type Av.567 Static Altimeter with fixed pressure scale.

SMITH'S AIRCRAFT INSTRUMENTS
(Branch of S. Smith & Sons (M.A.), Ltd.)
AVIATION INSTRUMENT SPECIALISTS,
185, GREAT PORTLAND STREET, LONDON, W.1.
Telephone: Welbeck 7916 (4 lines). Telegrams: "Airspeed, Wesdo, London."
INCORPORATED BY ROYAL CHARTER

PLEASE SAY YOU SAW THE ADVERTISEMENT IN "THE AEROPLANE."

Smiths Instrument advert, 1930s. *[C. N. Dodds]*

de Havilland's Stag Lane airfield, 1934, looking north-east. *[British Aerospace (BAe)]*

Section 1 – Chapter 2: The de Havilland Aircraft Company, 1932

Since its formation in 1920, the aircraft design and manufacturing business formed by Captain Geoffrey de Havilland and a close group of like-minded colleagues had grown in size and capability, having produced many successful designs for both military and commercial customers, from their small airfield at Stag Lane.

By the end of 1932, the company employed around 1000 people, and was emerging well out of the world-wide depression. The following year, Chairman Alan Butler reported that the number of employees was then around 1200, and great improvements in turnover and profits were being made, with the Tiger Moth in full production and the Leopard Moth being introduced. There were many overseas orders, and the new Gipsy Major in-line engines appeared to be unequalled for efficiency and price. Their subsidiaries in Australia, Canada, India and South Africa were progressing but not all yet in profit. A move away from Stag Lane to the new aerodrome and factory at Hatfield had been planned because of the increasing housing developments encroaching all round the old airfield, which were making flying unsafe. Also, if the expected increase in business actually occurred, then more space would be needed for manufacturing and testing the new, larger aircraft. Of course, the imminent sale of the existing Stag Lane property would bolster the company coffers by around £106,000, helping to fund the new buildings at Hatfield. Manufacturing work would start at the new factory early in 1934, but the engine manufacturing shops would remain at Stag Lane for the near future.

VIEW OF COMMERCIAL AVIATION

In order to gain an indication of the de Havilland company philosophy on aircraft design in the early 1930s, some comments from the Captain himself, made in a lecture to the Royal Aeronautical Society in 1935, give a good pointer to why de Havilland designs appeared the way they did.

Capt de Havilland made the key point that: "Types embodying simplicity, low power, light loading and low cost have achieved the objects for which they were produced".

On the choice of construction material, he commented: "There is a tendency now to look on metal as more suitable than wood, and any improvements in the strength/weight ratio are to be looked for in metal, (but) years of actual service under extreme conditions have proved that wooden construction gives little trouble, cannot suffer from the effects of fatigue, and is cheaper to produce and repair. For machines of moderate and small size, wood (is used) for reasons of cost and speed of production and has proved safe, light and reliable".

G de Havilland, A S Butler and C C Walker with another, Stag Lane, 1933. [Aeroplane]

Designers Arthur Hagg and Major Frank Halford alongside the prototype DH 86, 1933. [Aeroplane]

And finally, on the layout of the smaller types, he observed that: "Biplane construction is lighter and the monoplane is faster. (With a biplane) it is easier to take off with a large load. This makes the biplane suited to operations from poor aerodromes and high altitudes where light wing loading is called for".

So, for medium and small commercial types, the current de Havilland perception (as well as preference) was still towards wooden biplanes of simple structure and low power, with low wing loading, and low cost. These characteristics were certainly followed very closely in the design of most of the commercial types which came out of de Havillands between 1931 and 1935 and were applied to the DH 83, DH 84, DH 86, and the DH 89. The DH 88 and the DH 90 were the only aircraft which began to move away from the strong principles, in that they were for more specialised uses, and being much more complex in their structure, were therefore more costly. The more complex wooden laminated structure of these latter types was, of course, the basis for other de Havilland designs, the DH 91 Albatross and the DH 98 Mosquito. But that is another story.

THE DE HAVILLAND TEAM

An insight into the main personalities in the nineteen thirties team may help give a fuller picture of the decision makers at the head of the company.

Alan Butler, a wealthy businessman, was the company Chairman at this time, having joined the de Havilland team in its early days when he saw it needed a cash injection, and he became the wise, steady hand able to stand back, give a wider view of new projects and oversee the business from a non-technical viewpoint. He was, as were many of the team, a practising pilot, and owned several DH types over the years. Working closely with the Chairman was Geoffrey de Havilland himself, who was the centre-point of the company. When he set up the company bearing his name, he took the titles of Chief Designer and Technical Director, but from the beginning, he was in effect the chief executive. He later became Managing Director until retiring in the 1960s. Tall, slim, outwardly severe and unsmiling, but actually open, whimsical, inspirational and a real "people person", known throughout the company as "DH", he was the technical genius behind most of the DH products.

A short man of unassuming appearance but strong views, Charles Walker was the company's Chief Engineer and undoubted engineering expert. He was DH's closest colleague and confidante on the technical side. A modest and humble-minded man according to colleagues, he had exceptional technical skill and vision, as well as a subtle sense of humour. Frank Hearle, a tall, immaculately turned-out man who had much wider influence over company decisions than his title of Works Manager would suggest, had worked closely with his brother-in-law Geoffrey de Havilland since the earliest days of their joint aviation ventures. He was appointed Works Manager on creation of the company, and had done much to foster the hard-working but fair ethic within the Stag Lane works. Financial expertise behind the de Havilland Company from its outset came from Wilfred Nixon, who saw it through the recession in the early years. Another tall, quiet man, Nixon maintained, in Alan Butler's words, "the fundamental business well-being of the company". He worked closely with St Barbe on the business plans for expanding the company's sales worldwide in the nineteen thirties. Francis St Barbe was another dapper, well-presented man, almost always seen with a bow tie, who began at Stag Lane in 1920 as Business Manager, becoming Sales Director post-war. He had an infectious and likeable personality, which made him a most effective salesman for the company. This team formed the company's inner circle.

Much in tune with that inner circle while remaining just outside it, was the man with the title of Chief Draughtsman, Arthur Hagg, who had the responsibility of converting the new ideas into reality on paper. Having joined the company from Airco in 1920, Hagg was responsible for overseeing the majority of the design effort on the Dragon family in the nineteen thirties, as head of the Drawing

Arthur Hagg, 1949. *[C N Dodds (CND)]*

Office, and from 1936 as Chief Designer. His acknowledged artistic talents could be guessed from his charmingly eccentric appearance, always with large horn-rimmed spectacles, colourful shirt and tie, neat double-breasted suit and jauntily set trilby. Another key influence on the technical side was the engine designer, Major Frank Halford. While he was very closely connected to the de Havilland team, Major Halford remained an independent designer and consultant to the company, not an employee. He had already designed several famous engines with other engine companies, but was the designer as well as the main thrust behind the Gipsy and Gipsy Six engines used in the Dragon family.

STAG LANE AIRFIELD AND WORKS

Since the company's inception in 1920, the entire business had expanded to overflowing on the 76-acre company site at Stag Lane, just off London's Edgware Road, on the road out to the North West. Not only were the aircraft and engines and most of their components manufactured in a growing factory, but also all of the flight testing was completed on what was even then, a small airfield. Until 1930, it had to accommodate the company's own London Aeroplane Club as well as an ever growing set of 'Lock-ups' for private pilots wishing to fly their Moths from the airfield. Already relatively small for a training and experimental airfield, the landing area was not large even by contemporary standards. The maximum length was 600 yards, and there was a "pleasant valley" running across the prevailing wind direction, which could easily conceal a taxying aircraft. This was becoming less safe by the late 1920s, as the gradual expansion of the population of London was beginning to surround the airfield on all sides, as new houses were built.

Moving on to the day to day activities, what were conditions like on the shop floor? Incredible as it would appear seventy years later, the Stag Lane Works Rules (1936), signed by Frank Hearle, stipulated one hour's notice to be the minimum for the "Determination of an Engagement" (which was a polite term for sacking) by the company, but worse still, "Any breach of Rules, any disobedience to lawful orders or any misconduct renders an employee liable to dismissal without notice". So the work codes for their 47-hour week were pretty harsh for the ordinary employees. Despite this, the directors and senior managers of the company were highly respected by their staff, most of whom spoke very highly of their superiors.

William Phillips, who worked on the shop floor in 1933, believed "De Havilland's was a happy place. We all knew each other so well. We were a happy family; the directors all knew us, called us by our names, which was nice, wasn't it?" However, in a reference to the hard times post-recession, he commented: "...but there were lots of ups and downs. It was all most frightening in those days - shortage of work and so on".

Meanwhile, there was a wide variety of manufacturing work to be done, as potential new projects were appearing at a surprising rate, all of which were being addressed at the Stag Lane site. So, how was the process of designing and building such complex items as modern aircraft carried out?

Starting Point

With such a close-knit team as Geoffrey de Havilland had built around him over the previous decade, new projects were developed in an interesting way. The deputy Head of the Drawing Office, and later Chief Designer, Richard Clarkson, recently gave an interesting insight into the way the DH inner circle came to its decisions: "Tea was served every afternoon in Sir Geoffrey's office, and this event was attended by his closest colleagues, generally on the technical side, others being included as required. ...Most of the imaginative policy developments got their first airing at these daily informal meetings".

That collection of close colleagues usually included Frank Hearle, Charles Walker, Wilfred Nixon and Francis St Barbe.

The Drawing office

Once the inner circle had decided to go ahead with a new project, the next step was to put together some designs which would fit the concept roughly sketched out by "DH" and his technical team leaders. The drawing office was to remain at Stag Lane for some time, working on all the new designs for private, military and commercial buyers. The main factory and the majority of aircraft manufacturing processes were due to move to Hatfield when it was completed in 1934, but until then, the wooden buildings housing the Stag Lane drawing office continued as the practical starting

The Stag Lane Drawing Office, 1933. *[BAe]*

point of all new projects. A look at this department in the early nineteen thirties may help in understanding why the new Dragon appeared in the form that it did.

While the Head of the Drawing Office was in practical terms the company's chief designer, a new project's design principles were an informal but joint effort between Arthur Hagg, Charles Walker, and Captain de Havilland. The Captain, himself a designer of considerable flair, was still responsible for overall design policy. He did, however, tend to concentrate on the design and development of the types for which he had a greater affinity, the "private types" such as the various Moths. He left the major elements of the larger commercial designs to Hagg and his small team of draughtsmen. The de Havilland drawing office had already been a training ground for many aspiring designers such as Alfred Tiltman and Nevil Shute Norway, both of whom had recently set up the Airspeed Company at York; Harry Povey; Ronald Bishop and Richard Clarkson were there during that period. Young Richard Clarkson, Charles Walker's nephew, who had joined the company in 1926 as an aerodynamics specialist, carried out the stress calculations on the Dragon (as well as the Dragon Rapide wings and fuselage), as a member of the drawing office team. By the early 'thirties he had begun to concentrate on stress-work and aerodynamics and later managed to beg flights as an observer with Hubert Broad during flight testing of several of the new types.

In recent years, Clarkson remembered the regular but informal discussions on all new projects between "DH", Charles Walker and Arthur Hagg, and other key players and that the new "Dragon Moth" was very much a team effort, with elements and ideas coming from each of these senior men. Clarkson recalled working at his board one day, completely absorbed in the detailed draughtsmanship of the fin and rudder of a new design. He suddenly felt a presence behind him, then a large, thick pencil appeared, and a hand drew a heavy, sweeping line over Clarkson's delicate outline of the fin and rudder. The pencil's owner then said "Now that's what I would call a real de Havilland fin and rudder".

The speaker was of course DH himself, and the new lines were duly echoed in the finished aircraft.

Woodworking
De Havilland were rightly considered to be expert in wood construction by 1930, having used the medium for virtually all their aircraft to that point. One of the largest areas of the Stag Lane factory, the woodwork shop workers would cut, shape and build the parts for wings, empennage and fuselage, using jigs made in the shop, to ensure correct shape and size. The wood used was mostly selected straight-grain spruce for the spars and ribs, and 3-ply for various coverings and supporting parts. The prepared parts would then be assembled, pinned and glued, ready for removal to the fabric and dope shops.

Rib and decking manufacture in the woodwork shop. *[BAe]*

Dope shop girls spraying a DH 89 wing. *[BAe]*

However, most of the work on a new experimental type would in fact be done in a special secure section of the final assembly area, so that the department heads could keep a close eye on the construction as it progressed. Certainly, in late 1933, de Havilland Technical School apprentice (and later lest pilot) Geoffrey Alington remembers streams of parts being taken to a large canvas screen hiding a secret, new, "four-engined air liner" in the assembly area, and hearing the sounds of wood and metal being joined, but not being allowed sight of the new machine, until it emerged for engine tests. This was the new DH 86 Express Air Liner, undergoing its rapid-build programme in the winter of 1933.

Fabric and Dope Shop
The completed wooden assemblies would then be moved across to the fabric and dope shop, where most of the work was done by a very lively and efficient team of girls, who quickly sewed up the Irish linen envelopes for the wings, installed them, stitched and doped the fabric onto the wooden surfaces, then passed them on to the dope shop girls, who seemed quite happy to spend all day enveloped in the overpowering stench of taughtening dope, chattering away as they worked, apparently using the most colourful and un-ladylike language heard anywhere at Stag Lane.

Metalworking Shop
Much of the metal work at DH was completed in-house. For example, most aircraft being built at Stag Lane had cowlings, strut fairings, some undercarriage parts, and pilot's seats made out of the aluminium alloy known as Elektron. In the early thirties, each aircraft had its Elektron cowlings made up individually - the automatic pressing of aluminium was not started until a modern pressing machine was installed at Hatfield in 1935. So every Dragon had very similar, but slightly different, cowlings, which meant that fitting new cowlings always needed varying amounts of gentle persuasion with an engineer's hammer! Duralumin was the aluminium alloy used for many of the smaller metal parts of DH machines in this period. Such items as the ubiquitous control wheels, (which were basically the same on all Dragons, Rapides, Dragonflys and the Express Air Liner, and suspiciously similar on the DH 104 Dove and DH 106 Comet); trim wheels; sprocket cases, pulleys, and brackets were made up from duralumin, mainly because of its lightness, non-corrosive properties, ease of working and strength.

The crankcases, blocks and cylinder heads for the Gipsy and Gipsy Queen engines also used aluminium in the main. Engines for most of the DH types were still being built in-house, so the elements of the engines would be machined in the shop, then built up into complete engines on separate stands, usually with one man completely assembling an entire engine. That engine would then be wheeled down to the engine test bay on the edge of the aerodrome, to join the queue for testing. The engine bay foreman would then have the engine tested for satisfactory power figures for the Air Ministry inspector's records.

Inspection Department

After the departmental supervisors had satisfied themselves with the workmanship within their own areas, tested engines would be added to the almost complete machine then be wheeled out for the aerodrome foreman's team to make its own inspections. When the Inspection department foreman, then a man always known as Mister Morse, (only Arthur to his closest associates), had obtained his own team's satisfactory reports from their detailed examination and test runs on engines, fuel systems, electrical systems, controls, and general condition of the whole machine, he would then have any adjustments and repairs made. After checking these, he would make out his own report, probably working alongside the Ministry AID Inspector, and finally submit it to the Flight Test team for their air test. Arthur Morse's signature can still be seen on the original paperwork for quite a few aircraft still flying today.

Flight Test Department

Being a manufacturer of new designs, one of de Havilland's most important departments was the Flight Test department, whence came the critical comments and recommendations for all new types, and therefore the modifications which then appeared on the production machines. The flying side of the company was managed by the Chief Test Pilot, Hubert Broad, but some of the test flying was also shared with other pilots, including Captain de Havilland himself, and Bob Waight and later by Geoffrey de Havilland junior. A short, smiling, unassuming man who was widely acknowledged as a very skilful pilot, Hubert Broad completed the first flights of most of the de Havilland prototypes until he left in September 1935 to join Hawkers at Langley. His place was then taken by Bob Waight, who had been with the company for several years as assistant test pilot (and who was to lose his life testing the TK.4 in October 1937).

Support Department

This was a separate department sited on the north side of the Stag Lane airfield, responsible for setting up the customer support facilities as well as creating and amending all the manuals for the aircraft produced by the company. At first run by Albert Brant, who wrote all the 'Manuals of Instruction for the Operation, Maintenance and Rigging' of the four aircraft of the Dragon family, this department also made many visits to customers who had questions or problems with their aircraft or engines.

Hatfield airfield and hangars under construction in 1934. [BAe]

Chief Test Pilot Hubert Broad, 1934. [BAe]

Move to Purpose-built Site

In those mid-war years, the airfield was being squeezed, both by the need for greater production facilities on the east side, as well as by encroaching suburban housing estates on the north and west sides, so by 1929 the company had decided a move was necessary. A much larger, less congested area was needed, so company pilots were encouraged to explore, when airborne on other tasks, all the main roads leading North out of London. Eventually, they found an ideal site on the Great North Road near the small town of Hatfield, twenty miles north of Stag Lane, in Hertfordshire. Here, in open countryside alongside the new Barnet by-pass, was an ideal area for building a new purpose-built aircraft factory with a large aerodrome. The pilots could see that road and rail access to London were obviously good, so the company quickly bought the land. The de Havilland School of Flying had moved up in June 1930, and the manufacturing and testing elements transferred progressively to a 400 acre site alongside the Flying School over the next four years.

Stag Lane finally closed as an airfield shortly after the London Aeroplane Club also moved to Hatfield in September 1933 and the aerodrome licence was revoked in January 1934.

THE PASSING OF STAG LANE

Although not one of the oldest aerodromes in England, Stag Lane is very far from being the least known. For 12 years it has been the home of the De Havilland Aircraft Co. Ltd., and the birth-place of the celebrated Moth series of aeroplanes. Before that It was used by the London and Provincial Aviation Co. Ltd., which was a different affair altogether from the present company of that name.

The sale of the aerodrome by the De Havilland Aircraft Co. Ltd to Hilbery Chaplin Ltd., for building purposes, is now announced, and the principal reason given is the encroachment of residential building on this once rural site. All those who have flown much from Stag Lane will agree that the massed homes of the people, unlovely from any point of view, look their worst when seen from an aeroplane just taking-off over them.

About two years ago the company established a new aero-drome at Hatfield airfield where all the work of the De Havilland School of Flying and a considerable amount of testing is now done. Stag Lane remained in use for most of the testing, for the operations of the London Aeroplane Club and as a place where private owners might land and house their machines. The private owners and members of the Club naturally found Stag Lane more convenient than Hatfield as it is nearer the City and well served with public transport.

The De Havilland Aircraft Co. Ltd. will retain their shops and premises (about 15 acres) but flying will cease in about six months' time at the old aerodrome (by end 1933). The London Aeroplane Club has not yet selected its future home.

The purchase price is slightly over £100,000 and the site is town-planned for about 1,200 houses.

The Aeroplane, *June 1933*

Section 2:
The DH 84 Dragon

Prototype Dragon awaiting its first flight, Stag Lane, November, 1932. [BAe]

Section 2 – Chapter 1: Design and Initial Testing

THE DRAGON CONCEPT

The customer requirement which became the Dragon grew from de Havillands' perception of the need by small airlines and other developing transport businesses for an aircraft with the capability of carrying up to eight passengers for a minimum of about 300 miles, including over water, at greater speeds than hitherto available, for as low a cost as possible. A major influence in the creation of this perception was the commercial foresight of an existing customer, Hillman's Airways, who had begun operating a fleet of DH 83 Fox Moths from their airfield at Maylands, near Romford, Essex, only a few months previously, in June 1932. Hillman's larger than life owner, Edward Hillman, known to most as Ted, already wanted to have greater passenger capacity and greater speed than could be provided by the four-seat Fox Moth, for his projected routes to Paris. Hillman therefore went to Stag Lane in August 1932 to discuss the prospects with the Captain and his team. Would they have such a design available for sale within a matter of months?

Also in discussion with the de Havilland Sales team in the summer of 1932, was Flight Lieutenant H E Forrow, the surprisingly junior officer that the RAF had seconded to be adviser to the emerging Iraqi Air Force. Seeing that his customer Air Force had a need for a "Type Coloniale" in the currently popular language, Flight Lieutenant Forrow saw that a multi-purpose aircraft, adapted from a commercial design, could be an inexpensive yet suitable type for what *The Aeroplane's* editor, C G Grey, called "inflicting the benefits of western civilisation on a native population of turbulent habits". If a small, twin-Gipsy-powered aircraft could be fitted with a light gunnery and bombing capability, it would be useful as a personnel and cargo transport when not inflicting civilisation on a dissident population.

The small team responsible for new designs realised that the needs of these two potential customers confirmed their own ideas about future light transport aircraft. They could meet the differing requirements of Hillman and the Iraqis by starting with the key elements of proven Gipsy Major power plants, and combining this with low cost and other elements of current technology. If a name reflecting the provenance of previous successful models were used, this would also help build on the good reputation of the de Havilland company. Costs to the passenger should be comparable to those of luxury buses or taxis, allowing for a premium for the extra speed of air travel. Aircraft in use in Europe for short-range passenger transport up to the early thirties were considered to be somewhat slow, had poor climb, cruise and gliding performance, and with most having a single engine were not perceived as safe for long flights over water. In accordance with Captain de Havilland's stated "safe, step-by-step policy, taking as few risks as possible" the design team felt they could consolidate their success in small transport machines by developing their earlier designs, and incorporating them into a bigger, faster transport, with the added safety of twin engines.

The de Havilland Board agreed that a new small airliner should be built, and design work was started in September 1932. Hillman was delighted and with little hesitation ordered four aircraft without waiting for the type to fly. He also agreed to pay the maker's price, £2,700 plus £95 for the "chairs, carpet upholstery and decorations", with delivery of the first aircraft in the remarkably tight timescale of four months - by the end of 1932. Flight Lieutenant Forrow and his Iraqi masters were also delighted with an offer of the same design, but adapted to meet their special requirements, and ordered eight aircraft, for delivery in the Spring of 1933.

By late summer 1932, the British aviation press had already picked up rumours of the new design and began writing about de Havilland's type number DH 84, the "Dragon Moth", which was the name given to the new type by the aviation press, as a continuing reference to Captain de Havilland's habit of naming his designs after examples of British lepidoptery, but early in 1933 the makers shortened it to simply the "DH 84 Dragon".

Gipsy Major engine before installation. [BAe]

Hubert Broad taxying prototype G-ACAN c/n 6000, Stag Lane, 1933. *[CND]*

DESIGN PRINCIPLES

This new aircraft had to have two proven engines to carry an increased load and for added safety; it must also be light; had to be cheap to build, and finally must have good short-field performance for operations away from large airfields. But, wherever feasible, existing components were to be used; a policy which had parallels all the way through the "Dragon" family.

In de Havillands' view therefore, it had to be constructed mainly of wood, but with as many elements from previous types as possible. Needing to have either six or eight seats for a passenger version, or alternatively, provision for guns, bombs and aiming systems, a new cabin would be needed, as there was nothing similar in the recent portfolio. This meant that a new tail, larger wheels and a new undercarriage would also be required. The engine cowlings could be based on those of the Puss Moth, as they housed the same engines, and the wings outboard of the engines could be the Tiger Moth's. It was also decided to adopt the folding wing concept of the Gipsy Moth, so the new type could take up less hangar space! The rudder and tail empennage were simply larger versions of those on the Moth types, incorporating the now familiar DH swept-back fin and rudder.

Fuselage design would take most effort, but started with the Fox Moth's small ply-covered spruce box, much enlarged, to hold six or more seats, and with a cockpit up front, in place of the Fox's engine. A wooden box fuselage could be used for both the passenger and military tasks, provided enough strength could be built-in to allow for large cut-outs for dorsal and ventral gun positions, and a small opening for a bombsight. If the box frame was made strong enough for cut-outs for guns etc, it could also allow for a continuous window down both cabin sides, and a well-glazed view for the pilot, right up in the nose. So that was the basis of the new twin design, started in the Drawing Office by Arthur Hagg's team in September 1932, and completed and flown an incredible two months later, on 24th November. Chairman Alan Butler paid special tribute to the design and production teams that winter, when he said that "the 84 was an achievement, exceeding all expectations" by flying in such a short time. Very few changes were made to the initial design, indicating that the first ideas were very close to what the customer wanted.

COMPANY TESTING

All civil aircraft were required to hold a Certificate of Airworthiness (C of A) before being used commercially or privately. After the maker's own ground and flight tests, the official process of gaining the CofA for a new type involved three elements; inspections at the factory where the aircraft was being built by the resident technical officer from the Air Ministry's Director of Technical Developments (DTD) department; examination of the design in terms of materials and strengths by Air Ministry officials, and finally, flight tests on behalf of the Air Ministry by military test pilots at the A & AEE, Martlesham Heath, Suffolk.

The Stag Lane flight test, engine test and service departments completed their own new-type tests of all the systems in the first weeks of November 1932. When the Inspectors under Mr Morse were satisfied that their new charge was in good shape, they handed over constructor's number 6000, now marked as de Havilland Experimental aircraft 'E.9', doped overall in silver, to Captain Broad's flight test department for the first flight. Hubert Broad obviously spent some time on the ground checking the engines and systems on E.9, and then, on 24th November 1932, took off for the first test flight. This was successful, showing no particular problems, so he carried out the standard company flight tests into early December, checking the designer's performance figures and testing, stage by stage, the handling of the aircraft and engines, in flights from Stag Lane. These company tests, flown mainly by Broad, but also by Bob Waight, only took two weeks, despite the winter weather, and they confirmed the predictions of the designers. Unfortunately, no specific reports on these flights remain today, but no particular problems appear to have been found and certainly no major modifications were carried out after these first tests, which indicates general satisfaction with the aircraft. In early December 1932, with the aircraft still in its all-over silver dope, and 'E.9' down the fuselage sides, Hubert Broad took his new protégé across to Martlesham Heath for the Air Ministry Certification Trials.

AIR MINISTRY CERTIFICATE OF AIRWORTHINESS TESTS – MARTLESHAM HEATH.

The new DH 84 was tested in the first week of December 1932 by the Martlesham team in the same way as all similar types of commercial aircraft, at three Centre of Gravity (CG) positions; Intermediate first, then, if all went well, at the aft CG limit, and at the forward CG limit. The performance tests were completed first, at the 4,200 lb maximum all up weight given by the makers. Take off, landing, climbing and speed performance tests were completed; take off run in the test was 232 yards, and the initial climb figure was 42 feet after a slightly short 546 yards, but no mention was made in the official report of this shortfall of 8 feet, so it can be assumed that the figure was interpolated to relate to the 50 feet minimum after a take off distance of 626 yards.

In E.9's case, for some unstated reason, while the handling tests were completed with CG loadings in the three normal positions, only the first test was flown at the maximum weight, 4,200 lb, which included full fuel and oil, 6 passengers, and 367 lb of ballast, representing baggage in the cabin and rear compartment. The other handling tests were then carried out at slightly lower weights. For the aft CG test, ballast representing only 4 passengers, 367 lb of baggage and normal fuel and oil weights was carried, making a total weight of 3,860lb. The final tests were made at 3,854 lb, with ballast representing 5 passengers and 191lb of baggage, and with CG at the forward limit. There was likely to have been a small difference in the handling caused by these weight decreases, particularly in the asymmetric handling, but this was not commented on in the report.

The Martlesham pilots commented positively on the lightness and good harmonization of all the controls, and no unusual characteristics were detected, apart from a slight snatching at the stall. The aircraft was given the usual rudimentary check "with one engine throttled" where only the turning ability in both directions with either engine "throttled" was tested, and found to be normal. This was an unrealistic test, as, with failure of an engine, the propeller would be stopped, not at idle thrust as in this case, so the differing thrust levels would make quite a difference to asymmetric handling on an aircraft such as this, which had only marginal single-engine capability. However, in comparison with contemporary aircraft, the Dragon's asymmetric handling was considered satisfactory. E.9 was then checked at maximum weight for its handling at the stall and interestingly, in a "stalled glide" where the aircraft was "easily controllable laterally and directionally". Finally the aircraft controls were tested for correct functioning, before landings were checked.

An approach speed of 75 mph was recommended, at full load, and on touch down, "a very small backward movement of the elevator is required to effect a three-point landing, the elevator being very powerful at low speeds". This reference to three-point landings is still borne out by today's Dragon pilots, as the aircraft is quite happy to land on three points, but only on a grass field. On hard runways, not tested by Martlesham pilots, the aircraft is much more manageable when landed on the mainwheels first, in a "wheeler" landing.

The Martlesham team was not happy with the undercarriage. They described it as "very rough and harsh, and it jolts the aircraft very badly, making take off, landing and taxying.....extremely uncomfortable". They stated that its unconventional design, with its "overhung axle, [caused] the telescopic leg to be subject to considerable bending and torsion loads. For these reasons there is a danger of structural failure of the undercarriage". The rough condition of the Martlesham Heath land and heather-covered airfield, well known at the time, will have had some bearing on these comments about the Dragon's undercarriage, but the comments were made in relation to all the other aircraft being tested in that period, so would have to be taken very seriously by de Havilland, and a fix arranged. The right-hand brake cable on the floor of the cockpit was stated to need a guard over it, to stop the pilot tripping on it or catching it by accident.

In the second section, two more adverse comments on the construction were made, concerning the aluminium wheel fairings, which the Martlesham pilots considered unsatisfactory because "they have already become seriously deformed by mud and stones forced between the tyres and the fairings". In addition, the single Emergency Exit came in for criticism, as it was considered that while there was "provision" for a roof exit, there was only one narrow door for both pilot and passengers, and that an emergency exit in the roof should be provided.

MARTLESHAM RECOMMENDATIONS

Although personal comments were not allowed in the official reports, from the overall tone of their report, it appears the Martlesham pilots, over their few days with E.9, considered it capable of meeting the current Air Ministry standards, and in addition, were generally happy that the aircraft performed safely and capably enough for its designed task. The report therefore recommended the issue of a C of A in the Normal Category, at a maximum weight of 4,200 lb, with six passengers, and 367 lb of luggage and full fuel, "but only on condition that the four adverse points noted in the report were modified". A further test after the recommended modifications was not considered necessary.

The aircraft was soon collected by Hubert Broad, and returned to Stag Lane for painting, ready for its new owner. With the recommendation from Martlesham, the Air Ministry was content to issue a C of A, which it did on 16th December 1932. The modifications required by the Martlesham report were put in hand by the Drawing Office and the Support Department, and would take but a few days to check then incorporate. In the meantime, the paint shop rapidly transformed the newly certificated E.9 into 'G-ACAN', with Ted Hillman's striking blue and white colour scheme. They had to be quick, as the aircraft was due for delivery to Hillman's Airways at Romford on 19th December, a bare month after the first flight - what seems now an incredibly optimistic schedule.

SATISFYING THE MARTLESHAM RECOMMENDATIONS

No record remains of the company's actions following the return of E.9 from the Martlesham trials, but it can be assumed that the four adverse points were addressed, otherwise the Air Ministry's resident inspectors at Stag Lane would not have allowed the aircraft to obtain its C of A. The comment on the handbrake cable was almost certainly satisfied by placing the cable below the cockpit floor, where it was situated on all subsequent aircraft. On the point about emergency exits, the cabin roof opening, covered by a removable fabric patch, was now labelled as the emergency exit, as had always been intended, and the wheel fairings were enlarged slightly, in order to stop dirt and stones from distorting them. Rectification of the most serious criticism - of the harsh undercarriage - is less easy to confirm. No record is available to indicate what was done to make the system less harsh, and no apparent changes were made to drawings of the undercarriage. It can only be assumed that the harsh feel was eased by the use of softer rubber in the telescopic legs, which therefore made the shock-absorbing effect of the telescopic leg more pliable, and the ride much softer, so reducing the torsional and bending loads to an acceptable level.

DEMONSTRATION OF G-ACAO, HUBERT BROAD, 6TH MARCH 1933.

This aircraft, the second to be built, was given its C of A on 3rd March 1933, and was due for delivery to Hillman's Airways soon afterwards. However, de Havilland felt the need to publicise their new machine, for which they needed a Dragon demonstrator, so kept G-ACAO back at Stag Lane for the month of March.

One of a series of typical de Havilland demonstrations was set up by Francis St Barbe for stalwarts of the aviation press only three days after the aircraft had been awarded its C of A. Flown by the ebullient Chief Test Pilot, Captain Hubert Broad, it included a bold, and to modern aviators, a somewhat risky demonstration of the aircraft's single-engine capability. The company wanted to emphasise to the aviation world the safety elements of their new transport, so felt a demonstration of G-ACAO's single-engine capability would look good in *Flight* and *The Aeroplane*, assuming all went well. Captain Broad had now had nearly two month's worth of experience with his new toy, and even the Martlesham pilots had shown that the Dragon had adequate performance on one engine. However, the demonstration would still be tricky to handle, especially if there was a problem with the live engine, having shut down the other, and a failure would be less than impressive. A look at the figures might give an idea of the risk.

With pilot, six press passengers, 60 lb of baggage, one umbrella, two cameras, and presumably full oil in the engines, we can assume that the gallant Captain had taken on minimum fuel to give lowest weight, and therefore the most convincing single-engine performance. He had to fly for one hour with both engines, at about 7 gallons each per hour, and then a little over one hour on one engine at virtually full power (at around 9 gallons per hour). But as he had no method of cross-feeding his live engine from the other engine's tank, he had to give himself enough on both sides to cope with full power on either engine for over an hour, plus about 5 gallons for contingencies. That would give him around 32 gallons,

G-ACAN airborne from Romford in Hillman's colours with a full load, in early 1933. *[DHMC]*

or just over half fuel. He therefore would have started about 500 lb below his maximum weight of 4,200 lb on this flight. The Martlesham trials two months earlier had shown that the prototype E.9 could maintain a height of 1,000 feet at maximum weight, with one engine failed. So, in this case, Captain Broad was typically confident of his own and his aircraft's ability to give an effective demonstration of the Dragon's safety in the event of engine failure.

The flight took the party out of Stag Lane on 9th March 1933 and headed south-west, out over London into a moderate headwind, climbing to 2,000 feet in a cruise at 105 mph down to Southampton. The *Aeroplane* correspondent considered the flight to be comfortable, and he noted readings of 1,900rpm on the two gauges mounted on top of the engine cowlings. Reaching Southampton docks in 55 minutes, Captain Broad proceeded to circle the two ocean liners about to depart, headed the Dragon back towards Stag Lane, and then switched off the port engine. The Gipsy Major would not stop completely, the airflow merely forcing the propeller to windmill at slow speed, and therefore producing considerable drag. Broad then slowed the aircraft right down in order to stop the prop, in what was described as "a semi-stalled glide", ending up at 1,400 feet with the prop finally stopped. Full power of 2,000 rpm was then applied to the starboard engine, and a speed of 80 mph gained for the return cruise. Broad then skilfully but gradually eased the Dragon up using the starboard engine at full power, at the same speed, until they had reached 1,700 feet by the time they reached Stag Lane, some forty five minutes later. The port engine was then started up by diving to get the prop turning (there being no internal starter system), and the aircraft landed with the benefit of both engines. The reporters were certainly impressed, as the *Flight* correspondent was convinced of the "Dragon's conclusive proof of reliability". Whilst convinced of the aircraft's single-engine capability, he was somewhat critical of the vibration felt in the cabin from the straining starboard engine, which he considered to be underpowered! He did however concede that de Havilland had produced "a commercial machine of outstanding cheapness, efficiency and safety".

This apparently reasonable demonstration showed that a standard Dragon, at about 500 lbs less than maximum weight, could actually climb on the starboard engine alone. It also seemed to indicate that it would probably at least maintain height at full weight if it lost the starboard engine. In 1933 there were, of course, no rules for what performance a multi-engined British commercial aircraft must achieve if an engine failed at any point in flight. There was merely an assumption that an aircraft with two engines was statistically safer than one with only one. Makers were only required to show that a multi-engined aircraft could still fly subsequent to an engine failure, but did not have to meet any performance criteria. Along with other makers, de Havilland therefore kept to their low power, low cost ruling, so producing what would now be recognised as underpowered aircraft.

With most British engines of that period turning in the same direction (in this case anti-clockwise when viewed from behind), loss of the Dragon's starboard engine would take more effort to control, as the live engine, already having a natural gyroscopic tendency to yaw to the right, would also cause the airframe to yaw to the right. Counteracting this yawing motion would require considerable rudder force from the pilot and create extra turbulence and inefficient drag from the rudder. With an aircraft already just able to maintain height with full power on the favourable engine, this extra drag caused by the "critical" engine loss would probably cause it to lose height. The wily Hubert Broad knew which engine to shut down for the most effective demonstration!

By the time the aircraft had been in service for over a year, the Air Ministry, responsible for airworthiness of civil aircraft, was to question the validity of the Dragon's ability to remain safe for passenger carriage on one engine, but for now, they were able to accept the tests carried out by the company and by the military pilots at Martlesham Heath, who flew the certification flights in

1930s postcard showing a DH 84 on approach to St. Mary's, Scilly. *[M. Stroud]*

Section 2 – Chapter 2: Construction and Performance

STRUCTURE

The Dragon's main planes were of two-bay biplane construction, with engines mounted on the bottom stub planes. The plan form was tapered to the point of the extensions, and then parallel, as on the Tiger Moth, for top and bottom wings. Each mainplane extension consisted of spruce I section spars with spruce ribs, leading and trailing edges. Wing tips were of light alloy tubing, and internal steel struts were used for bracing. The wings were designed for folding, outboard of the engines - somewhat surprising, considering the company's desire for greatest efficiency from the available power, which meant the lowest weight for the structure. Stub wings were of similar construction, except that steel tubing was used for engine, fuel and oil tank mountings, undercarriage attachments and fuselage and interplane strut mountings. This was all covered with fabric.

The tailplane and fin were made of spruce spars, supported by spruce ribs and formers, and then covered in 3-ply, and rigidly braced to the fuselage by steel struts. All tail control surfaces were made in similar fashion, but were covered in fabric.

Fuselage structure for the Dragon was of similar style to the Fox Moth, consisting of spruce longerons and members, making up a shaped box framework covered on the outer side by 3-ply, joint plates and fittings all being made of steel. This whole ply surface was covered in fabric "attached in the first place with a cellulose adhesive and finally protected with a nitro-cellulose finish". Cockpit and cabin windows were made of transparent, "unbreakable" celluloid sheet, except the windscreen and cockpit side windows, which were of "safety glass". Control runs and piping were all fitted below the fuselage box, which was then protected by a fabric outer covering, having access for inspection via a zip fastener running down the centre of the fuselage.

A basic fuel system was fitted, consisting of a 30-gallon tank attached behind each engine, within the same nacelle, and protected by an asbestos firewall from the engine itself. The Gipsy engines had duplicated engine-driven fuel pumps, which fed fuel up and into the carburetters. Behind each fuel tank was a 2.25 gallon oil tank which again was fed via a filter by a single engine-driven pump into the engine. There was no interconnection of fuel tanks from side to side, so loss of one engine would mean that its fuel could not be used for the remaining engine.

A simple two-wheeled main undercarriage was used, being a rigidly-braced structure connected to the wheel axles, which had two piston tubes sliding in rubber compression containers, so providing a simple shock-absorbing and rebound process for the two main wheels, providing a combination of minimum weight and minimum maintenance. The tailwheel was a high-pressure pneumatic wheel with full castoring and once again, the shock-absorbing element consisted of rubber blocks in compression mounted in telescopic tubes.

STANDARD EQUIPMENT

The standard, very simple instrumentation included in the new price in the Dragon brochure can be seen in the contemporary *Flight* advertisement, showing the standard price (excluding cabin furnishings or equipment) was £2,800 per machine, or £4,025 for the Floatplane version.

At extra cost, you could specify extra-large engine instruments fitted to the engine cowlings; (for pilots with poor vision?); luminous instruments; illumination of instruments on the instrument board; an automatic Air Log, and two engine temperature gauges, which fitted alongside the other engine instruments on the engine cowlings.

INTERIOR

In keeping with the period, the Dragon's cabin was generally unsophisticated, yet reasonably comfortable for the duration of journeys expected of the aircraft. The company contracted with L A Rumbold and Co., who were then based in nearby Kilburn, to make and fit the cabin upholstery and seating for all Dragons. Only basic soundproofing materials were used in the fuselage sides and for the passenger, wind and engine noise were quite loud by modern standards, but as good as in any other aircraft of the time. Commentators report that only shouted conversation could be heard across the cabin in the cruise and that any journey longer than about two hours in a standard Dragon's cabin could become uncomfortable. But with the extra soundproofing and comfort of the special-order "De Luxe" cabins, longer journeys became more acceptable.

The Dragon's cabin could be set out for four, six, eight or even ten seats, depending on the customer's requirements. Ten alternative "Schemes" were offered in the 1933 price list, varying from the austere to the luxurious. At the top of the range, the Prince of Wales' first Dragon, G-ACGG, which was fitted out to his personal specification, had what de Havilland described as "Four De Luxe Adjustable Armchairs, and one fixed light seat (for the radio operator); a separate compartment with lavatory, wash basin, water supply and other toilet requisites; and a separate luggage compartment with external door". Without the special fittings and materials used on G-ACGG, but with special coloured upholstery, this de Luxe specification was called Scheme 8 and was usually charged at £190 per machine.

At the other end of the scale, the standard Scheme 1 was for "six comfortable armchairs, upholstered in royal blue leather with light blue piping; dark blue carpet for floors; lower half cabin walls covered with royal blue upholstery (probably leather) and upper half and ceiling covered with blue grey material. Interior painting and decorations to suit with rope pulls, ash trays and pockets". Rumbolds charged de Havilland £73.5s.0d (£73.25) for this package which was then recharged at an additional £105 to the customer, on top of the basic price of £2,800 per machine (ex works, unpacked). This aggregate cost equates to about £100,000 in today's money; good value for a ten-seater transport.

The forward-facing "fixed light seats" were made up by Rumbolds in Elektron tubular light aluminium alloy with three slotted feet which fitted into clamps on the wooden floor. The arms, seat and back were then padded and upholstered in piped leather, usually in the standard royal blue, but occasionally in the customer's own colours. When new these seats were surprisingly comfortable, but in due course the seats and backs tended to stretch and allow the metal frames to be felt through the cushions.

Most customers opted for the basic Scheme 1 with six seats and toilet, but some small airlines, such as Hillman's and Jersey Airways, also took the economy option of adding two more seats and removing the wooden bulkhead between the main cabin and the baggage compartment. This allowed them to alternate between six seats with toilet, or eight seats without toilet and separate baggage compartment, depending on demand. For Dragons adapted to the ambulance role, Schemes 9 and 10 provided for either two stretchers and attendant's seat or four stretchers.

Four "independent ventilating devices" (air scoops) were fitted above the windows in the cockpit sides and allowed some cooling for passengers, and for those unconcerned about the extra weight and complexity, a crude heating system using warm air ducted from the engine exhausts through the stub wings into the cabin could be fitted. Because of its propensity for leaks, this system was often blanked off by overworked engineers.

DH 84 cabin with tropical rattan seats and a toilet compartment. *[BAe]*

A chromed handhold was fitted inside the entrance door, small braided "rope pulls" fitted on the cabin walls above each seat and braided loops fixed to the transverse struts in the cabin roof to help passengers negotiate the steep slope of the cabin when at rest. Rather surprisingly for a wood and fabric aeroplane, a chromed ashtray was fitted below the window for each passenger, but de Havilland treated the cabin with "fireproof dope that conformed to Air Ministry regulations, allowing smoking to be indulged in". A fabric-covered circular escape hatch in the roof was the only emergency exit, other than the main entrance door.

Moving forward from the passenger compartment, the standard Dragon had a light wooden bulkhead attached to the upright metal struts immediately behind the pilot's seat, with an awkwardly-shaped wooden door enclosing the driving compartment. Because of its intrusion into the cabin space when open, and the difficulties larger pilots had in squeezing past it to enter the cockpit, this door was often removed, allowing the passengers a better view of what their driver was up to during flight.

COCKPIT

The standard Mark I Dragon's cockpit was a pleasantly uncomplicated place, and even later models had few alterations to the original layout. The view from the pilot's seat was remarkably good, with safety-glass panes ahead of and to the side of the seat. Above and behind the pilot, the clear panes were made of celluloid. Both side panes were hinged at the front, and could be let down to help with cooling on the ground, or visibility in the air.

The pilot sat in an "Elektron" aluminium shaped seat with thin leather cushions, placed centrally in his reasonably spacious cockpit, with a better view on both sides and ahead than in almost any contemporary enclosed-cockpit aircraft. On the triangular instrument panel in front of him, the early models had only seven instruments, starting with the all-important Air Speed Indicator at the top centre. Below that were a large Reid and Sigrist Turn and Slip indicator, an inclinometer, and a "fore and aft level". On either side of these were the paired magneto switches for left and right engines, and below these again were a rather insensitive altimeter; a clock or watch; and a large horizontally-mounted Hughes grid compass. The only engine information available to the pilot came from a tachometer and an oil pressure gauge on the top of each engine cowling. And that was it. Nothing fancy, nothing unnecessary for the type of flying expected. But quite a challenge for pilots forced to fly blind, in cloud or in bad visibility.

The controls available to the pilot were also fairly basic. On his left side, the cockpit wall had a fuel on/off cock for the port engine, and inboard of that, a long, ratcheted brake lever; a pair of elegant polished aluminium throttle levers with associated mixture levers level with his elbow, and below that a large black painted wheel coupled to the elevator trim cables. In the centre, between his knees was the vertical pole mounting for a large black metal control spectacle, again connected to cables running down the fuselage floor and out to the ailerons or back to the elevators. With true de Havilland economy, the same trim wheel appeared in all the later Dragons up to the Dragonfly, and the same full control wheel graced the cockpits of the DH Express airliner and the early Rapides, before being replaced in later Rapides by a less graceful 'W'- shaped wheel. Beneath the instrument panel were the adjustable, parallel-action rudder pedals - again virtual copies of those on most Moths, and aft of the right pedal, a small rotating handle for winding-on what de Havilland insisted on calling "rudder bias" to take out asymmetric rudder loads.

Most aircraft had a few switches and fittings either on a small panel by the pilot's left elbow, or on the instrument panel, controlling instrument and navigation lighting, but these were extras, as were a Rotax 150 watt wind-driven generator and an electrical system with an accumulator. There was no internal method of engine starting on the standard landplane, so all starting had to be controlled from outside, with manual engine priming and prop-swinging to start the engines. As a concession to modernity, however, the "1934 Type DH 84" (which became the DH 84 Mk II) had the option of using either a BTH inertia starter, or an Eclipse electric starter motor, either of which was supplied with 12 volts from a small accumulator. When the Dragon seaplane came along, also in 1934, the BTH inertia starter and an internal carburetter "tickler" were fitted as standard, because of the difficulty of priming the carburetters and hand-swinging the propellers with the aircraft sitting on water.

The standard Dragon was therefore quite usable without electricity, pneumatics, or hydraulics, all of which were becoming standardised on contemporary designs, particularly in the USA. This was one reason why de Havilland could sell their Dragon in 1933 at a list price of £2,905, including standard interior, or less if you could persuade the nice Mr St Barbe to allow a discount.

ENGINES

The engines were the same as those which powered the Fox Moth - the 1932-designed Gipsy Major, developed from the first inverted Gipsy, the Gipsy III. The Gipsy Major had the slightly higher compression ratio of 5.25, and produced 130 brake horsepower at full power, slightly more than the Gipsy IIIs 120 bhp. Apart from these changes, the Major 1 was the same inverted, in-line, air-cooled engine, with four bronze cylinder heads and twin-magneto ignition, with each engine fed by its own separate fuel and oil tanks.

RADIO EQUIPMENT

There were two main types of transmitter/receiver which could be specified, complete with engine screening parts, as optional extras; a Marconi AD 6N or a Standard Telephones ATR 4. The bulky transmitter, receiver and associated equipment weighed just over 80 lbs and usually fitted behind the pilot's bulkhead on the port side of the cabin, with a seat for a radio operator if required. They could also be used by the pilot if necessary, using a rather complicated system of cables fed into the cockpit to adjust the various controls on the radio.

In 1933, the sets could be provided for £220 (around £6,600 today) plus £60 for fitting. To make most efficient use of such a valve-operated radio set, of course, the electrical elements such as the magnetos, ignition harness and spark plugs would have to be screened, bonded and fitted as well, which cost another £100 (£3,000). So radios were a pretty expensive luxury in 1933.

Both the Marconi and Standard radios were long-waveband sets, usable for Morse telegraphy or voice telephony on direction-finding frequencies in Southern England and Europe. Both types of radio were fixed to a large wall tray, taking as much space as one passenger, so the commercial cost of installing a radio had to be weighed against the loss of a revenue-generating passenger. If the pilot was to operate the radio, tuning in the set and either tapping a Morse key or speaking on the low-fidelity telephony system took a considerable amount of physical and mental effort, thereby making concurrent lookout or instrument flying somewhat hazardous.

DH 84 cockpit with an unusual variometer on the right side. *[BAe]*

However, the weather factor on routes such as Croydon to Paris or Amsterdam was such that scheduled services would often be forced to fly in poor visibility or in cloud, and radio direction-finding was the only method of being relatively sure of finding one's destination. If atmospheric conditions were right these radios had an effective 100 to 150 miles air-ground range on telephony, and 150 to 200 miles for intermittent carrier wave telegraphy.

All radios need a power source, and the Dragon had no generators on its Gipsy Majors, as fitting generators to such low-powered engines would drain too much horsepower. So an operator fitting a radio would either rely on a well-charged accumulator, or on an accumulator plus a Rotax wind-driven generator, mounted on the leading edge of the top wing.

PERFORMANCE FIGURES
These figures for performance are taken direct from the Operation, Maintenance and Rigging Manual produced by de Havilland in 1933 for the DH 84 Dragon, so apply to the Mark 1 version only. The figures were subsequently amended for the Dragon Mark II in 1934, and for the 1942 Australian version.

WEIGHTS (approximate) - LANDPLANE (6 seater):

	lbs
Tare weight, including chairs, carpet, cabin heaters, ventilators	2,285
Petrol, 60 galls	462
Oil, 4fi galls	44
Pilot	160
Useful load	1,249
Maximum permissible weight	4,200

DIMENSIONS:

Length overall	34 ft 6 ins
Span overall	47 ft 4 ins
Span folded	25 ft 4 ins
Height overall	10 ft 1 ins

RANGE IN STILL AIR:
Standard 60 Imperial gall fuel 500 miles at 110 mph
Extra tanks can be fitted to meet special requirements.
NB - The above mileage is reckoned on a basis of all petrol being used. A safe margin must naturally be allowed when calculating for a journey.

A Mark II Dragon with a small wind-driven generator on the lower wing and a mounting for a larger generator on the upper wing-root. [CND]

Early Mark II Dragon G-ACOR Fiona, *c/n 6073, photographed in 1935 by Charles E Brown.* *[Aeroplane]*

Section 2 – Chapter 3: Mark II and Mark III Developments

"1934 TYPE DH 84" - DH 84 MARK II

By early 1934, just one year after the Dragon first flew, the Service and Design departments at Stag Lane had incorporated enough modifications to the aircraft for the company to re-name it "The DH 84 Dragon '34 Type". This change soon became known as the Dragon Mark II, which was a little easier on the pen and the ear. The notification to operators came in the form of amendment sheet 8 to the Manual of Instruction for the Operation, Maintenance and Rigging of the DH Dragon (Type DH 84), which was undated but must have been distributed after 8th January 1934, and before Amendment Sheet 9, which was dated 14th June 1934. There is some uncertainty about which aircraft was the first "Mark II", particularly as G-ACMC, 6053, was considered the prototype Mark II, but the definitive company answer is given in the Instruction Manual, which indicates that "the Type 1934 machines are 6066, and all subsequent". That made G-ACKU, built for William Lindsay Everard MP and given its C of A in November 1933, the first production Mark II.

Compared to the original Dragon, the 1934 Type had an increase in maximum permissible weight, from 4,200 lbs to 4,500 lbs. An interesting rider to the weight figures appears in the 1934 Type manual, where the single-engine performance is referred to for the first time, possibly as a result of the Martlesham tests which took place in March 1934. The maximum weight at which the aircraft was able to fly on one engine was given as 4,200 lbs, when the ceiling would be 1,000 feet.

Other changes included optional introduction of Eclipse electrical starters, with the alternative option of inertia starters if required, as usually fitted to the Seaplane version in Canada. Metal Fairey Reed propellers could now be fitted in place of the usual wooden de Havilland type. Probably the most visually obvious change was the welcome tidying-up of the cabin windows, each of which was rounded off and given the same type of external aluminium surround as on the new Dragon Rapide. Most of the new models had more aerodynamic aluminium spats around the mainwheel struts, and some had the position of the venturi altered to a position under the nose.

A somewhat premature report in the de Havilland Gazette of October 1933 indicated that the Dragon II would have ailerons on the top wings only, so eliminating the operating strut beween the two ailerons on the same side, and decreasing aerodynamic drag. In fact, no Dragons appear to have had this change, and no evidence can be found of any aircraft being so modified.

The Mark II was the last of the series built in England and production ceased in 1936, with three final specimens being sold in May 1937 to Portugal ex-store, and probably blocked Spanish aircraft.

THE DRAGON SEAPLANE

While only three Dragons were sent to Canada the DH Canada design work for skis and floats for these aircraft became the model for all future such modifications, including the later Dragon Rapide.

Phil Garratt and his team at DH Canada set about converting CF-AVD, a Mark II Dragon, to water-borne operations by first fitting Fairchild metal floats and water rudders, via a wire-braced metal framework of struts to hard points on the lower fuselage. A dorsal fillet was fitted ahead of the fin, to compensate for the aerodynamic effect of the long floats, and a luggage door was fitted on the starboard fuselage side, opposite the passenger door. Seating was arranged for five passengers, using the standard de Havilland dark blue leather seats and grey interior trim, with a toilet and luggage compartments. Electric inertia starters and heated air intakes were fitted to the otherwise standard Gipsy Major engines and a "heating device" was fitted in the cabin, presumably fed by hot air from mufflers around the exhausts. The propellers fitted had finer pitch than standard in order to provide better take-off performance, but this made for a slower than normal cruising speed. The fuselage was given extra protection against the wet environment with a nitro-cellulose finish.

RAAF female groundcrew unfolding the wings of A34-70 c/n 2059, No1 W&G School, Ballarat, 1943. *[RAAF]*

Apparently the water handling characteristics were good, helped by the twin engines and water rudders on each float. Control was reported as excellent at low speeds, and spray from the floats onto engine and fuselage on take off and landing was minimal. The floats made some difference to the flight handling characteristics but turns against a single live engine could be made without difficulty. On one engine, the Dragon could maintain 1,000 feet at 4,200 lbs, some 300 lbs below its maximum weight. In this configuration, the Seaplane cruised at 95 mph and had a creditable maximum range of 475 miles to dry tanks, using the maximum 60 gallons of fuel.

SMITH'S AIRCRAFT INSTRUMENTS DEVELOPMENTS
One unique development of a Dragon, Mk II G-ADOS, was bought in September 1935 by S Smith and Sons, the well-known aircraft instrument manufacturers trading as Smith's Aircraft Instruments. It was flown down to Heston, where it was fitted out by Airwork with a remarkable range of radios and many of the company's own equipment and instruments, to be flown by Hugh Samuelson as a demonstrator and test aircraft. Included for the engines were "Record" electrical rpm indicators, together with oil temperature and pressure gauges, mounted as before, on the engine top cowlings. The standard flight instruments were augmented by a useful electrical fuel gauge and a "fore and aft" and a "cross" level, both of which were supplanted by easier-to-interpret artificial horizons in later years. An altimeter incorporating a "pressure gauge"; an Air Speed Indicator; a rate of climb indicator and a turn indicator made up a much more modern instrument panel than usual for an aircraft of the mid nineteen thirties. Also unusual for the period, was a very bulky Smiths three-axis autopilot, which took up the area normally used by two passenger seats at the right hand rear of the cabin floor, and this had a myriad of tubes running up to the cockpit and to various control boxes. At the forward end of the cabin sat a long table, above which was an internal ADF radio aerial system, a Standard long wave radio transmitter and receiver, and a seat for the operator. The final luxuries from the instrument flying viewpoint were a Lorenz blind-landing system and a nose-mounted landing light.

A Williamson Eagle survey camera was fitted, which looked downwards through a hole in one side of the fuselage floor; a floor-mounted navigational drift sight was fitted on the other side, and a Wimperis course-setting bomb sight could be fitted in place of the Williamson camera.

In order to provide sufficient power for all this extra equipment, three extra generators were needed - one each in the normal position on the top wing roots, with a third one under the centre fuselage.

Smiths Aircraft Instruments kept G-ADOS at Heston, from where Airwork operated it on demonstrations in Britain and on the continent until 1940. Still with most of the equipment on board, the aircraft was impressed into RAF service in June 1942, appropriately enough, to No 3 School of General Reconnaissance at Squires Gate, but only lasted for two weeks before being written-off in a landing accident at Squires Gate on 24 June.

AUSTRALIAN PRODUCTION - MARK III
During World War Two, the Royal Australian Air Force had an increasing requirement for more radio and navigation training

Australian-built Dragon A34-59, returned to RAAF colours in 1986. *[J F Hamlin]*

aircraft, as the Dragons they had impressed into service from civilian companies were insufficient for the task. They wanted to buy new Rapides which could better cope with the higher temperatures and rigours of Australian operations, but de Havilland were unable to increase supplies of that type, with all their other wartime commitments. The Australian government therefore looked at finding new Dragons, which could use the Gipsy Major engines already being produced in Australia by Holden Motors for a Tiger Moth contract. De Havilland suggested that the relatively simple airframes could be built by de Havilland Australia, and the engines could come from increased production at Holden's factory. An order was therefore placed in September 1941 with de Havilland Aircraft Pty Ltd for an initial 50 Dragons, to be built at their Bankstown factory, near Sydney. A second order was placed in January 1942 for another 37. This aircraft was to be a utility machine, very similar to the British Mark I version, but with a few small changes. The cabin windows would be the continuous "glasshouse" type, and the usual wooden bulkhead immediately behind the pilot would be replaced by a tubular steel diagonal bracing strut. There would be no wheel spats and some of the navigation trainers had deeper rear windows and a small wind-driven generator on the top wing root. In service, most Dragons also had the top section of the cockpit glazing covered in fabric, to give the pilot some protection from the sun.

Luckily, all the jigs and tooling for the British Dragons were still at Hatfield, so they were promptly despatched to Bankstown, together with all the drawings, and the first Australian Dragon flew from Bankstown on 29 September 1942. The Australian version was usually referred to as the DH Type 84 Dragon Mark III. Despite the factories building both engines and airframes exactly to the DH specification, the performance was not as expected, and it took some time to tweak the rigging to obtain any sort of performance on one engine. It would also appear that the government and the RAAF had a slightly different view of the use to which their new aircraft would be put, as the factory turned out only eleven for the Wireless and Gunnery Schools; 30 for the Air Navigation Schools; 42 for transport squadrons and 4 for ambulance duties.

The last Dragon III was delivered from Bankstown to the RAAF on 28th June 1943. Several were later converted by Australian National Airlines at Melbourne (Essendon) to ambulance aircraft, with four stretchers and two seats for attendants, and in some cases, a large water tank in the roof.

The RAAF thus became by far the largest user of the DH 84, with the rather surprising total of 98 aircraft taken on charge, made up of the eleven impressed into military service and the 87 built from new by DH Australia. Of these, 42 were written-off in RAAF use but the type continued in military service until late 1945 and the fifty six survivors were all sold off to civilian operators in 1946, often for as little as £50. The second production aircraft, now VH-SNB, is on permanent display at The Museum of Flight, East Fortune, outside Edinburgh.

ITALIAN IMITATION

A rather intriguing aircraft appeared in Italy in 1934, which bore a striking resemblance to the Dragon. It was the Breda 44, and was reputedly a development of the DH 84, with a very similar fuselage, empennage and undercarriage, but with different wings and with 130 hp Alfa Romeo S63 engines. It was designed by Eng. Panzeri, and first flew in the spring of 1934, but after trials, the large, low-powered engines were reportedly replaced by 185 hp Gipsy Majors. There were of course no Majors of that power in 1934, so it may be that the most powerful Major which became available in 1935, the 140 hp Gipsy Major 1C, was actually the engine fitted. Eighteen Model 44s were produced by Breda, with most being used either on African passenger services by Ala Littoria or by the Italian Air Force, although three were exported to the Paraguayan Air Force.

An early example of the Breda 44, showing many similarities to the Dragon. *[M Stroud]*

An engineer hand-swinging Royal Dragon G-ACGG c/n 6025 in a Swanage field after a precautionary landing, 1934. [DHMC]

Section 2 – Chapter 4: Flight Comments

WHAT IS IT LIKE TO FLY?

Being a relatively basic design, with low-powered engines and high aspect ratio wings, the Dragon is fairly easy to fly. There are no systems to complicate matters, apart from the brakes, which are really only there to help with taxying in strong winds, and have little effect on landing. On the early aircraft, starting is very much the same as with a Tiger Moth, as both engines need to be primed from outside, by lifting the starboard cowling, then pressing the carburetter float button. Several turns of the propeller will suck fuel into the carburetters and the engine will be ready to start. All the pilot has to do is switch on the appropriate magneto switches and the groundcrewman swings the propeller.

Taxying the Dragon is straightforward in light winds, and the view ahead and to the sides is excellent, but the task becomes progressively more tricky as the surface wind increases, particularly when taxying across wind, as the aircraft is prone to weather-cocking into wind at even moderate speeds. The control column has to be held back to prevent the tail from rising, and the throttles moved continuously and often independently to keep the aircraft moving. There is insufficient rudder authority at slow speed to turn the aircraft, and only a castoring tailwheel, so differential brake has to be used, with rudder and brake in combination, and the brakes cannot usually be left partially applied in this situation. Unfortunately, the long brake lever is operated by the same hand as the throttles. A solution found by the old hands on the Dragon, as on the similarly configured Rapide, was to hold the control wheel back with the inside of the right elbow, then stretch the right hand over to move the throttle levers as necessary, while using the left hand on the brake lever, pulling it on and releasing it as the brakes take effect.

With so few instruments, the take-off checks are simple and quick. Wind direction is always critical with aircraft of this era, and the Dragon is very sensitive to crosswinds on take-off and landing, with a large keel surface and relatively little rudder authority at slow speeds. Take-offs into wind on grass runways are just what the Dragon likes, but attempting cross-wind take-offs on hard runways requires rapid yet sensitive hand- and foot-work. To aggravate the handling, the Gipsy Major engines both turn in the same direction, so compounding the turning moment to the right, when the maximum of around twice 2000 rpm is applied. Some pilots recommend leading with starboard throttle, slightly ahead of the port, to counteract this tendency, so enabling a straight take-off run to be achieved. Some rudder control becomes available soon after full power is gained, and can be used to counteract any drift or wind effect. The tail is lifted soon after achieving full power, and the take-off speed of around 55 mph reached soon afterwards. Climb-out on full power is quite comfortable at five mph above the single engine safety speed of 65 mph, and if an engine should fail, 70 mph should at least keep the aircraft level, or even achieve a slight climb at lower weights, until a landing can be made. Holding this single-engine speed is critical to achieving the best chance of climbing with a failed engine, and if conditions allow, a climbing speed of 80 mph gives a nice margin of safety.

Cruising in the Dragon is simplicity itself, and 1,950 rpm will give 105 to 108 mph for a consumption of around 7 gallons per hour at maximum weight. Instrument monitoring is pretty basic, with only engine rpm, oil pressure and fuel contents to watch, together with height and speed. The aircraft is well harmonised and can be trimmed at all speeds to fly "hands off". Apart from trimming and navigation, little else needs attention in the cruise. It is wise to be aware of a potential engine failure which will require careful flying to maintain height, as well as calculating the maximum remaining endurance, as a single live engine will be using around 9 gallons per hour, and there is no cross-feed facility.

Having no flaps or airbrakes, the Dragon is a surprisingly slippery machine, and short-field landings require an early reduction of

Torquil Norman landing G-ECAN c/n 2048 at the 2003 DHMC Woburn Abbey rally. [Gretton]

N43DH c/n 6096 in Chrisair colours over the American countryside, 1981. [G. Bain]

speed to 75 mph (at maximum weight); some old hands say as low as 65 mph. "Tail-down wheelers" are the landings favoured by most pilots and if the speed is correct at touch-down, reasonably short landings can be achieved. The favoured runways are into-wind and grass-surfaced, where you can achieve the most precise landings. Hard runways seldom have a direct headwind, and this makes the Dragon more skittish directionally, needing a level, "wheeler" type of touch down, on the main wheels. The square-tipped wing is not prone to tip stalling on landing, as with some tapered-wing DH aircraft, so in smooth air, slow touch down speeds are relatively safe, but as soon as the tail is lowered onto the ground, the aircraft can rapidly "weathercock" into the wind. Reliance on the brakes for shortening the landing run is unwise, because of their general ineffectiveness but in most cases, the landing run should be about 300 yards without their use.

Pilot Comments - Captain John Holmwood

In the opinion of a contemporary commercial Dragon pilot, Captain John Holmwood, flying Dragon II G-ADDI from Squires Gate airfield at Blackpool, it would perform

".... like a farm tractor - just take it out, fly it, refuel it and put it away again".

Captain Holmwood likens it to a Tiger Moth in flight, with much attention being needed to using rudder for properly-balanced turns and changes of power and speed. When taking off and landing straight into a headwind, everything was easy, particularly given the view from the glasshouse in the nose.

"It fairly leapt off the ground when empty and went up like a lift in the strong sea breeze at Squires Gate. On either side there seemed to be masses of struts and wires, and the note of the two Gipsies when synchronised was music indeed. Flying this aeroplane was a sheer delight. Take offs were achieved with little or no tendency to swing. With the throttles open the tail rose into the flying attitude and the Dragon's 376 square feet of wing floated it off the ground. Only with a full load was there any necessity to push the wheel forward to get the tail up. Glide approaches at 80 mph resulted in fairly long floats across the aerodrome before the rumble of the undercarriage showed that the wheels were there. Since there are no flaps, the only way to get a reasonably short landing run was to carefully nail the speed at 70 mph, when a three-point landing could be made, with brakes, in about 200 yards.

"Being sensitive to weather-cocking into wind at slow speeds, the take-off technique with any sort of cross wind is to lead with 'up-wind' throttle, feeding in the other throttle as speed increases, and as the rudder gains more authority. The brakes are of little use at any speed, as they were only usable to assist with steering on the ground and also means that landing in a cross-wind presents problems with keeping straight on the landing roll.

"Gusty cross-winds are the most awkward landing conditions for the Dragon. The aircraft could be crabbed with rudder into the wind, or flown with the into-wind wing down in order to achieve the correct track over the ground, but the aircraft has poor directional control as soon as the power is decreased, with little

Chrisair's G-ADDI c/n 6096 landing after another joyriding trip at Rochester, 1964. *[M Stroud]*

Paul van Longkussen demonstrating EI-ABI c/n 6105 over Littlehampton, 1998.

[G. Bain]

C/n 6105 G-AECZ at Biggin Hill 1948 with the Wiltshire School of Flying before becoming EI-ABI. [C Holland]

JJ Sullivan taxying EI-ABI into the Woburn Abbey park, DHMC Rally, 2000. [DHMC]

Stan Smith taxying ZK-AXI c/n 2057 at Ardmore, March 2003. *[DHMC]*

airflow over the rudder surface. The 'wheeler landing' technique, touching down on the mainwheels while in a horizontal attitude, is the only practical way of managing landings in these conditions. This technique, combined with asymmetric throttle handling, keeps some power on the into-wind side, provides reasonable controllability on the roll-out.."

EI-ABI, JJ Sullivan
Of the two airworthy Dragons in Europe, Aer Lingus' delightful EI-ABI is the one seen most over the past nineteen years and the first pilot to fly '*Iolar*' after refurbishment, was Captain JJ Sullivan, at that time a Boeing 747 captain with his country's airline. 'JJ' described his thoughts on flying the Dragon:

"In March 1985 John Molloy suggested to me that we should try to get the Aer Lingus DH84 restored for the 50th anniversary coming up in May 1986. I approached the company and after some hesitancy we got clearance to go ahead and were allocated a budget for our group of voluntary helpers from the Aer Lingus workshops. It was always exciting when I returned from a flight to go straight to the hangar to check the progress.

"EI-ABI is a Mark II Dragon, named '*Iolar*', Gaelic for Eagle, has a max gross weight of 4,500 Ibs and an empty weight of 2,336 lbs. After restoration we reduced the max take off weight to 3,800 lbs and we also restrict the load to 4 passengers out of respect for the old lady.

"On 10th April 1986, the aircraft made its first test flight with myself, and Johnny as engineer. She floated into the air at 55mph, climbed at about 500 fpm and attained 105mph at 1,950 rpm in the cruise. Approach speed 70mph, reducing to 60mph over the hedge. We had the engines reconditioned to zero hours 4 years ago and they now have 300 hours on them. The instrument panel and engine instruments are as original and the only mod to be carried out was to fit a 'windy' generator to charge the battery and to power the transponder required by ATC, plus a modern 720-channel radio, tucked away out of sight. All navigation is carried out in good VFR conditions and helped by a hand-held GPS.

"With experience on the type, the aircraft is very pleasant to fly. In ways she is very like the Tiger Moth, with her requirement for good rudder control at all times otherwise that big Reid & Sigrist (Turn and Bank Indicator) will quickly draw attention to what a poor pilot you are.

"I now have about 200 hours on EI-ABI and I totally enjoy flying her but at all times treat her with the respect she demands. She dislikes hard runways and three-point landings should not be attempted on them. On grass she is at home and loves to three-point. Her other big demand is a good approach - she is a 'floater' on approach and needs good speed control to get the touch-down point correct."

ZK-AXI, Stan Smith
Having spent 20 years restoring his Australian-built Dragon III in New Zealand, ZK-AXI, Stan Smith knows it inside and out and has spent many hours flying this aircraft, now fitted with more powerful Gipsy Major 10 Mark 2 engines. His comments about the tests he completed in 1997, after completely refurbishing the aircraft, are interesting when compared with comments from pilots of the early machines:

"My initial reaction to flying the Dragon was 'What a weird aeroplane!' There is no attitude reference and you have to watch the VSI all the time. That and the big Reid and Sigrist turn-and bank are the most used instruments. Rather than the pilot flying, it is a feeling of sitting in the pulpit pontificating. There are three main problems: the aeroplane does not take off, it levitates; it does not fly, it makes stately progress; and it is not landed, it does that all by itself.

"In descent the drag is such that the nose attitude determines the rate of descent rather than the speed. It is very light on the controls which just need subtle pressure and like so many pre-war designs the proper use of rudder is essential. The four ailerons, one on the end of each long wing, are so effective they are not used much, and cause massive aileron drag anyway. It has to be kept straight or there is a snatch, an occasional judder.

"On our Maximum All Up Weight test, with the cabin filled with sandbags for ballast, I started the single-engine climb test at 1,500 feet [at 70 mph and 2,200 rpm on the live engine] and was still going up. After five minutes I was at 1,900 feet and I found I could just maintain 3,000 feet. Mind you, that was a rare 1038 millibar day. In ISA conditions it will hold 700 to 800 feet, with a 200 ft/min descent at 2,000 feet."

Ted Hillman with one of his Puss Moths G-ABVX at Maylands airfield in 1933. *[CND]*

Section 2 – Chapter 5: First Commercial Users

AN AIR BUS FOR HILLMAN

"The de Havilland Aircraft Co. Ltd. is designing, to the order of Hillman's Saloon Coaches and Airways, a six-passenger twin-engined biplane which will be known as the type DH 84. Hitherto Mr Hillman has concentrated on operating a very successful domestic airline and taxi-service from his aerodrome at Romford with a fleet of single-engined D.H. Puss Moths and Fox Moths, but his order for a number of twin-engined aeroplanes would suggest that Mr Hillman has plans to extend his operations to points abroad. Persistent rumour says that he intends next year to sell return tickets to Paris at £5 per head - or seat."

This note in the normally accurate *Aeroplane* aviation magazine for September 21 1932 suggested that de Havilland were building the Dragon specifically for Ted Hillman's small airline, but the rest of the information was accurate, except that the Paris service standard return fare, when it was announced in April the following year, was £5.10 shillings!

Ted Hillman was an anomaly in the commercial aviation world of the thirties, but he certainly played a major role in the rapidly-expanding British commercial aviation world. He was the son of a farmer in Essex, had little formal education, and joined the army as a young man. Having served throughout the First World War, he was demobilised in 1918 at the age of 29, having achieved the rank of Warrant Officer - an indication of his strength of character and his skill with people and organisation. He then took several different directions including bicycle repairer and chauffeur, until, in July 1928, he bought his first coach to take holiday makers from the industrial areas around north-east London to the coastal beaches at Clacton-on-Sea. His tremendous energy, strong but rather blunt personality and desire to get best value out of all his business efforts helped to make this business a rapid success. By 1931, he had 300 coaches, but then came up against new government curbs and was forced to sell up his coach business to allow the nationalised coach service to flourish. At least he was able to benefit from £145,000 (about £4.3 million in 2003) as compensation. In November 1931, he took over a former joy-riding field at Maylands Farm, near Romford and started flying customers to Clacton in a de Havilland Puss Moth. In the following spring, he bought two DH Fox Moths, and used all four seats of these to whisk jaded London workers (at all of 100 mph!) on regular summer services to the seaside delights of Clacton. Renowned for being down-to-earth, Ted Hillman was not trying to emulate the state-subsidised Imperial Airways, but merely to make money by providing an economical air service without frills. Like Imperial, he employed mostly ex-military pilots, but his were mainly ex-non commissioned officers, because he paid them only slightly more than he had paid his bus drivers. He did not want "high falutin' pilots or toffee-nosed flying hostesses" or anything that would increase his costs. When shown by the sales staff at Stag Lane the various DH 84 cabin layouts, which included a "lavatory, interchangeable with the sixth seat", together with their prices, he is reported to have remarked "What, another thirty five quid for a bleedin' ****house!" He did, however, show enough interest in his crews' problems to learn to fly, and occasionally acted as a ferry pilot in order to keep the operation running.

Hillman initially ordered four Dragons for use on his planned Paris service and, rather surprisingly, paid the list price of "£2,800 per machine, plus Scheme Six cabin furnishing of six Comfortable

G-ACAN c/n 6000 at Redhill in 1940, after being taken over by the wartime National Air Communications organisation. *[BAe]*

Armchairs, plus interchangeable lavatory, at an extra £140 per Machine".

He took delivery of the first Dragon, the prototype G-ACAN, on 20th December 1932, and his next three, G-ACAP, G-ACAO and G-ACBW, in February, March and April, 1933, in time for his inaugural service to Paris that spring. The smooth, well-known London aviation press agent, Mr William Courtenay, who also represented and promoted the famous aviatrix, Amy Johnson, arranged for G-ACAN, the first Dragon to arrive at the Hillman base, to be met and ceremoniously named '*Maylands*' by Amy Johnson in a public ceremony. She even briefly became a director of Hillman's and occasionally flew for them.

Hillman's well-publicised Romford (Maylands) to Paris (Le Bourget) service began on 1st April 1933.They had decided to equip each with pilot-operated Marconi AD 6N radios mainly for obtaining navigational bearings, powered by a small 150-watt wind-driven generator fitted on the port lower wing, whereas most later Dragons had their generators fitted near the wing-root of an upper wing. Despite the cost, Hillman fitted toilets in addition to the six passenger seats, so his Dragons were well equipped. Chief pilot Harold 'Timber' Wood flew the first service in G-ACAN with only two passengers, and the afternoon service was flown in G-ACAP by Charles Allen. In May and June 1933, G-ACEU and G-ACEV were added to the fleet and the six-strong fleet were being used on what Hillman's somewhat cheekily called their "London-Paris, twice daily service", as well as passenger services to Castle Bromwich, and later to Liverpool.

In May 1934, the thriving airline moved into a new aerodrome a little further north at Stapleford Abbots and the Paris services were thriving, with a special day return fare of £4. 5s.(about £150 at 2004 prices). Despite the cost, a typical passenger count for one week in May 1934 on this route was 117 passengers, so the business was beginning to attract considerable attention. In addition to the continental service, the company continued to expand northwards, with daily services in conjunction with Midland and Scottish Air Ferries, to Glasgow and Belfast, which connected to the Paris service. With an expanding fleet and route structure, Hillman's Airways became a public company in December 1934 but sadly, a bare two weeks after that event, the entrepreneurial Ted Hillman died of a heart attack at the early age of 45. Whilst his son Edward 'Sonny' Hillman joined the board, and Major R McCrindle became chairman, soon afterwards, in September 1935, the company was acquired by Whitehall Securities and lost its identity when at the end of the year, it was amalgamated with British Continental, United Airways, and Spartan, into the first British Airways.

PRIVATE WEST COUNTRY ENDEAVOUR – NORMAN EDGAR (WESTERN AIRWAYS)

In September of 1933, another typically imaginative operation was set up at Bristol's Whitchurch airfield. Norman Edgar, de Havilland's local concessionaire, formed Norman Edgar (Western Airways) Ltd, having just bought a new Dragon G-ACJT. He believed that a shuttle air service from Bristol to Cardiff across the Bristol Channel was ideal for an eight-passenger aircraft, as the two cities were just fifteen minutes apart by air but several hours by road. Trial services had been carried out a year previously, using Fox Moths and the Norman Edgar Dragon service quickly proved popular. The company expanded with services to Bournemouth on the south coast the following May. In June 1935, another Dragon, G-ACAO was taken on, and two more, G-ACMJ and G-ACPX in July and September 1936 with the routes expanding to take in Le Touquet and Paris. By 1938 the company had a fleet of five Dragons, following the purchase of Dragon Mk II G-AECZ (which still exists today as EI-ABI). Then in February the company was taken over by the Straight Corporation, with a change of name in October to Western Airways. The next year saw an increase in services to Birmingham and Manchester, and other destinations in the west country, following a move to Weston-super-Mare, west of Bristol in 1936. In order to keep pace with the increasing number

G-ACMJ c/n 6058 at Western-super-Mare in 1938 when with Western Airways. *[CND]*

A delightful view of c/n 6027 G-ACFG over The Great Glen, when with Northern & Scottish Airways, 1934. *[DHMC]*

of passengers, Western had purchased three Rapides in mid 1937, with a further example in 1939 together with an Express Air Liner and a Dragonfly, making Western Airways the only company which operated all four of the types covered by this book. Other Dragons operated included G-ACAP and G-ACLE and all four types were used until the operations were closed down and the whole fleet requisitioned in March 1940, leaving only the maintenance side of the company to operate during the war.

SCOTTISH MOTOR TRACTION AND MIDLAND & SCOTTISH AIR FERRIES

In a remarkably similar way to the activities of Ted Hillman, another ambitious and enterprising coach operator up in Ayr in Scotland, John Cuthill Sword, also decided that air transport held great promise for the future. He had previously built up Midland Bus Services in southwest Scotland in the 1920s and merged this into Scottish Motor Traction, (SMT) in 1929, following which he was appointed director to manage their Western Area, operating 509 buses in the Glasgow and Ayr areas. In 1932, he persuaded the SMT board that investing in air transport would be a good move and, with two de Havilland Fox Moths, an air taxi and charter operation was started in July. A further eight Fox Moths were bought in 1933. By this time, however, in December 1932, Sword had formed his own separate operation, Midland & Scottish Air Ferries (MSAF), which commenced operations from Glasgow Moorpark in February 1933 with an Airspeed Ferry and a fleet of four more Fox Moths. Sword recognised the Dragon as the next step up and, wearing his SMT hat, two Dragons, G-ACDM and 'DN were ordered and delivered to the new SMT base at Turnhouse, near Edinburgh in May 1933, to be followed in June by G-ACET.

Meanwhile, at MSAF, he bought Dragons G-ACCZ and G-ACDL, also delivered in May, to be followed by G-ACJS in August. This latter Sword had fitted with six seats and a radio operator's seat and equipment, and used as his own personal transport, complete with "personalised" registration. The MSAF Dragons were used alongside their Fox Moths, and several other types, to operate charter and ambulance flights around western Scotland and daily scheduled flights from Glasgow to Campbeltown and the island of Islay. By mid-1934, the MSAF Dragons were also being used for an extended route from Glasgow to Belfast which Sword called "The Irish Scot", and then another service to Stornoway in the Western Isles. Rapid expansion continued later the same year with several services from a second base at Liverpool to Dublin, the Isle of Man and Blackpool, and other connecting flights with Sword's good friend Ted Hillman's services from Romford. They were also discussing joint services with the Dutch airline KLM. By the end of 1933, MSAF had carried 10,000 passengers, and they made plans to increase this to 50,000 in 1934.

London to Belfast in G-ACDL

A journalist's journey from London to Belfast, made in MSAF's second Dragon, G-ACDL, in the spring of 1934, gives an indication of the passenger's viewpoint. This was the first of a scheduled service jointly managed by Hillman's and Midland and Scottish, with a refuelling stop at Liverpool's Speke.

After breakfast in London, five passengers were collected at 7 am by a Hillman's coach from Kings Cross railway station and sped up to the East London airfield at Romford. Here they boarded the Midland Dragon, departing into a rainy sky at 8 am. As the aircraft cruised at 1,000 feet across the damp English countryside, the passengers employed themselves looking outside and identifying the towns they passed along the route. Following a good view of the Mersey River, they arrived at Speke one hour and forty-five minutes after take off, to meet their pilot for the next leg and down some light refreshment. The Belfast sector was flown in the same aircraft, this time with only three passengers, but the comment was made that "complete confidence was felt in putting out over 70 miles of open sea in a Dragon. The Gipsy Major has such a fine record, and the loading is arranged so that if one motor did fail, the machine could continue at an airspeed of 70-75 mph".

Fifty-three minutes after take off, the Dragon landed on the Isle of Man's grass field at Ronaldsway, amongst grazing cows. Two passengers were offloaded at Ronaldsway's cottage "terminal", and the Dragon was airborne again an impressive eight minutes after landing, en route to the RAF airfield at Aldergrove, west of Belfast. This time the route took the aircraft 500 feet above the top of the island's hills, then it was back down to 1,000 feet above the Irish Sea to Strangford Lough, 32 miles away. Overflying Belfast city on the way to Aldergrove airport, the Dragon climbed again over the hills to the west of Belfast before reaching the city's only airport. In August 1934, Lord Londonderry's small grass field at Newtownards, on the northern edge of Strangford Lough, was opened and used by MSAF, which made the journey to Belfast considerably quicker.

Despite a half-hour car journey into Belfast, a lunch was still taken in the city, with enough time to drive back out to the airfield to catch the Dragon's scheduled departure for Liverpool and London. Arrival back at Romford was just after six in the evening, which then allowed our passenger to reach London again in time for dinner. The average speed for this trip worked out at around 100 mph, including the stops at Ronaldsway.

It seems that the passengers on this round trip were more concerned about finding out where they were on their cross-country flight than they were about the comfort of the seats or the cabin. The only criticism voiced was that the airline provided no simple route maps they could use to identify their position over the ground. Another suggestion was that all towns should have large sign-posts, so air passengers (and even pilots) could identify the places they passed, "especially when the weather was thick".

This single trip from Romford to Belfast had only taken three hours and twenty four minutes, including stops at Liverpool and Ronaldsway, which was about seven hours less than the direct journey would have taken by rail and ferry, and saved the inconvenience of an overnight sea crossing. While the time for the round trip may have been a great improvement over surface travel, however, the cost of the return flight, at £10 (about £340 in current values), was more than twice that for the first-class rail and ferry journey.

Sword's management of both the bus and two competing air transport operations soon began to give rise to serious internal issues and conflicts of interest. Indeed, the two fleets sometimes became mixed, with two, G-ACDN and G-ACET, actually transferred from SMT to MSAF ownership. Despite his very successful initiation of MSAF, John Sword was still employed by SMT, and the railway-orientated board and shareholders of that company gave him the ultimatum of remaining as SMT's Western general manager and stopping his aviation activities, or resigning from SMT. Sword, being basically a motor-transport man, and realising that Railway Air Services were beginning to take a strong hold on the west coast and Scottish air services, agreed in July 1934 to cease all his and SMT's air operations and sell the aircraft, including G-ACRI , which had only been bought by SMT in May. Sadly, this meant the end of a very promising operation and all the Dragons had been sold to other operators by mid-1935.

JERSEY AIRWAYS

Another of the Thirties' most interesting examples of commercial enterprise in the air transport field involved Dragons as a key element. The island of Jersey, 100 miles south of the English coast, and the largest of the three main Channel Islands, had long been a venue for business and holiday travellers, but the Southern Railways' combined rail and boat connections were slow, inconvenient and expensive. A return journey from St Peter Port to Southampton cost £3. 6s. 9d (£3.34p) in 1933, and took ten hours, given fair weather. The Island's Chamber of Commerce had considered the idea of creating an airport on Jersey for several years, but much talking between interested parties had produced no results.

Jersey Airways 'Rozel Bay' G-ACNJ c/n 6072 airborne on a proving flight from Hatfield, Spring 1934. *[S Clark]*

Then, quite unexpectedly, in late 1933, at the same time that Ted Hillman was taking delivery of his first DH 84, another larger-than-life coach owner operating from Hillman's neighbouring county, Hertfordshire, was becoming embroiled in the government's mandatory licensing of 'bus and coach operations. Walter Thurgood had decided that his People's Motor Services could not compete with the London Transport Board's services, and sold out in November 1933. It so happened that a Jersey businessman, Louis Greig, became so convinced that such a service could succeed commercially, that he persuaded his friend Thurgood that the future lay in investing in air travel, and that the Channel Islands were just the place to start. The fact that Thurgood suddenly had around £200,000 available made the decision to create a new transport business easier!

The two moved quickly, registering "Jersey Airways Limited" with the Jersey Royal Court on 9th December 1933, and ordering from Stag Lane, two Mark I Dragons (G-ACMC and G-ACMJ), to be followed in early 1934 by another six (G-ACMO-ACMP and G-ACNG-ACNJ), this time the latest "1934 type DH 84s", later referred to as the DH 84 Mark II. Quickly poaching Scottish Motor Traction's dour chief pilot, Captain Bill Caldwell, to run the flying side, Thurgood moved rapidly. At a very early hour on 15th December he took over the log books of G-ACMJ, already named '*St Aubin's Bay*', from Mr Ward of the DH Sales Department, then Captain Caldwell flew them down to Portsmouth to check the Channel Islands weather, and to clear customs for the first route-proving flight of Jersey Airways Limited. After being joined by Mr Greig and one other passenger, Caldwell flew down to the beach at St Aubin's Bay, next to the port of St Helier, the only landplane landing site on the island, taking just under an hour for the flight. As none of the team had landed there before, and the mile-long, sandy beach revealed occasional rocks and soft patches when the tide was out, Captain Caldwell flew down low, looking for the best area on which to land, before opening up and completing a circuit to the south over Elizabeth Castle, descending over the harbour, and landing alongside the wall of the Victoria Promenade.

This first Jersey Airways proving flight took place within days of the registration of the airline, and only a bare three days before the first public service was due to start, on 18th December - an incredibly optimistic achievement in any business, and one almost unimaginable in the aviation business, even in those pioneering days.

A sceptical official view of this service was presented to his masters by the local Portsmouth Air Ministry Inspector, whose report after an early inspection of Jersey Airways facilities, said that Thurgood "shows complete ignorance of matters aeronautical; relies entirely on his pilots and engineers, and did not see any reason why it should be more difficult to operate an air service than it was to maintain a bus service between two adjacent towns. I fear we shall have just as much trouble with him as we have experienced with Messrs Hillman and Scottish Motor Traction".

So much for official support of struggling new airlines!

But these three airlines did in fact learn pretty quickly, building up practical and profitable businesses in the years before World War Two, until their successors were eventually metamorphosed into British European Airways in 1947.

Air Ministry Concerns

An interesting situation related to the Dragon's performance developed when the combative Air Ministry inspector at Portsmouth seems to have spent a goodly part of the next two years following up his prophesy of "trouble" with Jersey Airways. Back in March 1933, de Havilland had demonstrated to the aviation press that the Dragon was able to at least maintain height on one engine at a weight close to its maximum. The Air Ministry's own certification report of December 1932 from Martlesham Heath also pronounced the DH 84 "capable of maintaining level flight at 1,000 feet on one engine". However, despite 4,200 lbs being accepted by the Air Ministry as the maximum allowable weight of the Dragon, there were still apparently unquantifiable concerns in some areas of the Ministry about the safety of the aircraft at that weight. These concerns were to drag on for many months, the main protagonists being the Portsmouth Air Ministry inspector versus Mr Greig, who had become the General Manager of Jersey Airways, the latter supported by Francis St Barbe at de Havilland.

Soon after Jersey Airways had begun their Dragon services in December 1933, the Air Ministry inspector issued a statement to the airline that as they had had two engine failures on this route, a decrease in maximum weight for their over-sea routes to 3,850 lbs was recommended. This weight restriction appears to have been an arbitrary figure, being simply the Ministry's estimate of the Dragon's capability. As this restriction would mean decreasing their payload by up to two passengers, Greig wrote back to the Ministry saying that as it was only a recommendation, he would not accept it for commercial reasons. At Stag Lane, Francis St Barbe took up the case, and wrote to the airline stating that it was an indisputable fact that the prototype Dragon, G-ACAN, with a weight of 4,200 lbs, maintained 1,000 feet on one engine during the Air Ministry performance trials at Martlesham Heath in November 1932. The Ministry had officially accepted 4,200 lbs as the maximum weight for the Dragon Mark I, with no restrictions being placed on single engine weights or performance.

Despite this rebuttal by de Havillands, the Air Ministry inspector and his masters in London remained very concerned about the safety of the Dragon, in the event of single engine failure over water. The basis for their concern could not be quantified, so for the moment, they had to accept the logic of de Havilland and Jersey Airways, and allowed the airline to continue unrestricted operations. A close watch was, however, kept on the Jersey Airways loading procedures at Portsmouth over the next months and after much watching and discussing in March 1934 they required the situation to be tested, by setting up a further trial at Martlesham Heath. Jersey Airways magnanimously lent their first Dragon, G-ACMJ, for the tests, which were "required in order to determine the ceiling of [G-ACMJ] at various weights, with one engine stopped and the airscrew stationary".

Unfortunately for the operator, the trials, beginning on 13th March 1934 for a bare two days, were pretty disastrous. They were flown in the midst of the March gales sweeping the East Coast and the test report confirms that they took place in "very bumpy conditions, with a gusty wind", making readings by the pilot "erratic, [so] no consistent results were obtained". What was even more frustrating was that the trials were started, not at the maximum of 4,200lb, but at the lower weight of 3,860lb.The report stated that "tests at the greater weight were not made" because of a combination of the weather conditions and the "short period the aircraft was available". The trial could therefore only prove that in these "bumpy conditions", and at 3,860 lb, the aircraft could maintain height on one engine. Conveniently for the man from the Ministry, this weight was very close to the figure of 3,850 lbs that he had wanted to use as the maximum for over-water flights. Since the Report only referred to the maximum weight proved in the trial, this (minus 10 lb) was used for all subsequent discussions with de Havillands and Jersey Airways, requiring all DH 84 operators to limit over-water flights to this weight.

But the battle between Air Ministry and Jersey Airways was not over, as Jersey's Operations Director wrote to the Ministry requesting amplification of what the British Air Navigation Order (the legal rules for aircraft operations) actually required, stating his Dragons, at full weight, could still reach land in the event of engine failure. He did say that extra precautions would be taken, but would be pleased to receive further amplification of the requirements of the ANO. This argument took place over many months in 1934, and in the meantime, Jersey Airways continued to operate its Dragons up to maximum weight when the loads were available.

In a final masterly piece of technical logic, Francis St Barbe joined the fray again, pointing out to the Ministry in December 1934, that a Dragon Mark II, as used now by Jersey Airways, fully loaded to its newly-authorised maximum of 4,500 lbs, had a single-engined descent angle that would allow it to reach land 34 miles away from 2,000 feet, or 17 miles away from 1,000 feet. He therefore presumed that the restriction issued to Dragon operators was merely "cautionary advice". The Ministry eventually conceded that it was in fact only a warning, not an order, and the Dragon operators were in effect able to continue as before.

Despite many difficulties caused by weather, Air Ministry legislation, landing sites and mechanical problems, Jersey Airways progressed rapidly, and by the end of their first year, 1934, they had

Dragon G-ACMJ c/n 6058 attracting attention on St Aubin's Beach, Jersey, in 1935. *[BAe]*

Captain Eric Fresson handing over the first Scottish air mail, Inverness, 1934. *[CND]*

carried nearly 20,000 passengers in their eight-seat Dragons, with a splendid average of 5.32 passengers per flight. For a start-up venture which was, unlike Imperial Airways, completely unsubsidised, and which operated regularly into and out of sites notoriously affected by fog and high water, these figures are most impressive. Profits at the end of this first year were a surprising £5,150 (equivalent to around £170,000 today).

In line with the company's expansion plans, now financed by the ubiquitous Whitehall Securities, the pioneering Dragons were superseded in 1935 by the faster Dragon Rapides and Express Air Liners, and by February 1936, they had all been redeployed in other Whitehall companies.

HIGHLAND AIRWAYS

Way up in the Highlands of Scotland, Captain Eric Fresson, founder of the pioneering Inverness-based Highland Airways, enjoyed his own problems of weather and over-water flights. Formed in April 1933, Highland acquired their first of five Dragons, G-ACIT in July 1933. This was a Dragon Mark 1, and survives to this day, displayed at The Science Museum at Wroughton

The adventuring spirit of Eric Fresson and his team is reflected in the story of a Highland Airways flight arrival at Wick, on the Northern Scottish coast.

Low Cloud at Wick, 1935

One of Highland Airways' pilots, Captain Adam Smith, who had joined the airline in October 1935, was a bold young pilot who obviously felt that getting the job done was his most important objective, despite all the obstacles put in his way. The 25-year-old Smith tells of a typical weather-bound journey in G-ACIT in 1935. He was Highland's pilot based at Kirkwall on the far north Scottish island of Orkney, and was returning empty to Wick, on the mainland, on a misty winter's day. Despite a rather tricky cloud base of 50 feet at Kirkwall, he managed to take off and negotiate the short land crossing before heading south, back across the Pentland Firth to pick up some waiting passengers at Wick, for the journey down to Highland's main base at Longland, Inverness. The weather northbound had been clear, but on this southern leg over the sea, the cloud had lowered to about 100 feet over the sea. As he had no real blind-flying instruments on this basic Dragon, he found it safer to stay below cloud. The small airfield was just south-west of the cliffs of Sinclairs Bay, so he nursed the Dragon, still about 100 feet above the North Sea's surface, round the mainland to the east of Duncansby Head, towards the town of Wick, then turned south west into Sinclairs Bay, hoping the cloud would lift enough to hop over the cliffs and into the field. Unfortunately, the base remained a solid 100 feet all the way in, and as he later reported: "The only trouble was the field was 150 feet high, and the cliffs 200 feet." But "Having no passengers, I decided to have a go, and headed straight for the cliffs. After five months on that route, even the wave formations were familiar, so, about 50 yards from the cliff face, at full throttle, wheel hard back, into cloud, eyes tight shut for concentration. I closed the throttles after three seconds and slowed down to just above stalling speed. Jupiter Pluvius must have been sitting on that cloud, because he brushed it aside for an instant to show me a hawthorn hedge three feet below. This told me that we were at the second field, as the first had a wire fence. We trundled over 15 fields, hopping each hedge, luckily with no cows in the way, to land safely on the 17th,, our landing ground".

That is typical of the way the pioneers on the Scottish islands routes occasionally had to use their aircraft, and was the only way they could maintain any kind of service in the poor winter weather conditions. There are not many aircraft that one would dare to use in that way.

Winter in the Highlands and Islands produced strong winds in abundance, with very powerful westerlies blowing in low cloud from the Atlantic. Captain Smith's most memorable flight from his time with Highland, was in G-ADCT in 1936. The small island of North Ronaldsay, in the Orkneys, had had four weeks of extreme weather that Autumn, with high winds and heavy seas, and neither ships nor aircraft could bring desperately needed food for the islanders. The Orkney-based Captain Smith was called to help. While he knew the wind was likely to be well above his normal landing speed over the island's landing strip, he persuaded his engineer to load up the Dragon with sacks of bread, butter, flour, sugar, tea (of course), and medications, in an attempt to drop these on the island. Whilst he would be unable to land, the engineer might be able to release the cargo over the strip. For the 35-mile northbound flight to the island, the pilot struggled, through the gale

Dragon c/n 6075 G-ACPX on the Croydon apron, when with Railway Air Services, 1934. *[CND]*

force, turbulent winds for a very long 90 minutes. He recalled the special landing technique learned by Eric Fresson which was to approach the centre of the strip at a height of around 50 feet, then, with selective use of power, allow the aircraft to descend almost vertically, keeping the nose slightly down, until the aircraft touched down, and the waiting strong men were able to grab hold of wings, struts and tailplane, to prevent it lifting off again with successive gusts. Only then could the pilot allow the tail to come down, hoping to keep the aircraft on the ground.

In this case, he did not plan to land, but merely to deposit the provisions before climbing away back to his base. On reaching the centre of the landing strip, he descended into wind, then, still with three-quarter throttles, virtually flew the aircraft into the ground at around 70 mph indicated, with the aircraft almost stationary over the ground, albeit badly battered by the gusty wind. While Captain Smith tried to keep the aircraft approximately level, the engineer dumped the stack of sacks out of the rear door, occasionally interrupted by gusts taking the aircraft bodily up to 50 feet, before the pilot could carefully fly her down again to ground level, still with considerable power on the engines. The struggling islanders managed to catch all but two of the sacks, before the gale carried them away. At that, the hard-worked pilot put on full power again, slowly climbed, almost vertically above the strip, and, when clear of all obstructions, carefully eased the Dragon's nose round to the south, to race away with wind this time, back across to Orkney.

Going south, in contrast to the 90 minutes, the trip took just over eight minutes, giving an incredible 240 mph ground speed, probably a record for a Dragon! However, his troubles were not over for he had to get his machine back into its hangar at Kirkwall. Luckily, the field at Kirkwall had enough room to allow an approach to the northwest, directly into the gale, and close as he could safely get to the hangar. He very gradually reduced power over the field, allowing another almost vertical descent towards his struggling team of twelve men, who would hang onto his wings as soon as he was down and gradually ease the bucking aircraft back into its hangar, when he could shut down the engines and the doors be forced closed. Grateful Ronaldsay Islanders later presented the gallant Captain Smith with a silver cigarette box as thanks for his efforts that dreadful autumn.

Highland operated five Dragons; G-ACIT and G-ADCT (the latter delivered in June 1935) were transferred to the new Scottish Airways when Highland merged with Northern & Scottish Airways in August 1937; G-ACCE, delivered in April 1934, crashed at Kirkwall four months later; G-ACGK, delivered in July 1934 crashed in the Moray Firth in January 1935 and finally G-ACET was delivered in September 1934 to be traded back to DH in June 1937 in part exchange for Rapide G-AEWL.

RAILWAY AIR SERVICES

By the early thirties, coach and air travel were beginning to poach British travellers from the traditional railway companies. In response, four of the largest British railway companies - Great Western (GWR), London, Midland and Scottish (LMS), London and North Eastern (LNER) and Southern (SR) - jointly decided to set up their own airline, with a minority interest being held by Imperial Airways, who did not operate internal services. This airline, Railway Air Services Limited, was formed in March 1934 and its first aircraft, a Mark II Dragon, G-ACPX, was delivered on 3 May 1934 to operate scheduled west coast services from Plymouth to Liverpool via Cardiff and Birmingham.

The Aeroplane for 8th August 1934 commented that, for Liverpool people, a holiday in Devon was now a practicality, the journey being shortened by two half days and the flight taking just over 2 hours by Dragon. "The passenger is looked after in the business-like manner so dear to the British public. Courteous direction, help with luggage, convenient motor services etc are very important to air travellers, who pay ....first class fares." For this RAS return service the fare in 1934 was £6.0.0, or just under £200 today.

RAS's first aircraft, Dragon G-ACPX looked resplendent in silver overall with striking red and green cheat lines down the fuselage sides and green registration letters outlined in red. Circular RAS badges on nose and rudder finished off this restrained but attractive colour scheme. De Havilland's Hugh Buckingham handed over the log books at Stag Lane to Major Herbert Brackley, Railway's initial operations director and also Superintendent of Imperial Airways. This post was transferred to Wing Cdr Harold 'Daddy' Measures when he joined later that month. G-ACPX flew the inaugural service on 7 May1934, which became a daily route from Plymouth to Liverpool via Haldon, Cardiff and Birmingham, with the return flight leaving Birmingham at 3.30 in the afternoon.

From 1934, despite the high fares, RAS who were based at Croydon, rapidly expanded their services, to Plymouth, Cardiff, Birmingham, Liverpool, Belfast, Glasgow and the Isle of Wight. The company moved quickly on to larger aircraft, buying their first

DH 86 in August 1934, and their first DH 89 in March 1935. However, they operated seven Dragons, although some for relatively short periods. G-ACPX, G-ACVD and G-ACXI were delivered in 1934 but were sold later the same year or in 1935. Four were delivered new in 1935 - G-ADDI, G-ADDJ, G-ADED and G-ADEE and whilst the latter two were both written-off in accidents the same year, G-ADDI remained nominally in the fleet until 1938, having a long post-war joy-riding career, surviving to this day in the USA. G-ACHV was also delivered in 1935 as a replacement for G-ADED, being sold in 1936 and finally G-ACVD rejoined the fleet in 1936, to be sold to Australia in 1937.

An indication that the newly-developing internal airlines were beginning to coordinate their services was given by the fact that this new RAS service connected at Cardiff with Western Airways flights, and at Liverpool (Speke) with KLM flights. In addition to hosting RAS and KLM services, Speke was also the northern connection between Hillman's Airways, based at Romford, and their route partners Midland and Scottish Air Ferries, who used Speke as their home base.

AIR DISPATCH AND COMMERCIAL AIR HIRE, CROYDON

In 1930/31, the 35-year-old Mary, the Hon Mrs Victor Bruce, who had previously been a racing motorist, undertook a solo flight round the world in her Blackburn Bluebird, G-ABDS. The following year, she attempted to break the world endurance record in the Saro Windhover G-ABJP by using early in-flight refuelling from a pair of Bristol Fighters. In 1933, she spent from April to October flying with the British Hospitals Air Pageant, touring 150 British towns with her Fairey Fox G-ACAS, performing the terrifying vertical "Fox Dive". This very lively, adventurous and most tenacious lady happened to see an advert in *The Aeroplane* in 1934, which read "Aircraft required to carry newspapers to Paris". That sparked her interest, and after making rapid enquiries, she decided to tender for the work, despite having no organisation or aircraft suitable for the job at the time.

Surprisingly, she won the contract and on 9 July 1934, she formed Air Dispatch Limited at Croydon and began an early morning newspaper service from Croydon to Le Bourget. This service was required to leave South London by 5.00 am no matter what the weather, so that the newspapers would be on Paris breakfast tables by eight o' clock. By the end of August 1934, *Flight* was reporting that Air Dispatch were regularly flying 1,400 lbs worth of newspapers to Paris every day. With very few aids in the aircraft or on the ground, this was a risky business, but Air Dispatch seldom failed to make the deliveries in the five years it operated what was later named the "Dawn Express" to Paris.

Deciphering the facts of Mrs Bruce's convoluted business affairs has always been difficult. Her interesting autobiography "*Nine Lives Plus*" is somewhat inaccurate in places and leaves out much detail. Matters are also confused by her use of a number of different companies, including Luxury Air Tours Ltd (formed in July 1932) and Commercial Air Hire Ltd (formed in August 1934), which was either the subsidiary or parent of Air Dispatch. What does seem to be the case is that Air Dispatch's initial operations were contracted out to the short-lived Provincial Airways, also Croydon-based, which then operated two Dragons, G-ACBW and G-ACKD. By August 1934, Mrs Bruce was also operating Dragon G-ACCR, buying another Dragon, G-ACDL, in September 1934. This latter was sold to Provincial Airways in January 1935 then later bought back, in company with Provincial's G-ACBW. Various other Dragons were subsequently acquired by Air Dispatch; including G-ACAP in December 1935, G-ACKB in early 1936 and G-ACKC in April 1936. Her various companies also operated G-ACCZ, G-ACDN, G-ACEK, G-ACET, G-ACHV, G-ACKU, G-AEMI and G-AEMK - making this the largest fleet of Dragons anywhere.

Dangers of London-Paris Newspaper Flights

The Air Dispatch Dragon pilots, usually John Pugh and A P Hattersley (appointed chief pilot in August 1934), and their radio operators had to take considerable risks to keep the regular newspaper service on time, coping with night flying, low cloud and fog in particular. A very basic blind-flying panel consisting of turn and slip indicator, altimeter, airspeed indicator, magnetic compass and a crude "fore and aft level", was the only equipment the pilots had, together with a cumbersome, battery-powered direction-finding radio, operated by the aircraft's radio officer. The radio could only provide approximate bearings from the few ground radio stations then available such as Croydon, Droitwich, Le Bourget and Kalundborg in Denmark, and plotting the resulting bearings in a bouncing Dragon produced erratic results.

Typical of the difficulties experienced by the "Dawn Express" crews in those pioneering days was when one of the Dragons set off from Croydon into the misty darkness at 4 am on its ninety-minute cross-channel flight, the fuselage loaded to its maximum 4,200 lbs weight with heavy bundles of *The Times*, *The Daily Mail*, *The*

G-ACVD c/n 6084 in its Croydon hangar, 1936, when with Railway Air Services. *[M Stroud]*

Daily Herald and the *Daily Express*. Surmounting the first hurdle of the North Downs to the south of Croydon, the crew slowly eased the Dragon up above the mist, until it reached a very prudent 4,000 feet over the Kent countryside. Then, at the critical point over the Channel, approaching the French coast, and with about 80 miles to go to his destination, the pilot heard the port engine falter, run roughly for a few seconds, then fail completely. Being a conscientious pilot, he felt that if he could maintain enough height to clear the 2,300-foot hills to the south of Beauvais, he could make Le Bourget. But when he had slowed down to his single engine cruise speed of 80 mph, he was still descending, which was not very encouraging if he was to reach Paris. 'Snowy', the radio officer, was then told to dump some of the heavy newspaper bundles, in the hope of maintaining a reasonable cruising level. The *Daily Mail* went first, followed by *The Times*, and then the *Daily Herald*. Before the *Daily Express* went as well, the Dragon, labouring along with full power on the starboard engine, and having lost two thirds of its load, seemed to settle at an acceptable height and enough to clear the Beauvais hills. Despite their decreased cruising speed, Le Bourget was reached, somewhat late, but at least with an almost complete aeroplane. Of course, the only English newspaper available on the Paris breakfast tables that morning was the Daily Express.

Two Dragons from Air Dispatch's fleet, a Mark 1, G-ACDL and a Mark II, G-ACKC left Air Dispatch in more mysterious circumstances in August 1936. As the story goes, one evening, as she was about to drive off in her car, Mrs Bruce was stopped outside the Air Dispatch hangar at Croydon by a rather mysterious, foreign-sounding stranger who asked if he could buy her two Dragons. As Air Dispatch was having some difficulty surviving against strong commercial pressures, she replied that if he wanted aircraft fitted out for ambulance work, he could have them, "at a price". The stranger, giving away few clues, was quickly shown over the two machines in Air Dispatch's hangar, and said he would pay more than their usual value. Bearing in mind that when new, these two-year old Dragons had only cost £2,800 each, Mrs Bruce rather cheekily asked for £10,000 for the two. The stranger agreed to pay that amount in cash, on condition that they could be flown away at dawn next morning! To Mrs Bruce's amazement, a bundle of notes for the correct amount was handed over before dawn next morning. Customs officials at Croydon accepted the deal as being legitimate and the aircraft were flown away to France on 15th August 1936 by two pilots recruited by the mysterious purchaser.

In fact, while Mrs Bruce professed not to have known the purchaser, the Dragons were bought on behalf of the Spanish Republican Air Force. The "mysterious stranger" was most likely to have been their London-based agent, Commandante Carlos Pastor Krauel, a member of the Spanish Aviacion Militar. The Commandante had already bought several other aircraft from other owners, and was soon afterwards to buy several more from Air Dispatch, despite the British government's acceptance of the International Non-Intervention Agreement prohibiting sales of aircraft to Spain. The subterfuge which enabled Cdte Krauel to sneak the Dragons out of England was that they were officially to be taken to France for use by Societé Française des Transports Aérien (SFTA), with headquarters on the Champs-Elysées, Paris. However, this was a shadow company set up for the Republicans for exporting aircraft to Spain. It is almost certain that the pilot who flew G-ACDL was GW Haigh, and it is known he took a Dragon to Barcelona on 15th August, 1936. Two days previously, he had flown another Dragon to Le Bourget, where it was detained and forced to return to England. The 15th August flight was made non-stop from Le Bourget to Barcelona, from where the Dragon then became part of the Republican force at Sarinena. The other Dragon which left at dawn on that August morning in 1936, G-ACKC, was flown by another charter pilot, Alfred Jaffe, who took the same route to Barcelona, also to join the Alas Rojas Squadron at Sarinena. No doubt the pilots were paid handsomely for their risky journey.

This clandestine arrangement was typical of other deals occurring around that time, with several Dragons leaving from Croydon in August and September 1936, plus around nine Dragon Rapides and various other types. A number of others, including some in Mrs Bruce's fleet, were detained and, after various ownership changes to seek to get round the official restrictions, were restored to her fleet.. However, Mrs Bruce was able to use her windfall to buy some new aircraft to bolster up her business.

OLLEY AIR SERVICE (including Blackpool & West Coast and Channel Air Ferries)

Yet another entrepreneurial character set up his first operation at Croydon at the beginning of 1934. Captain Gordon Olley had flown with the RFC in the first War, and became one of the first airline pilots when he joined Handley Page Transport in September 1919. Joining Imperial Airways as a senior captain when it was formed in 1924, he was put in charge of its charter business in January 1928. As a result, he believed that there were good opportunities for another charter airline in the south of England.

With finance from Sir Hugo Cunliffe-Owen of British-American Tobacco and Lord Beaverbrook of Express Newspapers, he formed Olley Air Service Limited in January 1934 and bought two Mark II Dragons, G-ACNA and G-ACPY and began charter operations out of Croydon from March 1934. The first of these Dragons was fitted with auxiliary fuel tanks, giving it an extra 400 statute mile range in still air, which was put to good effect on an early two-month charter trip to central Africa. In September 1934 he was able to take control and became managing director of Blackpool & West Coast Air Services, which operated Dragon G-ACGU and two Fox Moths, G-ACFC and G-ACFF, on services to the Isle of Man from Blackpool and acquired further Dragons, G-ADCP and G-ADCR in March/April 1935. In May 1936 he formed a subsidiary, Channel Air Ferries Limited, to operate services from Shoreham Airport, whose management he had taken over in June 1935. There was considerable interchangeability in the fleets of these various entities.

Channel Air Ferries became the first successful operator to fly from the mainland to the Scilly Isles, 30 miles and 20 minutes' flying time south west of the Cornish coast. Initially using an eight-seat Dragon Mk 1, G-ADCR, the scheduled service began in September 1937, with a return flight each day from St Just airfield near Land's End, to the only area big enough to take an aircraft on the Scillies, St Mary's, which coincidentally comprised the fifth and seventh fairways of the Isles of Scilly Golf Club. For twelve months, this short but weather-affected route achieved a surprising 100% regularity, for a charge of 20 shillings (£1) single and 35 shillings (£1.75) return, which was only marred by the accident to G-ADCR on landing in fog at St Just on 25 June 1938 which resulted in the death of the pilot, Flt Lt David Dustin, and injury to the six passengers.

In June 1938, a financial reorganisation took place, when Olley Air Service merged with Air Commerce Limited, a Heston-based small charter operator, under the controlling ownership of British & Foreign Aviation Limited. Gordon Olley became a director of this new concern, which, two months later, arranged a 50:50 merger between Olley and Railway Air Services, to form Great Western & Southern Air Lines Limited, with Olley being appointed managing director. The railway companies eventually bought out British & Foreign Aviation's interest in 1942.

Channel Air Ferries Dragon, G-ACPY

In March 1938, Dragon Mark II, G-ACPY, that had previously operated for Aer Lingus as the first Dragon to be registered EI-ABI, joined the Channel Air Ferries service to the Scillies, and remained on that service until the operation was transferred to Great Western and Southern Air Lines in December that year. G-ACPY operated the Scillies route with the new company, and continued as part of the Associated Airways Joint Committee during the war, still on the Land's End to St Mary's route, but now in wartime camouflage. As a civilian aircraft flying under wartime regulations, its prominent civilian registration, underlined in red, white and blue stripes, was displayed on fuselage sides and wings. One of the regular pilots,

Captain W D Anderson, had brought G-ACPY across from Land's End on the morning of 3rd June 1941, and then took off again with five passengers at 1700 for the return to St Just. There had been an air raid warning on the mainland, but it was not in force at St Mary's, and the weather was reported as being hazy, with small fog patches over the sea. Despite the aircraft being fitted with radio, nothing was heard from it, and when it was 15 minutes overdue at St Just, an accident was suspected and a search begun. Nothing more was heard of the aircraft, and all that was ever found was the body of one of the passengers in the sea, two days later.

The mystery of G-ACPY's disappearance was only resolved many years after the war, when contact was made through the RAF Museum with the former navigator of a German Heinkel 111 from KG 28, based at Nantes in France. The navigator confirmed that his aircraft was returning to its base from a raid on Barrow in Furness on 3rd June 1941 at a little after 5 pm, when a small twin-engined aircraft in RAF colours was seen and subsequently shot down.

Olley Air Service and its subsidiaries supplemented their Dragons with Dragon Rapides from 1936 onwards, and were still using de Havilland aircraft when eventually nationalised into British European Airways in 1947.

Other British Operators
Space precludes mention here of 27 other operators who used Dragons in Britain in the 1930s. All were described in *'The de Havilland Dragon/Rapide Family'* by John F Hamlin, published by Air-Britain in 2003 and including all individual aircraft histories. Some of their stories will be told later, but the organisations are listed at Appendix 3.

OVERSEAS PRE-WAR OPERATORS

HOLYMAN'S AIRWAYS, AUSTRALIA
Having been assembled at de Havilland Australia in mid-933, Dragon Mark I VH-URD was fitted out with six passenger seats for its new owner, Tasmanian Aerial Services, based at Western Junction Airfield, Launceston and in July 1933 was given the name '*Miss Launceston*'. Soon afterwards, the company was renamed Holyman's Airways, to reflect the Holyman family's ownership and by late 1933, the single aircraft began flying across the Bass Strait to Melbourne on a regular three-times weekly service. By the end of 1934, this first Dragon was joined by VH-URG, which had been '*Golden West*' with the Western Mining Corporation.

An offshoot of the Holyman family's shipping business, the Dragons were a much quicker method of travelling than on the Holyman steamers. Stops were made alternately on Flinders Island and King Island, and the return fare was £12.10s (about £400 today). The company was an immediate success and the summer after the air service started, it bought another, larger DH aircraft, the second Express Air Liner built, VH-URN. The Holyman story is most interesting, and the unlucky saga of their Express Air Liners will be fully dealt with in that section. Both Dragons continued with Holyman's Airways until the company was taken over by Australian National Airlines in 1937.

GOLD SURVEYING IN AUSTRALIA
The third and fourth Dragons to go to Australia, VH-URF and VH-URG, were fitted out for survey work in October 1933, before being shipped out to DH Australia for the Western Mining Corporation. 'URF was named '*Gay Prospector*' and her sister '*Golden West*'. Intended for gold-mining exploration surveys in the Kimberley, and Kalgoorlie districts, they required modifications for special 10-inch lens Williamson survey cameras, and drift sights in the fuselage floor. In addition, Sperry directional gyros, Reid and Sigrist turn indicators and sensitive altimeter "statoscopes" were fitted to help pilots keep accurate headings and heights during the survey photographic runs. Marconi radios were fitted in order to take advantage of direction finding facilities. They each had an extra 24 gallon fuel tank installed in the fuselage, to increase the range from some 500 miles to around 800 miles, which was to prove useful for the long ranges required in Australia.

An interesting method of maintaining accurate tracks for the photographic sessions was employed once the aircraft began their tasks in Western Australia. Three trucks with wireless telegraphy and direction-finding equipment were sent out to the area to be surveyed, and after accurate positions had been established at each end of the survey grid, the aircraft were able to regularly check their tracking by obtaining bearings from the d/f trucks. In this way the position and height of each photograph taken made the survey very accurate. VH-URF and VH-URG were based in Kalgoorlie on survey work for over a year, and when the task was completed, they were "de-converted" by de Havilland Australia and sold on. '*Gay Prospector*' went to MacRobertson-Miller Aviation in November 1934, and '*Golden West*' to Holyman's Airways at Western Junction, in December 1934.

Other Australian Operators
Fourteen other Australian operators used Dragons in the 1930s, but space precludes their being mentioned in detail here. These operators are listed in Appendix 3.

CANADA
DH Canada only received three Dragons; CF-APJ in May 1933, then CF-AVD and CF-AVI in 1935, and all were fitted at some stage with Fairchild floats, modified engine cowlings, fine-pitch propellers and extended dorsal fins to compensate for the large twin floats. The maritime gear added weight, so the Canadian Dragons were heavier than the standard aircraft, and the economics of the float planes were thus not as good. However, both Canadian Airways and for a time, North Shore Airways, with CF-AVI, managed to provide very useful services along the St Lawrence seaway, until Rapides took over most of their routes, the greater power available from the Gipsy Six engines making the Rapides more able to cope with the extra weight of the float equipment.

CF-APJ was a Mark I Dragon, and the other two were both Mark IIs. Having served only with Canadian Airways, CF-APJ was eventually broken up for spares in 1942, shortly after the airline became a constituent part of Canadian Pacific Airlines. After a short period with Quebec Airways of Montreal in early 1935, CF-AVD was also bought by Canadian Airways, eventually succumbing to a crosswind take-off accident at Baie Comeau in May 1944. CF-AVI on the other hand was used from 1935 to 1937 by Consolidated Mining & Smelting Co in British Columbia and was, in late 1938, bought by North Shore Airways of Toronto. It had the dubious distinction of being the only de Havilland machine to be destroyed by being washed over a dam, during a storm at Godbout in the province of Quebec, in January 1941!

MISR AIRWORK, EGYPT
Misr Airwork SAE was a joint British-Egyptian company set up by Alan Muntz of the enterprising Airwork Limited of Heston with the Banque Misr of Cairo. The venture began in February 1931, and quickly built up a charter and taxi flight business, based at Almaza airfield and using five DH Gipsy Moths, a Puss Moth and a Fox Moth. By 1934, a scheduled route structure was created which covered Alexandria and Aswan, with more destinations to follow, and three DH Dragons were ordered. Capt Tony Spooner, a well-known character in the 1930s, who had previously been chief instructor of Montreal Flying Club, joined Misr Airwork in 1932 as chief pilot. He had once been a cavalry officer, which he maintained was proof that horsemen always made the best pilots. SU-ABH and SU-ABI, both Dragons Mark 1, were flown out in five days by Captain Spooner and Mr Figgins from Heston to Almaza in June 1933 , to be followed by SU-ABJ in October 1933. Unfortunately Captain Spooner was lost when flying SU-ABI on 15 March 1935, having been caught in a sandstorm which caused both Gipsy engines to fail and the aircraft to crash-land in the middle of the storm, killing all on board. SU-ABH returned to Airwork at Heston for sale in July 1936, but SU-ABJ continued working until 1938, when an internal signal rocket fired

The first DH 84 floatplane, CF-AVD c/n 6086, February 1935. *[BAe]*

accidentally, destroying the aircraft. One other Dragon, Airwork's G-ACIE, joined the fleet as SU-ABZ in September 1938 after being briefly used on the Martin's School of Navigation contract and gave service throughout the war.

INDIAN NATIONAL AIRWAYS, CALCUTTA

Typical of the way that aviation spread throughout the British Commonwealth in the 1930s, was the example of Indian National Airways, based at Dum Dum airport, Calcutta. In 1934, Calcutta, Dacca (as it was then spelt) and Chittagong were still part of a larger India, but are now partly in India and partly in Bangladesh. This new airline saw that an air service from the Bengali cities of Calcutta, Dacca and Chittagong would speed up business communications around the tortuous routes of the Ganges delta. While the train and boat trip from Calcutta to Dacca took a tiring 16 hours, a Dragon would only take one hour and twenty minutes, and to Chittagong from Calcutta would take around two hours.

Indian National Airways ordered two new Dragons in late 1933 and the aircraft, VT-AEK and VT-AEL, were flown out as a pair from Heston in November the same year by INA pilots A G M Cary and C E F Arthur. The wife of the Indian Viceroy, Lady Willingdon, baptised the aircraft '*Ruby*' and '*Emerald*' at Dum Dum on 20th November, ready for their daily services to Dacca, and their weekly services to Rangoon. This latter service made a tremendous difference to travel around the Bay of Bengal, as it only took ten hours, including stops at Chittagong and the Burmese towns of Akyab, Sandoway and Bassein, in comparison with two days by boat. These two Dragons, joined by another, VT-AES '*Sapphire*' in May 1934, continued to provide pivotal passenger and mail services around Bengal until VT-AEK crashed in 1937 and VT-AEL on a mail flight to Lahore just over a week before war broke out. The business was then closed down and VT-AES was transferred to Qantas Empire Airways in 1940. Some of the services flown by the Dragons were taken over by Indian National Airways' Rapides post war.

NEW ZEALAND ENTERPRISE - EAST COAST AIRWAYS

The capabilities of the Dragon were spreading south by 1935, as two had been ordered by a new airline which started on New Zealand's North Island in April 1935, part of the country's recognition that aviation could help make travel around the country much more practical. East Coast Airways was formed in 1934, with the intention of joining the two main east coast towns, Gisborne and Napier, 80 miles apart by air but much more by road. At that time there was no railway and the roads were subject to mud slips off the hills, so, in the words of Gisborne's mayor at the inaugural ceremony of the scheduled service between the towns, the air service would "bring Gisborne one day closer to the rest of the Dominion".

ZK-ADR was the first Dragon to arrive in New Zealand, having been shipped from England in February 1935, then taken to Hobsonville for re-assembly. Unfortunately, on a maximum weight air test by the new chief pilot, the tail was kept low, the aircraft failed to become airborne properly, subsequently stalled and was badly damaged, requiring considerable repairs. It may have been a coincidence, but the date was 1st April, 1935. The second aircraft, ZK-ADS, arrived a little later and was used for the inaugural Gisborne to Napier flight on 15th April.

One of East Coast Airways' pilots, Captain Ron Kirkup, had an unusual problem with ZK-ADS in December 1935, when the starboard undercarriage collapsed due to a broken supporting strut. The aircraft had been operating from the rough and fairly short Darton Field, and had hit a particularly rough patch on take-off. Ron Kirkup continued on to Napier where he had a smoother and larger landing ground, and he considered the undercarriage to be still intact. He landed very carefully, and tried to keep the weight off the starboard undercarriage for as long as possible. Towards the end of his run, the leg buckled, the aircraft slewed to the right, ending up on its nose and starboard wing tips. All four passengers and the pilot were shocked but unhurt, and the damage to ZK-ADS was repaired in two weeks. The problem was put down to continuous operation from the bad surface at Gisborne, and resulted in the airfield being closed for levelling at the end of that season, which took nine months to complete.

UNION AIRWAYS, NEW ZEALAND

Although badly affected by the Gisborne airfield closure, the Dragons continued to serve East Coast Airways until 1938 when the company was taken over, along with two other small airlines, by Union Airways of New Zealand, which was itself a division of the larger Union Castle Steamship Company. The Dragons continued to operate, now in the striking Union Airways colours of

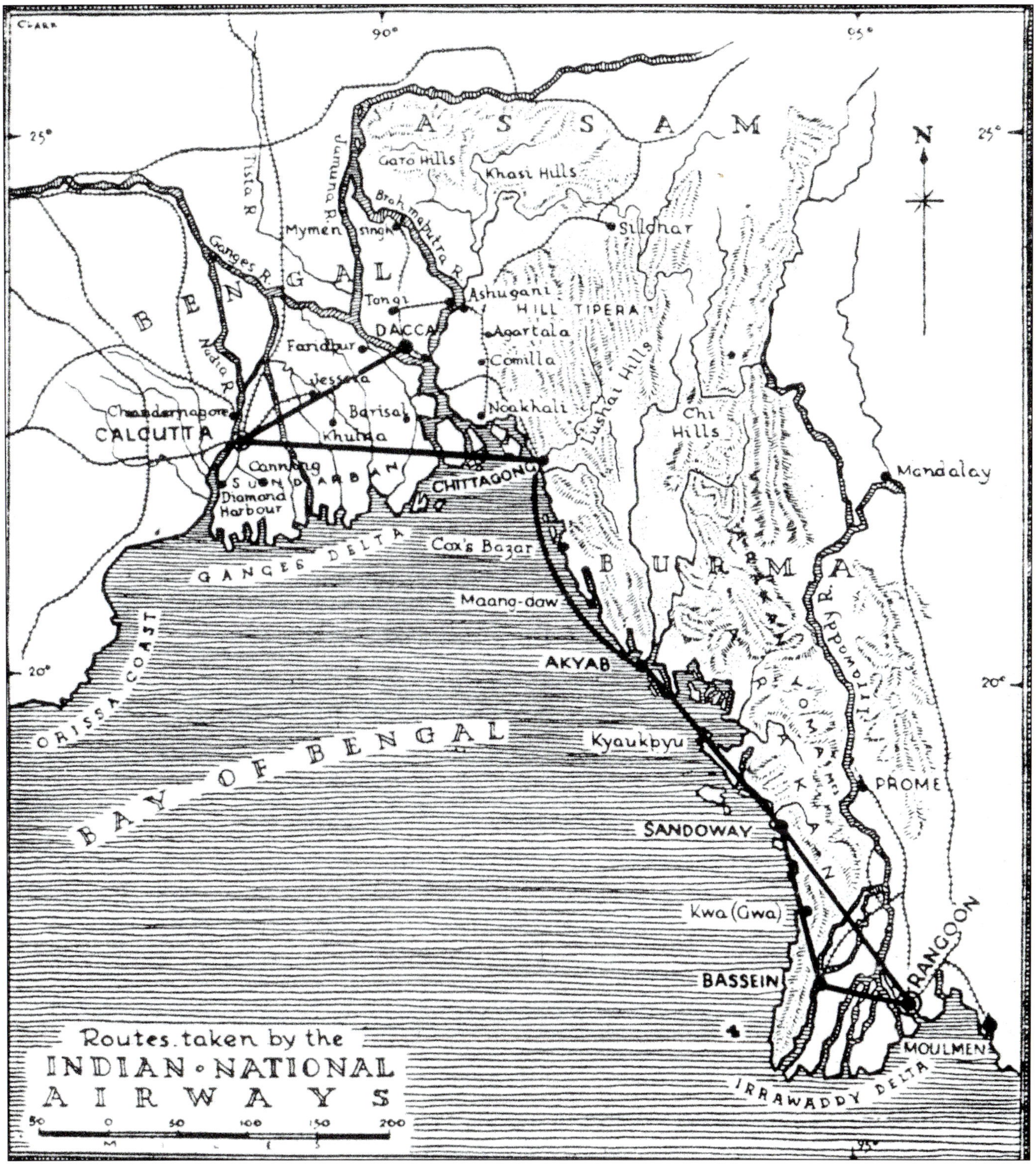

A 1935 drawing of Indian National Airways' Dragon routes. [CND]

red and silver fuselage and engines, with black cheat lines and contrasting registration letters.

The weather on the East Coast routes made an interesting contrast to the severe weather often experienced on the South Island's west coast. Most times of the year the schedules were easily met and they achieved a 98.4% regularity in 1937. George Harvey, a 23-year old Union Airways pilot, flew the Gisborne to Napier schedule when not flying as co-pilot on the company's DH 86s. Many years later he recalled:

"The worst weather was in south-easterly conditions when we encountered very low cloud, thick drizzle and poor visibility. Strangely enough, there was often a slight improvement at Waikokopu, possibly due to the shelter from the Mahia peninsular. One's local knowledge quickly built up and I do not recall cancelling or aborting a trip."

The routes were the same as with East Coast Airways, but with some additional flights to Palmerston North, where passengers could connect with the so-called Express Route to Wellington and Auckland, for which Union Airways used their DH 86s. Around this time, the two Dragons were fitted with a venturi below their noses for powering the suction instruments, and a unique wind-driven generator sitting on a pylon high above the cockpit, to re-charge the aircraft battery.

The Union Dragons (ZK-ADR having become ZK-AER when it was noted that international rules had 'ADR' as a distress signal),

ZK-ADR (6090) and ZK-ADS (6091) over Auckland in 1935 with the newly-formed East Coast Airways.

[R Waugh]

A pleasing view of East Coast Airways' two new Dragons, Gisborne, New Zealand, 1936. *[R Waugh]*

Ron Kirkup surveying the results of his 1935 undercarriage collapse in ZK-ADS, Napier, New Zealand. *[R Waugh]*

continued in civilian service until October 1939, when they were impressed into Royal New Zealand Air Force service, ZK-AER as NZ551, and ZK-ADS as NZ550. When the RNZAF sent NZ550 to Fiji in September 1942, the climate apparently did not suit the wooden structure and it was written-off in July 1943. NZ551 served for four years with the Electrical & Wireless Flight at Wigram and was "demobbed" in 1944, to become ZK-AHT with Air Travel (NZ) Ltd. Unfortunately, it crashed on Mt Hope, near Nelson only three months later. Bert Mercer, the pioneering commercial pilot who owned the company but was that day travelling as a passenger, died from his injuries. The Company Secretary, Maurice Dawe also died and the pilot, Flt Lt PC Lewis and five other passengers were injured, but survived.

VASP, BRAZIL

A new airline, based in Sao Paulo, west of the capital Buenos Aires, which had set up operations with government help in 1933, Viacao Aerea Sao Paulo SA (VASP), began services between Sao Paulo and Rio de Janeiro with two GAL Monospar ST-4s in the same year. While the Monospar had only three passenger seats, VASP felt that the service was capable of expansion, so took delivery of a single DH 84 the following year. This was a Mark II Dragon, PP-SPC, with the identification 'VASP 3' painted on its nose, and it was delivered in November 1934. It continued the same service for the next five years, before being given to the Brazilian Navy, where it saw two more year's service as D4H-178. The airline later expanded, taking on more aircraft including Junkers Ju-52/3Ms and seven Dragon Rapides in 1946.

OTHER OVERSEAS OPERATORS - PRE-WAR

In Europe, apart from Aer Lingus in Ireland, which operated EI-ABI and single corporate examples in Czechoslovakia (OK-ATO with the Bata Shoe Company) and the Austrian Aero Club's OE-FKD, which was effectively in military use, the only country to operate Dragons was France. Five were registered there, three being used initially by wealthy individuals and two by the small airline, Lignes Aériennes Nord-Africaines (LANA) set up in Algiers by Henri Germain in 1933. LANA bought F-AMTR from new in November, although it was originally registered to a British nominee as G-ACLP, presumably whilst French certification problems were overcome. This was followed by F-AMUZ in March 1934 and second-hand F-ANES in January 1936. However, the airline collapsed in late 1936 and its assets taken over by the French Government within a few months and services were continued by Régie Air Afrique. F-ANES survived the war in North Africa and resurfaced in Casablanca, where it remained until fading away in 1957. Of the other two French Dragons, F-AMTM crashed in the Gironde in November 1938 killing its owner André Garric and five of his family, whilst F-ANGE disappeared during World War Two.

Stewarts & Lloyds' ZS-AEH c/n 6054 at an aviation picnic, Karkloof, South Africa, 1934. *[BAe]*

In Africa, only those stalwarts of DH products, South Africa, Kenya and Rhodesia acquired Dragons. In South Africa, four were acquired - the first in July 1933, ZS-AEF for The Aircraft Operating Co of South Africa, for use on a 20,000 square-mile air route survey of Northern Rhodesia. Unfortunately, on 26th September, this aircraft crashed following a steep turn after take-off from Johannesburg's Baragwanath Airfield, killing Sir Michael Oppenheimer and also Major Charles Kennedy-Cochran-Patrick, the founder and managing director of AOC. ZS-AEG initially went to a private owner in Bechuanaland but later operated for African Air Transport and was then leased to Rhodesia & Nyasaland Airways, becoming VP-YBY and serving it and its state successor, Southern Rhodesia Air Services until an accident in 1944. The third was ZS-AEH, which was used as a corporate transport by Stewarts & Lloyds of South Africa from November 1933 until it was taken over by the South African Air Force as 1414 in 1940, where it ended its days as an instructional airframe. ZS-AEI was the replacement for ZS-AEF and was delivered in March 1934, again serving until its transfer to the SAAF for use by the School of Photography as 1570 in 1940, until suffering the same fate as its fellow Dragon in 1942.

In Kenya, Wilson Airways, the pioneer airline ordered VP-KAW in 1933 and it was delivered by air in September. Unfortunately, it crashed following engine-failure on take-off near Mombasa on 8 December 1933 and was replaced by VP-KBA, delivered over the New Year. This gave many years good service until hostilities required it to be transferred to the Kenya Auxiliary Air Unit in late 1939. Wilsons also bought VP-KBG in November 1934 but this also suffered a take-off crash at Nairobi on 14 April 1937.

In the Middle East, Airwork had ordered a Dragon for operation in Iraq in 1933. Registered YI-AAC, its delivery flight was overtaken by Airwork obtaining an urgent charter enquiry from the Maharajah of Nepal. Pilot Neville Stack, accompanied by a Harley Street surgeon, his anaesthetist and a nurse left Heston on 17th September bound for Bombay, arriving nine days later in order for the passengers to undertake an urgent operation on the Maharajah's nephew's wife. The operation successfully completed, they all returned to Britain on 22nd October by which time it was discovered that use could be made of the aircraft for charter work in Britain. It was thus never delivered to Iraq and was simply taken on to Airwork's books as G-ACLE.

ZS-AEI c/n 6017 of the Aircraft Operating Co landing at Baragwanath in 1935. Note the unique small round cabin windows. *[DHMC]*

Amy and Jim Mollison at Hatfield before departure for their Atlantic crossing, June 1933. *[BAe]*

Section 2 – Chapter 6: Special Dragons

In the early days of the Dragon, several owners used the aircraft for special work. The first of these were the husband and wife record-breakers Jim and Amy Mollison.

THE MOLLISONS WITH '*SEAFARER*' ACROSS THE ATLANTIC

Much has already been written about the 1933 Atlantic record flight of the Mollisons in their Dragon, '*Seafarer*', but a short mention of the aircraft and its flight will help give a broader view of the Dragon's story.

After their marriage in July 1932, Jim Mollison and Amy Johnson were persuaded by the notorious London publicist, Bill Courtenay, to announce that they would in the near future attempt an Atlantic crossing together to New York, and then return to the Middle East via Europe in an attempt on the world's long-distance record. Having had success before with de Havilland aircraft, they opted for one of the new DH 84s. In early 1933, the adventurous couple went to discuss with Francis St Barbe the sort of modifications they would need for a long-range version, and in March 1933 they ordered the fifteenth aircraft, G-ACCV. Since it would need as much fuel as possible, the team agreed to make special fuel tanks giving a total of 612 gallons, including the standard 60-gallon tanks. The enormous tanks would fill most of the cabin, and would be supplemented by enlarged oil tanks at the rear of the engine cowlings, in place of the normal fuel tanks. The increased fuel load was estimated to give a still air range of 6,525 statute miles, with around 60 hours' endurance. This extra fuel and oil alone would equal the normal maximum weight of the aircraft, so the total weight would increase to 7,334 lb. To cope with this increased load, strengthening of the undercarriage by adding extra bracing to the legs would be required. There would only be room for the Mollisons to crawl from the normal entrance door, through a narrow gap between the three enormous fuel tanks and the cabin floor, up to the cockpit, where the pilot's seat would be supplemented by a small seat for the non-flying pilot. A rather nice double entendre in a contemporary *Flight* report said "The cockpit is so arranged that the pilot on duty may be relieved without difficulty".

In the first week in June, G-ACCV, now named '*Seafarer*', was ready for departure and the Mollisons took the rather risky decision to leave from Croydon. The heavily-overweight Dragon would require a much longer take off run than normal, but Croydon's longest run had only a modest 2,200 feet of take-off distance available. Croydon had been chosen because of the greater publicity to be gained by departing from London's principal airport, but it turned out to be an unhappy choice. On 8th June, watched by an enormous crowd all round the airfield, Mollison taxied beyond the normal operating boundary to get the greatest possible length for his take-off, which meant he had to enter rough ground before turning into the easterly wind. Soon after he began his take-off run, while still in the rough ground, the wheels hit a deep rut, causing the aircraft to bounce, which in turn caused the undercarriage to collapse, thereby bringing the departure attempt to a rapid and ignominious halt. It would seem that this mishap was not all bad, as the combination of '*Seafarer*''s heavy weight, a relatively short take-off length and obstructions immediately

The Mollisons' aircraft G-ACCV c/n 6014 on a proving flight from Hatfield, June 1933, before their Atlantic crossing. [DHMC]

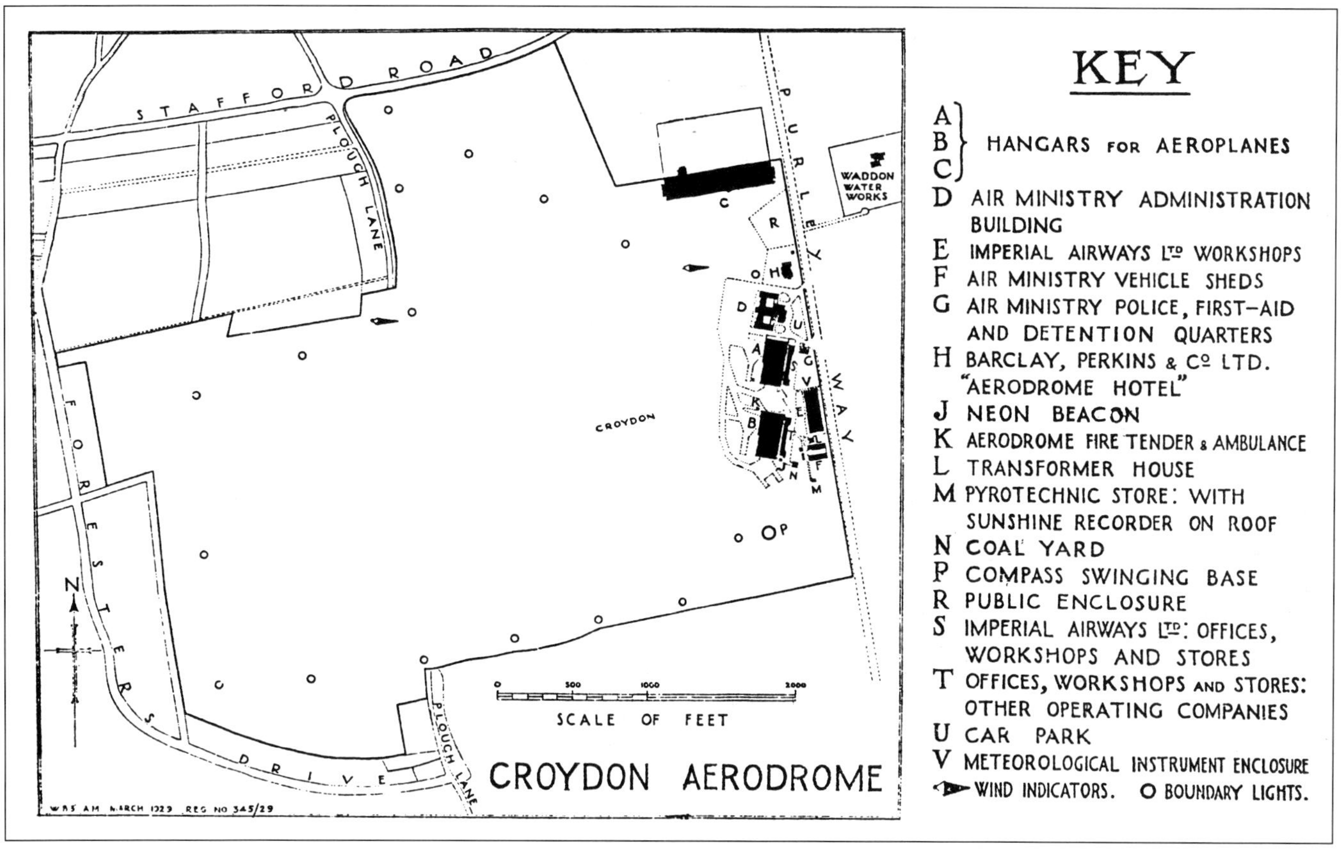

1929 diagram of Croydon aerodrome layout. *[CND]*

beyond the airfield boundary would probably have prevented a safe take off anyway. The sudden stop had caused extensive damage to the Dragon's undercarriage and all four wings, so the attendant de Havilland engineers rapidly dismantled the remains, and took them away to Stag Lane for repair. Meanwhile a chastened Jim Mollison retired with Amy to the Grosvenor House Hotel, while Bill Courtenay returned to the Croydon terminal to tell the disappointed crowds that the Mollisons would try again as soon as the aircraft had been repaired, but this time from a longer runway.

It took six weeks to repair the damage to '*Seafarer*', and during that time a better take-off site was investigated. Pendine Sands, on the west coast of Wales, where there were several miles of straight, smooth surface, would allow plenty of space for the overloaded aircraft to ease up to take-off speed and make a safe climb-away. Towards the end of July, the Mollisons took her across to Wales for the second attempt. The fuel and oil tanks were filled to capacity and, at noon on 22nd July, 1933, the Dragon finally managed to gain enough speed to take off and climb out over the Irish Sea.

A stronger than expected headwind kept the groundspeed low, so by 9 pm on the second day and after around 39 hours' flying, the tired couple had reached the area of Bridgeport, Connecticut, only 50 miles short of their destination. By this time their fuel state was becoming dangerously low and they were both exhausted, so they decided to land there. Fatigue, poor weather, and uncertainty of the layout of the airfield caused Jim, who was flying at the time, to approach Bridgeport's grass field downwind and in the dark. Just short of the field, he caught the Dragon's wheels on a small dyke, which once again broke off the undercarriage and tipped '*Seafarer*' on her back. Luckily there was no fire, but Mollison was knocked unconscious whilst Amy scrambled clear of the wreckage, unhurt but badly shaken. Both were taken off to hospital, and next day given a great welcome in New York, their hoped-for destination. Sadly, '*Seafarer*' was so badly damaged that she was never repaired. Interestingly, DH Canada, who were supporting the North American side of the effort, were saved the expense of recovering most of the wreckage by an enterprising Bridgeport store, which collected the broken wreck and during a massive publicity sale,

G-ACCV after crashing on take-off from Croydon, June 1933, with newsreel cameras in attendance. *[Green]*

A rather dishevelled Jim Mollison attempting to start 'Seafarer's' engine, Pendine Sands, July, 1933. *[Aeroplane]*

gave away items from Seafarer with each purchase. The long range fuel tanks, engines, instruments and some of the special items were saved by DH Canada for use in a possible replacement aircraft.

Not to be beaten by a mere written-off aircraft, the Mollisons managed to gain the support of that great supporter of aviation venturers, Lord Wakefield (whose family controlled the Castrol oil company) generously offered to provide another Dragon for an attempt on the Canada to Baghdad record. The new Dragon, G-ACJM '*Seafarer II*', was registered to Amy Mollison, issued with a C of A in early September 1933, then crated for transfer by sea to DH Canada at Downsview, Toronto where G-ACCV's long-range tanks and strengthening elements were incorporated by the hard working DH Canada staff. By the end of September, Leigh Capreol, de Havilland Canada's test pilot, had successfully air-tested the completed '*Seafarer II*', and the Mollisons had agreed with DH Canada's recommendation of using a suitable take-off site for the west-to-east attempt. Wasaga Beach, on the long lakeside shore of Georgian Bay, north-west of Toronto was considered by the Canadian experts to be ideal for a heavy-weight take-off and climb-out. The Dragon was therefore flown up to Wasaga Beach on 2nd October, for refuelling and preparation by the DH Canada team. While the prevailing wind was across the beach, DHC advisers Bob Loader and Leigh Capreol together with the Mollisons, hoped for a light enough wind for the take-off. During several take-off attempts on the morning of 3rd October, the crosswind proved too strong during the first two runs, and then on a third attempt, one of '*Seafarer II*'s wheels dropped into soft sand and once again the overladen undercarriage buckled with the jolt, causing the structure to collapse. This time, the Mollisons admitted defeat, and the salvaged aircraft was crated up once more and eventually shipped back across the Atlantic, to be stored at Hatfield.

REID & AYLING'S ATLANTIC CROSSING

But de Havilland Canada had not seen the last of G-ACJM. Captain Leonard Gillespie Reid, an Englishman who had spent many years in Canada, had been bitten by the flying bug when working with de Havilland Canada at Downsview and decided that he would try to succeed where the Mollisons had failed. He planned to try for a world distance record over the same route as envisaged by the Mollisons, leaving Toronto in the summer of 1934 for Baghdad, to beat the current record of 5,657 non-stop miles. Reid, who happened to be the brother-in-law of the chairman of de Havillands, persuaded Alan Butler to provide sponsorship for his scheme. He then co-opted another Englishman, James Ayling, another ex- World War One soldier, to join him in buying the damaged Dragon, still lying unused in a shed at Hatfield. Reid renamed G-ACJM '*Trail of the Caribou*' and had it repaired by the team at Hatfield, prior to shipping it back across to Canada in June 1934.

Once again, DH Canada set about preparing G-ACJM for a long-range expedition. It seems that there was a slightly more practical

Reid and Ayling at Hatfield with G-ACJM c/n 6049 after their arrival from Canada, August 1934. [BAe]

G-ACJM being dismantled at Hamble after Reid's landing accident. [DHMC]

approach to this journey, as several of the problems experienced during the earlier record attempts were addressed properly by the pilots. Reid understood that one of the greatest dangers in an Atlantic crossing was icing, even at low altitudes, and in particular, engine carburetter icing, so he devised a system for selecting a flow of hot air onto the carburetters whenever he wished. He used a simple pair of cables which ran from the cockpit to the normal carburetter heating gates, and this system worked well on test. He also believed that the technique and timing of the earlier attempts could be improved on, so he planned an early morning departure, to take advantage of lower temperatures. Having observed the Mollison's attempts at Wasaga, he thought that Jim Mollison had kept the tail of his overweight Dragon too low, thereby keeping the wings in a semi-stalled condition. The struggling engines were therefore not given the chance to accelerate the aircraft properly to flying speed. Reid felt that getting the tail higher on take-off would give the aircraft a better chance of building up to flying speed, and allowing a safe take-off.

Once the team had taken the Dragon across to Georgian Bay, the weather again caused some delays. The crosswind was judged by Lee Murray, an experienced de Havilland Canada pilot, to be too strong, so the take-off was postponed until 8th August. Early that Wednesday morning, '*Trail of the Caribou*' was refuelled and Reid and Ayling climbed aboard. Soon after sunrise, despite a slight crosswind, they opened up for another attempt to take off. The Dragon's tail was noticeably higher than on the Mollisons' attempt, and after a long run down the beach, the aircraft was eased into the air at a high 90 mph, carefully eased over the treetops, and gradually turned towards the east, Quebec City and the Atlantic. They were seen five hours later over Quebec, but nothing further was heard until next day, 9th August, when the Toronto team learned that they had landed at Heston, west of London, at 6 pm. The crossing had not been easy, as icing had caused the usual worries to the pilots. When they had tried out Reid's ingenious de-icing system, the cables had merely jammed, leaving them with no control over the air going into the carburetters, so they could not feed hot air into the manifolds when needed. During the night, over a thick fog bank that extended down to sea level, they spent a six-hour period entirely on instruments, were forced to descend each time the icing affected the carburetters, then tried to "pump" the throttles to clear the ice. Most of the night was spent descending then climbing back up to a safe height, and they were forced to keep the throttles on full power for much of the time, in an attempt to regain height. Fuel was therefore consumed at around 16 gallons per hour, about 6 gallons per hour more than expected. By the time they had reached central England, fuel consumption was such that they decided to abandon the attempt to reach Baghdad, and simply land in England. Reid and Ayling did however achieve the first non-stop flight from Canada to England, having flown an impressive 3,700 miles in 30 hours 50 minutes. Despite the heavy use of full throttle on the Gipsy Majors, they still had 198 gallons of fuel remaining after landing at Heston.

Being short of money, Reid decided to attempt to earn enough to keep the Dragon by travelling around Britain giving joy-rides. However, this plan was soon dashed when, arriving at Hamble only three days later, he caught the undercarriage on the boundary hedge when landing and caused moderate damage to the Dragon. Sadly the aircraft was never repaired and its fate is unknown, although it was reportedly in store at Hatfield when the war broke out in September 1939. Reid himself was killed in a car accident in Northampton in October 1939.

A ROYAL DRAGON, G-ACGG

On 12 June 1933, the twenty-sixth Dragon went to an illustrious owner, His Royal Highness the Prince of Wales. The air-minded Prince had already spent many hours at Stag Lane with his earlier de Havilland aircraft, so it was not surprising that, once the Dragon had had time to prove itself with commercial and private customers, he sent his personal pilot, the urbane Flight Lieutenant EH Fielden, to arrange for a Dragon to be bought and fitted out for His Royal Highness's use. Prince Edward was no stranger to aircraft ownership, as altogether he had owned eight de Havilland machines before ordering G-ACGG. He was also a regular visitor to Stag Lane, where he flew his various Gipsy Moths, Puss Moths and Fox Moths on pleasure flights and official business trips, with 'Mouse' Fielden at the controls.

The Prince of Wales' Dragon over the Welsh coast, 1934. [CND]

G-ACGG was only the second Dragon to be fitted out to the luxury Scheme Eight standard, with separate toilet, wash basin and separate luggage compartment. William Lindsay Everard, MP had been the first with G-ACEK, a month earlier. G-ACGG's leather "armchairs" were similar to the normal aluminium-framed seats, but were taller and more fully padded than standard and were trimmed in red with fawn piping. The cabin upholstery was tastefully carried out in a fawn and red colour scheme "with red fittings and bulkheads", and matching "clock and aneroid" on the cockpit bulkhead, according to contemporary reports. The cabin was specially sound-proofed, and cooling air ducts were fitted adjacent to each of the seats. As befitted the heir to the throne, this cabin undoubtedly cost more than the quoted £190 for the "De Luxe scheme 8". Outside, the aircraft was painted in the Prince's favourite, very striking Guards Regiment colour scheme of deep red and dark blue fuselage and tail, with white outlined fuselage registration letters. Wings and tailplane were silver, with red registration letters. The Prince of Wales used this Dragon more than he had his previous aircraft, keeping it in use for many of his official visits around Britain until February 1935, when it was sold to Richard Shuttleworth, (who later was to create the now thriving Shuttleworth Collection of historic aircraft at Old Warden, Bedfordshire).

INSURANCE COMPANY TRANSPORT

One customer who chose a Dragon for his own and his company's use was Mr Graham Mackinnon, who was senior partner in his father's insurance underwriting business at Lloyds of London. As a result of Mr Mackinnon Junior's passion for flying, the firm had recently moved into aviation insurance. He had bought an old Cirrus II Moth in order to gain his pilot's licence, and when he needed transport for his family and his developing business, throughout Britain and the continent, he decided that de Havilland were the right people to approach. He laid out his criteria quite succinctly in an article he wrote for Airways and Airports magazine in 1934:

"To begin with, two engines were a necessity. I have never relished a long sea crossing behind a single engine, and, for business reasons, I am never very keen on others doing it!

Following the paramount question of safety and reliability, the other factors for consideration were :

Initial Cost
Operating Cost
Maintenance
Service
Appearance
Roominess and general comfort.

"I do not think I am exaggerating when I say that the Dragon scores all along the line with these features. The initial cost (£2,800) is moderate for a luxurious air-yacht that will carry six people speedily, safely and comfortably to the very ends of the earth. The operating cost is a figure undreamed of in pre-Dragon days, for which we have to thank the rare overhauls that the Gipsy Major engine needs. Folding wings reduce the storage charges. Maintenance is a matter of simple routine. From a pilot's point of view, the machine is ideal. It provides as perfect a view in all directions as can be desired, and is a delight to handle either in the air or on the ground. Wheel-brakes and electric starters are refinements no pilot would be without once he has used them, and the completeness of the instruments is a joy."

The object of this effusive praise was G-ACOR, a very pretty Mark II Dragon named '*Fiona*' (after Mr Mackinnon's eight-year old daughter), and delivered in May 1934. It was fitted out with six de luxe seats to Scheme Six but with lavatory and wash-basin, and had Marconi radio, ADF and a PB autopilot. The total cost of the aircraft plus this equipment, at current de Havilland prices, would have been around £3,500, or about £120,000 at 2004 values.

Mr Mackinnon went on to become a director of British Continental Airways soon after buying his Dragon, and it is not surprising that this company took over '*Fiona*' eighteen months later, but presumably using it for Mr Mackinnon's staff and customers as well.

Several airline mergers saw G-ACOR with Scottish Airways in August 1937, and in a change of continent, sold to Australia in 1938. Here, as VH-AEA, it joined the fleet of Wewak Air Transport, of New Guinea. Kevin Parer, the owner of this small airline, was caught in the aircraft on the ground at Salamaua during a Japanese raid on New Guinea on 21 January 1942. VH-AEA was set on fire and Captain Parer became trapped in the burning machine. One of the ground staff, Mr WE Clarke, managed to drag Capt Parer to safety, being badly burned in the process, and was subsequently awarded the George Medal for his bravery. Unfortunately, Capt Parer was fatally wounded in a second strafing attack and the aircraft was completely destroyed, a sad end to a well-travelled Dragon.

Handover of c/n 6073 G-ACOR to a British Continental Airways crew, 1935. [Aeroplane]

The seven Iraqi DH 84s lined up at Hatfield for a press demonstration, April, 1933. *[BAe]*

Section 2 – Chapter 7: Military Service

IRAQI AIR FORCE

While Ted Hillman was putting together his plans for the Romford to Paris passenger service in 1932, a team of officers from Iraq was visiting Stag Lane and Hatfield to see if the company could provide their Air Force with a suitable machine for local defence purposes, or what some of the aviation press preferred to call a "Type Coloniale". Being an emergent air force, advice on equipment was being given by Britain, and the Royal Air Force had seconded Flight Lieutenant H E Forrow and Flight Lieutenant G L Carter to help set up the operational activities. Flt Lt Carter had led a party of Iraqi pilots to Stag Lane in 1930, when five Iraqi instructors were trained at the de Havilland Flying School, and the Gipsy Moth was selected as the first aircraft for the Iraqi Air Force. Following on from this strong de Havilland connection, Flt Lt Forrow had naturally returned to Stag Lane in August 1932 to discuss the next type for Iraq's needs.

A multi-purpose type was needed, in order to control insurgents within and outside Iraq, with the primary ability to attack ground forces but also to carry personnel, evacuate casualties and co-operate with friendly forces. These differing requirements pointed to a multi-crew aircraft, with space for light bombing and gunnery equipment, as well as room for able and injured personnel. The space and weight specification also pointed towards a multi-engined aircraft, as there were no convenient engines capable of powering an aircraft of the size dictated by such needs. So, an aircraft with a sizeable fuselage, probably two engines and enough space to mount light machine guns and bomb racks was dictated. There was not likely to be a large market in 1932 for such a military aircraft, so de Havilland's business and sales teams had to find other potential uses for the same airframe, the only other likely role for such a type being that of a light passenger carrier. It was therefore quite fortuitous that an operator of Fox Moths came along at that time asking for a similar aircraft, but with twice as many seats. Building a new design capable of fulfilling both of these requirements would obviously make commercial sense, so de Havilland agreed to produce a new type to satisfy both the Iraqis and Ted Hillman.

Starting with a relatively large fuselage, Arthur Hagg's draughtsmen set about fitting a considerable selection of military hardware into their new design. They felt they could accommodate one Lewis gunner standing on a platform adjacent to the rear cabin door, firing a "manoeuvrable gun" mounted on top of the fuselage roof; a second gunner lying on the fuselage floor, firing a Lewis gun forwards and downwards through a sliding hatch in the floor; and a pilot-operated, fixed Lewis gun firing through a slot in the fuselage nose, to the right of the pilot, and aimed through a ring and bead sight in front of his seat. A bomb rack holding sixteen 20 pound bombs could be fitted on a rack below the centre fuselage, aimed from a bomb sight and release gear just behind the pilot's seat; a retractable message hook would fit below the left side of the fuselage, sliding windows at the rear of the cabin would be used for oblique cameras and fittings for four stretchers within the fuselage and four retractable seats would be placed around the fuselage walls. These fittings were all specified for the Iraqi aircraft, and the customer was happy enough with the designs to order eight aircraft off the drawing board, to be delivered in May, 1933. De Havilland designated the aircraft the General Purpose DH 84M, and set about building them at Stag Lane, alongside the civilian DH 84s for Hillman's Airways.

In addition to the military equipment, the Iraqi customer specified the fitment of Standard radios. As the aircraft were to be flown out to Iraq by its own pilots, the two lead aircraft, flown by Flt Lts

An Iraqi pilot hand-swinging a colleague's DH 84, Hatfield. *[BAe]*

Three Iraqi DH 84s airborne from Hatfield, April 1933. [DHMC]

Forrow and Carter, had the larger ATR4 transmitter/receiver sets, and the others were fitted with the Standard AR I receive-only, short-wave sets. The only other modifications from standard on these DH 84s were an enlarged dorsal fin, two 12-gallon auxiliary fuel tanks fitted in the roof of the cabin and use of Fairey Reed metal propellers. Fin extensions were fitted to compensate for any instability caused by open hatches above and below the fuselage, and by aerodynamic effects of various bomb loads.

The eight aircraft, the fourth to ninth built, and the thirteenth and fourteenth built, were all completed, equipped and resplendent in their white military paint scheme, ready for presentation, together with their crews, to the aviation press on 5th May on a rain-soaked Hatfield airfield. The party left next day for Iraq in two groups, transitting via Paris, where the poor weather held them up for two days.

The journey onwards to Baghdad took two weeks, the Dragons arriving safely at their new base on 13th May. No feedback was formally received by the makers on the effectiveness of the aircraft or their military equipment, but the Dragons then began a short but varied service in the Middle East. Basic information of the Dragons' work then filtered back through the attached RAF personnel. The aircraft began their service in Iraq at Baghdad West, later moving to RAF Mosul and then Arbil, and six were reported as being used in operations in 1933. One "stalled and crashed" in September of the next year near Hinaidi, killing all five on board, and from then onwards, the fleet gradually diminished. By November 1938, only one Dragon was reported as serviceable, with four others out of use for unexplained reasons. '19', c/n 6006, was awaiting write-off in August 1939 after an unspecified incident. Several were written off by August 1940 and the last report from the British Air Attache in Baghdad indicates that only one aircraft was still serviceable with No 2 Squadron by May 1940. Neither the identity or the fate of that last aircraft are known.

ROYAL AIR FORCE

Of the total of 115 Dragons built In Britain, 46 served in military colours for several air forces, either as original military equipment, or as wartime impressments. While the Royal Air Force never bought Dragons specifically for military service, quite a few civilian Dragons had been used since 1938 for military cooperation, flown by commercial companies, and after being impressed into RAF service, many were used for the same tasks - working with anti-aircraft gunnery and searchlight units around London, Manchester, Birmingham and Bristol for (simulated) target practice. Much of the anti-aircraft unit cooperation work was done at night, so that searchlight operators and gunners could gain practical training with reasonably-sized targets, ready for the expected blitzkrieg - tedious for the pilots, but essential for those on the ground. Aircraft impressed into the RAF and the Commonwealth Air Forces between 1939 and 1940 were mostly used by the RAF, which service took 20 Dragons, but sadly two crashed before being given RAF serials, so only 18 actually saw military service. In addition to those used for gunnery work, five saw some service as station communications aircraft, and another five served as staff transports with the ever-expanding 24 Squadron, nominally based at RAF Hendon, but actually spread over many airfields in southern England and western France from 1939.

One Dragon in particular had a very short but exciting time with 24 Squadron. Having been built in 1933, registered as Dragon Mark I G-ACIU, and fitted out with the luxury company Scheme 8; this was a comfortably-configured VIP aircraft, bought by Viscount Furness for his family's use, and flown by Tom Campbell-Black (later to be the winner of the England to Australia MacRobertson Race). It had been loaned to racing motorist and aviator Whitney Straight and flown to South Africa over Christmas 1934, where Straight won the Border 100 Motor Race and then had two further owners before "joining"the Air Force. Still in its smart civilian VIP fit, it had been impressed into RAF service as X9395 in April 1940, and taken over by 24 Squadron, the premier communications squadron based at Hendon. When the 24 Squadron French detachment at Rheims damaged one of its two Rapides in an accident, at Arras, another VIP aircraft was needed, so, still wearing its civilian registration, G-ACIU was sent out to Rheims for Army staff communications work. The Dragon was kept very busy for the whole of that month, as the battles around the Ardennes were intensifying, but, just ahead of the advancing German forces, was damaged during an attempted take off from Mourmelon, about 50 miles from the Belgian border, on 29th April. Because of the proximity of the enemy forces, there was no time to repair the aircraft, so on 9th May, 24 Squadron ground crew set fire to the unfortunate Dragon on the airfield, alongside several other aircraft which could not be salvaged, to prevent their use by the enemy.

In addition to the 18 Dragons which entered RAF service, about ten others remained in various civilian guises in Britain. Air Force conditions were obviously not conducive to long life for the Dragon, as only two of the 17 survived the war. Nine of the others were written off by the DH CRU at Witney as being beyond economical repair; six had accidents of one type or another, so that, by early 1942, the RAF had stricken all but the two survivors,

AW171 and AV982, off their records. This explains the paucity of DH 84s in the 21st century. Of these survivors AW171 ex G-ACET, is still on long-term rebuild but AV982 returned to its former marks as G-AECZ and then went to Ireland in March 1950 as EI-AFK. Bought by Aer Lingus in 1967 as a replacement for their original EI-ABI, it was used initially for static display, but was then restored in 1986 to flying condition by an Aer Lingus team as the second EI-ABI *'Iolar'*. This Dragon Mk II is still very much airworthy and appears at events around Ireland and Britain throughout the summer months, flown by a team of Aer Lingus pilots.

THE SPANISH CIVIL WAR

By May 1936, the Mark II production line, by then moved up from Stag Lane to Hatfield, was slowing down, with 109 aircraft built. At the same time, the troubles in Spain between the Republicans and the Nationalists were reaching a state of Civil War, and both sides were desperately attempting to increase their air fleets. In August 1936 most of the major countries signed a "Non-Intervention Agreement", which prohibited sale of war materials to Spain, intended to prevent further escalation of the civil war. However, the two factions resorted to all sorts of subterfuge to bypass the international ban on sales. The Republicans voted money for aircraft purchases, and then set up several agencies in Athens, Brussels and Prague and even a direct purchasing commission in Paris. These agencies together managed to transfer, mainly by clandestine means, an impressive 1,120 aircraft to the Spanish Republicans during the two years of the war. The majority of these came from USSR. Meanwhile the Nationalists were even more successful in breaking the embargo, importing around 1,520 aircraft, mostly from Germany and Italy.

Given these surprisingly large numbers of illicit aircraft winging their way to Spain in 1936, the numbers that escaped from Britain were quite small, but still significant, with de Havilland machines seeming quite popular with the "cloak and dagger" agents. Five Dragons are known to have passed into Spanish Republican hands - G-ACKC, G-ACNA, and G-ACDL, all bought from Air Dispatch; and G-ACEV, which was sold in August 1936 by Airwork. EC-TAT, c/n 6020, which had been used from Barcelona by Sociedad Aerotaxi since 1933 was also taken over by Cdte Diaz Sandino of the Republican force as LD-001. All of these Dragons went to the Alas Rojas Squadron at Barcelona. At least five other Dragons belonging to Air Dispatch and Airwork, G-ACHV, G-ACDN, G-ACMC, G-AEMK and G-ACKB, were sold to Spain in August 1936, but were refused permission to leave and were impounded in Air Dispatch's hangar at Croydon for several months before being released or sold on to other buyers.

ROYAL AUSTRALIAN AIR FORCE

Eleven civilian-operated Dragons already in Australia were impressed into military service by the Royal Australian Air Force, between January 1940 and March 1941, as a result of an urgent need for radio and navigation trainers. They were then were given the type prefix 'A34-' for DH 84, with numbers from 1 to 11. Seven Mk I and four Mk II versions were taken over by the Air Observers Schools at Cootamundra and Mount Gambier. Several were converted into air ambulances and others later served with communications squadrons from 1942 until the end of the war.

As an indication of the variety of tasks undertaken by Dragons in the RAAF, A34 -3, ex VH-UZZ, a Mark II version, was impressed into the RAAF in January 1940, used at No 1 FTS at Point Cook, then Central Flying School, Camden before going to No 1 Air Observers' School at Cootamundra in October 1940. It was then converted, along with six others, to ambulance configuration in 1942, until being withdrawn from service in October of that year, and stored until sold to Airlines of Western Australia in 1945. Interestingly, another Dragon, A34-6 ex VH-URY, flew for No 2 Air Observers' School, Mount Gambier for two years before being passed on to the Flying Doctor Service at Cloncurry in 1943, once again as VH-URY, *'John Flynn'*. It remained with the Queensland Division of that service until it crashed on take-off at Cheviot Hills Station in North Queensland on 20th October 1953.

RAF survivor G-AECZ c/n 6105 at Biggin Hill in 1948, when with the Wiltshire School of Flying. *[C Holland]*

C/n 6105 next became EI-AFK, seen at Woolsington, Newcastle, on charter to a greyhound racing syndicate, 1957. *[DHMC]*

One of the Dragons impressed into RAAF service had already had an impressive history, and was to continue to survive despite many attempts to finish it off. G-ACMO was the third Dragon bought by Jersey Airways in Southern England in February 1934 serving as *'St Ouen's Bay'*. Sadly, when attempting take-off from Jersey's notoriously tricky St Aubin's Bay sand during the summer of 1934, it swung to the right, towards the sea wall, where several children were still playing, and hit ten-year old Denis Dust. The aircraft was undamaged, but unfortunately the boy died. The aircraft later went up to Glasgow to become part of the Northern and Scottish Airways fleet, where it remained until an Australian company, South Queensland Airways, of Archerfield, bought it in July 1938, when it became VH-ABK. After two years it was impressed into the RAAF as A34-4, for use by No 3 EFTS, then No 1 and No 2 Air Observers Schools before being converted to ambulance configuration in 1942. It was then loaned to MacRobertson Miller Aviation for four months in 1943 and eventually struck off RAAF charge in September 1944, and put into storage. Parts re-surfaced again at Murwillumbah in 1999, probably from deep storage in Queensland and it is being restored by Mothcair, for John Sinclair.

Australian-built Dragons

As the Second World War progressed In Europe in 1941, the training of replacement bomber crews became a high priority. The Commonwealth Air Training Plan began to get underway, with increasing numbers of pilots, observers and wireless operator/gunners being trained in Australia, Canada, South Africa and Rhodesia, at schools which replaced those originally formed in Britain. In Australia, with a rapid expansion of training facilities, particularly for observers and wireless operators, there were not enough suitable aircraft with which to train these new aircrew. The Dragon was considered a suitable aircraft for the conditions in Australia; it was not expensive; and it was British, so the Australian government ordered 87 Dragons in two batches from September 1941, to fulfil the requirement. The requirement in this case was for mainly light transport and ambulance work (45 aircraft), with 30 for use by the Air Observer Schools and 11 for Wireless and Gunnery Training Schools. Due to slight differences from both earlier British-made Dragons, these new Australian Dragons became known as the Dragon Mark III.

The task of building these new Dragons was given to de Havilland's Australian subsidiary, de Havilland Aircraft Pty Ltd of Mascot, near Sydney. As this factory had only built Tiger Moths

Australian-built c/n 2019 VH-AON, painted as 'Puff The Magic Dragon' in 1985, remains airworthy at Wangaratta. [M Stroud]

VH-AML back in its old RAAF colours as A34-92, at Kyabram in 1990. *[B Winley]*

and erected kits of other types sent from the UK company, they decided they needed more information about the DH 84, so in 1942 they bought VH-URE, a Mk I, from Australian Aerial Medical Services at Sydney. The Dragon was an ideal vehicle to use as a guide for the new Dragons, so it was duly dismantled and the parts used as patterns, despite there being differences between this early Mark 1 and the new Mark IIIs for the RAAF. When the Mascot production line came to an end in 1943, VH-URE was re-assembled and returned to medical work, this time with the Flying Doctor Service at Broken Hill, later becoming VH-FDB in 1948.

By the time the war ended, the sale of RAAF Dragons had already begun, mainly to smaller airlines in Australia, New Guinea and New Zealand. Surprisingly, 42 had been written off or reduced to spares in service, partly because of accidents in the rough conditions on the primitive airstrips from which they were flown. Over half of the causes appear to have been operating problems such as swing or damage on take-off and landing, or merely getting lost and crash landing. Technical problems caused a third of all accidents, with the remainder being due to bad weather conditions or, in the case of A34-9, the aircraft being destroyed by an incendiary bomb at Wyndham on 3rd March 1942.

Several of the survivors of wartime service have remained extant up to the present day, Australia having the same number as Britain - four Dragons each.

TURKISH AIR FORCE

While the Turkish Air Force was only a minor user of the Dragon, with five of the type being sold in the country, an interesting insight into military procurement methods in the 1930s can be gained from comments made by a de Havilland engineer. In October 1934, Phil Haggar had just finished his two-year apprenticeship at Stag Lane and gained his Ground Engineer's licence, when he was approached by Wing Commander Clem Pike, the Chief Flying Instructor at the De Havilland School of Flying. A DH 84 was being sent to Turkey to try to interest their Air Force in the type, and Pike had been tasked to take it. Would the young Haggar like to go along as engineer and general dogsbody? The answer was an immediate "Yes, please", and so it was agreed.

The Turkish Air Force had accepted an offer from de Havilland to demonstrate a Dragon to them for use as a photographic and navigation trainer, and it had been decided that the CFI of the Flying School was the right man for that job. It is interesting that no member of the Sales team joined this attempt to persuade a new customer to buy a number of aircraft, and neither was there a permanent de Havilland agent in Turkey. Francis St Barbe presumably felt this to be an unpromising prospect, as no operational requirement had been received from Turkey, so practical demonstrations by the head of the company's own training school should suffice in this case.

It was decided that G-ACXI, a Mk II Dragon, should be used for the trip to Turkey. This aircraft had been loaned for two months to Railway Air Services from August and was available at the beginning of November. The flight out to Stamboul, as Istanbul was then called, left Hatfield on 1st November and involved 16 hours and 45 minutes' flying over nine days via the scenic eastern European route, with stops at Belgrade to meet T G Mapplebeck, de Havillands' agent for Yugoslavia and East Europe, and then over the Bulgarian mountain range to Sofia, before heading south-east into Turkey and on to Istanbul. Once in Turkey, Clem Pike and Phil Haggar spent several busy weeks showing the various elements of the Turkish Air Force what the Dragon could do as a VIP transport, a staff transport, or a navigation and photographic trainer, flying into the air bases at Ankara, and the rough field at Eskisehir, south of Istanbul. It would appear that the Air Force and government officials were undecided on how to use the Dragon, and much questioning of the gallant Wing Commander at interminable meetings still produced no decisions until finally, after six weeks of demonstrations, briefings and discussions, the British team was told that the government would buy G-ACXI, with the possibility of further purchases later. Financial arrangements were apparently unclear, so the cautious Phil Haggar removed components from the ignition system of the Dragon, requesting a trustworthy American engineer to replace them only when payment had been confirmed!

The lucky de Havilland pair then took a luxury train ride back to Paris, followed by an Imperial Airways flight back to Croydon, just in time for Christmas. The demonstration of G-ACXI had certainly been successful as, the following year, an order for three more standard model Dragon IIs came from the Turkish government, for use by the Turkish Air Force.

IRISH AIR CORPS

Another military user of the Dragon was the Irish Air Corps, which bought a Mark II from Airwork at Heston in March 1937. This

Irish Air Corps' only Dragon c/n 6071 serialled 18, dropping a towed gunnery target at Baldonnel, 1937. *[DHMC]*

aircraft, G-ACNI, had been used first by Jersey Airways as '*Piemont Bay*' in March 1934, then used by United Airlines, Railway Air Services and the newly formed British Airways, until Airwork Limited were given that airline's disposal contract in August 1936. Through their international connections, Airwork sold the aircraft to the Irish government for use by the Irish Air Corps and converted it from the passenger role to a general-purpose military aircraft. The seats were removed, and replaced by a radio tray with an operator's seat, a camera aperture, a bomb rack below the fuselage, and equipment for streaming a towed target for ground to air gunnery.

This work was completed by March 1937, and the aircraft was handed over to the Irish Air Corps at their Baldonnel base, near Dublin later that month, with serial 18. The IAC used the aircraft mainly as a target tug for the next four years, until it was written-off in an accident at Baldonnel on 16th December 1941.

OTHER AIR FORCES

Other military users include the Portuguese Air Force, who took three Dragon IIs in 1937 as crew trainers and communications machines at Sintra air base, near Lisbon. Denmark used two as transport and aerial survey for the Danish Army, and on the outbreak of war, Kenya, New Zealand, Southern Rhodesia and South Africa all took over one or two Dragons each for military purposes, which usually meant light transport and aerial survey. The Brazilian Navy even used one, ex-PP-SPC, in 1940, which had been used by VASP since 1934. This Dragon was used for a naval mail service, but only survived in naval hands for 7 months, before crashing near Sao Paulo in December 1940.

One of the three Portuguese DH 89Ms built in 1937, seen at Hatfield before delivery. *[CND]*

Dragon G-ACIT, c/n 6039, was used by Sir Peter Masefield in Beagle Aircraft colours, 1962-1964. *[CND]*

Section 2 – Chapter 8: Post-War World-Wide Operations

BRITISH OPERATORS

With the relaxation of the wartime flight restrictions, many small airlines sprang up in 1946, some from the remnants of pre-war operations and some to start from new beginnings. In Britain, Dragons only played a small part in this renaissance, since just three had survived in airworthy condition. Scottish Airways, by now based at Renfrew, Glasgow, continued to operate G-ACIT, still proudly bearing the name '*Orcadian*' on its nose, on the Inverness to Orkney and Shetland, as well as a service to Stornoway in the Western Isles, until its fleet was folded into the new British European Airways in 1947.

A new company was set up in 1947 by a man who was to become famous in later years - Freddie Laker. His first airline, Air Charter Ltd, was started at Croydon to carry out ad hoc charters of freight and passengers, using a Dragon (G-ADDI, which had been used by Vickers Armstrong at Castle Bromwich during the war) and a Rapide. The business flourished, but after three years of hard work, the Dragon and several Rapides were sold off, with Freddie buying up a much larger fleet of Avro Yorks.

Air Taxis Ltd, also at Croydon, was a pre-war company which re-commenced operations in 1946 and introduced G-AECZ, a Mark II, for charter work, including some flights to Paris during a French rail strike. A downturn in business caused the company to fail in 1948, and the Dragon was sold, eventually ending up with Aer Lingus. But that part of this Dragon's history will be completed later.

Air Navigation and Trading, Blackpool

An entrepreneurial Blackpool family, the Whyhams, led by Russell Whyham, set up the grand-sounding Air Navigation and Trading Company at Blackpool in 1947 and operated holiday services from their base at Carlisle to that other popular destination, the Isle of Man. The company bought two rather tired Dragons in 1951, had them overhauled at their Squires Gate base and set them to work on passenger and pleasure flight services. The Dragons were a Mark I, G-ACIT, latterly being used by BEA's and BOAC's in-house flying club at Denham, and a Mark II, G-ADDI, from Air Charter. Both of these gave ten years of further service in ANT colours, before being sold in 1962.

Joy-riding round Blackpool Tower, G-ACIT
Captain Gordon Edmondson

One of the joys of "Sunny Blackpool" for the thousands of holiday-makers who flocked to this north-west coast holiday centre in the early nineteen fifties was taking a ride round the famous Blackpool Tower in an aircraft from the town's Squires Gate airfield.

By 1954, Dragon G-ACIT was looking somewhat elderly in its silver with red and white striped scheme. It had just come off a short-notice maintenance job, prompted by a final edict from the unpopular airfield Senior Telecommunications Officer (STO) that "in future, not only must all aircraft operating from Squires Gate have a wireless fitted, but the radio must work, without interfering with other radio traffic". As elsewhere, Air Navigation and Trading were forced to use "economy" in their maintenance work, and while complying with the ruling by actually fitting radios to their aircraft, had for many months skilfully avoided the protestations of the STO about their questionable serviceability. But finally the STO would accept no more prevarication, and from this particular week, insisted on grounding any aircraft attempting to operate without a serviceable radio.

With a frantically busy maintenance schedule, the engineer on the previous evening's shift had had to work fast to fix the problem of making poor old Item Tare's radio work without interference, along with all the other repair work for the rest of the fleet. If the Plessey crystal set were to function properly, then the engines would have to have the old ignition wiring completely replaced with electrically-screened wiring and plugs, to prevent engine noise interfering with the radio reception. In keeping with the company's financial stringency, the engineer measured up the length of the existing wiring, went off and scrounged the bare minimum of screened harness lead. Unfortunately, each lead end had to be cut short to fit into its new plug connector, and by the time he got to the starboard engine, he discovered that the last set of four leads was slightly short. He could not, at that late hour, obtain any more screened lead, and the Boss would develop apoplexy if he missed a morning's flying, so he just managed to squeeze the last

G-ADDI c/n 6096 landing at Rochester, June 1967, after a Chrisair joyriding flight.

[M Stroud]

connectors from the distributor round a very tight routing and into the plugs. The engine ran properly when tested, so he released it for the morning's joy-riding.

That next morning was a warm summer's day. The first eight (no room for a toilet in a joy-rider's cabin) of an eager crowd had paid their five shillings to the company's traffic clerk in Blackpool's rather seedy terminal, and trooped across the tarmac where the old Dragon, with its newly-rated 20 year-old pilot sitting up in the small cockpit, eagerly awaiting his first flight of the day. The engine runs had worked normally on the way across from the company's hangar to the terminal, so he was looking forward to using a workable radio for the first time.

The passengers weighed and the load pronounced within limits for the trip, all was looking well on board during start-up and the short, rather rapid taxi to runway 31. Take-off was into the light North-Westerly breeze, over the housing estate bordering the airfield, and all appeared to go as normal as they slowly climbed towards the sandy beach.

At 300 feet, just as the pilot began a right turn towards the 200 foot-high Tower, several of the short leads on the starboard engine finally shook themselves free, and the starboard engine began to "bang and crash". Without enough flying distance left to land back on the short runway 31, and knowing the reputation of the elderly Dragon on only one engine, in summer with a full load of passengers on board, he took the only actions available to him. He pushed both throttles even harder against their forward stops, eased the nose down to maintain something like 75 mph, and turned, very gingerly, away from the houses ahead of and below him, towards the misbehaving engine. His one priority at that moment was to keep the aircraft in the air long enough to find an acceptable landing place, knowing the likely outcome of an engine failure. Hoping that the banging and crashing would not turn to silence, he headed about forty degrees right, into a gradual but inexorable descent, aiming between the control tower and the large black hangars, gently turning all the while, with the misbehaving engine still producing intermittent power, until he saw the reciprocal runway to the one he had just left, appearing through his right cockpit window. Skimming past the top of the northerly hangar, he managed to ease the aircraft, close to the stall, into an erratic, descending turn, and then, almost unbelievably, found himself back on the ground, on the runway, with a largely intact aeroplane and eight intact passengers. With much use of throttle and brake, he managed to coax the misfiring machine back to the company hangar, where he disembarked his lucky passengers, then rather quietly told the engineers that he would not be flying that aircraft again today.

He had at least proved to himself that this normally very reliable aircraft would in fact fly on one engine, even if only for a short time.

G-ACIT is today on static display in the Science Museum's outstation at Wroughton airfield, Wiltshire.

Chrisair Ltd - G-ADDI

In 1960, taking advantage of the emerging interest in aviation in post-war Britain, the husband and wife team of Chris and Claire Roberts, formed a pleasure flight company with the rather unoriginal title of Chrisair. They began flying a Leopard Moth (G-AIYS, still airworthy today) and a Proctor (G-AHGJ) from Luton airport on joyrides in 1961, but soon decided to expand the number of passengers they could carry. They took over Air Navigation and Trading's Mk II G-ADDI in November 1962, repainting it in a bright red and white colour scheme, and initially operated from Ramsgate until moving to Sywell, near Northampton. Pleasure flying with the eight-passenger Dragon at air shows throughout the country was augmented by passenger and light freight work, including hauling cigarette stocks to Belfast and continued until 1968, when its C of A lapsed. G-ADDI then languished at Sywell, until it was bought by Irving Perlitch, a Californian collector in November 1970, and shipped out to the USA the following year, where it took the new registration N34DH.

Sadly, she was not restored or flown in Mr Perlitch's ownership, and was found in a Californian museum by Mike Kimbrell, a Delta

N34DH in the United States in the 1990s, still displaying the Chrisair colours that it wore as G-ADDI. *[Green]*

Airlines captain, who bought her in 1981, and took her back to his home in Oakville, Washington. Restored and now named '*Sir Geoffrey de Havilland*', Mike maintains her in airworthy condition, still with her red and white Chrisair colours.

AUSTRALIA
Out of the 98 Dragons used in Australia, 50 survived the War, and 47 went back into civilian service. The companies which took up the type included such well-known names as QANTAS, who took over 10 Dragons at various times; Mandated Airlines of New Guinea, which operated a total of seven into some very primitive strips in both Australia and New Guinea, and W R Carpenter of Sydney, who also bought seven Dragons. The Australian Flying Doctor Service based at Broken Hill acquired five to augment several taken over during the war, but in other areas, other operators were contracted to fly Flying Doctor services when necessary. In the Alice Springs area, for example, Connellan Airways operated the services; Trans Australian Airlines flew them in New South Wales, and the North Queensland Ambulance Transport Brigade flew for the Flying Doctor in Queensland. All these services used Dragons or Ansons for their ambulance flights.

Ambulance Flights, VH-AGI
Other operators of "Mercy Flights" on behalf of the Flying Doctor Service had little choice other than to use Dragons well into the 1960s, as no other aircraft were available or could be afforded by the service. One of this band of small operators of Dragons was the Bush Church Aid Society of Sydney, which flew its Dragon, VH-AGI, out of Ceduna, in South Australia, where it ran a Bush Hospital. This Mark III Dragon was the seventeenth built at Mascot in December 1942, and had been flown by No 5 Communications Flight, RAAF as A34-28, before being sold in 1945 to the Bush Church Aid Society for £750. It had been modified to carry four stretchers with four attendant seats on the port side, and had a small extra hatch behind the main door on the port fuselage side, to enable stretchers to be inserted more conveniently than through the main cabin door.

VH-AGI had a very arduous thirteen years of ambulance and clinic work in the outback, until being sold in 1959. The well-respected pilot Macarthur Job, who later worked for the Department of Civil Aviation as an accident investigator, flew for this small organisation in the mid-1950s, helping to save the lives of many outback patients, often flying their DH 84s in appalling weather, at night, without proper instrumentation, radio equipment or landing aids. VH-AGI soldiered on until it was badly damaged in a forced landing at Bateman's Bay on 1st October 1961.

Other Operators
The Royal Aero Club of New South Wales and Newcastle Aero Club took over five Dragons between them, for touring and parachute work, and other such diverse organisations as the Sydney Shark Patrol bought two for patrol and joy-riding work. A total of 26 different owners operated Dragons after they had been retired from military service.

New Guinea Operations
Many of the ex-RAAF Dragons served in New Guinea, either with WR Carpenter and Co. and its 1947 successor Mandated Airlines Limited, or with QANTAS, most of them operating from Lae and Madang. WR Carpenter is believed to have bought a lot of seventeen Dragons for $A50 each from the Australian Disposals Commission in 1946, and used most of them for charters from Lae to other sites in the area, keeping some unregistered for spares and later selling off another five to QANTAS, also for use in New Guinea. Mandated Airlines continued to fly the Dragons over the next 15 years, and its engineering department had the benefit of having Fred Bird as their Chief Engineer. Fred was well versed in de Havilland construction and maintenance methods, as he had gained his licences with de Havilland at Mascot towards the end of the war, before going to New Guinea as an engineer initially with Socony Vacuum, then to Lae, on the north east coast, with Mandated Airlines.

Fred Bird remembers many of the Dragons that passed through his hands in New Guinea, and also recalls the harsh flying conditions, which caused many accidents in the post war years.

One incident in particular concerned Dragon VH-AKX, a Mark III which had been sold to Mandated in 1946 after RAAF service. On 11 May 1948, the Dragon had begun the 2,200 mile journey back to Sydney from Lae, a hazardous flight entailing mountain, jungle, coastal, ocean and outback sections. The route was south east from Lae, on the Soloman-Sea coast, then over a 6,000- foot gap in the Owen Stanley mountains near Wau, down to the south coast of Papua, and along the very ill-defined, island-strewn coast towards the southern tip of Papua near Daru. The route then headed south over the 100 mile-wide Torres Strait, which was again strewn with difficult-to-identify islands. By this time the pilot, J Spiers, was becoming unsure of his position, but continued southwards, aiming for the west coast of the Cape York Peninsula. Unfortunately the weather had deteriorated, with a winter storm covering the Cape York coast, right across his route, so, being unable to penetrate the low storm cloud, the pilot turned back northwards, aiming for one of the sparse Papuan coastal towns. Becoming concerned about his fuel state on this northern heading, on seeing a small island in the Torres Strait which appeared to have a flat field near the coast, he made an approach, and made a very short landing on a surprisingly soft surface, almost overturning due to the forced retardation. He discovered that he had finished up at low tide on a coastal mud flat on the appropriately named Turnagain Island, towards the north of the Torres Strait. All was not lost however, as he worked out his approximate position and managed to get a message out on his radio, which still had enough battery power. He then sat up on the roof of his Dragon, hoping for rescue, while the aircraft sank further into the mud with each succeeding tide. The RAAF rescue service had a series of Catalina flying boat stations around the coast, but could only make an attempt to rescue the poor Dragon pilot at high tide, and it took two further days before they could get a Catalina to Turnagain Island. VH-AKX was abandoned to sink into the mud flat, and Fred Bird considered that it had gained the dubious honour of being the only Dragon to have been destroyed by mud.

Of the fifteen Dragons owned by WR Carpenter and Mandated Airlines at Lae and Medang post-war, the harsh climatic and operating conditions contributed to seven being written off in crashes or ditchings while in service between 1947 and 1954, and five were sold on to other companies. By 1960, DC-3s and other de Havilland types, the Beaver and the Dove, were coming into service in New Guinea, and the Dragons were retired.

There are still four Dragons in Australia. The earliest is VH-ABK the first Mark II, built as G-ACMO, which is now on rebuild with Mothcair at Murwillumbah for John Sinclair. The next is Stag Lane-built Dragon II VH-UXG originally with Portsmouth, Southsea and Isle of Wight Aviation as G-ACRF, which went to Australia in 1936, owned by Des Porter. This was rebuilt by Mothcair between 1996 and 2003 and was reflown on 20 March 2003. Two Australian-built Dragon IIIs are VH-AON, until recently on display in the Air World Museum at Wangaratta but now acquired by Harvey McBain of The Nelson Aeroplane Company, Nelson, Victoria and delivered to him on 20 April 2004 and secondly VH-AML, airworthy at Point Cook, and belonging to Mike Hockin.

AER LINGUS, IRELAND
Captain JJ Sullivan, a great Irish character happily flying Aer Lingus' Boeing 747s around the world in 1985, felt that the DH 84 which his company owned, but which had been hanging, neglected and unairworthy, in the lobby of Dublin Airport for many years, could form the basis of celebrations for Aer Lingus' 50th Anniversary the following year. 'JJ' (nobody ever uses his real name) persuaded Johnny Molloy, a company Quality Assurance engineer, that they could make the old girl airworthy again, and use her for publicity flights around Dublin, as long as the company would cover the costs. "After some hesitancy" as JJ remembers,

VH-AML c/n 2081 prior to restoration as A34-92. *[M. Stroud]*

VH-AON c/n 2019 as 'Puff The Magic Dragon', parked at Drage's Airworld, Wangaratta, 1990. *[B. Winley]*

"the company gave us clearance to go ahead and we were allocated a budget for it". He and Johnny then set about getting together a group of voluntary helpers from the Aer Lingus workshops; removed a tired old EI-ABI from the roof, and set about returning her to the air, ready for the May 1986 celebrations.

In fact this 'EI-ABI' was not the original EI-ABI, but was a later, Mk II DH 84, built at Hatfield in 1936 as G-AECZ, then brought to Ireland in March 1950, as EI-AFK. This Dragon had a very busy and diverse life even before arriving in Ireland. As G-AECZ, it was briefly used as a charter aircraft by Amy Johnson after her divorce from Jim Mollison, with finance from a French hotelier and friend, Francois Dupré. It was sold to the Straight Corporation and used on passenger schedules by Western Airways and probably also joy-riding at Ramsgate until being impressed into RAF service in 1939 as AV982. Following repairs after an accident in September 1940, it was used as a communications hack by English Electric before being sold to Air Taxis of Croydon in 1946. The next owner was the Wiltshire School of Flying at High Post in 1948, who sold it in 1950 to Mr J Cleary of Mullingar in Ireland, where it became EI-AFK. Another well-known Irish aviator, the irrepressible Captain Darby Kennedy bought it five months later for use by his company, Weston Ltd, from Weston Park aerodrome, west of Dublin. Darby Kennedy used the Dragon for flights around Ireland for the next 8 years, before putting it into store at Weston in 1959. The Irish national airline, Aer Lingus, bought it in 1967, painted it as their original EI-ABI, and later exhibited it in the Dublin Departures Hall. Restoration to flying condition was then undertaken by an Aer Lingus team and it was officially re-registered EI-ABI, to commemorate '*Iolar*', the first Dragon owned by Aer Lingus in 1936. It was then flown again by Captain Sullivan on 10th April 1986. The new '*Iolar*' has been used to promote the airline ever since, appearing all over Ireland and also occasionally in England and Scotland, lovingly maintained and flown by the same team who have looked after her since 1985.

Captain JJ Sullivan

Captain Sullivan's views on flying the Dragon, after over 200 hours of experience on EI-ABI, are of interest:

"The aircraft performs very well on two engines but the single engine performance is very poor and I always aim for a speed of 80 mph after take off just in case we might have an engine failure. On test flights I have found the VMCA (minimum control speed in

J J Sullivan flying EI-ABI over Woburn Abbey, 1998. *[DHMC]*

flight) to be about 63 mph. In cruise, with one engine at idle, the aircraft will maintain level flight at 75 mph, with the other engine at full power and hopefully you will not be too far from an airfield, height to spare and settle for a very slow descent - it will make all the difference.

"My most memorable flights will always be our visits to Woburn Abbey for the de Havilland Moth Club annual rally, arriving there in the still evening air on the Friday and wondering if she will be safe from the park deer during the night. Then the departure on Sunday afternoon with little or no wind and temperatures in the high 20s. Trying to avail of as much runway as possible, with fuel for Liverpool, with at least 2 passengers (on one occasion I had 4) and convincing myself - of course she will make it over all those trees at the end of runway 19! Then relief - sit back and enjoy our flight back to Dublin, via Liverpool for fuel."

The second EI-ABI airborne over the English south coast, with JJ Sullivan at the wheel, 1998. *[G Bain]*

ZK-AXI c/n 2057 parked at the Auckland Flying School, April 1967, before refurbishment by Stan Smith. *[D A Noble]*

NEW ZEALAND DRAGON, ZK-AXI

One Australian-built Dragon is still flying from Dairy Flat airfield, north of Auckland, New Zealand, in the hands of Stan Smith, as ZK-AXI. This aircraft has had a hardworking life, having been built in 1943, and after service with the RAAF, was sold into civilian service in 1945 as VH-AEF, with Butler Air Transport, then QANTAS in New Guinea. After several more owners in Australia, the aircraft went in 1953 to Palmerston North in New Zealand.

After being owned by the Nelson Aero Club from 1954, the Dragon was due for its C of A renewal in 1962, but the club decided not to spend the money on the old girl, so put her back in the hangar where she stayed until bought in 1964 by Mr Arthur Bradshaw. Bradshaw was a legendary figure in New Zealand commercial aviation, having flown from many places on South Island with his own Puss Moth and Fox Moth fleet before the war, then in the RNZAF, and after the war with several other organisations and clubs. Despite nearing retirement, 'Brad' as he was generally known, carried out most of the refurbishment work on ZK-AXI himself, finishing up with a bright red paint job and the name '*Puff*', after the children's story-book Magic Dragon, on the nose. He then used it for the next four years on a task not often undertaken by Dragons - aerial mapping photography, covering most areas of the country. Brad describes the work in his entertaining book '*Flying by Bradshaw*':

"All photographs had to be taken from as high an altitude as possible. At the beginning of each flight old '*Puff*', loaded with three adults, cameras and six hours' fuel, could only struggle to 12,000 feet, but as fuel was used, she would reach 15,000 feet. It was quite rugged flying, for there was no heating and the cockpit windows often froze over on the insides. After two flights of 5 hours in the one day, under these conditions, we knew we had been doing something! When the weather was suitable, we would fly hard, and when it became unsuitable, we would return home. I flew nearly 500 hours on the Dragon for aerial mapping flights until the end of March 1967, when the survey company purchased their own aeroplane and employed their own pilot."

Soon afterwards, Bradshaw sold ZK-AXI to the Auckland Flying School, but two weeks later it had a take-off accident at Ardmore and was then donated by the insurers to the Auckland Museum of Transport, where it was put into store. In 1983, a former Air New Zealand air engineer, Stan Smith and his wife Gilly arranged to buy the resting Dragon in exchange for a Fox Moth, ZK-APT, and set about restoring the aircraft to flying condition.

The irrepressible Stan, being no stranger to restoration of de Havilland machines, then spent the next 14 years and much effort in bringing ZK-AXI, now named '*Taniwha*', back to airworthy condition. The engines had to be completely overhauled and many parts re-made, including the instrument panel and control cables, but all was finally completed in 1997, allowing the first flight for almost exactly thirty years to be made on 22nd April of that year, by Stan Smith himself. '*Taniwha*' is now immaculately turned out in a scheme very similar to that of East Coast Airways, with dark blue instead of black on the fuselage top; neat blue cheat lines on the fuselage sides; silver on all other surfaces, and smart gold registration letters. The immaculate interior is set off by cream leather seats for pilot and passengers. She is used for pleasure flights and occasional sightseeing trips round North Island, from Dairy Flat airfield, near Auckland.
Two Australian-built Dragons have been imported to Britain and remain here today. VH-SNB, built in October 1942 was used as an air ambulance by the RAAF as A34-13 and later as VH-ASK at Darwin, before being used by an Evangelistic Mission in New South Wales. In 1975, Sir William Roberts' Strathallan Aircraft Collection near Perth, Scotland, bought her in dismantled state for static display. In 1981 she was moved on again, this time to the Museum of Flight at East Fortune, east of Edinburgh. A more recent Australian import is that of G-ECAN.

RESURRECTION OF MARK III DRAGON, G-ECAN

A Dragon III which has had a rather intermittent flying career is the newly-registered G-ECAN. This aircraft was built half-way through the de Havilland Australia contract, and handed over to the RAAF in March 1943, complete in its foliage green and earth-brown camouflage colour scheme as A34-59. It served for short

R Waugh blessing ZK-AXI at North Shore, 1997. *[R Waugh]*

periods at four different units, including No 5 Service Flying Training School at Uranquinty, finishing its military service at No 6 Communications Unit, Batchelor, in December 1944. Along with most of its RAAF sister ships, it was then sold into civilian service, in December 1945, being one of several going to Syd Marshall at Bankstown, with the registration VH-AQU. Then began a series of flying and storage periods as it was withdrawn from use then restored by four owners, finishing up in 1985 with Hawker de Havilland at the Bankstown factory where it had been constructed, for repainting in its original RAAF camouflage colours as A34-59, with the unit codes 'XJ-A' in sky grey on the fuselage sides. A change of registration then came in 1986 to VH-DHX, in deference to its de Havilland successor company ownership. It seems that the intention was to keep the aircraft for static display at the Power House Museum in Sydney around 1993, but in the event it was sold on to restorer Nick Challinor in 1996, who removed it to his Murwillumbah facility.

British collector of de Havilland machinery, Torquil Norman, had by this time decided that he needed a DH 84 in his growing collection, so arranged to take over the project in 2000 and have it shipped to his delightful airfield at Rendcomb, in the rolling Cotswold Hills. It then became a British Dragon for the first time, taking on a period registration, G-ECAN, close to that of the prototype DH 84 and being registered to the Norman Aeroplane Trust. The work of refurbishing the Dragon back to the high standards required by Torquil was entrusted to the well-respected restorer, Cliff Lovell, who set to work with G-ECAN in January 2001, with the intention of putting the Dragon into the colours of one of the first operators of Dragons, Railway Air Services. The restoration plan was to have Torquil fly the aircraft to the de Havilland Moth Club Rally at Woburn Abbey in August 2003, and this was achieved with several months to spare. Torquil duly flew an immaculate G-ECAN to Woburn, to take the prize for the best restored de Havilland aircraft. The Dragon is now based at Rendcomb alongside the other superb machines of the Norman Aeroplane Trust.

Dragon VH-AQU c/n 2048 in RAAF colours as A34-59 coded 'XJ-A' in 1986. *[DHMC]*

The immaculate G-ECAN at the 2003 DH Moth Club Rally, Woburn Abbey. [DHMC]

Section 3:
The DH 86 Express Air Liner

The DH 86 prototype c/n 2300 marked as E.2, parked at Stag Lane, 1934. *[CND]*

Section 3 – Chapter 1: Design and Build

ORIGINS

In the early 1930s, de Havilland's fertile business was turning out new types at an impressive rate as well as being embroiled in new engine designs, and in preparations for the transfer of aircraft production to the new airfield and factory at Hatfield. The DH 84 Dragon, developed in line with the DH evolutionary approach to new designs, also required more design effort because of increased complexity compared to the simpler Moths. The emergence of the next major project, the DH 86, required a modified approach. This project required not only incorporation of new design elements, but also some new, untested equipment. This willingness to take financial and manufacturing risks was encouraged by the company's chairman, Alan Butler, with his progressive, adventurous attitude to new business. The company had only had two years of experience with "modern" multi-engined aircraft in the autumn of 1933 and had never built a four-engined machine.

The largest DH aircraft to go into production by this time, the three-engined DH 66, had been built in 1926, and had weighed over 15,600 lb all up, cruised at about 105 mph and employed three Bristol Jupiter engines of 420 hp each, to carry the small total payload of 2,260 lb, which included seven passengers and mail. However, by 1933 the DH 66 was a product of an earlier generation in terms of design. A "long range" aircraft in its day, it was now considered slow, heavy, aerodynamically inefficient, and carried a small payload when compared to the "modern" metal aircraft then beginning to come out of America. The Boeing 247, then entering service, showed a quite different philosophy when compared to de Havilland thinking. It was an all-metal monoplane, carrying 10 passengers and 3 crew at 170 mph using two engines on a total of 1,100 hp. In comparison, Armstrong Whitworth in Britain were about to bring their modern-looking new Atalanta into Imperial Airways service, using 4 Serval engines which produced a total of 1,360 hp. This monoplane gave the 20 passengers a 130 mph cruising speed, and a moderate 400-mile range for a rather heavy 21,000 lb all-up weight.

PIONEERING EMPIRE AIR SERVICES

In the summer of 1933, the de Havilland factory was visited by a pioneering Australian pilot and businessman, Captain Hudson Fysh. This persuasive Australian had a powerful effect on the de Havilland team, as their usually conservative approach was swept aside in their desire to accept a quite different design challenge. The entrepreneurial Mr Fysh was managing director of Queensland and Northern Territory Aerial Services Limited (QANTAS), which company was creating a joint venture with Imperial Airways under the name of Qantas Empire Airways (QEA) to bid for the Australian government's competitive tender, due in September 1933, to operate a subsidised extension of the Imperial Airways mail service from England to Singapore. This would require an aircraft to take the mail on from Singapore to Australia, thereby completing the "Empire" route from Britain to Australia. Imperial Airways had extended the eastern end of the Empire route as far as Calcutta, India, and by December 1933, were expecting to complete their part of the network to Singapore. The successful bidder would complete the service from Singapore to Brisbane in Australia.

Hudson Fysh felt very strongly that Australia should have a chance to expand its influence outside Australia, but there was a major difficulty in QEA's view. The Australian administration maintained a strict "buy British" policy, yet no current British aircraft was capable of meeting the specification for the notoriously dangerous 2,200-mile journey from Singapore to Darwin.

Armstrong Whitworth Atalanta prototype G-ABPI over Coventry, 1932. *[M. Stroud]*

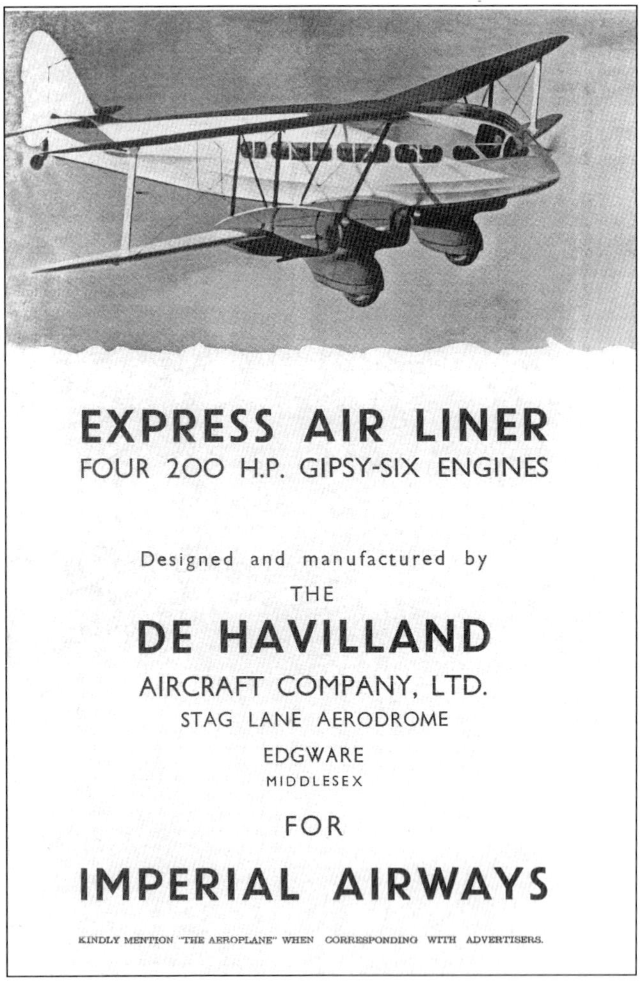

De Havilland advert for the DH 86. [CND]

The QEA/Imperial collaborators needed an aircraft which could meet what was then quite a high performance specification. Together they agreed a surprisingly simplistic specification. It must carry ten passengers and at least 1,800 lb of mail at a cruising speed of around 135 mph and must have "adequate" range without refuelling, although no figures for range were quoted. It should have "considerable reserves of safety in the event of engine failure", particularly because of the long Timor Sea crossing, and it should have low initial and operating costs. No mention was made of crew numbers or on-board equipment but the bidder for the contract must have a certificated aircraft available by the end of January 1934.

As the driving force in the collaboration, Hudson Fysh was determined to find a suitable new aircraft and travelled up the Edgware Road to see the de Havilland Company. The fact that QANTAS was an Australian agent for de Havilland no doubt had some bearing on the choice of Stag Lane for his exploratory visit.

With no aircraft in the current de Havilland inventory that could cope with the long range, moderate payload, reasonably high speed and multi-engine safety requirements of the Australian government, the de Havilland directors were intrigued by the challenge of designing and building a contender for this prestigious programme. Captain Fysh had introduced requirements which were pretty revolutionary for the normally conservative team, which would force de Havillands to accept several untried elements in the design. A rapid design-and-build programme such as this would also entail considerable technical and financial risk. However, despite these major difficulties, they were enthused by the challenge, and agreed to offer the joint QANTAS Empire Airways an entirely new, four-engined design for the imminent tender.

The Australian government's tender document for the route operation appeared on 23rd September 1933, and one of its conditions was that the winning aircraft for the contract must have a Certificate of Airworthiness within four months, namely by 31st January, 1934, which was an incredibly tight schedule for any bidder proposing an unbuilt new design. After perusal of the initial de Havilland design specification, however, Imperial Airways and QANTAS both agreed that their proposed aircraft should comfortably exceed the requirements, so, despite the tight certification timescale and the risks of ordering a new aircraft "off the drawing board", they placed an order for six new DH 86s.

DESIGN OF THE NEW TYPE

As seen by the Stag Lane team in September 1933, there were major hurdles to jump if they were to get this new aircraft into the air in the four short winter months. The critical question, as well as being the crucial factor of the design, was that of the engines to be used for the aircraft. Then, in order to gain greatest efficiency for the "long range, reasonably fast" requirements, the aircraft should weigh as little as possible, in the region of 10,000 lbs, and certainly be lighter than the inefficient 15,600 lb DH 66. That would mean wooden construction, the only material they were familiar with and, in keeping with company philosophy, design strengths would be "just enough, but no more".

The design needed three or four engines of around 200 to 250 hp in order to meet the "engine out" safety elements, but there were no such engines in the present DH stable. The Gipsy Major was too small, producing only 130 hp and whilst other engines were available in Europe from various manufacturers, none produced the relevant power output. Most other British engines of the period like the Armstrong Siddeley, Bristol, and Napier engines were rated around 400 to 500 hp; French or American engines could be available, but since they were not familiar to the teams at de Havilland, getting to know them would be rather risky in the timescale.

THE ENGINE

However, the de Havilland company strategy in the early months of 1933 included a plan to develop their existing four-cylinder Gipsy Major of 130 hp into a more powerful engine through the evolutionary process of adding two more cylinders, thereby gaining fifty percent more horsepower, while still using many well-tried components from the original engine. Major Frank Halford, in discussion with Captain de Havilland, had been working on a private-venture engine design with a rating between that of the Gipsy Major and the other heavier engines then available - around 190 to 200 hp. Here was an immediate vehicle for this proposed engine, and if an aircraft could be designed around this project from de Havilland's own engine department, the costs could be kept down to a minimum, and the programme achieved in the time allocated. There would still be major technical risks, but they could be minimised if all elements of the programme came from the in-house team. If the engine was based on an existing, successful engine and the airframe built on lines already used for existing de Havilland machines, then the

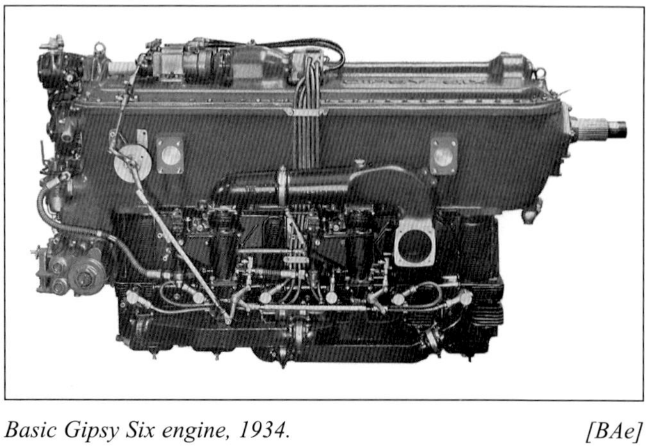

Basic Gipsy Six engine, 1934. [BAe]

whole project could be controlled by the same team which had together built many new designs in the same factory. A lot of "ifs", but it was the least risky and potentially the least costly proposal.

The de Havilland board therefore decided to go ahead with a new aircraft designed around Halford's expanded Gipsy Major engine, which he confidently predicted would produce 200 hp. The aircraft was to be the company's 86th design, to be called the "Express Air Liner", and the new engine, using normal de Havilland logic, the "Gipsy Six".

Major Halford and his Engine Department Head, Mr R H Hutchinson, accepted the task of building enough of these new extended Gipsy Majors to allow full ground- and air- testing in time to fit four engines to the new aircraft and bravely promised that they would have nine Gipsy Sixes, tested and ready for installation of four into the prototype DH 86, by the last Saturday before Christmas 1933.

With great urgency, the engine shop set about producing an engine which had as much in common with the Major as they could possibly manage. While the machined crankshaft, forged in nickel-chrome-alloy steel, and the crankcase, made from the now well-tried "Elektron" aluminium alloy, had of necessity to be completely re-designed, much of the running gear was simply transferred from the smaller engine. The cylinders, cylinder heads, valves, valve gear, pistons, rings, gudgeon pins, connecting rods, and big-end bearings were, at first, all the same as on the smaller engine. Changes were inevitably made as the engine was developed, but these initial similarities allowed the Gipsy Major engineer to quickly become familiar with the Gipsy Six. The nose of the engine was only increased in length by about six inches, and yet it had the same diameter and only slightly greater height than its smaller sister. The air-cooling ducts for all six cylinders had to be more efficient than with the four-cylinder version, and so did the carburettor heating, so these two elements required some re-design. In order to leave more space for the carburettors and various linkages on the side of the engine, the two magnetos were moved to the top casing of the engine, which actually fitted quite neatly into the ideal cowling shape. Drive gears were made available for use by items such as generator, electrical tachometer and constant-speed propeller governor, but none of these were fitted to the early engines. Care was taken to screen the high-tension ignition leads from the magnetos to the spark plugs, so that radio interference was minimised and the heavy braiding was kept as short as possible to save weight. All up, the new engine produced a very creditable figure of 2.11 lbs per horsepower, at a weight of 432 lbs, which

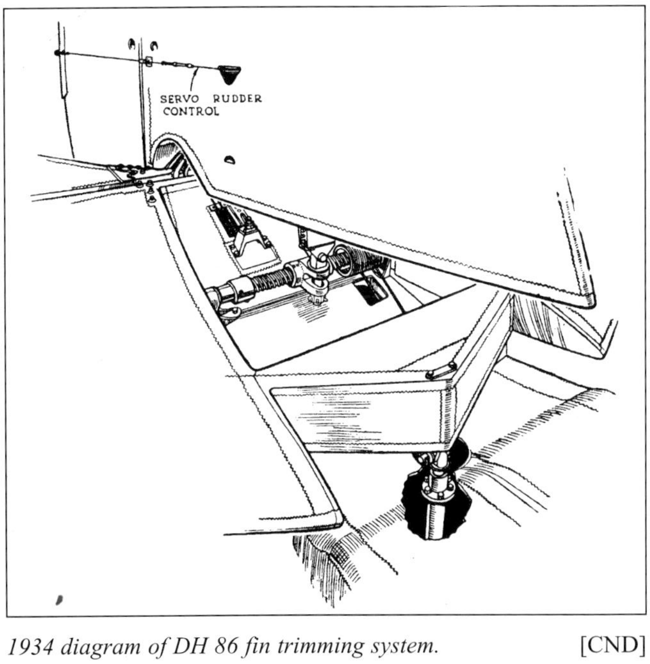

1934 diagram of DH 86 fin trimming system. [CND]

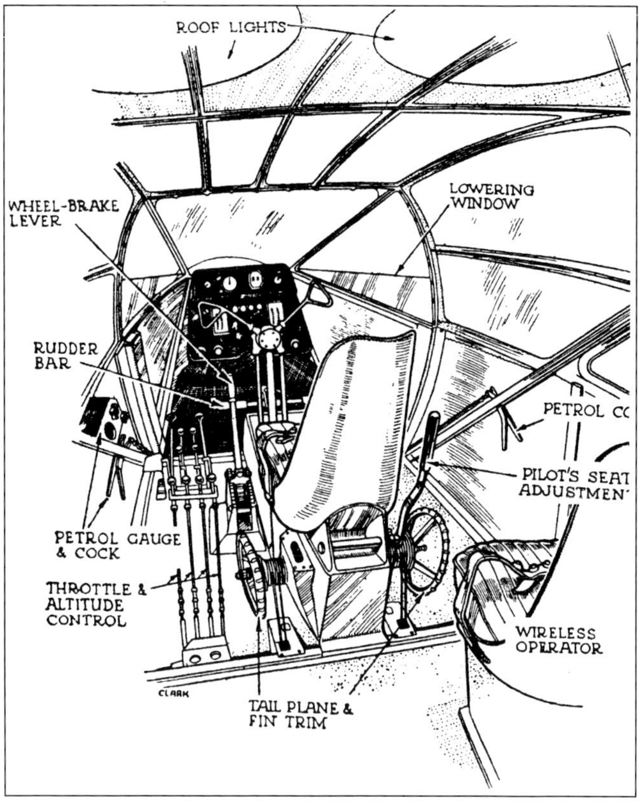

Single-pilot DH 86 cockpit drawing from a contempoarary aviation magazine. [CND]

compared well with the smaller Gipsy's 320.5 lbs and 2.4 lbs per horsepower.

Through the expertise and prodigious efforts of the experimental section of the engine department, Mr Hutchinson had nine shiny new Gipsy Sixes, all satisfactorily tested in the Stag Lane test sheds and merely awaiting Type Test certification by the local AID inspector, by lunch time on the Friday before Christmas, 1933.

THE AIRFRAME

In the meantime, the sketches seen by Captain Fysh were rapidly converted into a full design by the Stag Lane drawing office, with Arthur Hagg at the helm. In addition to the engines, the other element of the design which would give the relatively high speed required by the specification was the wing. Remembering their Technical Director's well-known philosophy that span was the most important factor in producing better lift/drag ratios, proffering higher aerodynamic efficiency, and producing higher overall cruising speeds, the draughtsmen drew up a wing which was fairly thin, was well tapered, had a high aspect ratio and a wide span. In order to keep the wing span within reasonable bounds and still produce enough lift to take the weight, this was a braced biplane and in line with previous designs, the wings were a two-bay biplane set-up, based on I-shaped spruce spars, spruce leading and trailing edges, with internal bracing by steel drag struts. Flaps were excluded to save weight, as the landing speeds would be quite low with a biplane wing, giving reasonably short field performance. All surfaces were fabric covered, but the leading edges were covered with three-ply wood for extra strength. Four of the new Gipsy Sixes were fitted to the lower wing, extra support being provided by a short steel spar running through the stub wing, and two main fuel tanks, holding 57 gallons each, were fitted behind the two inboard engines. With sensible forethought, but not requested in the specification, a modification to provide two auxiliary fuel tanks, to be fitted within the inboard bottom stub planes, was also drawn up.

A relatively simple fixed Dowty undercarriage, with steel coil compression-sprung cylinders supporting a single wheel on each side of the aircraft, was fitted to the inboard engine bearers.

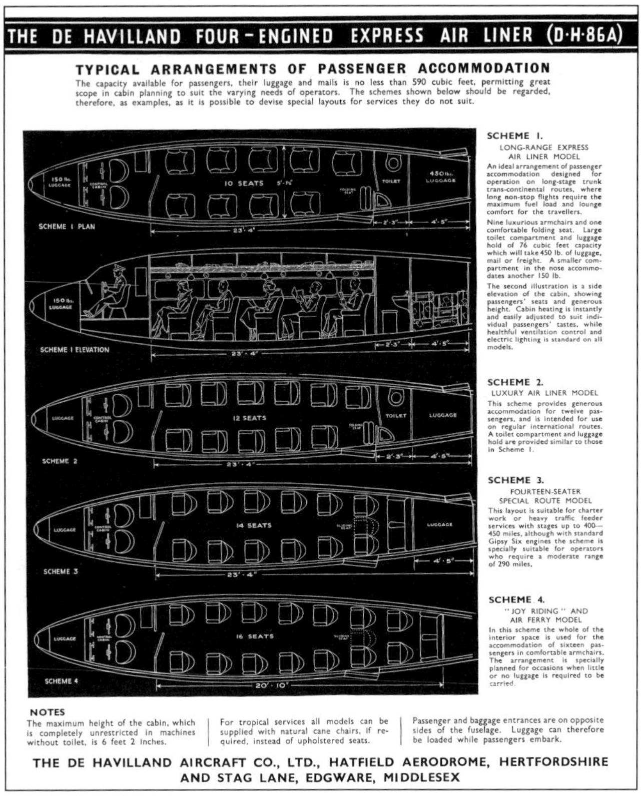

THE DE HAVILLAND FOUR-ENGINED EXPRESS AIR LINER (D·H·86A)

TYPICAL ARRANGEMENTS OF PASSENGER ACCOMMODATION

The capacity available for passengers, their luggage and mails is no less than 590 cubic feet, permitting great scope in cabin planning to suit the varying needs of operators. The schemes shown below should be regarded, therefore, as examples, as it is possible to devise special layouts for services they do not suit.

SCHEME I.
LONG-RANGE EXPRESS AIR LINER MODEL

An ideal arrangement of passenger accommodation designed for operation on long-stage trunk trans-continental routes, where long non-stop flights require the maximum fuel load and lounge comfort for the travellers.

Nine luxurious armchairs and one comfortable folding seat. Large toilet compartment and luggage hold of 76 cubic feet capacity which will take 450 lb. of luggage, mail or freight. A smaller compartment in the nose accommodates another 150 lb.

The second illustration is a side elevation of the cabin, showing passengers' seats and generous height. Cabin heating is instantly and easily adjusted to suit individual passengers' tastes, while healthful ventilation control and electric lighting is standard on all models.

SCHEME 2.
LUXURY AIR LINER MODEL

This scheme provides generous accommodation for twelve passengers, and is intended for use on regular international routes. A toilet compartment and luggage hold are provided similar to those in Scheme I.

SCHEME 3.
FOURTEEN-SEATER SPECIAL ROUTE MODEL

This layout is suitable for charter work or heavy traffic feeder services with stages up to 400—450 miles, although with standard Gipsy Six engines the scheme is specially suitable for operators who require a moderate range of 290 miles.

SCHEME 4.
"JOY RIDING" AND AIR FERRY MODEL

In this scheme the whole of the interior space is used for the accommodation of sixteen passengers in comfortable armchairs. The arrangement is specially planned for occasions when little or no luggage is required to be carried.

NOTES

The maximum height of the cabin, which is completely unrestricted in machines without toilet, is 6 feet 2 inches.

For tropical services all models can be supplied with natural cane chairs, if required, instead of upholstered seats.

Passenger and baggage entrances are on opposite sides of the fuselage. Luggage can therefore be loaded while passengers embark.

THE DE HAVILLAND AIRCRAFT CO., LTD., HATFIELD AERODROME, HERTFORDSHIRE AND STAG LANE, EDGWARE, MIDDLESEX

Passenger seating schemes, August 1936. *[BAe]*

Bendix wheel brakes were fitted to both main wheels operated, via cables, by a lever to the left of the pilot's seat. Engines and undercarriages were closely cowled in Elektron alloy sheeting for minimum drag. Tailplane and fin structure were spruce-based, similar to that of the wings, then covered in ply, but a tailplane-trimming device, using a single screw jack, was fitted at the elevator front spar. In the interests of withstanding greater asymmetric loads, the rudder was a welded steel tube structure, again covered in three-ply and fabric.

In order to allow for better directional controllability in the event of engine failure, the drawing office somewhat boldly introduced a new method of compensating for directional loads associated with engine failure in flight, a system previously untried on DH machines. A trim tab was fitted at the trailing edge of the horn-balanced rudder, linked to a lever in the fin, which in turn applied a balancing force to the pilot's rudder movements. In addition, directional assistance was incorporated, consisting of a trimming device, operated by a screw jack, which allowed the angle of the fin to be adjusted from the cockpit, with the objective of trimming out asymmetric flight loads. This innovative rudder balancing system was to produce problems in practice, almost certainly because insufficient time was available for flight testing under all conditions, before the aircraft entered service.

The fuselage was made from a spruce-formed box frame, similar to that of the DH 84, but in this case, shaped longitudinal stringers were fitted outside the ply box, over which was stretched a medapolam fabric covering, giving a more rounded appearance to the fuselage. It had smooth plywood interior surfaces measuring a comfortable 16 feet by nearly 5 feet wide and an average of 6 feet 3 inches of headroom. For sound-proofing and insulation, Cabot sound-proofing material was fitted between the ply box and the exterior. There was a choice of seating arrangements, but the main format was for ten comfortable blue leather-covered "armchairs" made by Rumbolds, and for the eight-seater, walnut panels along the cabin walls. There was a controllable ventilator above the windows, supplying cool air for each passenger, and later models would have a basic heating system. At the rear of the cabin was a lavatory, and aft of that, with an external door on the right side of the fuselage, a separate luggage compartment. The single pilot had quite a spacious cockpit, with a thwart-ships seat for a radio operator behind and to his right and particularly for the long sectors on the Singapore to Darwin run, a medium-frequency radio would be fitted as standard. There was to be a major change to the crew seating arrangements before QEA took delivery of their first DH 86, but the design agreed with QEA only required a single pilot, and that is how the first four aircraft were built.

PERFORMANCE ESTIMATES

Using the expected all up weight of 9,200 lbs, and a payload load of 1,915 lbs, de Havilland's performance calculations predicted a reasonable cruising speed of 140 to 150 mph, and a range, with the two standard 57-gallon tanks feeding all four engines, of 450 statute miles to dry tanks. With optional auxiliary tanks, the potential range increased to 758 statute miles. The maximum ceiling would be around 20,000ft and the stalling speed would be a very reasonable 66 - 68 knots.

THE RACE TO CERTIFICATION

The DH 86 had to be assembled very quickly in order to meet the contracted timescales, and there was virtually no time for the extensive development work normally accorded to a new aircraft before it was submitted for Air Ministry certification. However, all the Stag Lane departments put in frantic efforts to get the work finished. The efforts of the drawing office team to convert the basic design into working drawings could be seen from the big wooden skeleton expanding daily behind canvas security screens in the main assembly area. The sub-assembly shops translated those drawings into wood and metal; the electrical and pipe shops fitted their own elements of plumbing into the growing structure; the dope-and-fabric and paint shops covered and sprayed the wings, fuselage and empennage, so that by the first days of January, 1934, functional tests could be carried out by Mr Morse's Inspection Department. By the end of the first week of the New Year the precious new aircraft was handed to Mr Woodhouse, the aerodrome foreman, for pre-flight tests.

Captain Hubert Broad, the Chief test pilot, finally signed for the prototype, sprayed silver overall and wearing de Havilland's test marking 'E.2.', on Sunday, 14th January 1934. Despite it being a weekend, a small crowd of company workers had gathered on the airfield to watch with great excitement on that cold winter's day. Captain Broad climbed aboard, ran up each engine in turn and, satisfied, waved the chocks away, taxied to the north-eastern corner of Stag Lane's diminishing airfield, then turned back towards the south-west for the first take-off. The aircraft was airborne quickly because of its light load, and flew off to carry out the main parts of the first proving flight. Only a portion of the flight tests could be completed that day, as the light metal nose bowl had caved in during the speed runs, so Captain Broad returned early and further flights followed over the next few days, before the aircraft was submitted to the Martlesham Heath test pilots, for Certificate of Airworthiness testing.

THE INITIAL MARTLESHAM TESTS

When it appeared at Martlesham ready for testing, E.2 was ballasted up to its initial maximum weight of 9,200 lbs all-up, which included ten passenger seats, and crew seats for the single pilot and a radio operator. The test reports revealed a maximum level speed of 171 mph, a cruising speed of around 145 mph, a landing speed of 72 mph, and that the aircraft could maintain 15,000 feet with one engine out, and a creditable 3,600 feet with two engines on the same side out. In terms of handling, little was said, except that the controls were considered heavy above 170 mph (above maximum level speed) but otherwise handling was good. No mention was made of any adverse aspects of directional or lateral stability. These tests indicated that the DH 86 carried the same load as the current American mail aircraft, at approximately the same speed, with half the engine power, and was able to continue at a safe height even if two engines failed - and all at around one third of the price. The main requirements of the Australian contract had therefore been exceeded and the Airworthiness Certificate was signed by the Air Ministry on

Hubert Broad landing E.2 at Stag Lane after its first flight, 14th January 1934. *[LNA]*

30th January. DH had met the contractual timescale with one day to spare.

That the DH 86 was reported as behaving as well as it did in its early life is rather surprising, considering the faults that were inherent in the aircraft as first flown. None of the major difficulties often associated with a new and markedly different aircraft showed themselves within that sixteen day period, which was just as well, as there would have been no possibility of correcting any structural or design faults before the contract deadline. There is a possibility that the tests were less rigorous than usual because of the great pressure on the makers and the Air Ministry to achieve certification for this prestigious project by the key contract date of 31st January. While there is no indication of incomplete testing from the detailed Martlesham flight test reports, there must have been considerable pressure to gain a satisfactory result in the few days that E.2 was at Martlesham Heath.

Despite stability problems that undoubtedly were inherent in the design, and which existed during the Martlesham trials, but which were only to came to light after some time in service, the award of a Certificate of Airworthiness was quite justified, bearing in mind the flight testing methods of the period. The problems would certainly have been discovered by the more searching tests which were introduced a few years later, but in 1933 this aircraft was fully tested to the levels then believed to be acceptable for all commercial types. More radical handling difficulties were discovered later in the aircraft's life, but at this stage none were discovered that would prevent the aircraft going into airline service in the summer of 1934, a bare six months after the grant of the first Certificate of Airworthiness.

The few minor criticisms identified during the Martlesham Heath tests required only small changes which were promptly incorporated in the prototype, to be followed by further modifications recommended as a result of company and airline development trials. These trials were carried out by Hubert Broad, Bob Waight and Major Hereward de Havilland, on the prototype, which was now registered G-ACPL. Over the summer of 1934, changes began to appear, initially on G-ACPL and later on the second and third aircraft, VH-URN, and G-ACVY which had appeared in July 1934. By the end of December, drawings had been produced for as many as 30 modifications. Most of these were minor, and began with a changed shape for the "trouser" cowlings below the inner engines and surrounding the undercarriage, to "minimise drag, give greater accessibility to the power installation and to facilitate maintenance" in the words of the DH manuals, but also to give a much neater appearance to the whole engine/undercarriage area. Landing tests had also brought out criticism of the landing performance of the type, despite the quite creditable test figure of only 260 yards . As a result of tests, hydraulically-operated split flaps were fitted as standard inboard on the upper wings to the fifteenth aircraft, G-ACYF and all subsequent aircraft, from early 1935. This modification gave an increased angle of descent in the glide from "1 in 9.5 to around 1 in 6.5", and slightly decreased the stalling speed, but more importantly, a 5 mph slower landing speed coupled with decreased float on landing, thereby giving a reduced landing distance of 239 yards. Temporary use of Fairey Reed metal propellers with a different pitch compared to the usual wooden type was also tried, but as no noticeable benefits were gained, the lighter wooden type remained as standard.

QEA-REQUESTED CHANGES

In the Spring of 1934, QEA's chief pilot, Captain Lester Brain, came over to familiarise himself with his new charge, looking at the design from the operational view point. His first request to de Havilland was to look at the possibility of changing the cockpit to accommodate two pilots, instead of one, as the aircraft would need to fly long distances, often at night, when a two-pilot operation would be much safer. This request was backed up by QEA, so the drawing office team set to work to modify the cockpit, nose, and

Hubert Broad at the controls of G-ACPL on a press demonstration flight, 1934. *[Flight]*

The interior of G-ACPL on the press demonstration flight, 1934. [Flight]

control systems in order to comply with what was a major change of specification. Captain Brain also asked for longer range than the published "450 miles to dry tanks" of the basic aircraft, which meant fitting two extra fuel tanks in addition to the 57-gallon tanks specified. Provision for two auxiliary tanks holding 38.5 gallons each had been built into the design, and these were later fitted to the QEA aircraft, increasing the range to a more practical 750 miles (to dry tanks). Such basic changes showed a remarkable lack of planning on the part of the customer, as they required drastic alterations to an aircraft which was already flying and certificated. At this point in the production of a new aircraft, such major changes to the original specification were bound to cause extra costs and significant delays to the in-service date of the new machines. It would appear that the aircraft required by QEA had not been specified with much regard for its actual task, as surely the need for two pilots and for a greater range than 450 miles, when the distance from Koepang to Darwin was just less than 500 miles, should have been included in the original specification?

The drawing office team, still working from Stag Lane for a few more months, were by now heavily embroiled in designing the DH 87 Hornet Moth and the DH 89, both of which were to fly within the following four months. Despite these pressures, they produced a complete re-design of the DH 86's forward fuselage with a wider, higher, longer nose with separate luggage compartment; new windscreen; two seats with dual control system for two pilots; two auxiliary fuel tanks, holding 38.5 gallons each, positioned in the inboard lower stub wings; and larger oil tanks to cope with increased engine running time. With the auxiliary tanks, the aircraft had a total fuel capacity of 191 gallons, giving an extra 300 miles' range, increasing the "ultimate range, with no reserves" to 750 statute miles. With all these modifications, the all-up weight inevitably rose, until it rounded out at 10,250 lbs for the two-pilot DH 86 model. The price quoted for the standard DH 86A, "ready for flight", in the May 1936 de Havilland Price List, was £8,750.

The new nose was quickly applied to the prototype, G-ACPL, and this shape then became the standard, until further changes were made in 1936, to create the DH 86A. Because of the time needed to re-design the new nose, the second, third and fourth aircraft, VH-URN, G-ACVY and G-ACVZ were completed as single-pilot models and the first aircraft to be built from new with the two-pilot nose was the fifth, G-ACWC, which was completed in March 1935, for service with Imperial Airways in the spring of that year. G-ACVZ was later converted to two-pilot status in March 1936. At around this time, the aircraft was given a name rather than just a number - the aviation press had initially called it the "Double Dragon" and even suggested it be called "Caravan" because it housed so many Gipsies, but the name announced by the makers was "The de Havilland DH 86 Express Air Liner".

REVISED COCKPIT LAYOUT - TWO-PILOT

Dominating the space in front of each pilot was the heavy, electron-moulded control column, agricultural in style, which sprouted from the central cockpit floor and which branched out into a Y-shaped yoke to provide smart black control spectacles for the two pilots. Despite the change of seating arrangements compared to the single-pilot version, the trim wheels remained in virtually the same central position, usable by either pilot, and the single long brake lever was somewhat awkwardly placed between the two trim wheels. The

Prototype G-ACPL had been painted in Imperial Airways colours in June 1934 prior to conversion to two-pilot configuration. [D.Fox]

Modified prototype G-ACPL airborne from Stag Lane, 1933. *[CND]*

simple alloy "petrol taps" were fitted, as on the earlier version, on the left and right cockpit walls. Probably the most inconvenient change from the single pilot-version was the re-positioning of the neat handful of elegant alloy throttle and mixture levers from the left cockpit wall to a position, sprouting on long unwieldy stalks from the centre of the instrument panel. This position tended to disturb the flying pilot's throttle hand whenever the heavy control column mounting moved fore or aft. When the split flaps were fitted as standard from 1935 onwards, the control box and rather awkward operating lever were placed behind the left hand seat, usually operated by the co-pilot, whose seat could be rotated to facilitate flap and radio controls. On the bulkhead behind the pilot's seats were the large radio control boxes, containing a choice of radio aids, depending on the wishes of the purchaser.

VH-UUA c/n 2306 for QEA on airborne air test from Hatfield, February 1935. *[DHMC]*

Single-pilot version G-ACVY c/n 2302 on a test flight over Hatfield House, August 1934. *[CND]*

As an example, British Continental Airways ordered a comprehensive radio fit for their first aircraft, G-ADYC, in the spring of 1936. In addition to the usual flight instruments, the airline requested a Marconi medium-wave transmitter-receiver, together with trailing aerial, hand-winch and Morse key on the co-pilot's side panel, as well as a Lorenz short-wave "blind-landing" set, the precursor of the modern instrument landing system. This set, with three large boxes behind the co-pilot's seat, and selection controls on the Captain's left wall, fed a crude "direction indicator" in the centre of the instrument panel, and provided signals to assist in making approaches to airfields in poor weather conditions, assuming, of course, the airfield was fitted with the equivalent ground equipment. These two sets of bulky, valve-driven radios themselves took up a good deal of space in the cockpit, and also weighed close to 500 lb, which brought the CG even further forward, and reduced the payload to only 1,635 lb with full fuel and radio sets fitted.

The Qantas Empire Airways board approved the purchase of a fleet of seven DH 86s for their Singapore to Cootamundra service, and following the award on 19th April 1934 of the contract from the Australian government to QANTAS for the new service, orders were placed by Imperial Airways on their behalf. In addition, orders were beginning to appear from British airlines as well as another Australian company, Tasmanian Aerial Services (soon to become Holyman's Airways) of Tasmania.

Left: DH 86 two-pilot early cockpit arrangement, 1935. *[BAe]*

VH-USC c/n 2307 refuelling at Singapore, January, 1936. *[DHMC]*

Section 3 – Chapter 2: In-Service Problems and Development

INITIAL SETBACKS IN AUSTRALIA

Holyman's Airways and QEA began operations in the summer and autumn of 1934, and all appeared to go reasonably well for the first few months.

However, two accidents occurred to Australian DH 86s in quick succession in late 1934, which caused the Australian authorities, the Air Ministry in England and de Havilland to become concerned about the type's safety. First, on 19th October, Holyman's Airways' VH-URN, the second DH 86 built, and still a single-pilot model, disappeared near Wilson's Promontory, Bass Strait, with the loss of the owner, Victor Holyman, the designated pilot and nine passengers. This accident was then followed a month later, on 15 November, by the loss of QEA's VH-USG on take-off from Longreach, still on its delivery flight, with the loss of its British crew and an Australian engineer. The Australian Department of Civil Aviation promptly suspended the Certificates of Airworthiness of all indigenous DH 86s, pending an inquiry by the Department and the makers. The Australian inquiries found no positive causes for the local accidents, but, in December, a joint British investigation was agreed between the Air Ministry and de Havilland, so the DCA in Australia awaited the outcome of this before allowing their DH 86s to fly again.

In England, QEA's fourth aircraft, VH-USF, was held back at Hatfield for practical tests, centred around possible engine failures and the subsequent behaviour of aircraft and crew. Asymmetric handling trials were flown by de Havilland at Hatfield, and on behalf of the Air Ministry at Martlesham Heath in December 1934, concentrating on examination of handling characteristics during all combinations of engine failure. The company concurrently set up structural tests, but found no apparent weaknesses. The flying tests identified no obvious handling problems and no conclusion was reached on the likely cause of the Australian accidents, but as a precaution, to assist with gaining full rudder authority in the event of engine failure, de Havilland re-designed the rudder with a metal rather than a wooden structure and the fin was also strengthened, but no further changes were made to the design at this stage.

Following the completion of these trials, with the conclusion that the aircraft structure appeared satisfactory, the Australian DCA reluctantly re-instated the aircrafts' Airworthiness Certificates, and clearance was given to recommence DH 86 operations, subject to the modifications set in hand by de Havilland.

THE DH 86A

After two years of service with Holyman's Airways and QEA in Australia, British Continental Air Services, British Airways, Imperial Airways, Jersey Airways, Olley Air Services, Railway Air Services and Wrightways in Britain; Misr Airwork in Egypt, and Union Airways of New Zealand, de Havilland offered two modified versions of the "New De Havilland Express Air Liner" in 1936, both to be known as the DH 86A. The first model was to be powered by standard 200 hp Gipsy Six engines with standard wooden fixed-pitch propellers, and the other was offered with 210 hp Gipsy Six Series II engines, complete with de Havilland controllable-pitch propellers, very similar to those used on the DH 88 Comet Racer of 1934. Both

Imperial Airways' G-ACWD c/n 2305 at Kai Tak, Hong Kong, March, 1936. *[CND]*

airframes were to be identical, and were to incorporate "desirable improvements" permitting a higher payload than the standard DH 86. In fact, no customers opted for the Series II engines, and no DH 86As were produced with these engines, with operators seemingly happy with the standard, slightly lower-powered engines.

In their Express Air Liner publications, the company described the modifications incorporated into the "New DH 86A model for 1936" as :

1. Modifications to the main structure of the airframe to allow a higher maximum weight.(now up to 10,250 lb).
2. A completely different undercarriage, the "Turner compressed-air Landing Leg", is introduced, incorporating pneumatic compression legs, and a larger and more powerful braking system.
3. An improved tailwheel, with larger Dunlop "Ecta" tyre.
4. Redesigned inner engine cowlings, for lower drag and easier accessibility to engines and undercarriage.
5. Dual controls are again fitted as standard, but the general comfort of the crew has been the object of particular study in the new model. The commander and first officer's seats have undergone certain improved changes, while the cockpit windows and windscreens have been modified to reduce the entry of wind and rain when opened, and to improve visibility during bad weather. In addition to luminous instruments, the instrument panel is indirectly lit, while the general lighting of the cockpit has been carried out on more scientific principles.
6. A change in the profile of the wing tips, to give a higher degree of lateral stability and increased lift at low speeds.
7. Improved cabin sound-proofing, heating and ventilation.
8. The use of a rudder servo-flap in conjunction with the adjustable fin entirely counteracts the effect of uneven thrust occasioned by one or two engines out of action, and enables the machine to be flown with full load in this condition without undue muscular effort on the part of the pilot. The servo flap is now operated by the fin trim gear and not by the rudder.

An important part of the "modifications to the main structure", was the strengthening of the drag tubes and the internal wing bracing wires and spars, in an attempt to counter the wing flexing reported earlier by the Australian DCA. These stronger elements were incorporated on all DH86s from early 1936 onwards.

Imperial Airways house magazine cover, 1936, showing the unfortunate G-ADCM 'Draco' c/n 2317 which was written-off in October 1935 in Austria. *[P Edmonds]*

EUROPEAN ACCIDENTS

By the summer of 1936, with over forty DH 86s and DH 86As in service, several more had been lost in accidents. While no clear causes had been found for the two earlier Australian accidents, two occurred in Europe neither of which could be fully explained. Understandably, the Air Ministry, de Havillands and the Australian DCA were becoming increasingly concerned that structural or handling problems might be associated with some of these accidents.

The first of the British-operated aircraft to crash was an Imperial Airways DH86, G-ADCM, which crashed during a forced landing at Zwettl, Austria on 22 October 1935. Then, in the following month, a false alarm was raised when Holyman's VH-USG made a forced landing on Flinders Island, after a suspected structural failure. In fact the problem here was simply a loose plastic cover at the base of an interplane strut, and the structure was completely intact. The following year a British Airways' DH 86, G-ADEB,

First production DH 86A, c/n 2333 G-ADUE "Dardanus" parked at Gatwick in 1936, alongside G-ADUF 'Dido'. *[CND]*

British Airways' G-ADYJ c/n 2348 parked adjacent to Gatwick's new railway station, 1936. *[CND]*

crashed into a mountain at Altenkirchen on 12 August 1936, whilst on a night mail flight from Hanover. In the light of later knowledge, these two European accidents can probably be attributed in the first instance to flight through severe icing, to which the DH 86 was particularly prone, with so many wings, wires and excrescenses sitting out in the airflow. But, these incidents, coming so close together, with the same type of aircraft, aroused much public concern in Britain and Australia. British Airways became very concerned about the inherent safety of the type, and requested an urgent investigation into the handling qualities of the type, offering another of their DH 86As, G-ADYH, which had been delivered in August, for tests by Air Ministry pilots. The Air Ministry agreed that the recent accidents warranted fuller investigation into the type's handling characteristics, and at the end of October 1936 requested de Havilland and Martlesham to cooperate in a further series of tests, in an attempt to isolate the cause of the accidents.

MARTLESHAM STABILITY INVESTIGATIONS

While the flying tests were underway, de Havilland carried out their own in-house structural tests and concluded that there were no indications of weaknesses in the design or the structure of the aircraft. The Air Ministry flying trials with G-ADYH at Martlesham Heath were completed in November 1936 and in complete contrast to the initial Air Ministry C of A tests, this report certainly came up with some very disturbing results. The flying controls were found to lack harmony to different degrees. Aileron response was "erratic, and not well proportioned to the amount of aileron movement; at low speeds it was inadequate. Rudder response was inadequate for small movements. Larger movements of the rudder gave a sudden and rapid response and a decrease in the force on the pilot's foot".

This is symptomatic of classic rudder over-balance. More unexpected and surprising comments were to follow: "When rudder was applied without ailerons, the aircraft swung violently and dropped its nose. If, in calm air, bank was applied by the ailerons alone, the rudder being held fixed, then the aircraft would slowly turn in the opposite direction". Leading on from this test, if right rudder was applied in a climb, then released, the aircraft was initially seen to swing to the right, then recover and, rather alarmingly, turn to the left, together with a significant dropping of the nose.

On general stability, the report stated: "In normal flight at speeds up to 235 mph, the aircraft tended to move bodily from side to side. With the C of G on the aft limit, this movement in sideslip was accompanied by a rolling motion in which the outer wing dropped".

Another disturbing aspect was that in the pilots' opinion, should an outboard engine fail suddenly on take-off, temporary loss of control might well result. This was almost certainly a function of insufficient rudder authority at slow speeds. However, they considered that failure of an inner engine would not cause such an uncontrollable swing, so would probably not lead to loss of control.

The handling comments concluded with the opinion that because of the control features exposed in the tests, the aircraft was: "extremely difficult to fly in disturbed air conditions.....lively in its reaction to bumps, and the lag in response [to controls] made it impossible to keep on a straight course in such conditions".

Finally, the Martlesham report's damning conclusion was that the aircraft was "not satisfactory in flight except in calm air and very gentle manoeuvres".

Such a drastic result was astonishing, bearing in mind that nearly two years had passed since the aircraft had first flown; that it had by then been quite thoroughly tested both by the makers and a team from Martlesham; that pilots from ten different operators had flown the aircraft in commercial service, yet none of these had made official complaints about its handling until the QANTAS and British Airways requests for investigation into the aircraft's handling. It would almost seem that this was an entirely different aeroplane from that tested by A&AEE's own pilots in January 1934.

G-ADUH c/n 2336, one of the DH 86s grounded after the 1936 Flight Tests. *[M Stroud]*

AIR MINISTRY RESTRICTIONS

Immediately after the Martlesham report (M363B) was published in December 1936, the Air Ministry took the drastic action of withdrawing the Certificates of Airworthiness of all British DH 86As, announcing that each was to be tested and categorised before being considered for re-certification. The categories were to be:

"Group I, Grounded" as being considered unsafe to fly, or
"Group II, Restricted to being flown only by day, and, if passengers were carried, by pilots with at least 50 hours on type".

Imperial Airways G-ADUG, airborne, 1936.

All sixteen of the DH 86As then on the British register were quickly tested at Gatwick and Croydon by the same two Martlesham pilots, so that a standard level of assessment could be made. Rather illogically, despite the essentially similar configuration and handling qualities of the two models, the 27 DH 86s by then operating worldwide were not affected by this Air Ministry edict, and so they were allowed to continue in service.

Of the DH 86As, those grounded as Group I were :
G-ADYG, G-ADYH, G-ADYI, of British Airways;
G-ADUH, of Imperial Airways;
G-ADYC, G-ADYD, G-ADYE, of British Continental Airways.
These aircraft were quickly modified to DH 86B standard in early 1937, and went back into service.

Those aircraft categorised as Group II were:
G-ADFF, G-ADUE, G-ADUG, G-AEFH, G-AEAP, G-ADUF, and G-ADUI, belonging to Imperial Airways;
G-AEJM, of Wrightways;
G -ADVK, of Blackpool and West Coast Air Services.

In addition to the precaution that this Group could only be flown by day and only by pilots with at least 50 hours on type, the Air Ministry also required them to have "the spring loading removed from the elevator", which seems unusual, but was aimed at improving speed-keeping and making the aircraft "more manageable in bumpy weather" as found during the Martlesham pilots' tests. Once again, as with the Group I aircraft, all these Group II aircraft were returned to de Havilland and modified to DH 86B standard by mid-1937.

UNSTABLE DESIGN?

A test pilot who had considerable experience of assessing the handling qualities of many wartime multi-engined designs, particularly when a Tutor at the Empire Test Pilots School, Air Commodore 'Cyclops' Brown, was recently asked to comment on the apparent stability of the single-pilot and extended-nose DH 86s, and their likely handling qualities, when seen from a test pilot's viewpoint. He had not flown the DH 86, nor had he then seen the Martlesham reports, but had considerable experience of handling and stability tests on aircraft such as the DH 89, Stirling, Halifax and York.

His immediate reaction on looking at photographs of both versions was that this aircraft was very likely to have stability problems. From the appearance of the aircraft, with its four wide-spread engines on narrow-chord wings; the small-area single fin and relatively small rudder, and the short nose, this test pilot believed that there would be a probability of directional instability causing serious de-stabilising effects on the aircraft's handling. The fin and rudder were considered to be too small to prevent any directional disturbances from exaggerating the tenuous directional stability, and this would be made worse by any over-balancing effects from the rudder and its servo tab. The weight of the outboard engines would also make any directional disturbances more pronounced. If this directional sensitivity were to be coupled with poor aileron control, particularly at slow speeds, then the already poor lateral stability would compound the handling problems. And this was only by looking at elements of the design.

These comments proved to be very closely in accord with the actual stability problems discovered by the Australian and Martlesham pilots during their belated handling tests. If these problems had been seen earlier, either by the designers or the Air Ministry testers, then his aircraft would have been much safer and may have had a more successful service life.

MODIFICATIONS LEADING TO THE DH 86B

The November 1936 Martlesham report, being an official pronouncement, had obviously to be acted upon by de Havilland, in the interests of safety and their own reputation. They therefore set to work very quickly to find a solution. But they first had to define the problem.

From the Martlesham pilots' serious criticisms of the aircraft's handling, it was obvious to the de Havilland design team that the main problem was one of stability, both directional and lateral. The root of this instability was probable over-balancing of the rudder, not helped by the over-active rudder servo-tab, together with less-than-effective ailerons and wing flexing. Could there also be a directional stability complication caused by the longer, wider, heavier nose built onto the original DH 86 design, which certainly provided more lift than the original shape, but may also have required compensating aerodynamic balancing by a larger fin and rudder? Was the rudder servo-tab too powerful, causing the over-balance situation? Was the reported "side to side and rolling motion" in some way related to the weight of the heavy outboard engines and the small vertical tail surfaces? They set about searching for aerodynamic solutions, as quickly and simply as possible. A major change, such as enlarging the ailerons or rudder, would involve complicated, costly and time-consuming calculations and modifications, so the most cost-effective solution was to first pursue greater directional stability through other aerodynamic means. They needed a solution which would enhance both directional and lateral stability, particularly during turbulent flight, so instead of increasing the size of the existing fin and rudder and including ventral and dorsal fillets, they looked at increasing the vertical surface area, but outboard of the elevators, and within the slipstream from the engines.

Working closely with the Drawing Office team, the Hatfield Experimental Department in Autumn 1936, made up trial fittings and attached them to a newly-produced DH 86A, c/n 2342, which then became the second E.2, and used for test flights. Auxiliary fins were initially fitted over each tailplane of the aircraft at half-span but were soon changed to larger elliptical fins, four feet in height, (later nicknamed Zulu shields by the Hatfield workers, for obvious reasons) which were moved to the outer ends of the tailplane spars. Both elevators were also slightly increased in area for better

SU-ABV c/n 2342 at Hatfield in early 1937, after completing DH 86B trials, before delivery to Egypt. *[Hawker Siddeley]*

controllability at low speeds. The auxiliary fins were offset by 3 degrees to starboard in order to assist rudder effort in the case of failure of a critical engine. A lower-powered spring gear was fitted to the elevator control system, and the rudder servo-tab was disconnected from the rudder pedal circuit, and made to act only in concert with the fin bias system, thereby making the removal of rudder loads easier under asymmetric conditions. In order to address the wing-flexing problem, the top and bottom outer wing lower surfaces were completely covered with 1.5 millimetre 3-ply and the incidence of the outer section of the wings was altered to give better lateral control at slow speeds. In an attempt to gain more effective aileron response to control input, the gearing in the aileron system was also altered. Despite the adverse comment in an earlier Martlesham report, there was insufficient time to fit a guard between the two sets of rudder bars in E.2's cockpit, to prevent the possibility of either pilot accidentally applying rudder when turning in his seat, but all later DH 86Bs were fitted with this guard.

DH SOLUTIONS

E.2 was flown to try out these modifications and to the delight of all, these company tests showed that these aerodynamic fixes produced much better stability and vastly improved handling, especially in turbulent air. These modifications became the basis of the new designation DH 86B and with only 12 hours' flight in its log book, E.2 was submitted for further testing by the Ministry pilots at Martlesham Heath in mid-December 1936. These tests were as thorough as for an initial airworthiness test, covering performance, handling, diving, take-off and landing trials at maximum weight, and three CG positions, but of course the emphasis was naturally on handling and stability.

Controls were reported as being better harmonised and effective all-round. The aileron adjustments were not quite right, as full movement was necessary to raise a wing when taking off and landing. The rudder was heavy but effective throughout, and the elevator was light, but its trimming gear did not give sufficient range for gliding, although there was sufficient control for landing. The pleasing result was that directionally, "the aeroplane is stable with engines on or off, the application of rudder followed by release resulting in a quick return to the original course".

Laterally, it was not quite neutrally stable as, after a small disturbance, the depressed wing remained down, but there was no yaw. There were comments on the harshness of the undercarriage; the low gearing of the ailerons; the slightly less-effective tail trimming range; and the need for a partition between the pilots' rudder bars, to prevent fouling by the 2nd pilot, when turning rearwards to operate radio or flap controls.

Finally, the main concerns of de Havilland were covered by the summary of the flying qualities: "In general, the stability of the aeroplane is satisfactory and it is not unpleasant to fly in bumpy weather. The tail is difficult to raise when taking off and although there is not quite enough tail trimming range to trim for gliding when the CG is at the foremost limit, there is sufficient elevator control for landing purposes".

The report's overall conclusion was that the modifications made to this aircraft had produced "a marked improvement in the handling qualities" of the aircraft, and that a C of A should be issued for the type as tested.

This then meant that the Air Ministry's operating restrictions to all DH 86As could be lifted, as soon as the fin, fin bias, aileron gearing, elevator spring modifications and a rudder pedal guard could be fitted. De Havilland's Support Department at Hatfield rapidly issued modification kits for all the existing DH 86s and DH 86As in May 1937 and sent these off to all operators, for incorporation in the field by the operators' own engineers. With these changes incorporated, de Havilland re-designated the aircraft as the "DH 86B Express Air Liner".

At about this time, another minor change was made to the aircraft, which should have helped to alleviate some of the problems caused by icing. Instead of the usual system of using suction from several venturis sitting in the slipstream to power the flight instruments, an engine-driven vacuum pump was fitted to the inboard Gipsy Sixes, thereby eliminating the potential loss of vacuum pressure and therefore instrument indications, through ice accumulation on the venturis. These were the last major modifications made to the DH 86 series during its life. The final production run of the type,

Jersey Airways' G-ACZP, 'Belcroute Bay' c/n 2321, parked at Portsmouth, 1936. [M Stroud]

for ten DH 86Bs, beginning with G-AENR in February 1937, had an additional adjustment of the gearing of the ailcrons and as a final check on the satisfactory operation of the DH 86B specification, G-AENR was flown by Martlesham pilots for "handling and diving tests" in February 1937.

FINAL MARTLESHAM TESTS - DH 86B

For this series of tests, G-AENR had the definitive wide-chord tailplane; the now standard outboard "Zulu shield" auxiliary fins; and a more highly-geared aileron system, but not the rudder pedal guards. Interestingly, the ply covering on the outer mainplanes which had been tried out on E.2 was not fitted on this or any other DH 86Bs, so the wing flexing problem was probably considered to have been resolved by a combination of the other modifications to ailerons, fins and strengthening of the internal bracing struts.

G-AENR was loaded to the new DH 86B model's maximum weight of 10,250 lbs and tested at forward, central and aft CGs and the handling qualities checked. This time the longitudinal stability was satisfactory, with decreasing stability at slower speeds and the lateral stability was neutral. There were no tendencies for bank to increase with depression of a wing, and the directional stability was now normal, with behaviour after rudder application and release allowing the aircraft to return quickly to the original course. In summary, the aircraft was considered to be easy to fly in "bumpy" weather, and the controls were now considered to be well harmonised, making turns easy. However, the elevator trimming system was felt to require greater range, to allow for the gliding case. The tail was still felt to be difficult to raise for take off.

The Report recommended that the tail trimming gear required higher gearing, that a partition should be fitted between the pilots' rudder pedals, and that the undercarriage design should be reviewed , to provide better shock absorption and rebound damping. Subject to "consideration of the [above] comments", the issue of a C of A was recommended, so finally clearing the type to operate again in commercial service.

Virtually all the existing DH 86As had the DH 86B modifications applied, but interestingly, only one of the earlier standard DH 86s, SU-ABF of Misr Airwork, was so modified, as the Air Ministry had not required standard DH 86s to be modified, for reasons unexplained. One of the unmodified DH 86s was the long-serving G-ACZP, one of Jersey Airways' pre-war aircraft, which joined the Royal Navy during World War Two. It later worked for the Lancashire Aircraft Corporation at Blackpool, before ending up as the longest-serving as well as the last-surviving Express Air Liner, when its undercarriage finally succumbed to side load collapse at Barajas, Spain, on 21st September 1958.

WEAK UNDERCARRIAGE?

Throughout the aircraft's life, considerable numbers of incidents on take-off or landing, indicate that there was a general weakness in the undercarriage, particularly if side loads were applied. From the records which still exist, indicating the fate of 51 of the type, it is apparent that 21 major Express Air Liner accidents occurred during take-off or landing and which were serious enough to cause major damage or write-off. While only five accident reports specifically mention undercarriage collapse, another nine can be connected to undercarriage problems. So, of the 51 DH 86s whose fate is known, around one quarter were badly damaged due to problems related to the undercarriage in some way. That is a particularly high proportion of serious damage occurring during take-off and landing incidents, but what could have been the cause?

All of the reported incidents of undercarriage problems involve comments about some sort of swing off the intended track being experienced during the landing, and sometimes the take-off run. A most significant factor is that pilots contacted in recent years who have flown the aircraft all commented on its tendency to be difficult to control once a swing started at slow speeds, either on take-off or landing. This difficulty is usually attributed to poor directional control from the rudder at slow speed and a strong

G-AENR at Hatfield, undergoing weight and balance measurements, 1937. *[BAe]*

weathercocking tendency, exacerbated by crosswinds, possible differing rates of acceleration of the four engines and the usual lack of specific visual references on all grass airfields with which to maintain a precise track over the ground. The aircraft's in-built tendency to swing off track required first of all a sharp eye on the distant horizon to detect any slight swing, then "a good pair of feet" on the rudder pedals to counter, assisted in most cases by " a good pair of hands" on the throttles to apply asymmetric power to counteract the swing. It is not surprising that there were many instances of slow responses to incipient swings resulting in "ground-loops", where wind and inertia completely took over the aircraft's behaviour. Such rapid reversals of direction of a 10,000-lb aircraft inevitably placed a good deal of sideways stress loading on the undercarriage legs, for which they were not designed. It is almost certain that the design of the legs of the DH 86 was such as to provide adequate strength for heavy loads applied in a fore and aft and vertical sense, but the evidence indicates that many of the accidents involved some swinging off the intended track, which then resulted in the collapse of the undercarriage.

It would seem that the DH 86's poor directional control at low speeds could allow mishandled take-offs and landings to deteriorate to a point where strong side loads were imposed on the undercarriage legs which they were not capable of withstanding. Changes made to the undercarriage in 1936, which constituted part of the upgrade to the DH 86A series, included the replacement of the original Dowty "patent spring legs" by Turner "compressed air landing legs", but the reason for the change was to gain better shock-absorbing and damping effects, not to increase strength, as there was little indication at that time that there might be a problem with the undercarriage. Beyond that period, it is most unlikely that de Havilland connected the cause of the gradually increasing number of landing incidents with the aircraft's design, but instead assumed the accidents to be generally due to mishandling by the pilots, allowing their aircraft to swing off course and putting abnormal strain on the normally adequate undercarriage.

This undercarriage problem, easy to see with hindsight, would appear to be a manifestation of the de Havilland desire to build aircraft "strong enough, but not over-strong", so that the greatest weight could be saved and thereby the greatest efficiency gained, as long as calculations indicated safety factors to be adequate.

ANTI-ICING MODIFICATIONS

Dunlop "Anticers" were fitted to an Imperial Airways DH86 in 1937, and subsequent tests at Martlesham Heath showed that the extra fittings gave no deterioration in aerodynamic handling qualities. The system forced ethylene glycol anti-icing fluid from a tank through rubber tubes fitted along the leading edges of all wings and struts. Vents in the tubes allowed fluid to flow over the surfaces likely to be affected, melting the ice. Difficulties were experienced in the early tests with poor distribution of the fluid,

Impressed HK 829 at Nefatia North, after undercarriage collapse, March 1943. [DHMC]

Wing anti-ice system on DH 86B, 1937. [CND]

and the system was not widely fitted. Another method tried out at the same time used "Kilfrost" paste smeared on the parts of the airframe most likely to be affected, including airscrews, and was claimed to be capable of preventing water from freezing during extended flights.

PERFORMANCE FIGURES

These figures are for the 1936 Type DH 86A, powered by the standard Gipsy Six engines, and are taken from the official de Havilland Express Air Liner brochure (slightly revised by the de Havilland sales department in August 1936 as a result of service experience) giving details of this modified aircraft. The figures are very similar to those for the single-pilot DH 86 and the later DH 86B.

WEIGHTS	lbs
TARE WEIGHT, including electrical equipment, lighting, accumulator, generator, standard removable equipment	*6,200*
DISPOSABLE LOAD	*4,050*
Crew of two	340
Fuel, standard tanks (114 galls)	878
standard plus auxiliary tanks (191 galls)	1,471
Oil, standard tanks (12 galls)	108
long range tanks (16 galls)	144
Wireless equipment	120
Passenger fittings (average weight)	310
Lavatory	30
Pay load 114 galls fuel	2,264
191 galls fuel	1,635
Total All-up Weight	*10,250*

DIMENSIONS	
Length overall	46 ft 1.25 ins
Span overall	64 ft 6 ins
Height (tail down)	13 ft 0 ins

PERFORMANCE	
MAXIMUM SPEED at sea level	166 mph
CRUISING SPEED at 1,000 feet	141 mph
FUEL CONSUMPTION	
cruising as specified above	35.5 galls per hour
ULTIMATE RANGE	
With 114 galls	452 miles
With 191 galls	758 miles
TAKE-OFF RUN in a 5 mph wind	340 yards
HEIGHT at 656 yards from rest in 5 mph wind	100 feet
LANDING RUN with wheel brakes and flaps in 5 mph wind	175 yards
GLIDING ANGLE	
With flaps up	1 in 11
With flaps down	1 in 8.5
RATE OF CLIMB at sea level	925 ft/min
TIME TO CLIMB	
to 5,000 feet	6.5 minutes
to 10,000 feet	15 minutes
ABSOLUTE CEILING	19,500 feet
CEILING WITH ONE ENGINE STOPPED	13,000 feet
CEILING WITH TWO ENGINES STOPPED	2,000 - 4,000 feet According to combination

12-seat interior of British Airways DH 86, 1935. [BAe]

Section 3 – Chapter 3: Handling and Flying Impressions

THE INTERIOR OF THE DH 86

As with most de Havilland aircraft of the nineteen thirties, opening the cabin door of the Express Air Liner produced a gentle aroma of leather, with the seats and linings all being covered in the usual dove-grey leather. Depending on the particular task, there were either ten or sixteen leather seats in the sloping cabin, with its sumptuous light fittings; simple On-Off cooling vents, claimed by the makers "to prevent the cabin from becoming in any sense stuffy, since the air is being constantly and automatically changed"; grab handles and on some aircraft, curtains at the windows.

The first four aircraft were built for a single pilot and a radio operator or navigator in a separate cockpit, closed off from the cabin by a central door. The roomy single-pilot cockpit resembled a wider, more substantial version of the Dragon's cockpit, but, in keeping with the new aircraft's longer range, had more instruments and controls. Notable were the long throttle and mixture levers immediately at the pilot's left elbow, and the two wheels on the sides of his seat, the left one for the unusual "fin bias" system (used to trim out assymetric loads - in effect a rudder trimmer), and the other for the elevator trim. Despite the 758-mile ultimate range of the aircraft (with auxiliary tanks), it was not fitted with an autopilot, despite such devices being available at the time. Some of the aircraft were modified with autoplilots from 1937 onwards.

With aircraft number five, the cockpit design was changed to accommodate two pilots and the new nose became standard with only small changes to the shape being made for the DH 86A in 1936.

DUAL-CONTROL COCKPIT

A pilot's assessment in the June 1935 '*Aeroplane*' of the two-pilot cockpit indicated that it provided an air of pleasantness and light not frequently met. Dominating the space in front of each pilot was the control column mounting, branching out to provide single, or optionally, dual-control spectacles for the pilots. The early single-spectacle version could be swung over in flight from one side to the other. Despite the change of seating arrangements, the trim wheels remained in a similar central position, usable by either pilot, and the long brake lever was placed centrally between the two trim wheels. Two pairs of simple aluminium "fuel taps" were fitted on the left and right cockpit walls. The handful of throttle and mixture levers were centrally positioned forward of the control yoke, which disturbed the flying pilot's throttle hand whenever the control was moved fore or aft. When the new flap system was incorporated, its hydraulic reservoir and selector were fitted behind the Captain's seat, with a long lever facing inwards towards the centre of the cockpit. This lever had to be pumped to gain pressure to operate the flaps, and was more convenient to the co-pilot, while being reachable by the Captain only with an awkward movement. The large radio station behind the Captain's seat was usually operated by the right-hand seat occupant, who had the convenience of a rotatable seat.

The minimal instrumentation was allowed more space on the wider, but shallower "instrument board", with the rudimentary flight instruments on the left side, leaving the right-hand seat pilot to look at all the engine controls and instruments. Rudimentary electrics for the radio, engine starting and lighting were provided by a single battery under the left seat, pumped up in flight by a wind-driven generator on the leading edge of the port wing, all switched and indicated on the right-seat pilot's panel. One less beneficial result of this new cockpit was that, while it still provided ample view, there was considerable diminution of visibility for either pilot, compared to the panoramic view provided for Hubert Broad during his first flights in the single-pilot aircraft. Entry to the cockpit for both pilots was much less easy, as they both had to negotiate the central brake lever, the trim wheels then the heavy central control column, before being able to gain their seats.

DH 86 later cockpit, with dual-control yoke. [BAe]

Being built as a long-range transport for use over sparsely-populated regions of the British empire, the Express Air Liner incorporated a comprehensive radio outfit for its day, the standard set weighing 310 lb. The early aircraft carried a HF transmitter and receiver, with its trailing aerial and winch, plus an attachment and aerial for direction-finding. Fitted into the roof of the cockpit behind the pilot's seats, the manual DF aerial could be rotated to find the best signal, therefore the direction of the transmitting station. On post-war aircraft, a Radio Range system and a Selectable Beam Approach system were often fitted, in order to help with navigation and with bad weather approaches to the few airfields fitted with the relevant transmitters. Few of the remaining DH 86s were fitted with voice radios.

With more space than provided in the original single-seat cockpit, the two-seat version took on a much more substantial and modern appearance, looking more like the contemporary American and later British multi-engine cockpits, while still maintaining its basic simplicity.

Following a 1935 demonstration flight in the aircraft, '*Aeroplane's*' correspondent commented that: "When sitting in the pilot's cockpit, on either side, there is ample view and an air of spaciousness and light not frequently met. The attitude on the ground is such that the pilot can clearly see the lower strata of air behind, which is enormously convenient just before taking off or during taxying. One could, for example, easily see a control tower signal although taxying straight away from the buildings." He went on to say that: " The controls are well laid out and are full dual. The rudder pedals are unobtrusive enough for the inactive pilot to be able to stretch his legs in comfort, and as the wheel control is of the swing-over dual pattern (as in the early two-pilot DH 86A) the spare pilot can rest easily. The layout of the instruments is good despite the necessity for a large number of instruments entailed by four motors and the business-like equipment in the way of blind-flying indicators of various sorts.

"The designer deserves credit for the fact that all switches, including the self starter buttons, are disposed clearly and visibly. Indeed, the whole of the auxiliary controls could not be better arranged. A neat arrangement enables the pilot to start the motors from a ground source of current if he wants to save his batteries. The engines do not hesitate. The petrol taps are simple, and obviously though unobtrusively placed; r.p.m. indicators are on the dashboard, which considerably facilitates synchronising and is also very convenient when so many motors are to be looked after."

He finishes with a surprisingly positive opinion on the aircraft's asymmetric handling, which contrasts with views expressed by other test pilots the very next year: "The aeroplane is delightfully stable in all three senses and can be trimmed to fly by itself; what is more, it can be trimmed to fly by means of the trimming gears with any two of its motors out of action - and this is remarkable."

CHIEF TEST PILOT'S HANDLING COMMENTS

As a result of a report in '*Flight*', February 1934, summarising E.2's trials at Martlesham, Chief Test Pilot Hubert Broad wrote the following response to points raised in the report:

"On reading through your excellent description of the de Havilland four-engined Express Air Liner this morning, I notice that you have quoted the landing speed as 72 miles per hour, which is considerably in excess of the actual stalling speed or alighting speed.

"During the trials at Martlesham Heath, the stalling speed in a fully-loaded condition was established at 66 mph. As the performance figures you print will certainly be widely read all over the world, I would be grateful if you would insert a correction in your next issue. In practice, of course, an aircraft is very rarely landed in with full load, as on the conclusion of a flight, weight has been reduced by reason of the fuel consumed in flight.

"Having flown the D.H.86 during all its trials, under all conditions of load and with every combination of engines, I am very glad to report that I have found it delightfully light and positive on controls, straightforward in landing and, if anything, easier to fly than the "Dragon," which, as you know, is very highly regarded in that respect.

"It may interest you to know that during its trials I took off and flew the D.H.86 on the power of two engines only, with the propellers removed firstly from the two inboard engines and then from the two outboard engines. During these flights the aircraft carried 80 gall. (363.7 litres) of fuel and was loaded to 6,940 lb. (3,147.9 kg), which included one passenger, 260 lb. (117.9 kg) of ballast, and the weight of two dead engines and their installation gear, amounting to over 1,000 lb. (453.6 kg), equivalent to a pay load of nearly 1,500 lb. (680.4 kg), with a range of over four hours.

"In this (two-engined) condition the top speed, even with the standard propellers, which are naturally very inefficient and under-revving, averaged about 127 m.p.h. (204,4 km/h), and the take-off would have complied with I.C.A.N. requirements. The object of these tests was to determine the relative propeller efficiency of the inboard and the outboard engines."

Hubert Broad. February 1934.

While few modern test pilots would have the pluck to remove two of their propellers for a performance test of a new aeroplane, at least this shows that some aspects of the engine-loss case were trialled in these early days of the DH 86. However, the symmetric cases tested and noted here by Hubert Broad were much less relevant in practical terms than the more serious asymmetric case of loss of one or two engines on the same side. Testing the behaviour of the aircraft following an asymmetric power loss is more critical, as this is when rudder and aileron control must be sufficient to enable the pilot to retain full control of his aircraft. De Havilland would almost certainly have tested asymmetric cases with the prototype by simply reducing power to idle on the relevant engines. There are no company reports still in existence to indicate the outcome of such tests.

CRU TEST PILOT COMMENTS
As general manager of the wartime DH Civilian Repair Unit at Witney and being, as were most de Havilland executives, an experienced pilot as well, Philip Gordon-Marshall flew all the types his team took in for repair. Witney was a small grass field, not designed for large aircraft, so when needing to bring in a DH 86 for overhaul Philip had some concerns.

"I remember taking off in a DH 86 (I'd never flown one before) and tried a couple of landings at Brize Norton, which persuaded me that I could not safely land the machine back at Witney. It seemed to need a long landing run, it was bouncy on rough ground, and the brakes could not be used until nearly all speed had been lost. However, it would have been a great bore *not* to return the machine to Witney: working parties etc, etc. So I thought I'd have a careful try, opening up again if things seemed unsafe. By concentrating hard on getting the approach etc. right, the '86 settled down smoothly enough (it must have dodged the bumps) and stopped with plenty in hand."

EARLY INSTRUMENT APPROACHS
Despite the death of the founder of the company, Edward Hillman Jnr carried on his father's enterprise, with orders for three DH 86s; the first, G-ADEA being handed over at Hillman's new Stapleford airport in May 1935, ready for services to the continent. On a mid-November morning in 1935, Captain Pelly and his radio operator, Alan Wood, flew the Paris schedule in Hillman's smart new flagship, and their report gives an interesting insight into bad weather operations with the instrumentation fitted into G-ADEA and her sister ships.

Croydon and Heston had that week suffered worse than usual November fogs, with Railway Air Services and Jersey Airways having to divert aircraft away from the two main London airports. RAF Kenley and Hillman's Essex airport had only been slightly better, yet the Hillman's DH 86s had managed to achieve all their schedules to and from Le Bourget. G-ADEA had a Marconi MF radio telephone system and a short-wave Lorenz beam approach system installed, so Le Bourget's Lorenz approach equipment could be used to help line up the aircraft for landing. Captain Pelly spoke to his passengers before leaving the departure lounge at Stapleford, and discovered that they were an entire Canadian ice hockey team due in Paris for an important match, so he told them that he would do his best to get them to Le Bourget in time for their game, despite the poor weather. Radio Officer Wood had picked up a Le Bourget forecast giving only about 650 yards' visibility in fog, but Captain Pelly decided that his newly-installed approach system would give him a reasonable chance of finding his destination, so boarded his passengers and took off.

His Express was fitted with what a modern pilot would consider a very basic flight instrument panel consisting of artificial horizon; air speed indicator; altimeter with a new-fangled barometer setting knob; a rate of climb indicator; a small directional gyro, and the all-important Lorenz direction and glide-path indicator. Gyros were supplied from a venturi sitting in the airflow on the outside of the cockpit wall. The key instrument for this blind approach would be the Lorenz indicator, which was in 1935 considered revolutionary, but was quite difficult to use, as it required varying interpretation depending on its relationship to the ground beacons. The first indication in azimuth of the aircraft's position in relation to the final approach path was a combination of dots or dashes heard in the pilot's earphones, and shown as a flick on a horizontal indicator, to either the "dot" or left side of the ideal approach beam, or a flick to the "dash" or right side of the beam. If the aircraft was in the centre of the approach beam, the indicator would move to a central position. The vertical pointer on the instrument gave a guide as to the aircraft's vertical position in relation to a series of glide-paths leading to the edge of the airfield. Each segment of the vertical pointer showed a different glide-path angle, depending on the distance from the beacon and the height of the aircraft, so was open to incorrect interpretation. The pilot had to interpret the aircraft's position in relation to both the horizontal pointer and which vertical scale to follow to fit his required

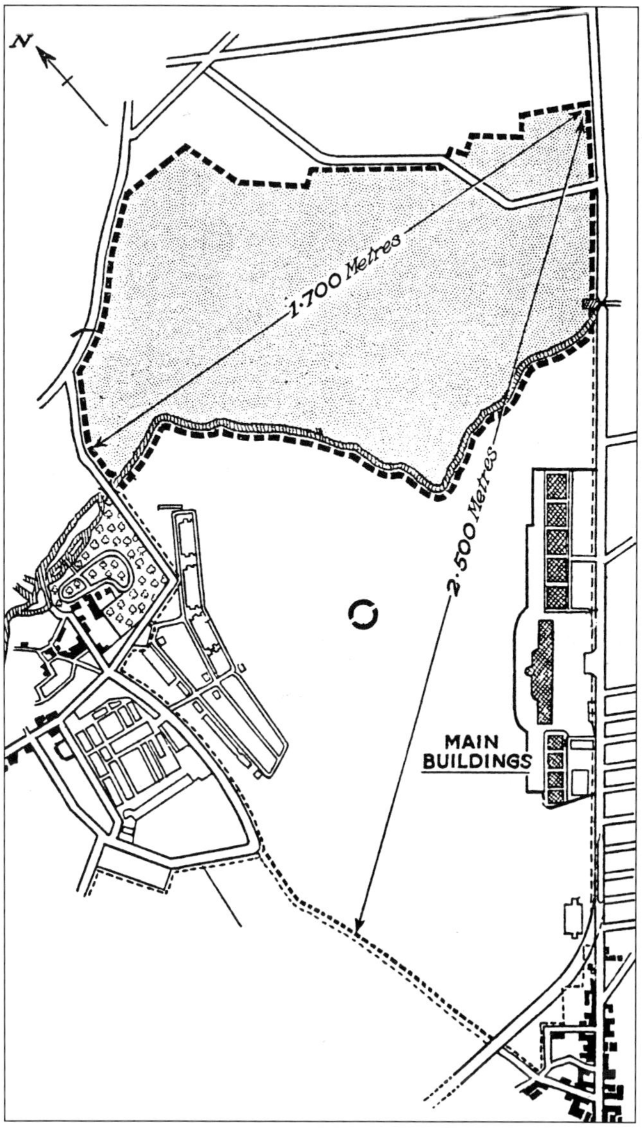

1930s plan of Le Bourget airfield. [CND]

rate of descent. While following the critical Lorenz signals, the pilot had also to correlate those with the headings of his gyro compass, and maintain balance with his artificial horizon, altimeter, air speed indicator and rate of descent indicator. So, making a beam approach in the Express was not an easy task, even if all the equipment was working correctly, and it required considerable skill on the part of the pilot. Finally, ground marker beacons at 2.5 miles and a quarter of a mile from the airfield lit up neon lights on the Lorenz instrument as the aircraft passed over them.

As G-ADEA approached Le Bourget's grass field towards the north-east on the inbound approach leg, a slow descent was made to the initial approach height, and the approach beacon's six-second azimuth signals gave Captain Pelly his position in relation to the beam. Settling at 1500 feet, he waited for the first marker to signal his glide-path point. Making small heading corrections on his compass as he settled on the approach path, he throttled back to his approach speed of 80 mph, then cruised on until he saw the glide-path indicator begin to move. Then the marker beacon told him he was 2.5 miles out, so he called for the flaps to be set, and began his final approach. Descending at about 500 feet per mile, both crew members strained to see the ground through the front windscreen, to no avail. As the final marker beacon flashed its signal, there was still no sight of the ground through the midday mist, so after a short pause, Captain Pelly moved all four throttles up and climbed away for another attempt.

Settling down again at 1500 feet, he then turned back to the main beacon and set up a south-westerly outbound heading for another attempt, hoping that the fog might have lifted a little this time.

Captain's seat of G-AEJM, showing the Marconitrack 66 blind landing receiver, 1939. *[Marconi]*

Turning in towards the north-east again, the Lorenz signals were coming in well, and there was little drift in the still air, so another approach was made, with the aircraft keeping well on the approach beam. The glide was followed again, and both crew began straining for a sight of the ground as they approached the second beacon, but as it began flashing its neon signal on the cockpit indicator, there was still no sign of the ground in the swirling fog. R/O Wood then glimpsed a ploughed field below, and both sets of eyes strained to see the airfield lights ahead. Suddenly a dark object flashed past, just to the left of the nose - a large tree! As it passed slightly higher than the port wingtip, Captain Pelly decided that this was not a healthy place to be, so rapidly pushed the throttles open and pulled up into an urgent climb.

There was now no alternative but to head towards their diversion airfield of Beauvais, where the visibility was much better. The Express and the crew settled down on a heading for the Beauvais D/F beacon and this time found the airfield in quite clear weather. Beauvais was not far from Paris, so a coach was quickly arranged for the Canadians, and they were still in time for their match. They were not asked if they had seen the Le Bourget tree.

A NARROW ESCAPE WITH G-ACZO ON JERSEY.

A series of incidents that occurred from 1935 onwards began to indicate that there was something not quite right with the DH 86's undercarriage. One incident experienced by Jersey Airlines at St Aubin's Bay illustrates an example of a growing problem. Captain A T Orchard had converted onto the DH 86 in the early summer of 1935, and at five o' clock on an August afternoon of that year, he flew the recently-delivered G-ACZO from Southampton onto the beach at low water.

After a normal approach over the harbour, the aircraft touched down on the damp sand, and immediately the aircraft's port brake for some reason appeared to seize. The resulting rapid swing to port pulled the aircraft round towards the south and the sea, causing the right wing to drop and putting a heavy sideways load on the starboard undercarriage. The undercarriage leg promptly gave way, allowing the starboard lower wing, both propellers and engine cowlings to contact the hard sand, while still moving at some speed. The aircraft skidded to a halt some distance down the beach, obviously unable to move on its own undercarriage, and thereby presenting a major problem for the Jersey airlines staff in the face of the approaching tide. It so happened that the spring tide that day was due to produce an impressive 38 foot variation from low- to high-water, and the high tide at 9.30 in the evening would be expected to lap right up against the sea wall by the Victoria Avenue Promenade, next to the island's railway line.The next day's *Jersey Morning News* told a thrilling story about the battle to get the stricken Air Liner up the beach and onto the slipway at the western end of the promenade, using two trucks under the wings for support, and beating the high tide only by minutes. The aircraft had to be shipped back to the mainland weeks later for repair and was out of service for several months.

Jersey Airways' G-ACZO c/n 2318 'Ouaine Bay' parked at Portsmouth, 1936. *[M Stroud]*

PASSENGER VIEW

One of QANTAS' passengers on the tedious 2,000-mile journey from Sydney to Port Moresby in New Guinea gave his impression of long-distance travel by DH 86 just before World War Two. Despite each of the legs on this journey up the Australian east coast being between 350 and 450 miles long, there is no mention of the discomfort or otherwise of the cabin, so presumably they must have been satisfactory. This is his account :

"It took most of the first day for the DH 86 to fly from Sydney to Townsville, with stops for refuelling at Brisbane (Archerfield) and Rockhampton. The runways were gravel strips in what seemed to be farm paddocks. During refuelling, we passengers waited in small sparsely-fumished rooms in modest weatherboard cottages adjoining the runway, while airline staff attended to the paperwork relating to our flight.

"The DH 86, like all aeroplanes of that time, was unpressurised, and to ensure that passengers did not suffer the effects of lack of oxygen, it rarely flew above 10,000ft. As a result the aircraft often flew between or through cloud and passengers were frequently subjected to convective turbulence resulting in the more vulnerable passengers needing to use the brown paper airsickness bags provided.

"After overnighting in Townsville in hotel accommodation provided by Carpenters we flew first to Cooktown where the aeroplane was refuelled. We then made what was, at that time, a long flight of about four hours to Port Moresby over the sea. The first glimpse of Papua was of coral reefs, a hinterland of dry-looking hilly country with straggly eucalyptus and, in the distance, high mountains shrouded in cloud. The Kila Kila aerodrome was even more primitive than those in Australia. Within a few hundred metres of a native village, a grassy undulating field contained a short narrow strip of gravel and one small solitary building housing the meteorological and radio offices. The radio room was staffed by RAAF signals personnel from whom we obtained most of our weather reports from the Australian mainland."

VH-USC c/n 2307 at QEA's base, Archerfield, 1936. *[CND]*

VH-USF at Croydon en route Australia, after the Martlesham trials, 1935. *[CND]*

Section 3 – Chapter 4: Into Commercial Service

FIRST AUSTRALIAN OPERATOR

The "Double Dragon", as it was initially dubbed by '*The Aeroplane*', was ordered to a Qantas Empire Airways specification, but the first Australian operator was a much less well-known airline. Part of the 1934 Australian government air route plan, which QEA hoped to win for the northern sector, was to subsidise a service in the south, over the difficult Tasmania - Melbourne route. This contract was won by a new company called Tasmanian Aerial Services, operating out of Launceston on the island of Tasmania. Captain Victor Holyman, a larger than life character, ex-RNAS pilot, current captain of one of the Bass Strait sea ferries, and operator of a well-known shipping line based in Launceston, had decided to buy out the other partner in TAS in mid-1934, and had given his family name to the new airline. Anticipating success in the government's competition for the Launceston-Melbourne route, TAS had in early 1934 ordered two new DH 86s for delivery towards the end of 1934, in order to augment their DH Dragon service from Launceston to Flinders Island and Melbourne. It was thus that Holyman's Airways were the first operators of DH 86s in Australia, and their first DH 86, VH-URN, the second aircraft built, arrived in Australia by sea, to be delivered to its new owner in September 1934. It then began operations across the rough-weather Bass Strait on the Launceston to Melbourne service the following month.

Into QEA Service

Captain Lester Brain, QEA's chief pilot, flew his company's first aircraft, VH-USC, from Hatfield out to Australia, arriving at his Archerfield, Brisbane home base on 13th October, 1934. The second and third aircraft for QEA were shipped out to Australia, VH-USD arriving in November, for de Havilland Australia to erect at Laverton and fly up to Brisbane. VH-USE was due to arrive by sea in December, also to be erected before flight up to the QEA base at Archerfield. However, barely a week after Captain Brain arrived at Brisbane, Holyman's had a major problem with their Express Air Liner.

Disappearance of *Miss Hobart*

DH 86 '*Miss Hobart*' was registered VH-URN in September 1934, being fitted out by DH Australia at Laverton, near Melbourne. Significantly, as an early model, it had a single-pilot cockpit, but, in keeping with Australian government advice, had a medium frequency Marconi AD36 radio fitted, together with a radio operator's station fitted athwartships behind the pilot's seat. There were twelve passenger seats in the spacious cabin, unlike the standard QEA ten-seat cabin, as Holyman's would only use the type on the 300-mile Bass Strait service. A much-publicised inaugural flight from Launceston to Essendon Airport, Melbourne, took place at the beginning of October 1934, with Holyman's senior DH 86 pilot, Captain Frewin at the controls. It is interesting to note that the company chief pilot was nominally Captain Victor Holyman, a principal shareholder of his family's airline, but his pilot's licence had not been endorsed for him to act as pilot or radio operator of a DH 86.

Just over two weeks later, on 19th October, 1934, when the daily service was settling down well, the Holyman's flight left Launceston at the usual 9 am for Laverton, Melbourne's slightly larger Air Force airfield. Captain Gilbert Jenkins was in command, and Captain Holyman was understood to be acting unofficially as radio operator. Normal radio calls were made by the crew to the Melbourne maritime radio station, at 0950 and 1050, but no more calls were made and nothing was ever heard or seen of '*Miss Hobart*' again. A full search of the Strait and the land area to the south of Melbourne was initiated, using ships and aircraft, but still nothing was found. The government Air Accidents Committee set up an inquiry soon afterwards, but with very little evidence, was unable to find a satisfactory conclusion to the puzzle of the aircraft's disappearance.

There were of course several theories about the cause. Structural failure of the aircraft was considered but discounted, as there was good weather at the time, and there were no radio calls indicating any problems. The main questions considered by the Inquiry focused on the possibility that the aircraft had run out of fuel, or that the pilots had attempted to change seats when airborne and lost control. However, the Inquiry did hear evidence that pointed to a possible reason for the loss, and one which seems to fit known with forecast winds as usual, '45 miles an hour headwind on the ground, decreasing to nil at 11,000 feet; 10 miles an hour tailwind at 13,000 feet'. Pretty good that, when you realise the winds have been projected from a point 500 miles away. Two hours out; three hours out; wonderful weather, all clouds left behind, clear as a bell, from the sea to the stratosphere...Is it? Yes, there comes that faint darkening, away on the edge of the world, - Australia!"

After the investigations into these accidents, all appeared to be settling down to normality in 1935 for QEA with the new Darwin-Singapore route. Holyman's also managed to recover quickly from the loss of their first Express, and took delivery of two more DH 86s, VH-USW and VH-UUB, in May and September 1935. These two-pilot Expresses were then set to work in October 1935 on the Melbourne (Essendon) to Sydney route via Canberra, as well as continuing the Launceston to Melbourne service.

Further Problems in Australia

But then, in October 1935, the second of Holyman's DH 86s, VH-URT '*Loina*', disappeared inexplicably over the Bass Strait while flying on the Melbourne-Flinders Island-Launceston route. That unfortunate occurrence re-kindled all the worries of both operators and administrators once again and, of course, the reputation of the DH 86 was severely damaged. Once more, however, no evidence could be found as to the cause of the loss, and neither could indications of structural problems be found, so clearance was given by the Civil Aviation Branch for the type to continue operations. A subsequent conference arranged by the Civil Aviation Branch and involving all interested parties in Australia, decided that there was no positive indication of the cause of the DH 86 accidents, but that some of the attending experts felt that either torsional flexibility of the wing structure or unusual flutter characteristics could possibly have contributed to the accidents. The Branch therefore decided to carry out its own investigations into some of these areas on Holyman's remaining Express Air Liner, VH-USW.

Once again, the Inquiry into the latest accident concluded that no definite cause for VH-URT's disappearance could be determined. The report did indicate that structural failure possibilities were to be investigated by the CAB in flight tests with another DH 86.

For this set of in-house trials, special protractors and indicators were set up on VH-USW's wings and cameras were arranged in the fuselage to film the movements of wings and ailerons, so that flight tests could take place on 2nd November 1935. The flight test was carried out by Holyman's chief pilot, Captain Frewin and a small test team, with manoeuvres being filmed at 12,000 feet for more than an hour, near Essendon airport. Apparently the film showed that the wings twisted quite distinctly with application of aileron, and this suggested that aileron reversal, coupled with the known poor directional stability, could be a potential contributory cause in the unexplained accidents. The CAB chief engineer, Gordon Berg, then travelled to England to discuss the findings with the makers and the Air Ministry.

VH-USW refuelling at Archerfield with ANA. This aircraft was used for CAB handling trials in 1935. *[J. Peterson]*

The last Express Air Liner, c/n 2361 VH-UYW, when with WR Carpenter at Archerfield in 1938. *[J. Peterson]*

There were further discoveries in Australia. QEA's chief engineer, when examining the structure of the crashed Express Air Liners, had found that the fin post attachment, which was used as part of the "fin bias" system of adjusting the angle of the fin to compensate for asymmetric directional forces, had shown splitting in the wooden attachment post. This seemed to be an inadequately designed fitting, as the wormscrew-to-fin attachment mounting, when moved to its extreme left or right full bias positions, had inadequate room to allow for the wooden post to also move fore or aft without causing splits in the post. These splits could possibly cause failure of the fin post and therefore possible detachment of the fin. In fact, virtually all the Australian aircraft were found to be in this condition, with cracked fin posts. In addition to the fin problem, the CAB chief pilot recommended that the directional stability problem found in their flying trials could probably be caused by the over-sensitive rudder servo-tab, and suggested that a test be flown with the tab disconnected, and the tab taped over to prevent it moving. QEA therefore devised a fix for the fin problem and eliminated the mechanism for the rudder servo-tab, also taping over the tab on the rudder, preventing any movement. The CAB chief pilot and QEA's chief pilot then flight-tested an aircraft with these modifications, after which both agreed that the modified Air Liner showed directional stability that was then equal to any other type of aeroplane.

As a result of the findings from the trials in Australia, de Havilland decided to take remedial action to attempt to correct the fin attachment weakness and the apparent wing flexing. Changes were made in early 1935 to the fin bias worm drive attachment, and the outer wings were stiffened with extra ply covering, in an effort to resolve the reported problems. While the fin bias gear modifications were fitted into the Australian aircraft, it would seem that the modifications which brought about the DH 86A and the DH 86B were not incorporated into the QEA and other Australian aircraft. Only the three DH 86s which were bought by W R Carpenter of Mascot airfield in 1937 were the DH 86B model.
After the de Havilland modifications had been incorporated into their aircraft, QEA settled down to years of normal operations with their fleet of DH 86s until the type was eventually overtaken by newer machines in the mid nineteen forties. As an example of the hard work eventually completed by Australian DH 86s, VH-USC, the first of the type flown out by Captain Brain in 1934 had, by 1944, flown 11,664 hours and covered 1.5 million miles over that ten year period, with not only its original buyer, but also the RAAF and MacRobertson Miller Aviation. Unfortunately, this veteran met its end after swinging into a ditch on landing at Darwin, and was cannibalised for spares and the remains burnt in early 1945.

Lack of Communication?

A final intriguing element in the Australian Express Air Liner story involves a pilot who was present and very influential in the formative months of the DH 86's initial testing and development period. Captain Lester Brain, who QEA had sent to Hatfield in 1934 to look after QEA's interests while the first aircraft were being built, gave an interview towards the end of his life, reported by a retired Australian Inspector of Accidents, Macarthur Job, in his detailed commentary on the DH 86 accidents - '*Air Crash*'.

British Airways' Gatwick night mail run to Stockholm being prepared, 1935. *[DHMC]*

Lester Brain apparently had been unhappy about the handling of VH-USC, the first DH 86 for QEA, on his delivery flight to Australia in 1934. But it also seems that nothing about his concerns was fed to his employers or to de Havilland, despite the fact that the experiences he gained on that ferry flight would almost certainly have helped solve some of the handling difficulties experienced in Australia and England with the type.

Lester Brain's journey had begun badly. VH-USC had been loaded by de Havilland staff at Croydon before his departure, with a spare engine bolted to the fuselage floor, and boxes of spares stacked around the aircraft, which was loaded up to its maximum weight, with the CG limits "carefully calculated". When Brain began his take-off run, he found 'USC's tail to be so heavy, he had to push the control column with both hands hard up against the instrument panel in order to raise the tail enough to gain flying speed - what was almost certainly an aft CG problem. At his first stop, he then had many of the spares moved forward to get a more central CG. This seemed to make the take-off handling easier, but he believed there was still a problem associated with the aircraft's aft CG.

When cruising across the Mediterranean at 6,000 feet, he put his engineer in the left hand seat and slipped back to "check the plumbing" in the rear toilet. He then sat in a cabin seat to admire the view, and watched as the co-pilot turned from the right hand seat to operate the radio. The Air Liner yawed to the left as his co-pilot turned in his seat, and then quite suddenly yawed to the right, increasing in rate. Just as quickly, it then changed direction and rapidly yawed back to the left again, as if entering a spin. These manoeuvres were enough to throw baggage about the cabin, so Brain rushed back to regain his seat, and by the time he was able to get the aircraft under control, it had lost "two or three thousand feet" in height. The co-pilot felt that the controls had simply been carried away, as he was unable to correct the initial yawing motion.

This combination of aft CG, an inexperienced pilot being distracted and a slow recovery to a yawing movement, followed by rapid divergences in yaw, was almost exactly what seems to have happened to Captain Prendergast and his crew after take-off from Longreach, only a few weeks later. But VH-USG, flying at 1,000 feet, had insufficient height to recover, and crashed. If the problems seen by Captain Brain had been reported and investigated, then the subsequent accidents may never have happened. But that does not alter the fact that the DH 86 obviously had a major problem with directional control in certain situations.

IMPERIAL AIRWAYS

Back in England, Imperial Airways had settled down to steadily increasing activities with their own DH 86s. In March 1934, they had ordered 6 new DH86s and called them the '*Diana*' Class, with the first, the single pilot prototype, G-ACPL, being delivered to Croydon (in Railway Air Services colours) in May 1934. The remaining five aircraft for Imperial were to be delivered between June and August 1934. Some would be for Railway Air Services, which was to be operated by Imperial, and the others were for Imperial's own continental services. Each was designed to have a single pilot cockpit, a maximum of ten passengers and a freight compartment. By August that year, G-ACPL had been modified by de Havilland and was then returned to Imperial Airways markings, despite being used for several months by RAS, before that company took delivery of its own second aircraft, G-ACVZ, in December 1934.

Imperial Airways gradually took delivery of their Express Air Liner fleet until they received a total of twelve, the last of their second batch of six being received in January 1936, and which they used for passenger and mail services to Europe. The type was initially used for government-subsidised services from Croydon by the European Division to destinations in France, Germany and Switzerland, alongside their Handley Page Hannibals and Armstrong Whitworth Atalantas. The DH 86s were later used on middle-eastern routes, and for some years, on a connecting service between Penang, (then in Malaya) and Hong Kong, the DH86s being based at Bangkok. By mid-1936, in addition to QEA, Imperial Airways and Holyman's, the type was already entering service with British Airways, British Continental Airways, Jersey Airways, Misr Airwork, Railway Air Services and Union Airways in New Zealand.

Icing Problems

But the British operators were not to escape their own set of problems with the aircraft. After unexplained accidents to one of Imperial Airways' own Express Air Liners, '*Draco*' (G-ADCM) at Zwettl, Austria, in 1935, and a British Airways aircraft, G-ADEB, at Altenkirchen the following year, Imperial Airways became concerned about the type's difficulties in winter flying conditions. Some of their pilots had complained that the braced biplane configuration of the aircraft made it very prone to picking up ice, particularly on the route to Cologne, in northern Germany. While no different from any other of the large biplanes currently in use, the aircraft was certainly prone to both carburettor and airframe icing, caused by ice build-up on wings, struts, bracing wires and in the engine and carburettor intakes, and this can now be considered the likely cause of several of the "unexplained" winter accidents. And then, on the night of March 15th/16th 1937, Imperial Airways' European Division manager, the well-known pioneer aviator, Captain Wolley Dod, took an Express Air Liner on the Cologne route in part to experience the conditions for himself, which he unfortunately did, by flying into a severe snowstorm en route. Sadly, the aircraft subsequently crashed, without survivors.

Trial installation of tail de-icing tape. *[Aeroplane]*

The reason for these accidents could be partially explained in a report which Captain Israel of Jersey Airways made after an Express Air Liner flight test he made from Southampton on a wet February day in 1936. Captain Israel was returning to Southampton after the test, which had involved initial flight at higher levels, where the temperature had been well below freezing. He had no passengers on board, and was then flying with an air temperature slightly above freezing, but below cloud, when he entered a heavy rain shower. The rain rapidly turned to ice on contact with the leading edges of the mainplanes, and built up with a rapidity which the Captain had never experienced before, and certainly never out of cloud, in clear air. He saw the ice build-up on the leading edges of all flying surfaces and struts, as well as on the engine intakes. Despite applying full power on all four engines, he could not prevent the aircraft from slowing down, nor could he maintain height, despite applying power on all his engines. Luckily he was by then close to Southampton, and he managed to touch down on Eastleigh's runway at the moment his suction-powered instruments froze up, giving him erroneous attitude information, and incorrect speed indications. The biplane wings, bracing wires and other excrescences of the DH 86 were very prone to picking up icing, and therefore flying in icing conditions could affect this type to a greater extent and more rapidly than other, more streamlined machines.

Because the phenomenon was not fully understood in 1936, there were no effective anti-icing devices available to manufacturers, so pilots simply had to avoid icing conditions, or expect to have problems. The de Havilland engine company had attempted to provide a method of preventing carburettor icing on the Gipsy Six, by ducting intake air through an intake which drew warm air from around the cylinder heads, but at this stage in the engine's life, it was an automatic system, which worked only in cruising flight. At full throttle, a blanking flap operated automatically, giving only ambient unheated air to the carburettors directly from the external scoop. This system would be particularly prone to ice accretion in icing conditions, and could rapidly restrict the amount of air being fed to the engines at full throttle, so causing increasingly rich mixture which would eventually cause the engines to stop. This situation would certainly add to the pilot's problems in icing conditions, and if the temperature could not be increased, usually by descending into warmer air, and allowing warmer air back into the engines, the combination of airframe and engine icing could prove irredeemable. Post-war, a modification was introduced to the Gipsy Queen, the later name given to the Gipsy Six, which provided manual control of the hot air intake to the carburettors.

In addition, Imperial attempted to combat some of the icing problems by covering the leading edges of wings, tailplane and fin with tape, which was resistant to ice formation. A modification was made for the DH 86B whereby the venturis used for the airspeed indicators were recessed into the inboard lower wing roots so would be less prone to icing, and later still, engine-driven vacuum pumps replaced the venturis.

Captain Israel's incident gives a very strong pointer to the likely cause of the loss of the three DH 86s which crashed while flying over mountainous country, in winter weather conditions. As these flights were at night, the crews were probably not aware at first of the severity of the ice build-up, until it was too late to turn back out of the bad weather. The ice would have affected the flying surfaces, as well as the engine carburettor intakes, and the suction venturis used to power the flight instruments. It is likely that the aircraft were all forced to descend, by a combination of loss of

Single pilot G-ACVY in RAS colours at Croydon in 1934. *[CND]*

performance, partial or complete engine failure caused by carburettor icing and also loss of orientation through erroneous flight instrument indications, so causing the inevitable accident.

RAS - CROYDON TO BELFAST IMPRESSIONS

The second British operator, Railway Air Services, was building its own fleet during 1934, eventually receiving four Expresses and operating routes from the south of England through to the Midlands, Northern Ireland and Scotland. While RAS operated the prototype, G-ACPL, for the last months of 1934, this aircraft then reverted to Imperial Airways at the beginning of 1935, when RAS had received more of its own aircraft. G-ACVY and G-ACVZ, both single-crew versions and G-AEFH, a DH 86A, were brought into RAS service by August 1936. Two other DH 86s joined the fleet when they were transferred to RAS by the AAJC in 1940.

In 1934, however, RAS' main base was Croydon and a daily schedule leaving Croydon at 0945 served Birmingham, Stoke, Manchester, Liverpool, Blackpool, The Isle of Man, Belfast and Glasgow. The route split at Liverpool, then the Belfast Express Air Liner arrived at Aldergrove at 1245, and the alternate landed at Glasgow at 1400. For this surprisingly rapid service, the unsubsidised fares were very expensive in terms of modern air fares. For example, RAS' 1935 single fares from Croydon were £5.50 to Belfast or £6.00 to Glasgow. The return fares were £9.25 and £10.00 respectively, which at modern prices was certainly not cheap. That Belfast return at today's equivalent values would have been more than £350.00, which would have been prohibitive to many individuals or companies. Yet the service continued right up to 1939, when war-time restrictions began coming into force.

A contemporary RAS advert described their DH 86s as "luxuriously appointed four-engined express air liners, each seating ten passengers and provided with every modern wireless and other device. The aircraft are double-manned, carrying both a Captain and a First Officer". An insight into the passenger's view of that journey to Belfast in a DH 86 was given in a September 1934 report in '*Flight*'. This was on a Railway Air Services proving flight from Croydon to the new Ulster grass airfield at Newtownards, east of Belfast, and this passenger certainly felt that the aircraft's extra cost was well offset by having a journey time, including intermediate stops, of less than five hours from central London to his Belfast hotel, compared to the twelve hour rail and sea journey. As might be expected from a company used to providing comfortable travel for railway passengers, these RAS aircraft were fitted out in plush style, in what de Havilland's brochure called the "Airliner model, with ten comfortable armchairs with adjustable backs,.... and a toilet with wash basin at the rear". The cabin was luxuriously equipped, with carpeted floor, leather fuselage sides and seats, netting roof-racks, individual lights and air louvres above each seat and an engine-heated air system to help keep passengers comfortable. Sound-proofing, consisting of layers of sound deadening material between the ply inner fuselage and the outer fabric, was considered to be good for the period.

'*Flight*''s correspondent considered "...the interior of the DH 86 to be such as to give confidence to the most nervous new passenger, for whom there is a great impression of solidarity. Detail comfort, too, has been considered. Each passenger has his own ventilator, and folding table, and the usual comfortable Rumbold chairs are fitted with adjustable headrests. At cruising revolutions it is only necessary to raise the voice slightly above the tone used for normal conversations, and, in the hands of a careful pilot, the machine is just about as comfortable as anything could be. The passenger remains imperturbable."

Channel Island Services

The fifth purchaser of the new, "safe" four-engined airliner was Jersey Airways, a company already well-known to de Havilland through their entrepreneurial use of the DH Dragon from 1933 onwards. They bought direct from Hatfield, the fourteenth DH 86, G-ACYF , named it '*The Giffard Bay*' in February of 1935, and then quickly put it into service on the routes from the mainland to the Channel Islands. Jersey

Railway Air Services 1936 timetable. *[P. Edmonds]*

Airways was to become one of the greatest supporters of the DH 86, as they bought another five two-pilot DH 86s in early 1935, and then another two, DH 86A, G-ADVK, in 1938, and DH 86B, G-AENR, the first DH 86B, in 1939. The airline soon found that the sixteen seat version fitted their routes and landing sites so well that they gradually sold off their other types, concentrating on the DH 86s as their main aircraft from 1936 right up to the time that the Channel Islands were occupied by Germany in 1940. Few other operators of the DH 86 kept the type in reasonable numbers as consistently as did Jersey Airways. Considering the difficulty of Jersey's operating weather and landing sites, this is quite a compliment to the aircraft.

G-ACYF was put into service on the old DH 84 route from Portsmouth and Southampton to the beach landing site at Jersey's St Aubin's Bay on an inaugural flight on the 7th February, 1935,

Jersey Airways' G-ACZN 'St Catherine's Bay' c/n 2316 at Portsmouth, 1936. *[M. Stroud]*

fifteen months after the birth of the airline. Captain B A Blythe was at the controls, (with a certain Captain Hubert Broad in the right-hand seat, "for moral support", according to a contemporary '*Flight*' report). Some concern was expressed at the time about the capability of such a large aircraft as the DH 86 to cope with the quite tricky conditions of St Aubin's beach, with its notoriously high tides, and persistent cross-winds, so the first flights were watched with some trepidation by the airline staff, the Air Ministry and even the pilots themselves. However, the new aircraft was quite well able to manage the task, and the Jersey Airways pilots themselves soon became used to managing this larger sister to their old DH 84s onto and off the sands of St Aubin's Bay.

Of the six Jersey Airways new DH 86s, G-ACYF was sold to Wearnes Brothers in Singapore in 1938, and another, G-ACZN, crashed on Jersey in November 1938. They operated the aircraft in what de Havilland called the "14 seat short route" version, with no toilet, but a 40 cubic feet luggage locker behind the cabin. All the Jersey DH 86s had the, by then standard, two-pilot cockpit, and all had Standard MF transmitter/receivers for voice transmissions, and several were later were fitted with the airborne elements of the short wave Lorenz "blind landing system", which was a precursor of the post war Instrument Landing System. Two other aircraft, G-ADVK, a DH 86 modified to DH 86B standard in 1937, and G-AENR, a DH 86B, were bought in late 1938 and early 1939, G-AENR having been the first B model to be built.

Jersey's New Airport

On 1st June 1937, soon after the new airport at Jersey's St Peter opened, Captain Bill Caldwell, the chief pilot of Jersey Airways, achieved a proud ambition for his airline when he brought his favourite DH 86, G-ACYF, into the airfield with the first air mail for the Channel Islands from Southampton. The *Jersey Evening Post* described the event :

"At the appointed hour (just before 10 am) '*Giffard Bay*' was reported approaching the island and could be seen soon afterwards silhouetted against the almost cloudless sky, her hull shimmering in the sun's rays - a thing of beauty indeed. Flying just above the cockpit was the blue Royal Mail Air pennant and on the bow stood boldly out the words '*Royal Mail*' surrounding the crown. A perfect landing was effected, just before the appointed hour, and when the official party arrived, the 'plane taxied up in front of the main building', where the Lieutenant Governor and the Bailiff of Jersey waited for Captain Caldwell to shut down his engines and climb down from the aircraft to hand over the mail bags."

Six Express Air Liners still remained with the airline in 1939, when War was looming in Europe. By June 1940, with war now under way, the German army's approach westwards across France made evacuation of the Channel Islands a necessity. Under orders from the Air Ministry, which came on 13th June, Jersey Airways staff packed up and flew off to the mainland and the company ceased operations. Mr G O Waters, the company General Manager, had made plans well in advance for this event, and on the next day, Friday 14th, the plan swung rapidly into action. Of the six remaining Express Air liners, the first of the DH86Bs, G-ADVK, was in the middle of a major overhaul when the decision to evacuate was taken, and therefore had to be left behind in the hangar at St Peter's airport. The other five, DH 86s G-ACYG, G-ACZO, G-ACZP, G-ACZR and the only DH 86A, G-ADVK, began at first light to load up with the families of the airline staff, to begin a shuttle service to Exeter, on the mainland. On that Friday, over 100 families and staff were evacuated to Exeter, to be followed the next day by as much movable equipment as could be found. Mr Waters and his remaining two staff left on the Sunday, and then the DH 86s ferried 320 islanders across to Exeter and Bristol over the last two days before occupation. Before they left the island, the Jersey engineering staff, assisted by a Royal Air Force demolition crew, made certain that, as they could not fly G-ADVK, then neither would anyone else. It never flew again.

The five remaining DH 86s were all put up for disposal by the Air Ministry; four ended up as Royal Navy staff transports and the DH 86B, G-AENR, was allocated to the AAJC, which organisation loaned it to Railway Air Services for their west coast services based at Speke, where it remained for the duration of the war.

HILLMAN'S AIRWAYS

As Hillman's Airways had grown into a successful business since the introduction of the Dragon service to Paris, and their services to the Midlands, the company, now under the management of Ted Hillman's son, decided to enlarge their fleet by ordering yet another type from their neighbours at Hatfield. The first of three Express Air Liners, G-ADEA, was fitted out as a twelve-seater and delivered to Hillman's Stapleford base in early June 1935, and named by Lady Cunliffe-Lister in a very grand ceremony at Stapleford on 20th June. As seemed to have become the norm with Hillman's, the senior guests at the ceremony were then flown across

Jersey Airways' G-ACYG 'Grouville Bay' c/n 2314 landing at St Aubin's beach, Jersey, 1935. *[Le Sueur]*

to Paris in the new aircraft, with Captain W Anderson, the Chief Pilot, at the controls. The DH 86s, immaculate in their dark blue colour scheme, were used exclusively on the Stapleford to Paris service, until the company was eventually amalgamated at the end of that same year into British Airways.

BRITISH AIRWAYS, GATWICK

British Airways was formed out of several other small British airlines at the end of 1935, with financing from Whitehall Securities. The Air Ministry had prior to that year given precedence, not to mention subsidies, to Imperial Airways, its only "chosen airline instrument", in order for that airline to compete with the continental airlines, the flag carriers of which were assisted and subsidised by their own governments. By 1935, however, with Imperial Airways starting to make profits, and to develop into an effective company, it was felt by the government, and by the new Secretary of State for Air, Viscount Swinton, that the airline process should be expanded instead of perpetuating Imperial Airways' monopoly. The result of this freedom was the amalgamation of British Continental Airways, Highland Airways, Hillman's Airways, Northern and Scottish Airways and Spartan Air Lines. The Air Ministry granted the new British Airways a licence to operate, but unsubsidised, on some of the continental routes previously the prerogative of Imperial Airways, and the new airline rapidly expanded its fleet, routes, profits, and rather unusually, its pilot's salaries, much to the displeasure of Imperial Airways.

Among the aircraft inherited from Ted Hillman's recently acquired fleet were three DH 86s, G-ADEA, G-ADEB and G-ADEC, all built as DH 86As in 1935. The new British Airways soon placed orders for another eight DH 86s, and these were all delivered in 1936, making a total of eleven for a short time. The first batch of new DH 86s brought the British Airways total fleet to thirty, thereby making the new concern quite a challenge to the by now rather complacent Imperial Airways. The Airline called them '*Dianas*', and equipped the 1936 models with radio and navigation aids, including the Lorenz blind approach aid. Useful additions, bearing in mind the problems encountered by some other DH 86 operators in winter, were electrically-heated pitot heads and hot air bleeds from the engines to counter the carburettor icing to which the Gipsy Sixes were prone. There were still no practical methods of preventing airframe icing, so there was still a danger in flying the Dianas into icing conditions, and several aircraft were almost certainly lost during this period in such conditions, as enunciated later by pilots of both Imperial Airways and Jersey Airlines.

G-ADMY at Lympne in 1939 when with British American Air Services of Heston. *[B. Harding]*

NORTH SEA EXPERIMENT

> **Allied Airways (Gandar Dower) Ltd.**
> **to NORWAY**
> **Nature's Wonderland**
>
> *AS THE CROW FLIES ONLY FASTER!*
>
> **Swift, multi-engined Express airliners** by-pass tip-seeking porters, tiresome changes, crowded customs and the usual discomfort of travel over the sea.
> Fly to NORWAY once, you'll never think of going any other way again! Dozing or reading, writing or talking, comfortably ensconced in your armchair in the brilliant sunshine above the clouds, you'll be in NORWAY within three hours of leaving ENGLAND.

This exhortation to the travelling British (and Norwegian) public appeared in 1937 on the timetable for a service proposed by Allied Airways from Newcastle's Woolsington airport across the North Sea to Stavanger in Norway. The rather shaky rationale for this

British Airways and Hillman's crews, Gatwick, 1936, after the formation of the new airline. *[Aeroplane]*

New Wearnes Air Services crew ready to leave Jersey for Singapore, 1938 in VR-SBD 'Governor Murchison' c/n 2313. *[Le Moignan]*

Wearnes Air Services' VR-SBC 'Governor Ibbetson' c/n 2323 being refuelled, Kucking, Malaya, 1938. *[CND]*

Misr Airworks' SU-ABO 'Al Fostat' c/n 2329 posing over the Pyramids, 1935. *[CND]*

scared at the whole prospect", as he could not work out the identity of the warship. Meanwhile, his ecstatic captain took as many photographs as he could, before running out of film. After three low level circuits of the ship, Titch put away his camera and climbed the aircraft up to cruising height again. When Guy managed to speak to his Captain again, it was to discover that the ship was a highly suspicious Spanish warship, one of "Franco's Raiders" which were causing concern around the British coast. Captain Titch thanked Guy for his help, but apparently was not willing to share the *Daily Mail's* impressive £500 fee for the photographs which the newspaper duly published.

WEARNE BROTHERS, SINGAPORE

One Express Air Liner which by 1938 had already had a fascinating history, was to continue its itinerant career by becoming part of a new air service in the Far East, as the first aircraft for Wearne's Air Services in Singapore. G-ADEA, was the first DH 86 delivered with great ceremony to Hillman's Airways at Stapleford in May 1935, and then became one of the amalgamated British Airways fleet the following year. A lightning strike later that year entailed considerable repair work before the aircraft was sold in October 1937 to Airwork at Heston. Airwork then sold G-ADEA to the new Singapore company, and Wearne's Chief Pilot, Flight Lieutenant John Pugh, arranged to fly their acquisition, newly-registered VR-SBC, out to Singapore in the summer of 1938, in company with the second Express for Wearne's.

G-ACYF was sold by Jersey Airways to Wearne's in June 1938, becoming VR-SBD. Before its ferry flight, it was overhauled by Jersey Airways then flown up to Hatfield for fitting with Fairey Reed propellers and a Marconi radio together with direction-finding equipment. The "Ferry Scheme" seating was altered to remove the two rear seats and install a toilet in their place. With the aircraft, rather conveniently, went one of the ex-Jersey Airways pilots, Captain Rodney Beresford, who flew G-ACYF out to Seletar from Heston in July 1938, where he remained as one of the new company's pilots.

Captains Pugh and Beresford met up at Heston and left from there in company for their flight to Singapore on 7th July 1938, taking only a week for the task. On arrival, VR-SBC became '*Governor Ibbetson*' and VR-SBD became '*Governor Murchison*', both working Wearne's scheduled route from Singapore to Penang as well as charter flights around what was then still Malaya. Both aircraft then continued to have interesting careers, as they both left Singapore for Australia in 1940, becoming VH-UZX and VH-AND respectively, with W R Carpenter and Company, of Sydney, and both going to the Royal Australian Air Force on impressment later in 1940. VH-UZX, as A34-7, continued its exciting career as part of the RAAF Air Ambulance Unit in Egypt, but VH-AND finished its career as A34-2 in the more mundane training and transport roles in Australia.

Two DH 86s in build for Misr Airwork, Stag Lane, May 1935. [BAe]

DH 86B L7596 c/n 2348, formerly G-ADYJ, for the Royal Air Force, October, 1937. *[Flight]*

Section 3 – Chapter 5: Military Service

PEACE-TIME MILITARY SERVICE

Being built for a specific civilian transport role, the Express Air Liner was not an obvious choice for military use, but four aircraft were bought by the Royal Air Force before wartime requirements demanded an increase in its passenger fleet. Airwork Limited, of Heston, had made an astute move in 1937, buying up twelve DH 86As from various sources and selling them on to British and overseas customers. Four of these aircraft, recently converted to DH 86B standard, were sold to the RAF; G-ADYJ, as L7596, G-ADYG as N6246, G-ADYC as L8037 and G-ADYD as L8040. The first two went as VIP transports to 24 Squadron at Hendon in 1937 and 1938. L7596 then wrote itself off and nearly wrote off the Secretary of State for Air, Sir Kingsley Wood and his Assistant Chief of Staff, Air Vice Marshal Sir Sholto Douglas (later Lord Douglas of Kirtleside) on 28 June 1939 when it struck a hill outside Ulverston whilst flying in cloud taking the eminent gentlemen to open the new Belfast Airport. L8037 and L8040 went to Cranwell for use by the Electrical and Wireless School, which later became No 1 Signals School, and which was the only unit to use the type as a radio trainer. Airwork themselves converted the two aircraft to radio trainers and they joined two Rapides already in service. For radio operator training, the DH 86s were fitted out with six stations for student "W/Ops" and two for their staff instructors. The students each had a receiver and a table at their own stations, but only one station had a transmitter - they took turns at the transmitter. In addition to the transmitters, the aircraft were also fitted with an ADF receiver and, a rather puzzling extra for a radio trainer, a very bulky RAE-designed autopilot.

RAF AND RN WAR SERVICE

Surprisingly large numbers of the type actually served with the British and Commonwealth forces after impressments from 1940 onwards. In total, thirty seven Expresses were used for staff transport, navigation training, wireless operator training and air ambulance work on three continents, for the British, Indian, New Zealand and Australian forces. One of the ex-Tata Airlines Expresses, VT-AKZ now with RAF serial AX800, was even modified to drop bombs in the unlikely anti-submarine role, when at No 2 Coastal Defence Flight at Juhu Bay near Bombay in 1941.

Three ex-Jersey Airways DH 86s and one from British-American Air Services served the Royal Navy, most as staff transports with 782 Sqn from its base at Donibristle or 783 Sqn at Arbroath. They were all arranged for ten passengers and pilot, plus radio operator, for naval staff work around mainland Britain. One unfortunate DH 86, AX841, was destroyed at RNAS Lee-on-Solent before it could be put into service. It was parked in July 1940, the former G-ACZO, awaiting conversion when the airfield was attacked by German bombers, and was among several aircraft damaged or destroyed in the raid. One other DH 86, AX840, was hit by the RN's own guns on 8 July 1942 near the Bell Rock, off Dundee, during a live gunnery exercise, when a minesweeper's small gun managed to hit it, killing Midshipman Dennison but the aircraft made it safely back to Arbroath and was repaired. Several of the 24 Squadron DH 86s were transferred to RN service and the last ones retired in early 1945.

Two DH 86As which had been converted to DH 86B standard in 1937, G-ADYI and G-AEJM, joined up in 1940; G-ADYI to Farnborough as AX795, for a camouflage paint scheme and fitting of radio equipment, before becoming part of No 1 Signals School at Cranwell as a wireless operator trainer, joining L8037 and L8040. G-AEJM was impressed into the Royal Air Force from Wrightways Ltd, going to the premier transport squadron, No. 24 at Hendon as X9441. Unusually for an RAF aircraft, X9441 was named '*The Cathedral*', and served as a well-known VIP transport until accidentally destroyed by fire on 17 February 1943, tragically killing a fitter who ran into the propeller whilst trying to put out the flames. These RAF transports were fitted-out in the de Havilland Scheme One, with eight seats and toilet, with a 90 cubic feet luggage compartment behind.

MIDDLE EAST SERVICE

Ten DH 86s, mainly from the Imperial Airways and Australian civilian fleets, were impressed into military service for use as transports or ambulances in the Middle East; five with 117 Sqn at Bilbeis; one at RAF Lydda and three as ambulances with No 1 Air Ambulance Unit in Iraq. One other, HX789, ex Tata's VT-AKM, served at Cochin on the Indian West coast with No 5 Coastal Flight as part of the Indian Air Force Volunteer Reserve. Three Australian DH 86s, VH-UYU, VH-UZX (an ex-Hillman's aircraft, G-ADEA), and VH-UUB, became A31-8, A31-7 and A31-3 and were converted to the ambulance role; crated up and sent across to the eastern

HK843 c/n 2349 with No.1 Air Ambulance Unit in Iraq, 1942. *[CND]*

RAAF A31-4, with No 2 Air Ambulance Unit, 1940s. [CND]

Mediterranean, they joined three RAF DH 86s. All served No 1 Air Ambulance Unit, based initially at Heliopolis in Egypt, but then moved to other bases as the fighting required. Interestingly, four of the Ambulance Unit aircraft were written off by undercarriage failure on either landing or take-off, from which it can be inferred that even the strengthened undercarriage of the DH 86B was not man enough for the rigours of poor landing strips. Regrettably, one of No 1 AAU's Australian aircraft, A31-8, was shot down by a German Bf 110 on 8 December 1941, in the Western Desert, despite being liberally painted with red crosses on all surfaces. However, records show that there were no casualties despite the aircraft being written-off.

FAR EAST OPERATIONS

Of the DH 86s owned by QANTAS and WR Carpenter Airlines in Australia in 1939, apart from the three that had been converted to ambulances, five others, a combination of DH 86As and DH 86Bs, were used by the RAAF, serving mainly with No 35 Squadron at Essendon and No 36 Squadron at Maylands on transport operations. The fleet had a sad ending, as only one of the impressed machines, A31-4, survived beyond 1945, all others having accidents and being written-off. The survivor was sold in damaged condition by the RAAF to MacRobertson-Miller Airlines in February 1945, and was repaired and restored as VH-USW before being sold on again in November 1946 to Universal Flying Services at Kidlington. Unfortunately, ferry pilot Tim Bowen considered it was suffering from excessive tail flutter whilst on its flight to England, and he decided to abandon it at Allahabad on Boxing Day 1946.

The three civilian DH 86s which had been delivered to New Zealand's Union Airways in 1935, were impressed into the RNZAF as NZ552, NZ553 and NZ554 in 1939 and were used as observer and gunnery trainers at Ohakea. All three were damaged in accidents and their components were used by de Havilland New Zealand to rebuild NZ553 over an extended 20 months in 1943/44; it did not return to service with the RNZAF but did return to Union as ZK-AHW in 1945.

NEW GUINEA ESCAPADE

A little known adventure during World War Two involved DH 86s, a team of pilots from QANTAS and Guinea Airways, and rather surprisingly led by a missionary priest from New Guinea, Father Glover, who also happened to be a pilot.

In 1940 QANTAS had handed over to the RAAF two of their of the DH 86As, VH-USC and VH-USF on impressment for military service. However, the RAAF had little need of the aircraft, so Captain Lester Brain persuaded the authorities to pass them back to QANTAS in March 1942, for the airline to use in the Northern Territory. For the next few weeks, the Expresses were used for transporting equipment to northern Australia. But then a very strange request for help arrived from a missionary who had made a hazardous journey to Melbourne, all the way from Japanese-held northern New Guinea. Father Glover had been organising the evacuation of western civilians in the northern area, to a safer inland area at Ramu, using his mission's own light aircraft, but he had an accident at the Ramu strip, which wrote off the aircraft. Not wishing to leave the 90 evacuees to the probability of capture by the Japanese, he arranged for them to be moved to another hill station at Mount Hagen, 7,000 feet up in the Bismarck mountains, while he tried to find another way of helping them escape to the safety of Australia. He then set out to make his tortuous way back to Australia, using an amazingly varied series of transport methods, and after several weeks of hardship, Father Glover eventually arrived in Melbourne to ask for government help. The government officials in turn approached QANTAS to find a possible solution.

Because of his knowledge of the New Guinea area, Captain Orme Denny was given the job and his solution was to use the two Express Air Liners, with Father Glover and a team of pilots, to fly the 90 refugees out of the Mount Hagen strip back to mainland Australia. Both DH 86s had long-range tanks so had a maximum range of about 700 miles, and the ability to fly over the 9,000 foot Bismarck Range. A field on Horne Island, north of Cape York, the northern-most tip of Australia, was considered suitable as a base, so the aircraft were flown up there together with stocks of fuel. The distance to Mount Hagen from Horne Island was around 300 miles, depending on route and weather diversions, so the round trip, given no fuel in New Guinea, would be close to the aircraft's limit of range.

The first rescue DH 86 took off from Horne Island on 13th May 1942, flown by Captain Denny and Captain Sims, who normally flew for Guinea Airways. The Bismarck mountains were covered by cloud when they arrived in the area, but the pilots took the hazardous chance of flying up numerous cloud-topped valleys until they eventually found their way into the Mount Hagen strip. But, as he tried to taxi in after landing, Captain Denny found that the grass surface was so moist, the 10,000 lb aircraft's wheels sank in quite deeply, making taxying difficult and take-off almost impossible. The good Captain then came up with a clever solution, by suggesting to the local native population that they hold a "sing sing" on the airstrip that evening. With 2,000 people dancing over the grass strip all night and much of the next morning, the surface became almost usable, such that the pilots decided to risk flying out the first group of passengers that afternoon. Originally intending to take out ten passengers, they were still not happy with the weight they could carry, so they limited the passengers to seven per flight, and hoped that the more solid ground would allow the Express to accelerate to flying speed. The Gipsy Sixes produced enough power for take-off, so the reverse flight departed through the mountains to Horne Island and safety.The rescue then began in earnest, with the DH 86s taking-off at 7 am every morning and returning by about 3 pm. Several flights were caught in heavy cloud build-ups and the subsequent carburettor icing caused one aircraft to lose power on all four engines, only being able to recover after losing several thousand feet in an undemanded descent into warmer air. After eleven days, the evacuation of Mount Hagen strip was completed, with 78 people rescued, much to the credit and courage of Father Glover and his fellow pilots.

The three DH 86s impressed into RNZAF service, Ohakea, about 1940. From left to right NZ552, NZ554 and NZ553. [CND]

C/n 2321 G-ACZP being loaded at Croydon post-war, had operated the first peacetime service there in November 1944. *[M. Stroud]*

Section 3 – Chapter 6: Post War Civilian Service

COMMERCIAL OPERATIONS

Many of the DH 86s used by military forces during World War Two were written-off before they could be returned to civilian life, with records indicating that only 16 survived beyond 1944. One DH 86 of Railway Air Services, still in its camouflage scheme, but with its civil registration on fuselage and wings, had the honour of operating the first "post-war" civilian flight into Croydon. This was G-ACZP, which had been allocated to the Royal Navy in 1940, but not used and returned to RAS at Speke in August 1940, for use under the auspices of the Associated Airways Joint Committee, which arranged all civilian flights on behalf of the government. RAS had four Express Air Liners which was the largest post-war fleet of DH 86s anywhere, and they were kept busy until the company was absorbed into BEA in 1947.

G-ACZP flew this first commercial post-war service into Croydon on the morning of 13th November 1944, re-introducing commercial flights to Liverpool, Glasgow and Belfast. Each morning thereafter, an Express would leave Croydon at 0945, reaching Speke an hour and forty minutes later, very much as on the pre-war timetable. It would then cross the Irish Sea direct to the new Belfast airport close to the centre of the city at Sydenham (now Belfast Harbour), one hour and twenty minutes later. From that date, the DH 86s, G-ACVY and G-ACZP; DH 86A G-ADYH and DH 86B G-AENR kept up the service until they were sold to Skytravel in October 1946. Meanwhile, running in the opposite direction across the Irish Sea with Aer Lingus throughout the War, had been two DH 86Bs, EI-ABK and EI-ABT. These two aircraft had been bought before the War and flew daily services from Dublin to Liverpool, which continued until they were superseded by Dakotas at the end of 1946, when the Expresses were sold to British operators.

OTHER COMMERCIAL WORK

Amongst many post-war start-up companies, Skytravel Limited began in 1946 to operate charter flights out of Liverpool and Blackpool and in October 1946 took on RAS's well-worn Expresses G-ACVY, G-ACZP, G-ADYH and G-AENR, for holiday flights from Speke and Squires Gate to the popular holiday destination of the Isle of Man, for which the return fare was £5.00. Unfortunately, the financial burden of operating a large fleet rapidly overtook the company, and it closed down in summer 1947. G-ADYH was sold on as related below in October 1947, but G-ACZP remained stored by the finance company for several years and the other two were simply sold for spares. Union Air Services of Gatwick acquired G-ADUH in early 1947 for passenger charters to racecourse venues for the next year, but their business was unsustainable, and it was sold on to locally-based Bond Air Services, who had acquired ex Aer Lingus EI-ABK, which reverted to G-ADVJ. Bond's DH 86s eventually ended up with Gulf Aviation in Bahrain in the early 50s. Two other companies, Steiner Air and Travel Services and West Coast Air Services, also briefly used DH 86s from 1946 for only one season.

Holiday Flight to Jersey

For the summer season of 1954, a well-known charter operator operating in the industrialised north west of England, Lancashire Aircraft Corporation, obtained a licence to fly scheduled services from Blackpool to the holiday island of Jersey. The company used a fleet of de Havilland aircraft for this service, with several Dragon Rapides and one Express Air Liner, G-ACZP. Being a new route for this airline, there were no spare pilots from the Rapide fleet to fly the DH 86, so the company contacted Croydon-based charter operator Morton Air Services to find temporary aircrew. A very young John Holmwood remembers being told by his company to report at short notice to Squires Gate airport, to fly a "Rapide" on a schedule to and from Jersey for a few weeks. On arrival, he found, to his consternation, that the "Rapide" he had expected to fly was actually a DH 86. The inexperienced Captain Holmwood had never flown a DH 86 and was not rated on that type, so he made a hurried telephone call to his boss at Croydon, who rather dismissed the difference by saying that it was "...only a Rapide with two more engines, isn't it?"

In a matter of hours this young pilot, only recently qualified on Rapides anyway, found himself commanding a four-engined airliner on a daily return schedule from Squires Gate to Jersey - usually down in the morning, and back again in the evening. The single DH 86 operated in what de Havilland called the "Air Ferry" model, fitted out with 17 rather spartan triangular-backed seats with minimum spacing between; no tables, and, more significant for a full load of holiday-makers on a two-and-a-quarter hour journey, no toilet, since on this economy DH 86, the toilet area had been removed to make room for a double bench seat. As an early, dual-control model DH 86, it had not been modified to either DH 86A or DH 86B standard, so had no auxiliary fins or altered ailerons and thus had the inherent directional and lateral stability problems of the early machines.

To make matters even more interesting, the airfield at Jersey was closed for a period that summer. All services to the island therefore had to return to the previous operating "field", the wide beach at St Aubin's Bay, pioneered before the war by Jersey Airways. This was the operating base for our pilot during his tour of duty to Jersey. He usually had with him either a radio operator or a "pilot's assistant" in the right-hand seat, whose tasks were to work the flaps from the hydraulic box behind the Captain's seat, keep an eye on the passengers and to hand round the sweets, cigarettes and sick bags during the flight. He never had another pilot with him and operated the aircraft from memory, without a check list, which at least indicates the simplicity of the DH 86's systems, and their similarity to those of the later-designed Rapide.

Captain Holmwood's major concern on take-off was the aircraft's propensity to swing into wind if not carefully watched, followed by a resulting ground-loop, which would usually damage more than the pilot's pride. His opinion of the DH 86 was that the large keel surface of the fuselage, coupled with the small central fin and rudder, made it more prone than the Rapide to uncontrollable cross-wind swing into wind at the early stages of the take-off run. If the aircraft's direction was not very carefully controlled during the first 50 yards of take-off in a cross-wind, "it would swing like a pig", so his technique, also used by many other Express pilots, was to begin the take-off run by cautiously increasing power by leading with the "upwind" throttles, thereby tending to turn the aircraft slightly out of wind, monitoring the direction of the nose very carefully all the while, and adjusting for any incipient swings left or right. Once he had about forty mph of airspeed indicated, he would have enough elevator authority to lift the tail with a hefty push on the control column, and from that moment, with the rudder into more effective airflow, he could use rudder to keep the aircraft under directional control. At that stage, he could then bring up the remaining throttles to full power, and complete a normal take-off. All this of course also depended on the sand at St Aubin's being uniformly firm, as wet areas of sand tended to allow the wheels to dig in, slowing the take-off run, and probably causing a swing towards the softer sand. Luckily, the long strand available meant that he was never concerned with the longer take-off run caused by this cautious technique, because the Express Air Liner's performance was such that it would only use up around 340 yards (311m) for a normal take-off, providing ample reserves.

Once in the cruise, Holmwood considered the DH 86 to be pleasant and easy to fly, with nicely-balanced controls and effective trimmers, with no obvious difficulties, except for the one that occupied most of the pilot's cruise time - keeping the speed of the four Gipsy Sixes synchronised. The inaccurate vertical engine rpm indicators were only usable as a very rough guide as to engine speeds, so the normal technique was to listen to the two port engines first, moving the throttles fractionally until the thrumming "beat" of the two engines on that side disappeared. Then one leaned over to the starboard side to listen to the starboard engines, synchronising them to the other two. Speeds obtainable on the older DH 86s such as G-ACZP were by now well down on the maker's figures, as he could rarely coax more than 125 mph out of the Gipsy Sixes at cruising rpm, unlike de Havilland's Captain Broad, who gained between 138 and 142 mph in his cruise tests in 1934. Again, after eighteen years of service, G-ACZP consumed more than the official fuel consumption of 35.5 gallons per hour, time having increased her consumption to around 10 gallons per engine per hour, or 40 gallons total per hour at 1,000 feet.

Landing at St Aubin's Bay was not usually a particular problem at low tide, even with the beach's mainly East-West alignment, as the aircraft could be yawed partially into the wind, thereby lessening the effect of the cross-wind. If the wind was still across the landing direction, the usual method was to approach at about 80 mph, ten mph below the flap limiting speed of 90 mph, and to keep the aircraft "crabbing" its nose into the cross-wind. The power was then gradually decreased at the flare, but with some power left on the upwind engines, so countering the natural weathercocking tendency into the cross-wind. The aircraft was always landed on the mainwheels, in the "wheeler" attitude, in order to enable better directional control, to provide a better view of the runway, and to allow earlier appreciation of any apparent swing. The rudder was effective down to the point where the tail was lowered on to the runway at about forty mph, and directional control was then exercised by differential use of the outboard throttles, the Dunlop brakes being ineffective except for steering during taxying. In a five mph wind, the landing run was 200 to 230 yards (185m) - pretty impressive for such a large aircraft.

An illustration of the performance reserves of the DH 86 was given to Captain Holmwood when, due to fly a return schedule from the beach to Blackpool, he was unable to start his number two engine on the port side, despite trying all the usual wrinkles. Informing his ten passengers of a small technical problem, he climbed out to discuss the problem with the ground engineers, only to discover that they were as mystified as he was; probably "something wrong with the magnetos" on that engine, but they could offer no short term solution, as they held no spares. However, looking to the South from his vantage point high up the beach opposite West Park pavilion, the worried pilot could see the tide rapidly filling up the bay and he knew of course that there was no safe parking area at high tide, since the sea at St Aubin's Bay came right up to the sea wall.

A frantic telephone call to his engineering authority at Croydon gave him a rather dubious solution which he took with much trepidation. He dashed back to his 10 waiting passengers, apologised for the technical delay and told them that the flight would be leaving as soon as possible. Numbers one, three and four engines started once again without any difficulty, but number two still refused to do more than splutter with the twitching propeller returning to that infuriatingly static position. Deciding to go along with his chief engineer's solution, he therefore released the brake and aiming quickly for the end of the longest stretch of dry beach, he turned into wind, ran up the three serviceable engines, set up some right trim on the fin bias system, and set off across the beach for his first-ever three-engined take-off. Despite anticipating a swing to the left on the run, he hardly noticed any difference from a normal take-off, and had no difficulty trimming out the asymmetric power all the way up the climb to his 3,000 foot cruising altitude, where he obtained 120 mph as opposed to his normal 125 mph. Whether his passengers even noticed that they were only flying on three engines is not known, as no mention was made by either side after landing safely at Blackpool. The propeller of the rogue engine simply windmilled quite happily all the way home, giving a fair degree of extra drag, but making surprisingly little difference to the landing, so proving to this pilot that the Express Air Liner was safe to handle on only three engines.

DH 86B G-ADYH in the Far East

One Express Air Liner had an intriguing post-war existence. Built in 1936 as a DH 86A with a ten-seat cabin, G-ADYH had a conventional early career, being converted in 1937 to DH 86B standard, and serving throughout the war with West Coast Air Services, under the control of the AAJC, at Speke airport, Liverpool. After release from government control, in October 1946, G-ADYH was sold to Skytravel Limited for passenger services until they sold it on 27th October 1947 to Warren Penny, a visiting Australian charter pilot. Penny had recently built up a lucrative but risky business transporting British and European immigrants to Australia, owning an Australian-registered company called Intercontinental Air Tours, and was looking for a suitable but inexpensive ten-seater to add to his existing fleet - Lockheed Hudson

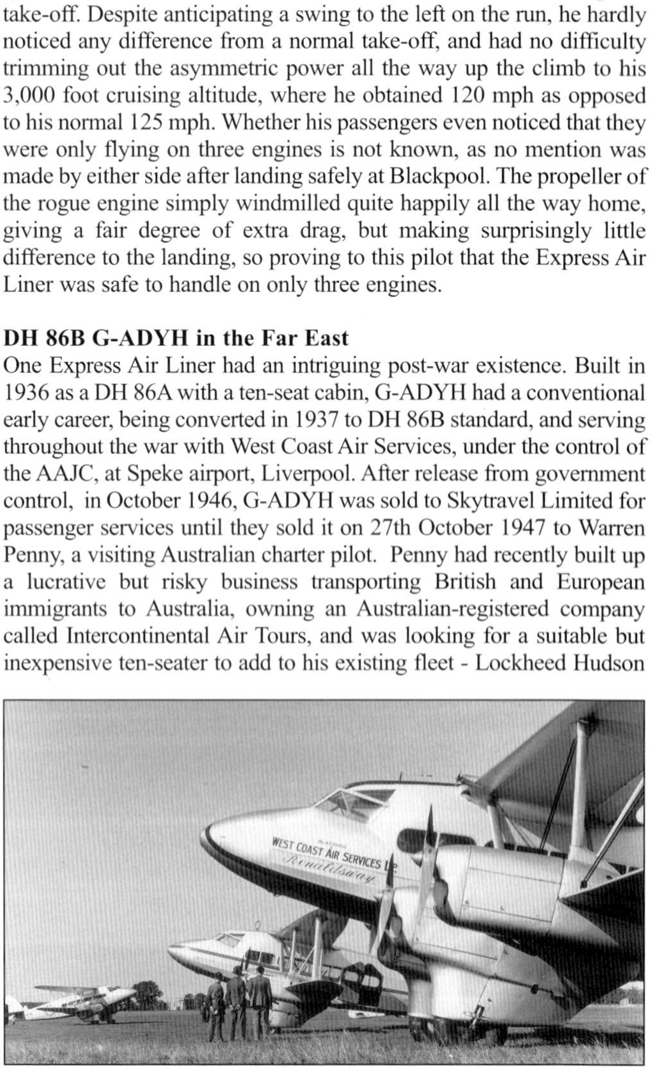

G-ADYH c/n 2344 of West Coast Air Services served with the AAJC in wartime and then with Skytravel and 'Intercontinental'. [CND]

VH-ASV and Lodestar G-AGBU. He needed an aircraft quickly, as he already had 10 immigrants eagerly waiting to leave for Australia, but he also needed a qualified pilot to fly it. The DH 86 soon had a new name, '*Denebola*' (a name previously used by Imperial on G-ADUI), painted on its nose, and 'Intercontinental' on the fuselage sides, and a suitable British pilot was engaged to join Penny's company and undertake the journey to Sydney - Captain Bill Mellor. The British, Greek and Italian passengers joined the Express at Croydon on 30th October 1947 and with Penny in the co-pilot's seat, they left that same day for Australia, a bare three days after the change of ownership. A fairly leisurely transit across Europe and Asia to Australia then followed, with the whole party arriving intact in Sydney, Intercontinental's base, on 28th November.

Penny's intentions for G-ADYH are unclear, for no application was made to re-register the aircraft in Australia, so she remained registered and certificated in Britain, with the Intercontinental name still on her side, despite continuing to be used occasionally for the next three months from Sydney. By early 1948, the Australian Director of Civil Aviation had refused permission for Penny to operate further immigrant charter flights into Australia, so he needed an alternative arrangement for the aircraft he had intended to use for those flights. He contacted an American who operated a similar rather shady immigrant charter arrangement from Manila, Francis Grigware, and persuaded him to take over ownership of the Express Air Liner, and use it to collect another 30 of Penny's customers waiting in Rome to be flown to Australia. Ownership was eventually transferred to Grigware's company, "South Eastern" on 13th April 1948 but in the meantime, G-ADYH had been taken to Darwin and was reported to have been hangared there from 1st March until 12th April, presumably being flown by Intercontinental staff. Australian records also show that the hangarage fees were not paid during this period, which indicates that Intercontinental were beginning to have financial problems. But finance was not Penny's only problem, as the Express had been damaged during an attempted take-off at Darwin, with the starboard undercarriage having collapsed "due to the brake seizing". This strained the axle and oleo legs and put the aircraft unserviceable, causing a series of questions from the Australian DCA about the aircraft's certification and safety. Repairs were eventually carried out, probably by unauthorised engineers, over the next six weeks, but the DCA remained very concerned about the aircraft's airworthiness, so they prohibited it from flying.

Eventually, on 12th May 1948, a restricted permission for a ferry flight to the UK was agreed between the Australian and British authorities, and the aircraft left Darwin "for Britain via Singapore" on 19th May, officially for renewal of its C of A, which actually expired on 14th May 1948. Liberties were obviously taken by the flight crew, as the DCA permission was not sent to Darwin until 21st May! However, it seems there was no intention of taking the aircraft back to Britain, as it was then operated without legal certification by a Captain Donati on behalf of ICAT from various airfields in Burma, Malaya and Indonesia, still in British markings, until late 1948. It was reportedly used as a personnel and cargo transport on behalf of the Indonesian rebel movement AURI during this period, with a 19th September report showing that it was unserviceable at Penang in northern Malaya and its registered owner, F Grigware, was currently in a jail in Rangoon, Burma! The next report on G-ADYH's whereabouts shows that it had been repaired and continued clandestine operations under rebel Indonesian control, possibly with Indonesian paperwork as RI-008, until eventually captured on 19th December 1948 by the legitimate Netherlands East Indies forces at Maguwo, Indonesia. A Dutch engineer, Hugo Hooftman, later reported that he had seen the Express Air Liner at Bandung airport, near the Indonesian capital, in poor condition, but still with its British registration, the name '*Denebola*' still on the nose and 'Intercontinental' painted on the fuselage. He also reported that sometime in 1949 the aircraft was broken up at Bandung, and the Gipsy Six engines were used on an indigenous aircraft built there. Warren Penny was declared bankrupt in Australia soon after the Australian government banned all immigrant charter flights in 1949, insisting that all future immigrants must use QANTAS or BOAC flights.

Gulf Aviation's G-ADUH c/n 2336 approaching Croydon in 1951.
[M. Stroud]

Gulf Aviation, Bahrain

Gulf Aviation was a successful airline set up in 1949 by a British pilot, Freddie Bosworth, to operate from Bahrain to other airfields around the Persian Gulf. Bosworth started with an Avro Anson, then expanded rapidly in 1951, buying up three rather elderly DH 86Bs, from Aerocontacts of Gatwick, for use on the lucrative 100-mile service between the Gulf island of Bahrain to Dhahran, the nearest port on the Saudi Arabian mainland. The first DH 86, G-ADUH, by then in rather poor condition, left Gatwick in May 1951, and eventually arrived at Bahrain after a broken tailwheel had been repaired at Beirut. Soon after it arrived at its new home, it was badly damaged in June 1951 by a runaway Auster Autocrat, G-AIBO at Bahrain and was declared a write-off. Before the second DH 86 arrived, Captain Bosworth had departed for Croydon for negotiations with BOAC for future representation activities in the Gulf, but also for him to gain a type rating on the Dove, which he intended to buy for the airlines' services. Sadly, he was killed when the Dove crashed after an engine failure, but the airline was kept in operation by chief pilot Captain Peacock, and Mrs Bosworth. Meanwhile, the second Express, G-ADVJ, which had served Aer Lingus as EI-ABK, arrived with Gulf on 9th August, to begin services from Bahrain. Another DH 86, G-ADUF, was bought from Air Navigation and Trading, to replace the damaged G-ADUH, and it arrived in November 1951. By March 1952, more Doves had been taken on by Gulf Aviation, making the tired old DH 86s redundant, so the remaining two were withdrawn from service when their Certificates of Airworthiness expired by the end of May 1952, then to be subsequently broken up at Bahrain.

Last Users

Other than Gulf Aviation, overseas companies which kept DH 86s in service after 1946 included Hurkus Airlines in Ankara, Turkey, which operated two ex-DHY Expresses, TC-ERK and TC-HEP, possibly up until the early 1960s, although very little is known as to their fate. Another rather shadowy company, Peacock Air Charter, nominally based in Alexandria, Egypt between 1947 and 1948, also operated two ex Misr Airwork Expresses, SU-ACR and SU-ABV, occasionally flying them, probably illegally, into Britain on charter flights.

With the incorporation of most of the established British airlines into BEA in 1947, and with increasingly bureaucratic restrictions, many of the enthusiastic start-up airlines had collapsed, their aircraft being sold on or scrapped. DC3s were also taking over many of the smaller services, and the large, wooden four-engined biplane had lost its appeal to passengers. By the mid 1950s, only one of the type, G-ACZP, was left to soldier on after the Lancashire Aircraft Corporation was taken over by Silver City Airways at Southampton. It was sold in February 1958 to the Hampshire Aeroplane Club, managed by that great aviation character, Viv Bellamy. The flying life of the DH 86 ended on 21st September that year when this early DH 86 model burst a tyre on landing at Madrid's Barajas airport, subsequently performing a slow ground loop, which caused minimal damage, but left the aircraft unable to taxi off the runway. An over-enthusiastic fire crew, rather unreasonably wanting to re-open their airfield, managed to cause further damage when removing it from the runway which put this unique aircraft beyond reasonable repair. It was reluctantly abandoned by Viv Bellamy, and was stored later to be used for fire practice by the airport fire service sometime in 1963, following which the type became extinct.

Section 4:
The DH 89 Dragon Rapide

Prototype E.4 awaiting flight testing at Martlesham Heath, April, 1934. *[BAe]*

Section 4 – Chapter 1: Design and Testing

WHY THE DRAGON RAPIDE?

The requirement which was initially known as the Dragon Six came from de Havilland's perception, in late 1933, of the needs of small airlines for an aircraft with the capability of carrying up to eight passengers for about 200 miles, where necessary over water, and to the continent of Europe, at greater speeds than available in such aircraft as their DH 84. Such an aircraft should have operating costs comparable to those of luxury coaches or taxis, but with an additional allowance for the extra speed of air travel. Aircraft which had been in use in Europe for short-range passenger transport up to the early 1930s were generally somewhat slow, had poor climb, cruise and gliding performance, and in particular were not safe on one engine. De Havillands decided to develop the capabilities and equipment they had already produced in their twin-engined Dragon, and the larger, four-engined Express Air Liner. They felt a safe, fast, small but more robust twin-engined transport would be in keeping with the company design policy of "evolution, not revolution". This policy dictated the direction which an improvement on the existing DH 84 airliner would take.

Richard Clarkson, an aerodynamicist in the Stag Lane drawing office, carried out the stress calculations for the wings and fuselage and recalled that, while the design of the DH 89 was the responsibility of Arthur Hagg, as head of the department, it was very much a team effort, with advice coming from Geoffrey de Havilland and Charles Walker in equal quantities.

DESIGN ELEMENTS

The de Havilland decision-makers felt they could improve on the Dragon formula in terms of maintaining existing load and range capacity, but with better cruising speed, better climb and gliding angles, a higher ceiling, better single-engine performance, and greater comfort, while using similar construction methods and materials to those already in use for other aircraft.

The critical element would be the power plant. The Dragon's 130 hp Gipsy Major was too low-powered to give the performance required without costly modifications, but by late 1933 Frank Halford and the engine factory manager, R H Hutchinson, had proved the new 200 hp Gipsy Six on the DH 86, so the design team now used this six-cylinder engine for the new design. As always, there were penalties to pay for the use of the bigger engine. The Major weighed only 305 lbs and consumed 6.5 gallons per hour for a 105-mile per hour cruise at 2,100 rpm on the DH84, whereas the larger Gipsy Six, at 468 lbs, was currently consuming around 9.5 to 10 gallons per hour, to produce an expected cruising speed of about 130 miles per hour at 2,100 rpm. Using the Gipsy Six, the better cruise performance would be offset by greater weight, higher relative fuel consumption and higher stall speeds, resulting in poorer short-field performance. The drawing office team therefore had the task of defining the best elements of the successful, but underpowered and relatively slow, DH 84, and of the larger DH 86 and incorporating them into a development of the Dragon to fit the de Havilland evolutionary bill.

PERFORMANCE REQUIREMENTS

The view of the DH Sales Department was that the market required a similar cabin and load capacity to the DH 84, so they agreed that up to eight passengers with around 40 lbs of baggage each, would be the aim for the new project. Taking a fuselage similar to that of the DH 84, adding to it a wing with similar chord but with greater span and with engines providing 50% more power at take-off a better cruising speed would be obtained than that of the Dragon. The outer section of the DH 86's wings, being thin, of long span and

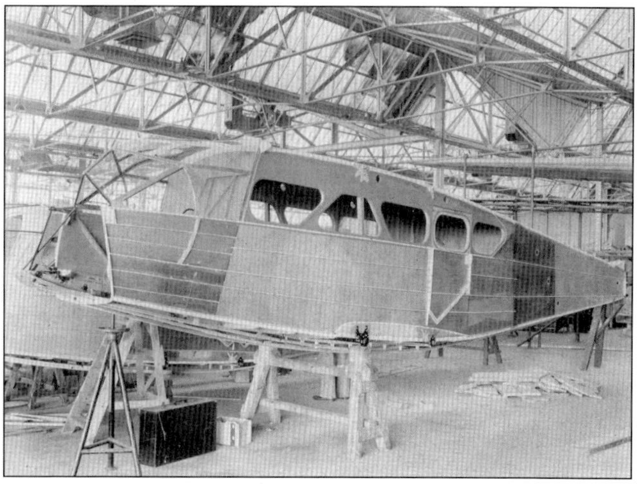

DH 89 fuselage construction, Hatfield, 1936. *[BAe]*

DH 89 wing during construction, Hatfield, 1940. [BAe]

minimal chord would, with little need for change, meet the often uttered desire of Charles Walker, to gain better cruising performance by combining as great a wingspan as possible with minimal chord. Walker often advocated to the de Havilland draughtsmen that span was the most important factor in producing better lift/drag ratios, thereby proffering higher aerodynamic efficiency, and so producing better overall cruising performance. There were trade-offs for this type of wing design, of course, as de Havillands were discovering at that time with their long-span, relatively thin, highly-tapered (but beautifully proportioned) monoplane wing planform for their MacRobertson Trophy Race Comet Racer. The major disadvantages were a tendency to uneven tip-stalling at low speeds, which could produce vicious stalls in some conditions, and a need for higher landing speeds, in the absence of high-lift devices to alter the camber for the landing condition. Use of high-lift devices such as slats and flaps would only decrease the landing speeds by a small percentage, but would increase the complexity and weight of the wings, and would also increase the cost of manufacture, so were not used on the original Dragon Six.

Slightly higher landing speeds were dictated by this wing design compromise, which meant that the excellent short-field performance for which the DH 84 had a strong reputation, would not be attainable on the new aircraft. On balance, however, these characteristics were felt by Arthur Hagg's drawing office team to be less problematical with a biplane than with a monoplane, so a slightly more symmetrical adaptation of the DH 86's thin, tapered wing, with maximum span and minimum chord, was chosen as the optimum solution for best cruising performance on the new aircraft.

On the matter of whether to make the new machine a monoplane or a biplane, the options available to the de Havilland draughtsmen made the choice easy. The close-knit DH team still held strong memories of the unsuccessful monoplane wing of the DH 29 of 1921, an experiment in aerodynamics which failed to produce the anticipated benefits, as well as the more recent structural problems with the monoplane wings of the otherwise successful DH 80A

Stag Lane engine assembly area, 1934. [Aeroplane]

Puss Moth, so they felt more comfortable with the familiar biplane designs. The Dragon and the Express Air Liner both used a biplane configuration with considerable success, and the weight versus drag argument favoured the biplane because of its lighter weight.

CONSTRUCTION METHODS

Construction processes were little problem, there being no reason to change current practices. As far as Hagg's team was concerned in 1933, being 'conservatively evolutionary', they could still provide lighter structures in wood than in metal. As the company's fabrication shops were expert in this medium, with very little experience in major metal construction, there was no need to change the currently successful construction materials. For the very commercially competitive DH team, cost was a major decider here, as metal construction was still more expensive than wood.

In keeping with the proven practices used on the DH 84 and the DH 86, the fuselage would be a stressed-plywood box, covered by outer stringers to give better shape and insulation, and then covered with Irish linen. Wings, being basically the same as the outer sections of those on the DH 86, would follow the existing factory construction methods, with spruce main spars and ribs, ply leading edges, and wire internal bracing, again covered in best Irish linen. In order to spread the flight and landing loads, the small central lower stub wing would be built around a metal main spar, connecting to the wooden main spars of the outer wings, and holding the engine bearers and undercarriage, and supported by a small wooden rear spar, spruce ribs and leading and trailing edges. 'Elektron' aluminium alloy sheeting would be used for the engine cowlings, which would be blended around the undercarriage legs, to form the streamlined 'trousers' which had proved attractive as well as functional on the Express Air Liner. An additional reason for keeping to the evolutionary process was the need to consider repair schemes, which in this case would be simple to set up, as DH maintenance agents around the world were used to repairing wooden DH structures, so no new skills would therefore be needed.

COCKPIT LAYOUT

An element of the Dragon Six's design which was not considered in great depth was the cockpit. The strengths of the de Havilland team were the efficient design, manufacture, production and in particular, sales organisations. For the smaller 'personal' aircraft such as the Moths, Captain de Havilland took a close interest, and added his own strong influence to the positioning of controls and the layout of the pilot's area. There is a family similarity with all the smaller Moth types, which owes much to the man who not only helped in the detailed design of the cockpits, but also carried out much of the development testing of the aircraft. With the larger types, the detailed layout was left more to the Chief Test Pilot, Hubert Broad, whose viewpoint differed from Captain de Havilland's. Broad was an extremely skilful pilot, whose orientation was much more towards the handling qualities of 'his' test machines. Being an outgoing extrovert, in contrast to his introverted, taciturn Managing Director, Captain Broad tended to take a wider view of aircraft development, and was able to overlook control difficulties experienced by other pilots.

This meant that he failed to allow for the fact that many pilots, being of only average ability, would have more difficulty in handling an aircraft than himself. He was also less concerned with cockpit design aspects such as the positioning of controls and instrument layout and tended to accept what had been designed into the cockpit by the designers. This acceptance by the test pilot of a cockpit produced by non-pilots would explain the less than ergonomic layout of the Dragon Six's controls.

Some elements were good, such as the superb view out of the cockpit, the comfortable spectacle-type control column, the neat instrument panel and the handy aluminium throttle levers. However, tall pilots had difficulty getting into and out of the cockpit, then in seeing directly ahead from the fixed seating position, because of the cockpit frames on a level with the horizon. The rudder pedals, while adjustable to three positions, could only

Early DH 89 instrument panel, showing engine starter buttons and early-type instruments. [BAe]

be moved by recumbent gymnasts under the instrument panel. One of the most difficult tasks with the Dragon Six is the control of the machine on hard surfaces in strong winds. This is partly due to the natural tendency of tailwheel aircraft to head into wind on the ground. With the Dragon Six, this tendency is difficult to control, because of the constant adjustments needed to rudder pedals, hand-brake, throttle and control column, all of which are some distance from each other. More effective positioning of the Dragon Six's controls could have been identified by a less dextrous test pilot in the development stages of the aircraft's life.

A minor irritation, not apparent for the first fifty years of the aircraft's life, manifested itself with the introduction in 1992 of shoulder harnesses for the pilot. In 1933, the only restraint considered necessary was a wide fabric belt simply fixed to the seat box by small bolts. With a tight, fixed shoulder harness, as is considered necessary by modern airworthiness authorities, the physical task of reaching forward and down to release the catch on the long flap lever's top is almost impossible, particularly for pilots with short arms. However, as only a lap strap was in use for the major portion of the type's service, the designers can be excused this ergonomic awkwardness.

PROTOTYPE BUILD

Despite a busy build programme at Stag Lane in the winter of 1933/34, with the DH 84 and the DH 86 both in production, work on the new Dragon Six began, with sub-assemblies being moved up to Hatfield, ready for a planned first flight in April. Time was not as critical as for the DH 86, so the schedule was less strenuous but by mid-April the prototype had completed all its inspections and ground tests at Hatfield, and was declared ready for flight. Still in its doped primer finish, but with the test registration on the fuselage sides, Hubert Broad took 'E.4' for its first flight on 17th April. No flight test reports still exist, but the time delay between that flight and the submission of the type for certification indicates that there were probably a few small items which needed rectification. The only visible modification made to E.4 was the addition of a fifth window on the starboard fuselage side, so the initial flight tests can be assumed to have been satisfactory. Twelve hours of testing were then flown by Broad and Hereward de Havilland at Hatfield, before the aircraft was ready for Air Ministry certification.

Prototype DH 89 airborne from Hatfield before delivery to Switzerland, July, 1934. [BAe]

FIRST MARTLESHAM TESTS

Seven weeks after the first flight, Hubert Broad flew the prototype across to Martlesham's broad heathland in June 1934 for its certification flight testing by the A & AEE. The Martlesham pilots commented in their test report M/643, that this new de Havilland was better than the DH84, as it had more power and greater seating capacity. With a maximum take-off weight of 5,000 lbs, they found a maximum speed in a dive of 195 mph; a short take-off run, achieving a height of 200 feet by their standard 656-yard point from start of run; a creditable 265-yard landing run with brakes; and 500 yards without brakes. This of course was before flaps were fitted, and as the DH pilots had found, the aircraft tended to 'float' on landing, making the landing run somewhat longer. A rather puzzling comment, made without any recommendation on how to rectify it, was that at about 175 mph, in a dive, "the extreme nose of the aircraft buckles with a loud report". No further reference to this rather alarming occurrence was made by Martlesham or de Havilland, so it can be assumed that this tendency to 'buckle' was remedied by using stronger metal or a different profile for the nose cone.

Martlesham's comments on handling were that it was pleasant to fly but that the glide was flat, and care had to taken with using the brakes on landing "or there is a liability for the aircraft to turn over"! Tail trimming was considered too low-geared; the electric starter buttons were considered insufficiently rigidly-mounted and it was suggested that the engines could be primed without having to remove part of the cowling. Apart from these minor recommendations, there were no other critical comments, so the type was recommended for a Certificate of Airworthiness, and flown back to Hatfield. After a total of eighteen hours and thirty-five minutes of flying, it was repainted in Swiss markings as CH-287, and flown on 18th July by Major Hereward de Havilland to the first operator of the type, Osterschweitz Aero Club, based at the delightful Altenrhein airfield, on the eastern shore of Lake Constance.

TESTING AT HATFIELD

Incorporation of modifications to satisfy the Martlesham recommendations was quickly put in hand, so that, by 5th July 1934, the second Dragon Six was given its C of A, as G-ACPM, for Hillman's Airways. Flight-testing of the aircraft was carried out by Hubert Broad, Bob Waight and Geoffrey de Havilland Junior.

The Aerodrome Foreman was the man responsible for the preparation of the aircraft for production fligh-testing, which initially involved the functional checks of all the aircraft equipment. He would have the aircraft trestled up in the flying attitude for checks of the engines, propellers and controls. The first of these was the fuel-flow check, which ensured that each fuel pump produced at least twice what the engine could consume at full throttle. Next, the engines were started, to confirm satisfactory running, and adjustments made to controls and instruments at all speeds. At this point the Foreman would check the aircraft over again to confirm all altered items and adjustments had been completed. The Inspection Department then completed a final check before "presenting his compliments to the test pilot" and requested a flight-test.

Geoffrey de Havilland Junior was asked by the persuasive editor of the *The de Havilland Gazette*, the company's informative house journal, to give readers his views on flight-testing the Rapide. The extract which follows appeared in the June 1938 edition :

"The pilot's intellect is roused from the semiconscious at this stage, because it is an unwritten law that he must find fault before he reaches the cabin door, moving at a normal walking pace. He grumbles and starts making notes straight away. Engine cowlings, doors, door handles, sliding windows, exterior finish generally provide the first opportunities for a normal scorn, and if all else fails he grumbles about the weather and the foreman then knows that the aircraft is externally alright.

It is a feature of the commercial aircraft business that the first thought is devoted to items which affect passengers' comfort - and I think it shows that the technical side is pretty well taped these days, as it should be.

Seated at the controls, the next thing is to check all lights - cabin, navigation, landing and signal lights - and the respective discharge rates on the ammeter. Then the flying controls and trims are checked for ease of movement on the ground. Notes are made for all such items, even if they only amount to the universal ' OK'. The engine starters are then used, engines are warmed oil pressures are noted, slow running checked and afterwards full-throttle static revs and oil pressures, smoothness of running while on the ground, and individual ignition circuits are checked.

Then the pilot takes off, observing his run and time and particularly whether the airscrews are giving correct r.p.m. (minimum 2,000) at the optimum climb speed of 95 m.p.h. The figures are entered down whether correct or not.

Geoffrey de Havilland Jr. handing over the documents of YI-FYA at Hatfield, 1938. [BAe]

Reaching calm air the first check is on rigging. Lateral trim - does she fly with hands and feet off without gradually dropping a wing? Is the differential aileron control perfect or is it a trifle too strong, causing excessive lightness to the feel? Then fore and aft trim - without a load on board is the control column centrally rigged or is it canted aft so that to land you have to pull it right into your breakfast? Directional trim - with neutral rudder bias does she fly straight indefinitely, checking on turn indicator, directional gyro and compass? Everything is noted on the form.

Electrical equipment is checked in flight; lights are put on to make sure there is no flicker due to imperfect contacts. Instruments; suction available for gyroscopic units is checked on a gauge. The mounting of the instrument board is examined for vibration and for setting - if it cocks forward then the artificial horizon will show descent when we are flying level. To check the airspeed indicator, the aircraft is stalled and then dived, and as speed is lost in coming out of the dive, even a slight time lag in the needle will be detected. The instrument has been checked for accuracy in the laboratory. R.p.m. gauges are checked for agreement by setting them alike on the throttles and listening for the tell-tale whirr-whirr which would prove imperfect synchronisation. Oil gauge readings are again taken for different engine speeds. The directional gyro is proved by flying a steady compass course for a certain period.

Then rigging wires - there are still one or two on the economical type of branch-line aircraft - are observed for possible vibration at all speeds.

Engine controls are next tried, particularly the drop in revs which must follow any coarse use of the altitude control when flying at low altitude. All being well the pilot then descends to 1,000 feet for a full-throttle test to enter down the r.p.m., a.s.i. and oil pressures.

Finally he checks two or three things that mean much to passengers - the proper functioning of the cabin heater and the ventilation system, the degree of cabin silence and freedom from rattles.

He lands, checks again the slow-running adjustment on the engines, hands in his 'snag sheet' to the ground team. Adjustments are nearly always trifling, and made within half an hour. If they are extensive, somebody is in trouble. The execution of all adjustments and work called for by the test pilot has to be passed by the Inspection Department.

The aircraft is then loaded right up to the full 5,500 lb limit and on the aft centre of gravity limit - worst of all for stability characteristics. He flies again now to test the stability in all attitudes and conditions of flight - a feature in which the Rapide excels and a test which is always a pleasure to do, even after one has done hundreds of them. He then checks the trim - with this adjusted forward, it must be possible to fly level with hands off the controls; if it is not, the tail-plane incidence has to be altered very slightly and another test made.

The Rapide is then loaded to the forward CG limit and flown to see that there is still enough trim in hand.

The radio manufacturer's engineer is then taken up to test his installation in the air.

Thereafter the aircraft re-enters the paint shop to be cleaned and finally touched up.

The pilot has one further job. He must record on a separate card the engine r.p.m. and a.s.i. reading noted during a 95 m.p.h. climb (which should give 2,050 r.p.m.) , during level flight at 2,000 r.p.m. (which should give about 132 m.p.h.) and at full throttle (about 156 m.p.h. at 2.350 r.p.m.). On this card are also entered the ground air temperature and fixed-scale aneroid reading, the tests having been done at a height corrected to correspond to a true 1,000 feet. This card enters the records of the technical department, is analysed, approved, averaged with other Rapides to make sure that the performance standard is being maintained.

Emerging from the paint shop, the aircraft is winged around once again for the final approval of every detail - and then the (customer's) acceptance pilot takes over, and away she goes to Singapore or Capetown or over those lovely pinewoods of Scandinavia to meet others of her kind and the merry boys who fly them."

General Reconnaissance competition aircraft K4772 c/n 6271 at Martlesham, 1935. *[CND]*

Section 4 – Chapter 2: Production and Development

PRODUCTION

As soon as the prototype had flown in April 1934, the Dragon Six production process began in earnest, as there were already orders for the type from two airlines and several private owners. That was the beginning of a ten-year production run of 728, both at Hatfield, and from 1943, under licence by Brush Coachworks at Loughborough, which company built 335 DH 89 Dominies for the Royal Air Force. Ted Hillman had ordered three off the drawing board for Hillman's Airways at Romford, and took delivery of his first, G-ACPM, after it had been a publicity entry in that July's Kings Cup air race, flown by Hubert Broad, but unfortunately had been withdrawn after hail damage over Waddington. Twelve were produced in 1934, increasing in 1935 to 49. Shortly after its introduction, de Havillands wanted to make the new type sound sufficiently different from the smaller Dragon, so it became the DH 89 Dragon Rapide. This name change applied to the eighth airframe onwards with G-ACTT, built for the Anglo American Oil Company.

THE MILITARY DH 89M

The second appearance of a DH 89 at Martlesham was in June 1935, when de Havilland responded to Air Ministry specification G18/35 for a Coastal Reconnaissance aircraft requirement. Avro had put up their new all-metal Type 652, later the Anson, and de Havilland entered a Rapide modified to carry a small bomb load below the fuselage, a bomb sight in the fuselage floor, and a rotating gun turret on top of the rear fuselage. It was given the designation DH 89M, and the RAF serial K4772. The crew would consist of Pilot, Bomb-aimer and Gunner. Both types flew at Martlesham in the summer of 1935, for evaluation by Martlesham test pilots.

During a comprehensive set of performance and operational tests, the de Havilland machine was clearly not liked as much as the sturdier, metal-built Avro machine, which was better suited to long flights at low level over water, and in poor weather. The DH 89M's performance was generally acceptable, but the time to climb to the ceiling of 15,700 ft, at 44 minutes, was not. In bumpy weather, the aircraft was not a steady bombing platform, and it could not be used for dive-bombing because of the position of the sight's controls. Location of the bombing and gun controls was considered adequate only for the bomb-aimer, but there was no inter-communication with other crew members and illumination for night bombing was inadequate. The bomb-aimer's position was "so uncomfortable, cold and draughty that accuracy is impaired." The ventral gunner's position was reasonable but extremely draughty, and could not be recommended, as the testers felt it should be totally enclosed. Several other areas and fittings came in for criticism for being too fragile, so would require strengthening. For these reasons, the DH 89M was not considered as suitable for the reconnaissance role and the Avro won the contract. K4772 did, however, serve several units as a communications aircraft and for various trials, until it was scrapped in 1942.

There were however a few customers for the DH 89M, with the same basic configuration as the RAF model, including three sold to Spain and two to Lithuania.

DRAGON RAPIDE DH 89A

Considerable changes were made in 1936 to the DH 89 Dragon Rapide which led the company to give the 1937 model a new type designation - the DH 89A. The 1937 amendment sheet to the 'Dragon Six Manual of Instructions', produced by Albert Brant of the de Havilland Service Department, put the reasons for this succinctly:

"With the knowledge gained by production and the accumulated experience of the world wide operators of the DH 89 over a period exceeding two years, it is succeeded in 1937 by the D.H. 89A."

The major operational difference for this type upgrade was the introduction of split flaps on the lower wing. The differences between this flap installation and that introduced on the

G-ACPO c/n 6253 in Hillman's Airways colours at Stapleford, 1934, after completing testing at Hatfield. [M. Stroud]

contemporary DH 86 are interesting. The DH 86 had been fitted with split flaps on the top wing centre section, operated by hydraulic hand-pump from the cockpit but there was little aerodynamic benefit from this installation, so when the need for flaps on the Rapide became apparent, they were fitted on the lower wing, between the fuselage and the engine nacelles, where the slipstream from the engines had greater effect. They were also operated by a simple system of mechanical levers and cables, without the DH 86's heavier and more complex hydraulic system. Installing the flaps required a re-design of the rear section of the stub wings, to allow a tubular flap-operating mechanism to be incorporated. The flaps themselves were made from aluminium, and were raised and lowered by links and levers connected to a torque tube, which in turn was rotated by cables attached to a long operating lever pivoting around a point near the pilot's right foot, and requiring a long pull to lower the flaps. Air resistance against the flaps made them very difficult to lower at speeds higher than the flap limiting speed of 80 knots.

One of the 'world wide operators' referred to in the type change notification was Captain Eric Fresson, the pioneer operator of Highland Airways. Fresson had borrowed the fourth Dragon Six, G-ACPO, in October 1934, with the intention of assessing the type for use on his services in the Scottish Highlands and Islands. He flew several services with G-ACPO, to Wick and back to Inverness, and concluded that the greater take-off power, single-engine performance and cruising speed, were better than with his DH 84 Dragons, but he was less happy with the higher landing speed and extra landing distance required by the new type. In his biography, 'Rivals in the North', he comments:

"The [Dragon Six] was faster than the Dragon and had a better reserve of engine power, thus giving better single-engine performance, which would be a great asset on the Shetland run over so much open sea, and it carried a better load, which was our immediate problem. I spent several hours testing this aircraft with particular attention to the distance this 'plane required for taking off with full load and the run required on landing. Our fields would accommodate the take-off run, but as this 'plane was faster and carried a higher wing loading, it required greater skill in landing and pulling up in still air on the existing small fields. The answer was, either lengthen the fields, ... or persuade de Havillands to fit landing flaps which would permit a slower touchdown. The proposition was submitted to the DH company, and within six months they had a flapped demonstrator for test. We tried it out and there was no question, our problem was solved! "

DH 89A G-ADWZ c/n 6309 at Martlesham for Air Ministry tests, 1935. [CND]

The Dragon Six Manual quoted the landing distance, with no wind and a full load, as 250 yards, whereas the Dragon could manage in about 180 yards. The take-off run, for the same conditions, was given as 205 yards. Fresson had to operate from some very small, limiting fields in the Islands, so this practical experiment told him he could not safely use the Rapide on these same services. Being aware of potential customers' needs, and after several similar comments from early operators of the type, split flaps were designed, fitted and trialled on the Rapide in 1936.

The other airframe alteration made for the DH 89A was the little-publicised change in area of the tailplane and elevators, which were increased in area by approximately 5% and 3% respectively. The reason given in the amendment notice for this change was to provide 'further fore and aft stability', and was probably related to a need to provide slightly more longitudinal control at slow speeds. A comment had been made by the test pilots at Martlesham Heath during C of A testing earlier in 1936 on the 'heaviness of the elevators' on take-off, so this increase in area was made in response to that criticism.

Feedback from world-wide operators, particularly those in Scandinavia and Canada, also indicated that a heating system was required, so the system as used on the DH 86 was fitted for cold-weather customers. Hot air was fed from a muff around the port engine exhaust and then to outlets in the cabin, with the pilot having a control cock on the cockpit rear bulkhead to control the flow of air into the cabin. Many of the aircraft still in service in the1960s had this heating system removed, because of British airworthiness authority concerns about possible undetectable leaks in the trunking, which could produce carbon monoxide poisoning. By the early 1990s, all surviving UK Rapides had their heating system either removed or made inoperative.

Another change was also brought about through operating experience, when the primitive, but simple, venturi-tube system of providing suction for the flight instruments was changed to cope with choking of the venturis by snow or ice. The new, more complex, system took tappings from the engine exhausts, where new 'Trumpet'-type rear exhaust tubes were fitted. The suction lines then fed through the cowlings and stub wings into the cockpit instruments.

The remaining changes were the choice of wooden Schwarz Finish or metal Fairey-Reed propellers; incorporation of more efficient material for cabin sound-proofing; minor changes to the instrument panel; some small changes in the cockpit, including lighting, and switch positioning; incorporation of an emergency exit in the pilot's roof, and finalisation of the nose landing lamp position and switch.

The final change from the 89 to the 89A was the increase in maximum permissible weight from 5,000 pounds to 5,500 pounds. Part of the reason for this increase was the increase in what was then called 'tare weight' (but is now known as basic weight) of 250 pounds, caused by the additional systems.

DH 89A PERFORMANCE

As a result of these changes, and the increase in weight, the performance figures were trialled at Martlesham in April 1935, and then applied to the 72nd aircraft (completed for the Imperial Iranian War Ministry in May 1936 and later registered as EP-AAA) and all subsequent construction. The test aircraft was probably under test markings, since it was used as a company aircraft then first registered G-ADWZ in November 1935. In the usual way, the de Havilland Service Department followed up the changes in due course, issuing Amendment number 9 to the Dragon Six Manual of Instructions in September 1937, to cover the 'new' DH 89A.

Post card view of DH.89A G-AEOV c/n 6342 after 1937 flap trials at A&AEE Martlesham Heath. [D.Fox]

This amendment to the only de Havilland-produced documentation for the DH 89A is revealing in its quantification of the performance differences between the earlier models and the new development. The amended Performance section gave an increased take-off run, with a five mph wind, to 285 yards, a surprisingly large increase from the DH 89's 205-yard take-off run. More surprising, however, was the decrease in the landing run, giving the DH 89A a stopping distance, with brakes and the new flaps, of only 190 yards. The use of the centre-section split flaps had reduced the stalling speed by all of one mile per hour, but more important, had reduced the ground effect 'float' which the flapless aircraft experienced on landing, allowing the aircraft to settle onto the ground sooner than before. The landing run decreased by a useful 60 yards, although the take-off run increased by 80 yards. Paradoxically, this made the maximum weight performance more limiting for the new model, since, for operations at maximum weight (and therefore maximum revenue), the minimum length of field that could be used had actually increased with the new model. No doubt pilots of the time were happier with the fact that the landing run was now demonstrably shorter, than they were concerned at the longer take-off run, for at least they could now get into a smaller field, and then, if necessary, take-off again at less than maximum weight, to allow for that shorter field length.

As might be expected, the new performance amendment also showed that the higher weight had caused a consequent reduction in rate of climb, which reduced to 867 feet per minute, compared to 1,070 for the 89. The cruising speed at 1,000 feet had correspondingly decreased to a quoted 132 mph, as opposed to the earlier model's 138.5 mph and the service ceiling was decreased marginally to 18,850 feet, down from 19,350 feet. But more significantly for a passenger transport aircraft, the single-engine ceiling, which had been a moderate 6,000 feet for the DH 89, was now down to a tricky 3,100 feet at maximum all up weight, providing only marginal safety in the event of an engine failure. It became apparent that an engine failure with the DH 89A would in some cases be inevitably followed by a forced landing. However, such low safety factors were common in the 1936 context, as most contemporary multi-engined aircraft had similar or worse single-engine performance.

MARTLESHAM TEST OF FLAP INSTALLATION

De Havilland incorporated all the changes which constituted the DH 89A into the 93rd Rapide, G-AEOV, in February 1937, and sent it across to Martlesham Heath as E.2 in March, mainly to gain official acceptance of the flap and tailplane modifications. Comments from the tests indicated :

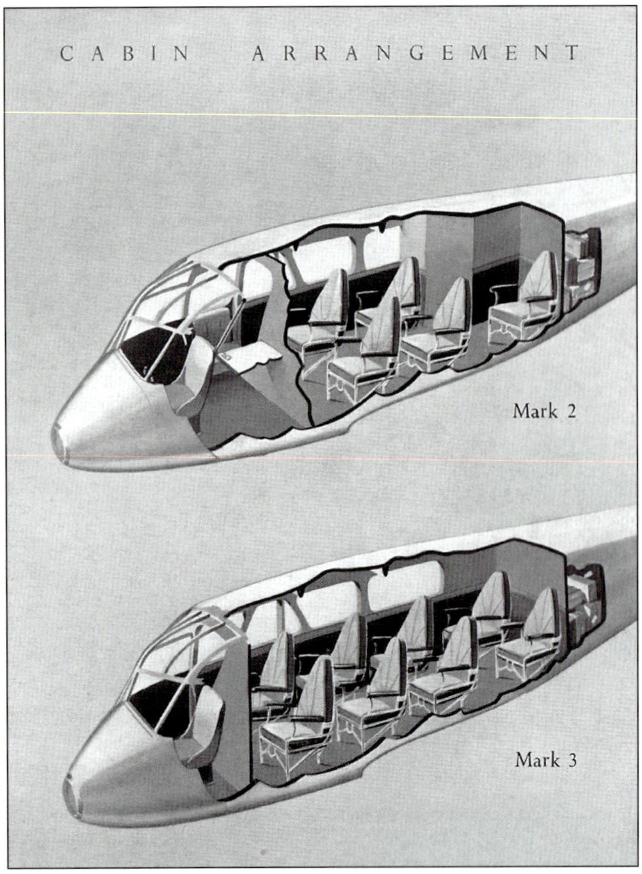

DH 89 Mark II and Mark III cabin arrangements. *[Bae]*

Extended cowling scoop, large spinner and variable pitch propeller on Mk 4 Rapide, 1994. *[CND]*

"The flaps are effective. They are difficult to operate because:

A. The lever has to be moved down to unlock it when the flaps are up and it is then so close to the floor that this is difficult.

B. The handle of the lever is too far from the pilot when the flaps are up.

C. The locking catch cannot be made to engage in the down position at an ASI reading above 80 mph.

D. The flaps cannot be raised at speeds above 90 mph as the catch cannot then be released."

While the effectiveness of the flaps was good news, the operating difficulty was only partly alleviated by the company, and the problem has been lived-with by Rapide pilots ever since. The tailplane modifications made to eliminate slight buffet under "certain conditions of flight" appear to have been resolved by the fitting of a plate above the flap operating jack, and changing the position of the tailplane bracing wires. No further trials were carried out on the Rapide by Martlesham pilots.

MODIFIED UNDERCARRIAGE TRIALS

One other airframe modification was tested by de Havilland in 1938. Some criticism had been levelled at the rather harsh ride of the undercarriage, so a new type of undercarriage was fitted to aircraft number 6420 in September 1938. A new type of oleo-pneumatic shock-absorbing system had been brought out by Dowty, the Cheltenham-based undercarriage manufacturer, was fitted to this Rapide, which became E.9 for the Hatfield trials. The new assembly was a development of that fitted to the Gladiator and the Lysander, with a single leg per side, but modified in order to fit the Rapide's existing twin telescopic legs. The main benefits of the new undercarriage were that it could provide up to 18 inches of vertical movement, had an in-built oleo-pneumatic shock absorber, and the shock-absorbing mechanism was adjustable by changing the inflation pressure. No reports of the success or otherwise of the tests on E.9 can be found, so it must be assumed that, as no other DH 89s were fitted with the Dowty undercarriage, the trials showed little benefit and the modification was abandoned.

After the Dowty undercarriage was replaced with the standard type, E.9 became F-ARII in December 1938 with Paul Legastellois, of Paris, an agent of the Spanish Republican Army, and was delivered despite the international Non-Intervention Agreement. However, it later fell into the hands of the Spanish Nationalists, who flew it as '40-6'. It survived the civil war to go to Iberia Airlines in 1942 as EC-BAC and later EC-AAR, before being scrapped in 1960.

DH 89A, MARKS 2 AND 3

According to de Havilland Service Department brochures, the Mark 2 and 3 designations were announced in November 1945 then published in March 1946, and applied to the civilianised Dragon Rapides sold post-war. The Mark 2 was simply a civilianised version of the Dominie C Mark II, fitted for pilot, radio operator and six passengers. It had a small cockpit extension behind the pilot's seat to allow room for radio equipment, a sideways-facing small table and a miniscule tip-up seat for a radio operator on the starboard side, immediately behind the pilot's seat. The usual bulkhead separating the cockpit from the cabin was moved rearwards by three feet, and seats were provided for six passengers, or five if the optional toilet compartment was fitted. This model had Gipsy Queen III engines, and an all up weight of 5,550 lbs with Fairey Reed X61186A/X4 propellers, or 5,750 lbs with Fairey Reed X61186A/X9 propellers. The Mark 3 designation differed from the Mark 2 by the absence of the radio operator's compartment and the installation of seven or eight passenger seats, with a toilet as an option. Despite de Havillands' attempts to classify Rapides from 1946, the Mark 2 and Mark 3 designations were seldom used in practice by customers.

DH 89A MARK 4 - AN INCREASE IN PERFORMANCE

The next mark number was introduced in 1953, when a commercial maintenance organisation, Vivian Bellamy's Flightways Limited of Eastleigh Airport, Southampton, decided to improve the Rapide's performance. By the early 1950s, de Havillands' Rapide successor,

G-AHGF c/n 6903 in the Flightways hangar, Portsmouth, after conversion to Mark 4, 1953. *[D.Fox]*

the all-metal DH 104 Dove, had become established in the world market, so DH naturally had a desire to promote the sale of this type, rather than assist in the prolongation of a wooden 1934 design. However, with several hundred ex-wartime Dominies and Rapides still in service, peacetime safety standards began to dictate greater performance levels, particularly in the single-engine case, than was obtainable with the standard Rapide. Flightways replaced the standard 200 hp Gipsy Queen Series III engines and fixed-pitch Fairey Reed metal propellers with the (paradoxically) more powerful Gipsy Queen Series II engines, driving de Havilland variable-pitch propellers.

Viv Bellamy considered that fitting the uprated engines and variable-pitch propellers would not only give a nominal five horse power increase in take-off power, but, more beneficially, also provide 2,400 rpm at take-off as opposed to the 2,000 rpm from the Queen III. The modification gave constant speed control over the propellers for optimum performance at take-off, in the climb and in the cruise and he rightly believed that while the simpler adaptation of the standard Queen III engines to use variable-pitch propellers, by adopting modified top covers with the necessary ancillary drives, would alone have provided a sensible increase in take-off power, the configuration of these slightly less powerful engines was not possible because of the configuration of the engine. In addition to the lack of the necessary auxiliary drives on the standard Queen III, needed in this case to drive the propeller's constant speed unit; the crankshaft and special oil system were not suitable for the larger propeller, and the engine was not designed to operate at the higher continuous speeds obtainable with a controllable-pitch propeller.

Bellamy knew, however, that de Havilland's Gipsy Queen II engine had the same approximate dimensions, the same general fittings, many common parts, and was easily obtainable in 1953. This engine was originally adapted for aircraft with controllable-pitch propellers, and a 225 hp version was used in the DH 88 Comet, winner of the England to Australia Race in 1934 and the Percival Mew Gull flown to Capetown by Alex Henshaw. The standard Queen II was usually teamed with a de Havilland PD 30/211/1

After conversion to Mark 4, G-AHGF went to New Zealand, then Australia, becoming VH-BIF in 1959. *[CND]*

C/n 6839 G-AHKA at DH Hatfield, as prototype Mark 5 with manual variable pitch propellers, 1949. *[BAe]*

variable-pitch propeller, and had special auxiliary take-offs at the rear of the top casing for the necessary constant-speed governor unit, but also for a vacuum pump and an electrical generator if required. Other special features on the engine included a modified oil system which was needed to control the pitch-changing mechanism, forged pistons, steel inserts in the cylinder heads, stellited exhaust valve seats, and an increase in the compression ratio to 6 to 1, compared to the earlier engine's 5.25 to 1. The only extra work required to fit the Queen II into a standard Rapide was to enlarge the nose air intake, to permit a greater flow of air round the cylinder head fins, for better cooling. This was already an optional modification for standard Rapides, and had already been fitted to some aircraft in service.

There were, of course, balancing disadvantages in this increased-power installation. The extra CSU mechanism, the more complex oil system, the modified crankcase, the larger propeller hub mechanism with its much bigger spinner and propeller all weighed more, and the procedures for setting up and maintaining the propeller system were more complicated. Some 'stiffening' of the undercarriage was also completed because of the increased weight. This weight increase countered some of the advantages of the Queen II's performance increase, but overall there was still an increase in performance and safety.

Having operated several Rapides for the past five years, and also converted several military Dominies to civilian standard, Bellamy knew the aircraft and its systems, and fitted two Queen IIs with DH PD 30/211/1 propellers into G-AHGF as a trial installation in 1953. This machine was a 1945 Brush-built Dominie, converted to DH 89A standard by DH Witney for Railway Air Services and used by several different operators before being bought by Flightways in March 1953. After successful installation and trials of G-AHGF, the modification was approved by the Air Registration Board in May 1953, as the first 'Series Four DH 98A Rapide'. A maximum take-off weight of 6,000 lb was approved soon afterwards, thus permitting a slightly greater payload than the 5,500 lb allowed on earlier Marks. Rather perversely, the maximum landing weight was limited to only 5,750 lb, which in practical terms meant that the new model could not legally land after a maximum weight take-off until it had lost 250 pounds weight of fuel, which equated to about 1.5 hours' flying.

The modification could be applied relatively easily to standard aircraft, and the performance benefits were felt worthwhile by many operators, particularly where take-off performance was critical. Bellamy soon sold G-AHGF to Ken Bloomfield in New Zealand as ZK-BFK, and his engineering team at Eastleigh converted a considerable number of other Rapides to Mark 4s over the next few years, before the type began to fade from the commercial scene, with the increasing popularity of newer, faster, more modern post-war designs.

One particular customer, Noon and Pearce Airways, operating in the hot and high climate of Kenya in the nineteen-fifties, wanted better performance from its fleet, to cope with airfields such as Nairobi, standing at 6,000 feet above sea level, and with high temperatures in summer. They bought several Mark 4 conversions from Flightways, including G-ALWJ, which had been Flight Sergeant Don Stoneham's mount at Cranwell's No 1 Radio School in 1945. On arrival in Nairobi, this new Mark 4 became VP-KLL and continued in use for some years in Kenya with successor Caspair before being withdrawn from use in 1965.

DH 89A MARK 5

In 1948, the use of small, inexpensive airliners was blossoming at a great rate, and the major proportion of military Dominies still in existence were being sold by the Air Ministry into commercial hands. These commercial operators were finding that the larger, more modern aircraft were more powerfully engined, and therefore safer to operate when one engine had failed. The more modern engines were also better at hot and high operations, such as those found in East Africa.

In an attempt to provide some improvements in Rapide performance in such conditions, and no doubt lengthen the life of the type, de Havilland fitted their own hack G-AHKA's existing pair of Queen III engines with modified top covers in late 1947. Unlike those of the standard Queen III, these engines already had built-in auxiliary drives at the rear for powering generators and other equipment. The engines were then fitted with what the company propeller workshop called '2/M/I' propellers, with a pitch-change range of 15 degrees. The official designation of these propellers was PD65/2WS/1. Cable controls connected the propeller pitch-change mechanism to an electric motor on each

LV-AER c/n 6609 is seen here in Argentina in 1968 with bathtub engine cowls and manual VP propellers. *[BAe]*

engine support framework. The pitch-change motors were in turn operated by switches on the pilot's instrument panel, which gave the simple choice of coarse or fine pitch. It is almost certain that the only engines that were modified were Gipsy Sixes or Queen IIIs, as the alternative Queen II which gave increased maximum rpm, was already modified to take the more complex hydraulic pump and ancillary equipment needed by the constant speed propeller system, as fitted to some Miles and Percival aircraft and later to the Mark 4 Rapide. As the 'manually-variable-pitch propeller' modification gave slightly better performance, but also weighed more than the standard Rapide, this model was certified with an increased all up weight limit of 6,000 lb for take-off, and 5,750 for landing, which limits later applied to the Mk 4 aircraft. The manual variable-pitch propeller modification was then considered radical enough to call for a Mark number change, so aircraft with the installation incorporated were designated Mark 5 Rapides. No explanation can be found as to why the Mark 5 pre-dated the Mark 4 by four years!

Although de Havilland archive information on the detail of the modification is non-existent, precise contemporary notes kept by an engineer in the Flight Test section at DH Propellers, J W Parker, are a guide to the actual situation. The change to the Mk 5 involved an attempt to achieve better take-off, cruising and single-engine performance through the use of variable-pitch propellers, while making minimal changes to the standard engine installation.

De Havilland's manual variable-pitch modification is known to have been incorporated on at least six Rapides, plus an unknown number modified elsewhere. The modification can be presumed not to have been particularly successful, since without an increase in engine rpm from the standard Queen or Gipsy engine, the only benefit of having variable-pitch was to provide a slightly finer pitch for take-off and single-engine cases, and then a slightly more advantageous coarse setting for the cruise case. The extra weight of the modification equipment would have tended to offset the benefits of being able to alter the propeller's pitch to suit the flight condition. There are also indications that the reliability of the propellers was not good, as several were found to have serious fatigue problems in service, in a similar way to the fatigue problems found on the Australian de Havilland Drover's variable-pitch propellers.

From J W Parker's notes made at the time, the Rapides modified with manual variable-pitch mechanism by de Havilland were the experimental aircraft G-AHKA, followed by G-AKZV, G-AFEN, G-AKNZ and G-ALAY, in December 1948; and G-AKDX, modified in February 1950. The four aircraft modified in December 1948 were part of a batch of ten sold by Rollasons of Croydon to ZONDA in Buenos Aires, Argentina. Another intriguing note from Jim Parker's records indicates that, in September 1950, de Havilland's propeller service department rectified a problem with another Rapide, G-ALWO, which had been modified to use manual variable-pitch propellers by an unknown agency, not by de Havilland. This indicates that there were probably other Mark 5 Rapides in service modified by outside agencies, without the knowledge or approval of de Havilland Propellers. The existence of at least two more Mark 5 aircraft is indicated by photographs of LV-AER (formerly G-ALAU) and LV-AES (formerly G-AKYY), two others of the ten Rapides sold by Rollasons to ZONDA in 1948, showing the

Mark 5 cockpit, showing pitch-change switches at centre left and boost gauges at lower right. *[BAe]*

Capt Ray Mackenzie-Blyth taxying G-AIDL c/n 6968 for another joyride, 1994. *[CND]*

props jerk to a halt. Now the comforting bellow of the Queens has died, the quiet whirring-down of the the air-driven gyros is interrupted by the clunk of the brake lever as it is released. This spritely sixty-year-old is once again left to her own silence.

For a pilot of a later generation, it is a privilege to accept, in part, the same flying challenges presented to the pioneers of British aviation seventy years ago, and to be allowed a practical insight into the demands and the fun inherent in flying those machines.

ASYMMETRIC HANDLING

Among the most experienced commercial Rapide operators in the 1990s was a dedicated devotee of the DH twin, Captain Ray Mackenzie-Blyth. He operated that stalwart joy-riding Rapide, G-AIDL, from the delightful coastal airfield at Caernarfon in north-west Wales, for around ten years, and his comments and views on the handling of the type are as valid seventy years after the DH 89's first flight as they were in 1934.

Engine Problems during Joy-Riding, G-AIDL

An early experience of Captain Mackenzie-Blyth serves as a salutory reminder that this old machine is not just a gentle old lady, but like some other old ladies, can be a real handful, with a mind of her own.

With over 10,000 hours and many years as a Chief Flying Instructor under his belt, Captain Mackenzie-Blyth climbed aboard his public transport DH 89A at Caernarfon on a hot summer day in 1986, for yet another joy-riding trip around the foothills of Snowdonia. He had a full load of holiday-makers aboard, all of them happily chatting about the fun of flying in this vintage biplane, a prudent 75 percent fuel load, and the August temperature up in the mid-twenties Fahrenheit, partially cooled by a moderate sea breeze from the south-west. Caernarfon now had only one 880-metre runway, and the duty runway, 26, had a cross wind from the left. Being a small ex-wartime airfield now used for farming as well as flying, there were several fenced-off grass fields laid out parallel to the runway, and a built-in ten-foot crash barrier of rocks on the seaward end. To the east, a bare ten miles away, loomed the conical 3,600 foot peak of Mount Snowdon, but immediately north of the airfield the wide Menai Strait lapped the sand banks around its edges.

The good Captain was quite satisfied with the power being produced by his Gipsy Queens on the pre-take-off run-up, so he lined up and put on full power for take-off. Before reaching the halfway point, he was airborne, and soon afterwards saw the speed climbing past his critical 75 mph single-engine safety speed, so he began easing into the climb, aiming towards the normal climb speed of 95 mph. As the crosswind took effect, and nudged the machine off the runway line, suddenly, the aircraft lurched further to the right, and stopped climbing - a very sickly feeling for any pilot. Captain Mackenzie Blyth immediately suspected engine failure. Being too close to the rocks to attempt a landing, and anyway by now heading way off the runway direction, no combination of maximum rudder, gentle aileron and cautious elevator could prevent the sickening, curving progress to the airfield boundary. Despite the screaming port engine doing its utmost to help, the speed rapidly fell to somewhere around 75 mph, (when directional control is lost), and the early climb had now become a relentless and apparently inevitable meeting with the ground.

The heavily-fenced field was dead ahead, so Captain Mackenzie-Blyth hauled back on the column, aiming to hop over the fence, but knowing that he could not stop the ensuing descent on the other side. Somehow clearing the fence, the Rapide staggered roughly down onto the grass, virtually out of control below single engine speed. But now the rocks were getting perilously close. A desperate pumping of the starboard throttle then brought a seemingly miraculous, momentary burst of power from that engine. Staying level just clear of the ground long enough to inch back up to single-engine speed again, the Captain balanced speed and flight path to squeeze a couple of feet over the rock boundary to the North of the field. Then he was out over the sea, at about 20 feet, and still flying. He quickly thought about what do next.

He could sometimes gain a few seconds of power from the sick starboard engine by pumping that throttle, so he may have a chance to remain airborne instead of ditching into the sea. If he could at least maintain height, he might be able to stagger round over the low-lying banks of the estuary, and attempt a landing back on the disused south-easterly runway. He could find no cause of the engine problem, but at least he could gain occasional bursts of

Air Caernarfon's G-AIDL landing at Caernarfon Airfield, 1994. *[CND]*

power, as if the carburettor jets were squirting intermittent bursts of fuel into the engine. But the engine would then die back to a tick-over once again.

By a delicate balance of rudders and elevator, on the knife edge of controllability at a speed of 75 mph, and then easing into a tortuous climb of one or two feet per minute, the Captain cautiously persuaded the old biplane foot by foot up to around 150 feet, out over the Menai Strait. He then felt confident enough, with his continuing throttle-pumping, to try a landing almost into wind on runway 26. After what was only another 15 minutes, but felt like a lifetime to the heavily perspiring pilot, he nursed the aircraft round onto a shallow final approach, and with incredible relief, gained the airfield boundary. Throttling back both the valiant port and the recalcitrant starboard throttles, that allowed both aircraft and pilot to sink gratefully back onto Caernarfon's tarmac.

In contrast with Captain Mackenzie-Blyth's twenty minutes of 'sheer terror', the happy passengers had believed the whole activity to be a normal part of the joy-ride, and were blissfully unaware of the danger. They all said the trip was great, and did not even notice that they could not see Snowdon from 150 feet over the Menai Strait. They were equally amazed to be offered free trips in the company's Cessna 172 as compensation.

BAD-WEATHER FLYING IN NEW ZEALAND

The west coast of New Zealand's South Island has very fickle and rapidly changing weather. On the coastal runs, the prevailing westerly wind from the Tasman Sea would often produce fog over the land within minutes of clear skies, and so the pilots on that run had to know what to expect, and how to cope with it, if caught out. Bearing in mind the lack of reliable ADF beacons and minimal flight instrumentation in the Rapide, the pilots had to be able to remain in contact with land or sea, in order to keep their services running. This usually meant flying very low below the cloud or fog layer, and using the narrow strip of surf along the beach for visual reference, while using the instruments to maintain level flight, on a specific heading. Careful timing was then used to give approximate positional information, confirmed by the changing colour of the water when a particular river mouth had been reached. Paul Beauchamp-Legg was the youngest surviving pilot on what was the longest serving airline in New Zealand - West Coast Airways, and he recalled that his first boss, 'Popeye ' Lucas, insisted on only taking experienced, skilful pilots on their challenging flight routes. Popeye required 2,000 hours total time, and an instructor's rating. He also made sure they could fly as low as 50 feet over the sea in something like 1,000 yards visibility, as they would need to in order to keep the service running. They ran a strictly visual regime because of the peculiar weather conditions and because of the lack of instrument flight or navigation equipment.

One safety factor on the coast was that the weather further inland was often better than on the coastal plain, so diversions could usually be made to the airstrips higher up in the slopes of the Alps, or even to an airfield on the eastern side of the Alps. The fact that the routes usually flown in this area included services to the short mountain strips at Fox and Franz Josef glaciers also meant that pilots had to be able to cope with other factors as well. The winds at 7,000 or 8,000 feet in the Southern Alps were often strong and in places, turbulent, so they had to be carefully studied before entering the mountains. Paul Beauchamp-Legg commented that he could "whistle up to 10,000 feet on the lee side of a mountain in the hope of crossing over the top, but then enter a strong down-draught and end up hill-sloping through the valleys" in order to get through to the other side.

The other main requirement for pilots on the New Zealand west coast was to be able to land first time on high, short strips, in a cross-wind, particularly when there was a mountain in the overshoot area. Again, Paul Beauchamp-Legg's advice is most informative:

Ritchie Air Services' ZK-ALB c/n 6655 over mountains to the east of Milford Sound, 1966. *[R. Waugh]*

ZK-ALB c/n 6655 of Tourist Air Travel, parked at Queenstown, 1971. *[R. Waugh]*

"There are two ways here. The old-fashioned way we used. Reduce speed on a long, fairly flat approach and let the aircraft down with power so that it touches down with the minimum flare. The 'petite' way is to approach with plenty of height , then reduce height and speed on the way down, so that you cross the fence at a much steeper angle than you do on the 'drag-em-in' method. In both cases you touch down at the minimum speed. Yawing the aircraft is done with the aid of the slipstream. The wings are kept level with the ailerons. It's all a matter of practice and staying in practice.The aircraft must end up sitting on all its wheels travelling along the runway, so think it out backwards and this is the best method."

Paul had more than his share of engine failures, and on flights from West Coast airfields, this required skilful actions.

"Of the nine single-engine flights I had in Rapides, two were due to piston collapses and the others were generally disappearing oil pressure. There is much more to learn from one I had at Milford Sound.

Each morning I went out to the airstrip at daybreak to get the aircraft ready for scenic flying amongst the fiord and Alps at Milford Sound. The aircraft would be covered in dew. I found the easiest, and in fact the very best way, all factors considered, was to take it for a short flight. I cleared enough of the window to see ahead and when I reached about 200 ft. there would be a sort of 'swoosh' with the inversion warming the air and the aircraft would be almost dry again. This made plenty of noise which echoed around the Sound and let the hotel guests and anyone in the motor camp know that we were flying. I returned to land on one engine. Today on the left, tomorrow on the right and, if the wind was agreeable, I would approach from opposite ends.

On April 15 1963, five passengers climbed on board and we started our take-off run in a slight tail wind out towards the sea. We always took off towards the sea. ZK-AKS stuck to the ground. 'I've boobed it,' I thought to myself as we passed the place where normally we would have been airborne. The high retaining wall/bank at the end of the airstrip rushed nearer. I was going too fast to stop. Hopefully I could bounce over the bank at the end of the airstrip and stay airborne in ground effect without hitting the water.

The port motor began to vibrate severely. A strong smell of smoke came into my cockpit and I knew immediately from previous experience that I had a collapsed piston or pistons in that engine. (When the pistons collapse they pump oil up through the breather and onto the exhaust pipe which makes for some very spectacular smoke if you could see it). The fumes came in through the heater pipe to the cockpit. My conscience eased slightly because the problem was now mechanical and not my misjudgement. There was nothing gained in closing that motor with the bank coming up so I left both throttles wide to get what help I could from it.

We became airborne and missed the bank by a few feet and flew out into the Sound. I turned the fuel off and eased the port throttle back. The trim changed and I glanced back to see the rear passenger walking forward. "Would you mind going back to your seat," I said. "No ". He replied.

"Would you mind going back to your seat," I said a little more firmly. " I bought a ticket and I'm going to take some photographs," he shouted back quite annoyed. "Get back to your seat." I ordered very firmly. " I'm going back to land." The man meekly went back to his seat.

I commenced a very gentle wide turn out to the right to give me sufficient room to turn inside the Sound and come back to the airstrip. "Mayday Mayday Mayday. This is AKS, AKS, AKS, Milford Sound. Engine trouble. Am attempting to return to the airfield. Six POB" I said on the radio.

I continued the very wide and low turn and lined up on the airstrip. Everything was exactly as I had done about half an hour previously. The approach was the same. The trees were at the same angle. The aircraft felt the same. The only difference was that when I landed I could not taxi because AKS, with only one motor working, wanted to go around in circles. We were using H.F. radio and the frequency was such that Milford Sound air radio, almost below me, did not hear it. It was picked up by Oamaru radio which is on the opposite side of the South Island. By the time they had relayed back to Milford Sound we were on the ground.

The most excited and most congratulatory person was the passenger I had ordered back to his seat. He went around telling all and sundry of his wonderful flight amongst the Alps and over the Sound on one motor and our successful landing. In fact he sold more passengers seats than I had had on any other day. Southern Scenic Air Services Ltd soon had another Rapide out from Queenstown for me to continue flying so all in all it was a very successful day."

Milford Sound airstrip at centre, viewed from the east.
[P. Beauchamp-Legg]

Railway Air Services' G-ACPR "City of Birmingham" c/n 6255 at Hatfield, 1934. *[CND]*

Section 4 – Chapter 4: Pre-War British Commercial Users

G-ADAH c/n 6278 parked at Romford with Hillman's Airways in 1935 before the merger with British Airways. *[D.Fox]*

FIRST OPERATORS

The Dragon Six entered service with Hillman's Airways surprisingly soon after the first aircraft had flown, indicating that the company's reputation for sound products was high in the British airline and charter field. After obtaining its C of A on 5th July, 1934, the second aircraft, G-ACPM, was briefly used for test flying at Hatfield, and was handed over to Ted Hillman's Hillman's Airways at the end of July. Hillman's put the aircraft, resplendent in their distinctive blue and silver colours and contrasting fuselage registration letters, into service from their new Essex airport at Stapleford Abbotts to Paris, charging £5 for a return trip. However, a little over two months later, on 2nd October 1934, 'CPM, returning from Paris, was caught out in autumnal fog off Folkestone, and crashed into the English Channel. The somewhat inexperienced pilot, Capt Walter Bannister, who had only joined Hillman's in August, and the six passengers were killed, and the qualifications of Hillman's crews was called into question at the crash enquiry. Hillman, in keeping with his policy of minimising his costs, used pilots without navigation or radio licences and often without instrument flying experience. The Air Ministry responded to this accident some months later by introducing new rules requiring all commercial pilots to hold navigation, radio and instrument-flying qualification as part of their licences. Hillman's took the third and fourth aircraft, and by the end of 1935, when they were merged into British Airways, they had six of the type working out of their small Essex terminal, flying to destinations in England and France.

RAILWAY AIR SERVICES

Railway Air Services, collected their first two machines, G-ACPP and G-ACPR, in March and April 1935, for use on a series of pioneering internal routes based on Croydon, Glasgow (Renfrew) and Liverpool (Speke) airports. These two were the last aircraft to come out as Dragon Sixes, as the type was now re-named 'Dragon Rapides', to differentiate it from the earlier DH 84, and no doubt to gain some sales benefits by emphasising the speed increase over the smaller-engined Dragon.

The RAS Rapides, in their smart white and silver scheme, with cheat-lines and company badge picked out in contrasting red, green and white, were to be seen from 1935 onwards throughout an expanding route structure covering Croydon, Birmingham, Plymouth, Bristol, Liverpool, Belfast and Glasgow. By 1939, RAS Rapides were flying from Liverpool's Speke airport to Belfast on a 95-minute weekday schedule, and another daily route to Glasgow, taking one hour. The fortunes of the airline changed during the pre-war years, causing routes and the fleet to be altered accordingly, but the Rapides continued to give safe, steady service.

The airline operated Rapides continuously from 1935, throughout the Second World War, and until it was taken over by British European Airways in 1947, operating some twenty different Rapides although the greatest number at any one time was eight, because of the numerous policy changes and wartime requirements and the occasional accident. The only pre-war accident was when G-AEBX spun in after take-off from Sydenham on 3rd July 1938, fatally injuring the pilot, Captain Alfred Larmuth and his engineer.

C/n 6254 G-ACPP in a damp Croydon hangar. *[M. Stroud]*

New Zealand entry ZK-ACO c/n 6259 at Heliopolis during the 1934 England-Australia race. *[DHMC]*

After the war, it suffered another major accident at Belfast when G-AERZ , which the airline had operated since 1943, crashed onto Belfast's Craigarad Golf Course while attempting to land at Sydenham airport in early morning fog on 1st April 1946. The pilot, Captain Tyrer and 5 others were all lost. RAS's G-ACPP is the oldest Rapide in existence, having served many owners before being sold in Canada in 1961, becoming CF-PTK. In 2001 it was transferred to the Reynolds Aviation Museum at Wetaskiwin.

MACROBERTSON RACE TO AUSTRALIA, OCTOBER 1934

While airlines were preparing to operate Rapides on their domestic and European services, de Havilland took the opportunity of an international event to gain publicity for their new airliner. The event of 1934 was undoubtedly the England to Australia race sponsored by an Australian chocolate manufacturer, Sir Macpherson Robertson, of Melbourne. Known as the MacRobertson International Air Race, this brilliant example of international organisation and cooperation, was one which could provide considerable kudos for the winners. The most memorable de Havilland machines were of course the three specially-designed DH 88 Comets, which gained great fame during the Race, but also entered was a single example of their other new DH aircraft, the DH 89, still called the Dragon Six.

Soon after its first flight, the tenth DH 89 was ordered by the New Zealand Centenary Air Race Committee, as ZK-ACO which showed the Committee's great confidence in the ability of the de Havilland company to build a new aircraft type capable of competing in this gruelling race. Delivery was going to be tight as it was due for handover at the end of September, a bare two weeks before the last reporting date for the race.

The pilots appointed by the Race Committee were James Hewett, an ex-RAF New Zealander, who managed an airline in Auckland, and Cyril Kay, another ex-RAF New Zealander who had already flown a light aircraft from England to Australia. ZK-ACO was nominally a standard DH 89, but the description in the Race entry forms, as a 'Dragon Six biplane, with a Maximum weight of 5,500 lb, a fuel capacity of 240 gallons, and an oil capacity of 24 gallons', indicated that it was considerably modified for the race. The maximum weight was increased by 500 lbs, the fuel increased by a 160-gallon cylindrical tank stowed in the centre cabin, and the 17-gallon increase in oil capacity was achieved by use of larger tanks with blister extensions.

In the event, the New Zealand aircraft was certificated on 9th October, just in time, had an exciting race including a forced landing at Boulogne, and finished in fifth place, arriving at Melbourne with a flying time of 106 hours and 51 minutes. A flight to New Zealand followed soon after where it was intended that the aircraft would be sold, but there were no takers and, in 1935, it was returned to Australia for West Australian Airways at Perth, and completed a long life flying there for various Australian airlines and the RAAF, finally succumbing to bad weather on 23rd May 1952, in the mountainous region north of Tooraweenah, New South Wales, when operated by Butler Air Transport.

OIL COMPANY TRANSPORT

Several of the larger British oil companies, including the Anglo-Iranian Oil Co.; the Asiatic Petroleum Co (Shell); Anglo-American Oil Co and Iraq Petroleum Transport Co quickly took up the new Rapide for company transport from 1934.

Typical of these companies was the Ethyl Export Corporation, which had interests throughout the world, and bought the twenty-sixth DH 89, in April 1935. As G-ADAO, the Ethyl Rapide was then flown to the company's blending facilities in Europe, the Middle East and the Far East for the next 18 months. The Ethyl pilot was Flying Officer DW 'Tommy' Lucke, a recently-retired RAF pilot, who arranged to have some extras fitted, including metal Fairey Reed propellers, a comprehensive radio fit and an air log, together with a full set of Shell Air Route maps, made up in

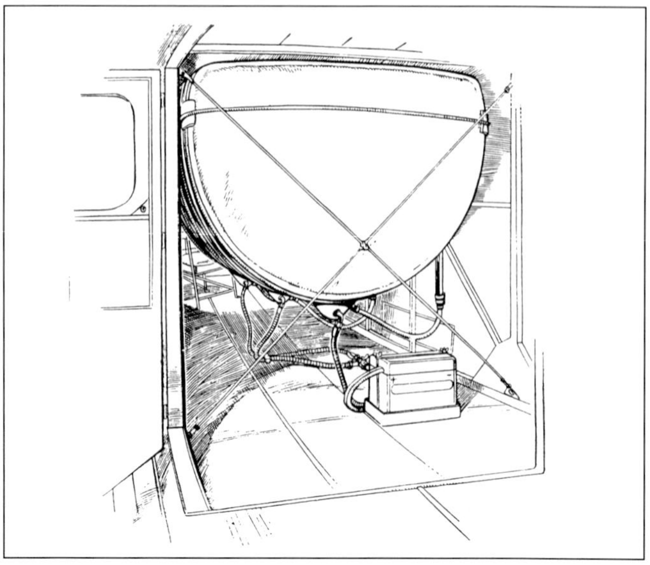

Extra fuel tank construction used in ZK-ACO *[Flight]*

C/n 6367G-AEWL in later life, with C Allen at Croydon in 1948. *[D.Fox]*

very practical strip format. Lucke planned and flew all these trips, with various teams from the company, from the company base at Brooklands.

Immediately after taking over this aircraft, an Ethyl company director, Air Commodore FR Banks, another ex-RAF pilot, set off with Tommy Lucke for a visit to Prague, on a blustery spring day. On the way to the first stop, the weather became worse, with lowering cloud and increasing wind, until they struggled through to Cologne. There they met an Imperial Airways crew who had flown in from the east, who told Tommy and his passenger that the weather was not too bad in that direction, so the Rapide team set off on their next leg, away from the Rhine valley and up over the edge of the Sauerland hills towards Kassel, then south of the 3,000-foot Harz range and on to Leipzig on the lower ground beyond. While turbulent, the cruise appeared to go reasonably until, in the approaching darkness, the senior passenger looked up to see Tommy Lucke peering rather worriedly from side to side. The Air Commodore went up to the cockpit and discovered that he was in fact lost; the aircraft was down to about 500 feet above ground; the hills were getting higher; the cloud base was getting lower, it was getting dark and they had no navigation aids.

Being an experienced aviator, the Air Commodore suggested (quite forcibly) that the only sensible thing to do was to find a flat field and land. As night fell, the situation became serious, but then the pilot saw some lights and told his passenger to move to the rear of the cabin to keep the CG as far back as possible and prepare for an emergency landing in a field. Lucke set up for a landing in what he later discovered was a ploughed field, but unfortunately, according to his passenger, he rounded out at 20 feet, stalled, and hit the ground in a nose-low attitude, turning the Rapide on its back within a few feet. Lucke was unhurt, but his passenger was knocked unconscious, having been thrown from the rear of the cabin right up to the cockpit, collecting a deep scalp wound on the way. He awoke to the sound of dripping fuel and, confused by the inverted cabin, eventually managed, with Tommy's help, to open the door and escape, compounding his troubles by landing in a bed of mud. However, the aircraft did not catch fire, and locals quickly came to help, whisking the battered Air Commodore off to hospital in nearby Halberstadt.

After having his skull patched up, Air Commodore Banks discovered that he had an old friend living nearby, who arranged to have the Rapide dismantled by the local gliding club and whisked off to Hatfield for repairs. The head wound took a week to repair, and in that time the Rapide's occupants had time to reflect how the aircraft had ended up, lost, in the Harz mountains, 45 miles north of their expected track.

G-ADAO was quickly repaired at Hatfield, and went on to serve Ethyl well, even completing a 19,000-mile trip to Indonesia from September to November 1935, and a 28,000-mile tour of Africa between May and August 1936. On its return it was sold, via several dubious deals, to the Spanish Nationalist forces, where its history is somewhat obscure but it may have become 40-1, which Rapide survived the war to join Iberia as EC-AAV or EC-ABG.

HIGHLAND AIRWAYS 1936-1940

Captain Eric Fresson of Highland Airways had pioneered routes from Inverness' Longman field to the remote Orkney and Shetland Islands, using DH 84 Dragons and a Monospar. With a view to the future he borrowed Hillman's Dragon Six G-ACPO from de Havillands for an extended trial in October 1934, and in 1936 leased G-ACPN from Airwork. After this he bought Rapides G-ADAJ and G-AEWL then continued to operate the type on the difficult routes to the Orkney and Shetland islands, until the airline merged with Scottish Airways in 1937. As the northern division of Scottish Airways, Fresson's pilots continued to operate Rapides of the Scottish fleet from Inverness throughout the Second World War, under the control of the AAJC.

BRITISH CONTINENTAL AIRWAYS

British Continental Airways was one of the privately-owned airlines which sprang up in the 1930s using three Rapides and a DH 86, patriotically named St Andrew, St Patrick, St David and St George. Graham Mackinnon initiated in 1935 what was termed "a fast new service to Ostend, Knokke and Brussels", despite Imperial Airways previously arranged subsidised schedule on the same

British Continental Airways' very smart G-ADAK c/n 6281 at Croydon in 1935. *[D.Fox]*

Olley Air Service Rapide G-ACYR c/n 6261 which carried General Franco back to Spain in 1936. *[BAe]*

King Edward stepping out of the Royal Rapide G-ADDD c/n 6283 for the Royal Review of the RAF, Mildenhall, 1936. *[BAe]*

route in cooperation with SABENA, the Belgian airline. Sir Percy Mackinnon, the founder's father, took a high-powered party in Rapide G-ADAK, 'St Patrick' to Ostend for lunch in July 1935, to inaugurate the service. The bearded Captain J K Morton flew the aircraft on the short hop over the Channel, reaching Brussels after only sixty minutes, despite a slight headwind. On the return leg, a stop was made at Knokke for tea, and the return to Croydon then took another hour. The company's Rapides had a full radio outfit, and operated with pilot and radio operator on all their return services, which ran on alternate days throughout the summer of 1935.

This attempt to expand the independent air routes to the continent did not last long, as BCA was merged into British Airways the following year.

OLLEY AIR SERVICE

> "Olley's Air Services sent off a machine, [Rapide G-ACYR] piloted by Captain Bebb, on Saturday morning to the Canary Isles on some mysterious mission. Perhaps it is to fetch a canary back for Capt Olley, who is not to be outdone by Major Brackley, (Imperial Airways' superintendent) who recently brought some rare birds from Australia."
>
> *[News Report, 'Flight', 16th July 1936.]*

An early and loyal user of the DH 89 was Olley Air Service, managed by the pioneering Captain Gordon Olley, which flew mainly charter and special flights. They took delivery of their first Rapide, G-ACYR, the eleventh aircraft off the Hatfield line, in February 1935, to be followed by five others over the next two years. This first aircraft was nominally chartered in July 1936 to take four holidaymakers, including the conspiratorial Spanish journalist Luis Bolin on a trip to the Canaries, but in fact, the aircraft dropped the passengers at Las Palmas, to make their own way home later. G-ACYR was then used to collect the exiled General Franco from Las Palmas, then return him to Spain via Tetouan in Morocco, to command the rebellion which became the Spanish Civil War. It stayed on to carry General Franco and Senor Bolin to meetings in Europe before being returned to Croydon, and remained with Olley until 1945. It was later presented in 1957 to General Franco and is still on display in the Museo del Aire, Madrid.

G-ACYR c/n 6261 preserved at Sabadell for the Spanish Museo del Aire. *[D.Fox]*

BRITISH AIRWAYS, 1935

In October 1935, British Airways was formed from an amalgamation of several independent airlines - Hillman's, United Airways and Spartan Airlines, followed by British Continental Airways in July 1936. Thirteen Rapides operated by these founding airlines were taken over by the new company, including the third aircraft, G-ACPN and the twenty-ninth machine, G-ADAH, both from the Hillman's fleet. The Rapides served alongside other British Airways types until most were transferred to associates or sold to Airwork in 1936. G-ADAH had a very long career with BA, Northern and Scottish and Allied Airways, before being taken out of service and stored at Aberdeen in 1947. It was refurbished in 1966 and is now displayed in the Manchester Museum of Science and Industry - the oldest surviving example in UK.

ROYAL FLIGHT 1936 - 1940

The Prince of Wales' personal pilot, Flt Lt E H Fielden, advised Prince Edward on all matters relating to his aircraft fleet. After successful use of the Prince's Dragons, a Rapide - G-ACTT, the

An immaculate Royal G-ACTT c/n 6257 completing engine runs, Hatfield 1935, before delivery. *[BAe]*

Interior of Royal Rapide G-ACTT, 1935. *[BAe]*

eighth to be built - was ordered and registered in Flt Lt Fielden's name in February 1935. A second Rapide, G-ADDD, also joined in June 1935, as it had been envisaged that King George V's Silver Jubilee celebrations in 1935 would require the use of two aircraft. However, The Prince of Wales became King in January of 1936, and the Air Council agreed to regularise the operation of Royal aircraft by instituting the King's Flight at Hendon, operating under the auspices of 24 Squadron, RAF. It was to be commanded by the newly-promoted Wing Commander Fielden, (who had been granted the title of Captain of the King's Flight) and maintained by the same civilian ground crew, who were now given RAF ranks. In the event, there was not enough work for two Rapides, so in April 1936, the first Rapide, G-ACTT was sold to Olley Air Services at Croydon. Knowing how meticulously the Royal aircraft had been maintained, Captain Olley had certainly gained quite a prize with this aircraft, which he used on airline and charter services before handing her back to 24 Squadron in 1940 as X8509, for war service. Sadly she did not survive the war, as in July 1941, X8509 was damaged beyond repair and struck off 24 Squadron's charge.

G-ADDD soldiered on alone with her royal duties, being used extensively as Royal transport for His Majesty the King, and his brothers the Dukes of York, Kent and Gloucester until 1937. King Edward had abdicated, and while the new King George had retained the King's Flight staff, the Rapide had actually been the personal property of Edward, who understandably decided to sell the machine soon after his abdication. The buyer this time was Western Airways of Weston super Mare, who operated her until she also was impressed into military service as AW116 in June 1940. However, restless as ever, Wing Commander Fielden had been investigating potential new royal aircraft for some time and, in 1937, persuaded the Air Council to specify an Airspeed Envoy to replace the Rapide as the King's Flight aircraft.

JERSEY AIRWAYS

Having used DH 84s and DH 86s for their first mainland to Channel Islands services for several years, a move to the Dragon Rapide was natural for Jersey Airways. The company bought two Rapides, G-ADBV and G-ADBW, in June 1935, and continued to use them and their other DH types charging 105 shillings (£5.25) for the return trip from Shoreham to Jersey. However, they were not a success and were sold in 1937 and 1938 respectively.

WRIGHTWAYS OF CROYDON

A charter operator formed at London's Croydon Airport in 1934 with a single DH 84 G-ACHX, Wrightways Limited was one of the first small companies to recognise the potential value of the larger DH 89 as a short-range economical transport. The company specialised in carrying newspapers, mail and occasional passengers on the Croydon-Le Bourget route, with the emphasis on early morning delivery of newspapers, so that the British community in Paris could enjoy *The Times* with their petits dejeuners. After the Rapide began to make its name in the British aviation scene, Wrightways' Chief Pilot, Captain Jack Duggan, realised that it would suit the company's needs better than the Dragon, and recommended to his board the purchase of two Rapides. G-ADAL was flown down to Croydon from the Hatfield production line in June 1936, to be followed in September by G-AEML, with a further Rapide, G-AFEZ, joining them in June of 1938.

Wrightway's newspaper deliveries

Arthur Morse, who in mid-September, 1936, was the de Havilland Deputy Chief Inspector at Hatfield, completed his usual series of thorough post-production inspections, before handing his latest Rapide, number 6337, over to the company Aerodrome Foreman for initial flight testing . The Aerodrome Foreman set about completing his engine and functional checks until, on 23rd September, he in turn handed the new machine on to the test pilots for air testing. Captain de Havilland was himself available on this particular day for flight test duties, so he took the new machine, as yet unpainted, on its first flight. This test took only thirty minutes, and there was insufficient time to fly the maximum weight test that day, so Captain de Havilland flew a twenty-five-minute, heavy weight, aft Centre of Gravity test the following day, followed by a shorter, forward Centre of Gravity test. Further test flights, probably for radio testing, and to check rectified snags found on earlier flights, were then undertaken by Mr Bob Waight over the

G-AEML c/n 6337 taxying out from Panshanger when with Neil Tool Co, 1963. *[CND]*

next two working days. The aircraft was then returned to Mr Morse, who signed off 6337's logbook on 26th September. Two weeks then elapsed while the new machine was finished off by E W Knightley's experts in the paint shop, with Wrightways unusual colour scheme of primrose yellow fuselage, silver wings and empennage and chocolate brown cheat lines and with registration G-AEML.

Captain Jack Duggan collected his sparkling new aircraft from Hatfield on the 11th October, 1936 and so began a flying history which continues to the present day. Being the Chief Pilot, Jack Duggan could choose his own aircraft, and he formed a liking for this new Rapide, using it as his flagship on many charter and special trips, particularly when he had interesting VIP passengers to take to interesting places. The Wrightways fleet grew until in 1938, there were two DH 86s, used most effectively on the Le Bourget newspaper runs, and three Rapides; the last Dragon having been written-off in April. The company's offices were in the main Croydon terminal building, next to those of The Hon. Mrs Victor Bruce's similar airline, Air Dispatch Limited, and across the hall from the old British Continental Airways office.

The Wrightways traffic clerk and general fixer, young Jim Dowdall, used to ride from home by motor bike, leaving at three am every working day in order to reach Croydon in time to supervise the loading of his aircraft for the Paris run. Hatchett's, the large London newsagents, delivered the newspapers each weekday, and Jim Dowdall would arrange the loading of the large bundles into the bare cabins under the glare of the Croydon terminal floodlights, before handing over to Captain Duggan and his colleagues, Captain Stead, Captain Fair and their Radio Officers, for the night take-off for Le Bourget.

Fog was a hazard often encountered on these early morning flights, and this often caused delays or cancellations to regular airline schedules, but Croydon was moderately well equipped at that time, with airborne radio direction-finding equipment and airfield landing floodlights. These aids were some help in guiding suitably equipped aircraft back to Croydon, and then assisting with providing visual references for landings in poor visibility. The system was inaccurate and not particularly reliable, but it did increase the regularity of some of the airlines. In times of forecast poor visibility, Captain Duggan made sure that his aircraft were filled with enough fuel for about four hours' flight in case they could not land in France, and had to make a distant diversion to an airfield clear of fog back in England.

For this reason, G-AEML was fitted with a single 30-gallon auxiliary fuel tank in March 1937, thereby providing another ninety minutes' range in case of bad weather. This modification was unusual, as the normal auxiliary fuel system consisted of two 18 gallon tanks, one on each side of the forward cabin, immediately behind the pilot's bulkhead, and each feeding its own engine. G-AEML's system, to drawing number WL 624A, was for a single tank positioned in the luggage area at the rear of the cabin, which would have a considerable effect on the centre of gravity, and the complication of extra pipe-work and selection methods. G-AEML had no rear luggage compartment during this period, with no separate door on the starboard side, so the large tank tucked away at the rear of the cabin would not have been quite so intrusive as if it had taken up the bulk of the separate small luggage compartment, as is the present configuration.

Captain Duggan always used 'ML when he had one of his many 'VIP' trips to the races with His Highness the Aga Khan, who was a devotee of horse racing. The smart primrose and silver Rapide had to be spotless for the Chief Pilot on these flights, with its leather seats and interior carefully cleaned and engines warmed up before being handed over to Captain Duggan, himself always immaculate in white flying overalls when flying his important passengers. The Aga Khan and later his son, Prince Ali Khan, used G-AEML for many of their journeys to the major race meetings

G-AFEZ c/n 6408 at Portsmouth with Hants and Sussex in 1954, was first with Wrightways in 1938. *[CND]*

around Europe - Deauville, Le Bourget and Liverpool (Speke) being some of the airfields noted in the log book for these outings.

After four years of quite intense use with Captain Duggan and his team at Croydon, averaging a very creditable 475 hours each year, G-AEML succumbed to the requirements of wartime, and was impressed, alongside her sister ships into service with the Royal Air Force. Following the outbreak of war, Wrightways carried out an extensive overhaul of the aircraft over the Christmas holiday, and in accordance with the Air Ministry instructions, re-sprayed the whole aircraft in the standard camouflage scheme, adding the civil registration in black, outlined in white, on the fuselage sides. 'ML continued in civilian service for some months before Requisition Order 336 finally called for delivery of the aircraft to No. 6 Anti Aircraft Cooperation Unit, Royal Air Force, at Manchester (Ringway) on 9th April, 1940. G-AEML was not painted with its service serial until she had served with the AACU for a further three months, when she became X9450. Her sisters, G-ADAL and G-AFEZ, became X9448 and X9451 at the same time.

The story of X9450 is taken up in another chapter, but she survived the war, and having undergone an extensive re-build between 1988 and 1993, this lovely old Rapide still graces the skies in the 21st Century, over sixty years after Geoffrey de Havilland first flew her at Hatfield.

Wrightways' three Rapides had been heavily involved in the company's operations, each flying a creditable average of about eighteen hours per week, carrying 214 passengers and 858,143 lb of freight in 1937 on the Paris run alone. The service built up, with regular newspaper and freight routes to Le Bourget interspersed with charter flights all over Europe for the next two years until the wartime shut-down of commercial flying at Croydon caused Wrightways, along with most other aircraft operators, to move away to other sites or simply finish off outstanding work, pay off staff, and close down. Wrightways actually moved their engineering and overhaul work up to Barton, near Manchester, in late 1939, but by mid-1940 had ceased all operations, as most of the flying and engineering staff were required for military service elsewhere.

SCOTTISH AIRWAYS

Up in Scotland, there was much feuding in the smaller airlines, mainly as a result of the amalgamation of the pioneer airlines. Northern and Scottish Airways and Highland Airways joined together in August 1937 to form Scottish Airways, continuing services to the Western Isles, the Orkneys and Shetlands, from Glasgow and Inverness. But there were other interests involved at the same time. The shareholding of the new company was held by British Airways, the LMS railway and the Western Isles ferry company, David McBrayne Ltd, so there were many conflicting interests at play, despite the nominal amalgamation. Rapides were beginning to replace Dragons and Spartan Cruisers, with G-ADAJ, ex Highland Airways, G-AFEY and G-AEWL being the first.

This Inverness Post *cutting shows Scottish Airways Rapides at Longman's Field, 1942.* *[D.Fox]*

G-AFEY was delivered new on 15th April 1938 to the Southern division at Glasgow's Renfrew airport.

Airline operations being fairly simplistic in the nineteen thirties, the pilot who was due to fly the first scheduled service from Renfrew to Inverness, Captain David Barclay, was given a 25-minute 'check' by his operations manager on the day the Rapide arrived, and that was his conversion to type. The next day the 'converted' Captain Barclay flew G-AFEY on his first schedule with passengers to Campbeltown, to be followed three days later by a flight to Inverness via Perth, taking 3 hours and fifteen minutes for the round trip. The return fare for that trip would cost a passenger £4 and 5 shillings, or about £170 at 2004 values, which is considerably more than the equivalent rail fare. Business for the Rapides began to build up over the next two years, scheduled services being interspersed with the most important ambulance work to and from the islands, and some army cooperation work around the Glasgow area.

A rather nice but apocryphal story about how the Scottish crews coped with poor visibility approaches into Renfrew was recently re-told by one of their radio operators, Andrew Ruthven. Normally, when running into Glasgow for an approach towards the west, the radio operator would obtain bearings from the airfield, which then confirmed their approach path, and then the last part of the approach could be flown visually. However, if the visibility was poor, they could still obtain the radio bearings to give directional guidance, but they had no way of knowing their distance from the airfield, and therefore the heights they should be passing in the descent. That was left to the crew's ingenuity. R/O Ruthven claims that both he and his favourite pilot, Jock Young, would then, on a poor visibility approach, apply their favourite distance-measuring method. They would open their side windows, and keep popping their noses out into the ambient airflow. As the approach progressed, Jock would prepare the aircraft for the final descent into the airfield, keeping the speed well back. As soon as both Jock and his R/O smelt the sharp odour of cornflour in the air, Jock would select flaps down and start a final descent, which they claimed always gave them a well-judged landing. The secret was that Brown and Poulson's custard factory lay one mile from the airfield, exactly in line with the westerly approach, and its powerful chimneys gave off a precisely-defined olfactory signal to crews passing overhead.

By 1939, the two Scottish Airways divisions had six Rapides, three Dragons and four Spartan Cruisers in their fleet, and the services were settling down well, providing what was now becoming an essential part of the Scottish way of life, particularly for the islanders.

Weather Diversion, G-ADAJ Captain Vallance
An example of the type of flying necessitated by the west of Scotland weather was given by a flight by Captain Henry Vallance in Scottish Airways' Rapide G-ADAJ. Flying the evening schedule from the small field at Wideford, on the northern island of Orkney, in August 1939, he set off for his home base at Inverness, the grass airfield at Longman, on the northern edge of the Moray Firth. There was fog forecast for the north of Scotland, and sure enough, Captain Vallance's radio operator, R/O MacGill, obtained a report indicating that Longman airfield had become fog-bound. The young captain decided to divert to the east, hoping that Aberdeen would still be usable, and he could get his six passengers to somewhere on the mainland, so continued with the flight. There were no radio aids at that time at Aberdeen's Dyce airfield, but at least the captain had spent several years flying out of that airport, and knew the area intimately. So they flew on, descending out over the North Sea, then flying west towards the airfield, which was to the north of the city. But the fog had beaten them to Dyce, and they could see no breaks in the weather anywhere near where the airfield should have been. Captain Vallance then began making a series of low level sweeps to the south of the city, and around the low lying land near the river Dee, hoping he would see some sort of clearance. After several circuits of the Cults area, on the northern bank of the Dee, the captain saw a brief glimpse of what he knew to be a reasonable field just south of the river. He quickly flew a circuit of the field and put G-ADAJ safely down on what turned out to be Easter Ardoe farm, near what the locals called the 'Shakkin' Briggie'. His passengers disembarked, thanked their pilot for his safe landing, and soon embarked in taxis sent down from Dyce airport.

G-ADAJ was flown out of the field the next day, ready for the Scottish Airways schedule to Glasgow. The aircraft went on to serve the AAJC during the war to be sold in France in 1948 and finishing up in Indo-China as F-BAHY in Hanoi, near where it finally crashed into trees on take-off on 20 August 1954.

WESTERN AIRWAYS
Norman Edgar, a pioneering aviator based in the west country at Weston-super-Mare in North Devon, began his operations to other west country airfields with DH Dragons, and then took on three early-built Rapides, G-ACTU, G-ADBV and G-ADDD in 1937. The following year his company was amalgamated into the Whitney Straight organisation. The Rapides, which had all had interesting careers by this time, were especially popular on the short hop across the Bristol Channel from Weston to Cardiff, which ran hourly during the summer holiday season, took all of eight minutes by Rapide, and cost 6 shillings and 6 pence in 1937, which equates to around £10.00 today. The first service began at 0730 and the last return landed at Weston at around 2015, so the company managed to get their money's worth from their pilots. The fare was actually reduced that year, because of the better utilisation of the Rapides, and was less than the third class rail fare, which took two and a half hours from station to station. The Rapides, joined by G-AFSO in 1939, did move on to wider-ranging services, but then were taken over, as were most others, by the AAJC when War broke out in 1939 and were impressed into RAF service shortly after. A small point of interest is that Western Airways was the only British company to operate all four of the Dragon types, as it used one DH 86B and two Dragonflies, as well as seven Dragons and the four Rapides mentioned above.

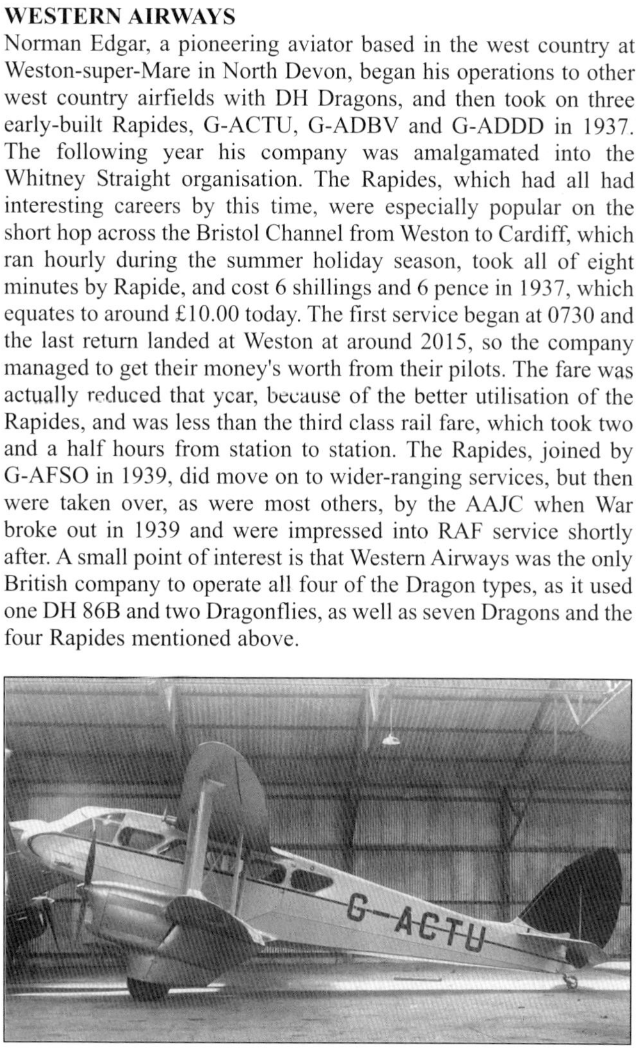

Western Airways' G-ACTU c/n 6258 in its Weston-super-Mare hangar, 1938. *[D.Fox]*

British Continental Airways' Rapide G-ADAI c/n 6287 at Croydon, 1935. *[CND]*

Airwork-operated c/n 6288 G-ADBW in RAF markings, No 6 AONS, Staverton, 1940. *[D.Fox]*

Other companies
Fourteen other companies used a total of 54 Rapides in the 1930s, building up a strong internal network by the time the Second World War began. Again, descriptions of these will be found in companion volume '*The de Havilland Dragon/Rapide Family*'.

CIVIL AIR NAVIGATION SCHOOLS
With the increase in armed forces decreed by the British government in the mid nineteen thirties, there was a concurrent need for increased training facilities. The Martin's School of Air Navigation, run by Mr C W Martin, was set up at Shoreham to train navigators for civilian and, later, military duties, using Rapides adapted to give the trainees practical training. Initially using a Dragon G-ACIE and three Rapides, including G-ADAI and G-ADIM, which were owned and operated by Airwork Limited, this school taught military pilots and observers from 1937 onwards, involving about 36 hours' flying per student. Each Rapide had a staff pilot, radio operator and navigation instructor, with two student navigators working from their own plotting tables. The pilot flew in accordance with the students' instructions, and the radio operator, using Marconi WT and a radio compass with its loop aerial, took bearings as requested by the students. Most exercises from Shoreham took place over the English Channel, and were aimed at making landfalls around the coastlines and on small targets such as the Owers light ship or one of the cross-Channel ferries plying between England and the Channel Islands. In May 1939, this school became a military unit, No.6 Civil Air Navigation School, renamed three months later as No.6 Air Observer & Navigator School, and moved to a safer base at Staverton, using many of the same aircraft and staff, but soon operating a total of ten Rapides or Dominies. By the end of 1940, most Rapides at this and other AONSs had been replaced by Ansons, which had more suitable facilities for pilot, radio operator, a staff navigator and three student navigators, as well as having greater endurance.

No 2 Civil Air Navigation School, Yatesbury
Set up by the Bristol Aeroplane Co. in September 1938, alongside their pilot training school, No 10 EFTS, at Yatesbury. This school mainly provided air experience to trainee wireless operators, and also used Airwork-owned Rapides, as well as RAF Ansons. This school became No 2 AONS in November 1939, but closed in December 1940, when most primary navigation training was transferred to the Commonwealth air forces in South Africa and Canada.

DE HAVILLAND CIVILIAN REPAIR DEPOT, WITNEY
In mid 1939, war was imminent, and it was obvious to de Havilland that they must find ways of coping with the impending increase in work-load at Hatfield, and complying with the Air Ministry requirement for dispersal of manufacturing facilities. By then the factory was becoming overloaded with new-build aircraft, including the Tiger Moth, Rapide, other Moth types, Dragonflies, Oxfords, and not far into the future, the Mosquito variants. In addition, all the repairs to, and servicing of existing de Havilland machines was undertaken at Hatfield. This work-load required considerable use of workshop space and so the company board first of all arranged for the Tiger Moth production line to be dispersed to the Morris Motors works at Cowley, near Oxford. They next sent a senior member of the Sales department, C S Thom, off in an aircraft to search about 50 miles west of Hatfield for suitable sites where the Service and Repair Departments could set up new shops. After some hours of searching, Mr Thom found an under-used, sleepy little airfield just on the western edge of Witney, about ten miles west of the city of Oxford. On the site there were some hangars and accompanying buildings, and a small grass landing area. He investigated further, then recommended that Witney should be used for the company's repair depot. After he had conducted urgent contractual discussions with the Air Ministry, a team of service department engineers, led by an enterprising young DH executive, Philip Gordon-Marshall, moved into Witney beginning in October 1939.

Philip Gordon-Marshall was a 27-year old, short, immaculately dressed man of distinguished appearance, but also of great managerial ability and was given the task of managing the Witney repair unit. He was a remarkably well-liked and efficient leader, and it seems that there was not one member of DH Witney who would not "follow him to the ends of the earth" in the words of several Witney people who worked with him. He managed to imbue his new factory with the typical 'de Havilland Spirit', a fact still remembered with great pleasure fifty years later, by the surviving characters of the very lively de Havilland Witney 1939-

de Havilland Civilian Repair Unit airfield, Witney, 1947. *[CND]*

1945 Association. He had the reputation, which it is suspected he enjoyed, of resembling a certain Royal personage who was of similar height and bearing. A well-known de Havilland story tells how P G-M, having had a pleasant dinner in a dimly-lit Parisian restaurant in the nineteen thirties, stood up to leave, whereupon all the other clients immediately stood up as well, as a mark of respect to His Royal Highness the Prince of Wales.

As Works Superintendent of their Civilian Repair Unit, de Havilland sent another well-respected engineer, Ken Brown, to run as a strict disciplinarian deputy to the easier-going General Manager what was soon to become a high-pressure, complex, and very successful factory organisation. It returned to service 700 Hurricanes and Spitfires, 800 de Havilland aircraft of various types, as well as returning to stores thousands of repaired components, taken from those machines pronounced irreparable.

In the Rapide story, Witney plays a very critical part. It was here that all damaged Dominies and Rapides impressed into military service for the war, which were 'not repairable on site', were brought, usually by Queen Mary road transport, to be given careful attention by the makers' experts, before being flown out again. There were other repair tasks at Witney, as de Havilland already repaired Hurricanes, various Moth types, and later, Spitfires and Mosquitoes. From contemporary reports by the Works Manager, backed up by the logbook of Witney's loaned Royal Air Force test pilot, it would seem that in the region of 600 of the 800 DH types repaired were Dominies, and that Mosquitoes did not appear at Witney until late in the war.

The airfield itself was not large, and had a line of high power-cables stretched rather inconveniently across the western edge of the field on the most favourable take-off direction. As a result, most take-offs and landings were made in a south-south-west direction, which, at about 600 yards, gave a shorter run than the westerly direction, making landings in the larger and faster types interesting for the pilots. After three Dominies had been 'nosed over' on landing at Witney, the ATA pilots on delivery flights preferred to land at Brize Norton, five miles to the south west, and fly their collection aircraft out from there.

Speaking from experience as the pilot who flew all the early test-flights out of Witney, Gordon-Marshall commented : "... it was certainly a poor aerodrome, small and uneven, and thinking back, it is surprising we did not have more accidents : there was little or nothing to spare. But I suppose that where there's less room for error, you take even more care. "

Flight Testing

As the numbers of aircraft coming in for repair began to increase, Philip Gordon-Marshall who had initially carried out all test flying, found that managing the factory as well was too much of a burden, so the Air Ministry sent a Royal Air Force pilot to help. Flight Lieutenant Richard Jones arrived in 1940 and stayed on until the end of the war in Europe, sharing with the general manager the task of testing all the repaired aircraft. Jones loved his flying, but also his fun, joining in the social activities at the factory and enjoying a nourishing glass or two down at 'The Bull' at Burford, where Philip Gordon-Marshall lived during his five years at Witney.

Being a fighter pilot, Richard Jones flew virtually all the fighter air tests, but also completed a fair percentage of the Dominie work as well, although the General Manager particularly enjoyed flying Dominie tests himself, having a soft spot for the type, and enjoying the chance to get away from the hustle of the factory for an hour or so. The two Witney pilots had, of necessity, a different philosophy on testing their Dominies from the pilots at the main factory. The machines coming out of the repair factory were not expected to perform exactly as new, so were simply tested to a minimum performance level, in keeping with a normal squadron aircraft, and if they met that liberal standard, were pronounced fit for service.

Testing of the Dominies was carried out in two phases at Witney, in contrast to the full testing done when they were first manufactured. First, the pilot would take a newly-arrived aircraft up after a basic engineering inspection, without any load, and with minimal fuel, to carry out simple checks of the flying controls and engines, and find any outstanding problems. Any faults would then be passed to the flight inspection team for rectification. After completion of the major repairs, and a re-spray, the test pilot would then take the aircraft for a full air test, consisting of an hour's worth of stalling, climbing, performance and landing checks, using Witney's simple 'Guide to flight testing aircraft after repair'.

On the full air tests, the flight-test staff would use house bricks to make up the necessary ton of ballast, but occasionally Flight Lieutenant Jones preferred to use selected human ballast on his air tests, as a reward to factory workers for their hard work. It was no mistake on his behalf that most of these passengers came from the 'Dope Shop', which was well known as containing the prettiest girls in the factory. One day, having collected their 'blood chits' exonerating de Havilland from blame in the case of an accident, Flt Lt Jones welcomed eight of the Dope Shop's best aboard his little airliner, and took off for a routine performance test. Feeling pleased with this more responsive than usual ballast on board, he was soon to reflect that it was a good job that he had remembered to collect the blood chits that day. What was normally a routine, totally uneventful flight test, was about to give him a real test of skill. As soon as he tried an airfield circuit after a normal take-off, he discovered to his alarm that he could not rotate the control column laterally. The ailerons just would not move despite every effort on the control spectacle, and so the aircraft would not bank and turn. The column would move fore and aft, but could not be budged an inch in the lateral sense. A forced landing ahead was out of the question as he apparently could not make

Demonstration to the Press of the Dominie's ambulance role, Hendon, May, 1941, using Z7261 "Women of Britain" c/n 6436 which de Havillands had converted the previous month. *[CND]*

any adjusting turns at this stage. Keeping full power on the engines, he climbed away straight ahead from Witney, in order to give himself some height and some time to think. There were no radios at Witney, so he could not tell anyone about his problem - he was on his own.

When he reached a reasonable height, he experimented to see what he could use to control the machine. The elevators and rudders worked normally, so he could climb and descend, but, as the inherent stability of the aircraft kept bringing him back onto an even keel, he could not turn. He tried asymmetric throttle, to see if that would give any help with turning. By using rudder to initiate a skidding turn, and by throttling back the engine on the same side, he found that he could overcome the natural stability of the aircraft, and force a very gentle turn away from the aircraft's original heading. The changes of power meant that the pitch would change whenever he tried to throttle into or out of a turn, so he had to carry out a continuous juggling act with rudder, throttles, elevators and trimmers. It was certainly very precarious, but by careful combinations of rudder and engine power, balanced by elevator and trimmer, he felt he might be able to complete a slow turn all the way round the airfield and with a long, straight run-in, attempt a landing. Working very hard at the unnatural turns, after twenty five minutes, he eventually found himself back on a long extended run into Witney's westerly runway. Luckily there were no other aircraft in the circuit, and very little wind to cause him to veer off heading. He managed to juggle the rudder and throttles to give himself something like the right speed and height, making skidding turns to compensate for changes of direction throughout the long careful approach, eventually managing to get his wheels on the ground reasonably close to the beginning of the grass runway. With

After restoration to civilian use, c/n 6436 G-AFMJ, ex Z7261, with Air Enterprises, Croydon, 1947. *[D.Fox]*

Three Air France Rapides awaiting delivery to Madagascar following civilianisation and refurbishment at Witney, 1948. All three were formerly Scottish Airways machines pre-war; F-BEDY ex G-ADAJ, F-BEDZ ex G-AGIC, F-BEDX ex G-AGDG. [DHMC]

enormous relief, he allowed the Dominie to trundle slowly to a halt with the now irrelevant ailerons still stuck solid. This time he really felt he had earned the admiration of those lovely girls in the back , but they had been totally unaware of any problems, merely enjoying the pleasant break from the factory routine.

Royal Air Force Dominie Mk II (ambulance) Z7261, Flt Lt Richard Jones

On the morning of 18th April 1941, Richard Jones found he had another Dominie on his list of tests for the day. The engineering records showed it to be Z7261, the same aircraft he had given the usual short preliminary test the day before, so this time he was to complete the longer full test of performance. From the serial newly painted on the sides and wings, he knew that this was a pre-war Rapide impressed into service for the duration (it was in fact the former G-AFMJ, one of Airwork's School of Navigation machines). When he arrived at the aircraft, ready for the test, he saw that it was now fitted out for stretchers and seats, and a double cabin door, extra air scoops on both sides of the cabin, but without any of the medical equipment.

He was not to know that this was to be a well-publicised machine, photographs of which were seen in all the national newspapers when it was demonstrated at Hendon as one of two ambulance aircraft presented to the Royal Air Force on 21st May by the Silver Thimble Fund at a cost of £5,000. It was personalised at that ceremony with the name 'Women of Britain' painted on the nose, and with two large white-backed red crosses on the fuselage sides. As far as Flt Lt Jones was concerned, it was just another standard Dominie, with nothing inside the fuselage but a loose pile of bricks. He did hope that the flight-test staff had prepared this aircraft with no more than the standard ton of brick ballast into this one, as he always harboured a fear of the potentially embarrassing results of a vicious stall, or a particularly heavy landing in a Dominie with more than the statutory load on the fuselage floor. He also hoped that the repair workers had inspected the integrity of the fuselage floor.

After the usual checks of the Gipsy Queens on the ground, he took off for his usual check of handling, and took an hour to complete his performance checks, with timed climbs, stalling, maximum speed and controllability checks and engine checks. He then brought Z7261 back to the small field for a careful, gentle landing despite the somewhat bumpy surface, being relieved at preventing any landing embarrassments and incidentally returning Mr Brown's bricks without any additional scratches. 'Women of Britain' was soon painted up and delivered to Hendon and then, in August, flown to Wick in Scotland, to serve nominally with the Communications Flight. One notable flight was from Scatsta on Shetland, to collect six crew members of a Catalina which had crashed at Scapa Flow, and return them to hospital in Edinburgh. She completed her war service from Wick and Kinloss, before continuing a fascinating series of adventures after the war. She became G-AFMJ again in 1947, and joined Air Enterprises Ltd's fleet of Rapides at Croydon, where she was converted back to a passenger transport before joining Captain Bolte's United Nations Rapide fleet in Palestine, (of which more later). On return in May 1949, she operated a holiday service from London to the Isle of Wight for several years as 'The Shanklin Flyer'. From 1953 to 1956 she took on another role change coincidentally back with her initial owner working as a training aircraft with Airwork Training Services at Perth, north of Edinburgh. Airwork sold her on to Paraguay in 1956 for yet another role change, this time as a cargo carrier for Aero Carga in Asuncion, registered ZP-TDH. She soldiered on in South America for another six years, until she came to an unfortunate end in October 1962, when her hangar at Stroessner airport, Asuncion, collapsed, damaging this gallant Rapide beyond repair.

Before leaving the story of the repaired Dominies at Witney, a somewhat belated admission from the DH Witney flying fraternity, to the protectors of a certain Hertfordshire airfield, presided over by the late Captain de Havilland, a professed devotee of Hertfordshire mushrooms, would seem appropriate here.

It seems that, when an unmarked Dominie Mark II was pronounced ready for flight-test on a particularly bright autumn day, a certain Royal Air Force officer would order his flight test team to prepare the aircraft the night before, ready for a very early morning air test. Arriving at the flight shed soon after dawn, he would then load the aircraft up with five trusted flight-test staff, all laden with large wicker baskets, take-off, without radio or other notification, and head due east at low level. After flying for 47 miles, (the last few miles at about two hundred feet above the north Hertfordshire countryside), he would hop over a line of trees, and pick an appropriate area on the northern part of the airfield that appeared ahead, well away from the hangars far away on the south side of the airfield. The pilot would throttle back early and quietly land on his chosen spot, near a line of trees bordering the northern edge of the field. Leaving the engines running, he would quickly order his crew out onto the airfield, where they rushed around the aircraft, gathered as many mushrooms as they could pile into their baskets and then dash back aboard the Dominie, gently ticking over in the middle of the field. The pilot judged that two minutes was the critical time, for that was what experience said it would take the airfield's defending RAF Regiment guards to wake up to the fact that they had been invaded. As soon as his team was aboard again, the pilot would open up, getting airborne straight ahead, well away from the buildings to the south, and, keeping low over the easterly boundary, turn back onto a westerly heading at very low level. A few miles away, over St Albans, the pilot would climb his unmarked aircraft back up to a reasonable cruising height and speed back to the Witney canteen for a delicious breakfast of Hatfield mushrooms. Despite many dawn raids, the Witney Raiders were never caught, and Captain de Havilland never complained to Witney about losing his mushrooms, or of the misuse of His Majesty's property. This is the Witney team's first public confession to their sin!

TJ-AAE c/n 6961 "Moab", in Arab Airways' bright orange scheme, parked at Amman in 1946. *[D.Fox]*

After the War, many of the DH Witney staff were laid off, as the flow of aircraft for repair was almost completely cut off, and the few that were passing through the factory required a much smaller team. However, another important stage in the Rapide's history began in 1945, when de Havillands decided to buy all the remaining Dominies that were still being completed to Air Ministry contract at Brush Coachworks at Loughborough, and convert them to civilian standard, for sale to the companies planning to join the rush for the post-war revival of civil aviation. This move was commercially very successful, as virtually all the hundred or so conversions completed from 1945 to 1947 were sold to airlines and charter companies throughout the world, and were a major element of small airline work for the next fifteen years.

Most conversion work involved removing the military fittings and radios, re-installing six or eight civilian seats, fitting the interiors with civilian materials and colours, and re-spraying the exteriors, if required, to customers' instructions. Typical were the first post-war aircraft sold from Britain, three dark blue and silver Rapides for the Portuguese airline, CTA, in November 1945, (CS-ADI, -ADJ and -ADK) and the five vivid orange and black Rapides, TJ-AAA to TJ-AAE, that went to Arab Airways Association of Trans-Jordan in July 1946. However, most of the conversions went out of the DH hangar in the more anonymous civilian all-over silver dope scheme, as standard Mark II or Mark III Rapides, depending on whether they had six or eight seats. Some customers required specific radio and direction-finding equipment, but most aircraft left Witney without radio. A young engineer who had come across to Witney in 1946 from the de Havilland Technical School, 'Pop' Bilkey, particularly remembers one of the conversions completed in that year.

The Fairey Aviation Company of White Waltham had bought one of the 'new' Rapides, and the son of Sir Richard Fairey was due to fly the new aircraft. Richard Fairey was a very tall, well-built man, who had lost his lower limbs during the war, so Witney were asked to modify the cockpit and controls to make his entry and exit a little easier. Bilkey and his team met the requirement by inverting and shortening the 'W' shaped control column; moving the P11 compass from the left-hand instrument panel to a central position, and making cut-outs in the bottom of the panel where the pilot's legs fitted. This aircraft, G-AHJS, continued in use with Fairey for nearly twenty years, when it passed to the Three Counties Aero Club in the mid-'sixties, although soon after it was used for spares to keep the Army Parachute Training Association's fleet of Rapides airworthy.

C/n 6967 G-AHJS, modified for Richard Fairey in March 1946, photographed at Llanbedr, 1960, with Fairey Aviation. *[D.Fox]*

VT-AJB c/n 6381 at Juhu Bay, 1937, served by more primitive transport, when with Tata & Sons Ltd. *[Aeroplane]*

Section 4 – Chapter 5: Pre-war Civilian Activities world-wide

The de Havilland sales team, headed by Francis St Barbe, ably assisted by CS Thom and Hugh Buckingham, kept expanding their horizons with sales of Rapides to Australia, Belgium, Canada, Chile, China, Egypt, Finland, France, Ireland, India, Iran, Iraq, Italy, Jugoslavia, Kenya, New Zealand, Netherlands, Norway, Portugal, Portuguese East Africa, Rhodesia, Romania, Singapore, South Africa, Spain, Switzerland, Turkey, and Uruguay. By April 1936, there were already twenty-three operators of Rapides world-wide.

Many of the airlines overseas used the Rapide for straightforward land-based passenger flights, usually for flights of up to three hours, which was close to the maximum endurance with safety margins applied. Direction-finding and communications radios were often fitted by airlines, sometimes with a radio operator, but this limited the revenue-earning seats, so many companies relied on the pilot to operate the radio as well as fly their aircraft. Some later aircraft were fitted to receive Lorenz airfield approach aid signals, which gradually became available at major European airports.

Activities of some of the overseas countries with their Rapides make interesting reading.

TATA SONS LIMITED, INDIA

A successful Indian industrialist and avid aviator, Jehangir R D Tata (more commonly known as 'J R D') had been infected by the flying bug, and at the remarkably early age of 26 had been persuaded by a British barnstorming pilot, Nevill Vintcent, to create a small postal and passenger airline covering peninsular India during 1932. The grandson of the founder of the indestructable Tata family steel and banking empire, J R D Tata had started small with his airline, known generally as Tata Air Lines, but actually registered to 'Tata Sons Ltd', operating from the commercial capital of India, Bombay. By mid 1937, however, he was ready to expand further. Tata Sons Ltd had been using DH 83 Fox Moths for their services, but the progressive J R D could see that a larger aircraft was needed, to cope with his increased passenger loads. He therefore ordered three Rapides direct from de Havillands, and had them shipped out to Bombay in September 1937. The first Tata aircraft were registered VT-AIZ, VT-AJA, and VT-AJB, and were soon operating surprisingly long-range routes to the main centres of commerce in India, with the proud title 'Tata Sons, Bombay' inscribed on their fuselages, while the airline's ground equipment still carried the legend 'Tata Air Lines'.

As with all the early Tata Sons' fleet, the Rapides were based at Bombay's small coastal airfield at Juhu, just north of the city, which is now disarmingly known as the resort of Juhu Beach. This airfield had been first used by J R D Tata and his small team in 1932, when this enterprising young pilot discovered an area on the Juhu mud flats, outside the sprawling city's northern limits. With the sea on one side and a row of protective palm trees on the other, he felt this could be used to operate their two DH Puss Moths. Unfortunately, during the monsoon season the muddy 'airfield' became inundated and unusable, being situated slightly below sea level. J R D had built a small hangar on the edge of the mud flats, with the help of Vintcent, a rather unreliable engineer called MacWade, a promising young apprentice called V G Gadgil (who later rose to be the Air India chief engineer) to assist with the maintenance, and a chowkidar to do the rest of the work. This little team had begun an enthusiastic scheduled air mail and occasional passenger operation, and beat all the government and official opposition and developed the airline over the next few years with considerable and surprising success.

By the time Captain Vintcent had led the ferry flight of the three Tata Sons' Rapides to Bombay in mid-1937, the business had expanded considerably. The new Rapides had auxiliary fuel tanks fitted, giving a range of nearly 700 miles, and were used to fly passengers and cargo north to the government capital at Delhi and

Tata & Sons' hangar, Juhu Bay, Bombay, 1930s. *[Aeroplane]*

Delhi (Drigg Rd) terminal and airfield, 1936. *[Aeroplane]*

to the north-western city of Karachi (now in Pakistan). Later, they flew south to Colombo, in what was then Ceylon, a total north-south route distance of around 1,900 gruelling miles flown by an expanded team of pilots led by J R D and Captain Visvanath. An engineer who later joined the team at Juhu, A S De Sa, later described the airline's 'headquarters' as :"a small hangar with the smell of oil and grease mingling with the mud and slush all around. It was not the riches we were after. We loved aviation and we were a happy family.... Mr Tata was very close to us then.... We worked very hard."

One of De Sa's charges, VT-AJA, did not last long, even with his hard work in the Tata hangar, as it is reported to have crashed in unknown circumstances at Juhu in November 1938, the year after it went to India. The remaining two Tata Sons Rapides were handed over to the Indian government at the end of 1939, to be used as military transports by the Royal Air Force. VT-AIZ went initially to Air Command South East Asia, as AX 806, based up in central India, at Delhi, where at least eight Rapides or Dominies served. AX 806 then became a trainer with Number 2 Flight, Indian Volunteer Reserve from 1941, but on a return to its former home at Juhu demonstrated that this was not a safe operating base for the type, as it too succumbed to the airfield's hazards when landing there in October 1942, when still in IAF service. It was written off in the crash. The other pre-war Tata Rapide, VT-AJB, served with the Air Force as HX 790 for three years before being transferred to the Indian Civil Aviation Department based in Delhi, as a transport in September 1943, possibly with the new registration VT-ASC, and then it too was struck off DCA charge in 1945. Its subsequent survival is not traced, so it presumably expired when struck off charge.

Indian civil aviation records are sketchy for the immediate post-war period, but at least two more Rapides, VT-ARZ and VT-CHZ, were bought by the re-formed Tata Airlines company in 1947, and were part of J R D Tata's build-up towards what was to become the international airline, Air India, in later years. Little is known about

C/n 6308 VT-AHB, for the Maharajah of Jammu and Kashmir, Hatfield, 1935. *[BAe]*

Interior of VT-AHB, including pith-helmet stowage. *[BAe]*

these aircraft, as the airline at that period was expanding rapidly, with many aircraft types and routes, the rather insignificant Rapides gaining no mention in the airline's story. VT-CHZ was known to have been sold by a British company, Kennings, in 1946, and finished life as a write-off in Vientianne in March of 1961.

Among the private owners of Rapides was HH The Maharajah of Jammu and Kashmir, who bought the 58th DH 89 in December 1935, for use in his travels from his charming palace at Srinagar in the North of India. The Rapide's interior was one of the most sumptuous built, with special upholstery by Rumbolds. It contained four luxurious leather armchairs, complete with headrests, reclining backs and 'expanding armrests' as well as fitted curtains all round, and windows either side of the pilot's bulkhead, allowing the passengers a view ahead. Each seat had an adjustable cooling duct above it to provide some relief from the hot Indian air, and the cabin had thick carpet and extra sound-proofing to lessen the external noise. A special walnut cocktail and luncheon cabinet was fitted opposite the cabin entrance, and notable among other fittings were the elastic holders for pith helmets and a set of brass-bound entrance steps. The aircraft fuselage and fin were painted in a 'biscuit' colour, with trim lines in the Maharajah's own colours. Unfortunately the aircraft was only kept at Srinagar for two years, as it was transferred to Air Services of India in 1937, presumably without its luxurious fittings.

CHINESE AMBULANCE AIRCRAFT

Moving north and east, a rather mysterious order for six Rapides was placed with de Havilland in mid-937 by the 'China National Aviation Corporation'. The aircraft were known only by their constructor's numbers, which were 6385, 6388 to 6392, and were painted white with red crosses in circles on the fuselage sides. No other markings were requested, and no Chinese markings or serials are known to have been given to them. The aircraft were nominally to be used as ambulances, and were fitted-out with four purpose-built stretchers which sat on specially made racks on the starboard side of the fuselage. A large water tank was fitted into the forward

Guinea Airways' VH-UFF c/n 6270 at Adelaide, 1943, after initial service with ANA. *[DHMC]*

cabin roof and a hand-basin and water tank were placed in the rear area, along with four retractable seats for attendants and an unusual set of retractable entry steps. The Rapides were delivered initially to Kai Tak airport, Hong Kong, in two batches in late 1937, and handed over to the Far East Flying School instructors, who flew them into China to an unrecoded site in February 1938 and July 1938, for use "for the rapid conveyance of wounded in the war in China". Very little is known about their service in China, but contemporary photographs show one aircraft in a simple camouflage paint scheme, still retaining the red crosses, when operated by CNAC from 1938 until about 1941. Their subsequent fate is unknown.

AUSTRALIA

Assisted by de Havilland Aircraft Pty at Sydney, 10 Rapides were delivered to Australian operators from 1935 onwards. Most went to small airlines, including Holyman's Airlines of Tasmania; Adelaide Airways, which had VH-AVI and VH-UVT; W R Carpenter and Co who flew VH-UZY out of Cairns from 1938, and West Australian Airways of Perth. I addition, a Shell Petroleum company, Asiatic Petroleum, put VH-UVS into service from Melbourne in January 1935. Adelaide Airways used two eight-seat Rapides from 1935 for their services from Adelaide to Melbourne, as well as to Port Lincoln. Australian National Airways, based at Essendon, took over five Rapides, including VH-UFF, VH-UXT and VH-UXZ, after its formation in 1936, using them for services to Tasmania and Sydney from Melbourne. Most Australian Rapides still in service at the outbreak of World war two were impressed into the RAAF in 1940.

NEW ZEALAND AIRLINES

Down in New Zealand, the Rapide began a long involvement in that country's aviation, which continues today. The first Rapide to have a New Zealand connection was the one which took part in the 1934 England to Australia Race - ZK-ACO. Flown by two New Zealanders, Jim Hewitt and Cyril Kay, it finished fifth in the Race, then continued to make news by being the first aircraft to fly from England to New Zealand and the first twin-engined aircraft to cross the Tasman Sea. After another year in its home country, ZK-ACO was sold to West Australian Airlines, as VH-UUO, and it flew in Australia for another ten years before being destroyed by fire in 1952.

In 1934, a group of influential businessmen in Nelson, on New Zealand's South Island, felt the time had come to provide a service across the natural divide between the country's two Islands. Cook Strait is a bleak stretch of often turbulent water, 23 kilometres across at its narrowest point, with rugged, hilly coastlines on either side. But with major towns on both sides of the Strait, efficient trade required better communication across the watery divide than was currently available by boat. Gaining considerable local support, Cook Strait Airways was created, centred on Nelson on the southern side, and the new company quickly ordered the first of five Rapides from de Havilland in 1935. Rapides 6305 and 6306 were duly shipped out from Hatfield, assembled at Hobsonville by the de Havilland agent, Air Survey and Transport Limited, before being handed over to the airline at their Nelson base on 21st December 1936, as ZK-AED and ZK-AEE. Cook Strait's first Chief Pilot was Captain George Bolt, a well-respected pilot who by then had 7000 hours' flying and had recently been the Chief Engineer at the Wellington Aero Club. Cook Strait Airways then used their Rapides, appropriately, on scheduled services from Nelson across Cook Strait to Wellington's Rongotai airport for the next five years. The aircraft were given an attractive colour scheme, with black fuselage top and engine cowlings, light blue lettering and struts, with the rest of the aircraft silver. They were fitted with radio for contact with those airfields which had radio installed. An impression of the first flight south from Wellington on Boxing Day 1935, both Rapides flying together, was given by Cook Strait Airways' Company Secretary:

"Climbing above the blanket of fluffy white clouds that now covered Wellington to the west and stretching for miles to the north, we witnessed a sight that can best be described as one of the beauties of flight. Fourteen minutes after taking off from Rongotai we were across the Strait, passing the Brothers on our right. The flight over the Sounds opened up to us a most glorious land and seascape. We were ahead of time and speed was slackened. During

ZK-AEC c/n 6334 of Cook Strait Airways over the impressive Marlborough Sound, 1936. *[R. Waugh]*

Scene at Hokitika before the first Cook Strait schedule to Wellington, 1937. *[R. Waugh]*

C/n 6423 ZK-AGT on a flight for West Coast Airways from Hokitika over the Alps, 1939. *[R. Waugh]*

the journey, the wireless telephony on the 'plane was well tried out, the pilot conversing and 2YA (local radio) was also tuned in. The seating is very comfortable and there is ample room for the six passengers and conversation is easily carried on."

When their third Rapide arrived a year later, the airline began a service from Blenheim to Wellington, to be followed soon after by a daily schedule from Wellington to Hokitika, on the stormy west coast of South Island. Cook Strait Airways' fifth Rapide, ZK-AGT arrived in 1938, and mainly flew a Wellington-Blenheim-Nelson-Greymouth-Hokitika route, until all the airline's Rapides were impressed into the RNZAF in 1939. The only one to survive the war was ZK-AGT, which had been used in New Zealand, unlike its sisters, which went to Fiji. This aircraft survived the war; became ZK-AKU again; flew for several Aero Clubs; and took part in the London to Sydney Race in 1969, finally being based with David Gray and Harry Norton at North Shore, Auckland, where it remains in airworthy condition today.

Other small airlines were blossoming soon afterwards in New Zealand, including West Coast Airways centred on Hokitika, Southern Scenic Airlines of Queenstown and East Coast Airways, based at Gisborne on North Island. Most had started off with smaller aircraft, and then moved onto Rapides as business increased. Wartime government requirements then forced most of these small companies to hand their Rapides over to the RNZAF in 1940, so forcing most to go out of business. Several started again after the war, often with the same aircraft.

DUTCH EAST INDIES 1935

In 1935, the Netherlands New Guinea Petroleum Company (NNGPM) was formed out of a consortium of major oil companies which had obtained a 75-year drilling concession in the Dutch East Indies. The objective of this new company was to explore the practicality of large-scale oil production in the Netherlands East Indies, before setting up an expensive drilling and production scheme. The area of interest covered 10 million hectares of New Guinea jungle, and as no reliable maps had been made of the area, the NNGPM decided to make their own.

A Dutch aircraft operator already working in the region, the Royal Netherlands East Indies Aircraft Company (RNEIAC), was asked to arrange for an aerial survey. Captain G A Koppen, an experienced survey pilot, was given the task of directing the operation on behalf of RNEIAC and of finding suitable equipment. He looked at several machines, including the Ford Trimotor, the Fokker F VIII and the DH 89. After several false starts with different types of aircraft, he decided on the de Havilland aircraft, on grounds of performance, price and availability. In July 1935, Captain Koppen went off to England to buy three of de Havilland's new Rapides, straight off the Hatfield line. He was allocated DH 89As 6292, 6294 and 6296, being built either side of a Rapide for British Continental Airlways at Croydon, and another for Canadian Airways. De Havilland were to fit the aircraft for survey work, with intercom and radio equipment, and making fittings and apertures for cameras and visual sighting. A contemporary DH report indicated that one of the aircraft was fitted with a PB autopilot, which would be of use during the photographic survey work, but no details of which aircraft was fitted can be found. KLM planned to install the survey equipment in Holland after delivery.

When KLM's paint shop sprayed on the Dutch registrations PH-AKU, PH-AKV and PH-AKW at Schiphol, they set up a mystery for the DH Support Department, as the three new aircraft then disappeared from the de Havilland customer records. Usual de Havilland customers maintained regular contact with the makers in order to receive information and technical bulletins, but these particular aircraft were flown away to Holland in September 1935 and not heard of again by the service department, until they were all removed from the Dutch register four months later. All the DH service department knew was that the aircraft had left Holland, but they had no indication of their continued existence or location until a translation of a Dutch report on an East Indies escapade came to light in the 1990s. The simple reason for the mystery was that the aircraft left Holland with normal Dutch national 'PH-' registrations for the East Indies, but they were then re-painted with Dutch East Indies 'PK-' registrations as soon as they arrived in the KNILM hangar at Bandung, Indonesia. The three 'PH-' Rapides simply ceased to exist from January 1936, when they were officially removed from the Dutch register, without cross-reference to their new registrations.

While he was waiting for his new aircraft to be completed at Hatfield, Captain Koppen hired Aberdeen Airways' Rapide G-ADDE, known by its pilots as '*The Violet*', for use in July and August as a trainer for himself and his pilots, Lt P G Tideman, Lt Joop Vonk, and Lt J Meininger, and to give his Chief Radio Officer, P G L Hegener, practice with the CW and radio direction-finding kit he would be using on the forthcoming long ferry flight.

After the compulsory photographic session with all three new aircraft together on the Hatfield grass, the first two, PH-AKU and PH-AKV, were flown to Schiphol on 2nd September, to be followed four days later by PH-AKW. KLM then fitted the cameras and prepared the aircraft for the journey to New Guinea, with the first stage ending at Bandung, the airport for what was then Batavia, in Indonesia, a journey of around 10,000 miles. Because of the inexperience of the junior pilots in Captain Koppen's team, two de Havilland pilots from the Flying School at Hatfield, Captains Cox and Fulford, were offered the chance of helping ferry the aircraft. As it would obviously make a pleasant change from the humdrum Hatfield circuit, they both accepted. The team, with Captain Koppen, Lt Meininger and Hr Hegener (radio operator) in the lead aircraft, PH-AKW; Captain Cox, Lt Tideman and a Dutch engineer in -AKU and Captain Fulford, Lt Vonk and a de Havilland engineer, Mr S J Cope, in -AKV, set off from Schiphol on 11th September, 1935, on what was to be a fascinating episode in the story of the Rapide.

The journey progressed without incident until the 20th of September, on the route from Akyab to Rangoon in Burma. Flying in loose formation behind the leader in the radio aircraft for mutual navigational assistance, the team encountered a line of tropical thunderstorms which they could not circumnavigate. The three pilots were forced by low cloud to fly closer to the jungle, experiencing violent turbulence, flooding of the cockpit by rain being forced through the leaky direct vision windows, a drastic reduction in flight visibility caused by the torrential rain, but more significantly, producing the virtual blanking of forward visibility through the windscreen which afflicts the Rapide in heavy rain. There were no windscreen wipers on these early Rapides, and as the view through the forward windscreen panels reduced to zero, the pilots following the lead of Captain Cox were forced to slow down and pull back, so that they would not collide with each other. Captain Koppen and Captain Fulford were then on their own, probably separated by at least a mile from Captain Cox in the radio aircraft, and also separated from each other. Each was now forced to navigate individually through the storm, with little idea of their position, without any recognisable features in the incessant jungle terrain, but also without the benefit of radios to obtain bearings to their destination. Captain Cox managed to struggle through the storms to land at Rangoon, followed soon after by Captain Koppen. But there was no sign of the third machine. Captain Fulford had obviously had problems as, several hours after the others had reached Rangoon, he had still not appeared.

Koppen and Cox then decided to back-track their route in search of their colleagues, so they set off from Rangoon in PH-AKW, searching through the thunderstorm line again, but without success, until their own fuel ran short, when they were forced to turn back to Rangoon for a worried night.

Captain Fulford, in PH-AKV, had meanwhile had great difficulties with the bad visibility and strong winds, being unable to obtain any navigational clues over the featureless jungle. He could find no landmarks to confirm his position despite searching for several hours so, before his fuel supply ran out, which would result in a short-notice crash landing, he decided to make a precautionary landing on the only piece of flat land he

Allied Airways' G-ADDE c/n 6282 was used for training by Capt Koppen prior to his delivery flight of three Rapides to KNILM in the Dutch East Indies. *[D.Fox]*

could find. Having earlier seen what appeared to be a stretch of beach beside a small lake, he made a safe landing, and parked the Rapide with a great sense of relief. The three crew members had no idea where they were, so decided that they should remain in the aircraft overnight, in the hope that a search might be set up for them next day. However, with no signs of any activity on the 21st, it was decided that the younger, fitter pilot, Lt Vonk, should leave the other two with the aircraft, while he walked out in search of habitation and help. Some hours later, he walked into a native Burmese village, which he later discovered to be Haingui, south of a town called Bassein, some thirty miles from the west coast of Burma and about one hundred miles from Rangoon. The villagers had no English, no outside communications and only oxen for transport, so he persuaded the inhabitants by sign language to lead him to the coast, believing that this was the only means of gaining contact with civilisation.

After reaching the coast, and by an incredible stroke of luck, Lt Vonk then managed to attract the attention of a passing coastal freighter which, even more incredibly, stopped, then sent a boat to pick him up. The freighter eventually dropped him off at a town called Ngaputaw, some fifty miles further down the coast, which he reached on the 22nd, two days after the forced landing.

This town at least had a telegraph office, so the gallant Lieutenant managed to send a telegram to Rangoon airport, informing his very worried colleagues that all was in fact well; that the aircraft was undamaged, and giving details of the position of the lake landing site. On the next day, the 23rd, an aircraft was sent from Rangoon with a load of fuel cans to the landing beach, where the thankful Captain Fulford and his engineer filled up PH-AKV's tanks and took off with great relief for Rangoon.

A grateful reunion, a period of rest and recuperation, and no doubt a small celebration or two, then took place in Rangoon, and it was not until 28th September that the Rapide formation departed Rangoon on its next leg. For ever after this incident, PH-AKV was called '*Vera*' by her pilots, after the heroine of a Dutch story "who had strayed from the right path". History does not recall if her crew were also given appropriate nicknames.

By 1st October, the team had arrived in Indonesia, and soon afterwards moved down the Indonesian coast to the KNILM base at Bandung airport, near Batavia. At this point the three Englishmen left the aircraft in the hands of Captain Koppen and his team, and departed for home in more relaxed style. Here also, the aircraft were repainted with their new 'PK-' registrations and given a thorough inspection, before flying across Indonesia to the coastal naval air base at Surabaya, with the three Dutch pilots at the controls. From this point, another Dutchman, rejoicing in the title of Artillery Captain R N de Ruyter van Steveninck, who was the leader of the surveying expedition, joined the flying team. Van Steveninck flew PK-AKU, Captain Koppen PK-AKW, and Lt Vonk PK-AKV, on the last flying stage, which took the team across the Flores Sea to the southern tip of the Island of Celebes, where they ended the flying part of the journey at Makassar, the main port on Celebes. The expedition leader had decided that the possible

C/n 6296 PK-AKU destroyed by fire after crash-landing at Ketapang, Borneo, in 1938. *[D.Fox]*

flying routes from Makassar to the survey headquarters at Babo, on the northern New Guinea peninsular, at around 1,100 miles, were too long and had insufficient airfields, and that the Rapides would therefore be embarked on the SS '*Baud*', to be carried across the Banda Sea to the small harbour at Babo.

The dismantled aircraft and their crews reached Ambon, on the most southerly of the Moluccas on 23rd October, and then finally arrived in New Guinea two days later. The journey was not yet over, however, as there was no dock at Babo, so the 'Baud' had to anchor offshore, and the three aircraft had to be carefully loaded onto flat-bottomed lighters for transfer to the beach. A light railway had been specially constructed to carry the bulky machines from the harbour area up to the small airfield outside the town, where the journey ended and the real work began.

Over the next eighteen months the aircraft operated from their base at Babo, and from two other small landing sites built out of the jungle on the small island of Jefman, north-west of the Vogelkop peninsular, about 200 miles from Babo, and another on the island of Japen, in Geelvink Bay, to the north of the peninsular, also about 200 miles from Babo. There were many problems with the weather, as the daily thunderstorm build-ups only allowed an hour each day for cloud-free photography, and then the aircraft had to quickly return to one of the airstrips before it became too waterlogged for a safe landing. Lt Tideman was caught out in March 1936, when attempting a landing at the Babo base in PK-AKW, with a photographer and a navigator on board. Heavy rain had so softened the ground that, before he could stop, Tideman found his wheels were rapidly sinking deep into the mud, causing such a deceleration that the aircraft executed the well-known 'Rapide somersault', ending on its back, with such extensive damage that the engineers declared it a write-off. That was therefore the end of PK-AKW's seven-month life. Interestingly, this was yet another example of a Rapide being broken up around its occupants, without any human damage being done.

The two remaining Rapides were soon augmented by two Sikorsky S-38s, and together they carried on the survey work throughout 1936, interspersed with some light transport flights around New Guinea for government officials. By November 1936, ahead of schedule, most of the survey had been completed, so the expedition leader decided to reduce his aircraft fleet by sending the remaining Rapides and most of the surveyors back to Batavia by sea. After they arrived back at Bandung in early 1937, the aircraft were taken over by the KNILM, the Dutch East Indies section of KLM, and they carried out further small surveys of Java and the surrounding archipelago. After this survey work was completed, they were again used as light transport aircraft, from bases at Bandung and Surabaya, on Java. On August 16th, 1938, during one such communications flight, KNILM Captain L J Fritz was over the island of Madura, some 50 miles north of Surabaya, when he noticed a gradually decreasing oil pressure indication on one of PK-AKU's engines. This was a strong indication of impending engine failure, so he immediately turned south towards the distant airfield at Surabaya, in the hope of reaching there before the engine stopped. The oil pressure continued to decrease, indicating imminent seizure of the engine, so he closed down the engine. With high ambient temperatures, a relatively heavy weight, and a drag-producing propeller, he failed to gain either height or comfort, despite maintaining full power on the remaining engine. Captain Fritz then ordered his mechanic, van der Putten, to throw out all the freight, luggage and fittings, to try to slow down the descent. Even with this weight-shedding, Captain Fritz realised that he was not going to reach Surabaya at his current rate of descent, so he found a reasonable-looking stretch of beach near Ketapang Daja, and attempted a forced landing. Unfortunately, during his landing run, Fritz was unable to avoid large rocks on the beach, contact with which tore off both sets of the Rapide's wings, and ruptured the fuel tanks, which in turn sprayed fuel over the hot engines. The engines quickly ignited the fuel and the whole machine was soon completely destroyed. Fritz and his mechanic escaped, slightly injured, but the aircraft was damaged beyond repair, thereby ending the career of the second Dutch East Indies Rapide.

PK-AKV, meanwhile, continued to serve KNILM on various flights from Java and later from Timor. One rather special flight she undertook, on 1st February 1938, was to celebrate the birth in

Amsterdam of Her Royal Highness Princess Beatrix. In keeping with a typically Dutch naval tradition, PK-AKV was fitted with fifteen-foot long orange-coloured 'wimpels' on the rear of her outer wing struts, and flown slowly round the celebrating colonial capital of Batavia.

By 1941, war was creeping closer to the Dutch East Indies, and PK-AKV had by then taken over a short KNILM service on the island of Timor, flying daily from the main city, Dili, the 180-mile route to Koepang, on the southern tip of the island. On 26th January 1942, PK-AKV was in use as part of an air defence exercise on Timor, carrying a party of officers between military airfields. Just before departure from Koepang airfield, the KNILM pilot, Captain de Gioxa Salvi, reported to his passengers that the aircraft was not serviceable, so they transferred to a KNILM Grumman and departed. Immediately after take-off, a Japanese air raid took place, and the attacking fighters pounced on the Grumman, shooting it down, destroying both the aircraft and all board. In the attack, the grounded Rapide was also damaged, but not enough to prevent Captain Calvi from hurriedly collecting his wife and limping off to his base at Andir, where repairs were begun. By the date of the capitulation of the Netherlands East Indies on 8th March 1942, PK-AKV was still awaiting repair at Andir, and her subsequent fate is not known. The most probable contemporary report indicates that she was destroyed by Dutch Army forces later in 1942, to prevent the invading Japanese from making use of her, but she has never been heard of again.

MALAYA
Further north, in Malaya, Wearne's Air Service bought two new Rapides, VR-SAV, and VR-SAW, in 1937 for their operations from Singapore to Kuala Lumpur, Ipoh and Penang. These aircraft were operated alongside two DH 86s which were already in Wearnes' service, and in their first year of service the Rapides flew 258 scheduled flights, with only one late departure, one cancelled departure, 1,643 passengers flown and 25,240 lb of freight carried. Both Rapides were impressed in 1941 to play a short but valuable part in the defence of Malaya, before the Japanese invasion, during which VR-SAV was destroyed. VR-SAW continued for another year, but was then damaged beyond repair in a taxying accident in Sumatra in 1942.

CANADIAN RAPIDES
Sixteen Dragon Rapides were imported into Canada from 1935 up to the Second World War and several were subsequently imported during and after the War. Three were in active use from 1936 to 1951, and at least seven were used regularly from 1939 to 1946.

The first Rapide to fly in Canada was CF-AEO, which was shipped out to the de Havilland Canada factory at Downsview, Ontario, for sale at the DHC price of C$23,000 to Canadian Airways Ltd, operating from Vancouver. Canadian Airways' subsidiary, Quebec Airways used this first Rapide, then took on a further two in later months, and one more on lease, for use along the North Shore of the St Lawrence river. They flew with floats in the summer months, changing to skis when the hard Canadian winter froze the waters of the St Lawrence, then converting back to landplane configuration in the summer. A well known French-Canadian pilot, Romeo Vachon, from Sept-Iles, provided such valuable service to the communities along the St Lawrence with Quebec Airways Rapides including CF-AEO and CF-AVJ in the years up to 1937, that he was awarded the prestigious McKee Trophy for services to aviation in that year.

Floats and Skis
De Havilland Canada specialised in converting English-built Rapides to the use of floats and skis, producing fittings for American EDO floats, then later experimenting with different types. The lower section of the engine cowlings had to be cut down and resealed, the tailwheel removed and the hole sealed, to prevent water ingress. On most Canadian Rapides, the pitot head was removed from the starboard wing strut to a point under the nose, out of the way of water spray from the floats, and common anchor

CF-AEO c/n 6279 was the first Rapide in Canada, shown here on floats at Trail, BC, in 1938. *[BAe]*

points were made on the fuselage and wings for the floats or skis and for their bracing wires.

Rapides adapted well to the skis and floats that were almost essential items for year-round work in Canada's wild geography and rugged climate, taking over a good deal of the business that had been previously carried out by earlier aircraft such as DH Fox Moth float-and ski-planes, and to a small extent by the three DH 84 Dragons. The Rapide's greater speed and load capacity started to provide the emerging small airlines with cost-effective transport to the remote settlements which abound in Canada. They remained in service until well into the post-war period, when the metal DH Canada Beaver and Otter became more practical than the older wooden machines.

In 1936, CF-AYE was used for trials of a new type of aircraft ski which had been designed by the Canadian National Research Council. The idea was to find a simpler and more aerodynamic mounting, with better balanced skis to be made of Canadian spruce, as opposed to the usual metal types which needed complicated bracing. The very neat, silver-doped skis were tried out towards the end of the winter by DHC test pilot Lee Murray from the snow-covered Downsview field, but unfortunately, the light wooden structure could not cope with the harsh torsional and shock treatment of taxying and landing on hard snow, so the conventional thin metal-clad wooden skis were refitted and the big wooden boots were never used again.

Other practical re-design work was completed by the de Havilland Canada team led by Bruce Douglas and Don Long and gave the Canadian aircraft quite a different, but sleek and pleasing appearance. In order to fit skis or the Fairchild floats, several bracing struts and support cables had to be fitted to the engine cowlings and fuselage strong points. Other modifications centred around keeping engines and occupants at practical temperatures. The cold-climate heating system was always fitted to provide hot air for the cockpit and cabin and an external quick-drain pipe fitted for removing engine oil, thereby permitting oil drainage during winter parking, so preventing the oil freezing in the engines. In order to allow for the bracing wires of both floats and skis, the standard undercarriage trousers, or 'pants'

CF-AYE c/n 6304 on DHC-designed wooden skis at the Toronto factory, 1936. *[BAe]*

Toronto Globe and Mail's *Rapide CF-BBG c/n 66354 at Toronto Air Harbour, 1937.* *[BAe]*

as the Canadians called them, were truncated by about 16 inches and re-formed into a bathtub shape. The de-stabilising aerodynamic effect of the large floats forward of the centre of gravity required some compensation, so all Canadian Rapides were therefore fitted during build in England with curved ventral fins, the same shape as on the DH 89M, which blended quite attractively with the lines of the rest of the fuselage, and gave a pleasing line to the side view of the machine. Again, as a practical requirement for the float-planes, an additional cabin door was fitted to the starboard side of most Canadian aircraft, which permitted entry to the cabin from the starboard float during water operations.

The performance of the Seaplane version was adversely affected by conversion for float operation, but not by a large amount. As could be expected, the basic weight increased by 300 lb, which decreased the cruising speed from a quoted 133 mph at 85% power to 123 mph. The take-off performance was obviously affected by the extra drag and weight of the floats and fittings, but a direct comparison is difficult to make, as the take-off, on glassy water with no wind, was given as 40 seconds. With increased weight and drag, the single-engine ceiling was also somewhat lower, at 2,500 feet, compared to 4,500 feet on the landplane version.

Floatplane CF-BBG

Quebec Airways had pioneered the adaptation of the Rapide to Canadian route work, attracting considerable attention to the type in the process. It was therefore not surprising that one of the most enterprising of the Canadian newspapers, the *Toronto Globe and Mail*, owned in the 'thirties by a wealthy industrialist, George McCullagh, decided that a reasonably speedy floatplane with some space in the cabin, could help them get to the newsworthy parts of the province quickly. The news could then be processed on board and the newspapers out onto the streets quicker than could their competitors. McCullagh's business partner, William Wright, was involved in mining in the wilds of Ontario, so a floatplane would also facilitate rapid travel to their joint business interests.

A new Dragon Rapide, built at Hatfield in May 1937 and converted to floatplane capability by DHC, was duly bought, then fitted out as a luxury 'newsroom', with two-way radio, interchangeable wheel, ski and float undercarriage, interior comprising desk and seats for six and a removable ambulance couch. Newly painted in smart *Globe and Mail* colours and registered CF-BBG, the new aircraft was christened with great ceremony at the Toronto waterfront Air Harbour the following month. Captain J G Crang, an ex-RFC pilot, and an engineer were taken on and several expeditions were flown to the northern mining towns over the next few weeks. Returning to the Toronto riverside mooring on 12th August, Crang brought the Rapide in to be greeted with much interest and publicity and then, with the aircraft still on the water, left the machine to be refuelled for the flights which had been planned for the next day.

The operation was awkward, due to the height of the filler caps above water level, but the first tank was safely filled, then one of the worst fears of any refueller or pilot of wooden aircraft occurred. Unfortunately, static electricity from the dry Canadian atmosphere had obviously built up so that, with no static bonding having been made from the refuelling line to the aircraft structure, as the metal refuelling nozzle was introduced into the filler, a static spark ignited the fuel vapour. The whole aircraft was alight in a matter of seconds, and so rapid was the conflagration caused by the combination of aviation fuel, dry wood and fabric that nothing could be done to save her. All the refuellers could do was push the inferno out into the stream, where within minutes she was completely consumed apart from the metal floats and a few jagged metal struts. She had been in service a bare month.

CF-BBG's sister ship, CF-BBH, was somewhat more successful, having arrived in Canada when the market for versatile utility aircraft was beginning to pick up in North America. DH Canada fitted Fairchild floats to this aircraft and sold it in January 1938 to a mining company in British Columbia, the Consolidated Mining and Smelting Company based at Trail, high up in the Selkirk Mountain range, near the Washington state border. A floatplane was particularly useful in the western-most Canadian Province, where there were many lakes, rivers and sea inlets accessible by floatplanes, so CF-BBH, named '*City of Victoria*', was seen in many places when with the mining company. A very young George Kent remembers photographing this floatplane on the water in 1938, near Zeballos, a small town on the remote west coast of Vancouver Island, where the company was mining gold in the nineteen thirties. As in many areas accessed by Rapides, there were no roads in that part of northern Vancouver then, so all people and equipment had to be transferred by boat, or, in Consolidated Mining's case, by CF-BBH. '*City of Victoria*' was sold on to Canadian Airways, also of Vancouver, in May 1939, and she continued to serve the British Columbian community for many years, becoming part of the Canadian Pacific Air Lines fleet when that company took over Canadian Airways in 1942. Sadly, CF-BBH was very badly damaged when her pilot made his third attempt to take-off from a 'sticky' snow surface at Pentecost, Quebec, in 1947, and was subsequently written off.

A scenic view of floatplane Rapide CF-BBH at Zemballos Harbour, Vancouver Island, in 1938. *[W Teague]*

CF-BBH c/n 6370, with Canadian Airways, on a British Columbian lake, 1939. *[BAe]*

CX-ABI c/n 6371 at Montevideo after transfer from Canada for Expresso del Plata, 1938. *[BAe]*

SOUTH AMERICA

One of the ex-Hatfield Rapides delivered to DH Canada in 1937 had an even more interesting career than the Canadian floatplanes, after being converted at Downsview. Arriving in Canada as a company demonstrator with the registration CF-BFM, this machine was used for part of that winter on skis, but then left the DHC factory, as a float plane, in the sub-zero temperatures of January 1938, to be re-assembled a matter of weeks later in the baking heat of a Uruguayan factory. The De Havilland South American representative engineer, Mr W Ballantyne, supervised the reconstruction at the naval aviation facility at Isla Libertad, near Montevideo, in a temperature of 97 degrees Fahrenheit. Mr Ballantyne discovered that a Canadian humourist had left a large sheet of brown wrapping paper in the packing crate in Toronto with the words:

HOPE YOUR
HANDS ARE WARMER
THAN OURS WHEN
UNPACKING -
THIS MACHINE
WAS PACKED
AT ZERO (Fahrenheit)

The wooden aircraft adjusted surprisingly well to the considerable change in moisture and size caused by the change in temperature and humidity, becoming CX-ABI. It was used for many years by Cia. Expreso del Plata for a unique ferry service across the wide estuary of the River Plate from Colonia on the northern side, to Buenos Aires on the southern shore. Expreso del Plata already operated a fleet of 'fast motor coaches' from Uruguay's capital, Montevideo, on the 100-mile route to the port of Colonia, from where passengers would pay the equivalent of 75 new pence for the forty-mile flight across the Plate to the Argentinian capital, taking a total of only three hours to complete the one hundred and fifty-mile journey.

One of Brazil's first airlines, VASP, centred on Sao Paulo, west of Rio de Janeiro, had begun operations with a Dragon Mk 2 in 1934, but no others used Rapides until after World War Two.

ROMANIA

In the important overseas market, buyers included both established and new airlines. In 1936, the Romanian Liniile Aerienne Romane Exploatate de Stat (LARES) took four Rapides, YR-DNC, YR-DRA, YR-DRI and YR-DRO in 1936, to join eleven other aircraft for internal passenger services from Bucharest. Initially the Air Secretary used YR-DNC under the banner of the National Department for Aviation as a personal transport for two years before handing it back to LARES for airline use. Only one aircraft, YR-DRO, survived to serve the Romanian Air Force during World War Two.

BALTIC STATES

A year after Romania took its Rapides, Hugh Buckingham of the Hatfield Sales Department and a Latvian pilot flew YL-ABC and YL-ABD out of Hatfield to the Posts and Telegraphs Department of the Latvian Ministry of Commerce in October 1937 for use on postal, freight and passenger routes. On the normal daily route between Riga and Liepaja, 125 miles away, these two Rapides were used for both postal and passenger work, with the remarkable charge for passengers of just over one penny per mile (1937 figures) for the single journey. The service soon expanded with services to Daugavpils in east Latvia and to take passengers as well as running the postal service. Two more aircraft were ordered in late 1938, but the Rapides carried on doing steady service until the

An indistinct view of the fourth Romanian Rapide YR-DRO c/n 6331 at Bucharest in 1936. *[D.Fox]*

The Latvian Rapides awaiting collection, Hatfield, 1930. [DHMC]

Hugh Buckingham about to hand over the Lithuanian Rapides' logbooks, Hatfield, 1937. [BAe]

country was overrun by Russia in 1940, when they were reported to have been stored at Riga. However, in an interesting turn of events, with the German invasion of Latvia the following year, the two Rapides were brought out of hiding by the Luftwaffe, and reports indicate they were used as staff transports by an Estonian unit and later by JG54 of the Luftwaffe until about 1942.

Not to be outdone in its modernisation, Latvia's southerly neighbour also bought two Rapides in 1937, but these were for the Lithuanian Air Force. Constructors numbers 6348 and 6349 were given the national marks 701 and 702 and delivered from Hatfield via Schiphol in April 1937. Both were constructed as DH 89Ms with a dorsal gun installation and the attendant dorsal fin extension. It is not known whether or not a front-firing gun was installed, but a radio installation was fitted in the cabin, and it is probable that bomb racks were also installed. Delivery was made to No 3 Light Bomber Squadron, at Shaulaj, and the aircraft were active when Lithuania was overrun by Russia in 1940. As in Latvia, the German Luftwaffe then took both DH 89s over after they invaded in 1941, and used them with Luftflotte 2 apparently as communications aircraft. One was later abandoned at Riga and operated in the Baltic area as SB+AH in 1942.

The delightful Bern Airfield in 1936, with Moths on the ground and the Alps in the background. [Aeroplane]

SWITZERLAND

After the prototype, CH-287, had been delivered to the Aero Club St Gallen at Altenrhein in 1934, it was to be five years before the next Rapides arrived in Switzerland. Two consecutive models came off the Hatfield line in March 1939 as HB-AME and HB-AMU, for use by the avuncular Captain Pierre Sauge and his pilots of the appropriately-named Alpar Schweizerische Luftverkhers A G. These machines, fitted out for five passengers and a radio operator, were employed on exclusive Alpine pleasure flights from their Berne base up to the mountain resort at St Moritz, as well as on twice-daily scheduled services to Zurich, Lausanne and Geneva. They were also held on standby for ambulance services from Berne. The first of these two Swiss aircraft, HB-AME, survived the war in Europe to become HB-APE, continuing to operate in Switzerland until it was bought in the 1960s by a German flying club. It then served several German clubs as D-IGUN before being put on static display in the 1980s at Frankfurt airport, where it was still substantially complete and on display in the airport concourse in 1995.

AERO O/Y, FINLAND

Further north, Flight Captain Leppanen, Chief Pilot of Aero O/Y, flew a new DH 89A out to Helsinki, Finland, for a prolonged trial period during the spring of 1937. With the opening of the expansive new Bromma airport at Stockholm, Aero O/Y were trying out new routes to land airfields between Stockholm, Abo, Helsingfors (now Helsinki) and Tallinn, and wanted to use landplanes instead of their earlier Junkers seaplanes. The Rapide was configured for a Marconi W/T radio set, a radio operator, seats for six passengers and the option of wheels or skis for use in the harsh Arctic climate.

Above: Tied down here at Frankfurt, c/n 6437 D-IGUN had begun service as HB-AME in 1939. [CND]

Left: Tidy HB-AMU c/n 6438 of Alpar parked next to the pleasant café at Bern Airport, 1939. [Aeroplane]

Aero O/Y's OH-BLB c/n 6401 "Lappi" on a sunny frozen lake near Helsinki, Finland, in 1939. [BAe]

The trials were considered successful, so Aero O/Y bought the trials aircraft and had it registered OH-BLA. She was christened 'Salama' (Lightning) at Hatfield in May 1937, returning for airline service immediately afterwards, to be followed a year later by a second DH 89A, OH-BLB, which was duly named 'Lappi' (Lapland). The two aircraft were used for unsubsidised scheduled services initially from Helsinki to Stockholm, but by 1938, to other internal Finnish airfields and frozen lakes. The Rapides were operated throughout the harsh Finnish year, from airfields on wheels in the summer, and converting to skis in the long arctic winter. The internal routes were from Tampere in the central region, to Helsinki then on to Viipuri, a distance of 435 miles, six days a week, at a cost of around two pence per mile (1937 figures). For the first year of this route, the remarkable figure of 99.3% regularity was achieved.

Two years later, Aero O/Y contrived to continue operations despite the German invasion of Finland. Lappi, the second Finnish Rapide, fitted with skis for snow operations, had a particularly charmed existence. On a flight in the winter of 1941 to Kiestinki to pick up some wounded Finnish soldiers, she was attacked by three German Bf 109s. In what would naturally be considered a one-sided battle, the radio operator and the Army doctor on board were both wounded by bullets from the Messerschmitts, but the pilot managed, by skilfully throwing the Rapide into tight turns at the critical stages of each attack, to evade the fighters long enough to make a landing on the nearby frozen lake. Rapidly taxying across to the lake's edge, he then managed to hide amongst the tall overhanging trees and bushes, so spoiling any further attacks by the Bf 109s and saving both occupants and aircraft from further damage. After repairs, Lappi was flown back to its base, where both Rapides were hidden for the remainder of the war, surviving to carry on serving several Finnish companies for the next twenty years. Both changed registrations post-war, to OH-VKH, then OH-DHA, and OH-VKI then OH-DHB respectively, and by 1953, the aircraft had each flown 3,300 hours. While both aircraft were still operating in Finland up to at least 1965, OH-BLB (formerly OH-DHB) ended up in Norway as LN-BFB, operating out of Sokna then Honefoss airfield, Eggemoen until 1960. It was then kept in open storage for four years before being burnt in 1968. OH-DHA was sold to Sylvest Jensen in Denmark in 1955, as O/Y-DAS, and then to a photographic survey company in West Germany the following year, being based at Hamburg, with the registration D-IGEL. It was finally sold to G Sueffert of Bremen in December 1966 and after its C of A expired in 1968, the remains were destroyed in a fire at Weser Wume in 1972.

MIDDLE EASTERN OIL COMPANY WORK

Some of the largest users of Rapides in the Middle East were oil companies, either British-owned or with British connections. By 1935, six companies used the type for transportation of material and people, as well as for survey work. The Anglo-Persian Oil Company, based at Abadan; the Iraq Petroleum Transport Company, based at Haifa; and the Ste de Transports du Proche-Orient based in Syria, all used the type around their areas, and between oil wells. In several cases, that ubiquitous aircraft operator, Airwork, which company had many of its own Rapides in Britain, used its expertise and crews to operate a small fleet pre-war from Abadan for the Anglo-Persian Oil Company. Included in that fleet were the fourteenth and eighteenth-built, G-ACZE and G-ACZF, which were bought new from de Havillands in November 1934 and February 1935. They were flown out to Airwork's joint facility at Almaza airport in Egypt by Captain L H Weedon, Anglo-Persian's Chief Pilot, and Airwork crews, then after servicing delivered across the Syrian desert to the oil company's base at Abadan, at the northern tip of the Persian Gulf. Both of these aircraft had interesting further lives, both surviving for several more years in Britain. Parts of G-ACZE were used in a re-build at Witney, using the c/n W1001, and this aircraft was then rather inappropriately given the registration G-ACZE in the nineteen nineties. Another of Anglo-Persian Oil Company's Rapides, G-AEMM, with its bright white fuselage, silver wings and prominent British registration, was delivered to Abadan in October 1936, to operate from Abadan into the foothills of the Zagros

D-IGEL at Hanover in 1966, owned by Uwe Reska. This Rapide c/n 6347 had originally been OH-BLA in Finland. [M. Stroud]

RANA passengers boarding Dragon Rapide VP-YAU c/n 6285 at a Rhodesian outstation, 1937. [BAe]

1957 by the Turkish engineer and designer Vecihi Hurkus for his new independent airline Hurkus Hava Yollari (Freebird Airlines), of Ankara. Hurkus had a hard struggle against the government bureaucracy, and after a few years of operations, the airline was closed. One of these Rapides re-surfaced in the Turkish Aviation Museum in Istanbul around 1997, with the spurious registration TC-ERK ,and is still stored in the Museum. This Rapide is most probably one of the three originals which arrived in Istanbul in 1936, but its correct identity is not known.

AFRICAN COMPANIES

Further south in Africa, Rapides, starting with VP-YAU, eventually went out to Africa for Rhodesia and Nyasaland Airways, (RANA), to be used for passenger services from Salisbury and Bulawayo, and for connections to Johannesburg in South Africa. The company had been formed in 1935, and was the only air service formed in Southern Rhodesia pre-war. By 1939, the company had nine aircraft, and nine pilots, and its routes extended to South Africa, Northern Rhodesia, Nyasaland and Portuguese East Africa. The company was shut down in 1940, when the fleet was taken over by the government on impressment, and the old RANA services were then run as the Southern Rhodesia Air Services.

In Kenya, Wilson Airways of Nairobi, a staunch supporter of de Havilland aircraft, took three; one, VP-KCL, being delivered personally in the spring of 1938 by Captain de Havilland, who took general manager Frank Hearle with him for company and no doubt some navigational assistance. The Rapides joined several other DH types, which served routes from Nairobi to Dar-es Salaam, Lusaka, and Mafia Island, and some of the same aircraft, after impressments during the war, went back to Wilson Airways to continue their operations after the War.

On the east coast, six Rapides eventually went into service in Lourenço Marques for a new company initiated by the Portuguese East African government in 1937. The airline became the Divisao de Exploraçao dos Transportes Aéreos (DETA), by 1938. They were used mainly for government transport work to Mozambique and Quelimane, but also for exploration of the country's hinterland. A twice-weekly, two and a half-hour return Rapide service from Lourenço Marques to Germiston airport, Johannesburg, was initiated in 1938, to connect with Imperial Airways' South African services.

Misr-Airwork

In Egypt, Misr Airwork, set up on behalf of the Egyptian government by the British Airwork company, and already a well-known user of de Havilland aircraft, had five Rapides by the end of 1935, beginning with SU-ABP, 'Al Kahira' from August 1935. All were used for scheduled and charter services from Almaza airport, Cairo, to Alexandria, Luxor, Beirut and Haifa, alongside their two DH 86s. In 1943, two further Rapides were bought by Misr-Airwork, but were lost at sea during their delivery voyage. These two were replaced by two ex-RAF Dominies, SU-ACS and SU-ACT, both of which were delivered in September 1943, and which served the company well until after the War.

Wilson Airways' VP-KCL c/n 6394 being loaded at Salisbury with mail for Cairo and London, 1938. [BAe]

Rex Hayter delivering c/n 6397 CR-AAM over barren country to DETA in Lourenço Marques, 1938. [BAe]

Happy Misr Airwork passengers at Almaza, Egypt, 1937. [D.Fox]

Section 4 – Chapter 6: Spanish Military Operations, 1936-1939

SPANISH MILITARY RAPIDES

The involvement of military DH 89Ms and civilian DH 89 Rapides in thc Spanish Civil War bctwccn 1936 and 1939 is a story of mystery, intrigue and subterfuge. Prior to the start of the Civil War, in early August 1936, the French government had reluctantly brought into effect an International Non-Intervention Agreement related to Spain, which the majority of the western countries had signed by the end of 1936. This Agreement effectively banned the sale of arms to the Republican and Nationalist Armies in Spain. However, the opposing Spanish sides were desperate to build up their military power, and had since 1935 sent out many representatives into Europe, Russia and the USA, to look for ways of buying armaments, including aircraft. The Non-Intervention Agreement was a severe blow to this effort, not only for the Spanish sides, but also to a good number of unscrupulous dealers, who aimed to profit from this buying spree. Over the next three years, many ways of by-passing the international rules were discovered.

While the DH 89 would not normally be thought of as a weapon of war, several buyers, acting on their own behalf, or "for companies in France, Belgium and Austria", but in fact working for the Spanish factions, approached British companies between 1936 and 1938, to buy British aircraft, including DH 89s, in defiance of the international ban.

Prior to the Civil War, which commenced in mid- July 1936, only one DH 89, EC-AZZ, had been ordered, through Senor Escario, the DH Spanish agent and it entered service in December 1934 with Lineas Aereas Postales Espanoles, the predecessor of Iberia, which organisation was simply a passenger and postal transport. In addition, the three well-known 'Moroccan Police' DH 89Ms had been manufactured in late 1935, and a December 1935 Flight report re-affirmed the British government official position that the aircraft were " for colonial police work in Morocco". No other DH 89s were officially delivered to Spain during the Civil War, but it is likely that as many as another 16 were involved in some way, mainly through third parties in Britain and France.

To make matters more mysterious, even the de Havilland order records are unclear, probably helped by the intentionally circuitous purchasing methods of the buyers. Available data shows that the three DH 89Ms built for the 'Moroccan Police', were at one stage allocated constructors numbers 6321 to 6323, but these aircraft were not built as military models, and were in fact sold to the Government of Iran as standard DH 89s. The aircraft actually involved in the Spanish order were three earlier aircraft registered to de Havilland Aircraft Ltd as civilian DH 89s, with constructors numbers 6310 to 6312, and registrations G-ADYK, 'L and 'M issued on 2 December 1935. They received Certificates of Airworthiness eight days later and are usually referred to in DH contemporary reports as standard passenger-carrying DH 89s, intended for the UK market. The most probable position was that the Spanish Republican government agents who bought the transports (with British civilian registrations) had them modified by de Havilland in late 1935 into special DH 89Ms, 'for Moroccan Police work'. This would have diverted attention away from what were obviously military aircraft, giving an outward appearance of their being for civilian, or at least police, purposes.

But inspection of the equipment on board these aircraft would have indicated that the Moroccan Police were either a very war-like force, or that the aircraft were actually intended for another

Spanish DH 89M, showing gun muzzle below the cockpit window, gun sight and bomb rack. *[CND]*

purpose. In fact, all three aircraft were almost certainly intended for use by the Spanish Republican Army against the Nationalist 'rebels' in the imminent Spanish Civil War. Photographs of the aircraft at Hatfield in December 1935, "waiting to depart for Spanish Morocco", show the machines devoid of registration marks, but apparently, British marks were later applied for the ferry flights. That was the beginning of an impressive series of adventures for humble transport aircraft.

DH 89M, G-ADYL

This was the second of the three, which were known to the de Havilland workforce only by their numbers 6310-6312 and were similar to the earlier DH 89M military model built in 1935. They were fitted out similarly to the RAF DH 89M, for a crew of three, and incorporated some ingenious equipment for a wide range of capabilities, of which the de Havilland designers must have been quite proud, considering the constructional problems that the modifications undoubtedly created. The customer had seemingly specified a true multi-role combat aircraft.

First the armament. The aircraft was fitted with three machine guns. One fixed Vickers E pattern gun sat in the cabin by the pilot's right leg, with its muzzle pointing forwards through the nose, being aimed by a simple bead on the nose cowling and a ring hung from the cockpit roof, being fired by a trigger on the control wheel. As if the cockpit were not already crowded enough, below the pilot's seat was a 200-round ammunition box, replenished by tipping up the pilot's seat. A drum-fed Vickers F-type gun was mounted in the rear fuselage floor, firing downwards towards the rear through a pair of sliding hatches, but with an incredibly narrow field of fire - 30 degrees in azimuth, and 60 degrees vertically. The positioning of this gun leads to questions about its practicality. Its extremely limited field of view could only permit it to be used for attacking

DH 89M c/n 6311 parked at Croydon in civilian colours as G-ADYL before transfer to Spain, 1936. *[M. Stroud]*

Spanish DH 89M, 1936, showing the bomb rack. *[CND]*

undefended ground targets, after the Rapide had passed over the target. Was this what the Republican Army intended?

The same hole, protected from the breeze by a canvas roller blind, doubled as the vertical camera hatch, whereas canvas-covered holes in the fuselage sides, protected by box-like surrounds inside the fuselage, were used for sideways-facing oblique photography. A swinging mounting allowed the camera to be swung to either side or vertically down for photography.

In the dorsal position, a second Vickers F-type gun was mounted on a swinging monopod system, designed with typical DH ingenuity, so that the whole contraption could be swung up and out of the normal stowage position inside the cabin, through a large opening

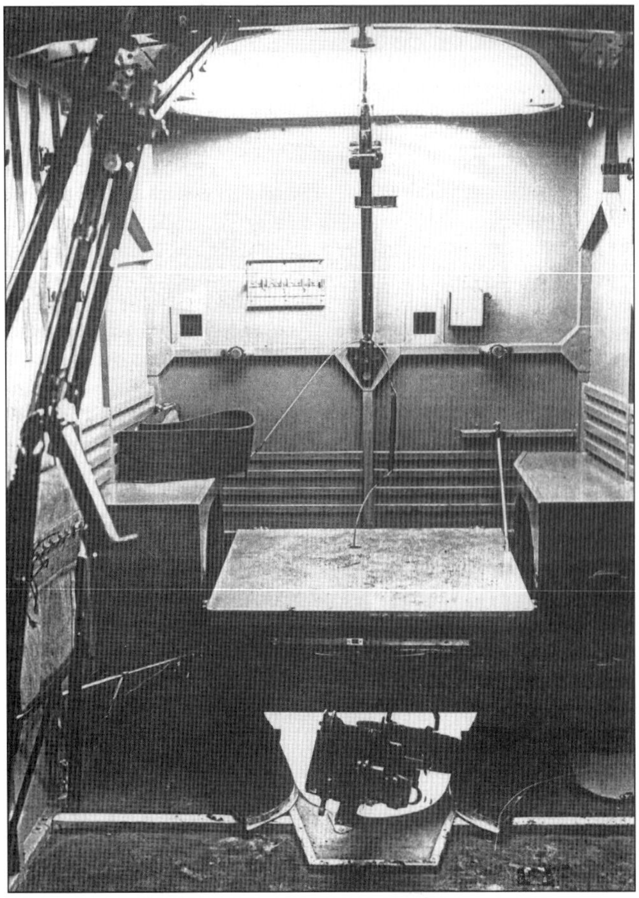

Spanish DH 89M, showing the rear gun positions, with the upper gun swivelled to the left. *[CND]*

in the rear cabin roof, and providing a wide field of fire sideways, above and behind. A detachable metal hoop device at the rear of the hatch prevented over-exuberant gunners from shooting off the fin and tailplane. The position was closed by a sliding hatch when not in use. This gun was fired by the operator standing on a raised platform and secured to the fuselage by a safety harness while in the hatchway.

The bombing system must have caused some problems with the designers, as the under-floor area of the standard Rapide is used up by control runs, pulleys and a complex of wooden framework. In this case the system consisted of a light bomb rack fitted below the normal belly of the aircraft, a Spanish-designed vertical bomb sight placed centrally in the forward fuselage floor, and a simple quadrant-type release system on the left side of the cabin, abeam the sight. Without a complete re-design of the under-floor area, the simplest solution for positioning of the bomb rack was below the normal floor, on an external rack. There would have been no simple alternative for the bomb sight, however, so a hole had to be cut in the centre floor, and relevant control runs moved outboard, to allow a clear view through the floor. A small canvas roller blind operated by draw-strings covered the bomb sight slot when it was not in use. Problems of drag, weight and ground clearance were minimised by having a small rack which could only take twelve 27 lb bombs, in three rows of four.

Another interesting and ingenious item of equipment, sometimes fitted to other DH machines, was the silent ground to air communication system. This consisted of a telescopic pole attached, with freedom to swing vertically, along the port lower fuselage, close to the wing root. The rear of the pole had a looped end, shaped like a musical bass clef, and near the rear end was a cable connection, feeding into the cabin through the floor, from which the crew member could collect message pouches from co-operating ground troops, after being hooked up by the pole. Simple, but probably very effective, if the pilot could fly low enough to scoop up the pouches.

For longer-range communications, the radio operator was provided with a folding radio table and seat, positioned immediately behind the pilot's bulkhead, and probably had a medium-wave transmitter/receiver of Spanish design, compatible with their own ground radio equipment, installed on arrival in Spain. Radios were not fitted at Hatfield, and photographs of the aircraft before departure show no any external radio aerials. Electrical power for radios and lighting came from a wing-mounted, wind-driven generator in the upper wing root, in a manner which was to remain in use throughout the life of all models of Rapide. This generator charged two internally mounted accumulators, one for the radio, and the other for lighting and engine starting. Interestingly, while the contemporary Flight description mentions navigation lights, photographs show only one downward identification light on this model, and no wing-tip or tail lights were fitted.

With all this equipment, the basic weight of the Spanish machine increased, but this was balanced by only having a crew of three, so the difference was not great compared to the passenger version. The empty weight was still only 3.230 lb, with a maximum allowable weight of 5.500lb. Contemporary reports give this model of DH 89M a cruising speed of 130 mph, compared to 132 mph for the DH 89; an initial climb rate at full load of 900 feet per minute, compared to 1000 feet per minute; and an endurance of four and a half hours, about ten minutes less than that of the civilian model.

The colour scheme of this aircraft, when in Spain, was black fuselage and engines, with ochre wings and tailplane and the serial 22-2. This scheme was later to earn it the nick-name 'El Avion Negus' (The Black Aircraft) when it took an active part in the Spanish Civil War on the northern front.

The three DH 89Ms were flown away from Hatfield in late December 1935, not to Morocco, but to the Republican government-controlled Air Combat Training School at Alcala de

OO-JFN c/n 6273 went via Belgium to Spain during the Civil War, 1936. *[V Jacobs]*

Henares, near Madrid, where they were given the serials 22-1 to 22-3. A minor coup by some senior officers was discovered at Henares in spring 1936, so an anxious military commander moved the valuable DH 89Ms, together with some Fokker VIII/3ms, to Getafe, in case the senior officers involved in the conspiracy were tempted to take the aircraft for anti-government use. On 31 July, a few weeks after hostilities started, 22-2 was moved again, this time to join a hastily-recruited Republican group ready to defend the Catalonian area, north-west of Barcelona. This was to be the first time the DH 89Ms had been used as offensive aircraft, and 22-2 was soon embroiled in the battle, acting in the somewhat inappropriate role of escort fighter to the Ajas Rojas (Red Wings) bombing group at Sarinena, north-west of Barcelona. The Republican Government forces had little option but to use a hotch-potch of aircraft for their combat tasks against the technically superior Nationalist air force at this point in the war. The aircraft of the Ajas Rojas were used for bombing, ground attack and fighter escort work. When employed on bombing missions, this improbable group (known quite descriptively as 'La Balumba' by the ground forces), was led by a single ex-civilian transport Fokker VIII/3m tri-motor, converted to carry bomb racks for 50 kg bombs; a Latecoere 28 with a single 50 kg bomb and some small, hand-aimed fragmentation bombs; two or three ex-commercial DH 84 Dragons, also with hand-aimed bombs; about six two-seat Breguet 19s, carrying two racks of 50 kg bombs, and sometimes a Vickers Vildebeest. This 'bomber' section was escorted by the only aircraft fitted with guns - the group's four Nieuport 52s, plus the single DH 89M, 22-2, with its fixed Vickers gun in the nose, and the upper gunner poking his moveable Vickers out of the fuselage roof.

While operationally not very effective, the Ajas Rojas crews were certainly enthusiastic, and flew against the rebels continuously until October, 1936, when the group was disbanded. One of the reasons for the disbandment of this incredible team was a battle in which 22-2 took an impressive role. On 19 October, La Balumba was airborne on another bombing mission, when a rebel Nationalist force of Heinkel He 51 fighters intercepted and attacked them. The incredibly gallant pilot of 22-2, Luis Aguilera Cullell, managed to distract the greatly superior and better-armed fighters away from the bombing group by counter-attacking them with his fixed machine gun, and with his gunner firing from above the fuselage. The bombers escaped into cloud and survived, but predictably, the gallant Cullell could not out-manoeuvre or out-gun the four fighters, and was shot down over Almudevar and killed.

OTHER RAPIDE ACTIVITIES

The other Rapides, mainly imported from England in July and August 1936, together with the surviving DH 89Ms, also had their own adventures. After the setback of the early battles in the north, nine Republican DH 89s were used at the multi-engine training school at Totana, near Cartagena, which remained a Republican stronghold. 22-1 was also used as a bomber in the northern front, but was destroyed on the ground by Nationalist bombs at La Albericia airfield, Santander on 6 April 1937. 22-3 had already been captured by the Nationalists at Zaragoza early on in July 1936, almost before the war started. It had been flown there in an attempt to persuade the military governor, General Cabanelles, to stay loyal to the Republicans. But the General declined and the three on board the Rapide, including General Nunez de Prado, were charged with 'treason' and promptly shot. 22-3 thus joined the Nationalist Air Force as 40-5, but was accidentally shot down and destroyed near Segovia by a Heinkel He 51 from its own side in late August 1936, killing Capitans Pouzo and Vela (whose names were then painted on 40 1 and 40 2 as memorials).

LAPE, the Spanish airline, had a mixed bag of about 16 aircraft at the outbreak of war, including its single Rapide, used for short-range routes and it would seem continued to operate it throughout the war. The various other Rapides which found their way into the Spanish conflict did so by more circuitous routes, sometimes through the hands of aircraft dealers like Airwork, who sold at least three Rapides through intermediaries.

One of the clandestine journeys completed by an ex-Airwork machine was that undertaken by G-ADCL, which was to become number 40-2 for the Nationalist Forces. This Rapide had a very active first few years, with several changes of owner and role.

It was completed at Hatfield in May 1935 for the Anglo-American Oil Company. Initially used as a personnel transport by the oil company, it was involved in an accident when it overturned on landing at Redhill on 26 June 1935, killing Brendan [Jimmy] Hanstock, the company's General Manager. It was rebuilt by de Havilland and sold to Airwork in December 1935. In late July 1936, it was sold on to Tom Campbell-Black, who was no stranger

40-2 had been G-ADCL (c/n 6277) before transfer to the Spanish Nationalist forces in 1936. *[CND]*

to long-range flights in de Havilland machines, and the well known Spanish autogiro designer, Juan de la Cierva. Campbell-Black and de la Cierva had bought four Rapides at the same time, each of which was eventually to reach Spain.

Campbell-Black had 'CL fitted out with five-gallon fuel and oil drums for its Spanish flight, and false Spanish registration marks painted on its wings and fuselage. Over these were painted, in soluble paint, the official British marks. Campbell-Black quietly recruited a team of British pilots keen to find some interesting flying, and this first aircraft was flown to Spain by Lord Malcolm Douglas-Hamilton, assisted by Airwork's Sales Manager, Richard Malone on 1st August. The plan was to fly to Spain direct, having Malone top up the main fuel and oil tanks in flight through hoses leading from the fuel drums to modified fuel and oil filler caps on the engine cowlings. The registration ruse was apparently designed to confuse the local authorities in case of a forced landing, when either the British or Spanish registration would be used, depending on the country of landing, and no doubt some pre-planned story passed over. G-ADCL did reach Burgos, in Nationalist Spain, and was then, as related below converted to fire a machine gun fitted in similar fashion to the 'Moroccan' DH 89Ms. It is likely that 40-2 was later converted to 'hand-deliver' bombs through a hole cut in the fuselage floor; although it later became a training aircraft and survived to be handed over to the Republicans when the war ended. In 1940, it was transferred to Iberia as EC-AAY and was later based in Spanish Guinea.

THE 'COMBAT' RAPIDES

Three other British Rapides, G-ADFY, G-ADAO and almost certainly G-ACPN, joined 'CL later in August 1936, on similar journeys to Spain, and it is likely that all but G-ADFY were also converted to carry guns and bombs, as they were used later in support of a fighting group led by Major Ansaldo. G-ADFY, which was flown out by A Rowley to Burgos on 4 August, was probably used in a less exciting role, as a troop transport or for casualty evacuation. All were painted in an ochre camouflage scheme, with Spanish crosses on fin and wings, and, whilst various sources are at variance, may have been given the Nationalist serials 40-1 (probably G-ADFY), 40-2 (G-ADCL), 40-3 (G-ADAO), and 40-4 (probably G-ACPN). In addition, the captured DH 89M, 22-3 (G-ADYM) was renumbered 40-5.

An interesting insight into the Rapide's involvement in the Civil War is given in a Spanish report of the activities of Capitan Angel Salas Larrazabal, who was a pilot in the Nationalist force in 1936. Involved as the leader of a trio of Breguet 19s attacking Pamplona in July 1936, he was captured by the Republicans and imprisoned in Pamplona later that month. A few days later he was released by Nationalist colleagues and then went to join a unit which had obtained Rapide 40-2, the former G-ADCL. Capitan Salas worked as a liaison officer between General Mola, who was leading the Nationalist forces in northern Spain and General Franco, who was still in the Canary Islands.

General Mola believed that his efforts to defeat the government forces would be helped if he had more fighter aircraft, but the Nationalist forces could not supply any more, so Capitan Salas decided he should do what he could to rectify that deficiency. He felt that Rapide 40-2 could be turned into a makeshift fighter. With the help of an old friend, Capitan Del Monte, who was an engineer in the artillery arsenal in Burgos, Capitan Salas obtained a Spanish version of a Vickers machine gun and mounted it in the forward fuselage, much as with the DH 89M, alongside the pilot, so that the pilot could have direct access to change ammunition belts. A hole was cut in the nose to allow the muzzle to protrude outside the fuselage. This became the first Rapide to be turned into a fighter-bomber during the Civil War.

The first aerial combat in the North took place over Somosierra on 27 July. Capitan Salas, in 40-2, was escorting a group of Nationalist Breguet 19s when they were attacked by a Nieuport 52. The Rapide received two direct hits, but Salas managed to fight off the attack and land safely. He continued to fly 40-2 as an escort for the next month, until a joint Dragon and Fokker group was formed at Burgos for escort duties. Eventually, on the 23rd of August over the Teruel front, Salas, in 40-2, gained his first victory in the war by attacking and destroying what is described as a 'light aircraft'.

By the middle of August, in addition to the Rapide, Salas had flown several other types in combat from Burgos and Zaragoza to battles at Teruel and Huesca. He had flown 50 operational sorties over 116 flying hours during the previous four weeks, and was taken into hospital at Zaragoza suffering from exhaustion. After several days of recuperation, Salas went to Tablada and then Talavera, to fly Fiat fighters and Heinkel He 51s supplied by Germany, and claimed a further kill in October. The Rapide was left at Burgos to be flown by other pilots.

HG644 was the first Dominie completed by Brush Coachworks and flown by BS Allen in 1943. [BAe]

Section 4 – Chapter 7: British Military Service

ROYAL AIR FORCE

Prior to the armament build-up to World War Two, the British government bought a few DH 89s; K5070 "for the use of the Air Council" in March 1935; K4772 for the April 1935 General Reconnaissance competition, and two more, P1764 and P1765, for light communications duties with No 24 Sqn at Hendon in 1938. But then, with the threat of war looming, two contracts were placed towards the end of 1939, for a total of five Rapide radio operator trainers (P9588/9 & R2485/7), to be used by No 2 Electrical and Wireless School at RAF Yatesbury, alongside the Tiger Moths of No 10 Elementary Flying School. More contracts soon followed, with another 14 Rapides (R5921/5934) in late 1939 for No 2 E&WS which became No 2 Signals School in August 1940. Larger contracts for both radio operator trainers and communications Rapides followed over the next two years, and these were designated Dragon Rapides Mk I and Mk II respectively. In 1941 the service name was changed to the more appropriate training name 'Dominie' but the mark numbers remained the same. Several other tasks were undertaken by the British military Rapides and Dominies, such as navigation training, ferry work by the Air Transport Auxiliary and by stations and manufacturers as staff transport. Eventually, the surprisingly large number of 529 DH 89s were completed under Air Ministry contracts, some of which were used by the Royal Navy, the Air Transport Auxiliary and foreign air force units attached to the RAF.

Because of higher priority work at Hatfield, after they had built 189 Dominies, de Havilland handed over type production to a Midlands woodworking company, Brush Coachworks at Loughborough. The first Brush Dominie, HG644, was flown by BS Allen in March 1943 from the Loughborough aerodrome close to Brush's 'Falcon' factory, the last of 335 being flown in March 1946. As well as the military purchases, some 75 were impressed from civilian service into government use, by radio and navigation training schools, manufacturers and the National Air Communications organisation. Eight privately-owned DH 89s which were being used by oil companies in the Middle East managed to escape impressments into military service, but several were seized from Iran in 1941 and others were impressed in India and Palestine. The larger numbers of Dominies were used by light communications squadrons of the RAF and RN, but then a considerable number of other units used the type in ones and twos for their own occasional personnel and cargo transport needs. While there is insufficient space here to cover all the British units that used the DH 89, some of the more significant units are described below, and a list of units using the Dominie is at Appendix 4.

An indistinct view of c/n 6421 P1764 at Hatfield, 1938, before handover to 24 Squadron, Hendon. [D.Fox]

K4772 c/n 6271, intended for the General Reconnaissance aircraft competition, showing pilot-operated gun, gunsight and drift-sight, 1935. [BAe]

K4772's cockpit, with the Vickers gun at lower right and trigger on the control column. *[BAe]*

THE RAF GENERAL RECONNAISSANCE COMPETITION

At the beginning of 1935, the Air Ministry issued a specification, G.18/35, for a new class of military aircraft, the General Reconnaissance class, which would be used for coastal reconnaissance and offensive action against enemy shipping, and for which manufacturers were asked to submit bids. A competition would then be held to decide a winner. De Havilland decided to respond to this request, and set the Drawing Office, by now installed at Hatfield, to modify the standard Dragon Rapide to compete for the new class. The specification required a three-crew type, with forward and aft firing guns; a light bombing capability; drift and bomb sights; flare dropping facilities, and a military radio installation.

As usual with de Havilland, work was completed quite quickly, and the twenty-second Rapide off the line was extensively modified to meet the G.18/35 specification. Many of the installations fitted to the DH 84M two years earlier were now applied to the GR competition DH 89, with fittings for a Mk III Vickers, belt-fed gun in the nose, along the right side of the cockpit floor, and a retractable gun sight on the cockpit centre-line. A box for 400 rounds of ammunition was placed under the pilot's seat. The dorsal gun position required a circular slot in the cabin roof, covered when not in use by a sliding hatch, plus an extended fin fairing to provide greater directional stability when the hatch was in use. The bombing capability required considerable adjustment of the plumbing and cabling under the fuselage floor, as two shallow bomb bays, covered by an internal box, and with spring-loaded external doors, were fitted on the centre fuselage floor. The bay could alternatively carry 4 x 20 lb bombs; or 4 x 11.5 lb bombs; or 4x 4 inch flares; or 4 x naval smoke floats. Forward of the bomb bay, another sliding hatch in the cabin floor was used for the bomb-aimer's sight, together with its internal bomb-release, selectors and switches. Ahead of the bomb sight, a small panel held an instrument panel with an altimeter, ASI and temperature gauge. To the right of this position was an external drift sight and sighting compass. The bomb-aimer doubled as the navigator in this model, so a table was provided on the port side, together with instruments and chart stowage.

The rear gunner was also the radio operator, and had his radio position on the starboard side of the fuselage, with transmitter, receiver and switchboard forward of his table. To the rear of the radio position were stowage space for parachutes, naval flares and fire extinguishers, while on the other side were stowage positions for eight 97-round ammunition drums. In the rear centre of the fuselage was the gunner's position, designed with typical de Havilland ingenuity. The swivelling seat and roller-race gun mounting, rotated smoothly and quickly, with the gun moving vertically as required by the gunner, while the gunner remained in the same position.

The other competitor for the class was the Avro 652A, which later became the Anson, and both Avro and de Havilland were asked to submit their entries for testing at Martlesham Heath in the spring of 1935. De Havilland's entry was serialled K4772, Avro's was K4771 and the de Havilland aircraft was taken over for initial tests by the A&AEE team at Martlesham Heath in April 1935.

The Martlesham report compared the two aircraft for performance and handling; the operational tests were to follow at the Coastal

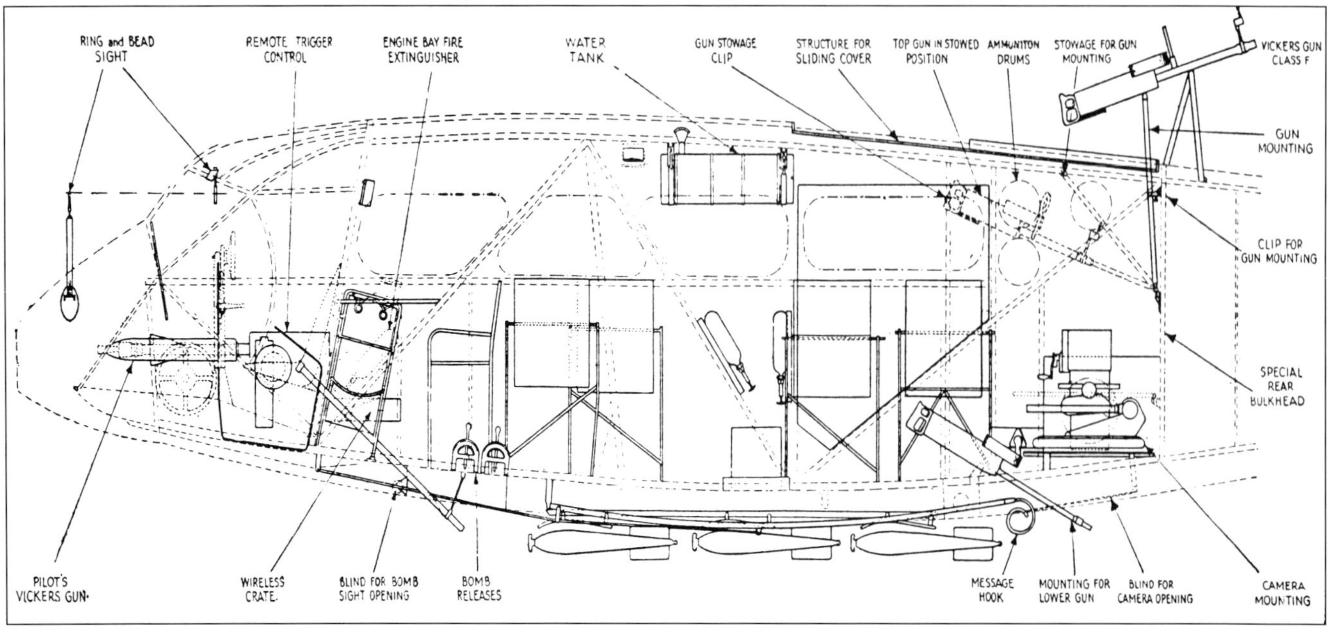

Contemporary diagram of the General Reconnaissance competition DH 89's weapons and equipment. *[BAe]*

The first communication Rapide, K5070 c/n 6267, 1935. [BAe]

Command Development Unit at Gosport. In terms of handling, the DH 89M was considered "...laterally unstable, but it is thought that this is due to inherent stiffness in the aileron system. As a bomber, it is a steady platform except in bumpy weather, when there is a tendency to over-correct."

From the weapon operation viewpoint, the Martlesham team considered that: "...location of controls is convenient for the bomb-aimer only. The position is so uncomfortable, cold and draughty that accuracy is impaired. No communication with other crew members was provided. The bomb-aimer's view ahead is inadequate. Dive bombing cannot be done. Illumination is inadequate for night bombing."

"The free gun position is slightly better but extremely draughty. It is considered that modifications are needed before this mounting can be recommended. The position should be totally enclosed. Clips to roof door release handles, etc. are too fragile and will require strengthening. The fixed gun position is good. There is no fitting for a camera gun, but the aircraft could have a free camera on the Lewis gun mounting."

The DH 89's ceiling of 15,700 ft was reached after a tardy 44 minutes and the maximum speed at normal revolutions was found to be 130 mph, some 30 mph slower than the Avro.The 652 was tested soon afterwards and its range, endurance, rate of climb and maximum cruising speed, together with its weapon operating capability, were all considered superior to those of the Rapide, so it won the competition. As a result, in July 1935, Avro was awarded a contract to supply 174 Ansons, and the DH 89M was not put into production for the RAF. However, the design work was not wasted, as examples of the DH 89M were sold to several other air forces in 1937 and 1938.

24 SQUADRON, RAF HENDON, 1935 TO 1945

No.24 (Communications) Squadron was based at London's main military airfield, Hendon, and was the senior communications squadron flying important passengers on duties throughout Britain and the nearer parts of Europe. Various aircraft types were used by the squadron, but confidence was shown in de Havilland's capabilities in late 1934 when the Air Council ordered a Dragon Rapide, for their use, only nine months after the type's first flight.

This first machine, K5070, was the eighteenth aircraft off the Hatfield line and was delivered in March 1935. Flight photographs show the aircraft to be immaculately finished all over in silver dope, but some special fittings were incorporated. The most conspicuous was the large Harley landing lamp fitted in the nose. An adjusting mechanism was fitted to this lamp, so that the pilot could find the angle of depression which most suited him for night landings. De Havilland later accepted the nose light as optional

Flypast of the two Women of Britain *air ambulances, Hendon, May 1941.* [CND]

equipment for all Rapides, but usually recommended a fixed mounting for the light, "so as not to distract the pilot when his attention is needed elsewhere". Other changes for this aircraft were the introduction of a second roof-positioned emergency exit, and an ingenious method of controlling the Marconi radio transmitter/receiver, which could be operated by the pilot or a radio operator. To enable the pilot to tune the transmitter/receiver, a system of cables was used, attached to the control panel of the radio, and feeding through into the pilot's cockpit. For the first time on a DH 89, a second wind-driven generator was fitted, this time on the leading edge of the starboard wing, to match that on the port wing. These generators supplied power to the radio, starting solenoids, and the lighting system, and for re-charging the aircraft accumulator.

No 24 Squadron also took the next two Rapides, P1764 and P1765, for an expanded light communication task, in November 1938.

Following the outbreak of war, 24 Squadron's fleet of transports expanded rapidly to include impressed Rapides, in order to take on the great increase in military transport needs around the British airfields. In particular, there was a rush of communications and mail flights across the Channel prior to and during the German occupation of France, and then for the evacuation of British troops from the continent. In that disastrous month of May 1940, at least seven of the Rapides were caught out by the advancing German forces; some, like P1765 and X8506, happened to be unserviceable on French airfields on 5th May and, there being insufficient time to repair them, the ground crews were forced to burn them, rather than let them be commandeered by the Axis forces. Another of the unfortunates was W6457, formerly Western Airways G-AFSO, impressed into 24 Squadron after only five months of civilian service. On a flight out of a bridgehead airfield, the Rapide had the misfortune to have an engine failure near the German lines, which necessitated a forced landing near Aneuil. The crew and passengers escaped the crash unhurt, but as they scrambled out of the aircraft, they were fired on by German ground forces. The people were not hit, but the aircraft was and, barely a year old, disappeared in flames within minutes.

After the dash back from France, and for the remainder of the war, 24 Squadron only flew communications flights within the UK and was the largest military user, as 25 different machines served with 24 Squadron at some time, with probably an average of about 15 at any one time, with others operated by its close neighbour, No.510 Squadron (also known as the Metropolitan Communication Squadron). By 1944, British and Allied pilots were being posted to 24 and 510 Squadrons as a rest from the more hazardous work of operational flying and in July of that year, enough Dutch, Norwegian and Belgian pilots had joined for there to be formed a

X7381 c/n 6541 in typical RAF camouflage at Boscombe Down, 1945, before civilianisation as G-ALZF in 1950. *[CND]*

separate flight, 1316 (Allied) Flight, from which beginnings the post-war Belgian and Dutch Air Forces emerged. In 1946, soon after the end of the war in Europe, 1316 Allied Flight split into two units based in Holland and Belgium.

The Squadrons maintained the bulk of passenger and mail flying tasks from the metropolis until, in 1946, after the war needs had decreased, the longer-range work of the Squadron moved to Bassingbourn. Some Rapides and Dominies were kept on until the spring of 1948 when the last of the type were pensioned off, having served throughout the country and the near continent for ten years, mostly in the hostile wartime environment.

An RAF 'Visual' flight to Germany, in NF 865

After Victory in Europe Day in 1945, 24 Squadron was often tasked for flights across the English Channel. One such trip was flown by Flight Lieutenant Loader and his navigator, Flight Lieutenant Bill Hickox in a Dominie, NF865. This aircraft was built as a Dominie Mk I at Loughborough in May 1944, but remained unused as a trainer and was, in July 1945, converted back to a communications aircraft, for service with the Metropolitan Communication Squadron at Hendon. Having had only one month in service, it was still nice and tidy and with Squadron code 'CB-P', so quite suitable for a week's trip by an Air Marshal and his party.

There were no ground radio facilities or direction-finding equipment available to Allied forces in this early post-war period, so continental trips were usually flown by pilot and navigator, using the old method of stop watch and rather outdated map, and strictly in visual contact with the ground. Bill Hickox had very wisely plotted, from a written list, all the known German landing strips on his pre-war chart. So when this 24 Squadron crew left Hendon in 'P for Peter' on an August morning in 1945 to take a Royal Air Force Air Marshal and two

NF865 c/n 6736 in later life as G-ALXT, in the Science Museum, Wroughton, 1981, painted in Railway Air Services colours. *[CND]*

interpreters on a journey to Bad Oeynhausen in North Germany, the first leg was easy, as it entailed an overnight stop at Brussels airport. Next day another easy leg to Frankfurt followed, but then the weather threatened to be a problem. This stage involved flying across the higher Westervald and Sauerland hills, which reached 3,000 feet, but with no meteorological forecasts for their destination available and a 500 foot cloud base at Frankfurt, they were not too hopeful. However, this was an important trip, so they planned to navigate over lower ground by a circuitous route, following the autobahn north-west along the Rhine valley, and then turning north east along another autobahn towards slightly higher ground, which then led to their destination.

Setting off from Frankfurt, they duly turned north-west and flew up the scenic Rhine valley, keeping below the low cloud base, until they crossed the Ruhr river near Duisburg and saw the north-east autobahn branch they wanted. However, after a few miles, the autobahn ended, despite being marked on their map. They searched around for other markers, and soon found a railway which went in the right direction, and began following it. Once again, the autobahn appeared again, so "things started to look rosy". Continuing east along the autobahn, just below the low cloud, Hickox and his pilot felt they were going to find their destination, but then, quite unexpectedly, about 20 miles short of Oeynhausen, they " came to a ridge and the autobahn went straight uphill into cloud. So did we!"

They had no choice, as there was no room to turn back below cloud. Turning back onto a westerly heading, the Dominie was then put into a gentle descent, with the intention of getting back below the low cloud on the western edge of the ridge. Bill Hickox then remembers suddenly seeing fir trees flashing past a few feet under their wheels, so it was back up into the cloud again for a few more minutes, to make sure they were clear of the high ground, before letting down again. This time they found the autobahn again and began looking around for the nearest airstrip Bill had plotted on his old map. Gutersloh was marked as suitable, being on the lower ground, so they headed north for about 25 miles, and found the strip, which looked excellent, but unfortunately was completely covered by army tanks. Off they went again to the next plotted strip, and on finding it, this one was covered in very shaky-looking pierced steel planking, which Loader considered would tear his tyres off on landing. By this time, having flown for around 3 hours, they were getting concerned about the Dominie's fuel state, so were anxious to find a landing site quickly, or they would have to try a landing on the autobahn they had just left. However, Bill Hickox then saw another spot on his map, showing that there should be an airstrip at Lippstadt, just north of the Sauerland ridge which they had failed to cross. Heading south again, they soon found Lippstadt, and on quick inspection, the pierced steel planking here seemed in good condition, so with great relief, Loader made an approach for landing. Bill Hickox said "On touchdown, we looked more like a flying boat, as there was a good inch of water on the surface. We taxied to the end where there was the only sign of habitation".

British troops camped near a farmhouse took the Air Marshal and his interpreters in hand, whisking them off to army accommodation at Buckeburg, while the pilot and navigator were taken into Lippstadt for the night. The next day, the Dominie was flown up to Buckeburg to collect the passengers, and a change of plan then took them all down to Le Bourget to continue the official tour from there.

'P for Peter' continued to serve the Metropolitan Communication Squadron until August 1946, when it was put in store, but in January 1949 it became a hack for No 5 Maintenance Unit at Kemble for a year before being sold off to become G-ALXT with the Herts and Essex Aero Club. It then continued its itinerant career, flying out to the Ceylon Air Academy in 1951 as CY-AAI, and returning to England in 1974 as 4R-AAI, in the hands of Gary Studd. It was later to be bought by the British Science Museum, who now display it at Wroughton, painted in Railway Air Services colours but as G-ALXT.

173 SQUADRON AND IRAQ AND PERSIA COMMUNICATIONS FLIGHT, 1942 TO 1944.

Formed as a communications squadron in 216 Group, 173 Squadron's B flight flew an assortment of light types on local VIP, passenger and freight services, from the RAF Middle East Command headquarters airfield at Heliopolis, Cairo. The Command's area of responsibility was quite extensive, as it had control over RAF units as far afield as the Sudan, Palestine, Trans-Jordan and Kenya, as well as those in North Africa. The aircraft operated were a diverse bunch, some in normal RAF service, but including others which had been impressed into service from civilian life. One such was Dragon Rapide G-AFEN, which had been with Sir William Firth at Heston before being sold to Palestine Airways at Lydda as VQ-PAC. Lydda Communications Flight took it over in early 1940 as Z7188 but, in August 1940, it needed to revert to its civil marks, as BOAC nominally used it for VIP work in Lagos. On its eventual return to Heliopolis, probably in early 1942, the aircraft became a Dominie Mark II, but with a new military serial, HK864. It was then used for transport flights from Heliopolis by Middle East Command, before transferring to the Iraq and Persia Communications Flight in October 1942, where it remained until 1946. Several attempts to purchase it locally failed and after acquisition by Rollasons of Croydon, it was flown back to their base for refurbishment the following year. Rollasons then sold it to ZONDA in Argentina as LV-AGV, along with several other Rapides. Several owners later, it was eventually withdrawn at Buenos Aires in 1960.

At Habbaniyah, G-AFEN/HK864 was to be joined by another Rapide, which had also been impressed into RAF service. Sister ship HK862 had also been in service in the area, in this case as G-AFFC with the Iraq Petroleum Transport Co at Haifa, until taken over in May 1941 by the British Military Force HQ in Jerusalem. Later allocated to No 206 Group Communications Flight based at Heliopolis, the two Rapides, disguised in Middle Eastern desert camouflage colours, flew the regular one-hour Habbaniyah-Baghdad-Habbaniyah round trips. The CinC Middle East, Major-General Selby and AVM R D Willock, AOC Middle East Air Forces, were often on the passenger lists, travelling to places such as Basra, Baghdad, Abadan, Rashid and Kirkuk. Even the Maharajah of Jodphur graced HK864 with his presence on a trip from Baghdad to Basra two days after Christmas 1944.

After two year's steady work in the heat of the Iraqi desert, HK862 was sent out in May 1944 on an unusual reconnaissance task - to search for a missing Boeing Fortress, somewhere south of the Qatar peninsular, along the southern coast of the Persian Gulf. The crew of the Rapide eventually spotted the Fortress, which had crash-landed about 100 miles east of Abu Dhabi, but obviously in a bad state, with the aircraft looking badly damaged. The Rapide crew decided that the Fortress crew was in need of urgent help, and considering the area to be acceptable for a landing by a light aircraft they took the risk. Unfortunately, the surface was not good enough, and the Rapide itself was wrecked in the landing attempt, now leaving two crews to be rescued. Eventually the Royal Navy

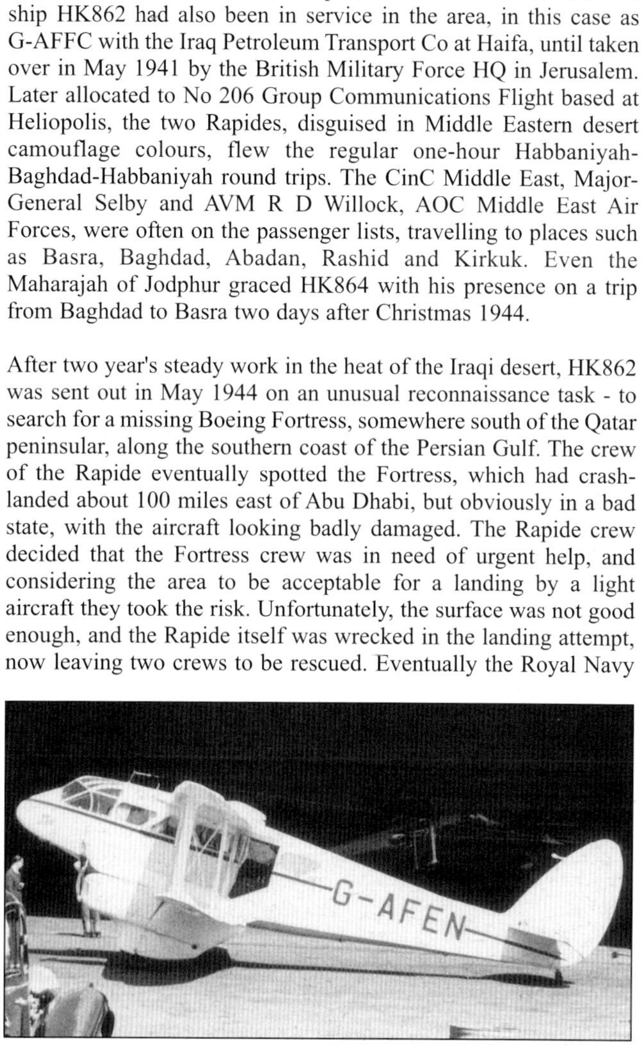

Sir William Firth's G-AFEN at Croydon in 1938, before use by BOAC in Egypt and transfer to the Iraq and Persia Communications Flight as HK864. The much-travelled c/n 6399 ended its days in Argentina! [CND]

F-BHCD c/n 6706 at Chalons sur Saône in 1962, having served 527 Squadron as HG721. *[CND]*

came to the rescue, taking off both crews several days later. Reports from passing aircraft, several days after the rescue, indicated that the local Arabs had quickly stripped the machines of any usable (and probably many unusable) parts, so the Rapide was formally written-off by Middle East HQ three months later.

271 SQUADRON, 5/42 TO 7/44.
This communications unit, based at Doncaster, operated as a light transport squadron with Harrows and acquired a number of Dominie Is in 1942 until 1944, when the type was replaced by Douglas Dakotas.

526 SQUADRON (RADAR CALIBRATION), INVERNESS. 8/43 TO 5/45.
526 Squadron was formed in June 1943 at Highland Airways' old airfield at Inverness, and operated a mixed fleet of Blenheims, Oxfords, Hornet Moths and Dominie Is for both radar calibration and communications services. Dominies were particularly used for transporting senior naval and military staff from the railhead at Inverness to Grimsetter airfield near Kirkwall in the Orkneys, and Sumburgh in the Shetlands. Several of the 526 Squadron aircraft were converted to ambulance standard, with fittings for carrying four stretchers, seats for two attendants, curtains, a water tank in the forward roof, and a small wash basin in the rear. Military units in the north of Scotland at Wick and Castletown were also served by the Dominies, the routes being shared with the civilian registered Rapides of Scottish Airways, flown under contract to the Air Ministry by Captain Eric Fresson. Interestingly, all the communications aircraft operating out of Inverness and Aberdeen had their cabin windows painted over, so that passengers would not see the disposition of the massive RN fleet in the Orkney anchorage at Scapa Flow. 526 Squadron was disbanded in May 1945, and its aircraft incorporated into 527 Squadron based at Digby. Three Dominies were left behind at Longman for communications duties, on behalf of the local Signals Wing. The Royal Navy's 782 Squadron was also a user of Dominies for a time at Longman from 1943, as they also used the airfield as a base for their Highlands and Islands communication flights, before moving down to RNAS Donibristle, north of Rosyth, in mid-1946.

527 SQUADRON
Initially formed at Castle Camps for radar calibration duties, before moving to Digby, this unit absorbed 526 Squadron's aircraft in May 1945 and in turn transferred its aircraft to the Radio Warfare Establishment at Watton in November 1945. One of their Dominies, HG721, became G-ALGB in 1948 and later F-BHCD in France, where it spent many years as a parachute club workhorse and is now on display in the French Musée de l'Air at Le Bourget.

HQSEA COMMAND, INDIA
In 1940, along with most of the civilian light aircraft then in use by Clubs and companies in India, at least five civilian Rapides, operating for Tata Airlines and Airlines of India, were taken over by the Royal Air Force, and impressed into service with serials in the series MA 963 to MA 968. The aircraft were used for military transport and occasional ambulance duties by the Headquarters of South East Asia Command, based in New Delhi. .

EMPIRE TEST PILOTS' SCHOOL, FARNBOROUGH
The Empire Test Pilots' School at Farnborough had a good supply of aircraft, many of which served long after most of the type had gone to the breakers.

One of its long-term servants was Dominie HG715, originally taken on strength at Boscombe Down in August 1945, moving to Cranfield in October and then Farnborough in July 1947. By this time it was painted in overall silver colours, with code '5' and fitted with six seats and a simple five-channel VHF radio, which was by then becoming a necessity for the busy area west of London. HG715 was popular with many sections of the Farnborough community and it was kept on the ETPS strength mainly for use as a communications aircraft for pilots moving around the various sites connected with ETPS course activity. It was also used as a 'test project' for students to evaluate the handling qualities of an 'ancient' machine and compare it with an early jet aircraft that the School operated. When the School's two Olympia gliders were towed across to Chilbolton by Tiger Moth for gliding evaluations by student test pilots as part of their course, the Dominie was a useful means of transporting the student test pilots.

But the Dominie was useful in other ways. One of the tutors on the ETPS staff, Squadron Leader 'Cyclops' Brown, who happened to live in Salisbury, near Boscombe Down, found that he always had a willing travelling companion on his journeys home to Wiltshire on Fridays and back up to Farnborough on Mondays. The School generally finished work at a civilised hour for the weekend so, after

HG715 c/n 6700 when with the Empire Test Pilots School, Farnborough, October 1953. *[D.Fox]*

completing his week's work at about four-thirty or five on a Friday afternoon, the Squadron Leader would walk across from the School to the ETPS flight-line hut, near Cody's tree, to pick up the Form 700 for his aircraft prior to the trip home to Boscombe, or Old Sarum, whichever was still open on that particular Friday. Coming out of the flight hut, he would invariably spot Pusher, his black Labrador, patiently sitting by the door of the Dominie, waiting for his ride home, having been looked after all week by one of the ETPS engine fitters. Pusher always seemed to know exactly which aircraft would be used for his homeward journey, and he was always waiting at the Dominie, ready for his trip home, and his own travelling place, up front behind his master on one of the passenger seats.

This particular Dominie continued to have an interesting life after leaving ETPS service in October 1953. Being in good condition, it was immediately civilianised by Hants & Sussex Aviation at Portsmouth as G-ANET and sold to Silver City Airways at Blackbushe. In 1955, it was sold to BOAC for use by their associate, Aden Airways as VR-AAL and converted as a mark 4 to take Gipsy Queen II engines with variable pitch propellers. It was then sold to two members of the Italian Consulate in Asmara, Ethiopia, Luigi Mascheroni & Christian Tonna in September 1958, and registered ET-P-22. Probably used for several years by the Consulate as transport around this former Italian colony, its C of A lapsed in June of 1960 at Addis Ababa, following the death of Tonna in a motor accident, and it was presumably scrapped soon after.

By 1955 the former ETPS Dominie HG715 had become Aden Airways' VR-AAL. *[CND]*

Air Ouest's F-BGIS c/n 6608, seen here in 1956, had served as X7491 with the School of Flying Control, Watchfield. [M. Stroud]

PILOT AND NAVIGATOR TRAINING

Several navigation schools had been set up by 1938, using Rapides and Ansons, but most were transferred to overseas schools with the worsening wartime conditions in Britain. Typical of the navigation schools were Numbers 1, 2, 6 and 9 (Observer) Advanced Flying Units. No 12 (Pilots) Advanced Flying Unit used Dominies for a short period, but the lack of dual controls made it an impractical trainer for pilots and the task was taken over by Oxfords and Ansons.

No. 2 Civil Air Navigation School, Yatesbury

This school opened at Yatesbury in September 1938 as a civilian-run organisation, alongside the Radio School, but despite its title, was mainly used for training military observers and occasional pilots, in navigational techniques. It was run by the Bristol Aeroplane Company and air experience was also given to trainee Wireless Operator/Air Gunners. With changing military requirements and equipment, this school became No 2 Air Observer & Navigator School in November 1939, and closed in December 1940, as most primary navigation training had by then been transferred to the Commonwealth air forces in Canada, Rhodesia and South Africa.

No. 6 Civil Air Navigation School, Staverton

This school originally operated from Shoreham from May 1938 as Martin's School of Navigation, using Rapides provided by Airwork Ltd. Along with the other civilian-run schools, this school became No 6 CANS in May 1939 on its move to Staverton, and was re-designated No.6 AONS in November 1939. The School trained RAF Observers in Rapides, but by the end of 1940 most of these had been replaced by Ansons, which had more room and greater endurance, while providing facilities for a radio operator, a staff navigator and three student navigators.

No. 1 Beam Approach School, Watchfield

Four Dominies were used at this unit from February 1942, initially called the School of Flying Control, to give student pilots beam approach demonstrations, before they moved onto Oxfords or Ansons for their own Beam Approach Training Courses, where they could handle the controls themselves. Dominie X7491 was one such aircraft, which served here in 1942 and then various other units, before becoming G-AHTY in 1946 with General Aircraft Ltd (later Blackburn) companies. One of many sold in France in the early 50s, it was operated by the engine manufacturers, Turbomeca for several years and ended its days as a freighter in North Africa in 1960.

ROYAL NAVY SQUADRONS AND UNITS, 1940-1962

The Royal Navy also received its share of the Air Ministry contract for Dominies and the first purpose-built machine, Dominie I navigation trainer X7394, came out of Hatfield in 1941, to be followed by a total of sixty two others, from both Hatfield and Loughborough. Several of the type were allocated to the Royal Navy as communications aircraft, including impressed Rapides G-AFEZ (Wrightways) and G-AFEP (North Eastern Airways), but then perversely allocated back to AAJC use for Air Commerce Limited and Isle of Man Air Services respectively.

RN Communications work

As Rapides and Dominies began to enter service, they were initially for use as staff communications aircraft, some with six seats and a radio operator, the others with eight seats generally allocated to the RN communication squadrons, Numbers 781, 782, and 712, at various bases including Lee-on-Solent, Donibristle and Hatston in the Shetlands. Detachments from these squadrons were sent to Scottish Airways' base, Longman's field, Inverness in 1945 and 1946. 782 Squadron was formed at Donibristle, on the northern side of the Firth of Forth in December 1940 and was a large squadron operating mainly Dominies, but with a variety of types including Oxfords, Beech Travellers, and Stinson Reliants. The unit disbanded in July 1953 but the RN Dominies stayed at Donibristle to be handed on to the newly-formed RN Northern Communications Squadron, with the aircraft flown and maintained by Airwork Ltd, until the station closed in April 1959.

RN Training

The other Naval Dominies came from the makers as Dominie IIs, for use by naval training squadrons for observer and radio operator training. Amongst others, 701 Squadron, based at Culham, Culdrose and later Yeovilton, took on the training tasks using the Mark I version of the Dominie, which was configured in the same way as the RAF Wop/AG trainers, with three receivers and one transmitter, for the three students and a small seat for the staff instructor.

The Royal Navy's last Dominie, delivered in June 1944 from Brush Coachworks as a Dominie I, was NF881. While it was nominally a radio trainer, it began its itinerant service career with 782 Squadron, a communications squadron at Donibristle, and it worked as a light transport for the rest of its RN service, staying with 782 until after the War, being temporarily detached to Eglinton in Northern Ireland and Lee-on-Solentin Hampshire. Subsequently it served at several other famous Royal Naval Air Stations, including Arbroath in Scotland, Brawdy in Wales, Lossiemouth in Morayshire, Scotland and Culdrose in Cornwall. This particular Dominie was typical of the Royal Navy's use of the type, as it served its various naval units for nearly twenty years, before being sold to The Anglo Diesel Company in June 1963 for reduction to spares.

Royal Navy Dominie X7341 in the post-war silver scheme, parked at Odiham, 1955. C/n 6514, it was never civilianised. [M.Stroud]

Dominies served the Royal Navy from 1940 until the mid-1960s, much longer than with the RAF. In 1961, there were still 14 on RN strength, still being used for communications and occasional air experience work, until the last of the type was finally replaced by the succeeding de Havilland light transport, the DH 104 Sea Devon.

AIR TRANSPORT AUXILIARY, 1939 TO 1945

The Air Transport Auxiliary (ATA) was formed in late 1939 in order to deliver new and repaired military aircraft from the manufacturers or repairers to their service units. This use of civilians, about one sixth of whom were females, released the operationally-trained RAF pilots previously used, to concentrate on front-line tasks. There were around 660 ATA pilots on strength at their busiest period, just before Autumn of 1945, and they were dispersed around the country, at Ferry Pilot Pools, (FPPs), of which there were 14 by 1945.

The last Dominie delivered to the Royal Navy, NF881 c/n 6752 seen as 901 with Brawdy Station Flight, 1952. *[D.Fox]*

The magnificent job done by these pilots, delivering all types of military aircraft, was an important factor in allowing highly-trained Royal Air Force pilots to concentrate on the operational part of the war. Most of the FPPs were centred near aircraft factories, so that new aircraft could be delivered more expeditiously. White Waltham was chosen as the first all-civilian Pool in 1940, becoming Number 1 FPP and incorporated the ATA headquarters, and the ATA Air Movements Flight. The ferry system sprang into action in 1940, delivering an impressive 260 aircraft in the first three weeks of operation.

The nature of the process meant that deliveries were mostly one-way, so an efficient means of collecting or delivering the ferry pilots was therefore essential to the process. 'Taxi' aircraft were the ATA's answer to this need. At first they were provided with small three-seaters like Puss Moths and the Fairchild Argus but, as the ferrying task began to escalate, the Air Ministry recognised that greater efficiency could be gained by the use of larger, but easy to operate, twin-engined aircraft like Oxfords, Ansons and Dragon Rapides. These types could carry six or eight ferry pilots who could be dropped off at the collection points first thing in the day, and then the 'taxi' could collect the pilots after they had delivered the aircraft to their bases, before returning to the Ferry Pool. Most FPPs used the first two types, but several, including the Headquarters at White Waltham, No 3 FPP at Hatfield and No 7 FPP at Sherburn in Yorkshire in particular, used impressed civilian Rapides, and from 1941, military Dominies, as 'taxis'. One of the aircraft taken over in 1941 by the new organisation, X9386, was a 1935 civilian Rapide, originally delivered as G-ADDE to Aberdeen Airways, and impressed into military service in 1940. As with most aircraft impressed into military service, X9386 was repainted in the RAF 1940 camouflage dark earth and dark green scheme, with its military serial on fuselage and wings. By the time it reached White Waltham, it had already had a busy military career, initially with the Ringway AACU before taking part in the scramble to return as much as possible in the way of people and equipment from France in May 1940. It had survived, unlike ten of the type, which had been destroyed by enemy action or by the retreating Allied forces to avoid their being taken over by the German Army.

By 1943, there were 14 Ferry Pilots Pools, many of which had Dominie Mk II air taxis, in addition to the Ansons, Oxfords and other smaller types. The Pools were all similarly tasked with ferrying aircraft from nearby manufacturing sites and factories; for example, Number 6 Pool at Ratcliffe, the small airfield belonging to Sir Lindsay Everard, was close to the Vickers factory at Castle Bromwich, where Spitfires and Lancasters were produced, so this Pool delivered the majority of the Castle Bromwich output.

Hatfield, from where the de Havilland-built Tiger Moths, Dominies, Oxfords and Mosquitos were sent out to Maintenance Units or Squadrons was, for the early part of the War, home to No 3 Ferry Pilots Pool, which was the first all-female FPP. An indication of the size of the task carried out by ATA pilots between 1940 and 1945 was that from de Havilland factories alone, the ATA delivered 1,075 Dominies, 14,367 Oxfords, and 12,480 Mosquitos. These numbers of course include aircraft delivered new and after repair, which explains why, in the case of the Rapide and Dominie, of which only about 450 were made during the war, so many were ferried.

Of the many stories from the ATA pilots one was that it was not only two-legged animals that enjoyed the Dominie. ATA pilot Douglas Fairweather was the father figure who jointly commanded No 4 FPP at Prestwick in 1941. A friendly, caring, but somewhat eccentric West Coast Scotsman, Flight Captain Fairweather found one day that he had no spare taxi pilots to do a 'Round Robin' to collect his pilots and return them to Prestwick. As he was the only pilot left in the office, he had no alternative but to take the trip himself. He duly worked out his route, checked the weather at the various destinations, then climbed aboard, taking with him his daytime office companion. Being a good Scotsman from farming stock, his quite sensible reason for taking an extra passenger was that this particular pet always received special care and attention, and there was nobody left to look after him. The story does not detail the domestic or safety arrangements for the carriage of goats in military Dominies, but the hope is that the return trip was short, both for the sake of the human passengers and the aircraft's interior fabric.

This same ATA pilot moved south to form a separate ATA Air Movements Flight at White Waltham in 1942, for the operation of internal passenger and ambulance flights. This was in effect a communication flight, in the same style as a Royal Air Force unit, as it used newly-allocated Ansons, Proctors and Dominies to carry government passengers on duty journeys throughout Britain. Additionally with specially-modified Ansons and Dominies, it flew inbound ambulance cases to the Canadian military hospital at Taplow, near White Waltham. The Air Movements Flight task was quite separate from the routine work of taking ATA pilots to and from airfields for ferry flights, as it concentrated on carrying military officials, service personnel and urgent freight to destinations in Britain and in 1945, to the continent. The unit was kept busy, and by 1944 a batch of new Loughborough-built, but Witney-converted, Mark II Dominies was delivered, including NF883, NF886 and NF888. These aircraft remained with the ATA until 1945, when NF883 was transferred to Prestwick, and NF886 to Ringway, subsequently being sold as G-ALPK, with the Lancashire Aircraft Corporation at Squires Gate, and later several air taxi companies. NF888 was sold to South Africa as ZS-AYG in October 1946, but crashed at El Adem during delivery.

One of the young female pilots of the ATA, who has written the definitive history of the ATA which included some of her own

The three Iraqi Aeroplane Society's Rapides airborne from Hatfield, 1938, before departure to Baghdad. *[BAe]*

three of these were later returned to the Government of India for civilian use in 1946, but retaining RAF markings. Of the six Indian Air Force Volunteer Reserve 'Coastal Defence Flights' which were formed from 1940, at least one, No 2 CDF at Juhu Bay, Bombay, had Dominies or Rapides on their strength. HX790 and HX791 were impressed, serving for two years before returning to civilian ownership. These Rapides were used, alongside two DH 86s, for coastal patrols around the sub-continent's coasts, assisting naval forces on the lookout for enemy vessels. Another eleven Dominies were diverted from RAF service during the war and provided to India for use by civilian-run airlines.

IRAQI AEROPLANE SOCIETY

This unusual name was given to an organisation set up by the Iraqi government in 1932, to encourage 'air-mindedness' in the country, but almost certainly it was simply a government-organised military force, through the auspices of a small commercial airline. By 1938, the 'Society' had gathered enough funds to spend £12,000 on three DH 89s direct from Hatfield, so YI-ZWA, YI-HDA and YI-FYA (officially registered in July 1938 to the Iraqi Aeroplane Society) were delivered to Baghdad on 1st October 1938. The RAF had for several years supplied advisers to the Iraqi Air Force and the Rapides were collected by the current adviser to the IAF Military Mission, Flt Lt Reed, together with two Iraqi officers who had been converted to type at Hatfield the previous month.

Soon after their arrival, the three aircraft were incorporated into a government-run airline which took the name Iraqi State Airline. It appears that all the pilots who flew the ISA flights were military pilots, and most of the flights were to take government officials to various appointments within Iraq and the region. After an initial spate of flights, including one to Egypt for a conference, where one of the Rapides was damaged on landing at the refuelling stop at Rutbah Wells, the ISA activity declined. One officer who did an impressive job of organising, maintaining and even flying the ISA Rapides was Rais (Captain) Jawad Hussain, a pilot known to de Havilland for several years, as he had flown one of the air force's DH Moths in 1930, and delivered a DH Dragon from Stag Lane to Baghdad in 1933. By February 1939, Rais Hussain had left the IAF to run this Aeroplane Society offshoot, and with one of the Rapides now stuck at Port Sudan having been damaged on landing, began to operate, single-handed, the two remaining aircraft. In an incredible feat of organisation, Jawad Hussain managed to fly a two-weekly cycle of mail and passenger services from Baghdad to Amman, Basra, Kirkuk and Mosel, while managing and maintaining the two Rapides. However, by the end of 1939, the irrational way of running ISA was finally changed, when the DH 89s were transferred across to the Iraqi Air Force, to be used for occasional government communications duties, until the final one of the trio was reported as being 'burned out while refuelling' in September 1943.

THE ISRAELI 'LIGHT BOMBER'

In December 1946 an ex-RAF Dominie NR718 was purchased for Aviron, a newly-formed Jewish airline, and after overhaul and conversion to civilian specification by de Havilland at Witney, VQ-PAR arrived in Palestine in early 1947. When the IAF's predecessor, the Shirut Avir (air service), was formed in late November 1947, this Rapide joined its ranks along with Aviron's other aircraft. The Rapide was the service's first twin engined aircraft at this stage and also the largest aircraft so far acquired by Jewish forces at the outbreak of Israel's crucial War of Independence on November 30th. Soon afterwards, on December 13th 1947, the entire Shirut Avir fleet left Lod Airport for Tel-Aviv's Sde-Dov, the Rapide being flown by Emanuel Tzur, Aviron's ex- chief pilot.

Other Rapides were meanwhile acquired in somewhat clandestine fashion by Haganah agents from overseas, despite an embargo on sales to the renegade Israel. In April 1948 G-AKTX was purchased in Britain in the first of at least six deals through a British broker, Mayfair Air Services of London, and in May this aircraft was reported as passing through Italy on its way to Tel Aviv, where it arrived on May 5th. Two more Rapides were reportedly acquired in South Africa by another pair of Haganah agents but only one, ZS-BYT, painted in 'Pan African Air Charter' colours, made it to Israel, also in May 1948. The other, G-AKOI, which had been shipped out to South Africa in May 1948 and was also painted in Pan African markings, was reported to have left South Africa on April 20th, and was then impounded in Cairo by British aviation authorities on April 29th. The reported dates may be slightly confused, but strangely, G-AKOI was released from Cairo in July 1948, to be sold in Jordan, only to suffer at the hands of the Israelis two months later. Also from Africa in 1948 came two other Rapides, both bought from Nairobi-based East African Airways Corporation - VP-KED and VP-KEE, which became respectively 1306 and 1310 with the IDFAF. Another example, G-AKMF, funded by the Jewish administration, was another Mayfair Air Services purchase which was flown from Croydon by Emanuel Tzur, arriving at Sde-Dov on May 5th 1948. In this growing collection of Rapides, VQ-PAR was damaged by an Egyptian Air Force strike against Sde-Dov on May 15th, the day after the Israeli Declaration of Independence, but this aircraft was later repaired, becoming an air ambulance. These Rapides and others that joined them later in the war were in service with Shirut Avir's first squadron, initially at Tel-Aviv and later at Ekron (Tel Nof). Some 13 Rapides were operated in the period up to 1955 and the

C/n 6955 TJ-AAB of Arab Airways in 1946, which was forced to land by the IDFAF in June 1950. *[D.Fox]*

early ones were given serials S-71 to S-77, later changing to serials in the range 1301 to 1310, which included later deliveries.

This small band of unlikely combatants played a surprisingly significant role during the birth of the Israeli nation, being the largest type capable of both striking against ground forces and delivering people and equipment to beleaguered Israeli outposts.

Rapides in Palestine 1948

The Shirut Avir's Dragon Rapides served mainly as light transports, but were also converted to act as bombers against small, undefended targets. The type's contribution was most important in the early stages of the war, when Israel could only muster a very basic, hastily-collected group of aircraft, none of which had been built as bombers. Bearing in mind the Israeli's innate ability to improvise, the aircraft were modified for light bombing, probably with bomb racks below the fuselage, incorporating a release mechanism and most likely a rudimentary bomb-sight installed in the cabin floor, all operated by a bombardier. During the early period of the war, Rapides took part in most of the major operations, bombing enemy forces and delivering supplies to besieged and outlying settlements. From March until October 1948, flights of Rapides from Sde-Dov took part in bombing raids on such varied targets as Amman, in Jordan, to Sasa and Malkia during Operation Hiram, as well as attacks on Egyptian vessels off Tel Aviv during their bombardment of the Israeli town. Rather surprisingly, Rapides continued to carry out bombing missions even after the arrival of the IAF's B-17s, probably because they were considered more effective and flexible against small tactical targets.

Rapide TJ-AAB, Captain C C Cloud

But the new air force was not only interested in its own Rapides, it also attacked or captured others intruding into its self-imposed airspace. On September 22nd 1948 a Shirut Avir Messerschmitt 109 intercepted TJ-AAQ, of Jordan's Arab Airways, which was ironically the former G-AKOI which had been seized in Egypt en route to Israel. Still being over Irbid in Jordan, the pilot of TJ-AAQ had refused to respond to attempts to make it land in Israel, so it was shot down by the Messerschmitt. It was carrying BBC correspondent John Nixon and *Daily Telegraph* journalist David Woodford, both of whom were killed. During 1950 other Jordanian Rapides were spotted several times, making their way from Amman in Jordan to Almaza airport, Egypt, occasionally straying into the Israeli-held Negev desert airspace. These aircraft had usually evaded interceptions, but on 13th June, 1950, the pilots of two Spitfires of 101 Squadron, Shirut Avir, on a routine training flight over the desert, spotted the bright red fuselage of a twin-engined aircraft flying low over the desert. Catching it up, they saw that it was Rapide TJ-AAB, of Arab Airways, which they later discovered was flown by an American, Captain C Cloud.

Initial attempts to intercept it failed, as Captain Cloud threw the old girl into tight turns and evasive manoeuvres. The fighters did not wish to fire on this unarmed aircraft, and eventually they managed to fly alongside the slower machine, indicating by hand signals and lowering their flaps and undercarriages, that they required it to land. So, no doubt remembering the fate of his unfortunate predecessor, Cloud reluctantly followed the Spitfires to Be'er Sheva, where they all landed safely. Cloud and his four passengers, together with a load of oranges for Egypt, were captured, and the passengers soon being released to return home. The fighter pilots, feeling they required some reward, impounded the oranges! Not being inclined to squander another valuable asset, the Shirut Avir also impounded the Rapide, and passed it on to 100 Squadron at Ekron (Tel Nof), for use alongside the six others as a communications aircraft and light bomber.

This windfall aircraft was not to serve for long with the Israelis, for on 18th December, 1950, it was being flown by a recently naturalised American-Israeli pilot, Meir Hoffshi, down the coast from Ashqelon, in Egyptian-held Gaza, with a load of seven passengers. Some sort of major emergency then occurred, and the aircraft crashed into the sea, killing all eight occupants. No cause for the crash was ever discovered, whether the aircraft had a major failure or was shot down by enemy action, but the bodies were recovered by the Egyptian occupying forces and returned to Israel.

Unlike many other types within the emerging IAF, up to twelve Rapides continued to serve for several years after the end of the War of Independence. From 1950, the type was operated by 100 Squadron, primarily out of Tel Nof airfield. There were still 6 Rapides in service during July 1950, with three more being added in 1953.

G-AKRS c/n 6952 at Blackbushe, 1953, before sale as 'VQ-PAR' to the IDFAF Museum at Hatzerim. [D.Fox]

IAF Rapides were finally withdrawn from service in 1957, a few having been passed on to Israel's Arkia Airlines in 1953 but by this time their condition was very poor and only two were used briefly by the airline. One airworthy example of the type, ex G-AKRS, which never actually served with the IAF, was bought from Arrow Aviation in Britain, delivered to Israel in May 1978, and is now maintained in good condition in the IAF Museum at Hatzerim. Originally painted as '002'; it now wears 'VQ-PAR' in commemoration of the Aviron aircraft.

MALAYAN VOLUNTEER AIR FORCE

Wearne's Air Service, which was based at Kallang airfield, Malaya, were unable to continue their services with the approach of the Japanese invasion in 1941, and their two Rapides VR-SAV and SAW were impressed into a new auxiliary force, the Malayan Volunteer Air Force, at the end of 1941 as '18' and '19'. The Rapides, still in the distinctive blue fuselage and yellow tail of Wearne's Service, were then flown by volunteer pilots on several duties, including a military service between Singapore and Batavia carrying passengers and official mail, as well as journeys up the Malayan west coast to Butterworth and Ipoh, carrying military cargo. Soon afterwards both aircraft were caught up in the Japanese raids on Malaya. On 18th December, 1941, Pilot Officer Gatenby had an exciting time when arriving at RAF Butterworth on the north-west coast, in VR-SAW. Realising an air raid was underway, and that his cargo of explosives for the British forces there would make an impressive target, he managed to evade the bombers, then land after they had departed. He had his dangerous cargo unloaded, and then another air raid took place, damaging two Blenheims parked either side of his Rapide, and probably causing damage to his aircraft as well. With some difficulty, he managed to start both the Rapide's engines, and attempted to return to his base. As he was some way down his take-off roll, a damaged 67 Squadron Buffalo crashed on the runway ahead of him. He had just enough speed to pull the Rapide over the broken Buffalo then gently ease his aircraft into a climb, before turning south towards his base at Kallang. But his troubles were not over, as another 'friendly' aircraft, a returning Blenheim, took a dislike to him and attacked him, shattering his instrument panel and putting his port engine out of action. Luckily, the aircraft was quite light as he had no cargo on board, so Plt Off Gatenby managed to keep enough height over the reasonably flat terrain to reach Ipoh, 90 miles south of Butterworth. He landed safely there and VR-SAW was repaired, to continue service with the MVAF.

The day after Plt Off Gatenby's adventure, the other MVAF Rapide, still painted as VR-SAV and resplendent in its blue and yellow Wearnes' colours, was hit by friendly ground fire, which disabled one engine, forcing the pilot to land at Ipoh. The MVAF engineers there decided that they should arm themselves against further attacks and, as with the DH 89M, they fitted a Lewis gun into VR-SAV, to be manned by a gunner, Sgt F H Robinson. Sadly, this aircraft was destroyed nine days later during another raid on Ipoh, when both the pilot and gunner were killed. With the invasion of Singapore imminent, the MVAF evacuated to Palembang in Sumatra in February 1942, the remaining Rapide then flying on to Batavia. Later that month, VR-SAW was ferrying troops and stores from Batavia to a small reserve landing ground near Palembang when it was hit by a taxying Hurricane and damaged to the point that it was irrecoverable without spares backing. It was therefore abandoned on about the 10th February 1942, before the airfield was attacked by a Japanese parachute assault force.

ROYAL NETHERLANDS AIR FORCE, 1944 - 1956

One military operation re-created towards the end of the Second World War was the Royal Netherlands Air Force, which had had many officers incorporated into the Royal Air Force after escaping from their own overrun country in 1940. The story of the Dutch military operation of the Rapide is fascinating but space only permits an outline to be told here.

Dutch pilots first became involved with the Dominie Mark II towards the end of the Second World War in early 1944, through postings away from the front line to the more leisurely internal communications flying of No 24 Squadron at Hendon. As communications tasking increased, the Squadron was renamed the Metropolitan Communications Squadron, and sub-divided into 'Allied Flights', with B Flight being manned by mainly Dutch but also some Belgian pilots. By July 1944, the Flight became independent, being re-numbered 1316 (Dutch) Communications Flight, and equipped with a variety of light aircraft, some new, but including many civilian machines impressed into service for the duration of the war. The Dutch pilots used a pool of aircraft consisting of Proctors, Austers, a Lockheed 12A, a Hudson, and four DH Dominies. The DH aircraft allocated to 1316 Flight, NF868, NF869, NF870 and NF877, were all newly-built by Brush Coachworks, coming off the Loughborough line as Dominie Is. Two of these Dominies later went to Holland as part of the re-formed RNLAF; one went to Belgium with the Belgian air force and the fourth, NF870 was damaged when it hit a fuel bowser at Hendon in December 1944 and was replaced by NR731.

RNAF Captain M Kamphuis was given charge of 1316 Flight, and his pilots were initially tasked to transport military and government passengers to and from airfields around Britain, but as the liberation of Europe came closer, the need for short-range transport routes into Europe became more obvious. Under their new commander, 1316 Flight therefore quickly took over an expanding network of flights to the newly-relieved continent, beginning with a daily service to Brussels (Melsbroek) in September 1944. At the Dominie's normal cruising speed of 130 mph, with full fuel and eight passengers, the Melsbroek leg would take about one hour fifty minutes, depending on the amount of dodging of defence zones and weather that was needed. Returning against the prevailing wind could be expected to take around two hours, all at around two thousand feet, down amongst the worsening autumn and winter weather. A week after starting the regular Brussels run, the Dutch pilots were delighted to go back home, when a regular schedule to central Holland was begun, using Eindhoven as the base. This route would have taken a little longer, around two and a quarter hours. These routes were flown by NF869 and the other three Dominies throughout the winter of 1944/45 - providing the military passengers with a graphic view of war-devastated Belgium and Holland, a view particularly poignant for the Dutch pilots, who had spent the last three years fighting for this home-land from English skies. Warm greatcoats, gloves and boots were essential for pilots and passengers for these two-and-a-half hour journeys to Eindhoven on cold, turbulent winter days, as these Dominies had no heating systems.

1316 Flight in Holland flew 723 passengers and 60 tons of mail and light freight on these routes up to the end of the year, but then a new Commander was appointed. Commander First Class H P Sobels, of the Dutch Military Transport Service, took over for the next five months, during the gradual handover of the unit and its equipment to Dutch control. Officially, NF869 was transferred to the Royal Netherlands Air Force in November 1944, and the other machines followed soon after. There were difficulties over the winter period, no doubt exacerbated by the weather, when a loaned Metropolitan Dominie HG712 suffering an emergency landing in May 1945 at

RNLAF V-2 in post-war silver colours, at Schiphol, 1946. [D.Fox]

Ex-RNLAF V-3, c/n 6740, now back in RNLAF colours at the Soesterburg Museum, 2002. [P Schmidt-Crans]

Eindhoven, with Captain F Lutz at the controls. While the aircraft was considered a write-off, Captain Lutz and his six passengers escaped unhurt, which gives an indication of the unusual properties of the aircraft. The flight continued to operate its transport services throughout 1945, and into another winter, without further casualties.

Spring of 1946 saw further developments, as the Dutch government was eager to restore normality to its ravaged country. As part of this devolution of control back to the government in Holland, the Royal Air Force handed over control of 1316 Flight to the Dutch government, which immediately disbanded the RAF Flight in May 1946 and re-created it as No 1 RNLAF light transport Squadron, (No 1 Transva), with Major J N Mulder in command. This new squadron combined the assets and personnel of 1316 Flight and No 6 (Auster) squadron, and took over some of the ravaged buildings at the old air force base at Valkenburg, on the North Sea coast. The Squadron's official formation date was 17th June 1946, and from this date NF869 and her three sister ships became the mainstay of the new squadron. The engineers quickly celebrated the re-birth of the peacetime Dutch Air Force by spraying over the Dominies' old camouflage scheme with silver overall; replacing the RAF roundels with the Dutch segmented red, white, and blue, with an orange central circle; and changing the RAF fin flash to the horizontal Dutch tricolour. RAF squadron codes were removed, and the logical Dutch engineers sprayed their four post-war aircraft with large black code letters 'V-1 to V-4'. NF869 became 'V-3'.

The task of the new squadron was the usual transportation of government and military personnel throughout the country. The hard North Sea coast winters created many problems for the long-suffering Dutch people, with many island and country communities being cut off by floods and snow in the winter of 1946. Even the sea froze over during particularly harsh periods, so no ferries could reach the islands. No 1 Transva therefore undertook many ferry flights to island fields and in particular to Schiermonnikoog, being based over that winter at the coastal airfield of Leeuwarden. The Rapides used by the new government Aviation Service also helped in this life-saving mission, and their story is told in the chapter on civilian operations. After a normal summer and autumn in 1946, the squadron again spent the following two winter periods relieving the stranded islanders of Ameland and Schiermonnikoog, working alongside the Rapides which were now flown and controlled by the newly re-born KLM. The four Dominies carried out short range government and military communications flights until, in January 1952, V-3, '*Gelderland*', was de-mobilised, to become a photo survey aircraft for KLM, and V-4 was sold for spares. Soon afterwards, in December 1952, the old Squadron numbering system was reinstated, so that No 1 Transva became No 334 Squadron, and remained the only transport squadron in the RNLAF.

The appropriately-registered PH-OTA c/n 6740 airborne from Schiphol, 1954, when with KLM Aerophotos. [CND]

C/n 6872 F-OBGE, ex Dutch V-2, at Croydon, awaiting delivery to STRA in Tunis, 1958. [M. Stroud]

The two remaining Dominies continued to serve well during the succeeding years, notably during more disastrous floods in early 1953, but by 1956, their task had been taken over by newer and larger Dakotas, so V-1 and V-2 were retired, to be sold to Aerocontacts at Croydon, becoming G-APBM and G-APBJ.

As an indication of the feelings of the Dutch people towards this first and most noticeable peacetime aircraft to be seen in Holland, NF869 and her three sister ships became known amongst crews and passengers by the nickname 'Dominee', which to the religious Dutch meant 'Padre'.

Dominie Mk1 NF869, '*Gelderland*'.
NF869 was a standard Dominie Mk I trainer which, in May 1944, was flown out from the small airfield at Derby Road, Loughborough with two other machines, to No.18 RAF Maintenance Unit at Dumfries. As the aircraft had been built as a Mark I Dominie, the MU teams had to fit it out for carriage of passengers, making mountings for ten lightweight alloy-framed three-point seats, covered in Air Force grey leather, and installing side and roof panelling, interior lighting and hand-grips to help passengers negotiate the steeply-sloping cabin floor.

At this stage, the '1942' camouflage scheme was still in force, so NF869 had been sprayed in overall camouflage colours, with yellow under surfaces, 1942-pattern roundels, fin flash and serial, but no squadron identity letters. There were probably many aircraft to prepare for service, for '869 was not available for delivery to its new home, Hendon, until September, when it was ferried to 1316 Flight within a few days of its Dominie sisters. The Squadron code of 'CB' plus an individual aircraft letter was applied soon after arrival, when the Dutch pilots had pre-war Dutch orange triangles applied to the noses of their new machines. As a reminder of the flight's origins, the four Dominies had the name of a Dutch province painted below the cockpit. NF 869 was named '*Gelderland*', and this name remained with her throughout her Dutch Air Force service. This aircraft had several small modifications compared to standard Dominies. There were two air-cooling vents in the nose, to help keep the cockpit cool in summer, and a downward-facing identity light below the cockpit floor, with a switch on the pilot's cockpit wall.

NF 869 became V-3 and in 1948 was briefly given civil marks PH-VNC for United Nations operations in Palestine, but it was not needed for that operation. In 1952, it went on to serve with KLM, where it had some more modifications incorporated, including a change to a 24 volt electrical system, re-painting of the instrument panel light grey and modification of the ignition switches to a rotary switch as on some continental aircraft. A non-standard artificial horizon and fuel gauge were fitted, and a grey electrical panel was installed on the left cockpit wall. The starting switches were also removed from the floor onto this panel, and the ground/flight switch was eliminated. The bulkhead between the rear cabin and the luggage bay was also removed at some stage, but this may have been done when the aircraft was in military service.

In 1954, its registration was changed to PH-OTA, to reflect its new service as a photo survey aircraft, which it continued until sale to Aero Ypenburg in 1962. It ended up, semi-derelict, in a children's' playground in Alphen a/d Rijn in 1966 but was rescued by the Dutch Military Museum , rebuilt and is now proudly on display, once again as 'V-3', in the KLu Museum at Soesterberg in southern Holland.

ROYAL NEW ZEALAND AIR FORCE
As part of the Empire Air Training Scheme which was initiated in 1939, New Zealand joined Australia and Canada to assist in training aircrew for Commonwealth air forces, well away from the dangerous skies of Britain. The main object of this scheme was to train pilots, observers, radio operators and gunners, and New Zealand used both impressed and new aircraft for the training task. In 1939, five Rapides were impressed into RNZAF service, nearly all from the Cook Strait Airways fleet, and they were flown to Rongotai, near Wellington, where de Havilland had been given the task of converting them for military operations. The RNZAF obviously believed the Rapides could be used as bombers, as the conversion consisted of fitting extra fuel tanks in the fuselage; bomb racks below the fuselage; providing the fittings for a bomb sight on the front starboard side of the fuselage, and repainting in RNZAF overall silver with small military markings as well as checking the overall condition of woodwork and fabric. The Rapides were given the RNZAF serials NZ555 to NZ559 and after

NZ557 c/n 6306 was impressed into the RNZAF in 1939, serving at Ohakea and Fiji. *[CND]*

The three RNZAF Dominies of the Fiji Flight at Nandi, 1940. *[D.Fox]*

the conversion work, they went off to Ohakea as observer and radio operator trainers at the Air Observer and Gunnery School. All five subsequently went to Fiji as transports for the New Zealand forces stationed there.

The weather and enemy actions took their toll on the aircraft and two were damaged beyond repair in a hurricane which hit Nausori airfield in 1941. Two others were used as RNZAF staff transports with No 42 Squadron at Nausori, but only one, NZ559, survived to return to civilian work as ZK-AGT. The next DH 89s for the RNZAF were nine new Dominies, from the batch HG648 to HG674, which were shipped out to Wellington between August and December 1943. They were given the RNZAF serials NZ523 to NZ531.

All of these Dominies later had a civilian life, five transferring to New Zealand National Airways in 1946, but three were kept in uniform until 1952 and 1953. NZ531 and NZ524 later emigrated to Australia, as VH-AAG and VH-BGP, and the latter Rapide spent nearly 30 years at Drage's Air World Museum, at Wangaratta, Victoria, before being repatriated in 2004 back to Colin Smith in New Zealand for return to airworthiness. There must have been something good in the New Zealand air from 1943, because, out of the batch of nine Dominies shipped to the RNZAF, five still survive today, - VH-BGP, ZK-AKS, ZK-AKY, VH-IAN (ex ZK-ALB), and ZK-AKU.

SOUTH AFRICAN AIR FORCE

Some use was made by the South African Air Force of the DH 89, with 14 aircraft being shipped out from Britain to provide platforms as part of the Commonwealth Air Training Plan. The first four were new machines shipped out in May/June 1941, to be followed by five more new aircraft in August 1942. Later another two were delivered from used stocks held at 18 MU Dumfries but a further three new ones were shipped out in 1944. There were also three Rapides impressed into SAAF service from civilian owners. Initially the Dominies were used as radio training aircraft for Wireless Operator/Air Gunners at No 64 Air School, Tempe, Bloemfontein, which began using the type from February 1941, but as in the RAF, the school soon found that the cabins were too cramped for the student wireless operators, so Ansons were used instead. Most Dominies were then handed over to other units as communications aircraft. Seven of the Dominies were taken over by the Flying Instructors' School at Tempe, and used for twin-engined instruction until 1945 and the twelve survivors were sold to civilian owners in 1946.

UNITED STATES ARMY AIR FORCE

Rather unusually for an aircraft manufacturing country like the USA, six Dominies are reported to have served with various elements of the United States forces in England during the Second World War. They

Officers boarding NZ531 c/n 6668 at Rongotai, January 1944. *[B Winley]*

C/n 6477 ZS-BCD of Owenair, Capetown, 1946, which had been impressed into the SAAF as 1414. *[D.Fox]*

were mainly used by elements of the 27th Air Transport Group, USAAC, which itself was formed from the Ferry and Transport Services in 1942, but some were used initially by other transport units. All were flown in US colours, but retained their RAF serial numbers. For example, Dominie X7522 was built as a Dominie I, initially serving with 24 Squadron in August 1942 for only four months, before transferring, alongside fellow Dominie X 7523, to the 8th Air Force Ferry and Transport Service in December 1942. It served as a personnel transport with that unit and its successor the 27th ATG until it was returned to the de Havilland CRU at Witney in May 1944. After some time in storage, it was sold in March 1948 to L E Gisborne of Denham, as G-AKTX. Shortly afterwards, it was delivered to Tel Aviv for the Israeli Air Force, where it became S-72 and later 1302.

The headquarters of the 27th ATG were at Heston, west of London, and the unit held a mixed bag of American and British aircraft, including several Dominies and some C-47s, mainly for rapid transport of urgent cargo and equipment for the American forces then spreading out in southern England. There were two flying units; the 86th and 87th Air Transport Squadrons, based at Hendon and Warton in Lancashire, both having detached units at Honington and Little Staughton in Cambridgeshire, and Burtonwood and Langford Lodge. As well as the straight carriage of freight, the units also ferried new and repaired aircraft from the repair depots to the front-line squadrons. Other units actually took over Dominies for personnel transport, such as the 482nd Bomb Group at Alconbury, which operated X7346 from May 1944 until it was damaged two months later. Another Dominie which gained publicity in several areas was X7454, much photographed as 'Wee Wullie' when in USAAF service, which it began with 27th ATG at Alconbury in April 1944 and No 5 Base Air Depot at Warton. By August 1944, X7454 had been returned to the RAF at 57 OTU and in June 1945 was delivered to Vickers Armstrongs at South Marston and Castle Bromwich, later becoming G-AHKB. It then went to Viv Bellamy for use by Hampshire Aeroplane Club at Southampton in 1959 to replace the DH 86 G-ACZP and in 1961 was exported to Rousseau Aviation at Dinard for operation by a parachuting club. The other USAAC Dominies were X7403 (which later became G-AKTY), V4724 (later G-AFNC and OO-CCD) and X7523 (later G-AIUK).

Following a post-war career in the UK, Ireland and France, N89DH c/n 6709, was painted by D Cotton of Tulsa to represent X7454 of the USAAF 27th Air Transport Group, Alconbury, April 1944. *[W.Henry]*

Possibly at Sandown, 1950, is Air Enterprise's G-ALWY c/n 6741, which was used for holiday flights. *[D.Fox]*

Section 4 – Chapter 9: Post-war British Civilian Operators

RESURGENCE OF COMMERCIAL OPERATIONS POST-WORLD WAR II

So many British companies and individuals bought Rapides after World War Two that it is not possible here to give details of them all. Instead, some of those with more interesting histories have been selected so that their stories can be told.

The eight airline companies providing services on behalf of the AAJC throughout the six years of the Second World War, plus the independent Allied Airways of Aberdeen and Olley Air Service (who flew only charter flights), had operated mainly, but not quite exclusively, Dragon Rapides. These companies had operated between them around thirty four Rapides, providing this service together with a handful of DH 84 Dragons and DH 86 Express Air Liners, and in 1945, a few Avro XIXs.

The war's end brought to these British airlines a release from the constraints of the AAJC, through a December 1945 government pronouncement that non-military flying would again be allowed over Britain. Unfortunately, there was only a brief period of commercial freedom, as the Socialist government made a second pronouncement at the same time. As soon as arrangements could be made, all the internal scheduled routes provided by the old AAJC companies would be taken over by a new, nationalised airline, to be called the British European Airways Corporation. The new Corporation officially began flying in October 1946, using not only the routes taken over from its predecessor companies, but also their aircraft, under charter to British European Airways until BEA was at last able to undertake its own operation, and took over the services from 1st February 1947. This major legislation forced all the existing airlines wishing to remain in business to turn to charter work.

Despite this legislative barrier, and no doubt spurred on by post-war optimism in Britain, a surprising number of airline companies decided to continue in the flying business, and many others sprang up, hoping to make a living from the charter industry. The natural aircraft for these companies to use, because of its simplicity, low operating costs, inexpensive purchase price, and of course, its familiarity and availability in post-war Britain, was that work-horse of the wartime communications flights, the Dominie. In the region of 327 of the type, consisting of both Dominies built for the RN and the RAF, and also the Rapides impressed into military service, were put up for sale by auction or tender between 1945 and 1952 at various RAF storage MUs - 5 MU Kemble, with its many outlying hangars, being the main venue.

De Havilland Witney Conversions

With the end of hostilities, many of the Dominies still being built under military contract at Brush Coachworks at Loughborough, but never used, as well as Rapides impressed for the duration, were stored at various RAF Maintenance Units but commonly 18 MU at Dumfries. Others had been formally taken on charge by the RAF at Witney, pending sale back to de Havillands, where they were converted to civilian standard by the de Havilland Repair Unit. Here the Dominies would have their camouflage schemes exchanged for specific company schemes; have any special military equipment such as radios, chart tables, and military seating removed, and have civilian seats and cabin trim fitted. When specified by new owners, baggage or toilet compartments would also be installed.

AIR ENTERPRISES LIMITED, CROYDON AND RENFREW

This company set up small charter operations at Croydon in 1947, starting with a Proctor, and later bought a total of eight Rapides and seven Airspeed Consuls. Charter business expanded rapidly from their Croydon base, and an additional base was set up at Glasgow's Renfrew Airport to cover charters from this Scottish airfield, then, in 1948, an unusual requirement was taken on by the company. The United Nations Commission in the Lebanon needed a fleet of communications aircraft, to help police their peace-monitoring task during the Palestinian dispute between Britain and Israel. Air Enterprises received an enquiry from the UN administrators through BOAC, to supply and manage the fleet. There was a complication however, as a requirement of the contract was that neither the aircraft nor the operators should belong to the countries involved in the dispute, as it was apparent that the presence of aircraft registered in one of those countries was liable to leave the UN force open to accusations of bias. Air Enterprises, in conjunction with Morton Air Services, also of Croydon, arranged with KLM to supply Dutch pilots and engineers, and together all three offered a fleet of five Rapides, for use by the Commission. The fascinating story of this UN operation is related later.

G-AJBJ c/n 6765 derelict at Blackpool, 1967, before removal to John Pierce at Chirk in 1978. [BAe]

Seen here in 1953, Airwork's G-AKTZ c/n 6482 had served the British Air Training Mission at Taif, Saudi Arabia, in 1949. [D.Fox]

AIR NAVIGATION AND TRADING, BLACKPOOL AND CARLISLE

This company, set up by the extrovert Whyham family from Blackpool, started freight services with one Rapide from Squires Gate airport, Blackpool, in 1948, then building up to four at one time. During their 19-year period of operations, they used a total of ten different Rapides. They also used a wide variety of other types, flying charter services from both Squires Gate at Blackpool and Kingstown at Carlisle, carrying hundreds of holiday-makers to the popular resorts on the Isle of Man. The company gained an Associate Agreement with BEA in 1951 for some Blackpool and Carlisle flights, and continued with these, and summer joy-rides from Blackpool, for the next eight years. The Rapide fleet decreased in the mid-sixties, as the emphasis of the company changed, until the last one was sold in 1967.

G-AJBJ was bought in July 1955 and used occasionally between then and 1961 for charter flights to the Isle of Man from Blackpool and later Carlisle. It was taken out of service and stored at Squires Gate until acquired in 1969 by a preservation society, before being bought in 1978 by John Peirce at Chirk and unofficially designated a Mark 7 to be fitted with Gipsy Queen 30 engines for a proposed but abandoned world flight. It remains stored at Chirk, pending long-term restoration to airworthy condition.

AIRWORK LIMITED, BLACKBUSHE, GATWICK AND PERTH

Airwork has been involved with British light aviation ever since its formation at Heston in 1928, and used Rapides for many of its British and overseas enterprises before, during and after the Second World War. Post-war, five Rapides were used for passenger and freight charter work out of Blackbushe and later, Gatwick, but three were used for contract work with Airwork Services Training at Perth in Scotland. Contract work for several oil companies in Iran and Iraq was also continued, as it had been before the war, and an interesting aircrew training contract was taken on at Taif, Saudi Arabia in 1949, using Rapide G-AKTZ alongside other training aircraft. Eventually most Rapides were replaced by aircraft such as Airwork's own Doves, Bristol Freighters and Vikings and their last Rapide was sold in 1962.

ALLIED AIRWAYS, ABERDEEN

That stalwart of Scottish airlines services, Eric Gandar Dower, had continued his operations throughout the Second World War from Dyce airport, Aberdeen, and he also continued after the war, using basically the same Rapide fleet he had used since pre-war days. Two Rapides had been sold before the outbreak of war, and one, G-ACZE, was written-off in an accident on Orkney in 1945, but the remaining four continued post-war, augmented in 1946 by another, G-AIDL, which aircraft is still in grand flying form in the twenty first century, now based at Duxford in Cambridgeshire. The Allied Airways Rapides carried passengers and freight from Aberdeen to the Shetland Islands and down to Edinburgh, connecting there with London services, as well as flying some charter work. The take-over by the government-owned British European Airways Corporation put paid to Gandar Dower's enterprise in 1947, and his company was eventually forced to cease operations. The last three Rapides, G-ADAH, G-AIDL and G-AJGS, were then put into long-term store. G-AIDL was seized for non-payment of a debt at Witney in 1950 and auctioned off by the High Sheriff of Oxfordshire to Goodhew Aviation at local Kidlington; the others remained locked away at Dyce Airport until 1966 and have, accordingly, also survived.

Atlantic Journey - G-AJGS

A survivor of the Scottish pre-war services continued its somewhat intermittent career in more recent times. After the demise of the Allied Airways business, G-AJGS was put into storage at Dyce airport in 1949, with only 47 hours flying time in its log book, and kept there for the next 17 years. Then in 1966, Mr A F Ward bought the neglected aircraft, and had it transferred to Doug Bianchi's

G-AIDL "The Wanderer" c/n 6968 awaiting collectioin by Allied Airways from DH Repair Depot, Witney, 1946. [BAe]

G-AJGS c/n W1001 with Aerial Enterprises, in 1968. [D.Fox]

C/n 6792 G-AHKV when used by the Automobile Association, parked on a wet dispersal in 1957. [M. Stroud]

G-AGSH c/n 6884 back in BEA colours, viewed over the South Downs, flown by Philip Meeson, 1980s. [G Bain]

Personal Plane Services at Booker in Buckinghamshire, for refurbishment. G-AJGS flew again in February 1968 and was briefly used as a skydiving transport. The following year, an American enthusiast from Florida, Fritz Ludington, bought the Rapide and arranged to have an intrepid pair of British pilots fly it across to his home base at Miami.

Bill Downes, a commercial pilot from Kegworth, agreed to fly the old girl, with navigational help from another pilot, Ted Wein, starting from their own base at East Midlands airport in August 1970. They using the well-worn Atlantic route Glasgow-Kulusuq-Narssarssuaq-Goose Bay, and then on down to Burlington and Miami. The route would take around two weeks and cover about 70 hours of flying, forty of them over water. The only extra equipment was a long-range fuel tank, which would be needed for the legs from the Faeroes to Iceland and from Greenland to Labrador. The pilots set off on 28th August, taking care to fly only when they could remain clear of cloud, as they had no de-icing equipment. This forced several waits at intermediate stops but eventually, after 77 hours and 44 minutes' flying, they arrived safely at Miami on 13th September 1970, to hand over the aircraft to its new owner. The Rapide was not given a US registration, and was flown very little, being sold on to another American owner before being returned by sea in 1984 for Brian Woodford, a British collector, who was setting up a delightful collection of de Havilland aircraft in Dorset.

On refurbishment by Ron Souch in Britain, the CAA was persuaded to allow the Rapide to re-use the registration G-ACZE, which damaged aircraft had donated some parts to DH Witney's build of G-AJGS in 1947. The aircraft spent some nine years flying around Britain in 'Prince of Wales' colours, but since 1995 has been stored without a C of A, latterly at Haverfordwest in Wales.

AUTOMOBILE ASSOCIATION

One Rapide which gained a fair amount of newspaper and radio publicity was the distinctive yellow and black- painted G-AHKV, bought in 1957 by the Automobile Association. G-AHKV had had an interesting career up to that date, having served the RAF as NR693, then the AAJC at Liverpool, before becoming part of the BEA fleet in 1947. After being sold by BEA in 1953, it was operated by Sky Neon Aviation Company of Croydon, which company fitted a framework of neon tubes below the lower wings in 1954, and flew over much of London at 1,000 feet, at night, displaying various advertisements. The sight of moving lights spelling:

'DRINK ….OVALTINE'

droning over the West End cannot have been commercially lucrative for the owners, as the aircraft was sold on again after only one season of airborne advertising.

The AA had previously used an Auster Alpine G-APAA for traffic reporting, but this had neither the seating capacity nor the range to cope with the task of reporting on traffic conditions for the Association' s members, so in November 1957, G-AHKV was bought. With the neon tubes removed, but with a new Bendix radio compass fitted, the Association used the Rapide out of Fairoaks, south of London, for reporting on road traffic conditions around the Home Counties. Over the six years of its ownership, the Association flew 2,000 sorties and 1,750 hours with the Rapide, until its place was taken by a Piper Apache in 1963.

BRITISH EUROPEAN AIRWAYS, HEATHROW

The Socialist government running Britain in 1946 believed that airlines in Britain should be nationalised, so they set about producing legislation which was to create, on 1st February 1947, a new national airline for internal and continental services, using the current fleets and staff of many of the post-war private airlines. By 1946, the independent airlines, consisting of Allied Airways, Channel Island Airways, Great Western and Southern Airlines, Isle of Man Air Services, Railway Air Services and Scottish Airways were all operating their own services on behalf of BEA, prior to take-over. Finally, amid considerable sadness and some anger, at the beginning of February 1947, all those airlines were completely absorbed into BEA. Among the aircraft compulsorily purchased were no less than 48 Dragon Rapides together with 13 Avro 19s, 2 DC 3s, a DH 84 and 10 Junkers 52/3ms. The Rapides were used by the Scottish Division for services to the Western Isles, and to the Orkneys and Shetlands from Glasgow, Inverness and Aberdeen. The English Division used some Rapides from Liverpool and Manchester to the Isle of Man, and from Southampton on the Channel Islands and Isles of Scilly routes.

G-AHXW c/n 6782 operated by BEA, at St Mary's, Scillies, in August 1950, in the early BEA colour scheme. *[M. Stroud]*

By the end of 1948, 3 had been written-off in accidents and 19 had been sold, so the Rapide fleet had been depleted by half. Two years later, BEA appropriately re-classed the survivors as 'Islanders', painting them in a neat silver scheme with red cheat lines, small airline titles below the cabin windows and a BEA badge on the fin. By now, the new corporation was modernising its national fleet, and Vikings, Dakotas and Ambassadors quickly took over from the Rapides, so that by 1956, only three remained in the fleet. For the next seven years, three pilots solely served the Scillies route with the Islanders, producing a remarkable regularity of 88%, with each aircraft averaging around 90 hours per month in 1959 alone. The last BEA Islander service was flown from the Scillies to Land's End in May 1964, and they were then sold off.

Rapide G-AHXW

One Rapide taken over by BEA in 1946 was G-AHXW, which had been built at Loughborough as NR683 in July 1944. It was completed as a Dominie Mk 1 and delivered to No.5 Maintenance Unit, Kemble, for storage, in the same month, where it remained until early 1946, as there was no further requirement for Dominie trainers at the Radio Schools. In March 1946, de Havilland flew the Dominie the few miles from Kemble to Witney, for conversion to civilian standard, as the Air Ministry had declared it surplus to RAF requirements. The Ministry of Supply then took charge of it, issuing it to the AAJC aircraft pool in August 1946, for their use on the nationalised air routes with a new CofA issued on 16th August 1946.

G-AHXW later became one of the Islander Class with BEA, being named '*RMA John Nicholson*', flying from Croydon on the old Railway Air Services routes to Manchester and Belfast. It then became part of BEA's DH 89 cull in 1952, as its CofA expired in January 1953, and it was sold off in April of that year. Overhauled as a Mark 4 in October 1954 with Queen II engines and constant speed propellers, as well as being given bubble-type front cabin windows and a radio-compass dome on the cabin roof, it was delivered to the Fairey Aviation Company as an air survey and communications aircraft. Based at White Waltham, it was then flown by Fairey Aviation pilots including the well-known wartime ATA pilot, Lettice Curtis.

G-AHXW was sold again in 1968, changing hands several times before being bought by Californian enthusiasts JR O'Brien and R Puryear in 1971. A BOAC pilot, Peter Benest, flew the aircraft, in July 1971, from Booker to Rotterdam, where it was crated and shipped to USA. Here it adopted the marks N683DH and was painted up in late BEA colours but now named '*Sir Robert Puryear*', and was used for several years before being donated to the EAA Museum at Oshkosh in 1975, where it was on display until 1998. It was sold again in that year to a pair of US commercial pilots, John Reed and Bud Field, who transferred it to San Andreas, California, where it is undergoing another long-term rebuild programme.

N683DH, ex G-AHXW, back in late BEA colours, at Oshkosh, USA, about 1980. *[DHMC]*

C/n 6835 G-AJHO taxying out for a parachute drop at Sywell in July 1963, when in Rothmans colours. *[M. Stroud]*

BRITISH WESTPOINT AIRLINES, EXETER

A late-comer to the post-war British commercial aviation scene was British Westpoint Airlines, which began operations from Exeter with Dakotas in 1961. In 1964, the airline bought out Mayflower Air Services and began flying a network of Scilly Isles routes with the two ex-Mayflower Rapides plus three others bought for services around the south-west of England. Financial problems hit the company by 1965, and all its operations ceased in early 1966, the Rapides being sold on in late 1965 and early 1966.

BROOKLANDS AVIATION LIMITED, SYWELL AND SHOREHAM

The name of this company rightly suggests its origins, as it was set up originally in 1928, as a Flying School at the famous airfield. In 1933, it had taken over the management of the club at Sywell, near Northampton, and two years later did the same thing at Shoreham. They then retained a presence at both fields throughout the war and post-war, started flying operations again at both locations. Part of the new company activity at Sywell had been to overhaul ex-military Rapides and Proctors, so it was a natural progression to take over some of these newly-overhauled aircraft themselves, and operate them for charter work. This began in 1947, and, with the help of four Rapides, they also undertook navigation training and air taxi operations from Shoreham. The following year, Brooklands obtained an Associate Agreement from the national airline, BEA, to operate from Shoreham to Southampton and the Isle of Wight. The service expanded in 1949 and 1950 to cover the Channel Islands, but by then the business, as discovered by so many of the entrepreneurial small airlines, had become impractical, forcing the termination of the services at the end of the 1950 season. Three of the aircraft were sold on, thereby ending another pioneering scheduled air service by the seemingly limitless Rapides.

Loss of G-AJHO

One of the Brooklands Rapides retained in 1952 after their brave foray into the airline market, retreating back from Shoreham to their flying training school at Sywell, was G-AJHO. The flying training was carried out by Brooklands Aviation's Tiger Moths wearing the very striking pre-war red, black and silver colours, and G-AJHO was also painted in this same scheme. With crimson upper fuselage and engine cowlings, black lower fuselage and cowlings, nicely balanced by the silver wings and empennage, this scheme seemed to suit the aircraft's shape particularly well, and was admired wherever it appeared. In these colours this long-serving aircraft continued to work for the company on charters and communications work for the next ten years.

Into the nineteen sixties, however, large pre-war biplanes were becoming less attractive for charter work than the new light American twins, which were more modern and practical and the

G-AJHO c/n 6835 back in Brooklands Aviation colours at Netheravon, March 1988, prior to its demise the following year. *[CND]*

G-AJHO and XS735 – Dominies from different eras over the North Sea in 1971. Each has been flown by the author. *[BAe]*

Rapide was put up for sale in 1963, having been replaced by a Piper Apache. A certain Major John Weeks, Secretary of the Army Free-Fall Parachute Association, handed over something in the region of £2,000 to the nice man at Brooklands, and she moved to the delightful rolling grass acres of Netheravon, in Wiltshire, the first Rapide to be owned by the British Army for sport parachuting. After twelve years of strenuous work for the Army parachutists, both in Britain and in Germany, she was damaged in a landing accident at Netheravon. Shortly after, she was sold to the East Anglian Aviation Society, who embarked on a long-term refurbishment programme, a process which was completed at Croydon Farm, Cambridgeshire, when with special permission from the CAA, she was reflown on 20th May 1987 in the colours of the Prince of Wales' G-ADDD. A year later, she was bought by Victor Gauntlett's Proteus Petroleum, and interestingly, returned to Netheravon, where this time she was used for private and Proteus corporate activities.

On a cold, sunny 5th February 1989, one of the earlier pilots from her parachuting days, Charlie Shea-Simonds, himself an active sport parachutist, was due to fly her on the second leg of a round-robin trip to Oxford, Shoreham and Rush Green, where she was to have some final small jobs completed for the coming summer's work. Now shining and resplendent in the old red, black and silver she wore in her Brooklands days, she looked as good as new, proudly perched on the edge of the open acres of her Netheravon base, reflecting the morning sun off her bright red cowlings.

As one of the few remaining Dominie IIs, this Rapide still had the original radio operator's compartment and thwart-ships seat installed immediately behind the pilot's seat, so Charlie sat on this 'tip-up' seat for the sunny hop over to Oxford, where he swapped seats, climbing up into the pilot's seat, while the other pilot went to collect the second aircraft for the ferry to Shoreham. After a few minutes' wait with the Queen IIIs happily ticking over, the availability of the other aircraft was confirmed, so Charlie opened up to taxi across to the East side of Oxford's grass for his departure to Shoreham.

" I reached the holding point, turned into wind and carried out both power and pre-take-off checks - again everything OK. I had to hold for a couple of minutes to allow two Cherokees to land and I remember idly pulling the shoulder straps a little tighter. Having received a take-off clearance, I lined up and rolled on Oxford's tarmac 'two-zero' at 1104 hrs - full power and oil pressure OK on both. She lifted gracefully into the air and once through 500 feet, I turned on track for Shoreham. I relaxed somewhat knowing that the excellent viz. was going to make the map reading easy and, on reaching 1500 feet, I lowered the nose and eased the throttles back to give a 2,000 rpm cruise setting.

"I was just in the process of synchronising the propellers when, without warning, I witnessed the revs die away on the starboard rev counter. 'HO yawed to the right and I applied left rudder to hold her straight. Without further thought I started a left turn towards the airfield and informed air traffic that I'd had an engine failure and was returning to the field. I don't remember the acknowledgement because that was the moment I glanced out to the right to see a large part of the starboard wing outboard of the engine well and truly on fire. I just had time to tell Oxford Air Traffic of the fire when there was a crack - the aeroplane lurched - the starboard lower mainplane moved perceptibly upwards and the upper mainplane bowed alarmingly upwards in the middle. (The fire had probably burnt sufficiently through the rear spar of the lower mainplane to cause the re-alignment of the starboard wings.)

"Oxford cleared me for an emergency landing but I replied that I was putting the aircraft down in a field as I didn't think the starboard wings were going to last much longer. I pointed 'HO downhill at my chosen field, mentally willing the wings to stick with it a little longer. Then the ASI went out - the pitot head on the Rapide is on the starboard inter-plane strut and the tubes had obviously burnt through. The field was certainly long enough - it needed to be as I was going downwind, albeit with only a five knot surface wind, but, as it was close to a river and was a wheat field with the crop about 2-3 inches high, it was obviously very wet. The wheels touched, she skipped into the air for a few yards and then settled on. I hauled back on the control column and with my left hand, pumped the brake lever. She slowed rapidly in the soft soil before, at I guess about 15-20 knots, the wheels dug themselves deep enough for the momentum to turn her over onto her back.

"The shoulder straps held and prevented any injury and I remember fumbling clumsily in my haste to undo the quick release catch. I thought initially of getting out through the windscreen, but this had remained intact so, with the intensity of the fire causing a high degree of panic, I crawled down the fuselage (with the seats above me) to exit through the door. By now I was disorientated and went for where the door would normally be - but, of course, it wasn't there - it was on the other side as the aeroplane was inverted! Mercifully the door opened OK and I stumbled out, moving about 50 yards away before I dared look back. When I did the majority of the fuselage was burning fiercely. Above, a Cherokee who had taken off behind me was circling overhead so I waved vigorously in order that he could see that I was OK. We all watched helplessly as the Old Lady burnt completely out in only a few minutes and before the local fire brigade (who had actually reacted and arrived very quickly) could do anything about it. Timings from the Air Traffic log revealed that the whole flight had taken just over four and a half minutes."

The Accident investigators apportioned no blame to pilot, operator or engineers but, more importantly, indicated that the cause of the fire was the failure of the number four cylinder head gasket, which had allowed the release of hot cylinder gases onto the fuel delivery pipe, which was then made of rubber with internal steel braid. The hot gas burned through the pipe, eventually creating a hole three-eighths of an inch wide, and thereby allowing fuel to escape under pressure, and cause an intense fire which was sufficiently hot to melt the steel braid on the hose, and even the steel cylinder fins. This burning fuel was then rapidly forced back down the engine cowling onto the lower wooden wing, causing a very rapid spread of the fire to the whole of the wing, and giving virtually no chance of it being extinguished.

Out of this very sad accident, from which Charlie Shea-Simonds was incredibly lucky to escape completely unhurt despite the complete destruction of the aircraft, came an important change for all existing Rapides, which the British airworthiness authorities introduced as a mandatory modification in 1989. The remedy, to be applied to all Gipsy Queen and Gipsy Major engines, involves replacing all existing fuel lines with fire resistant pipes, and the re-routing of fuel pipes. Hopefully, this modification will now prevent any further recurrences of the disastrous type of fire which destroyed G-AJHO.

Monique Agazarian at the controls of c/n 6517 G-AGJG on a flight from Heathrow, September 1955. *[D.Fox]*

ISLAND AIR SERVICES

Typical of the entrepreneurial spirit of post-war aircraft operating companies is the story of Island Air Services. Monique Agazarian, an attractive, business-like young lady, retired from the Air Transport Auxiliary after the war, and in keeping with many other pilots, male and female, could not get flying fever out of her system. Miss Agazarian had started the War as a Nursing Officer in the Princess Mary's Royal Air Force Nursing Service. When she heard that the Air Transport Auxiliary was recruiting for pilots of both sexes, she applied to join and was accepted in time to complete her training by June 1944. The ATA effort was by now running down, but as she was now bitten by the flying bug, Miss Agazarian decided to obtain a commercial pilot's licence so that she could continue flying after the war ended. In 1946 she managed to find a pilot vacancy with a small business called Island Air Services just starting up on the Isles of Scilly, flying boxes of flowers to the mainland in single-engined Proctors.

The business flourished, and soon expanded into charter work, centred on Croydon, and a Dragon Rapide, G-AGUF, was taken on strength in July 1948 to cope with the increased traffic. It seems that many of the passengers were jockeys who needed to have rapid transport to British race meetings, business men travelling to the continent, and some holiday-makers to European destinations as far away as Italy. The flower loads were still carried on during the summer, and a good deal of the other traffic was to the Channel Islands, which were starting to become popular with the British holiday-makers.

Monique became Chairman and Chief Pilot of the company, now incorporated as IAS (London) Limited, and took on other pilots, and two more Rapides, G-AGJG, in July 1953 and G-AFFB in April 1954. Wing Commander Ray Rendall, one of the new pilots, later became not only Chief Pilot but also the husband of the Chairman.

Press reporters, newspaper deliveries and race meeting passengers kept the company busy, but they also had the idea of operating pleasure flights from the new London airport at Heathrow, which was accepted by the Licensing Authority in 1948. This introduction to flight became immensely popular, and for a mere one pound, thousands of passengers took their first ever flight with Miss Agazarian or one of her pilots during the next eight years. Proof of the interest created by these fifteen-minute hops is given by the large number of observers of an airworthy Rapide in the 1990s who pass comments such as " Oh yes, I remember the Rapide - it was the first aircraft I ever flew in, from Heathrow, in about 1955".

In 1950, IAS started scheduled services to Deauville from Shoreham, in association with BEA, which sounds a reasonably ordinary progression in a small airline company's business, but the method of obtaining this concession is typical of the style of post-war Rapide operators. Believing that there could be a market for a route from southern England to the French resort at Deauville, Miss Agazarian flew one of her Rapides over to St Gatien airfield, and visited all the casinos in Deauville to sound them out for weekend gambling potential.The service began in July 1950, followed by similar services to La Baule and Le Touquet and operated for a season but sadly Captain Agazarian had miscalculated the desire of the post-war public to lose their money in France, and the uneconomic schedule was soon abandoned.

In the meantime, the enthusiasm of Britons to sample short joy-riding at Heathrow continued to grow. The summer months kept IAS's Rapides busy every day, often operating as many as 100 flights in a day, equating to over 800 passengers, making the pleasure flights a lucrative business. By 1956, however, Heathrow and 1930s biplanes were becoming less compatible, and with very little notice, the airport authority banned pleasure flights from Heathrow. Island Air Services thereby lost their main source of income and were forced to move elsewhere. The next season was worked from a new base at Ramsgate, Kent, but unfortunately there were insufficient joy-riders. Undoubtedly the crash of G-AGUF, on take-off from Ramsgate on 29 June 1957, also had a negative effect on the company fortunes. By the end of the next year the company had sold its remaining fleet and ended another example of aviation initiative, with the DH 89 at its centre. One of the mainstays of 'Aggie's Airline', as it was jokingly called, G-AGJG, recently completed a long-term re-build to a superb standard by David and Mark Miller, at the Imperial War Museum, Duxford, Cambridgeshire.

Rebuild of G-AGJG

The most impressive Rapide restoration in recent years is that of the immaculate G-AGJG, which flew again on 16 June 2004 at Duxford, Cambridgeshire, after a rather protracted restoration by father and son David and Mark Miller. As a schoolboy in the late 1970s, Mark Miller remembers his father negotiating to buy a very run-down Rapide with the intention of rebuilding it to flying condition. Twenty five years later, a rather more mature Mark brilliant Aegean-like sea over the top of the pointed instrument panel, he could distinguish another jewelled setting, larger this time, and more distinct. Beyond the small jewels of the outer islets, a larger stone began to form itself into the main island, with the slight Telegraph Hill to the north, and the inverted grass saucer of St Mary's airfield, perched on the southern edge of the island, with its three runways starting uphill and finishing downhill. As the weather on this morning was so clear and beautiful, he gently reduced power, descended down to five hundred feet, and flew a left-hand orbit of the island, partially for the benefit of his current passengers, partially for community relations with the Islanders, but mainly for his own enjoyment, on such a delightful summer day.

Turning gently then towards the north-westerly runway threshold, just inland from the southerly cliff top, the visual aspect of the sloping runway changed. The far end of the 1,800-foot strip disappeared disconcertingly and Captain Chalmers could only see the upward-sloping section of the available runway. He had to remind himself of his own ruling that he had to be down to walking speed by two thirds of the length of the short runway, where the uphill slope became a downhill one, or he would have to overshoot, and try again. He deliberately approached low, with plenty of power on the Queens, and at a reasonable 80 mph, ready to put on more power to cope with any turbulence off the craggy cliffs, and anticipating the confusing visual effect of the upward-sloping runway. Finally, throttling fully back, and placing the main wheels firmly onto the first few feet of the grass, he could feel the unusual retardation as he rolled uphill to the centre of the field. As with every landing at St Mary's, this was an entertaining one, and he could not afford to relax until he felt the speed down below his stipulated walking pace as he topped the ridge, then turned off left towards the tiny terminal.

Once again, 'A-hag' had served him well, and Captain Chalmers was soon filling up with fuel for the return trip, and looking forward to another sector of this extremely pleasant way of earning a living.

It was not long after this trip that 'A-hag' came to the end of her airline career, for in 1968 the airline went into liquidation, and she was sold. A few eventful years as a charter and parachute aircraft followed, with Monty de Cartier operating her out of Compton Abbas. Another period of storage followed, after which she was bought in 1980, in a rather dilapidated state by Ralph Jones, who took her to his Southern Sailplanes facility at Membury, in Wiltshire, for long-term restoration, and where she still remains.

Sadly, by 1968, problems with replacement aircraft were causing Scillonia Airways considerable operating delays, and without serviceable aircraft or revenue, the company was forced to close down in late 1968, and the Rapides sold off, the last two airworthy machines fetching the derisory prices of £125 and £250. This closure really marked the end of scheduled services with Rapides in Britain.

SCOTTISH AIRWAYS, RENFREW

The second largest fleet of Rapides after World War Two belonged to Scottish Airways, based at Renfrew airport, Glasgow. The company had been formed before the war with the amalgamation of Eric Fresson's Highland Airways and Northern and Scottish Airways and had continued operations as a member of the AAJC during the War, to begin commercial services again in April 1945, using ten Rapides. Very soon another six Rapides were purchased and services began to expand again, with daily services from Renfrew to Inverness and from Inverness on a two-hour daily service direct to Sumburgh on Shetland. Flights from Inverness to the Western Isles also began again, and flights from Glasgow expanded to Campbeltown, Tiree and Benbecula, as well as to Belfast and London, in conjunction with Railway Air Services. By the middle of 1946, there were fifteen Rapides in service with the airline, which had up to that point flown for nearly ten years with a surprisingly high 83% load factor, and a good safety factor. However, in September 1946 that was about to change.

Approach Problems, Glasgow, 1946

On 27th September 1946, ten days after joining Scottish Airways at Renfrew, Captain F Stephens, a 27 year-old pilot who had a total of about 1,100 hours during the war, and with commercial airlines, took Rapide G-AFFF to the island of Islay, just off the Scottish west coast, then set off back to Renfrew with his radio officer, AM Calvert, and five passengers. Renfrew was reporting typical Glasgow frontal weather which was poor but not unworkable, with a main cloudbase of 1,200 feet, some cloud at 1,000 feet, and a visibility of two miles in intermittent drizzle. Captain Stephens decided to fly above the cloud at 7,000 feet en route to Glasgow, and therefore needed to use bearings from the airfield direction-finding equipment for guidance. Using the bearings from Renfrew, G-AFFF approached the airfield from about 12 miles east, and then passed overhead the D/F beacon at 1310 hours, without having sight of the airfield. He then turned south and tried an approach from the south-east, this time descending to about 1,500 feet, but again not seeing the airfield as he passed overhead at 1320. G-AFFF then headed out to the north-west of the airfield towards high ground, and soon afterwards another Scottish Airways Rapide, G-ADAJ, called for bearings and its radio operator, without the authority of his captain, declared that his aircraft was running out of petrol. G-AFFF was therefore told by the D/F operator to wait while the other Rapide was given homings to the airfield and the call was acknowledged by R/O Calvert. Bearings were then given to G-ADAJ for its approach as a matter of priority, and that aircraft was descended to pass over the airfield at 1329, subsequently landing from a visual circuit five minutes later. The fuel state of G-ADAJ on landing was apparently sufficient for another hour's flight. The D/F operator then called G-AFFF repeatedly, but received no answer. No further contact was made and it was later reported by a farmer at Milngavie that it had crashed at about 900 feet above sea level on the side of the 1,150-foot Craigton Hill, about seven miles north of Renfrew, with the death of all seven on board.

The subsequent report from the Accident Investigation Branch of the MCA considered that, as the tracks of the two aircraft listening to the D/F bearings for G-ADAJ were remarkably similar, Captain Stephens probably mistook the bearings being given to the other aircraft for bearings being passed to him, despite his being told to wait, and despite the fact that he was then some way north of the airfield. That would seem the most likely reason for Captain Stephens taking the route which led him into Craigton Hill. The inexperience of the Captain and the radio officer was also considered to have been a contributory cause, as was the message from G-ADAJ's radio officer, indicating that his aircraft was short of fuel.

SPORT PARACHUTE AND DISPLAY FLYING

During the 1960s and 70s, the Rapide was used as a platform for parachute work, mainly by military teams, but also by some civilian teams based in the Midlands. The Rothmans cigarette company sponsored several teams, not only in the UK, but also in Norway, Germany and New Zealand, and several Rapides were painted in Rothmans' distinctive dark blue and white colour scheme during this period. The Rapide was popular with skydivers because it was not expensive to operate, could carry up to eight jumpers and could operate out of fairly small fields. A well-known 'Barnstormer' pilot, Barry Tempest, was one of the pilots who flew Rapides for both military and civilian parachute teams, as well as flying the aircraft in flying displays.

Parachute and Display Work, G-AKNN

One of Barry's favourite para-platforms was a Midlands-based aircraft, G-AKNN, owned by Bill Tomkins, a Northamptonshire farmer. The charge for hiring Mr Tomkins' toy for parachute work on those occasions was the "princely sum of £6.00 per hour, dry" which parachutists considered excellent value. Barry remembers one drop he undertook for a film company as part of an advertising campaign. An army free-fall team had been engaged to drop from 14,000 feet onto the army airfield at Waterbeach near Cambridge in

'The Brown Bomber', G-AKNN c/n 6598, making a flypast at Denham. *[D.Fox]*

1967, but the weather on the day was not exactly ideal. Barry managed to get 'NN up to the right height, but had great difficulty avoiding the towering cumulo nimbus clouds which were gathering right over the dropping point. Along with the cloud, the surface wind had also increased from light to about 25 knots - right on the limit for safe landings. However, the jumpers managed to drop clear of cloud, only to be swept off by the strong winds and distributed over many parts of the surrounding area. By the time Barry had landed, reports were coming in from all over the Waterbeach camp of parachutists being picked from tiny tennis courts to precarious flat-topped barrack-block roofs. There was no mention by the film company of any photographs.

Mr Tempest, being an old hand at display flying, sometimes used 'NN for solo performances, often having dropped a parachute team earlier in the day. In August 1965, for a Barnstormers Air Display at Podington, he flew a flour bombing routine which he still remembers with consternation. During the display, Barry was due to make 'flour bomb attacks' on a minivan driving up and down the centre of the display runway. A parachute instructor colleague, Tony Unwin, strapped a static line round his waist and then to a seat mounting inside the Rapide, and gathered a stock of two pound flour bags near the open cabin door, ready to make hand deliveries onto the target. Barry felt that the eager crowd would be impressed if he could fly fairly close to his target, so he descended low enough for Tony to lean completely outside the cabin door, balancing his heels on the door sill, then lobbing his flour bombs with amazing accuracy onto and even into the minivan. On one run, coming up from behind, the occupants of the van had left the rear doors open, and Tony's bomb flew through the rear of the van , bounced on the floor and smashed the rear-view mirror, as the Rapide's wheels shot past on either side of the van. Barry was right in thinking the crowd was impressed, but he remembers that the van driver was very pale and still shaking during the debrief. He also declined to drive for the repeat routine on the following day.

G-AKNN was usually known as 'The Brown Bomber' after this performance, not entirely because of its rather drab light-brown colour scheme.

Several other parachute teams used Rapides over the next ten years, including the Parachute Regiment's Red Devils and considerable numbers of French parachute centres, both in France and Algeria. One difficulty became apparent after the Rapides had been used for several years. As with all aircraft used for parachute work, the long full-power climbs, followed almost immediately by rapid descents with the engines throttled back to idle rpm, caused thermal stresses on the engines which began to cause problems. The Parachute centre engineers had to keep careful watch on the exhaust manifolds and gaskets, as well as all the spark plugs because of an increased tendency to 'oil up'. When turbine-engined parachute aircraft became more accessible in the mid-nineteen seventies, the Rapides were getting quite tired, so most centres sold them on, to be replaced by more modern machines.

Engine Problems, G-AGTM

An example of the problems handled by parachute-dropping Rapide pilots came for Barry Tempest when he took off from Sibson, near Peterborough with a load of parachutists in G-AGTM.

This aircraft had spent nearly twenty years in the Middle East before returning to England in 1964. The Army Parachute Association took it to its centre at Netheravon and later leased it to the Peterborough Parachute Centre, where Barry often used it for parachute work.

With six student parachutists and an experienced jumpmaster on board, he took off into a hot July sky, aiming for a drop over the airfield from 5,000 feet. Passing 1,200 feet in the climb, the port engine suddenly began to vibrate alarmingly, to the extent that Barry found it difficult to read his instruments. There was obviously a major problem with that engine, so he throttled it back to idle, began a turn back towards the drop zone, and gently let the speed decrease to a safe single-engine speed, while trying to maintain some height. He shouted back to the jumpmaster that he could only make one run at about 800 feet over the drop zone, and would everyone 'please vacate!' Barry managed to run over the drop zone at around 800 feet, and he was immensely relieved to see the jumpers all leave safely. He then tried to circle back with his unhappy aeroplane to make a landing on the 700-metre strip. As he turned back he switched off the port magneto switches, but the errant engine still continued to windmill,

OD-ABP at Beirut, 1953, with Arab Contracting and Trading Co, before returning to UK for parachute duties, as G-AGTM. *[CND]*

C/n 6746 G-AGTM in its current Air Atlantique blue colour scheme at Brooklands, July 2000. *[M. Stroud]*

although the vibration was less severe. As he turned onto a close final approach at around 100 feet, he was then horrified to see three of his recently-departed parachutists landing across the centre of the grass runway, which had standing crops close in on both sides, and tall trees at the far end. He had little option but to attempt an overshoot, as continuing would have meant a collision with the parachutists.

With great trepidation, knowing the Rapide's single-engine performance, he quickly moved the starboard throttle up to full power, eased the poor old girl into a climbing attitude and allowed the speed to decrease to his single engine safety speed. Almost unbelievably, the aircraft began to climb away, no doubt helped by the decreased weight since the recent departure of his passengers. Completing another circuit at a much lower height than normal, he made an easy landing with a feeling of what he later called 'a total anticlimax'. The student parachutists kept his glass full that evening.

The rocker gear on one cylinder had broken off and sheared its attachment bolts on G-AGTM's engine, but she was soon repaired and went on to continue a long life with several English owners, until being re-furbished by Ben Borsberry and Dave Evans for Dave Geddes between 1994 and 1996, and is now to be seen regularly flying with the Air Atlantique collection at Coventry airport.

SOUTHERN JOYRIDES LIMITED, BIGGIN HILL

Mike Warner of the Alouette Aero Club, gave a passenger's view of a typical Rapide joy-ride in autumn 1977 at Biggin Hill:

"It was the day we queued up for a whiff of the past, the day of a joy-ride into the pioneer days of grass-roots flying, with wind in the wires and, on this occasion, a touch of elegance.

"We had, of course, been oggling the Rapide since it arrived. One or two of us had even poked our noses into it, smelled the fabric, itched for a go at the controls. It was only a matter of time before we dug into our jeans for the grubby £1 notes which would buy our souvenir tickets-to-ride in a flying legend. A Saturday it was, appropriately warm and sunny for an aristocratic turn about the skies.

"Tony was doing a splendid passenger-recruiting job on anyone who walked through the Alouette Flying Club door. Fancy a ride in the Rapide? We needed eight....

"We needed eight because Tony had done a deal with the pilot: fill the plane and - to you- not £4, but £3.50 a head. Summer sale time at Biggin Hill! A snip of a sortie! And not just a circuit, either, but a spot of local - Edenbridge and return. Roll up, Roll up....

"We were cleared to runway 03 and we were off. Now this really was flying. This, surely, was what it was all about. This, definitely, was the life.

"You feel a bit of a toff in a gentleman's airborne carriage. It's the sort of feeling that no high-flying, jet-propelled cigar tube can duplicate. Did the well-heeled passengers of old tap the pilot on the shoulder and say: 'Home, James'.

"It was home too soon and money well spent. G-AIDL, one of the few Rapides in the land licensed to carry passengers - is a refreshing addition to the Biggin scene. We must wish the operator well. "

In the years after the Second World War, a small industry was created by demobilised war-time pilots who felt the urge to remain flying, but had no will, inclination or capital to create a large company, as this would inevitably involve the sort of complex regulatory restrictions they had left behind in the Royal Air Force. A surprising number of individuals, attempting to indulge their passion for aviating, set up small joy-riding companies quite cheaply using converted Dominies, themselves recently retired from R A F service.

One of the companies coming late into joy-riding with a Rapide was Southern Joyrides Limited, run with a certain quiet style and gentlemanly charm from 1977 by Captain Mike Hood, DFC, and his wife Pat. Captain Hood would not permit the British European Airways young-retiring-age policy for pilots to keep him away from doing some enjoyable flying at his own pace during his English summers. He had remembered the pleasure he had had when flying Dominies on a short spell with No. 1 Ferry Pilots Pool with the Royal Air Force, so decided to investigate the advert he had seen for three Dragon Rapides for sale by Major Stacey, of the Army Parachute Association at Netheravon. The Army's parachutists had outgrown their Rapides after around ten years of service, and had moved on to Islanders, which were more rugged and for which parts were easier to obtain.

G-AIDL c/n 6968 at the Biggin Hill Air Fair, with Capt Mike Hood in control, 1977. *[M Hood]*

Southern Joyrides, G-AIDL

After spending the early months of 1977 in a sort of civilised haggling process followed by a quick test flight of one of the aircraft for sale, Southern Joyrides acquired its major company asset, G-AIDL, built as one of the last Dominie IIs for the RAF contract. As TX310, she came out of the Brush Coachworks factory in 1946 and, without seeing military service, was converted to DH 89A Rapide configuration by the DH Witney factory as the personal aircraft of Eric Gandar Dower of Allied Airways at Aberdeen. From 1950, she had toured Europe for some eleven years as the executive transport of the Fox's Glacier Mint company and in 1967, the Parachutists took her over. Captain Hood remembered that one of the selling points was that the cabin still retained the famous glacier mint aroma!

The Netheravon engineers had taken good care of the mechanical aspects of 'DL, but parachutists are not renowned for their care of the interior fittings of their aircraft, so Captain Hood took his new machine down to Redhill to have eight smart new seat cushions and backs made in dark green leathercloth, and the interior upholstery re-covered in cream and green. He sensibly fitted antimacassars in vinyl to all the passenger seat backs, to prevent hundreds of grubby hands from ruining their appearance. At this point in its career, 'Delta Lima had had the heating system removed, and unusually, two oil temperature gauges fitted on the starboard cockpit wall, forward of the priming pump, mainly for the benefit of pilots operating maximum-rate climbs on behalf of eager parachutists. The instruments, the lighting and the 360-channel VHF radio were adequate for the day-time, fair-weather flying intended, and the mechanicals were looked over by the vintage virtuoso of Biggin Hill engineers, Cobby Moore.

With her slow speed, the interesting view for passengers, easy flying characteristics and relatively easy maintenance, the staff of Southern Joyrides (Captain Hood, Chief Pilot; his wife Pat, ground hostess and adjutant, together with occasional assistance from two British Airways pilots, and the Hood's son) decided that this was a suitable aircraft for their purpose. An Air Operator's Certificate was soon obtained, and they began operations in the spring of 1977. Biggin Hill was the base, where 'DL wintered, then the season began each year on the first of April, following the holiday-makers down to the Isle of Wight, initially at Sandown, but from 1980 the operation was moved to Bembridge airfield.

The silver Rapide soon became a familiar summer spectacle, fitting in very comfortably at Sandown's friendly grass strip, in a shallow valley to the west of the holiday town. Pat Hood would greet the passengers at the airfield fence, take the bookings and the fares, help the passengers strap in, and manage all the ground work. Trips offered were either a four-pound, ten-minute circuit of the airfield, turning east to pass over Sandown beach, before heading gently back into the Sandown circuit, or if enough people required the thirty five-minute trip, then a partial tour of the island would be laid on, at a cost of twenty pounds a head. The times were of course nominal, as the airborne time tended to be inversely proportional to the sum of the length of the passenger queue, and the lateness of the hour, as " the customers had to be allowed to fly if they had taken the trouble to trek down to the airfield, hadn't they? " But the passengers certainly seemed to enjoy their time with Southern Joyrides, and one of the trips Captain Hood remembers most was the flight on which he flew a young couple across to the Needles, overhead which inspiring landmark the young man proposed to his girlfriend! He obviously had confidence in his plan, as there was champagne waiting when they landed.

Flying from Bembridge was most remembered for the cross-wind operations, as they appeared to have built their tarmac runway across the direction of the prevailing summer wind. Captain Hood and the other pilots on his Air Operator's Certificate were often tested by cross-winds while flying from Bembridge, and they were appreciative of 'DL's ability to operate from Bembridge's tarmac in anything up to twenty knots across the runway on take-off and landing, which is better than most tailwheel aircraft of the era. The good Captain even equated the well-co-ordinated control handling near the ground with that of the de Havilland Mosquito he flew for several years with the Royal Air Force's No.1 Photographic Unit. There was certainly a family likeness in the behaviour of rudders and ailerons of the two types on take-off.

View of central London from Southern Joyrides' Rapide, 1977. *[M Hood]*

At the end of each September, Captain and Mrs Hood flew back up to Biggin Hill, where they continued for a few more weeks before putting 'DL back in the hangar for the winter. A few more trips were flown from Biggin on special occasions, such as the annual Biggin Hill Air Fair, the British Aerospace Hatfield Open Day in 1981, were Captain Hood flew a record 704 passengers in one day, or for two other £20 'specials' - the City of London tour, or the Stately Homes of Kent tour. The City tours were usually flown up the River Thames to Tower Bridge at a memorable 1,000 feet, well below the commercial traffic transiting in and out of London Heathrow, and with the helpful co-ordination of Heathrow Air Traffic Control.

After about 36,000 joy-riders and ten happy, trouble-free years of flying G-AIDL from Biggin Hill, Southern Joyrides were caught up in the proposed new legislation which the Civil Aviation Authority wished to introduce, preventing old-age pensioners from flying commercially. Captain Hood therefore decided to put his dear old aircraft on the market in 1986 and another good home was found for the old girl, as Ray Mackenzie-Blyth of the romantic-sounding Snowdon Mountain Aviation at Caernarfon Airport in Wales took her over, with a goodly stock of spares, late in 1987.

G-AIDL has certainly taken well to pleasure flying as, even now, she still continues to operate commercially from Coventry, the home base of her latest owners, Air Atlantique.

WINDMILL THEATRE TRANSPORT CO, CROYDON

This intriguing little company was set up as an offshoot of the famous London Windmill Theatre company, operating from Croydon then later Gatwick, with Miss Vivian van Damm as one of the directors. Well-known war-time ATA pilot Miss Zeta Irwin was Chief Pilot, and from 1948 she flew charters for the company in their Rapide, G-AKSD 'Windmill Girl', to continental destinations when not ferrying Windmill Theatre staff around various UK and continental airfields. Eventually after over eleven years' service, and unlike the Theatre itself, the charter company did actually close and the Rapide was sold, ending up in Senegal.

G-AKSD c/n 6949 at Portsmouth, 1950, when operated for The Windmill Theatre. *[D.Fox]*

G-AKDW c/n 6897 parked at Rochester when with Short Brothers in 1950. [D.Fox]

Section 4 – Chapter 10: Transport for Aircraft Manufacturers

Most of the major aircraft manufacturers in Britain during and after the second world war had factories spread around the country, as a result of the wartime dispersal concept. The teams of pilots, engineers and project staff who had to visit these outlying factories, which were usually co-located with test airfields, very often continued to use the military-owned aircraft they had been allocated during the war by the Ministry of Aircraft Production, in many cases buying the aircraft from the Ministry after hostilities had ceased. Armstrong Whitworth at Baginton, de Havilland at Hatfield, Fairey Aviation at White Waltham, Gloster Aircraft at Hucclecote, Hawker at Langley, Short's at Rochester, Vickers at Weybridge and Westland at Yeovil all bought their own Rapides in 1946 or 1947. The majority of flights tended to be short communications hops between company airfields, with test pilots at the helm, and with a few company staff or engineers who needed to do the same journey. Many of the photographs taken by company photographers from the period were taken from the company Rapides. As the aircraft industry expanded again after the War, most companies began to advertise their wares at the European exhibitions, and on the flight lines of the Brussels, Farnborough, and Paris exhibitions, rows of company Rapides could be seen every day, waiting to take their company teams back to base at the end of the show.

G-AKRP's cockpit area during restoration, showing the pilot's seat and navigator's area behind. [CND]

Armstrong Whitworth, Blackburn, de Havilland, Fairey, Gloster, Hawker, Shorts, Vickers and Westland all had Rapides or Dominies in use on company communications work from about 1942 onwards, until the end of the war. A typical example was Armstrong Whitworth Aircraft, based at Baginton, near Coventry, and later in the war at Bitteswell, which was allocated Rapide X9450 (the former G-AEML) in March 1943, for use by pilots and staff; it actually remained with them as a civil aircraft until 1962.

SHORT BROTHERS

A slightly different type of operation for aircraft manufacturers was when Short Brothers set up a small charter subsidiary in 1947 under the name Rochester Air Charter Service. Based initially at their Rochester airfield, it moved to Sydenham, Belfast in 1952, where it became known as Short's Air Charter Service. Their fleet, which was atypical of aircraft manufacturers' operations, began flying with an Anson, a Dragonfly and two Proctors, but expanded soon afterwards, building up to seven different Rapides between 1948 and 1958. For the ten years between 1948 and 1958, the Rapide fleet combined the carriage of company staff on communications work with charter flying and freighting around Europe.

An interesting quirk of fate recently caused two of Short's original fleet to be returned to England to be restored. Both G-AKDW and

The restored Fordaire G-AKRP c/n 6940 at Old Warden in 2002, after a flying display. [M.Stroud]

G-AEML c/n 6337 airborne over the Solent near Portsmouth, 1994. [G Lee]

Neat leather interior of G-AEML, 1993. [CND]

Armstrong Whitworth's Baginton airfield, looking south-east, from the company-owned Proctor 5 G-AHBD, c.1949. *[E Franklin]*

the real work took place at the flight test 'shed' at Bitteswell. A Proctor, an Anson 19 and a Dominie were used to get the pilots across to Bitteswell every morning and back again every afternoon after completion of test flying. The Dominie was favoured for these daily trips, as it was easy to start, easy to fly, and easy to land and also carried more people in reasonable comfort, for the day's work at Bitteswell. This Dominie was X9450, which had been sent to Baginton in April 1943, and which, in early 1941, had been repaired by DH Witney following 'Category B damage caused by AA shells' when at Ringway with No 6 AACU. The AWA engineers and pilots referred to the aircraft as a Dominie but in fact it was the 1936-built DH 89, G-AEML, impressed as X9450, given the external appearance of a military Dominie for the duration of the war. In March 1946, AWA bought the aircraft from the Air Ministry and it reverted to G-AEML.

This particular aircraft was Sqn Ldr Franklin's favourite transport which gave him much pleasure, particularly on longer trips from Baginton, such as down to see the A & AEE people at Boscombe Down. The feeling of comfort and stability, with the superb view from the cockpit, especially in poor visibility, and the easy operation of the machine, made a pleasurable contrast to the hectic test schedules on much more complicated aircraft.

He would drive to the airfield from home, park his car in the fire station (which the airfield fire crew had kindly vacated for the day) complete his early paperwork in the adjacent pilots' office, walk across to the 'Dominie' with his colleagues for the Bitteswell trip, climb in, start up and be airborne, heading 062 degrees for Bitteswell, all in minutes and with very little effort. There was no need to call anyone on the radio, as Baginton had no ground radio for many years, until an ex-WAAF control assistant was taken on to give some form of airfield information service. With G-AEML, the minimal electrical power provided by the battery, (nominally augmented by the puny 150-watt 'windy' generator when airborne). Therefore most of these short flights were simply made with the radio switched off, which made life much more relaxing.

The still-air flight time from Baginton to Bitteswell at an average of 100 knots was about seven minutes, but from 1946 until about 1953, G-AEML's log book shows many entries such as:

Mr Franklin (pilot)	*Bag to B'well - 10 mins*
Mr Else (passenger)	*"*

The pilots would swap seats at the end of their testing day, and the other pilot would have the pleasure of the hop home for tea. Curiously, if the aircraft's journey log is to be believed, 'EML became somehow faster with age, for in 1953 until she was sold in 1962, the log books show that she took only five minutes for the short hop to and from 'Bag to B'well', whereas for the ten years previously she had taken ten minutes for the same journey! Or was it that the pilots no longer needed the flying hours?

In 1946, when the ability of aircraft companies to rely on the Air Ministry to provide air transport at His Majesty's expense disappeared, X9450 was still considered by Armstrong Whitworth to be a practical mode of transport, so she was bought from the Ministry, for an undiscovered sum. She was given an overhaul by the Baginton engineers who had tended to her in her military guise, repainted in the AWA colours of Oxford Blue with a cream cheat line and her pre-war civilian registration, G-AEML, on fuselage and wings, issued with a civilian Certificate of Airworthiness, and put back into company service, doing exactly the same job, but now owned, not borrowed.

She was to remain with AWA for another sixteen years, and was then sold to a variety of owners, ending up back at Baginton with Stuart Filhol in 1969. Retired in February 1971, she remained in the Baginton hangar until Viv Bellamy bought her in 1978 for rebuild at St Just. After three further changes of owner she finally got back in the air again on 16 April 1993, owned by Proteus Holdings and air tested by the author from Rush Green, following a six-year re-build to an immaculate standard by Bill Bowker, Steve Evans and their engineers. She is now in the capable hands of Ken Whitehead at Rendcomb, Gloucestershire.

C/n 6541 F-AZCA in Blue Way cigarette company markings at La Ferté Alais in the 1980s. *[M. Stroud]*

Section 4 – Chapter 11: Post War Civilian Operators World-wide

F-BGON, ex X7381, at Le Bourget around 1952, when with DALS. It later became F-AZCA. *[BAe]*

THE RESURGENCE OF COMMERCIAL OPERATIONS POST-WAR

"The first civil aircraft to be sold by commercial contract and exported by Great Britain since the war have recently been delivered to Portugal. They will form the nucleus of the Companhia de Transportes Aereos (CTA) fleet to operate Portuguese internal air lines. Four aircraft have been supplied; three DH 89A Dragon Rapides, (CS-ADI, CS-ADJ, and CS-ADK) and a Proctor IV, (CS-ADN)."

This announcement in the November 1945 edition of *Flight* heralded the beginning of an upsurge of post-war interest in commercial aviation, and it is a credit to a relatively small nation that she should be the first to resume commercial flying with new aircraft. While several hundred Rapides were sold on as surplus to military requirements in the immediate post-war years, the fact that they were being overtaken by more modern designs meant a steady decline in the numbers. By 1965, de Havilland company records show only 36 active in Britain and another 53 world-wide, a total of 89. There were, of course, some with which de Havilland had lost contact, and others in museums and under restoration, but this figure gives an indication of the decline of the use of the Rapide.

A look at some of the post-war operators produces some fascinating stories.

The three Rapides for CTA (c/ns 6899 - 6901) about to leave Witney for Lisbon, 1945. *[BAe]*

FRANCE

One of the first companies to take civilianised Dominies from Witney in 1946 was Air France. This was the beginning of a positive flood of Rapides to France post-war, as around 84 were registered to France or its overseas territories from 1946 onwards, and many remained in service until the 1960s, most by then in the service of parachute clubs. However, around 14 of this total had several previous French registrations, so the total number actually serving in French territories was somewhat less. One of the best-known multi-identity aircraft still in France today is F-AZCA, which was built as Dominie X7381 for the RAF and sold to the Herts and Essex Aero Club at Broxbourne as G-ALZF in 1950. It went to France in 1952 with the registration F-BGON and was used for many years as a parachute club transport, finally ending up with the famous Jean Salis collection at La Ferté Alais, south of Paris, in 1977. In June 1981, it took part in the Air Transit Transatlantic Air Race from Le Bourget to New York. It has had several paint jobs, and now has a pseudo-RAF colour scheme with a vintage series registration as F-AZCA, still delighting the crowds at La Ferté Alais air displays.

Most of the post-war French colonies, including Madagascar, Vietnam, Algeria, Tunisia, Gabon, New Caledonia, Senegal, and Laos had some Rapides from around 1950 up to the 60s, mainly for light passenger and freight services. A particularly prolific user of Rapides was the Societe Air Madagascar (SAM), based at Ivato, which was founded in 1947 and ultimately took delivery of 13 Rapides. The three 'Air France' Rapides that were photographed leaving the DH Witney depot in 1948 were also destined for Madagascar, but returned to mainland France in 1949 for operation by the airline's civil aviation school, before the two survivors were shipped off to Vietnam in 1952. The romantically-named 'Aigle Azur Indochine ' based in Hanoi, Vietnam, was to use several Rapides from 1952, with only limited success, as three of their aircraft were reported as being burnt out on start-up - always a potential problem when trying to re-start hot Gipsy Queens.

By the early nineteen sixties, more modern aircraft were entering the French inventories, so the Rapides that remained were often put up for sale, and surprisingly large numbers were bought and sold by brokers such as Rousseau Aviation at Dinard, moving on to serve many of the very popular French parachute clubs spread around France. One of these parachute club transports, F-BHCD, which had been G-ALGB with Yorkshire Aeroplane Club in Britain, was used in France by three different parachute clubs, finishing up with the Centre Nationale de Parachutisme de Bourgogne at Chalon from 1962 until its C of A expired in 1966. After several years in store, it was transferred to the Musée de l'Air at Le Bourget and has been displayed there since 1981, with dummy parachutists leaping out of the cabin.

PORTUGAL
By Autumn 1945, European airlines were beginning to re-emerge from wartime restrictions. A new Portuguese company, Companhia de Transportes Aéreos, was set up that summer with the help of an old friend of de Havilland, Senor Carlos Bleck, who had been the DH representative in Portugal for many years. CTA was claimed to be the first company to buy civil-registered aircraft for export from Britain after the War. They ordered three Witney-converted Dominie C Mk IIs and one new Percival Proctor V, and all four departed Witney in formation on 8th November 1945 for Oporto.

These first three newly-civilianised Dominies to be sold were close sisters, built on the Loughborough line as NR835, 836 and 837, and they remained together with the Portuguese company, taking sequential civilian registrations. The training of the Portuguese pilots and their subsequent departure from DH Witney was well documented by the aviation press, even to the point of local papers showing Witney General Manager Philip Gordon-Marshall, enjoying an evening out in his adopted home, 'The Bull' at Burford. '*Flight*' magazine that month showed some memorable photographs of this first batch of exports flying from Witney in very tidy formation, with the three Rapides in vic, and the smaller Proctor 'in the box'.

After several years carrying passengers, freight and newspapers on the Lisbon to Oporto and Pedras Rubras routes, CS-ADI was transferred to the Portuguese Air Force in March 1950 as a 'Dominie 1' for staff transport duties, with the serial 2307. This aircraft was eventually retired in 1968 and, after storage, it was displayed for some years in the Museum at Alverca, north of Lisbon, but is presently back in store at Sintra. Also in 1950, the other two Rapides were sold to Sao Tome Aviation as CR-SAD/SAE, and then in 1970 further south to Angola as CR-LKR and LKS. In 1980 the Brazilian airline, VARIG, wanted a Rapide for their museum to represent the Rapide they used on their formation in the early 40s so acquired one of the Angolan specimens, which were by then in open store in Luanda. Refurbished at Porto Alegre, this is now displayed in the Aeroespacial Museum at Rio de Janeiro, painted as PP-VAN.

CS-ADK c/n 6901 being refuelled at Lisbon for Compania de Transportes Aéreos, 1946. [D.Fox]

G-AMAI c/n 6879 at Fairoaks in 1950, with W J Nobbs. [D.Fox]

GERMAN RESTORATION PROJECT, D-ILIT
On 21st July 1995, a long-inactive Rapide flew again, after many years of obscurity. This aircraft, which was built as Dominie Mark I NR803, by Brush Coachworks in 1945, had served at several RAF transport units in Britain before being loaned to Airwork in 1947 for two year's experimental work with The Sperry Gyroscope company. In March 1950, the Air Ministry sold it off from 5 MU Kemble and it became G-AMAI at Fairoaks, before being sold to Spain in 1952. Here, it operated as EC-AGP with Comercial Exportadora de Articules Perecederos SA (CEAPSA) at Sabadell, before being acquired and stored by the Spanish Air Force museum at Cuatro Vientos, near Madrid. She remained untouched until a German collector, Gunther Kurfiss, bought her in 1984 and transported her back to Frankfurt for his Air Classik museum. After a period of display, painted as 'G-RCYR' (presumably after the other Rapide at Cuatro Vientos, the famous G-ACYR), he sold her in 1987 to another German engineer, Josef Koch, who operated a fleet of delightfully-restored aircraft from his Fliegendes Museum at Augsburg. After some initial work, Herr Koch also had to put the Rapide restoration in a queue, as he had higher-priority restorations to complete, but in 1993 he re-commenced the tortuous route towards airworthiness, reserving the marks D-ILIT, and toured the European 'Rapide Centres' looking for advice, information and spare parts. The two Gipsy Queens that came with the aircraft had had an unwritten history, so Herr Koch sent them off to a British specialist, Deltair, to be overhauled and certified, before re-installing them in his aircraft.

In 1994, D-ILIT moved to Lahr, on the Rhine valley south of Strasbourg, where Herr Koch completed the restoration, absorbing parts from D-IGUN and finishing the aircraft in an attractive light grey scheme with dark grey cheat lines reminiscent of the scheme she last wore in Spain. He had asked the author to carry out the test flights from Lahr's two-mile long ex-NATO runway as, despite being a current tailwheel commercial pilot himself, he had not flown a Rapide before. The author had flown the first test after re-

D-ILIT at Lahr, Germany, after meticulous rebuild by Josef Koch, awaiting air test, 1995. [CND]

build of G-AEML two years earlier, and had worked with him on various aspects of the restoration over the previous three years. On the blisteringly hot afternoon of 21st July 1995, the flight was preceded by several engine runs to confirm the condition of the engines, followed by a taxi test to check the brakes and general controls. After adjustments and another set of high-speed taxi tests down the long Lahr runway, the author, with Herr Koch as flight-test observer, took the aircraft off the runway for an initial ten-minute flight, before some more checks and adjustments to the engines and a second flight the following day. Some uncertainties about the engines were discovered on this flight, therefore no more flights were made until a full check was made of the magneto system, and several other minor defects rectified.

This was the first flight of this aircraft for 43 years, as it last flew at Cuatro Vientos in Spain in 1952. Herr Koch is to be congratulated on an excellent restoration carried out surprisingly quickly under considerable technical and administrative difficulties. The next set of air tests went well, and then in October 1995 the Rapide joined Herr Koch's fleet of historic aircraft which was based at Sandown, Isle of Wight. For this purpose, the Rapide was restored to the British register as G-AMAI, and flew from Sandown for several years before Hr Koch decided to return to Germany with his collection in 1999, at which time, the Rapide reverted to the German registration D-ILIT. It is now kept in airworthy condition at Oberpfaffenhofen, near Munich.

BELGIAN SURVEY AIRCRAFT OO-CNP

Moving across to Belgium, one of the most comprehensively-modified Rapides continues under long-term restoration at the Brussels Musée Royal de l'Armée. DH 89B, OO-CNP, as it is now registered, was built as one of the first Dominie Mark Is for the RAF at Hatfield around the end of 1939, entering service with serial R5922. An unexceptional period of war service was followed by the sale in December 1947 and conversion to civilian standard by Lancashire Aircraft Corporation at Samlesbury, Lancashire as G-AKNV. LAC used up to seven Rapides in the early part of their charter operations, from Samlesbury, nearby Blackpool, and later from Yeadon Airport, Leeds.

When, in 1953, LAC were required to cease their Yeadon operations, there was less work for their Rapide fleet, so 'KNV was sold to Ireland, where it was used for charter work by Republic Air Charters as EI-AGK. Derby Aviation of Burnaston bought her in June 1955 and overhauled her for Fairey Aviation Limited, who then transferred her in September that year to their Belgian subsidiary, Avions Fairey SA at Gosselies. Probably her most interesting and intriguing period then followed, as extensive and very unusual modification work was carried out by Avions Fairey, in their Gosselies factory, before they flew the aircraft as an executive transport. The Rapide was reported by the Fairey publicity manager, Derek Thurgood, as being stripped down and completely rebuilt and while he indicated that some "modifications had been carried out by Avions Fairey at Gosselies", he did not expand on why they were needed, nor why they were so drastic. There were some very interesting changes to this aircraft.

The major external changes wrought by Avions Fairey began with a moulded Perspex top cockpit roof to replace the individual DH panels, presumably because spares were then becoming difficult to find. The next alteration was the removal of the characteristic curved cabin windows, removal of the fuselage longeron below the cabin windows on both sides, and their replacement by a continuous Perspex window, deeper by about twelve inches than the standard DH windows, and exposing to view the wooden fuselage framework. This gave a strangely semi-naked appearance to the fuselage, and significantly altered the typical de Havilland lines.

Internally, the changes were no less drastic. Behind the pilot's bulkhead was fitted a full-length wooden radio equipment bay, with a 44 channel radio and radio compass, together with an operator's seat. As these instruments required much more electrical power than the standard wind-driven generators could supply, the engines were both modified to run one 1,450-watt generator each, using the same drive system, position and cooling system as fitted to other Rapides in England. Another generator was apparently fitted in the cabin, alongside an alternator, to provide DC and AC power for the extra instrumentation. Another modification was a heater muff which was fitted over a lengthened exhaust pipe on one engine. Into the normal exhaust pipe, an extra tube was inserted, around which was another tube which carried a separate air supply, and then the normal end-fitting 'trumpet' was fitted, making the system about four feet longer than usual. The air, after heating by the exhaust pipe, was ducted back through the stub wing and into the cabin, to provide a simple heating system.

In the cockpit, sloping six-inch-wide instrument and switch panels were fitted on either side of the pilot's seat, making a cramped cockpit even more so, and requiring the removal of the flap lever and primer pump from the starboard side, and the repositioning of the throttle and trim wheels on the port side. The trim wheel was re-fitted on the bulkhead behind the pilot's left hand, and the flap lever was replaced by an electrical actuating motor, with accompanying switch and position indicator on the front

G-AKNV c/n 6458 at Blackpool, with Lancashire Aircraft Corporation, 1950, before sale to Ireland. [CND]

C/n 6458 as EI-AGK at Baldonnel, when with Republic Air Charter, 1953. [M. Stroud]

C/n 6458 with its first Belgian registration OO-AFG at Gosselies in 1962 after modification by Avions Fairey. [CND]

A dismantled OO-CNP at the Brussels Musée de l'Armée during a long-term rebuild. *[M Stroud]*

instrument panel, in the only known modification of a Rapide flap system The main instrument panel was completely rebuilt, with mainly electrical instruments and many more switches than usual, mostly to control the extra instrumentation. These major changes were carried out under the supervision of the Belgian airworthiness authority, and were not recognised by de Havillands, who almost certainly had no knowledge of the work, as none of the work is registered as a DH modification. Following all this, the Rapide emerged in February 1958, nearly two and a half years after original delivery into the factory, now finally with the registration OO-AFG (Avions Fairey Gosselies).

C/n 6622 G-AGEE in 1942, part of GW&S's fleet. *[R Waugh]*

Whether these modifications were worthwhile is unrecorded but four years later 'AFG was sold to Air Affairs SPRL, also based at Gosselies, and two years later the registration was changed to OO-CNP to reflect its new ownership by the Centre National de Parachutisme, Wevelgem. It was withdrawn from parachuting use in 1966, and for several years, OO-CNP stood outside at the small airfield at Wevelgem before being donated to the Brussels Museum in 1973.

Post-war view of G-AGEE when with Gibraltar Airways in 1947. *[CND]*

The interesting challenge which the Belgian Museum restoration team has been facing for several years is to de-modify their Rapide, which involves considerable remaking of wood, metal and Perspex parts to the original DH specification. The Belgian Air Museum Restoration Society, an enthusiastic team of around twelve led by Vincent Jacobs, continues to rebuild OO-CNP to wear the colours she had when with LAC at Samlesbury and Blackpool in 1950.

ICELANDIC COMMUNITY SERVICES

At the north western end of Europe, a small flight service, begun in 1937, was allocated two RAF Dominies in 1944 to serve another island population. The company was Flugfelag Islands HF , based in Iceland's capital, Reykjavik. Given British CofAs in April and July 1944, HG671 and NF859 became TF-ISM and TF-ISO and went into service as 5 or 7 seat landplanes to serve the coastal towns of Akureyri, Hofn and Egilstadir. The only scheduled service was the daily 160-mile route from Reykjavik to Akureyri, which took one and a half hours by Rapide, but "12 hours by motor bus in summer along difficult roads which are closed for most of the winter". If the direct route was not available due to weather, the rocky fjord route would take over two hours. From the capital to the market town of Egilstadir, which served about 10,000 people, mainly farmers, there was no road connection. Hofn served about 7,000 fishermen and farmers, and took about three hours flight time from Reykjavik.

TF-KAA, ex G-AGEE, at Reykjavik in 1953 where it was operated by Flugskolinn Thytur HF. *[CND]*

Other tasks were completed by the Icelandic Rapides, such as spotting herring offshore in summertime, and ambulance work for the island's hospital, in Reykjavik. Average hours flown by each aircraft were 600 hours in the first years of operation. One of the

Rapides, TF-ISO, succumbed to the atrocious weather round the Icelandic coast on 27th August 1945, crashing at the appropriately named Grimseyjarsundi, but the fate of the other is not known.

KLM IN HOLLAND

At the end of the Second World War, the Dutch government opened up the country for commercial aviation again in July 1945. The RLD, attached to the Ministry of Work and Energy, began to regulate aviation matters, and announced that services to the North, East and South of the country could begin again, initially for government staff. Four Dominies which had been ordered by the RAF were transferred to KLM and modified at DH Witney for civilian use. PH-RAA and RAB were delivered on 19th September 1945, and ten days later, the first post-war service was begun. Captain Van Ebsen initiated the service from Schiphol to Eindhoven and Beecke. At the beginning of October, the next two Rapides PH-RAC and RAD arrived, and soon afterwards began a thrice-daily service from Schiphol to Leeuwarden and Eelde. The Rapides were fitted out for pilot and radio operator, with an HF radio and six seats. The services were quickly expanded and so two of the Dutch Air Force Dominies were also hired for a few months as PH-RAE and RAF to assist in the commercial services. The Rapides were used until 1947, when they were sold on to East African Airways in Kenya, and the services were taken over by DC-3s.

United Nations Operations in Palestine, 1948

In 1948, the United Nations Organisation was asked by Britain to assist in controlling the dissidents in the political battle for the occupation of Palestine. On one side was the emerging Jewish nation of Israel, aiming to occupy as much territory as they could, and on the other were the Arab nations who wished to re-claim the area known as Palestine, which they felt was rightly theirs. Britain had the mandate to keep the peace between the opposing factions, but by early 1948, the British government felt that the worsening situation required a United Nations peace-keeping force to be positioned in Beirut to replace the British force.

UNO responded by sending an Observer force to monitor the activities of both factions, and this Observer force had a requirement for independent air observation of the disputed areas of Palestine, so asked the Netherlands to provide a team to manage the air activities. They were to ensure that the crews were not British, nor of the Jewish or Muslim faiths, because of the sensitivities of the sides in the dispute. The British government was asked to provide the aircraft, so it contracted British Overseas Airways Corporation to gather a selection of aircraft for the task. No details of the size, range, or capacity of aircraft were given, but it was assumed that the aircraft were to be used for carrying UN observers over the disputed area.

A contract was hurriedly arranged between BOAC and the Dutch KLM, to supply UNO with seven aircraft, sufficient pilots, radio operators, and engineers, for immediate service. Lacking precise information, BOAC presumed that the simplest, least expensive option would be to charter some short-range, twin-engined aircraft in the UK and ask the Netherlands to provide all the personnel.

Two Croydon companies had what appeared to be suitable aircraft available for charter, and were asked to supply five Rapides between them. G-AGWR and G-AGWP came from Morton Air Services, and G-AFMJ, G-AKOB and G-AKNX from Air Enterprises, being given the identities UN-1 to UN-5 respectively. In addition, the Dutch government offered to loan four more Dominies if they were required, from their under-used Royal Netherlands Air Force fleet, all by then based with 324 Squadron at Leeuwarden, to bring the United Nations fleet numbers up to nine. In the event only two Dutch Dominies were used by the UN, and these were PH-VNB/UN-8, and PH-VND/UN-9 (although the two others were given civil identities in case they were needed). The two Dutch aircraft were to join the expedition in a second wave, after delivery of the first five British aircraft.

PH-RAB c/n 6891 at Schiphol, 1946, before transfer to Kenya where it became VP-KEB. [CND]

G-AGWR c/n 6917 at Croydon, before becoming UN-1. [CND]

KLM provided the aircrew and engineers, except for one Polish-born British engineer supplied by Morton. BOAC were finally informed by the UN that the aircraft should be in passenger-carrying fit and the aircraft were to be sprayed in United Nations all-over white, with light blue UN titles and UN fleet numbers UN-1 to UN-5 on the fins. No mention was made of registration letters, so it was assumed that the national registration letters should be retained on wings and fuselages. In view of the requirement for there to be no British personnel on the expedition, the decision to allow the aircraft to be repainted with conspicuous British registrations was somewhat puzzling - the unfortunate aircrew were to be caught out by this decision when in the area of operations. KLM arranged for their crews to collect the aircraft from Croydon, fly them out to Haifa, operate them under UN orders and return them to Croydon on completion of the contract. It appeared to be a straightforward operation, but problems now began to present themselves.

A modification-state problem became apparent when two sheets of rapidly-prepared Operating Notes were handed to the KLM leader by Morton and Air Enterprises staff. The notes showed that each of the five aircraft was significantly different in some key aspects and were inadequate for operators who were to fly the quite different aircraft more than 2,000 miles from their base, over long stretches of water. The most important differences were that only 'GWP and 'KOB had additional 36-gallon fuel tanks and could be considered ‘long range’ Rapides; the others all had standard 78-gallon tanks, and therefore limited range. The crews were not to know it at the time, but the simple performance figures contained in the notes were also misleading. The figures claimed that the fuel consumption for all five aircraft was a realistic 20 gallons per hour, but that the endurance of the three standard aircraft was four hours, and that of the longer range machines was 5.5 hours for 'KOB, and 5 hours for 'GWP. In practice, only the figures for 'GWP were accurate, so with a ten per cent margin, the safe endurance figures would be around 4 hours and 50 minutes for the long-range aircraft and only 3 hours and 25 minutes for the standard aircraft. The Dutch crews did not know the aircraft well enough to be familiar with the actual consumption figures, so were in considerable danger of overestimating the range they could obtain on their ferry flights.

Captain Herman Bolte, leader of the UN expedition, at Schiphol with G-AGWP c/n 6918. *[Bolte]*

While four of the aircraft had Marconi 1154/55 MF and HF radios fitted, G-AFMJ had no radios at all. The Marconi MF/HF sets were heavy, unwieldy post-war radios, which were out of the pilot's reach, so could only be used by a radio operator and only two radio operators were to be carried between the five aircraft. The Marconi sets would give reasonable ranges for morse key operations with w/t stations, and could be used for obtaining M/F navigational direction bearings, but they provided no inter-communication between each other or air traffic stations. G-AGWR alone had a VHF radio, which could be used by the pilot for communications with airport controllers, but even this was of limited practicality, being a single-crystal set, it could only be used to transmit and receive on one frequency without having a change of crystal! Changing frequencies meant getting into the radio's workings to remove the crystal and replacing it with another.

At least some thought had been given to the nature of the task by the owners, as all aircraft were provided with lifebelts, emergency rations and first aid kits, and two had drift sights, for use in overwater navigation. All except G-AFMJ were six-seaters and, by chance, this aircraft was still fitted out to carry ambulance equipment, as used in its earlier Royal Air Force service as Z7261, '*The Women of Britain*', but had now been partially civilianised, being fitted with eight passenger seats.

KLM were able to find several pilots who had flown KLM Dominies and Captain Herman Bolte was appointed to lead the KLM team out to Haifa. Captain Bolte, a twenty eight-year-old KLM pilot had been one of the first pilots to be selected by Captain Parmentier, the Head of KLM Flight Operations, to join KLMs post-war operations. He had moved onto Dakotas in 1947, and was by now a 'Captain, European services'. For the Palestine task, he was joined by another young Dakota Captain, Henk Nijdam, who was the only other Rapide pilot KLM could make available. The other three pilots, Bob van Hoek, Dick Ranke and Frits van Vianen, were young senior-course students from the Rijksopleiding voor Verkeersvlieger (Dutch Civil Pilot's Training School), who needed only a few more hours before gaining their commercial licences. They had no airline experience, no experience outside Holland, nor any experience on the Rapide, but were considered suitable to operate the UN charter. A problem then appeared, for, in order to operate British commercial aircraft, the pilots required commercial pilot's licences, so KLM sent the three pilots to Croydon where they flew the requisite 10 hours on the Rapides, and that satisfied the legal licence requirements.

The expedition leader quite rightly believed he had a difficult task ahead. He had to lead a group of five small civilian aircraft the length of the Mediterranean, over long sector distances, with little in the way of navigational assistance, and varying levels of operational equipment. More worrying, he had himself not flown this type of aircraft for two years, and had never flown outside the European environment. He had, for company, one similarly experienced DC-3 captain and three pilots just out of pilot training with minimal overall experience and certainly no experience of night flying, long-distance navigation, formation flying or overseas operations. In addition, he had received no instructions about how or where the aircraft were to be used when they reached Palestine.

Two of the Rapides, UN-1 and UN-2, gleaming now in overall United Nations white, were flown by Captains Bolte and Nijdam across to Schiphol in late August 1948, where the KLM team made the final preparations for the planned departure for Haifa on 27th August. As leader, Herman Bolte decided to take the only aircraft fitted with a full radio suite, UN-1, as he could then talk on VHF to some of the airfields on the journey, and his radio operator would be able to obtain navigational bearings on MF and HF for the whole formation. This aircraft was not fitted with long-range tanks, but that was not important, as he could only plan on scheduling the formation for the aircraft with the shortest range.

After rapid consultation with the KLM planners, Captain Bolte decided that their journey should make use of KLM handling agencies wherever possible, using the following route: Amsterdam-Paris-Lyon-Marseilles-Pisa-Rome-Brindisi-Araxos-Athens-Rhodes-Nicosia-Beirut-Haifa. The journey was expected to take six days.

Unfortunately, the urgency of the operation precluded time for comprehensive planning, and this inadequacy now began to show. Despite hastening action, the Air Enterprises aircraft were still not ready on the 26th August, the day before the expedition was due to leave Amsterdam, but Captain Bolte was anxious to at least begin, so he decided to leave on time from Amsterdam with the first two aircraft, and instructed the three junior members of the team, who were still at Croydon, to attempt to meet up with the expedition at Marseilles as soon as possible on the 28th. They would be led there by an experienced pilot from Air Enterprises. Captains Bolte and Nijdam, the two KLM radio operators and the four KLM engineers met for the flight from Amsterdam to Marseilles on the planned day, but even this departure was delayed because of administrative delays with Captain Nijdam's papers, which in turn meant that the two aircraft had insufficient time to reach Marseilles, so they night-stopped at Paris. Captain Bolte had the feeling that this was not going to be an easy journey! The two Rapides carried on down to Marseilles the next day, where they waited for the three aircraft to join them from England.

After frantic work by the Air Enterprises engineers, the final preparations were completed at Croydon on the remaining three Rapides early on the 28th, so they set off to Paris and Marseilles, led by Captain Lowe, one of the company's own pilots. When he saw the rest of his team arrive at Marseilles, the anxious Captain Bolte began to feel the expedition might be coming together, so, saying goodbye to Captain Lowe, he met the KLM agent to arrange the departure for Pisa. However, he then discovered that two of the aircraft did not have valid outward clearance authority from Paris, and the other three were using invalid ship's papers. And these five aircraft were emblazoned all over in white with three-foot high United Nations markings! After a good deal of time and much argument, the French authorities settled matters by imposing a 600 Franc fine on the group. Then it was discovered that the fuel carnets were invalid, as they were not signed by the owners. Captain Bolte managed to get past that by signing all the carnets

The two lead UN Rapides at Lyon en route Palestine, 1947. *[Bolte]*

himself, which seemed to satisfy the customs and airport authorities, and the whole team set off at last, late and frustrated, for Pisa.

Once airborne, the bureaucracy was soon forgotten as the five pilots settled into a very pleasant Sunday morning flight at 1,000 feet, each Rapide following Herman Bolte's white biplane in a loose vic formation, and beginning to learn their own way of flying in formation. The relaxed flight along the craggy French and Italian coasts took them to what they believed was the civil airport at Pisa, where they landed after their first leg together. When an armed guard arrived at the aircraft, they thought that this was something unusual for a civil airport and the Italian Air Force officer in charge eventually managed to indicate to the non Italian-speaking Dutchmen that they had no permission to land at a military airfield without a special permit, and by the same token, neither would they be permitted to take off. He further said they could have no fuel, as there was none!

Captain Bolte now settled into what was becoming a routine of wasted time and frustrating telephone calls, until eventually, after two hours and several attempts to call the KLM agent in Rome, the base Commander was roused, and between KLM and himself, finally agreed to waive the normal landing permits. Then, after hearing that the local Shell agent was unavailable, it being Sunday, he rather unexpectedly arranged for fuel to be delivered from Air Force sources. While the large amount of water drawn off the fuel supplied made the Dutch engineers question the age, octane rating and storage methods of the fuel, they agreed that at least it was fuel, and it should probably mix with the fuel of known quality remaining in the tanks. Even more unexpectedly, the Italians accepted Captain Bolte's signature for the fuel, in lieu of payment, 'on behalf of KLM, Rome ', and the relieved team taxied out and took off, a few more hours behind schedule, for the 180-mile leg to Rome. There being no night-flying equipment on board the aircraft, and no experience or permission to fly in formation at night, Captain Bolte was again becoming anxious, as landing at Rome at night would be both outside the rules and experience of his new pilots. In the event all went well and the five landed at Fiumicino an hour after sunset, in the gathering dusk.

Rome presented no problems for the team, so after a good night-stop, they attempted an early departure for the thirty-minute flight across Italy to Brindisi. On arrival at the take-off point, the next problem was provided by the Gipsy Queens on Captain Bolte's aircraft, UN-1, which produced unacceptably high drops in rpm on testing the magnetos. Engine runs at high rpm would not clear the 'mag drops' so he reluctantly handed over the lead to Captain Nijdam, who took the rest of the team on the next leg. Captain Bolte and his engineer shut down their engines and set about changing the six plugs on the side which had given the largest rpm drop during the run-up. Happily, this fixed the problem, so G-AGWP was soon airborne and following the others to the coastal airfield at Brindisi.

By the time Captain Bolte arrived, however, more complications had emerged. Captain Nijdam had discovered that no permission had been received at Brindisi for the aircraft to land at Araxos, a military airfield, and they could not leave Brindisi without having this permission, as the Greek government applied strict control there, due to activity by rebel forces. Soon after this revelation, Brindisi airport was closed by strong crosswinds, preventing further take-offs. There was nothing else that could be done, except to find overnight accommodation and start the now familiar telephoning and telegraphing routine, first to the KLM agent in Athens. Responses were at last obtained from the Athens agent, but they were unintelligible to Captain Bolte, so he decided that the only way to obtain an understanding of the official position was to send Captain Nijdam, in the second Rapide with long range tanks, UN-4, direct to Athens, a range of around 370 miles, to try to persuade the Greek authorities to issue permission for the aircraft to use Araxos, the only airfield within practical range from Brindisi. Nijdam was allowed by the Italian authority to take off "at his own risk" despite the strong winds at Brindisi, and reached Athens over three an a half hours later. Eventually, later that night, the necessary permissions came through by telegraph to Bolte at Brindisi.

On the morning of 31st August, the wind had died down, so Captain Bolte and the four Rapides departed the Brindisi runway, heading across the Strait of Otranto for a sunny two and a half hour journey to Araxos, on the Peloponnisos peninsular. The Dutch team found the small military airfield at Araxos to be very war-like and

The five UN Rapides at Marseilles, having met up for onward transit to Palestine. *[Bolte]*

quite different from any other they had seen so far. An active army unit had its guns and artillery gathered all round the tented site which covered the grass airfield. Nonetheless, they were given a surprisingly friendly reception by the Greek soldiers, and the commanding officer invited Captain Bolte to his tent for a cup of Greek coffee. Another surprise met them when the requested fuel turned up in small tins carried on a horse-drawn trailer, but at least they had the luxury of a hand-pump to draw up the fuel, rather than emptying the cans individually into the aircraft tanks. Pilots and engineers took turns with the protracted procedure of filling the four Rapides to capacity using these small petrol cans, but at least it was a warm sunny day, which made the task more amenable. By early afternoon they were on their way again, this time for a relatively short flight across the Gulfs of Patras and Korinthos to arrive at Athens airport, one hour and twenty minutes later, where they again met up with Captain Nijdam. The local KLM agent had also managed to arrange suitable accommodation in the capital for another night-stop.

September 1st began well, as the five machines took off from Athens early without delays, for the 280-mile trip across the delightful Cyclades and Sporadhes islands, to the small airfield at the northernmost tip of the island of Rhodes, where they planned to stay for the night. Once again, not surprisingly by this time, there was no fuel. After a long wait and much chasing, some fuel arrived, but there was not enough for their next long leg, the longest of the journey, which would require all tanks filled to the brim. Six hours later, the last aircraft was eventually refuelled and the crews made their way to the hotel in Rhodes. To their surprise, on arrival, they discovered that the United Nations Middle East headquarters staff were based in the same hotel. Discussions with the UN staff revealed that they had no information on the operations or even the reason for the aircraft being there, so could give no practical assistance. But a UN official strongly recommended they did not fly beyond Beirut with the very conspicuous British registrations on their aircraft.

Captain Bolte then spent that evening in the Rhodes hotel planning and worrying over the next 330-mile leg - Rhodes to Nicosia in Cyprus, which included 280 miles over open sea, with no airfields for diversion. Even relying on the questionable forecast winds, which were generally westerly at this time of year, this distance was very close to the limit of safe endurance for his formation. KLM rules also stated that their Rapides must never fly more than 20 kilometres (twelve miles) from the shore because of their poor single-engine performance and here he was, in order to complete his company contract, being asked to lead five aircraft with no intercommunication, poor navigation aids, at the limit of their safe endurance, over 140 miles from land at the worst point! If one of the aircraft were to have an engine failure, there would be little hope of rescue for the crew. He was very unhappy with the situation, but felt he had little option but to forego company rules, attempt the flight, and simply hope that all five aircraft performed safely.

Bolte's plan was that they should take advantage of the cool morning temperatures and light winds for better performance. Therefore, on the morning of 2nd September, starting up the Rapides on the dark, silent island airfield, he led his four colleagues off the Rhodes runway, up into the lightening dawn sky, with the sun rapidly bringing its summer heat to the cool Mediterranean below. The five white biplanes climbed steadily out to the west over the wide, expansive yet inhospitable western Mediterranean, towards the island of Cyprus, a lonely two hours and forty five minutes away. As the dark speck of Rhodes finally faded into the morning mist behind the cruising Rapides, the pilots were left to contemplate two more droning hours of sitting up front in their glazed hothouses, the ever hotter East Mediterranean sun rising slowly up their windscreens. With the temperature increasing as the sun climbed, the cockpit side windows were opened to allow cooling streams of air into their cockpits and cabins; those lucky enough to have cooling ducts in the aircraft's nose opened them, and fuel conservation was attempted by careful use of the throttles and a slight easing forward of the mixture controls to lean off the fuel/air mixtures being fed to the Queens. The pilots found themselves hoping that the gentle summer wind and weather would hold, that the leader's navigation was accurate, and that their own Queens would continue their steady booming roar, as they had done for the past few days. It was an anxious flight for the leader and his pilots - one to be enjoyed only in retrospect.

After over three hours' flight, all five aircraft landed thankfully at Nicosia not long after breakfast time. Refuelling of men and machines was completed quickly and efficiently by Cyprus Airways staff on the baking tarmac and they were soon happily into the climb towards cooler air again on the comparatively short 150-mile leg across the Mediterranean to the Lebanese coast and Beirut. Here, they would surely be able to find out what lay in store for them and their aircraft.

On arrival at Beirut airport on 2nd September, the difficulties continued, one upon another. At passport control, before they could leave the tarmac, officials would not let the tired crews enter Lebanon without visas, which they did not possess. Several more hours of fuss and pleas that they were United Nations staff, together with calls to UN Headquarters in Rhodes, eventually managed to prevail, and the crews found their way to the local UN office. No help was available here regarding repainting of the aircraft, the movement down to Haifa or the tasking for the aircraft, and Captain Bolte was advised to contact Morton Air Services, to assist in having the aircraft painted. Morton were unable to assist in any way, having no representation in the Middle East, so the Dutchmen decided to carry out the repainting themselves. The next day, they borrowed a spray gun from local Air France engineers, sprayed out the British registrations on the fuselage and wings of all the Rapides, and then sprayed on four foot high light blue 'UN' letters. Having completed this in the heat of the Beirut hangars, they felt they could safely move down to their final destination at Haifa, but they were refused clearance to enter Haifa by the UN Chief of Staff there. They would have to "wait for further instructions" and clearance from Haifa.

By the third day in Beirut, the team was becoming very short of cash, and could find no help from their airline nor from the Dutch government, neither of which was represented in Beirut, nor from UN headquarters. The only KLM agent was in Haifa, and he could not supply money "as the country was in a war situation, and they were in hostile territory". Captain Bolte was by now feeling desperate with the lack of support, money and instructions. Having made great efforts to get here, it appeared to him that they were not expected or even wanted. Another day was wasted, while they awaited some instructions from their supposed masters in Haifa.
Finally, on 6th September, after five frustrating days in Beirut, someone who was expected to understand the situation and explain all to the beleaguered Dutchmen arrived from Haifa. He was the Head of UN Flight Operations, a seconded American Air Force captain, somewhat appropriately called De Angelis, and called to see the Dutch team at their hotel. The euphoria rapidly evaporated, however, as the good captain appeared to have a completely different operation in mind from that anticipated by the Dutchmen, and the BOAC/KLM contract.

Captain De Angelis had wanted the Rapides to be used on regular passenger flights from Beirut to Cairo (375 miles) and Alexandria, then back to Beirut (400 miles), with additional routes to Cyprus and Rhodes. A fleet of American Dakotas was currently being used for such 'milk run' flights in the region, and the Dutchmen were expected to be able to use their aircraft for the same tasks, with the probability that they would also be fired on by anti-aircraft guns when approaching Beirut, as had the American aircraft. If they met such hostile action, this would entail diversion back to Cairo, a further 375-mile journey. They were also expected to fly UN observers over the disputed areas in Palestine at 1,000 feet above ground level, take full loads of observers to various places, including over the 8,000-foot Jebel mountains from Beirut to places such as Baalbek and Damascus and down to Jerusalem.

C/n 6872 G-APBJ, ex UN-8, at Croydon in 1957 after sale to Aerocontacts but still in hastily-altered camouflage. [CND]

They were expected to use both morse and voice radios on HF frequencies, with a radio operator on board all flights.

It was obvious that nobody had considered the capabilities of the contracted aircraft. Captain Bolte then explained that he could not carry out most the tasks the UN were requesting because their Rapides simply had neither the performance nor equipment for that work. Captain De Angelis realised that they had the wrong aircraft for the job, and set about trying to resolve the problem through UN headquarters. On the sixth day at Beirut, the UN deputy Chief of Staff, Mr Seward, came back with Captain De Angelis to discuss the problems with the Dutch team, and left after agreeing to explain to UNO in Paris that they had requested the wrong type of aircraft for the UN task. To compound the complications, the two Dutch Dominies, wearing the registrations PH-VNB/UN-8 and PH-VND/UN-9 arrived at Beirut that day, having been sent by a well-intentioned Dutch government. They were flown by junior pilots Mas Jelier and Wim de Jong, under the supervision of KLM Captain Krouwel, who was due to return immediately to Amsterdam after the delivery. But yet again, there were no visas for the new arrivals, so another two hours were spent trying to persuade the immigration officers that these were bona fide UN pilots.

Over the next four days, the pilots waited frustratedly in Beirut for the UN system to resolve the problem of the Rapides, and for the KLM system to find some money to pay for their hotel charges. By now they felt like tramps, having been unable to obtain anything but food, and that on extended credit, so that, when a potential new KLM agent called Mr Aboujaoude came onto the scene with the offer of a loan of 300 Lebanese pounds to cover their expenses, he was warmly welcomed. This new contact was now asked to help with communications back to Europe, in the expectation of taking over the KLM agency. By the thirteenth day of frustration in Beirut, Captain Bolte at last received clearance for the two long range Rapides, UN-2 and UN-4, to carry out some UN tasks while they awaited the decision on the whole Rapide debacle.

In the meantime, the United Nations had other, more pressing matters in hand, as the Palestinian situation was rapidly deteriorating. The senior UN representative, Count Bernadotte, was murdered in Jerusalem by Jewish extremists on 17th September, and his place taken by his deputy, the UN mediator, Dr Ralph Bunge. Occasional Rapide flights were now taking place between Beirut and Haifa, and five days after his predecessor's death, the new UN chief was flown by Captain Bolte from Beirut to Jerusalem. As the Dutch pilot's diary later noted : "I had never seen such a heavily-guarded airstrip. Everywhere machine guns, armoured cars and some heavy tanks. A creepy sight."

Soon afterwards, one of the American Dakota pilots was forced to make an emergency landing near the Dead Sea and then, along with his passenger, was brutally murdered by Arab terrorists, who had wrongly believed the passenger to be the Commander of the American Seventh Fleet, then based in the Eastern Mediterranean. A Rapide flight was made into the war zone to bring back to Haifa, in some haste, an unidentified Englishman who had been sentenced to death by both Jews and Arabs, before he could be caught by either side. Later in the month, Captain Nijdam flew Rapide UN-4 in an attempt to take some passengers over the Jebel mountains to Damascus, east of Beirut. The mountain range here averages around 8,000 feet, rising just east of the town to over 8,600 feet. In the high Lebanese summer temperatures, the heavily-laden Rapide could only just manage to crawl up to the level of a mountain pass, and skim over the top on the way through, with only feet to spare, before cruising down to Damascus without further incident. For safety reasons, the aircraft were not permitted by the UNO to use this route again, so confirming Captain Bolte's concerns.

By the end of September, Captain De Angelis obtained UNO confirmation that the Rapide contract was to be terminated, so Captain Bolte planned his return journey with his little fleet on 1st October. This time he had seven aircraft to lead, and he discussed his concerns with the UN staff. The greatest worry was the navigation problem on the long leg from Cyprus to Rhodes, this time against the prevailing westerly wind. Without a chance of checking his position on the over-sea crossing, he could only rely on forecast winds for the leg, and would have no idea if the winds were correct until he saw the coast of Rhodes. Or not! However, Captain Bolte felt that if he could somehow obtain a range-check half way across the sea leg, before his Point of no return, he would be able to confirm the forecast winds, and decide whether to continue or to return. He asked Captain De Angelis to arrange to have a UN warship steam to a point halfway between Cyprus and Rhodes, and wait as a position check for the Rapides to overfly. The UN Operations Chief agreed to make an urgent request to the US Navy.

Captain Bolte could not wait for confirmation of his request for the ship, so led his team away from Beirut for Nicosia as planned on 1st October. The winds were forecast to be light, and just within the range of the standard Rapides, so the formation left Nicosia at low level towards the West coast of Cyprus. Careful checks on speed and wind effect indicated that the wind was as forecast, therefore they set off from the Cyprus coast for the lonely leg to Rhodes, willing the fourteen Gipsy Queens to run steadily for the next two and a half hours.

By half-way, there was no sign of the warship. Had the winds changed, or had the aircraft compass drifted off, giving false readings? Surely the other aircraft would have warned if there had been a compass problem, so Captain Bolte carried on, in the hope that he was right, and the warship was wrong. After an agonising three hours, the smudge of the Rhodes coastline was now becoming definite on the horizon, and he still had six aircraft strung out around him, so he began to feel that they might all make it after all. Soon after, he did see the UN warship - it was safely riding at anchor in Rhodes harbour.

Two of the Rapides had less than four gallons remaining in their tanks on landing - enough for maybe seven or eight minutes of flight. As Herman Bolte later commented "Never again!"

The rest of the return journey progressed well until Captain Bolte in UN-2 had a recurrence of his plug-fouling episode, and had to hand over the lead to Captain Nijdam for the leg to Lyon. Another set of plugs and an hour later, UN-2 left to catch up but on arriving in the Lyon area above cloud, Captain Bolte was puzzled to make out five circling Rapides. What were they doing following each other overhead Lyon? And where was the sixth aircraft? Was the leader, Nijdam, in the group? As soon as they saw Bolte, the other aircraft joined him in formation, but Bolte needed to know which was the missing aircraft. There was no communication between the aircraft, and when Bolte slowed down to try to make out who was missing, the others slowed down too, not wishing to lose their leader. Confusion all round. But what was he to do? The other five had almost certainly refuelled at Lyon, and eventually his engineer and radio operator managed to count all but Nijdam in the following group, which meant they had somehow lost Nijdam and were circling, trying to find him.

With their lack of radio and navigation skills, they would certainly have been lost above cloud, so Bolte would have to help them find their next destination. He had enough fuel in his aircraft to reach Paris, so indicating by hand signals for the others to follow him, he hoped to find his way to Le Bourget. He set off northwards with the other five following. When the cloud begun to clear, he set about confirming his position and descended to around 1,000 feet to see a large town with a cathedral. But was it Chartres or Orleans? He could not tell, as he only had a narrow strip map for navigation, and this town was not on it. Soldiering on northwards, he continued until he reckoned the other aircraft had only about 30 minutes' fuel left. They must find somewhere to land soon.

By now he "did not feel at ease", not knowing where he was, and with five inexperienced pilots behind him. He knew that he ought to be getting close to Paris, and hoped that he might stumble across one of the many old wartime airfields in the area. Then, to his great relief, a reasonable-looking runway came into view below the nose, and he made a low pass down the runway, followed by five other anxious pilots. There were no obstacles and there was a convenient wind-sock and a hangar, so he landed and thankfully shut down at the end of the runway, closely followed by another five white Rapides, all very glad to be on the ground. Whilst his colleagues came up to ask where they were, it was not until a farmer rode up on a bicycle that he discovered that they were at Dreux, some 45 miles west of Paris, and many miles west of the track on his chart.

After that hairy journey, they were all happy to be so close to home, and were welcomed by the members of the local flying club, whose field they had invaded. The local bar had a small hotel attached, so after a few phone calls to arrange fuel from KLM in Paris, and to make contact with Captain Nijdam, they had a great party with the Dreux Club members. Nijdam had in fact set off from Lyon in the lead, and climbed up through cloud on track for Paris, expecting the others to follow close behind. His less-experienced followers had, however, done their normal procedure of climbing overhead the airfield on departure, and had only seen each other, the leader by now being miles ahead, en route to Paris. Nijdam had continued on alone to Le Bourget.

Fuel arrived at Dreux next morning, so the six Rapides flew direct to Amsterdam together on 6th October, thus ending a fascinating

One of the UN Rapides being refuelled at Dreux on the homeward leg to Schiphol. *[Bolte]*

G-AHTT c/n 6966 at Kermanshah in 1948, with the Anglo Iranian Oil Co. *[BAe]*

but frustrating adventure. The British Rapides were flown back to Croydon two days later, to resume their quiet life as light transports, while the two Dutch-registered machines went back to their former tasks with the Klu.

MIDDLE EAST OIL COMPANIES

As the Middle East recovered from the effects of the Second World War, the oil companies which still had interests in the area recommenced exploration and drilling operations, operating from the same bases as before, and many with new or replaced British-registered Rapides. The Anglo-Iranian Oil Company took on seven Rapides in 1946 and used them from Abadan until 1951, when the four survivors were 'nationalised' following the Iranian take-over of the oilfields. One such was G-AHTT, one of the last Brush-built Dominies, which de Havilland sold direct to AIOC in June 1946 for service at Abadan, which after the take-over by the Iranian government became EP-AAX with the National Oil Company.

The Iraq Petroleum Transport Company had two Haifa-based Rapides, G-AESR and G-AFFB, operated by Airwork since before the war, but these were returned to England in 1946/47. This company also operated an aggregate of twelve Rapides from Tripoli airport, Lebanon, between 1945 and 1956. Of these aircraft, G-AGOP was written-off after crashing in the Syrian desert in June 1948, and G-AGUV was destroyed by fire after an accident at Tarif, in the Persian Gulf, in April 1954. The others were all sold locally between 1950 and 1956, including four to Air Jordan in late 1951. Five other Rapides, including Skyways' 'Sky Trail', G-AHFJ and Airwork's G-AJFJ, were operated under contract to the Kuwait Oil Company, in the late 40s.

CANADA

Unusually, one Rapide went to Canada late in its life, whereas most other Canadian Rapides went there soon after their construction. G-AKGV had been built as Dominie NR697 for the RAF, with which service it worked from October 1944 until 1947, when it was sold as a charter aircraft to Ciro's Aviation, based at Gatwick. William Dempster Ltd then bought it in 1948 , selling it on again in 1950 to the aircraft parts specialist Vendair at Croydon, who kept it for all of five days before moving it on to a French owner, Air-Caen, as F-BFPU, for use as a parachute club transport. Its C of A lapsed in 1971, and a few years later the British de Havilland specialist, Stuart Filhol, brought it to Coventry, but did not operate it. In 1976 Filhol sold it to George LeMay of Acme, near Calgary in Canada, for an asking price of £4,000. The Rapide

Arab Contracting and Trading's OD-ABL c/n 6672 at Beirut West after a fire while refuelling, 1955. *[CND]*

William Dempster's G-AKGV, c/n 6796, visiting a racecourse in 1949, was soon to be sold to France and later to Canada. *[D.Fox]*

was flown all the way across to Calgary in August 1976, some 6,050 miles, taking 60 hours 30 minutes for the journey. It then flew as C-GXFJ from LeMay's farm strip, where it was lovingly cared for alongside his Beech Staggerwing, a de Havilland Dove, a Tiger Moth in many pieces and several other aircraft. LeMay and his wife Bonnie had bought their first de Havilland aircraft, a Tiger Moth, in 1959, and kept his collection until 1996. In 1978, LeMay realised the Rapide was in need of a proper restoration, and set about the long process, finishing in 1982, at which time he changed the registration to C-FAYE, to resemble that of another Canadian Rapide, CF-AYE, the third Rapide in Canada, which fifty years earlier had flown for Quebec Airways.

The LeMay family continued to fly their Rapide, which last appeared at the Kamloops Airshow in 1991, before being placed into storage at Acme. George sadly died in 1996, and in 1999 Bonnie donated the aircraft, still in its red, white and blue colour scheme, and with the typical Canadian extended fin fairing, to the Ontario Bushplane Heritage Centre at Saulte Ste Marie, Ontario, where it remains on display today.

Six other Rapides survived post-war, several flying for Queen Charlotte Airways, using floats and wheels as necessary. Most were pensioned off in the 1950s and, apart from C-FAYE, the only other survivor is CF-PTK, which is with the Reynolds Aviation Museum at Wetaskiwin, Alberta. There is a possibility that Queen Charlotte's CF-BND, which had crashed on Digby Island in 1949 and remained stored until donated in the mid-1980s to the Western Canada Aviation Museum at Winnipeg, may still exist.

C/n 6796 as F-BFPU of Air Caen on a visit to Jersey, 1959, before transfer to Canada as C-FAYE in 1982. *[CND]*

CF-DIM c/n 6928, temporarily back on wheels after its floats had been replaced, 1951. *[CND]*

G-ALWI c/n 6703 when with Shorts of Rochester, 1951, before sale to Hanoi as F-BGPJ. *[D.Fox]*

DH 89s IN LAOS

There are reports from experts in Laos, including T Lee, that up to nine different Rapides saw service there, but details are sketchy and unconfirmed. It is probable that several government organisations flew Rapides from the mid-1950s to as late as 1966. Air Laos apparently flew at least 4; a company called Veha Akat operated 5, including some from Air Laos; and Compagnie Air Transport flew one at around the same time. A 1966 photo shows a severely-damaged DH 89 that nosed-over at Vang Vieng, with an obscured registration, but probably XW-TAJ, a Laotian registration from about 1962.

One Rapide that operated extensively in Laos had previously been G-ALWI with Short Brothers at Rochester. This was sold to Hanoi as F-BGPJ in 1952 and flown by Aigle Azur Indochine and then Societe Autrex before being transferred to Laos Air-Service in 1955. It went to Veha Akat at Vientiane for rebuild in 1963, and may have survived as late as 1976. Another Rapide, built as Dominie NR744, was sold as G-ALET to Mannin Airlines of Ronaldsway in 1948, then registered as F-OALD for service with The Far East Rubber Co in Saigon in 1952. Around 1960 it became XW-TAB for use by Royal Air Lao, which was the successor to Air Laos, but it probably only saw limited service.

After service in the Isle of Man, G-ALET c/n 6832 went to Saigon in 1952. *[D.Fox]*

Mike Kimbrell's N2290B c/n 6588 in silver colours, Oregon, 1979, after many years' service in India as VT-ASA. *[DHMC]*

INDIA
Tata Airlines, founded before the Second World War, became Indian National Airways, and continued operating its services throughout India during the war. One of its aircraft, VT-ASA, had been built at Hatfield for the RAF in 1941 as X7446, but after being held briefly at 18 MU Dumfries, was shipped from Liverpool to Karachi, then part of India, in March 1942 to begin a fascinating career.

First user in India was the Royal Air Force, when it worked as a staff transport aircraft for Air Headquarters India, based at New Delhi. In common with several of the RAF Dominies in India, it was sold on to Indian National Airways in 1944, becoming VT-ASA. From 1946, it took part in air survey work from Calcutta's Dum Dum airport, where it acquired some extra downward-facing glazing in the cockpit. After running into a monsoon ditch at Ondal on 24 March 1959, causing severe damage and being repaired, it spent another 19 years in India until it was bought by an American, Buzz Gothard of Washington State, being one of two shipped to Portland, Oregon for rebuild. An enthusiastic Mike Kimbrell, of nearby Oakville, completed the rebuild in September 1979 and then flew it, as N2290B, for the next 13 years, visiting many historic aircraft events in the USA. In 1992, John Schell, a recently-retired Boeing 747 Captain for Northwest Airlines, decided he wished to sample the old style of transport flying and bought the Rapide, for use from his home at Puyallup, near Seattle. Captain Schell kept the Rapide for another ten years, proudly displaying it at many West Coast air shows, before selling it on to Al Stix and John Cournoyer, of Creve Coeur, Missouri, in 2003. The new owners, operating as the Historic Aircraft Restoration Museum, keep the old girl in good airworthy condition, and are currently considering a more appropriate colour scheme.

SOUTH AFRICA
At least twelve Rapides served in South Africa post-war, most going to mining companies, and some later being taken over by Rhodesian companies. Of the aircraft that remained in South Africa, several were flown from the Natal province town of Ladysmith, near the east coast, and north of the Drakensberg Mountains. Drakensberg Air Services and African Air Services used Ladysmith as their main base and flew many communications flights south into the mountainous region often called the Roof of

ZS-CAB c/n 6411 at Mokhotlong, with locals, 1950. *[K Fuller]*

Africa, where the highest point, then in Basutoland, but now known as Lesotho, is over 11,000 feet high. An ex-SAAF pilot, Bill Teague, remembered some flights in 1952 by Drakensberg pilots into a remote settlement in Basutoland called Mokhotlong ('The place of the Bald Ibis' in Sotho), which took them over some spectacular scenery - not a nice place to have an engine failure in a Rapide. Drakensberg owner and pilot Peter Strong regularly had a magnificent view of the 'Barrier of Spears' as he headed south from Ladysmith en route to Basutoland, with Natal completely covered by low cloud. The Mokhotlong settlement was not an easy destination, and at 9,000 feet above sea level, was one of the highest airfields in Africa. There were no roads leading to it, the only access being by foot, horse or aeroplane. With the decreased air density at the airstrip, the Rapide pilots had to be very wary of speeds and power settings when flying into the strip, and even starting the Gipsy Queens was tricky at that altitude. Unfortunately at least two pilots misjudged the difficulties of flying into the Mokhotlong strip, as both ZS-AKT and ZS-DDX, two of

An impressive view of the Drakensburg 'Barrier of Spears' from a Drakensburg Air Services Rapide, 1950. *[K Fuller]*

ZS-DDI c/n 6658 joined the Air Brousse fleet in 1959 as OO-CJX, and is seen here at Leopoldville with her sister ship. *[BAe]*

Drakensberg's fleet of Rapides, were badly damaged in accidents there in 1955.

Associated Manganese Mines, a mining company based in the very barren and mainly unpopulated Postmasburg area in South Africa's Northern Cape Province, took on a Rapide in 1949 for use as a personnel and light freight transport. The aircraft was ZS-DDI, which had previously served as VP-YCI with Southern Rhodesia Air Services during the War, and which in 1946 became Central African Airways . A young Captain Ken Fuller remembers his first flying job in his home country, when he was taken on by AMM to fly ZS-DDI. His routine was to fly from Postmasburg to the other company mines at Black Rock, and Glosam, with occasional more interesting trips to Kimberley in the east or the civilisation of Rand airport.

Associated Manganese Mines, ZS-DDI
Captain Ken Fuller
Captain Fuller's first trip for his new company was to fly out solo to the company mine at Black Rock, land at the adjacent airstrip, to collect the manager, Mr Harris, and bring him back to Postmasburg. "Having never been there before, I was informed that the strip was next to the mine,. In those days, the area was still very isolated and bushy, and the railway line was yet to be built. I, of course, knew what a mine consisted of: headgear, reduction works, mine dumps, etc.... This was not so in a small outcrop mine. Without a care in the world, I took off, and at the due estimated time, flew over a bush strip. Surely this can't be it I thought. I saw no mine (as I knew it) and so decided to carry on a bit further. After a search, however, I decided that it must have been the strip and the mine, so landed.

In the meantime, Mr Harris, seeing his aircraft flying overhead, panicked. He thought that I was lost, and quickly instructed a fire to be lit, to guide me back in. On seeing Mr Harris many years later, he remarked, 'Oh, it's you! If I'd known you were coming, I'd have lit a fire'. "

ZS-DDI gave ten years service to AMM and was then sold to Air Brousse in the Belgian Congo as OO-CJX, fading away in the 'new' Zaire in the early 1960s.

Fred Zunckel and Peter Strong with Basutoair Rapide VP-YCI, which became ZS-DDI in 1949. *[W Teague]*

RANA Rapide over a Johannesburg mine, 1938. *[CND]*

Captain Brian Waugh with his mount, ZK-AHS, c/n 6423 at the scenic Franz Josef glacier airstrip. [R Waugh]

Hokitika to Haast in ZK-AHS, which had been one of Cook Strait Airways' aircraft, and had returned to civilian flying in 1944, after RNZAF service. The flight departed Hokitika at 1030 every other day, for the one-hour journey to Haast, at a cost, in 1956, of £4 for the single trip.

West Coast service, ZK-AHS
Captain Paul Beauchamp-Legg
"I drop the Rapide down to 200 feet, white surf slips by on the left. A grey nothingness on the right will get thicker on the headlands further south. Should turn back but the pommie manager would complain again...Drop down another 100 feet. Can see a little better now. Maybe a thousand yards ahead, certainly not a mile. Time and position, jot it down on the log.

Bring her down to 50 feet. Jaw tightens. The motors drone on, perfectly synchronised. Trim slightly back. A salty vapour rises from the surf. Can only see a dim suggestion of darkness where bush and hills should be on the left. No sign of mountains. Move further out to sea, nothing to hit out there. Inch her down a bit more. Should turn back.

Wipe sweat from my hands. I don't like it.... Slip a hanky under one hand. No sign of the Wanganui Bluffs. Move out some more. Surf has disappeared. I'm in a little grey world of my own. Isolated from reality. Daren't turn left, might hit the Bluffs. Stick to heading and watch the water for a change of colour beneath. A change to dark vinegar will be water from the Wanganui River beyond the Wanganui Bluffs and then slatey-grey Cook River. Move in to pick up the surf again. Feel safer with a reference. A minute seems like a lifetime. Okarito Cliffs will be hidden. Bruce Bay will be worse. It always is.

Drop down to 20 feet. Can see better now. A bit like driving a high speed car along the road - only difference is the white surf on my left disappears amongst rocks here and there. Death lurks out to the right where sky and sea merge.

Mouth is dry. I run my tongue around and force a swallow. What's it like ahead? Alan said he would let me know if it deteriorated at Haast. Perhaps this won't last much further. I'll wait a while. Turn a few degrees to the right, make a mental note of time and position. Navigating now by dead reckoning and the colour of the water beneath.

Too thick to see the Okarito Bluffs, but the water suddenly turns slatey-grey. Glacial water. I'm over the Cook River mouth. Time? Call Haast for present weather before the scheduled Bruce Bay call. Good bloke Alan. Climbs a ladder outside the Haast Post Office to have a look around.

'Can see about a mile up the coast', he replies and adds 'Mosquito Hill is covered. Over'

'Roger. It's a bit thick here. I'll call you again at Bruce Bay.'

I put the microphone back on its hook, without looking. Thickening ahead.

The sea and fog are waiting. Minutes seem an eternity. My mouth is dry; hands are sweating; muscles are tensing. Fear is on me.

Visibility is dropping. The cloud is forming a sinister shroud.... Worse than death. I'm almost in it. I've ventured too far.

Open the throttles; stand on the wingtip and turn back. Grey walls close around me. I am gripped by absolute fear.

Level the wings. Check the compass heading. Trained mind keeps the jellied body working. I peer through the open window, body exhausted, feet chattering on the rudder pedals. Where is the surf? Where are the headlands, all rocky and black? Turn a few degrees to the left to intersect the surf at a shallow angle. Praying fast

Ex New Zealand VH-BGP c/n 6648 airborne at Drage's Airworld, Wangaratta, Australia, 1984. [CND]

now..... The oily sea, usually my friend, watches. A primeval force turned against me with its offspring; the cloud waiting for one false move.

A whitish line appears. I've made it back to the beach.

In these conditions the Fox Glacier airstrip is sometimes open. Wait for the glacial water to show beneath, then turn right and follow the water course, could so easily hit the trees at the side. The ceiling lifts, can see ahead, better call Haast.

Firm and controlled voice... 'Haast Radio, this is AHS'. No reply.

Try again, ' Haast Radio, this is AHS. Diverting to Fox'. Still no reply. Too low. There is always a dead spot amongst these hills.....

Cloud firms and shelves upwards. Fox Glacier settlement ahead. The hotel with its sloping airstrip never looked more welcome."

New Zealand Southland Services
As it's name might suggest, Southern Scenic Airways was formed to operate tourist and scheduled flights to the spectacular scenery around the Southern Alps, based on the delightful Frankton airfield at Queenstown, on the edge of Lake Wakatipu, in the centre of South Island. The company grew steadily, with a fleet of Austers and Cessnas, moving on to Rapides in 1956. Rapides operated by Southern Scenic Airways were ZK-BAU, and the two from West Coast Airways, ZK-AKS and ZK-AKT, when that company was absorbed later that year. The company continued to expand their services, with several schedules and scenic flights from Queenstown to Dunedin, Invercargill and across the Alps to Milford Sound. While the mountain and lake scenery was most impressive for the SSA passengers, the high ground and changeable weather also had their effect.

ZK-AKY c/n 6653 parked beside its National Airways Corporation hangar, Wellington, 1950. [CND]

TAT Rapide ZK-AHS c/n 6423 at Queenstown airfield in 1969. *[R Waugh]*

Joy-riding, New Zealand West Coast
Paul Beauchamp-Legg, by then with West Coast Airways at Hokitika, remembers flying out of Milford Sound in the early 1960s.

"When Southern Scenic Airways were short of a pilot I sometimes based at Milford Sound with a Dominie, doing scenic flying for them.

After dinner at the Milford Hotel, I would show slides and sometimes films which I had taken, so that I could sell at least two planeloads for the next morning. This allowed for one load to take off soon after daybreak and by the time I came down from that flight the second flight would be waiting and with a bit of luck the first flight would sell the third flight. This would go on until around about 10 a.m. when cloud began to develop and many of the hotel guests would be leaving. There was then a lull and I would aim the longer flights for the afternoon when the buses came back in with more passengers.

At one of my slide evenings a retired RAF man remembered the 'little old Dominie.' "We used to trundle the mail out to France during the war with that," he said, somewhat downgrading our wonderful twin-engined biplane. I got the impression that he was after all an ex RAF pilot and I was just a mere postwar civilian pilot. I managed to sell him a flight for the morning. He sat on the seat behind me so that I could chat to him. Most people were very impressed as we flew over the deep black waters of Milford Sound, Mitre Peak towering up on our left and the other peaks on our right. The half-mile wide entrance in this magnificent area appeared almost too narrow for the aeroplane to fit through. In fact when I came in from the coast end I often banked the aircraft as we entered the Sound and I would say to the passengers, "Would you watch that wingtip while I watch the other one." Some of them really believed me.

My ex-RAF passenger did not seem to be at all impressed - I think he had flown in Norway.

We flew out to the entrance and turned around to the right and climbed up near the top of Mount Tutuko where there is a narrow little cul-de-sac with a glacier and lots of snow and ice. On this morning, near the very top proudly stood a thar, lord of all he surveyed. This was absolutely magnificent and with the aeroplane flying in this relatively narrow confine most passengers were ecstatic".

My ex-RAF man sat mildly interested.

We carried on with the flight until we came to the top of the Sutherland Falls. Flying around the lake at the top just above the water in the very narrow confines was, even to pilots, spectacular. I used to sweep around then do a very steep diving turn at the very top of the falls and head off descending along a narrow valley. This allowed the passengers on the left hand side to look straight down from the top of the waterfall and if they were quick, take some photographs. The passengers on the right usually started to get out of their seats to look down the left hand side too. 'Will those of you sitting on the right hand side stay in your seats,' I would shout 'because in a moment those of you on the right hand side will be able to look back up the waterfall'. My ex RAF passenger, somewhat awestruck at long last, asked in a very humble voice, somewhat tinged with anxiety, ' Are you going to turn around in here?'

'There's no choice, mate,' I replied. 'There is just a blank wall at the end of this valley'."

Typical of the smaller New Zealand airlines, SSA was merged with Tourist Air Travel in 1965, and then into Cook Strait Airlines in 1968. The Rapides continued to serve, with occasional accidents diminishing the numbers, despite all the company changes. New Zealand Tourist Air Travel, Trans Island Airways, West Coast Airways and Ritchie Air Services all used the type post-war. There are still five DH 89s in existence which have seen service in New Zealand - ZK-AHS, now at Auckland; ZK-AKS, at Mandeville; ZK-AKY also at Mandeville; ZK-ALB, which is now VH-UTV in New South Wales; and ZK-BCP, which is now VH-BGP. This remarkable longevity is certainly a tribute to temperate climate, good flying, good maintenance and tremendous enthusiasm on the part of the New Zealand aviation fraternity. There is also another Rapide under rebuild in New Zealand - ZK-SWR - which Captain Gerald Grocott and partners recovered from Belgium via England in 1996, and which is also at Mandeville.

Joy-riding from Queenstown to the Southern Alps
One of SSA's most exciting regular trips (for both passengers and pilots) was the journey out of Queenstown's valley airfield, to the Southern Alps, Sutherland Falls and Milford Sound. The cost in 1961 for the return flight was £6 10s, and it was certainly worth it for a most impressive experience. Flying first across the 6,000-foot Humboldt and Ailsa Mountain ranges, then heading west to the Sutherland Falls, where the river drops 1,904 feet down a sheer cliff face, the Rapide flight then turned north towards the short strip perched below the Milford Sound Hotel, on the edge of the spectacular Lake Ada. This was where the pilots had most of their excitement, as the strip was narrow, short and one-way, with a steep-sided cliff at the eastern end. Once committed to land here, there was no possibility of making a missed approach because of the very restricted terrain.

After a cup of tea at the remote Hotel, passengers returned to the Rapide for a take-off in the opposite direction, sweeping out over the 12-mile long, steep-sided Milford Sound, and usually keeping well below the height of the 5,500-foot Mitre Peak to the south, and the 6,700-foot Pembroke Peak to the north, until well outside the Sound. The return trip was then to the north, across more lakes and valleys, finally crossing the 6,000-foot Richardson Mountains and back into Frankton.

Russell Troon, one of SSA's Rapide pilots, remembered a flight from Queenstown, north-east to Taieri.
"I encountered much lightning when flying over the Lammerlaw range, just as a southwest cold front hit us. A bright ball of about ¾ the size of a basketball struck the Dominie around the DF loop aerial and travelled along the flying and landing wires then exited with a bang at the starboard wing tip. This was a rare occurrence during my flying career but quite spectacular and alarming for the passengers. When I landed there was damage to the discharge wicks and one aileron hinge.

Russell was always on the lookout for fun when flying on the west coast area :

"On a flight, early in the morning, I came across the [Royal Australian Navy] aircraft carrier Melbourne, just off the Milford Sound. I decided to try a 'touch and go' on the deck, and as the Dominie descended on approaching the carrier's deck, just a few hundred yards off, I suddenly saw a gun being trained on me and then there was a bright flash! I don't know if it was a blank but I got the message, turned away and rapidly descended to sea level and scampered back to Milford as fast as I could"

In 2004, around forty-nine Rapides still exist world-wide, with about fourteen maintained in airworthy condition. The extant aircraft are widely spread, and to be found in Argentina, Australia, Belgium, Brazil, Canada, Denmark, France, Germany, Great Britain, Holland, Israel, New Zealand, South Africa, Spain, Turkey and the USA. The aircraft and their current sites are noted at Appendix 2, their individual histories described in our companion volume.

Section 5:
The DH 90 Dragonfly

Section 5 – Chapter 1: Design and Development

With all the design expertise available in the smart new Hatfield offices in 1935, it is not surprising that yet another new de Havilland design idea came to fruition that summer. The Dragon, Dragon Rapide and Express Air Liner were still in production, but the concept of a smaller aircraft, for use by the private owner for long-range, reasonably quick journeys, using the same basic principles as the Rapide, was investigated. This would be the 90th de Havilland design, and, endorsing its relationship to the other members of the Dragon family, was to be called the Dragonfly.

The intention was to produce a five-seat, twin-engined 'Air Saloon', with the basic qualities of speed, range and safety to enable the private owner to make continental trips in comfort. Range would be around 625 miles with full payload, or as much as 885 miles with reduced payload, using the same twin-engined, aerodynamic format as the Rapide, but with less power, lower weight and a smaller cabin. The engines could be smaller and less thirsty, so the 130 hp Gipsy Major would provide enough power for a 125 mph cruise, while still allowing twin-engined safety factors. The designers wanted to make use of newer construction methods, so using experience from the DH 88 Comet racer, the fuselage was to be a three-ply monocoque construction, with double curvature back to the luggage compartment, then simpler single curvature aft from that point. Considerable experimentation had by this time taken place in the Hatfield woodshop, to find the most effective method of using dies to press the newly-cemented plywood sheets to the desired shape. A synthetic resin cement was used on the sheets, then they were heated and pressed into shape on the dies while still wet. This was the process to be used on the Dragonfly and also the much larger DH 91 Albatross airliner, which was then taking shape on the drawing boards.

The wing bracing would be simpler and less cluttered by thickening the section of the lower wings and the main spars, so eliminating the need for wire bracing of the inner bay. The extra space in the lower stub wings was therefore made available for 30-gallon fuel tanks, one in each lower wing. Following lessons learned from the DH 86, a Turner compression-strut undercarriage and engine mountings were attached to the ends of these thicker spars, giving greater strength to the whole assembly. A tapered wing planform was to be used, but this time with shorter-span lower wings, ailerons only on the upper wings, and with split flaps on the lower wing, running across the lower fuselage. A nice practical touch was the small, aerodynamic step below the port wing stub, which dropped down when the aircraft was at rest, to help with entry to the cabin door, but which then flew itself neatly into a wing root slot when sufficient airflow passed over it. The tail assembly and control layout were to be virtually standard de Havilland, with wooden spars and ribs, covered in three-ply.

COCKPIT LAYOUT

The main difference from the Rapide was to be the cockpit which was designed for two pilots and dual controls but with a narrower cross-section, so was more cramped for two pilots. The Dragonfly's instrumentation and layout were comprehensive, the night-landing and blind-flying equipment being described in contemporary reports as being 'absolutely complete', consisting of the following illuminated instruments:

- Airspeed indicator,
- Aneroid (altimeter),
- Husun Mk III compass,
- Sperry artificial horizon,
- Sperry directional indicator,
- Air log, type P3,
- 8-day watch,

Prototype E.2 c/n 7500 completing engine tests, Hatfield, August, 1935. *[BAe]*

- 2 rpm indicators,
- 2 oil pressure gauges,
- and 3 'petrol meters' for the fuel tanks.

Dual controls, finished in black Doverite, were fitted, but the narrow cockpit made two spectacle type control wheels too cumbersome, so a removable spade-handled wheel was fitted in front of the co-pilot's seat if required. Engine starting was by Rotax Eclipse electric motors, powered by an internal aircraft battery, which was in turn re-charged by a wind-driven generator fitted into the port top wing root. Wheel brake, flap and landing controls were fitted around the centre of the cockpit area, and throttles and mixture controls were positioned on the left of the pilot's seat, and to the right of the co-pilot's seat. A new brake control was fitted, resembling the American design, with a car-type handle placed rather awkwardly below the port instrument panel, and duplicated flap levers were positioned between the pilots' seats. For the first time on a DH machine, the fuel in any of the three tanks could be used to feed either engine, through a complicated selection system, using a three-way Vickers cock, and this allowed all the fuel to be used in the event of an engine malfunction.

Behind the pilots' seats was a single seat on the right of the cabin, opposite the door, and what the DH brochure later described as a 'broad lounge seat for two passengers' at the rear. In keeping with the style of an executive transport, the whole cabin was soundproofed with 'Cellocol' material, all seating was "upholstered in light grey cloth, with grey headlining and floor carpets to match", and a light luggage and hat rack was placed at the rear of the cabin. There were four fresh-air vents adjacent to the passenger seats, as well as a modest heating system. In a separate compartment behind the cabin was a luggage compartment, containing the aircraft battery and a 25-gallon fuel tank

In this standard format, de Havilland quoted the aircraft's cost, in January 1936 as '£2,650 (Unpacked, ex-works)' which, at current values would equate to around £106,000. This was only £50 less than the price of the larger Dragon, which made the Dragonfly

Standard cockpit, showing spade-grip on right side. *[BAe]*

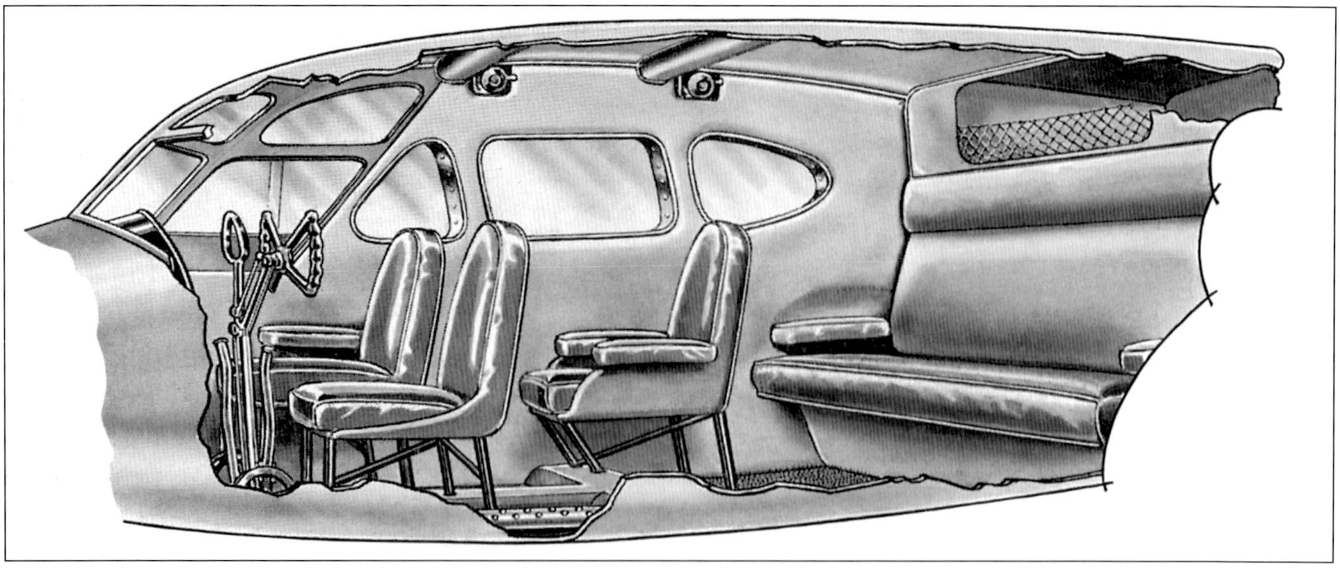

Above: Drawing of DH 90 cabin layout. *[BAe]*

G-AFVJ with Airwork at Heston, 1939. *[BAe]*

relatively expensive. However, the 1936 Dragonfly brochure justified the price by indicating that the aircraft was "designed as the most practical compromise possible to modern technical methods with the deliberate purpose of making available a thoroughly up-to-date aeroplane at a reasonable price".

The design progressed rapidly into reality and the prototype Dragonfly first flew, as E.2, on 12th August 1935, to be registered G-ADNA three days later.

PRODUCTION
By the time the Dragonfly was first certificated in early 1936, twenty-five aircraft had already been ordered by mainly British but also French individuals for personal transport, but five others had been marked down for use by companies for transporting senior company staff. The first year saw a very high rate of production, with forty-three aircraft handed over by the end of 1936. Production then dropped markedly, with only twenty being sold in 1937, a very poor total of four leaving Hatfield in 1938. Production was therefore halted with the sixty-seventh aircraft, ZK-AGP, which was certificated in September 1938.

GIPSY MAJOR 2
The second Dragonfly, G-AEBU, completed in February 1936, just after the prototype had completed its certification flights, was somewhat different, and it was designated a DH 90A. The main difference was in the initial fitting of two Gipsy Major Series II engines, which were slightly more powerful, producing 136 bhp at 2,400 rpm, with an increased compression ratio of 6 to 1. The cylinder heads on this version were changed to aluminium, allowing use of leaded fuel, and a new accessory cover was fitted, permitting the fitment of variable-pitch propellers. The maximum weight of 4,000 lbs was the same for both the DH 90 and DH 90A. In the event, G-AEBU was fitted with the standard Schwarz-finish wooden propellers, so the power output and performance were very similar to those of the standard model. In later years, a few DH 90s also had the Gipsy Major II fitted.

MINOR MODIFICATIONS
Very few changes were made during the three-year production life of the Dragonfly. After de Havilland had used the prototype for some months, its windscreen was modified to a rounded shape to assist in rain dispersion, in place of the original flat panels, which were prone to collecting rain water, considerably decreasing forward visibility. Larger 'eyebrow' clear panels were fitted at the same time, making upward visibility much better but, as far as can be ascertained, no other Dragonflies were modified with this curved windscreen.

The only other minor change by de Havilland was to a Dragonfly destined for use in Kenya by Wilson Airways as VP-KCA, which was fitted out at Hatfield for use as a stretcher-carrying ambulance with an opening panel in the starboard fuselage side, just aft of the co-pilot's seat, into which could be inserted, with some squeezing, a single stretcher. Post-war, several DH 90A operators fitted slightly more powerful Gipsy Major 1C or 10 Mark 2 engines to their Dragonflies, and at least two were modified with toe brakes and a lockable tailwheel, which considerably improved handling after landing.

DH 90A
Despite a general belief that the first 47 aircraft were designated DH 90 and subsequent aircraft then became DH 90As, recent careful research by de Havilland Support Limited, which company holds the design authority for the type, indicates that this is incorrect. Examination of the individual loading labels for each aircraft has now shown that only the first aircraft, G-ADNA, was designated DH 90, and all subsequent aircraft were given the DH 90A designation, although most were fitted with Gipsy Major Series I engines. The designation change to DH 90A of the second Dragonfly, G-AEBU, was almost certainly because it was fitted with the slightly more powerful Gipsy Major Series II engines and this may have caused some confusion with subsequent models, but the recent DHSL research can be taken as the correct situation. Interestingly, despite the different engines in the first two aircraft, de Havilland published the same performance figures for the DH 90A as for the DH 90, so the changes in climb, speed and consumption were presumably too small to note.

PERFORMANCE FIGURES
These figures for performance are taken direct from the Manual for the Operation, Maintenance and Rigging of the de Havilland Dragonfly (Type DH 90) with Gipsy Major Series I engines, produced by de Havilland in June 1936.

WEIGHTS, DIMENSIONS AND GENERAL DATA

WEIGHTS

	lbs
Tare weight, (including standard removable equipment)	2,500
Pilot	160
Fuel, normal, 60 gallons	462
Oil, 7 gallons	68
Luggage	160
TOTAL ALL-UP WEIGHT	4,000

Note: The machine is fitted with 85 gallons fuel tankage as standard - when the whole of this is utilized the pay load will be reduced by 193 lbs.

DIMENSIONS

Length overall	31 ft 8 ins
Span (upper main plane)	43 ft
Span (lower main plane)	38 ft 6 ins
Height	9 ft 2 ins

GENERAL DATA

Wheel track	10 ft 8 ins
Engine centres	10 ft 8 ins
Top wing incidence	2 deg
Bottom wing incidence	2 deg
Top wing dihedral	3 deg 30 min
Bottom wing dihedral	4 deg 30 min
Wing area (including body)	288 sq ft

PERFORMANCE LOADED TO 4,000 LB.

NOTE: All performance figures quoted are based on the most accurate possible tests carried out in England and reduced to International Standard Atmospheric Conditions. It must be borne in mind that local conditions of temperature, humidity and barometric pressure have an important influence on aircraft performance.

Maximum Speed (at sea level)	144-147 mph
Cruising Speed	
At 1,000 ft and 2,100 rpm	127-130 mph
At 1,000 ft and 2.050 rpm	122-125 mph
Cruising fuel consumption at 2,050 rpm	12 galls / hr
Ultimate Range	
With 60 galls at 2,050 rpm	625 miles
With 85 galls at 2,050 rpm	885 miles
Take-off run in 5 mph wind	295 yds
Height at 656 yds from rest in 5 mph wind	110 ft
Distance to standstill from altitude of 50 ft in 5 mph wind	340 yds
Gliding Angle - Flaps up	1 in 10 1/2
Gliding Angle - Flaps down	1 in 8
Rate of Climb at sea level	775 ft/min
Time to Climb to 5,000 ft	7.5 min
Time to Climb to 10,000 ft	19.5 min
Absolute Ceiling	16,000 ft
Service Ceiling	15,700 ft
Ceiling on one engine – On full load	2,100 ft
Laden to 3,750 lb	3,800 ft
Laden to 3,500 lb	5,400 ft
Laden to 3,250 lb	7,400 ft
Laden to 3,000 lb	9,500 ft

Prince Chichibu of Japan, after flight in c/n 7501 G-AEBU, Hatfield, May 1937. This was the only DH 90A, being fitted with Gipsy Major Series II engines. [CND]

VP-KCA c/n 7528 at Hatfield before delivery to Wilson Airways, Kenya, in 1936. *[CND]*

VP-KCA's unusual hatch being used to load a stretcher case, Hatfield, 1936. *[BAe]*

Section 5 – Chapter 2: Testing and Flight Impressions

COMPANY TESTING

The prototype was marked initially as E.2 for company tests from Hatfield and Hubert Broad, still Chief Test Pilot, took the aircraft for its first flight on 12th August 1935. Unusually for a de Havilland aircraft of the period, it was another five months before the aircraft was taken for its C of A tests, but there is no indication in company records of the reason for this delay. It is most likely that all the engineering and testing staff were tied up with other higher-priority projects, such as the DH 86 modifications; design of the new DH 91 Albatross and testing of the DH 92 Dolphin, all of which were underway at the time. It had been entered in the King's Cup Air Race in September 1935, but was withdrawn, presumably because the flight testing had not been completed.

CERTIFICATE OF AIRWORTHINESS TRIALS

The prototype, by now marked as G-ADNA, was eventually flown across to Martlesham Heath in January 1936 for the A&AEE pilots and engineers to check its suitability for a Certificate of Airworthiness. By this time, it had flown 56 hours, so the company test pilots had already completed more than the usual amount of test flying.

Martlesham Test report M/685, dated February 1936

As was standard practice, the tests were carried out at normal, full aft and full forward CGs, and at the maximum 4,000 lb weight, except for the forward CG case, which was flown at only 3,530 lb. Performance figures matched those given by the company, and the take-off and landing runs were given as 355 yards and 195 yards respectively. The controls were judged to be light and effective, becoming slightly heavier with increased speed, as was to be expected, and the aircraft was considered pleasant and easy to fly. The trimming was easy to operate, but there was insufficient trim available for the CG forward. As with the Rapide, the flap control was not considered easy to operate, but only because "the thumb locking device is too stiff".

On stability issues, the aircraft was considered just stable laterally, and it was slow to right itself after lateral disturbance. It was longitudinally stable under all conditions but, as with other recent DH types, was judged to be directionally unstable under all conditions, with power on or off. Having commented on this instability, the report does not mention it again, so the Martlesham team were obviously not concerned about this slight shortcoming. The stalling characteristics section gave a warning that the starboard wing dropped "rather quickly when the flaps are up", but "if immediate action is taken, to prevent entry into a spin, recovery is rapid and certain". Once again, no further comment was made about this rather unpleasant feature, and no recommendation was made about alleviating it.

Most of the comments then came in relation to the take-off and landing qualities. Rather unusually, landings were discussed first, probably because they were considered "easy and pleasant". The elevator control required careful handling, as it was very sensitive, and "owing to the harsh undercarriage, it is difficult to avoid slight bouncing when landing". No mention was made about directional control problems on landing, which is rather surprising when the comments on take-off are examined.

Surprisingly for a de Havilland machine, take-off was considered "difficult, especially on a rough aerodrome". Initially there was insufficient elevator control to lift the tail, which caused poor

Hugh Buckingham demonstrating G-ADNA for publicity photographs, 1936. [Lord Trefgarne]

acceleration. "Full left rudder is necessary at this period to prevent swing. As speed is increased, the elevator controls take effect and being very sensitive, make the aircraft want to porpoise; while violent use of the rudder is necessary to keep the aircraft straight. The aircraft then requires pulling off the ground which gives the pilot the impression that his speed is too low, although if he does not pull it off, the take-off run is unnecessarily long". This paints a pretty drastic picture of the handling characteristics of the aircraft, and makes the lack of A & AEE recommendations to alleviate the problem rather surprising.

Handling on either engine was easy and the rudder trim system felt to be effective. In the 'diving trials', to a limiting speed of 180 mph and 2350 rpm, the aircraft handled steadily and the controls were satisfactory. The final comments concerned the cockpit, where the pilot's seat was considered to be too clo0se to the side of the cockpit, but the view forward and sideways was felt to be good but poor upwards and to the rear.

The trials were judged to be satisfactory, despite the adverse comments related to directional stability. Somewhat unusually, bearing mind the adverse comments on stability, there were no recommendations for modifications, so the Martlesham team recommended the DH 90 be granted a Certificate of Airworthiness in the transport category. The first C of A was then issued for G-ADNA on 17th January, 1936.

COMPANY DEMONSTRATIONS

Once the Dragonfly prototype had completed its testing period in early 1936, the Sales Department began to use it and the second aircraft, G-AEBU, which had been certificated in February, for demonstrations to potential customers at Hatfield and by flying them to events where they would be given wider publicity. Sales Manager Hugh Buckingham took G-AEBU to the opening ceremony of the new airport at Stockholm in May and G-ADNA took part in the King's Cup Air Race in June 1936, flown by Captain de Havilland and his son Geoffrey into eighth place.

G-AEBU continued to serve as a company demonstrator, transport and for use by the members of Hatfield's London Aeroplane Club until May 1938. One of the Service Department engineers, Phil

C/n 7545 VT-AIE for the Maharajah of Indore, 1937. *[BAe]*

Haggar, who was also an A-licensed pilot, remembers going with the urbane Jimmy Buckingham in that aircraft on the eight-hour trip across Europe to Stockholm's new airport at Bromma, south of the city, where there was to be an air show as part of the opening ceremony. The Dragonfly, with only two on board and with 85 gallons of fuel on board, was well-suited to the 1,000-mile journey, so with a single stop at Hamburg, just under half-way, the trip was comfortably completed in a day. Young Phil Haggar, having completed his apprenticeship with the respected de Havilland Technical School two years earlier, went along as engineer and spare pilot. He modestly attributed all the "serious and demonstration" flying to Jimmy, but using the small spade control on the right-hand side, was able to fly much of the transit flights, while Jimmy dozed off to recover from the usual exertions of a demonstration pilot.

FLYING IMPRESSIONS

Having noted the A&AEE comments in 1936, particularly about the difficulties related to poor directional control, it is interesting to see the views of other pilots flying the type in later years.

Hugh Scanlon, Shell Aviation News

One of the Shell Aviation pilots, Hugh Scanlon, used several of the company's Dragonflies, on many occasions in the pre-war period. He considered it "a slippery, flapped, close-coupled biplane with full-gap side cabin areas and sharply tapered wings. The DH 90 was a potential swinger when three-pointed on landing, or if flown off in that attitude - a common enough technique between the wars. In perfectly calm weather you could trim it, retire to the wide back seat and leave the aeroplane to fly itself for an hour hands-off! In a tail-down attitude, though, the slender fin got blanketed and there is evidence that contemporary pilots found the type more difficult than they expected."

Shell had a lot of trouble with their Singapore-based Dragonfly, VR-SAX. "This machine had a malign sense of humour; it swung itself into a knot on no less than three occasions, shearing off just about every load-carrying member at the bottom end and smashing the all-important lower centre-section spar."

Another experienced professional pilot reckoned that: "Given large aerodromes and good weather, the Dragonfly was generally a fine machine. While differing greatly from the Moth class, it should not present difficulties to pilots of average ability. But it is under-powered, with an extremely long take-off run and slow climb with a full load. The pilot's view is restricted especially on the ground, and to starboard at any time, and not much in the way of rain is needed to obscure vision. Nothing like a downward view, so useful in most conditions of poor visibility, can be obtained.

Except in rain, I found the machine easy to land from the start. One cannot, however, take liberties with it, and in my opinion slow-all-the-way-down lift landings are not the most suitable, as it tends to drop quickly the last bit, especially in the tropics" (by this I presume he means that a relatively flat maximum drag approach with a little throttle is preferable to the RAF approved power-off glide.) "Given the normal precautions, the touch-down is quite simple but every now and again it becomes vicious ... As a rule this does not develop gradually but absolutely suddenly and once a real swing starts, it seems almost impossible to stop. At best, flat windshields were a hampering nuisance. It is possible in the DH biplane twins to reach through the clear-view panels with a cloth, but the blast of wet air chills the wrist and soaks one's watch; you can't get at the throttles and altogether the chances of a good arrival diminish somewhat. The Americans adopted curved windscreens long before the Dragonfly's great-grand-daddy the DH 84, or else fitted good fast wipers.

Then again, wheel brakes. American designers fitted early heel or toe brakes and without them, many a pilot would have lost it in a crosswind, or as the airflow got tired around the tail. Why were the British so shy of using their feet?"

Peter Harrison - Flying into Woburn Abbey airstrip in G-AEDT

"When Brian Woodford bought Dragonfly G-AEDT, it was suggested that I would be one of the pilots who could take it into the short Woburn Abbey airstrip during the Moth Club Rally in 1988, and I felt some trepidation at the prospect of being responsible for an almost unique aircraft with its reputation for ground-looping and being easily broken. Then Ron Souch (who restored the aircraft) asked me to go through some engine runs and taxi the aircraft around a bit. This was done, and my first impressions were that the ground handling was somewhat easier than the Rapide, but that the view, particularly to the right, was not as good, due to the side by side seating.

I then flew the aircraft a few days later. The advice had been to keep the tail up in order to keep the rudder in the slipstream, as long as possible, both on take-off and landing, and that the take-off is the danger-point. In fact one venerable ex-pilot of Dragonflies says that in one in every twenty take-offs it will get away. The Dragonfly rudder is definitely not as effective as on the Rapide, and possibly because the CG is quite a long way behind the wheels, if a turn is made on the ground at high speed, either by accident or by attempting to clear the runway too quickly, then the aircraft is prone to 'getting away' from the pilot. Also, with two Gipsy Majors and fairly coarse-pitch props, it does lack the power that one feels when opening the throttles on the Rapide. The approach glide is rather steeper than the Rapide, so the arrival over the Woburn trees should be easier, but the undercarriage suspension is by rubber blocks, which makes the touch-down easier - less tendency to bounce, but the tolerance of bumpy surfaces is much worse.

Following a good number of approaches (over 20) and landings onto grass, I came to the conclusion that it would be easier than the Rapide to approach and land over the tall trees, but any go-around would have to be started early. Several go-arounds were simulated at a safe height to check that engine response was good, and also matched between engines. I didn't want to be stuck at the top of a bounce with full power on one side, nothing on the other, and no speed!

The day of the Rally arrived, with a forecast of fresh north-westerly winds - straight across the strip at Woburn. A decision was made to fly to Cranfield, offload passengers then proceed to Woburn if we were happy. By the time we were overhead Woburn, a shower was in progress, and the cross-wind had all but gone. The problem then was that a Moth with a technical problem was stuck at the edge of the strip, so my intended diagonal approach was not prudent. An approach was made over the trees, aiming for a speed of 68 mph, 8 mph over the stall. In fact it was a little faster than that, and I was a bit further down the strip than ideal. It settled onto the ground well, but I saw a bump ahead, and rather than hit the bump hard with a lot of weight on the wheels, I held it neutral so when we hit the bump, we ended up airborne again. There was nothing for it but to go around for another try. On the next attempt, a little slower over the bump, but the aircraft was thrown into the air again, below flying speed, so full power and round again.

Peter Harrison flying Brian Woodford's G-AEDT c/n 7508 near Shoreham, 1989. *[G Bain]*

One more attempt, no more, and if no landing this time, return to Cranfield. Over the trees again, 65 mph this time, sideslip to lose height, over the fence, gently onto the ground, ready for the bump. Just a little power to catch it this time, wings level, gently off with the power, back down on the mainwheels. All OK. Enough room left, so tail down, gently on with the brakes. Phew! Don't relax, she's a Dragonfly, remember. Keep straight, or she'll bite! Gently off the edge of the strip, to be met by a beaming Brian and all the crowd."

One Dragonfly that had a fascinatingly itinerant life was c/n 7526, which came out of Hatfield in October 1936. Going straight to Lourenço Marques in Portuguese East Africa with what might be considered the prophetic registration CR-AAB, this Dragonfly joined DETA, a company which had used mostly DH types since its inception several years earlier. After operating with DETA for twenty five years, the aircraft moved west into South Africa, where A G Mechin used it as ZS-CTR for the next 13 years, before it was taken out of service at Baragwanath in 1974. Five years later, the tired remains were bought by two British de Havilland collectors, Martin Barraclough and Tony Haig-Thomas, and brought back to well-known restorer Cliff Lovell at Walkeridge Farm. Cliff and his team of DH experts brought the aircraft back to life, and on 1st July 1981, with the period registration G-AEDU, she was flown again by Martin Barraclough. Sold at the Christie's auction at Duxford in April 1983, the Dragonfly was soon on its way west again, having been bought by an American, Charles Osborne, of Clark County, Indiana, so it was flown across the pond in June, to become N190DH.

Unfortunately, the Dragonfly later succumbed to the well-known take-off swing, as it was extensively damaged at Clark County Airport on 22nd September 1987, and put up for sale. By the following July, another British DH collector, Torquil Norman, had bought the remains and had them transferred once again to the capable hands of Cliff Lovell, for a second rebuild at his new facility at Lower Upham, Hampshire. This time the work was more extensive with damage to wings, fuselage, engines and undercarriage, and required a complete strip and rebuild of many parts. By August 1992, the Dragonfly was once again complete, resplendent in its smart red and silver colours as G-AEDU, and ready to fly.

C/n 7526 CR-AAB with DETA, Laurenco Marques, 1939, before becoming G-AEDU. *[CND]*

Post-Rebuild Air Test, G-AEDU

Martin Barraclough was asked to carry out the air test, and continues the story:

"According to Cliff, the only mod incorporated into the current rebuild was a pair of Dunlop hydraulic toe-brakes fitted to the left set of rudder pedals. This was Torquil's solution to the Dragonfly's notorious reputation for ground-looping and was a quantum leap forward from the old system. The original hand-operated cable brakes needed several lightning-fast transfers of the left hand between throttles and brake lever just when you needed to operate both simultaneously to correct the onset of the dreaded ground loop. With a lockable tailwheel this had to be an improvement!

And so it proved on the afternoon of August 4th when taxi trials on Cliff's Lower Upham strip reminded me of the aircraft's utterly

Dragonfly G-AEDU at Old Warden, 1997. *[M Stroud]*

ineffectual rudder when the tail is blanketed by the fuselage and there is no puff from the props. After some engine runs, I taxied out for the take-off. The strip is a convex 700-metre north/south grass strip with pronounced climb for the first / of the distance and a long downhill slope the rest of the way. If we weren't airborne by the highest point, and needed to abort, only the hedge would stop us at the end of the downhill slope. An immediate left turn and climb out were needed to avoid overflying a housing estate.

When you have lined up at the end of this sort of strip in someone else's immaculate, beautiful vintage aeroplane, of which there are only two others left in the world, you daren't dwell on the results if something just might go wrong. This is the moment of truth.

Walk the throttles open until two Gipsy Majors are giving full welly and in no time the tail is up, then the wheels are off and we are airborne - drop the left wing and a touch of left rudder and climb away - Bless you, Cliff - and she handles exactly the same - that rather underpowered heavy Rapide feeling - stunningly graceful - but no match for the handling of her more powerful and greatly loved older sister. A gentle 360-degree turn and a low pass to show Cliff and his merry men that she really does fly and we are on the way to Old Sarum in company with Henry Labouchere in Torquil's Cessna 180. The flight was uneventful - several vintage instruments failed to record what they should, but the engines and controls behaved perfectly. The usual Dragonfly features were still there - back pressure on the stick as well as full aft trim to keep straight and level because there was no weight in the back - heavy ailerons - marvellously complex fuel cross-feeds - and the flap lever which at full extension suddenly feels as if it has come adrift - all unique to this old executive twin. Thirty-five minutes later, the main wheels hit the grass at Old Sarum and I nudged the spectacle forward to keep the tail high in the undisturbed airflow and gently pedalled the rudders and toe brakes to keep her straight. Now all that was needed was to check out Torquil!

The immaculate G-AEDU in its hangar at Rendcomb, May 1995, operated by Torquil Norman. *[CND]*

VP-YAX airborne from Hatfield before delivery to Rhodesia and Nyasaland Airways (RANA), Salisbury, in July 1936. *[BAe]*

Section 5 – Chapter 3: Worldwide Operators

FIRST USERS

The first two Dragonflies were taken on initially by de Havilland for further development and demonstration work, but also for use as company transport between sites and for customer visits. Captain de Havilland and his son Geoffrey used the prototype in the 1936 King's Cup Air Race, which was a typical de Havilland publicity process for their new types, and in the event the father and son team managed eighth place in the two-day event, so their objective was probably met.

King Ghazi of Iraq was the first commercial customer for the type, ordering 7502 in late 1935, before the prototype had gained certification. YI-HMK was a standard DH 90A with normal equipment, minus the extra 25-gallon fuselage tank, but it had one or two extras befitting a royal aircraft. The cabin had the usual four passenger seats, but according to a contemporary report, also had a table, a luncheon basket, a bookcase and ashtrays fitted and the fuselage and wings were painted in a gold finish, with the royal crown on either side of the nose, with the registration in Arabic script on the rear fuselage. It was delivered to His Majesty's private landing ground at Akerkuf near Baghdad during April 1936, and named 'The Golden Eagle'. A second Dragonfly, YI-OSD, was ordered by the Iraqi government six months later, nominally for use by the Director of Railways, but both aircraft were probably used by the Iraqi Air Force.

While many of the first users had been attracted by the concept of a five-seat, long-range personal aircraft, a large number of those bought in 1936 had been sold on by 1938, often to companies as executive transport. There is no obvious reason for so many of the 'private' aircraft being sold on, but one possible reason was simply the general belt-tightening as Europe prepared for the approaching war.

AN INTRIGUING SPANISH EXPEDITION

One of the many de Havilland aircraft to become embroiled in the war-like activities in Spain from 1936 onwards was the sixth DH 90, which became G-AECX in April 1936. It was sold to a typical Dragonfly buyer, Gordon Selfridge, of Selfridges department store in London. Mr Selfridge's son-in-law, Viscomte de Sibour was a French nobleman, a pilot and a European agent for the American Socony-Vacuum Oil Company. It was he who was to fly the Dragonfly on most occasions, from its base at Heston. What purported to be a "pleasant European air tour" for the Viscomte, his mother-in-law and Gordon Selfridge and "a lady from Rochester", Peggy Shannon (who was almost certainly an employee of the Socony-Vacuum company in New York) was arranged for late July 1936. The party of four set off from Heston in G-AECX and headed south. After a brief stop in France, they passed Biarritz on the south-west coast, crossed into the politically-turbulent area of northern Spain, and headed south towards the Mountains of Oca, landing soon after at Gamonal, close to the town of Burgos, where the Nationalist leader, General Mola, had set up the Nationalist Army headquarters.

For tourists, this was a volatile place to be, with the Nationalist army actively mobilising forces throughout the area, but what the Viscomte was actually doing was a little business as well as admiring the scenery. It is known that he had a meeting in Burgos with General Mola, and he was allowed to take some of the precious motor fuel that the general's forces had been hoarding for the forthcoming battles with the Republican armies. It seems likely that, as oil company agents, he and Miss Shannon were actually arranging clandestine shipments of sorely-needed fuel to the Nationalist forces from the Socony-Vacuum company, but against generally accepted international policy. After the meeting with General Mola, the tourists topped up the Dragonfly's tanks to the maximum 85 gallons with Nationalist Army petrol, and set off south to Granada, in the Sierra Nevada, near the Spanish south coast. The Dragonfly took only three hours for the journey across Spain, to be met at Granada by suspicious British and American diplomatic staff, who questioned their presence at such a dangerous time. Apparently the Viscomte charmed the diplomats with the story that they were there to help evacuate Socony-

Stylish 1930s PLUNA brochure showing DH 90 cabin layout. *[BAe]*

Vacuum staff, so were accepted. G-AECX was then used to take four of the Socony company's American employees from Granada across the Mediterranean to Tangier, before the tourists re-embarked for their return flight to Heston and a more stable existence.

AIRLINE SALES

Interspersed with sales of new Dragonflies to private owners in 1936 and 1937, were those to small airlines, such as Western Airways in England; RANA in Rhodesia; Qantas Empire Airways in Australia; Misr-Airwork in Egypt; DETA in Portuguese East Africa; Wilson Airways in Kenya; Air Travel in New Zealand and PLUNA in Uruguay, who all bought the type to supplement their normal services, usually flown with larger de Havilland types. The Dragonflies were mostly used on charter work or for training, but PLUNA deserves special mention, as they used their two DH 90s, CX-AAR and CX-AAS, for scheduled services.

PLUNA, URUGUAY

The story of the Uruguayan airline, Primeras Lineas Uruguayas de Navegacion Aerea, (PLUNA) is told in more detail in the DH 86 section, but in summary, the airline's young founders, brothers Jorge and Alberto Marquez Vaesa, had the foresight to inaugurate internal services with two Dragonflies, bought new from Hatfield in 1936. The two aircraft arrived in Montevideo in October 1936, and were then erected ready for use in November. They were painted in a striking vermilion colour scheme, prompting the first, CX-AAR, to be named 'Churrinche' (Robin), and the other 'San Alberto' after their father. They had one extra, lifting seat made for each Dragonfly, which they placed adjacent to the door, giving seats for two pilots and four passengers, and providing what their brochure described as "Splendid Pullman saloons, with excellent ventilation and heating, and the ability to maintain a cruising speed of 205 kph." Scheduled services began on 20th November, flying three days a week from Montevideo to Salto and the other three days to Rivera from Montevideo. By the end of their first year of service, the airline reported back to de Havilland that they were very pleased with their aircraft, having flown them for 2,000 hours; carried 2,600 passengers; over 2 tons of cargo; 20,000 letters; 70,000 newspapers and 1,700 kgs of parcels, and had gained a modest subsidy of £4,500 per year from the government. PLUNA kept their Dragonflies in use, augmented by two DH 86s from 1937, until they were retired in about 1949. One, CX-AAR, was then presented to the Uruguayan Air Force Museum in Montevideo, but it was unfortunately destroyed in a fire on 4th December 1997.

ROYAL CANADIAN MOUNTED POLICE

Soon after the DH Canada factory moved to Sheppard Avenue in Toronto, the Commissioner of the Royal Canadian Mounted Police, Major General MacBrien, visited the factory while investigating a new patrol type for the RCMP. Gen MacBrien was an enthusiastic pilot, and in late 1936, he flew in the demonstrator DH 90, CF-BBD, which was the second DH 90 in Canada. The Mounties were at that time fighting a hard battle to defeat the 'rum-runners'

Leigh Capreol starting up c/n 7538 CF-MPD for delivery to the RCMP, Downsview, June 1937. *[NArchCanada]*

proliferating in the Eastern Provinces, and the Commissioner believed that the aircraft was well suited to the patrol requirements of the RCMP, with two engines and a long endurance. As a result of this demonstration, the Royal Canadian Mounted Police ordered four Dragonflies from DH Canada, at a price quoted as C$ 8,000 each. The aircraft included the demonstrator, now given the appropriate registration CF-MPC; the others were CF-MPA, CF-MPB and CF-MPD. No doubt the eight Mounties who took over the flying task, operating from North Toronto airfield in 1937, were severely ribbed by their colleagues when the names on the new aircraft were made known. They were called 'Crocus', 'Anemone', 'Buttercup', and 'Dandelion'- names not quite in keeping with the tough Mountie tradition. At least the Dragonflies were easily recognisable, as they all had smart dark blue fuselages and tails, with gold wings, and they served the Mounties well from May 1937, three being passed on to the Royal Canadian Air Force in 1940. CF-MPD escaped impressment, as it had gone as a company hack to Noorduyn Aircraft in 1938.

Eight Dragonflies went to Canada between 1936 and 1938; but the last two, 7557 and 7558, were delivered without Cs of A and were stored until taken over by the RCAF in 1940. Floats and skis were fitted to many of the Canadian aircraft, in a similar way to the Canadian Rapides, but then several had accidents during RCAF service. By the late 1940s most had been taken out of service, and the last one, CF-BFF, which then belonged to Gold Belt Air Service of Rouyn, Quebec, finally succumbed to the icy Ottawa River on 20th December 1949. One which crashed into Indian Lake in the North West Territories the year before, CF-BZA, still partly survives. Its rear fuselage and tail are displayed in a tableau in the Alberta Aviation Museum at Edmonton City Airport.

SHELL COMPANY TRANSPORT

Various elements of the Shell Petroleum Company used Dragonflies from 1936 until the beginning of the Second World War. Five were bought by different elements of the company for use in Singapore, Argentina, the Netherlands East Indies and Nigeria. The first was bought by the Asiatic Petroleum Co, a subsidiary of Shell, for use by the Shell Aviation department manager in Singapore, Peter Vines. This was the twelfth aircraft and it began its rather erratic service life, as VR-SAX, just after Christmas, 1936.

Solo to Singapore

Rather bravely, Mr Vines had decided to send his engineer on to Singapore by sea, so he was alone, apart from a few spares, when he set off with full tanks from Croydon. The first two days went well, but by the time the Dragonfly, having refuelled at Gabes in Tunisia, was tracking east down the Libyan coast on the 550-mile leg direct to Benghazi, the expected checkpoints were difficult to make out in the featureless terrain, and the late time checks began

The first DH 90 in Canada, CF-AYF c/n 7506, seen here on skis at Trail, BC, in 1936. *[BAe]*

Consolidated Mining and Smelting's CF-BFF c/n 7543 on floats, at Trail, BC, 1938. *[CND]*

The RCMP Dragonfly fleet and crews on handover, Toronto, 1937. *[BAe]*

to indicate an increasing headwind. Then, up ahead, severe thunderstorms were becoming visible out of the haze, right across his track. The turbulence began to increase, and rain began to obscure the forward view out of the left windscreen. With the increased turbulence, making any sense out of the fuel gauge for the 25 gallon rear fuel tank, from which both Gipsy Majors were then feeding, became almost impossible, so, despite estimating Benghazi to be reachable with the estimated fuel remaining, Vines was becoming increasingly concerned. He knew the ground in the next 100 miles before his destination was mountainous, with few safe landing areas, and the weather was closing in badly in that direction, so he considered diverting to Gemines, about 50 miles short of Benghazi, close to the coast road. But when he reached the area where he believed Gemines should have been, there was no sign whatsoever of an airfield. He could see nothing looking like an airfield anywhere near the coast road, which he had followed at low level for many miles, and the weather ahead was looking increasingly unworkable.

When he spotted a smooth-looking area alongside the road, Vines decided that he would land there and wait out the weather, so he put down the flap and made a tidy landing on three points, alongside the road. The Dragonfly slowed down nicely, but then, it suddenly started a swing to the right, and Vines was unable to stop it with rudder or brake, there being little slipstream over the tail surfaces. The aircraft lurched into a ground loop, finishing up facing down the road the wrong way, with the right wing at a slightly lower angle than the left. On inspection from outside, Vines then saw that the cowling was creased and the undercarriage leg looked distorted after the strain caused by the ground loop. Soon afterwards, Vines had some good luck when a bus appeared on the road, and he managed to have a note passed to his Shell colleague in Benghazi, to come to his aid.

Many hours later, a truck appeared from the direction of Benghazi, with the Shell superintendent and some petrol cans. The aircraft was refuelled that night, and a few days later the experts at Misr-Airwork, from along the coast at Almaza, in Egypt, had a chance to look at the undercarriage and repaired the compression leg. That allowed Vines to continue on to his destination, and he eventually reached Penang airport in Malaya, on 27th January, three weeks late. Vines was unhappy about the incident, and unsure about the reason for it. He had many hours' RAF flying experience, without incident, so attributed this problem to something like a hole or rut in the ground, which had caused the Dragonfly to spin round on its starboard wheel. But he was still unsure whether it was him or the aircraft.

Landing Problems in Asia

On settling in at Seletar, the Singapore airport, Vines slowly managed to overcome VR-SAX's occasional forays off the required straight path, but he could find no reason for the swings. Interestingly, he always attempted to land the Dragonfly as the RAF had taught him - in the three-point attitude, which would have contributed to his control difficulties, but there were no Dragonfly experts in Singapore to advise otherwise. He had never before experienced an aircraft which, when slowing down normally, with its tailwheel on the ground, occasionally developed an uncontrollable swing to one side, which he had great difficulty countering because of insufficient rudder authority. He therefore had every element of the undercarriage, wheels, suspension and brakes checked very carefully, looking for faults. No problems were found over a period of months, and everything was just as the makers had specified. Then, at the end of 1937, he had to make a tour around the Shell agencies in Indo-China, using VR-SAX for transport. The route over the Gulf of Siam from Kuantan, on the Malayan east coast, to his first port of call, Saigon, in what is now Vietnam, was just over 500 miles, well within the range of the Dragonfly. Therefore Vines set off, this time with his well-qualified engineer, Claude Sculfor, who had been trained at that great seat of aircraft engineering expertise, RAF Halton.

The journey up the Malayan coast and across the Gulf was most pleasant and relaxing, under clear skies all the way to Saigon. On touchdown, all went well until, when slowing down still in a straight line, once again VR-SAX decided to suddenly take a swing to one side and Vines could not get enough rudder or brake to prevent it. This time, the swing was not too vicious, and on inspection in the Saigon hangar, engineer Sculfor found only that the right hand compression leg seemed a little low. He had wisely brought spares with him, and added another rubber block to the leg and all appeared well again. An Imperial Airways engineer, passing on the way to Hong Kong in a DH 86, told Sculfor that the DH 86, with a very similar Turner undercarriage, seemed to have similar problems, but they had no answer either. For the next few days, VR-SAX behaved herself, and the Shell inspection went well. There were several difficult strips to test Vines and his aircraft, including a strip at Pakse, in Laos, close to the Thai border and on the edge of the Boloven Plateau, which, at only 900 feet long by about 30 feet wide, was tight for a Dragonfly.

There were no problems here, so the tour continued north to Vinh on the Vietnamese coast, and then on 20th November, back south again down the coast to Tourane, south of Hue. From the air, the hard rock surface at Tourane looked good, and there was only a gentle breeze off the South China Sea. Vines brought the Dragonfly in to a graceful three-point landing and all seemed well as the aircraft slowed in a good straight line towards the end of the strip. But then, without warning, the nose started coming round to the right, and Vines could not get the brake lever on quick enough to prevent or even slow the rapid turn. Neither urgent application of left rudder or right throttle made any difference - VR-SAX continued on round and off the runway, with accompanying bending noises, ending up facing the opposite direction - again. This time the damage was serious, as both undercarriage legs had collapsed and both engines appeared to have come adrift from the strong main spar, which also had a deep spanwise split. There were other signs of damage to the fuselage as well, but the crew had switched off the engines and there was no fire, just physical damage.

Vines and his engineer were devastated, as this damage would require considerable expert work to enable the aircraft to fly again. However, Sculfor, in true Halton tradition, managed to have the aircraft removed to a hangar on the edge of the airfield, and immediately set to work assessing the damage and the required spares to make it fly again. The engines, wheels and brakes were eventually tested using gantries and jigs made by Sculfor and a helpful local team, but all worked well, so they could find no reason for the swing on landing. Vines set off back to Singapore after a few days with a long list of requirements, leaving his poor engineer to attempt the repair. The decision was made to do all the work in situ, so Sculfor remained at Tourane for the next three months, scrounging materials such as the correct grade of spruce with which to make a new main spar, to DH specification. A unit of the French Air Force was locally based and gave considerable help, even down to arranging for Claude Sculfor to spend his Christmas with a French family in Tourane.

Airborne Again

By mid-February 1938, Sculfor had worked his magic on VR-SAX, and had it ready for Vines to come up from Singapore to try out the aircraft and possibly continue the company visits. Vines spent many hours inspecting the aircraft and declared it "as good as new", so they tried it out over several days and were entirely happy with repairs. Vines then decided to continue his tour and they climbed aboard, setting off on 27th February for Vientiane, 400 miles away in Laos, just north of the Thai border. VR-SAX behaved faultlessly again on the flight over the mountains, and across Laos to its south-western border. The airfield at Vientiane had a strong, gusting wind blowing down the main runway, but all was well, until, once again, after making a good (three-point) touchdown, and beginning to slow down, the aircraft veered suddenly off to the right. Rapid corrective rudder and brake then pulled the nose round to the runway direction again, but the action was so rapid that the nose continued to the left and could not be stopped. Throttle, rudder and brake in the opposite sense were all tried, but still the Dragonfly continued left and slid off the runway into the mud at the side of the field. The thoughts of both Vines and Sculfor can be imagined, as they sat and contemplated the result of this second landing accident in three months.

The damage was almost a repeat of the last accident, and the pair had great difficulty summoning up the motivation to begin the repair sequence once again. This being a much smaller airfield, they had to build a bamboo shelter against the Laotian rainy season, then Vines went back to Singapore and left his engineer to start the repair sequence once again. Spares were ordered, and this time came via Imperial Airways to Bangkok and up to Vientiane by train, where they were collected by the hard-working Sculfor. Some of the more complex metal repairs had to be completed in Singapore, but then by May, another three months later, Claude Sculfor had yet again managed to put everything back together, and called his Manager to come back to look at his work. The Shell pair were happy everything was in excellent shape, so they set off on 30th May 1938, for Bangkok, where they made a safe landing on the Air Force grass runway at Don Muang airfield, not trusting hard runways anymore. One or two adjustments were made at Bangkok to the engine bearers, then they were off again to Penang, on the Malayan west coast, before flying down to Seletar, their home base on Singapore island. After one or two frustrating adjustments to the engine bearers, Sculfor was satisfied with his charge, and VR-SAX behaved happily for almost the rest of the year.

The finale for Shell came at the end of 1938, when Vines was asked to fly VR-SAX home to London. All arrangements were suitably made, and pilot and engineer left Seletar for their first stop, Alor Star, just north of Penang, on 1st December 1938. A gentle, 400-mile flight took Vines and Sculfor for their last Dragonfly trip together, and onto a smooth, easy landing on three points at the small airfield at Alor Star. It seems almost superfluous to say that the Tourane incident then happened again. As the speed was decreasing, VR-SAX decided to veer rapidly off to the right, and even this practised pair of hands could not stop the swerve, which took the aircraft off the runway, breaking the starboard undercarriage leg once again. They climbed out wearily. Then it began to rain.

At least Claude Sculfor knew by now how to dismantle his aircraft for its journey back by junk to Seletar, which task was completed a few weeks later. Not unexpectedly, Shell sold the aircraft the following year, and it was rebuilt by Wearne's Air Services for their operations out of Singapore until impressed along with all the Wearne's fleet in 1941. It was finally destroyed in a Japanese air raid on Kallang in January 1942.

SLOW-SPEED GROUND HANDLING

Peter Vines' disastrous relationship with his Dragonfly cannot all be put down to the aircraft's design foibles. It must be admitted, as the 1936 Martlesham test pilots had noted, that the aircraft was directionally unstable, particularly at slow speeds, and would have benefited from a more effective fin and rudder. The awkward positioning of the brake lever, under the left-hand instrument panel, and also below the control spectacle, made life more complex in an incipient swing situation, when rapid and effective corrective action was needed. It seems that rudder authority was seriously degraded when the tailwheel was allowed to drop onto the runway too soon, at which point the deep fuselage tended to blanket the fin and rudder. Later operators, after conferring about the directional stability difficulties of the type, were able to alleviate the problems experienced when taking-off and landing the Dragonfly. Poor Peter Vines had no such contact with other Dragonfly pilots, so continued to use his RAF-taught technique of landing on three points with the tailwheel down, thereby removing much of the rudder's already inadequate effectiveness. 'Wheeler' landings, with the tail kept high, in a more effective airstream, would almost certainly have alleviated his problems.

In more recent years, Peter Harrison would appear to have found the right technique when flying Brian Woodford's G-AEDU, as he specifically kept the tail up on take-off and particularly on landing, so that the rudder always had as much balancing slipstream from the engines as possible, and was not blanketed by the wings. This meant that when a wind gust or a discontinuity on the runway caused the aircraft to start deviating directionally, there was sufficient rudder authority to counteract the incipient swing, before a ground loop began in earnest. Torquil Norman's recent toe-brake modification also made controllability much more effective, as it meant that rudder, throttles and brakes could all be used concurrently if needed. In addition, the lockable tailwheel first found on the Australian VH-AAD (later G-AEDT) in the 1960s helped with handling at slow speeds, and was also incorporated in G-AEDU to very useful effect. Torquil's own technique, used on his own aircraft with its toe-brakes and lockable tailwheel, is to lock the tailwheel before take-off and then feed on power, correcting very carefully any slight deviation from the desired track, using rudder and brake if necessary. He usually uses a three-point landing technique, making sure his tailwheel is locked, but then watches very carefully for any swing, correcting it quickly with rudder and brake, before it can develop.

Two pilots in the rather cramped DH 90 cockpit. [BAe]

Peter Vines was not alone in finding the Dragonfly difficult on the ground, as 19 out of the total of 67 built are reported as being written-off in landing or take-off accidents caused by loss of directional control - surely a sign that there was a serious flaw in the aircraft's directional controllability at slow speed.

BATAVIA AND BACK, PH-KOK

Another arm of the Shell company, based at Ypenburg in Holland, used a DH 90 for a long-range tour soon after VR-SAX left for Singapore. The Dragonfly was the fortieth aircraft built, registered, rather aptly, PH-KOK, to Ingenieur J E F de Kok, the Director General of the Royal Dutch Shell company. The aircraft was delivered to its base at The Hague and Rotterdam Aero Club at Ypenburg in November 1936, and after use as a personal transport around the continent, Hr de Kok decided to use it for a combined business and pleasure visit to the Shell oil wells in the Dutch East Indies, via what was then called Batavia, but is now Djakarta. Hr de Kok was by this time an experienced private pilot and the President of the Dutch National Aviation Association, had flown several aircraft to European destinations, and also on one occasion to North Africa. KLM engineers at nearby Schiphol airport carried out a complete check and service of the Dragonfly ready for its long flight. For such a long trip, Hr de Kok felt it would be prudent to take with him a professional pilot, so he asked Hr H M Schmidt-Crans, the Chief Instructor of the Netherlands Civilian National Aviation School (NLS) to join him. The Dragonfly had the standard fuel tanks on board and, with a maximum range of just over 800 miles, the team believed they could manage up to 10 hours' flying and around 1,250 miles per day. Assuming no delays or complications, they could therefore reach their destination of Tjililitan, on the south coast of Java, in ten days.

Shell Director Hr de Kok with his crew and helpers, at Batavia, 1937. *[PS-Crans]*

PH-KOK duly left Ypenburg at 8.15 on 3rd February 1937, into a cold, overcast sky. Hr de Kok brought the Dragonfly back for a low pass, in front of the considerable crowd which had gathered to see them off. Accompanied by much waving of hats, they were then on their way in what the Dutch newspapers called 'the elegant bird', to their first refuelling stop at Lyon. What forecasts they could obtain in 1937 indicated that the weather was good for most of their route, but any forecasts were notoriously unreliable in those early days.

After Lyon, the weather was not good over Italy, so they headed further north than intended, and landed for the night at Milan, having covered about 850 miles. The Italian weather still affected them next day, as they were delayed by fog at Brindisi, but still managed the 550-mile leg to Brindisi in the afternoon. The next legs gave them no weather problems, and their comment on the run from Brindisi along the Greek coast to Rhodes was that they had beautiful weather. February 6th then saw a good run of nearly 1,000 miles to Baghdad, followed by further untroubled legs to Bushir, Jodhpur, Calcutta, Bangkok, and Medan, on the Indonesian east coast, adjacent to Kuala Lumpur. They wanted to visit Medan to see the Shell agent for Sumatra, and they were welcomed on arrival with flower garlands in the usual Indonesian style.

Their final leg to Tjililitan was anticipated by the Batavian press with great drama, as the weather just before their expected arrival time of 5 pm was becoming quite bad. With increasing layers of cloud cover, "a heavy storm ensued, and darkness fell. ...it was feared that a landing would not be possible,... when the aeroplane appeared overhead the field and made a swift landing."

Poor quality newspaper cutting of crowd welcoming back Hr de Kok to Ypenburg, March 1937. *[PS-Crans]*

That last leg was a tribute to the capabilities of the pilots, as it entailed a total of 1,100 miles, with a refuelling stop at Singapore and a battle through thunderstorms to find the small grass airfield at Tjililitan. Even with a still-air ground speed of 120 mph, and a one hour refuelling stop at Singapore, the two pilots would have had over ten hours in the air, and several more in pre-flight and post-end activities. With their arrival on 12th February, they had achieved their very ambitious goal of a ten-day trip, and their 'elegant bird' obviously served them well.

After two weeks of business and sight-seeing around Indonesia, the two pilots set off on 1st March on their return to The Hague. This time, they made it in even better time, as they arrived at Ypenburg 7fi days after leaving Batavia, which was a record for a private flight. They landed on the snow-covered grass at Ypenburg on 8th March to a great welcome.

PH-KOK had a change of registration the following year, becoming PH-ATK, and was impressed into the KLu in September 1939, with the serial 962. Sadly, it was destroyed in May 1940, still at Ypenburg. Hr Schmidt-Crans' son, Piet, continued the family flying tradition, by becoming a pilot in the post-war Royal Netherlands Air Force, and was often to be seen flying the British Army Rapides in Germany for parachute work during the 1960s.

NEW ZEALAND AIRLINE WORK

One of many small New Zealand airlines which sprang up in the 1930s, Air Travel (NZ) Ltd, bought two DH 90As, the first ZK-AFB in 1937 and ZK-AGP (the last DH 90A built), a year later. This airline was based on the remote west coast of New Zealand's South Island, at Hokitika, and provided the country's first scheduled flight service. Captain Bert Mercer initiated his airline in May 1934, and began services up and down 'Westland' despite the very fickle weather, which provided fog, rain and brilliant sunshine in roughly equal amounts. By 1937, he had expanded to more reliable twin-engined aircraft, and the first Dragonfly, ZK-AFB, was from October 1937 used on schedules and charters from Hokitika to Westport and Nelson to the north, as well as to Haast in the south. Trips to the mountain airstrips at Franz Josef Glacier and Fox Glacier, in the highest area of the Southern Alps were also undertaken, alongside the company's three Fox Moths. The second Dragonfly arrived in 1938, and the two twins worked regularly until the latter crashed in the sea off Westport in December 1942 and the latter was replaced by larger aircraft in 1944.

ZK-AFB c/n 7560 airborne over the New Zealand west coast, 1955. *[R Waugh]*

Post War Activities

Only twenty Dragonflies survived after 1945, and these were well spread out in countries as far apart as Australia, Canada, Uruguay, Egypt, Portuguese East Africa, South Africa, Spain and New Zealand. In Britain at that point, war service had decimated the population to one, but then several more were brought back in succeeding years. SU-ABW, which Misr-Airwork had used at Almaza, Egypt, since 1937, was brought back to Gatwick by DH Technical School graduate Geoffrey Alington in November 1946. He then had it overhauled, registered it G-AIYJ and used it as a company hack for his new Anglo-Belgian company, Air Transport SA, which, amongst other charters, undertook the unique task of flying missionaries to and from China on behalf of the Vatican. Another Dragonfly, retired from the RAAF as A43-1 in 1945, went on to serve several owners as VH-UXS in Melbourne and New South Wales, before being withdrawn from use in Darwin as late as 1968 and was reportedly stored as a derelict at Nowra in 1990 for rebuild. Four others survived in Australia; VH-ADG was written-off in a take-off crash in December 1947; VH-UXB, the ex-QANTAS Dragonfly, had a surprising series of six major accidents before being withdrawn at Alice Springs in 1951; VH-UTJ was sadly destroyed by fire when refuelling at Tennant Creek in August 1955 and VH-AAD is still in great form, having been successively G-AEDT, N2034 and G-AEDT again, and now in New Zealand as ZK-AYR with that stalwart collector, restorer and pilot of de Havilland machines, Colin Smith on behalf of owner Barry Donovan. In 2003, it was up for sale at £160,000.

New Zealand Mountain Flying, ZK-AFB

In the late 1950s, Captain Paul Beauchamp-Legg was flying Airlift (NZ) Limited's long-serving DH 90A, ZK-AFB, on services out of Wellington and Paraparaumu. Some of the routes flown with the Dragonfly on charters involved crossing the North Island mountain ranges, and Captain Beauchamp-Legg remembers some of the hazards of such flights:

"When the Rongatai airport at Wellington closed for re-building as what is now the Wellington airport, all of the normal Wellington flights went in and out of Paraparaumu. If one was flying south from Paraparaumu to Masterton, where I was based with the Dragonfly ZK-AFB, it usually meant an overnight stop in Wellington one way or another. We at Airlift (NZ) Ltd, started an as-required air service from Masterton to Paraparaumu and back. The flight time was around 30 minutes. This was through what could be the roughest area I have flown in during my 42 years as a pilot.

Dragonfly c/n 7513 VH-UXB at QANTAS' Archerfield base, 1937. *[CND]*

The turbulence in the Wairarapa and Ruahine area, where the tops vary between 3,000 and 5,000 feet, can be extreme at times and lenticular waves can stack up on each other to perhaps about 30,000 ft. This is due to the proximity of Cook Strait acting as a huge funnel for unobstructed westerly winds blowing across the Tasman Sea. When there was a westerly blowing, which was far too often, I would use wave lift from a line of lenticular clouds on the Masterton (western) side of the ranges. We would rapidly get to perhaps 10,000 ft. in smooth air in front of that lenticular in the hope of going over the top of the turbulence to the west and then descending in the clear through some holes which were usually over the Hutt Valley area and in the lee of Kapiti Island. We flew strictly Visual Flight Rules, so were not officially allowed to enter cloud. Anyone who entered cloud in the NZ mountains had a limited future.

Once well above the height of the cloud on top of the ranges, I would fly at maximum permitted power, either in climbing attitude, or more often in level attitude, then enter a few miles of downdraught, theorizing that the less time I was in the

G-AEDT became ZK-AYR in April 1998, with Colin Smith at Mandeville. [JF Hamlin]

downdraught, the less height I would lose. Occasionally I won, but at other times the downdraughts were so severe that I would end up hill-sloping at five hundred to a thousand feet or so through the Turanekau Valley. As the valleys were not terribly wide it was not always possible to do a 180-degree turn to fly back out.

Flying through the Turanekau Valley was a route I treated with great respect. It was not very wide. I would fly close to the up-wind side of the valley; trees could be seen waving in the wind and the thick bush was always ready to hide any aircraft which crashed into it. As the valley changed direction it was necessary to fly along the other side from time to time to stay in the updraught and out of the turbulence. Once through, we were at the head of the Upper Hutt valley and would then fly below cloud, out to Titahi Bay and so along the coast to Paraparaumu.

Under good conditions, the flight could be made direct, which would take around 30 minutes. An alternative route was to fly from Masterton along the lenticular waves all the way southwards to the coastline and then west around Wellington and back north along the coast to Paraparaumu. This of course took around about three times as long and there was usually severe turbulence at the southern end of the North Island. To go north was often difficult because about halfway to the Pahiatua Track near Palmerston North, where there is a low saddle, there is a high area which is usually clagged right in.

On December 14th 1958 I managed to fly the Dragonfly above the turbulence with two passengers from Masterton to Paraparaumu. While awaiting there I took five passengers for a joyride around Kapiti Island, then, as there was neither freight nor anyone wanting to go back to Masterton, I took off empty and was able to climb in the clear directly north-east towards Masterton. Because I was going downwind I had the speed reduced to reduce the severity of the turbulence.

'Thank God I'm through that lot,' I said to myself, relaxing as the air smoothed.

Without any warning there was a terrific thump. I felt as if I'd been hit on the head with a hammer, a large hammer. Fortunately, I did not have any freight on board and apart from cushions on the empty passenger seats being a little tossed around, all seemed well. I landed back at Masterton and as I was getting out I discovered that the middle seat was loose. An engineer's Inspection then showed that the critical main spar, running across the fuselage to both engine cowlings, had split, and would have to be completely replaced."

New Zealand West Coast Work

After it had been repaired, two other owners used ZK-AFB, until it was bought in 1961 by Captain Brian Chadwick of Christchurch, on the south-eastern side of New Zealand's South Island.

ZK-AFB, Captain Brian Chadwick

Brian Chadwick was a well-known and very experienced pilot who had operated scheduled and charter flights on South Island for many years by the time he set up his own charter company, Air Charter (NZ) Ltd, and bought the Dragonfly in 1961. He had it painted in a striking colour scheme, with blue fuselage with a white stripe; white fin with silver wings, and kept the name Kiwi Rover on the nose. His speciality was taking tourists around the spectacular scenery of the Southern Alps, particularly around the 12,300 foot Mount Cook; the airstrips at the two glaciers and another difficult steep-sided strip, over the top of the Southern Alps and towards the coast, at Milford Sound.

The year after buying his Dragonfly, on 12th February 1962, Captain Chadwick took off with the intention of showing his four

ZK-AFB at Haast, 1958. *[P Beauchamp-Legg]*

C/n 7560 as ZK-AFB of Air Charter at Christchurch, August, 1961. *[D A Noble]*

passengers the Alps and then landing at Milford Sound. The weather on the western side of the mountains on that day was unusual, in that it was clear and bright on the west coast, but all along the foothills of the Alps, was described by one pilot as 'pitch black' with complete cloud cover. The same weather continued on the eastern side of the mountains as well, and that is where Captain Chadwick had to transit on his way through one of several mountain passes at around 8,000 feet, across to Milford Sound.

An hour after the Dragonfly was due at the Milford Sound strip, the other operators on the west coast were alerted to the fact that ZK-AFB had not arrived, and they were all asked if it had been seen. None had, so after waiting a short while longer, the Search and Rescue unit at Christchurch asked pilots on both sides of the mountains to begin a search for the aircraft. Despite a comprehensive search which lasted for a week, involving 34 aircraft and 400 hours of flying, nothing was ever found of ZK-AFB, its pilot or its passengers.

One of Captain Chadwick's friends, Captain Brian Waugh, who was flying his Rapide from Hokitika on the same day, spent many hours searching for his friend, and in his book about his time flying in South Island, 'Turbulent Years', gave the view that the Dragonfly had probably succumbed to carburettor and airframe icing when trying to climb through the bad weather, and may have crashed somewhere in the Alps. Several expeditions have subsequently been mounted to search for wreckage, but still nothing has been found.

Long-Range Transport

It would appear that the Dragonfly was considered a suitable vehicle for long journeys for one or two people, even in modern times, as a good number of inter-continental flights have taken place in the type. With its internal tankage of 85 gallons; seats for two pilots; twin engines; a ceiling of about 15,000 feet and moderate room for baggage, it is a better bet than many other pre-war aircraft. Admittedly, the pilots' accommodation is tight, with a very rapidly-tapering nose and little sideways room, especially for tall or broad people cramped up for a ten-hour flight. The vacuum-driven instrumentation is not the most efficient for prolonged instrument flight; there is no de-icing equipment; it cruises at a slow 107 knots at heavy weights and the usual power supply is by wind-driven generator feeding a lead acid accumulator, but pilots have still not been put off. Two flights in particular give an insight into what the Dragonfly is like on a long flight.

Australia to England - G-AEDT

One particularly adventurous pair of young pilots undertook a very brave adventure in 1963, with a flight by Dragonfly from Sydney to Gatwick. They were two friends, Charles Masefield, son of Peter Masefield, then Chairman of the British Aircraft Corporation and another twenty-three year old, Lord David Trefgarne, son of the first Baron Trefgarne of Gleddeu, who had himself been an RFC pilot in the First World War. Charles Masefield was working for Beagle Aircraft, and the two of them agreed to fly a single-engined Beagle Airedale, on delivery to Australia, leaving London in May 1963 and arriving in Adelaide four weeks later.

A Means of Getting Home

Having spent some three months exploring Australia, and arranging one or two deals with local aircraft agents, the two adventurers then had to find a way home. Rather than the boring sea or airline routes, they felt it more appropriate to fly themselves home again. The Australian Beagle agent at Camden, near Sydney, suggested several aircraft for sale, and they looked at a Walrus, but felt that was too cumbersome and had not the range required. Then they looked at two ex-RAN Sea Furies, which they bought, but sold them on, for a profit. In August, they heard about a DH 90A, VH-AAD, the ninth Dragonfly built, which had been used by an aero club out in the area of the Murray Basin, but was not in use at present. They agreed to have a look at it with a view to buying it, but only if the aircraft could be demonstrated to them. Borrowing an Auster from the Camden Club, they set off via Cootamundra to Griffith, NSW, which was a 4-hour and ten minute flight away in the Auster. After speaking to the owners, the Griffith Aero Club, they asked about the air test, and after much muttering and discussion amongst the Aero Club staff, it was agreed that a certain pilot would arrange to demonstrate the Dragonfly.

The chosen pilot taxied out for take-off, with Charles Masefield alongside him in the right-hand seat and Lord Trefgarne standing behind. Being the Australian summer, the temperature was well up, so the tired old Dragonfly ambled on down the runway, but it seemed none of the gauges were working. Eventually the aircraft staggered off the ground, and at about ten feet, there was "a terrible noise from the port engine". The propeller ground to a halt and the

Brian Woodford's G-AEDT over Hampshire, 1989, again in the hands of Peter Harrison. *[G Bain]*

pilot pushed the aircraft back onto what remained of the runway, losing directional control soon afterwards, swung round into the bush, and with twigs and branches flying in all directions, came to a halt some way to one side of the runway. "Well that's it - you've had your test flight" said the Aussie pilot's voice " it's been airborne, hasn't it?"

Reluctantly, after agreement had been made to check over the aircraft and correct any other faults, approximately £1,500 was handed over, and the Dragonfly was flown, still without a C of A, back to Bankstown, Sydney. There the good Mr Nottley, the Beagle agent, had agreed to give the aircraft a complete overhaul, assisted by our two gallant airmen, on completion of which he would recommend the grant of a C of A to the Australian Department of Civil Aviation, which would in turn advise the British Authorities that the aircraft could be given a British C of A for the ferry flight and allowed to wear its old British registration, G-AEDT. That was in the first week in August 1963. It was subsequently discovered that the reason for the heated discussion on who should fly the demonstration flight at Griffith was because the only pilot who had flown the Dragonfly was the CFI, and he had been released from "Detention at Her Majesty's Pleasure" the previous week after "imbibing too much of the Amber Nectar". However, the Club's directors agreed to re-instate the CFI if he flew the demonstration and if the sale went through!

Preparation

Much hard work and paperwork were then applied to the Dragonfly at Bankstown, and our two aviators went to the Bankstown Aero Club to take multi-engine ratings on the Club's Apache. The engines were tired, so two Gipsy Major 10 Mk 1 engines were fitted into the aircraft, as they gave slightly more power and could take accessories, therefore the port engine was fitted with a generator to replace the wind-driven unit on the port wing. The pair found that a tailwheel lock had very wisely been fitted by a previous operator, so this remained, and was found to be very useful in keeping the aircraft straight at slow speeds. The major concern was to gain as much range as possible, "so we did not have to keep stopping", so an old Anson tank holding 40 gallons was fitted into the centre fuselage and a 50-gallon tank fitted above the standard 25 gallon fuselage tank. All these tanks required a complex system of cocks and pipes, to allow them to feed at the appropriate time. This gave a capacity of 175 gallons and an endurance of about twelve hours, with a range of around 1,500 statute miles in still air. To cope with the extra endurance, a 5 gallon oil drum, hand-pump and attendant piping were fitted into the cabin, which allowed both oil tanks to be re-filled by the non-flying pilot through a system of pipes leading to the tank caps. The weight with all these tanks brought the laden weight somewhat above the normal maximum, so the use of the uprated engines would be important in the event of an engine failure. A King VHF radio was fitted, together with a VOR and an ADF set, all of which would help with navigation in populated areas. But then, in October 1963, the whole package had to be tested to the satisfaction of the Department of Civil Aviation.

When the DCA test pilot was told that he would be flying the Dragonfly on its C of A air test he was heard to say "Ahhh, a Dragonfly - the last time I flew one of those, I pranged it!"

So the Bankstown team were particularly interested to watch when he climbed aboard on a baking hot summer's day and set off on his test flight. He took off safely enough and then, almost unbelievably, at about twenty feet off the ground, the port engine failed - again. He put it rapidly back on the ground, and, just like his predecessor, could not stop it swinging to the left off the runway and into the scrub, but luckily without any major damage. The pilot, in a vile temper, stomped back over the airfield, to where the new owners were waiting, and then said "OK, its passed!" When the incredulous listeners asked how it had passed its air test after this short but alarming occurrence, he said "If I don't pass it, I'll only have to fly it again".

So the Dragonfly was repaired once more over the next two weeks and Charles and Lord Trefgarne managed to get in a few hours flying. Then it was time to leave.

The return journey began on 1st December 1963 in the heat of summer, from Bankstown. The planned route was to be up the Australian east coast to Townsville, then inland and north to Darwin. Although the Indonesian Confrontation was underway at the time, our aviators took little notice of it, and in due course the protagonists ignored them on their way through Indonesia. The rest of the plan took them through Malaysia, Thailand, India, Pakistan, the Persian Gulf, Syria, Greece, Italy and France then home to Gatwick - an expected total of about 120 hours' flying. The basic plan was to make the best possible time, taking advantage of G-AEDT's long range, and even to fly at night if weather and route were suitable. The two pilots would take it in turns to fly each leg, and the spade control column in the co-pilot's position was not used, mainly because of its unnatural method of operation, which required vertical movements to move the ailerons. The non-flying pilot was also needed to make regular injections of oil into the engines from within the cabin. Most of the flying was done at 6,000 to 8,000 feet, when the weather permitted, cruising at around 110 knots and the general policy was to use the radio as little as possible, relying on the flight plans to keep people informed of their position.

The legs up the Australian coast went well, with each leg averaging about four hours. Then the terrain changed as the Dragonfly headed west towards Mount Isa, crossing the Great Dividing Range and then past Cloncurry and over the Selwyn Range. Almost west again to Tennant Creek, the pilots really began to see the Australian outback, with the very barren areas of the Northern Territory to their Australian departure point, Darwin, which they reached after four days and 22 hours of flying. The next psychological leg was the 500-statute mile transit across the Timor Sea to Koepang, well-travelled by all Australia-to-England pilots. Again there were no difficulties on this leg and on 5th December they arrived on the Island of Timor, which was largely unaffected by the Indonesian Confrontation. Skirting to the south of the Indonesian archipelago, they flew up to Denpasar for a night stop after a 5-hour fifteen minute trip. Then came a 650-mile leg to Jakarta, where the British Air Attache met them and advised them not to stay in Jakarta any longer than necessary because of the troubled situation. Despite having just flown their longest leg so far, they changed pilots and set off again as soon as they had refuelled, for another six-hour slog to Changi airport, Singapore. That was the longest day so far, with twelve hours in the air. Singapore made a welcome break, and the next leg was an easy 400 miles the next day to Penang. They had already passed the monsoon season, so the weather continued to be kind as they went on to Bangkok and then set off on the longest leg of the trip,

G-AEDT passing through Koepang en route UK, December 1963. [Lord Trefgarne]

At Penang, Malaysia, for refuelling. [Lord Trefgarne]

Bangkok to Calcutta, about 1,050 miles and an estimated nine and a half hour's flight from Don Muang airport up the Thai and Burmese coasts and across the mouths of the Ganges to Calcutta's Dum Dum airport.

The weather and the Dragonfly were both quite settled, and there were no bad landings, despite its brakes, which seemed to get weaker with every sortie. As expected, the time to clear customs and immigration became ever-longer as they flew further north into Asia. Another long leg took the team across the breadth of India, with another 1,000-mile leg from Calcutta to Ahmedabad in western India. The first real difficulty with the aircraft then occurred, when an hour out from Calcutta, their engine-driven generator failed, so they turned back to have it repaired. Indian ingenuity soon sorted out the problem and they were then off again, stopping at Ahmedabad, crossing into Pakistan and along the coast to Karachi. A small contretemps with the Pakistan ATC system then took place as they were told by the irate controller at Karachi that they had approached Karachi down the wrong route, so he demanded that they turn round, fly back down the route and come back up on the correct route. A common sense solution was eventually agreed, and they continued on their approach to Karachi airport for another night stop.

They then moved quickly on for their last long leg, right across Pakistan, into Iran, across the Gulf of Oman and then out over the Persian Gulf to Bahrain, taking just over ten hours. Moving on again to refuel at Kuwait, they crossed the Iraqi and Syrian deserts to night-stop at Damascus. On landing there, a rather casual remark from Charles, who was at the controls on that leg, that the brakes were now so bad that they were unlikely to stop before the end of the runway, prompted Lord T to open the cabin door, rush round the wing and physically persuade the Dragonfly to stop, before it hit the boundary fence. Finding a friendly Syrian engineer, they managed to have the brakes adjusted again in order to get a small amount of braking, and set off next morning across the Mediterranean to Athens, and that was when the European weather started to make its presence felt. G-AEDT had no ILS equipment, so the low cloud and poor visibility made the official instrument approach slightly less than standard. The depression and

Home at last! Charles Masefield and Lord Trefgarne safely home to Gatwick, 23rd December, 1963. *[Lord Trefgarne]*

thunderstorms affecting Northern Greece and Italy were obviously going to be a problem next day, so Charles and Lord Trefgarne decided to divert south, and land in Malta, instead of at Rome, so avoiding most of the bad weather. The 720-mile leg up to Marseilles was going to be another long slog mainly over water, so the navigation had to be by dead reckoning, until they could make landfalls on Sicily and Sardinia. Luckily, the French coast came up nicely on time, and the tailwind on the edge of the bad weather gave them a shorter than expected seven and a half hour trip. After all those long legs, the final one from Marignane to Gatwick was relatively easy, at only 600 miles, which took six and a half hours, before a timely arrival to a surprisingly large welcome by family and press on the tarmac on the evening of 23rd December, nicely in time for Christmas.

G-AEDT and her pilots performed remarkably well on the whole trip, with only minor difficulties, and the engines both survived 130 hours of running with only a small problem with the generator. The aircraft was then given another complete check and after the extra fuel tanks had been removed, and a new Rapide-type brake system installed, it was given a full British C of A. The next year, in July 1964, after being flown around Britain, it was bought by an American collector and flown to San Francisco by the same two pilots. But that is another story.

USA to England, G-AEDU

Another pair of gallant aviators, Torquil Norman and Henry Labouchere, also had a desire to take a Dragonfly on a long journey, but some years later. Torquil is a member of a famous British aviation family, his grandfather having been Nigel Norman,

G-AEDT passing through Prestwick en route USA July 1964 for the Tallmantz Museum. *[Ellis]*

who founded Airwork, the wide-ranging training, airport operating, maintenance and brokerage company. Torquil, having flown with the Royal Navy, had begun a collection of vintage de Havilland aircraft and in 1988, bought a wrecked DH 90A from the United States. This was the already well-travelled G-AEDU , which had originally been CR-AAB with DETA in Portuguese East Africa, in 1936. This aircraft's first rebuild story has already been told, but after its second rebuild by Cliff Lovell in 1992, Torquil decided he wanted to visit the American Experimental Aircraft Association annual fly-in at Oshkosh. But he felt it would only be appropriate to arrive in a vintage de Havilland aircraft, so he persuaded a great friend, Henry Labouchere, who was not only an expert engineer, but also a commercial pilot, to accompany him in the Dragonfly. They made the trip in July 1995, but mechanical problems prevented them from reaching their destination that year. As a result, the Dragonfly was left in the States and the two pilots went back in the summer of 1996 to complete the journey back home to Torquil's atmospheric little airfield at Rendcomb, in Gloucestershire.

Henry sorted out the mechanical problems, and the pair took the Dragonfly to the 1996 Oshkosh event in early August, with the intention of flying it back home in time for the annual de Havilland Moth Club Rally, two weeks later. Not surprisingly the Dragonfly won a prize at Oshkosh, then Torquil and Henry set off for the long slog across the Atlantic. The only radio and navigation equipment they had were a main and a spare VHF radio; a VOR receiver, a small but very reliable GPS set and an HF set which never produced good results while consuming enormous amounts of power. They had taken the wise precaution of carrying the normal ocean survival kit, including immersion suits, which they both wore for their ocean-crossing legs.

On departure from Oshkosh, on the 3rd of August, the delightful DH 88 replica was photographed alongside the Dragonfly, then Henry and Torquil set off to Ottawa on the first leg of their journey. Torquil takes up the story:

Ottawa to Goose Bay

"We had decided to take the shortest route home, which involved long legs over the sea from Goose Bay to Narsarsuaq on the southern tip of Greenland then on to Iceland and Stornoway. On paper the two ocean legs were almost identical lengths-about 675 nm (about 7.5 hours in still air) - but in practice the Iceland leg is an hour and a half longer, as Narsarsuaq is 95 nm inland up the fjords, with mountains to 9,000 feet on all sides. With the 67-gallon long-range tank on the back seat, we reckoned our endurance to be over eleven hours, and going east we should have favourable winds. But we'd need all our fuel if we were forced to divert to Godthaab, 360 nm up the west coast of Greenland, the nearest alternate!

We had a pleasant flight to Ottawa in fine weather, except for 1½ hours over fog on Lake Huron. Henry was pleased that he had flown the longest leg so far of the two-way trip, about six hours twenty minutes, but it felt like a trot round the block compared with what was to follow. When we took off the next morning, Ottawa

Torquil Norman flying G-AEDU over cloud, 1993. *[G Bain]*

Tower asked us to do a low fly-past, which I agreed to with pleasure. The run to Sept Iles took five hours ten minutes; the weather was perfect until we hit fog in the St Lawrence Estuary, 130 miles from our destination. We flew over it for an hour and were beginning to think about a diversion when we raised Sept Iles on the radio to find they had five miles visibility in haze and 1,500 feet, which was more than adequate.

After a short refuelling stop and a sandwich, we took off the same afternoon for the two-hour fifty minute run to Goose Bay over very inhospitable mountains and lakes. The landscape was dotted with forest fires caused by lightning strikes, which were common because of the exceptionally dry summer. We saw a huge fire fifty miles from Goose Bay itself.

In the morning there was a low pressure system over the southern tip of Greenland, and Narsarsuaq was socked in and forecast to stay that way. Henry and I took advantage of the kind loan of our agent's van and spent a restful day visiting the local seaplane base-and catching up on sleep. We wanted to make an early start the following morning.

Tuesday's forecast was for broken cloud with tops around 3,500 feet until 50° West, rising to 8,000 feet for the last half of the journey. Narsarsuaq was forecast to have 3,500 feet broken and more than ten km visibility. We were promised a following wind the whole way. As usual, things worked out rather differently. For the first three hours or so we were above fairly low cloud with an occasional hole in it, and the following wind gave us 112 knots TAS, which was terrific - about twenty knots following component. Then the wind veered to the north and became a slight headwind for the last three hours into Greenland. After 50° West the cloud became solid with tops at 6,500 feet, so when we were an hour from land we agreed we would prefer to approach the coast from below cloud. We took advantage of a fortuitous hole to spiral down to sea level. What we found was a fierce northerly wind and a wild sea with a cloudbase of 800 feet. It was gloomy and cold and very bumpy and our drift angle was twenty degrees, a typical Greenland welcome!

After 45 minutes the first island appeared, and thanks to our trusty GPS we entered the right fjord with the weather station on the starboard side to make our approach to Narsarsuaq. The weather over the land was much improved. With the sun coming through the clouds, it was a glorious evening as we swept by the fishing village of Narsarsuaq itself, past the sugar loaf mountain and the old wreck, waving our wings at the fishing boats, and then banked round the corner to the airfield. The wind was a six-knot tailwind down the runway so the simple thing would have been to land straight in off the water, downwind but uphill towards the glacier, i.e. no overshoot with a following wind. I wrongly chose to do a tight circuit to the left of the field against the mountains and land down the hill, into wind, with a good overshoot.

It worked out fine and we had plenty of runway, but the downhill slope is much steeper than it appears. The flight had lasted seven hours 25 minutes. We received a warm welcome and a quick refuel, then found that the hotel was full. But happily, patience and gentle persuasion finally got us a couple of rooms,

The evening forecast implied that, with a late start, we might get away the following morning, but the 0530 visit to the weather office showed that the weather had deteriorated badly and we would not only have a strong headwind but also low cloud with tops around 20,000 feet plus rain. So it was straight back to bed!

The pilot's seat in the Dragonfly is very narrow and cramped and was never designed for an old, brittle six-foot seven-inch pilot immobilised in an immersion suit, so a day of rest was very welcome. We spent it walking across the next-door island through the old settlement of Eric the Red, who apparently landed there 1,000 years ago after a misunderstanding with the authorities in Iceland over the small matter of murdering his wife.

We ran up the largest bar bill (on a price/alcohol ratio) of my life. An Israeli friend whom we met on our walk, our tour guide, Henry and I consumed the completely reasonable total of four Dry Martinis and two Bloody Marys at the astronomical cost of $275 and I'd thought that nothing could make the $1,000 fuel bill look reasonable! We spent four nights in Narsarsuaq watching the low pressure and the high bar bills.

The weather was still hanging around, the winds had become more easterly and the exit fjord was completely socked in. We even had snow on the Thursday night. The forecast from Sondestrom was confirmed by an actual report of conditions in the fjord from the local Air-Sea Rescue helicopter patrol.

Greenland to Iceland

Finally, on Saturday, it looked possible. A large front was still lying two-thirds of the way along the route, but Reykjavik should have broken cloud at 3,500 feet, and although there was the usual low cloud over the airfield, the Sea King reported a 400-foot ceiling in the fjord (provided we stuck to the south side) and broken cloud 25 miles south.

We always had a feeling of slight unease taking off in the heavily overloaded and somewhat under-powered Dragonfly in restricted visibility, but it would have taken more than that to suffer those bar prices for another day! In fact the take-off was fine and the cloudbase on the south side was more like 600 feet, rising soon to 1,000 which enabled us to take a left turn down the parallel fjord, past Jacobshaven. The question was how soon we could go the whole hog and cut the corner onto the direct route for Iceland. Every mile further south added to the journey, but some of the mountain peaks were around 9,000 feet so we couldn't take liberties. When we did climb through the broken cloud, at 200 feet per minute, which was all the old lady could manage, it was painfully slow. It had become clear, even before Oshkosh, that the port engine was not delivering full power. With the port throttle fully open and the starboard throttle 1½ inches back, the difference was clear. But the engine was smooth and the mag drop within limits, so we had taken the decision to proceed.

We eventually reached our full-throttle height at 6,500 feet, in brilliant sunshine above beautiful, snow-white cloud tops with black mountain peaks poking through. We tried to turn east and managed it for a while, but the cloud tops were rising faster than we could climb. Having left it rather late, I had to make a gingerly and surprisingly nerve-racking 180-degree turn, skimming through the cloud tops at full throttle to get back to a more comfortable clearance. The thought of icing, if we got forced into cloud, was very much in our minds, as the terrain was utterly deadly and we had absolutely no margin of power. The freezing level was 4,000 feet. So it was back to a southerly heading for half an hour before we could turn east again. All this must have added 1½ hours to our journey time. But the moonscape of black mountains, brilliant white glaciers and stratocumulus was breathtakingly beautiful. We reported 'Oscar Zulu November (the coast at Prins Christian Sund), and then the FIR boundary, through a friendly German Air Force relay, whilst enjoying a wonderful ride in glorious sunshine over broken cloud for close to 3½ hours. Our airline friends up in the jet stream at 30,000 feet, had the benefit of a following wind of over 130 knots. At 9,000 feet, we were making 115 knots, with the help of wind and engines!

All good things come to an end, and sure enough, the cloud became solid and the tops higher, until we had to let down through a providential hole and tough it out at sea level. The freezing level here was 6,000 feet, so the hole was very welcome. Below cloud it was dark and rainy and the cloudbase slowly lowered. We ended up flying at between 100 and 250 feet for 1½ hours below the front. We had the option of climbing to 1,500 feet and doing it on our rather limited instruments, but the visibility was always just enough to make the lower level more comfortable.

My only moment of fear came when Henry let out a terrific shout from the back seat. I assumed that something huge had fallen off the plane, but it was only a whale he had seen just below us. I flashed a quick look back, but never saw it.

An hour out of Iceland the weather improved, and at the coast it was 1,500 feet broken and 5,000 overcast. We arrived in Reykjavik on a lovely evening after nearly nine hours flying. We were pleased to find that, yet again, the weather would be bad the next day, which meant some relief from the aches and pains of that cockpit. Further relief was supplied by an affordable dry Martini and a delicious bottle of red wine to celebrate completing the longest leg of the journey.

Iceland to Home

By Monday the weather had improved and, after a slightly sticky start below low cloud, we left the coast and climbed gently to reach 10,000 feet three hours out. We had a clear, sunlit run above cloud until a hundred miles from Stornoway, when we let down between cloud layers to 2,500 feet. During this leg we were helped by Britannia Airways and American Airlines to relay our position, and then overheard a general discussion about who was going to take over whom in the next months.

Stornoway was giving 800 feet and rain with strong winds and, anyway, was about to close for the day, so we took a deep breath and asked about the weather at Glasgow. To our joy, this turned out to be 3,500 feet broken and all the nines. Our approach to Glasgow was behind a Hercules and we were asked to widen our circuit to 'allow the required six minutes separation'. Henry and I wondered how they would have coped with the 85 Bonanzas on simultaneous finals that we had witnessed at Oshkosh. Our elapsed time on this 720-nm leg was another bladder-straining eight hours 25 minutes.

I can't say enough for the speed and efficiency of our turn-round at Glasgow. After barely half an hour we had stripped off our immersion suits, cleared Customs, refuelled and were airborne again, as Henry was determined to get home to Langham before dark. We had a lovely flight and arrived over Henry's house just as the sun went down. A few minutes later we arrived with a perfect Labouchere landing. Our flying time from Reykjavik was 11½ hours - not bad for a 1936 aeroplane.

I had a lovely run to Rendcomb, punctuated by someone doing a courtesy barrel roll round the Dragonfly halfway down the route -a gesture I much appreciated. We also made it to the DH Moth Club Rally at Woburn at the weekend. It was a perfect summer's evening as the Dragonfly touched down at Rendcomb after a brilliant adventure.

Postscript.

Henry later found that the timing on one of the port magnetos had slipped twenty degrees and was in danger of shearing completely. At least our timing was a lot better! ”

There are only three Dragonflies still extant, with ZK-AYR in New Zealand, G-AEDU in England and allegedly the remains of VH-UXS at Nowra, in New South Wales, awaiting possible rebuild.

C/n 7552 serialled S-24 for the Danish Army Air Force, 1937. *[BAe]*

Section 5 – Chapter 4: Military Users

At least thirteen military forces have used the Dragonfly, but only three ordered them from new as military aircraft. The others were passed on from civilian operators to military arms, for use as transports in wartime.

BELGIUM

The only Dragonfly to be used in pre-war Belgium went into military service with the approach of the German invasion. The Aeronautique Militaire took possession of the civilian Dragonfly OO-JFN which had been bought by Louis Jean Mahieu, a director of the Banque Nationale de Belgique in August 1937. This Dragonfly replaced a Rapide which had been bought by M. Mahieu in 1935, and was also registered OO-JFN. The Rapide had been used for two years, before being sold via a French agent to the Spanish Republican Army in May 1937. After buying the Dragonfly, M. Mahieu flew it on Bank Nationale business, including a visit to the Belgian Congo in 1938. The Belgian Escadrille Estafette took over the Dragonfly and, most unusually, its pilot, M. Mahieu, in September 1939, to serve as a 'liaison transport' for the Belgian Army. After use in Belgium, and following the invasion, the aircraft was evacuated to Montpellier, France, in May 1940, and was handed over to the Vichy government in August 1940 at the time of the Franco-German armistice. Its subsequent fate is not known, but it seems the aircraft was abandoned at Montpellier.

RCAF's 7623, c/n 7543 impressed in 1940, at RCAF base Trenton after delivery from DH Canada. *[NArchCanada]*

CANADA

The only other military first user was the Royal Canadian Air Force, which bought two stored DH 90As from DH Canada in 1940. These were 7557 and 7558, which had been built in 1937 and shipped speculatively to Canada, as orders were drying up in Europe. The two Dragonflies remained in store in Toronto until the RCAF order, when they became serials 7624 and 7625, to join the four Dragonflies impressed into military service in the same year. The Dragonfly was given a very stylish paint scheme by the RCAF, with a silver overall fuselage and wings, with contrasting black engine cowlings, a neat RCAF badge on the nose below the cockpit, and an elongated red, white and blue fin flash.

Of the aircraft impressed into RCAF service, three were taken into multi-engine pilot training roles, with No.3 and No.4 Training Commands and the others were presumably used as staff transports. The type was not a success with the Air Force as none lasted more than five years in military service. 7623, 7625 and 7627 had crashed by 1942, and only 7623 was repaired to be revert to CF-BFF in 1943. Of the others, 7626 was reduced to spares in 1943; 7624 was sold from Winnipeg in 1945 to become CF-BXV but was written-off in a ground-loop within two months and 7628 which had returned to the Mounties in 1941 and became CF-BXU in 1945, to expire in a forced landing in Alberta just before the year end.

DENMARK

The Danish Haerens Flyvertropper (Army Air Force) were the first military customer, taking delivery of two DH 90As in April 1937. The aircraft were given the military identities S-23 and S-24, and were based at Vaerloese, at some stage with No 3 Squadron. They were used for blind flying and navigation training for pilots, and for senior staff transport, until the German invasion in 1940. S-23 was then reported as being stored, and unconfirmed reports indicate them both to have been taken over by the Luftwaffe in 1943, possibly being used at the experimental establishment at Rechlin.

Section 6:
The DH 92 Dolphin

Section 6: The DH 92 Project

AN UNSUCCESSFUL PROJECT

This design project was a low key attempt by de Havilland in August 1936 to develop the Rapide into a more practical aircraft, using the best elements of the DH 89 and the DH 90, then incorporating some useful additions. Company information on the project is very scarce, with little documentary or photographic evidence being still available. The de Havilland archive does still hold five partial photographs of the Dolphin in various forms and some performance and stress estimates from October 1935, but no reports on the handling or performance can be found. It would seem that the company wanted to keep information on their experiments very private, almost as if they expected the project to not to proceed to production. The information available today is derived from the few de Havilland papers and from individuals working at Hatfield during the mid nineteen thirties, who have searched their memories for details of the project.

The new project was given the constructor's number 6400, and was given the name Dolphin, and the design number DH 92, which implies that it was put on the drawing board after the DH 90 Dragonfly and the DH 91 Albatross, probably in late 1935. It seems that the fuselage structure was very similar to the DH 90, but with obvious influences from the DH 86, DH 88, DH 89, and even the DH 91. It had a fuselage of similar size to the Rapide, but a wider nose and dual controls for two pilots in a side by side configuration, with seating for six in the cabin, but using the Dragonfly's wooden monocoque construction method. Power source was slightly more powerful than the Rapide, with two Gipsy Queen Series II engines, together with variable pitch propellers and a new type of retractable undercarriage. The only model built was constructed in the Experimental Shop in the spring of 1936, amid considerable secrecy, and then first flown as E.3 on 9th September, with Series II engines, but for some unknown reason only fixed-pitch propellers were fitted, which would have entailed the complication of blocking off the oil lines to the which normally lead to the constant speed mechanism on the Series II engines. At the rear, the tail surfaces were similar to but slightly larger than those of the Rapide.

Photographs from the de Havilland archive at BAE Systems, Farnborough, show elements of the aircraft in its various undercarriage formats, but no written reports on handling or rationale for the various changes to undercarriage and engines is available. Constructor's number 6400 was built in the early summer of 1936, fitted with two Queen II engines and, strangely, a fixed undercarriage was initially fitted, despite the indication that the undercarriage was to be retractable. After several trial flights, a retractable undercarriage was substituted, using Turner twin shock absorbing legs, which pivoted at the top of the legs, so that they folded neatly rearwards into a modified engine nacelle, powered by combined gearbox and screw jacks, which in turn were driven through extension tubes by a single electric motor housed in the fuselage. A manual operating system was also employed for emergency use, with a handle mounted between the pilots' seats and a system of cables leading to the electric motor. As no reports have been found, the company views on 6400's success cannot be ascertained. However, during the summer of 1936, de Havilland tentatively entered the aircraft in the Schlesinger African Air Race from Portsmouth to Johannesburg, due to take place in September 1936, with Business Manager Hugh Buckingham nominated to fly it.

STRESSING ASSUMPTIONS

One document which has survived the cull of Dolphin papers is an unsigned, typed note from the Stress specialist in the Drawing Office, dated 27th October 1935.

First iteration, with fixed undercarriage and full cowlings. [BAe]

This gives an interesting insight into the planned capabilities of the proposed type 92.

Parameter	*DH 92*	*DH 90*	*DH 89*
Engines 2 x	Gipsy VI Series II	Gipsy Major 1	Gipsy VI Series II
Horse power (each) at 2400 rpm	215 hp	130 hp	198 hp
Max weight	6,000 lbs	4,000 lbs	5,000 lbs
Weight of structure	4,119 lbs	2367 lbs app	2, 910 lbs app
Weight of fuel + oil	780 lbs	530 lbs (60 gall)	684 lbs
Tare weight + fuel + pilots	5,099 lbs	3370 lbs	3,960 lbs
Payload	901 lbs	630 lbs	1,040 lbs
Span of upper plane	50 ft 6 in	43 ft	48 ft
Area of upper plane	194 sq ft		
Span of lower plane	45 ft	38 ft 6 in	48 ft
Area of lower plane	170 sq ft		
Total wing area	418 sq ft	288 sq ft	340 sq ft
Fuel capacity	80 galls	60 galls (plus 25 aux)	80 galls
Oil capacity	8 galls	7 galls	7 galls
Aerofoil section	Mod RAF34	Mod RAF34	
Top speed	170 mph	145 mph	163 mph
Cruise speed	153 mph	125 mph	138 mph
Stalling speed			
- flaps up	65mph	64 mph	63 mph
- flaps down	60 mph	59 mph	61 mph
Fast glide	229 mph		190 mph
Up and down gust	25 ft/sec		
Load grading	As for DH 90		

From the figures used in this Stressing Assumption, it would seem that the extra weight of the wooden monocoque structure, plus the weight of the larger engines (even without their heavier propellers) and the extra weight of the retractable undercarriage system, show the Dolphin to be much heavier than the Rapide, which had a greater carrying capacity. If a second pilot is added, as was intended for the aircraft, but no account taken of cabin furnishings, which were not fitted in the prototype, then the Dolphin weighed 1,139 lbs more than the Rapide. This figure gives only another 901 lbs for payload, but if cabin furniture and the heavier propellers, both of which were planned for the type, are added, then the payload comes down to around 600 lbs. If a radio were then to be installed, the payload would work out at around 500 to 550 lbs, which would only allow three passengers with minimal baggage to be carried, instead of the planned six passengers plus baggage.

If these assumptions are anywhere near the actual figures for the Dolphin, there was certainly a weight problem, but there were difficulties with development of a completely new undercarriage as

Les Vowles' impression of a potential DH 92 project allied to Wilson Airways of Nairobi, 1936. [L Vowles]

well, demonstrated by the three different installations which were tried out in the summer of 1936. Another potential complication was likely to be the fitting of the constant-speed propellers to the Gipsy Queen II engines, which had not been done before. The only similar combination of engine and propeller had been on the DH 88 Comet racer, which had similar engines, but a simple, pneumatically operated pitch-change system, not the constant-speed units later fitted to Rapides to make them into the Mark IV model. These problems, appearing when the company was very much involved in producing five of their own designs, plus another two on the drawing board, would seem to be a very good reason for the cancellation of the rather unpromising Dolphin project.

Early in the summer of 1936, the aircraft was registered as G-AEMX, but then an application for a Certificate of Airworthiness, which had been made on 16th September 1936, was cancelled by letter from A H Morse, by then the Chief Inspector, to the Air Ministry on 30th September 1936. An intriguing report from an engineer working for de Havilland in the mid-thirties, that the Dolphin project aircraft was sent out to Kenya in 1936 for trials with an African company, seems rather unlikely. Wilson Airways were very strong advocates of DH machines, and had a strong relationship with the company, but would be unlikely to have a requirement for a more complex, two-pilot, retractable-gear development of the Rapide for their harsh operating conditions. Why would de Havilland take an untried development project all the way out to Central Africa for trials, where there were no facilities for testing or making possible modifications? Surely, in their usual way, the company is much more likely to have carried out basic practical trials only at Hatfield, where configuration changes could rapidly be made to assess the suitability of the project for future sales.

An article published in *Flight* for 10th September 1936, gave de Havillands' official reason for the cancellation. It said that "development of the four-engined Albatross, important contracts contributing to the expansion of the Royal Air Force, and other urgent activities impose a heavy load on certain sections of the Company's organisation, making it impossible to devote the personnel and time necessary for the early production of the Dolphin." It was soon decided that "It did not come up to expectations" according to DH design staff, so the whole project was abandoned as impractical and scrapped. The sole unpainted airframe was reported as hanging in the roof of the Experimental shed for several months, before disappearing, probably to the fire dump, before being scrapped by November 1936.

Front view of the last iteration, with retractable undercarriage and wide spinner base-plate for a variable-pitch propeller, 1936. [BAe]

APPENDIX 1
De Havilland Dragon Types - Chronology

1920		De Havilland Aircraft Company registered its Stag Lane premises.
1930		London Aeroplane Club moved to Hatfield airfield.
		New De Havilland factory construction begun at Hatfield
		No 1 RAF Elementary & Reserve Flying School moved to Hatfield.
	26 Oct	DH 82 Tiger Moth first flight at Stag Lane.
1932	29 Jan	DH 83 Fox Moth first flight, Stag Lane.
	24 Nov	**DH 84** (E-9, G-ACAN) first flight by Hubert Broad, Stag Lane.
	Dec	First **DH 84** delivered to first customer, Hillman's Airways.
1933		HRDC building for DH workers begun at Birchwood.
	23 Sep	Australian government ITT for Singapore route operation, with closing date 31st January 1934.
	Late 33	**DH 89** design begun at Stag Lane.
		First **DH 86** ordered by Imperial Airways for QANTAS use.
1934	14 Jan	**DH 86** first flight (E-2, G-ACPL), by Hubert Broad, Stag Lane.
		DH 86 (E-2, G-ACPL) C of A issued.
		Hatfield factory completed.
	17 April	**DH 89** (E-4, CH-287) first flight, by Hubert Broad, Hatfield
	9 May	DH 87 Hornet Moth first flight, by Capt de Havilland, Hatfield.
	8 Sep	DH 88 Comet first flight by Hubert Broad, Hatfield.
	Oct	DH 88 Comet won MacRobertson Race to Australia.
1935	25 Feb	First QANTAS **DH 86** flight on Empire route, Darwin - Koepang.
		First RAF **DH 89** Rapide entered service.
	June	King's Cup Air Race at Hatfield
	12 Aug	**DH 90** first flight (E-2, G-ADNA) by Hubert Broad at Hatfield.
1937		Last **DH 84** built at Hatfield.
		DH 89A introduced, with flaps and other mods.
	30 Dec	Last **DH 86** built.
1938		Last **DH 90** built.
1940		DH 98 Mosquito first flight from Hatfield.
		First **DH 89B** Dominie built for RAF at Hatfield.
		DH 82 Tiger Moth production transferred to Morris Motors, Cowley.
1941		DH 98 Mosquito production begun.
1942	29 Sep	First flight of Australian **DH 84**, Bankstown.
1943	April	First **DH 89B** Dominie built at Brush Electrical, Loughborough.
	June	Last Australian **DH 84** built.
		First flight of Brush-built **DH 89B** Dominie.
1944		DH Engine Company formed.
1945		Last Brush-built **DH 89B** Dominie completed.
1946		DH Propeller Company formed.
1947		Last two **DH 89** Rapides built from spares by DH Witney.
1948		Single DH 89 Mark 5 conversion at Hatfield.
1953		First DH 89 Mark 4 conversion made by Flightways of Southampton.
1955	June	Last **DH 89B** Dominies sold by RAF.
1958	21 Sep	Last flight of a **DH 86**, crashed at Madrid.
1960		DH Holdings incorporated into Hawker Siddeley Group.

APPENDIX 2
De Havilland Types Production

This is a simplified Listing as comprehensive details of all aircraft histories are given in our companion Air-Britain volume, 'The de Havilland Dragon / Rapide Family', by John Hamlin.

Existing aircraft are denoted throughout by **bold** *lettering.*

DH 84 PRODUCTION

Production started at Stag Lane in November 1932, then from spring 1934, all production transferred to the new Hatfield factory. Australian production began at Bankstown, NSW, 1942.
Total Hatfield build 115. Total Bankstown build 87.
TOTAL built 202.

6000 E.9, First flight 24 November 1932, G-ACAN Crashed Dunbeath, Caithness 21.5.41.
6001 First production DH 84, G-ACAO, C of A issued 3 February 1933, X9398 Crashed Ollerton, Notts 21.10.40.
6002 G-ACAP Crashed nr Lyndhurst, Hants 26.3.36.
6003 Iraqi Air Force 16.
6004 Iraqi Air Force 17.
6005 Iraqi Air Force 18.
6006 Iraqi Air Force 19.
6007 Iraqi Air Force 20.
6008 Iraqi Air Force 21.
6009 G-ACBW, BS816, 2780M.
6010 G-ACCE Crashed Kirkwall, Orkneys, 29.8.34.
6011 G-ACCR Crashed nr Ault Lighthouse, Le Treport, France 22.1.36.
6012 Iraqi Air Force 22.
6013 Iraqi Air Force 23.
6014 G-ACCV Crashed Bridgeport, Connecticut, USA, 24.7.33.
6015 G-ACCZ, AW154, 2820M. Soc 20.12.42.
6016 G-ACDL Spanish Republicans LD-002.
6017 G-ACDM, ZS-AEI, SAAF 1570, Instructional IS13.
6018 G-ACDN, AW170 Crashed St Wenn, Cornwall 27.11.40.
6019 G-ACEK, AX867 Soc for spares 21.7.41.
6020 EC-W14, EC-TAT, Spanish Republicans LD-001.
6021 G-ACET, AW171, 2779M, G-ACET On rebuild, Southampton.
6022 G-ACEU Sold abroad 3.37, Spain.
6023 G-ACEV Spanish Republicans.
6024 CF-APJ To spares 10.42.
6025 G-ACGG, VH-AAC, A34-10, VH-AAC Crashed Slate Creek airstrip, New Guinea 29.1.51.
6026 ZS-AEF Crashed Baragwanath, Johannesburg, South Africa 26.9.33.
6027 G-ACFG, VH-UZG Crashed nr Cairns, QLD, Australia 7.5.37.
6028 SU-ABH, G-AEKZ, AW163 Crashed Castle Bromwich, Warwicks 18.11.40.
6029 VH-URE, VH-FDB, VH-DMA Crashed nr Katherine, NT 11.12.57.
6030 ZS-AEG, VP-YBY, SRAS 260. Wfu .44.
6031 SU-ABI Crashed nr El Arish, Egypt 15.3.35.
6032 G-ACIE, OK-ATO, G-ACIE, OK-ATO, G-ACIE, SU-ABZ . Wfu Almaza 12.46.
6033 G-ACGK Ditched Moray Firth, nr Inverness 8.1.35,
6034 G-ACGU Crashed Heston, London 16.7.35.
6035 G-ACHV, G-AEGK, G-ACHV, X9379 Soc for spares 7.8.40.
6036 G-ACHX Crashed Purley, Surrey 25.4.38.
6037 VH-URD, A34-7, VH-URD Crashed Menyamya, New Guinea 24.12.51.
6038 G-ACIW, F-ANGE
6039 G-ACIT Preserved at The Science Museum, Wroughton.
6040 G-ACJH, F-AMTM Crashed La Reole, Gironde, France 3.11.38.
6041 G-ACIU, (X9395) Damaged Mourmelon 29.4.40 and dbf.
6042 G-ACJS Cnx 11.36, to Spain?
6043 G-ACJT Crashed Weston super Mare, Somerset 20.12.39.
6044 YI-AAC, G-ACLE, X9397 Struck by runaway bowser Odiham, Hants 8.4.41.
6045 VH-URF, A34-9 Destroyed by incendiary bomb Darwin, NT 3.3.42.
6046 VH-URG Crashed Wenlock, Queensland 4.2.42.
6047 VP-KAW Crashed nr Mombasa, Kenya 8.12.33.
6048 VT-AEL Crashed 40 miles from Lahore, Pakistan 26.8.39.
6049 G-ACJM Crashed Hamble 12.8.34.
6050 VT-AEK Cnx 6.5.37.
6051 SU-ABJ Dbf Almaza 22.6.38.
6052 G-ACKD Crashed on take off Akaki, Ethiopia 23.3.36.
6053 G-ACMC, VH-UXK Crashed Innisfail, Queensland 29.8.38.
6054 ZS-AEH, SAAF 1414, Instructional IS12
6055 G-ACKB, AX863 To spares 1.2.41.
6056 G-ACKC, Spanish Republicans.
6057 G-ACLP, F-AMTR Destroyed 2.38.
6058 G-ACMJ, X9396 To spares 12.11.41.
6059 VP-KBA, KAAU K15.
6060 Danish Army S-21 Crashed Ringsted, Denmark 24.2.36.
6061 Danish Army S-22 Crashed Vaerlose Air Base, Denmark 9.8.39.
6062 G-ACMO, VH-ABK, A34-4, VH-ABK, A34-4 On rebuild Murwillumbah, NSW, Australia.
6063 G-ACMP Crashed near Splott, Cardiff 22.7.35.
6064 F-AMUZ Crashed 45 ml from Constantine, Algeria 13.6.38.
6065 VT-AES, VH-UZF, A34-8 Crashed 8.6.42.
6066 First production DH 84 Mk II, G-ACKU, C of A issued 24 November 1933, AW172 Crashed near Wantage, Berks 10.2.41.
6067 G-ACNA, Spanish Republicans LD-....
6068 VH-URO Crashed in the Bitol Ranges, New Guinea 30.9.35.
6069 G-ACNG Crashed Hatston 19.4.40.
6070 G-ACNH Wfu 1.37.
6071 G-ACNI, Irish Air Corps DH-18. Crashed Baldonnel, Eire 16.2.41.
6072 G-ACNJ Wfu Dyce, Aberdeenshire 28.5.43.
6073 G-ACOR, VH-AEA Destroyed in air raid Salamaua, New Guinea 21.1.42.
6074 VT-AFF, VH-USA Destroyed in air raid Salamaua, New Guinea 21.1.42.
6075 G-ACPX, X9399 [ntu] Crashed Castle Bromwich, Warwicks 22.4.40.
6076 G-ACPY, EI-ABI(1), G-ACPY Shot down near Isles of Scilly 3.6.41.
6077 G-ACRF, VH-UXG Current, Murwillumbah, NSW, Australia.
6078 G-ACRH Crashed Dyce, Aberdeenshire 13.7.34
6079 G-ACRO, VP-KBG Crashed Nairobi, Kenya 14.4.37.
6080 VH-URW Crashed Wau, New Guinea 30.1.40.
6081 VH-URX, A34-1 Ditched off Dongarra, WA 14.6.42.
6082 VH-URY, A34-6, VH-URY Crashed Cheviot Hills Station, QLD, Australia 20.10.53.
6083 F-ANES Wfu .57
6084 G-ACVD, VH-UZX Crashed near Croydon, Surrey, 26.2.38
6085 PP-SPC, Brazilian Navy D4H-178 Crashed 28.12.40
6086 CF-AVD Crashed Baie Comeau, PQ, Canada 26.5.44.
6087 G-ACXI, Turkish Air Force.
6088 VH-URU, A34-2 Cr nr Cootamundra, NSW, Australia 11.11.40.
6089 VH-URV Crashed Yarramunda, New Guinea 13.12.51.
6090 ZK-ADR, ZK-AER, NZ551, ZK-AHT Crashed into Mount Hope, near Nelson, NZ 30.6.44.
6091 ZK-ADS, NZ550 Wfu Nausori, Fiji 7.43.
6092 G-ADCP, X9440 Scrapped Belfast, NI 12.41.
6093 CF-AVI Torn from moorings and washed over dam Godbout, PQ, Canada 13.1.41.
6094 G-ADCR Crashed St Just, Cornwall 25.6.38.
6095 G-ADCT Crashed Longman, Inverness 14.2.40.

6096 G-ADDI, N34DH Current, Oakville, WA, USA.
6097 G-ADDJ, VH-UZZ, A34-3 Crashed Musgrove Station, QLD, Australia 13.10.42.
6098 G-ADED Crashed Ronaldsway, IoM 1.7.35.
6099 G-ADEE Crashed nr Garstang, Lancs 26.10.35.
6100 G-ADFI Crashed Thurso Aerodrome, Caithness 3.7.37.
6101 OE-FKD, Austrian Army Air Force 64.
6102 VH-UVB Destroyed in air raid New Guinea 21.1.42.
6103 E.4, G-ADOS, HM569 Crashed Squires Gate, Lancs 24.6.42.
6104 VH-UTX, A34-11 Wrecked in gales Oodnadatta 15.2.43.
6105 G-AECZ, AV982, G-AECZ, EI-AFK, EI-ABI(2) Current, Dublin, Eire.
6106 G-AEFX, VH-UVN Crashed Broome, WA 7.1.42.
6107 G-AEIS, Turkish AF.
6108 G-AEIT, Turkish AF.
6109 G-AEIU, Turkish AF.
6110 G-AEMI, AW173 Crashed Pillerton Hersey, Warks 14.12.40.
6111 G-AEMJ, Portuguese Air Force 504, 2304.
6112 G-AEMK, VH-AAO, A34-5, VH-AAO Wrecked in storm Coonamble, NSW, Australia 20/21.12.47.
6113 Portuguese Air Force 505, 2305.
6114 Last Hatfield DH 84 Mk II, C of A issued 20 May 1937. Portuguese Air Force 506, 2306 Wfu .50.

DH.84A DRAGON III (Australian Production)
All crash sites are in Australia except where noted.
2001 A34-12 first flight 29 September 1942, Crashed Berry Strip, NSW 9.12.43.
2002 A34-13 VH-ASK, VH-SNB On display Museum of Flight, East Fortune, East Lothian.
2003 A34-14 Crashed Popondedda, New Guinea 17.1.43.
2004 A34-15 Crashed Terapo 19.6.43.
2005 A34-16 Wfu 6.4.44.
2006 A34-17 VH-AOS Crashed Mount Kerigomna, New Guinea 29.1.47.
2007 A34-18 Wrecked in storm Katherine Strip, NT 1.11.43.
2008 A34-19 Crashed Toogoolawah, QLD, 17.9.43.
2009 A34-20 Crashed Marami Station 25.8.43.
2010 A34-21 VH-AOP Crashed Heyfield, New Guinea 9.8.54.
2011 A34-22 VH-AOQ Wfu 9.60.
2012 A34-23 Crashed Darwin, NT 21.3.46.
2013 A34-24 Crashed nr Crystal Cascade, QLD 7.3.43.
2014 A34-25 Crashed Croydon, QLD 6.12.43.
2015 A34-26 Crashed Merets Island 16.1.44.
2016 A34-27 Crashed Darwin 2.12.44.
2017 A34-28 VH-AGI Crashed Batemans Bay, NSW 1.10.61.
2018 A34-29 Crashed Terapo 11.9.43.
2019 A34-30 VH-AON, Current, Wangarratta, Vic, Australia.
2020 A34-31 VH-ASL, VH-SJW Crashed nr Charters Towers, QLD 16.8.57.
2021 A34-32 Crashed Bulldog Strip, New Guinea 17.1.44.
2022 A34-33 VH-ALL Crashed near Windora, QLD 6.2.51.
2023 A34-34 VH-AMB Crashed Palmerville Station, QLD 23.2.49.
2024 A34-35 VH-AFK Crashed Bena Bena, New Guinea 7.9.48.
2025 A34-36 Crashed in swamp Higgins Field, QLD 13.5.44.
2026 A34-37 Crashed N of Limeburner's Creek, NSW 14.10.43.
2027 A34-38 VH-BAF Crashed Zenag, New Guinea 14.7.47.
2028 A34-39 VH-ARI Crashed Wewak, New Guinea 31.8.46.
2029 A34-40 Crashed NE of KB Mission, Milne Bay, New Guinea 16.6.43.
2030 A34-41 Crashed 30 Mile Strip, Papua 3.7.43.
2031 A34-42 VH-AYM Dbf Canobie Station, QLD 24.11.48.
2032 A34-43 Crashed Terapo, New Guinea 12.7.43.
2033 A34-44 Crashed Berry Strip, NSW 26.7.43.
2034 A34-45 Crashed N of Tennants Creek, NT 1.4.43.
2035 A34-46 Crashed Wedau, NT 27.7.43.
2036 A34-47 Missing, Mascot to Wagga Wagga, NSW 17.4.43.
2037 A34-48 Crashed Parafield, SA, 11.3.43.
2038 A34-49 Crashed nr Toowoomba, QLD 2.3.43.
2039 A34-50 VH-ASN, VH-ASX Wfu Lae, New Guinea 28.8.54.
2040 A34-51 Crashed off Goulburn Islands, NT 31.5.43.
2041 A34-52 Crashed off Mindil Beach, Darwin, NT 3.9.44.
2042 A34-53 VH-AOR Crashed nr Brisbane, QLD 23.10.54.
2043 A34-54 (VH-API) Not civilianised.
2044 A34-55 VH-BJH Wfu 11.9.60.
2045 A34-56 VH-ASO, VH-FDA,VH-AGC Crashed Point Cook, VIC 13.12.79.
2046 A34-57 VH-AGJ Wfu 14.6.51.
2047 A34-58 Crashed Toowoomba, QLD 20.3.44.
2048 A34-59 VH-AQU, VH-DHX, G-ECAN Current, Rendcomb, UK.
2049 A34-60 VH-GAU, VH-BMX Crashed Atemble Mission, New Guinea 14.2.50.
2050 A34-61 VH-AOT Crashed Togoba, New Guinea 2.8.55
2051 A34-62 VH-APL Crashed Chimbu, New Guinea 23.9.52.
2052 A34-63 Crashed Bathurst Island, NT 12.3.45.
2053 A34-64 VH-AYZ Wfu 22.6.64.
2054 A34-65 Crashed between Plumbton & Mount Druit, NSW 5.1.45.
2055 A34-66 VH-BAH Crashed Brewarrina, NSW 1.7.56
2056 A34-67 VH-AOK Wfu 6.8.51
2057 A34-68 VH-AEF, ZK-AXI Current, North Shore, New Zealand.
2058 A34-69 VH-AOE Crashed Madang Harbour, New Guinea 29.10.55.
2059 A34-70 VH-AMN Crashed Jurien Bay airstrip, WA 12.11.60.
2060 A34-71 Crashed nr Daylesford, VIC 21.7.44.
2061 A34-72 VH-AKX Crashed Turnagain Island, New Guinea 12.5.48
2062 A34-73 Crashed Maryborough, QLD 19.9.43.
2063 A34-74 VH-BDB Crashed Kerowage, New Guinea 3.4.51.
2064 A34-75 VH-APJ, VH-RSZ, VH-PSZ Crashed nr Rutherford, NSW 10.6.61.
2065 A34-76 VH-AYB Crashed off Lae, New Guinea 20.8.47.
2066 A34-77 VH-AOM Crashed Mackay, QLD 20.7.46.
2067 A34-78 VH-AMO Crashed Mingende, Central Highlands, New Guinea 31.12.48.
2068 A34-79 VH-AQW Wfu 6.61.
2069 A34-80 Crashed Weatlock Strip 21.9.43 .
2070 A34-81 Crashed nr Vivigani, Goodenough Island 22.12.43.
2071 A34-82 VH-AXL Crashed nr Koranka Airstrip, New Guinea 21.9.51.
2072 A34-83 VH-APP, VH-CPP, VH-DMB Crashed Darwin, NT 27.2.59.
2073 A34-84 VH-AHY Crashed Hope Creek, New Guinea 20.5.48.
2074 A34-85 VH-AVU Wfu 5.51.
2075 A34-86 Sold 22.2.46 but used as spares.
2076 A34-87 Sold 21.2.46 but used for spares.
2077 A34-88 Crashed Coffs Harbour, NSW 23.12.43.
2078 A34-89 Crashed nr Batchelor, NT 3.2.45.
2079 A34-90 VH-ASU, VH-APJ Wfu 10.64.
2080 A34-91 VH-ARJ Wfu 9.60.
2081 A34-92 G-AJKF (ntu), VH-BDS, VH-AML Current, Perth, WA.
2082 A34-93 VH-AGM Wfu 7.46.
2083 A34-94 VH-BDC Wfu 7.57.
2084 A34-95 VH-AOL Crashed Orange, NSW 10.5.53.
2085 A34-96 VH-AFH Crashed Sleisbeck, NT 31.8.56.
2086 A34-97 VH-AIA Wfu 9.63.
2087 A34-98 Handed over 23 June 1943. Crashed Daru Island, New Guinea 27.9.44.

DH 86 PRODUCTION

Production started at Stag Lane in September 1933, then from spring 1934, all production transferred to the new Hatfield factory. First prototype E-2/G-ACPL, c/n 2300 completed January 1934, with single-pilot nose; 2-pilot nose fitted July 1934.

4 DH 86 single-pilot nose built 1934. c/n 2300 to 2303.
28 DH 86 2-pilot nose built 1934-1935. 1st G-ACWC, c/n 2304 to 2332. 1 converted to DH 86B.
20 DH 86A built 1936 - 1937. 1st G-ADFF, c/n 2328 to 2351. 19 converted to DH 86B.
10 DH 86B built 1937. First G-AENR, c/n 2352 to 2361.

1934 production 10 DH 86 and mod nose DH 86.
1935 production 21 DH 86.
1936 production 19 DH 86A and DH 86B.
1937 production 11 DH 86A and DH 86B.
TOTAL built 62.

2300 E.2, G-ACPL, HK844. Soc 1.12.42.
2301 VH-URN Crashed in Bass Strait, Australia 19.10.34.
2302 G-ACVY Wfu with main spar failure prior to 8.46.
2303 G-ACVZ Crashed 20mls W of Cologne, Germany 16.3.37.
2304 G-ACWC Crashed Minna, Nigeria 17.6.41.
2305 G-ACWD, HK829 Crashed Nefatia North, Egypt 17.3.43.
2306 G-ACWE, VH-UUA, VT-AKM, HX789 Crashed Cochin, India 15.9.42.
2307 VH-USC, A31-5, VH-USC Crashed Darwin, NT, Australia 9.10.44
2308 VH-USD, VT-AKZ, AX800, VT-AKZ Wfu 11.44.
2309 VH-USE Crashed into Mount Pirie, near Belmont, QLD, Australia 20.2.42
2310 VH-USF, A31-6, VH-USF Crashed Geraldton, WA, Australia 24.6.45.
2311 VH-USG Crashed nr Longreach, QLD, Australia 15.11.34.
2312 VH-URT Crashed into Bass Strait, near Flinders Island, VIC, Australia 2.10.35
2313 G-ACYF, VR-SBD, VH-AND, A31-2 Crashed nr Maryborough, QLD, Australia, 1.5.44
2314 G-ACYG, AX840 Wfu for spares 4.3.45.
2315 VH-USW, A31-4, VH-USW, A31-4, VH-USW Wfu Allahabad, India 26.12.46.
2316 G-ACZN Crashed near Jersey Airport, CI 4.11.38.
2317 G-ADCM Crashed Zwettl, Austria 22.10.35
2318 G-ACZO, AX841 [ntu] Destroyed by bombs Lee on Solent, Hants 16.7.40.
2319 G-ADCN Destroyed in hangar fire Don Muang airport, Bangkok, Thailand 3.12.38.
2320 SU-ABN Damaged RAF Lydda, Palestine 23.4.42.
2321 G-ACZP, AX843, G-ACZP Crashed Barajas Airport, Madrid, Spain 21.9.58
2322 G-ACZR, AX844 Crashed Donibristle, Fife 31.3.43.
2323 G-ADEA, VR-SBC, VH-UZX, A31-7 Wfu Heliopolis, Egypt 9.43.
2324 G-ADEB Crashed nr Altenkirchen, Germany 12.8.36.
2325 G-ADEC, CX-AAH Crashed Artigas, Uruguay 22.10.45.
2326 VH-UUB, A31-3 Destroyed by fire Heliopolis, Egypt 19.4.42.
2327 G-ADMY, X9442 Soc 4.4.44.
2328 G-ADFF, AX760 Damaged taxying Lydda, Palestine 26.11.41.
2329 SU-ABO.
2330 ZK-AEF, NZ552 Badly damaged taxying Nausori, Fiji 7.12.43.
2331 ZK-AEG, NZ553, ZK-AHW Wfu 31.8.46.
2332 ZK-AEH, NZ554 Crashed Ohakea, NZ 13.11.40.
2333 G-ADUE, AX762 ('AX672'). Crashed Siwa, Egypt 23.6.42.
2334 G-ADUF, HK828, SU-ACR, G-ADUF Wfu 3.5.52.
2335 G-ADUG, HK831 Shot down 12.41.
2336 G-ADUH, EI-ABT, G-ADUH Collided on ground Muharraq, Bahrain 22.5.51.
2337 G-ADUI, HK830 Damaged taxying Bilbeis, Egypt 11.3.42.
2338 G-ADVJ, EI-ABK, G-ADVJ Wfu 18.3.52.
2339 G-ADVK Lost to German occupation of Jersey 6.40.
2340 G-ADYC, L8037 Soc post-2.45.
2341 G-ADYD, L8040 Damaged taxying Hatston 22.1.44.
2342 E.2, SU-ABV, G-AJNB wfu Wadi Halfa, Sudan 8.5.48.
2343 G-ADYG, N6246 Destroyed in hangar fire at Hendon 21.4.43.
2344 G-ADYH, Indonesian RI-008 [ntu] Scrapped Bandoeng, Indonesia .49.
2345 G-ADYI, AX795 To spares 27.5.43.
2346 G-ADYE, CX-ABG Scrapped .49.
2347 G-ADYF Crashed nr Gatwick 15.9.36.
2348 G-ADYJ, L7596 Crashed nr Ulverston, Lancs 28.6.39
2349 G-AEAP, HK843 Destroyed by fire Pachino, Sicily 23.7.43.
2350 G-AEFH Abandoned Bordeaux, France on evacuation 18.6.40.
2351 G-AEJM, X9441 Dbf Hendon 17.2.43.
2352 G-AENR, AX842, G-AENR Wfu Speke, Liverpool 21.7.46.
2353 G-AETM, OH-SLA [ntu], OH-IPA, Finnish Navy DH-1 Badly damaged on ground Malmi, Finland 27.5.40.
2354 G-AEWR Abandoned Bordeaux, France on evacuation 18.6.40.
2355 G-AFAJ, TC-ERK
2356 G-AFAK, TC-FER.
2357 G-AFAL, TC-GEN.
2358 G-AFAM, TC-HEP.
2359 VH-UYU, A31-8 Shot down 2 mls S of LG.138, Libya 8.12.41.
2360 VH-UYV, A31-1 Crashed 15.8.44
2361 VH-UYW Ditched off New Ireland, New Guinea 15.3.40.

DH 89 DRAGON RAPIDE PRODUCTION

Production started at Hatfield in spring 1934. then transferred to Brush Coachworks, Loughborough.

Total Hatfield build 393.
Total Loughborough build 335.
Two final DH 89s assembled at CRU Witney in 1947.
C/n 89232, built Downview, Canada, from spares, CF-BNJ, June 1942.
TOTAL built 729.

6250 E.4, CH 287, HB-ARA, HB-APA Wfu Kloten, Zurich, Switzerland 5.61.
6251 G-ACPM Crashed off Folkestone, Kent 2.10.34.
6252 G-ACPN, Spanish Nationalists 40-4. Possibly shot down 27.8.36.
6253 G-ACPO, VH-UBN, A33-5, VH-UBN. Crashed Mount Kitchener, SA, Australia 20.7.44.
6254 G-ACPP, CF-PTK. On display Reynolds Alberta Museum, Wetaskiwin, AB, Canada
6255 G-ACPR Crashed Burford, Oxon 19.2.40.
6256 ZS-AES, VP-YBZ, SRAS 302, VP-YBZ Crashed 11.43.
6257 G-ACTT, X8509 Damaged beyond repair 14.7.41.
6258 G-ACTU, AW115 Crashed Cardiff 15.2.41.
6259 ZK-ACO, VH-UUO, A33-1, VH-UUO Crashed/dbf Warrumbungle Range, nr Tooraweenah, NSW, Australia 23.5.52.
6260 I-DRAG, Spanish Republicans.
6261 G-ACYR On display Museo del Air, Cuatro Vientos, Madrid, Spain.
6262 EC-W27, EC-AZZ.
6263 G-ADAL, X9448 Crashed Standish, nr Wigan 25.3.41.
6264 G-ACZE, Z7266, G-ACZE Crashed Grimsetter, Orkney 27.12.45; completely rebuilt as G-AJGS (c/n W.1001), G-ACZE Current with Brian Woodford and stored Withybush.
6265 VH-UVS Dbf on start up Mascot, NSW, Australia 12.5.37.
6266 G-ADAG, Z7264 To spares Witney 20.8.43.
6267 K5070, VP-KCK, KAAU [probably] K11 To spares Nairobi .46.
6268 G-ACZF CofA expired 18.5.47 and scrapped Witney.
6269 G-ACYM, X9320 [not used]. Crashed Moyenville, France 12.2.40.
6270 A3-1; VH-UFF; A33-3 (callsign VHCRP), VH-UFF, F-OAVG Wfu Noumea Magenta, New Caledonia 3.3.59.
6271 DH.89M K4772 To spares Witney 15.6.42
6272 G-ADAE, OY-DIN, G-ADAE To spares Ronaldsway, IoM after CofA expired 28.7.47.
6273 OO-JFN, Spanish Republicans.
6274 G-ACZU Sold abroad 7.37 - probably Spain.
6275 G-ADAO, Spanish Nationalists, possibly 40-5. Destroyed 26.8.36. [Or 40-1, EC-CAQ, EC-ABG Crashed Guinea 30.7.53].
6276 G-ADAJ, F-BEDY, F-OADY, F-BAHY Crashed Seno, Savannakhet, Indo China 20.8.54.
6277 G-ADCL, Spanish Nationalists 40-2, EC-AAY Crashed Spanish Guinea 22.6.46.
6278 G-ADAH On display Manchester Museum of Science & Industry.

6279 CF-AEO Crashed Moncton, New Brunswick, Canada 18.7.35.
6280 G-ADBU Crashed c.11.36.
6281 G-ADAK, AW155 To spares Witney 11.9.44.
6282 G-ADDE, X9386 Sold 24.3.47 but to spares at Dyce, Aberdeenshire.
6283 G-ADDD, AW116 To spares Witney 7.4.41
6284 G-ADDF, Spanish Republicans.
6285 VP-YAU, SRAS 301, VP-YAU Soc 8.44.
6286 G-ADBV, X8511 To spares Witney 22.10.41.
6287 G-ADAI, Z7262 (not used), Crashed Shawbury, Shropshire 31.7.40.
6288 G-ADBW, Z7265 Soc 17.11.41.
6289 G-ADBX Crashed Ronaldsway, IoM 16.5.36.
6290 G-ADFX, X9457 Crashed nr Sywell, Northants 17.5.43.
6291 G-ADFY, Spanish Nationalists probably as 40-3. Destroyed 9.36.
6292 PH-AKV, PK-AKV Destroyed/captured by Japanese, Andir, Dutch East Indies 2.42.
6293 G-ADIM, Z7263 Crashed Doncaster, Yorks 11.4.42.
6294 PH-AKW, PK-AKW Crashed Babo, Dutch New Guinea 7.3.36.
6295 CF-AVJ Dbf on start up St John, New Brunswick, Canada 17.5.39.
6296 PH-AKU, PK-AKU Crashed Ketapang (Madura), West Borneo 16.8.38.
6297 G-ADNG Crashed 30 ml East of Rutbah, Iraq 10.3.36.
6298 SU-ABP Crashed nr Maruit Airport, Alexandria, Egypt 6.2.45.
6299 SU-ABQ Crashed 18 ml N of Port Sudan, Sudan 9.10.41.
6300 G-ADNH, W6423 Damaged Coullomiers, France 16.5.40 and abandoned.
6301 G-ADNI, W9365 Damaged nr Nantes 5.40 and abandoned Bouguenais, France.
6302 SU-ABR Believed sold to Jordan or Yemen?
6303 SU-ABS Believed sold to Jordan or Yemen?
6304 CF-AYE Wfu Vancouver, Canada 8.51.
6305 ZK-AED, NZ556 Soc after hurricane damage Nausori, Fiji 20.2.41.
6306 ZK-AEE, NZ559 Soc after hurricane damage Nausori, Fiji 20.2.41.
6307 CF-BBC Crashed in St Lawrence River, near Mont Joli, Quebec, Canada 23.12.46.
6308 VT-AHB Crashed Kanpur, India 30.12.45.
6309 E. (?), G-ADWZ, F-APES, G-ADWZ, X9449 Crashed Llanrhaeadr-ym-Mochnant, Denbighshire 2.8.40.
6310 DH.89M G-ADYK, Spanish AF 22-1 Destroyed by bombing at La Albericia Airfield, Santander, Spain 6.4.37. (Also reported to Spanish Nationalists as 40-1 and destroyed early 9.36).
6311 DH.89M G-ADYL, Spanish AF 22-2. Shot down Almudevar, Spain 19.10.36.
6312 DH.89M G-ADYM, Spanish AF 22-3, Spanish Nationalists 40-5. Shot down nr Segovia, Spain 26.8.36.
6313 SU-ABU Scrapped .48.
6314 VH-UVG, A3-2 Crashed Laverton, WA, Australia 3.2.38.
6315 G-ADUM, TC-ARI, TC-ALI Wfu .59.
6316 G-ADUN, TC-BAY Probably wfu .59/60.
6317 G-ADUO,TC-CAN, Probably wfu 59/60.
6318 VH-UVI, A33-2 Crashed nr Cootamundra, NSW, Australia 20.6.41.
6319 G-ADUP [ntu], VH-UVT Wfu Alice Springs, NT, Australia 28.1.54.
6320 G-AEAJ, W6425 To spares Witney 7.9.44.
6321 EP-AAA, HK917, EP AAA.
6322 EP-AAB, HK916 W/off pre .45.
6323 EP-AAC, HK915 W/off pre .45.
6324 G-AEAK Crashed Speke Airport, Liverpool 25.4.39.
6325 G-AEAL, F-OAUE wfu Algiers, Algeria 9.1.62.
6326 G-AEAM, W6424 (not used] Damaged St Philbert, nr Clisson, France 23.2.40 and abandoned Amiens, France 16.5.40.
6327 G-AEBW Abandoned Bordeaux, France 18.6.40.
6328 G-AEBX Crashed nr Belfast Harbour Airport, NI 3.7.38.
6329 YR-DRA Crashed 29.4.37.
6330 YR-DRI Wfu .42.
6331 YR-DRO, Romanian AF
6332 G-AEKF, YU-SAS Captured by Germans .41.
6333 CX-ABL Wfu Naval Base No.2, Durazno, Uruguay 8.49.
6334 ZK-AEC, NZ555 Wfu Fiji 19.9.45.
6335 G-AEGS Crashed Affule, Palestine 30.12.36.
6336 G-AEMH, X9387, G-AEMH Stored Ipswich after CofA expired 15.4.60 and scrapped mid-70s.
6337 G-AEML, X9450, G-AEML Current with Ken Whitehead, Rendcomb. Mk 4
6338 YR-DNC Crashed 17.7.42.
6339 G-AEMM Mid-air collision 3.5.40.
6340 G-AENN, W6455 Crashed nr RAF Fraserburgh, Aberdeenshire 13.12.42.
6341 G-AENO, EI-ABP, G-AENO, EI-ABP, VH-ADE, A33-7, VH-ADE Cr on beach 13 ml S of Cape Sidmouth, QLD, Australia 26.1.44.
6342 E.4, G-AEOV, W6456 Damaged beyond repair taxying Hendon 11.4.42.
6343 ZK-AEW, NZ557 Wfu Nausori, Fiji 4.7.43..
6344 G-AEPE, BD143 Crashed nr Glengall Hospital, Dalmellington, Ayrshire 20.4.42.
6345 G-AERN, EC-AKO On display Museo del Air, Cuatro Vientos, Spain, painted in Spanish Republican c/s as '40-1'.
6346 VH-UXT, A33-4, VH-UXT Crashed Wynyard, Tasmania 13.8.43.
6347 OH-BLA, Finnish AF, OH-VKH, OH-DHA, OY-DAS, D-IGEL Dbf Weser-Wumme, nr Bremen, Germany 27.4.72.
6348 Lithuanian AF 701, Luftwaffe
6349 Lithuanian AF 702, Luftwaffe
6350 G-AEPW, X8510 To spares Witney 7.11.41.
6351 YL-ABC, CCCP-L20, Luftwaffe
6352 YL-ABD, CCCP-L21, Luftwaffe
6353 G-AEPF Abandoned Bordeaux, France 18.6.40.
6354 CF-BBG Dbf refuelling Toronto Air Harbour, ON, Canada 21.8.37.
6355 G-AERE Crashed Ettersgill Fell End, nr Forest in Teesdale, Co Durham 20.6.39.
6356 G-AERZ Crashed Royal Belfast Golf Course, Craigarad 1.4.46.
6357 VP-KCG, KAAU [probably] K16. Wfu .45.
6358 VP-YBJ, SRAS 303, VP-YBJ Crashed & soc 8.44.
6359 VP-YBK, SRAS 304, VP-YBK Crashed Balovale, Northern Rhodesia 3.12.47.
6360 VR-SAV, MVAF 18 Destroyed Ipoh, Malaya 18.12.41.
6361 CR-AAD
6362 CR-AAE
6363 G-AESR Crashed Gerdes El Abid, Libya 22.7.56.
6364 VR-SAW, MVAF 19 Destroyed Palembang, Sumatra 10.2.42.
6365 VH-UXZ Crashed Tanners Bay, Flinders Island, TAS, Australia 29.5.42.
6366 VP-KCJ, KAAU K4, VP-KCJ Crashed Entebbe, Uganda 7.10.62.
6367 G-AEWL, F-OATT, F-BJUY Crashed Gaillac, France 29.7.62.
6368 G-AEXO, X8507 Soc 13.6.41.
6369 G-AEXP, X8505 [not used] Damaged St Omer, France 21.5.40 and abandoned.
6370 CF-BBH Crashed Pentecost, Quebec, Canada 19.3.47.
6371 CF-BFM, CX-ABI Crashed Colonia, Uruguay 6.40.
6372 G-AFAO, TC-DAG Wfu after 7.50.
6373 CF-BFL Crashed Matane, Quebec, Canada 23.2.38.
6374 CF-BFP Dbf on start-up Walker Lake, Quebec, Canada 5.7.45.
6375 CF-BND Crashed Digby Island, BC 29.7.49. Stored pending rebuild Western Canada Aviation Museum, Winnipeg, MB, Canada.
6376 CF-BNE Broke through ice and sank Lake George, Manitoba, MB, Canada 3.12.43.
6377 G-AFAH, X8508 Damaged Merville, France and abandoned 21.5.40.
6378 VT-AIZ, AX806. Crashed Juhu Bay, India 22.10.42.
6379 VT-AJA Crashed Juhu Bay, India 20.11.38.
6380 ZS-AKT, SAAF 1560, ZS-AKT, OO-CJU, 9O-CJU, 9Q-CJU
6381 VT-AJB, HX790, VT-AJB. Regn cnx 20.6.45.
6382 F-AQIL, Spanish Republicans
6383 F-AQIM, Spanish Republicans.
6384 VH-UZY, A33-6, VH-UZY Crashed Coolibah, NT, Australia 21.10.49.

6385 Chinese Government
6386 G-AFFF Crashed nr Milngavie, 7 mls N of Renfrew, Scotland 27.9.46.
6387 ZS-AME, SAAF 1402, ZS-AME, VP-KHJ, ZS-DFL, CR-ADH Regn cnx 17.7.56.
6388 Chinese Government
6389 Chinese Government
6390 Chinese Government
6391 Chinese Government
6392 Chinese Government
6393 F-AQIN, Spanish Republicans.
6394 VP-KCL, KAAU K10 To spares Nairobi, Kenya .46.
6395 F-AQJH, Spanish Republicans.
6396 F-AQJI, Spanish Republicans.
6397 CR-AAM
6398 CR-AAN
6399 G-AFEN, VQ-PAC, Z7188, G-AFEN, HK864,TJ-AAI not taken up, G-AFEN, LV-AGV Wfu Buenos Aires, Argentina on CofA expiry29.4.60.
6400 DH 92 Dolphin G-AEMX
6401 OH-BLB, Finnish AF, OH-VKI, OH-DHB, LN-BFB Wfu Eggemoen Airfield, Honefoss, Norway 30.12.60.
6402 G-AFEY Crashed Wideford, Orkney 18.3.40.
6403 F-AQOH, G-AGDP Wfu Wolverhampton, Staffs on CofA expiry 24.7.58.
6404 VP-YBT, SRAS 305, VP-YBT Scrapped 12.44.
6405 G-AFEO, X8506 [not used]. Captured intact by Germans at Bricy, France 6.40.
6406 G-AFEP, X9388, G-AFEP, VP-KFV Dbf Masindi, Kenya 29.11.49.
6407 F-AQOI Destroyed in allied invasion of Syria 5.41.
6408 G-AFEZ, X9451, G-AFEZ, F-LAAL, F-OBHI Crashed Fort Flatters, Sahara 24.8.60. **Mk 4**
6409 G-AFFB CofA expired 23.6.62 and burned at Baginton, Coventry 12.8.67.
6410 G-AFFC, HK862 Soc by MAAF 31.8.44.
6411 ZS-AOM, SAAF 1401, ZS-CAB, ZS-DDX Crashed Mokhotlong, Basutoland 24.6.55.
6412 VP-YBU, SR8, VP-YBU, SR8, SRAS 300, VP-YBU, SR23, RRAF-23, VP-YNJ, F-OBOD Wfu Libreville, Gabon 27.4.65.
6413 VP-KCR, KAAU K8 Crashed Tanganyika 16.5.43.
6414 YI-ZWA, Iraqi AF Dbf 30.9.43.
6415 YI-HDA, Iraqi AF Dbf 30.9.43.
6416 YI-FYA, Iraqi AF Crashed Mosul, Iraq 31.8.40.
6417 G-AFHY Sold Belgium 9.6.50 but wfu Brussels prior to registration.
6418 G-AFHZ, VP-UAX, VP-KFH To spares Nairobi, Kenya 8.52.
6419 G-AFIA Dbf Abadan, Iraq 20.8.42.
6420 F-ARII, Spanish Republicans, Spanish AF 40-6, EC-BAC, EC-AAR. Scrapped .60.
6421 E.9, P1764 Abandoned Coulommiers, France 16.5.40.
6422 P1765 Crashed/soc 4.4.40.
6423 ZK-AGT, NZ558, ZK-AHS On display Museum of Transport & Technology, Western Springs, Auckland, NZ.
6424 F-ARIJ, Spanish Republicans, EC-AAS, F-OBAQ wfu Libreville, Gabon 5.11.57.
6425 F-ARIK, Spanish Republicans '7', EC-AAV Wfu .55 or .57.
6426 G-AFLY, Z7253 soc scrap 18 MU Dumfries, Scotland 22.12.45.
6427 F-ARIL, Spanish Republicans, EC-AAY. Crashed in Spanish Guinea 6.46.
6428 F-ARIM, Spanish Republicans.
6429 G-AFLZ, Z7254, G-AHPX, ZS-AYF, OO-CJS Crashed nr Dakar, Senegal 26.2.60.
6430 G-AFMA, Z7255, G-AFMA, CS-AEB, CR-LCO Wfu .61.
6431 G-AFME, Z7257 To spares Witney 20.2.45.
6432 G-AFMF, Z7256, G-AFMF Crashed on Stooprigg Fell, nr Hexham, Northumberland 19.2.54.
6433 G-AFMG, Z7259, G-AFMG, EI-AEA Crashed nr Hutton Cranswick, Yorks 4.10.49.
6434 G-AFMH, Z7258 Soc scrap Abbotsinch, Glasgow 25.7.45.
6435 G-AFMI, Z7260 Scrapped 63 MU Carluke, Lanarkshire 23.4.46.
6436 G-AFMJ, Z7261, G-AFMJ, ZP-TDH Wrecked in hangar collapse Stroessner Airport, Asuncion, Paraguay 10.62.
6437 HB-AME, HB-APE, D-IGUN Wfu Frankfurt 9.74 and to spares Lahr, Germany, 94 for D-ILIT.
6438 HB-AMU, HB-APU To spares Kloten, Zurich Switzerland 1.68.
6439 CR-AAT
6440 CR-AAU Wfu Lourenco Marques, Mozambique, early 70s.
6441 G-AFRK Wfu Christchurch, Hants on CofA expiry 10.3.59.
6442 G-AFNC, V4724, G-AFNC, OO-CCD Wfu Elizabethville, Belgian Congo 5.7.47.
6443 G-AFND, V4725, G-AFND, TJ-AAP, Arab Legion Air Force R301 Cnx 49/50.
6444 CNAC 38 Destroyed in hangar fire Chungking, China 27.1.40.
6445 G-AFSO, W6457 Forced landed nr Aneuil, France 31.5.40 and destroyed by German machine gun fire.
6446 R2485 To spares Witney 12.9.42.
6447 R2486, G-AKJY, F-OAPT Wfu Geryville, Algeria 2.3.60.
6448 R2487, G-ALZH, F-OAKF Wfu Ivato, Madagascar 21.4.62.
6449 PP-LAA, PP-VAN, PP-OMA Wfu after CofA lapsed 7.7.49.
6450 G-AFOI To spares Tollerton, Notts after CofA expired 20.9.57
6451 CR-LAV
6452 CR-LAU Wfu Luanda, Angola .56.
6453 CR-LAT, F-OAVZ Crashed 20 mls from Douala, Cameroon 18.9.56.
6454 VT-ALO, HX791, VT-ALO Regn cld 31.3.45.
6455 P9588, G-AGHI To spares Croydon, Surrey after CofA expired 31.8.50.
6456 P9589, G-AIYP Crashed nr Pentre Uchaf, Pwllheli, Wales 5.7.53.
6457 R5921, G-AJKX, AP-AGI To spares Biggin Hill, Kent .62.
6458 R5922, G-AKNV, EI-AGK, G-AKNV, OO-AFG, OO-CNP On rebuild for Musée Royal de l'Armée, Brussels, Belgium.
6459 R5923 Crashed Yatesbury, Wilts 22.4.41.
6460 R5924, G-AKFO Not converted Gatwick 8.49.
6461 R5925 Crashed 9.9.45.
6462 Static airframe.
6463 R5926, G-AGFU Sold Belgium 9.6.50 but withdrawn Brussels before local registration.
6464 R5927 Struck balloon cable and crashed Horton, Bucks 14.2.42.
6465 R5928 Crashed Carricknowe Golf Course, Corstorphine, Edinburgh 1.3.44.
6466 R5929 Crashed Bishops Cannings, Devizes, Wilts 27.5.41.
6467 R5930, G-AIUO, SE-BTT, OY-ACV, D-IDAK Wfu and to spares 15.11.62.
6468 R5931, G-AKOO, CC-CIC-0034 Crashed El Maizal Airstrip, Linares, Chile 23.3.53.
6469 R5932, G-AKNW, LR-ABH, OD-ABH Dbf on start-up at Airstrip H3, Syria 30.7.54.
6470 R5933, G-AKNY, F-OBRX, 6V-AAC Wfu Dakar, Senegal 4.70.
6471 R5934, G-AKSH, VQ-FAM Wfu Fiji after CofA expired 17.3.55.
6472 CF-BNG Crashed/dbf Great Lake, Quebec, Canada 9.3.46.
6473 R9545 Hit by fuel bowser Boscombe Down, Wlts 12.12.47.
6474 R9546, G-AKOK, F-BGPK Wfu Saigon, French Indo-China 15.9.53.
6475 R9547 soc 1.12.45.
6476 R9548, G-AKVU, F-BGPM Dbf on start-up Siem Reap, Cambodia 13.2.53.
6477 R9549, SAAF 1363, ZS-BCD, VP-YKJ, F-OBKH w/f Gabon 8.61.
6478 R9550, G-AHPT Struck lorry and dbf landing on St Albans By- Pass [M10] nr Leverstock Green, St Albans, Herts 7.7.59.
6479 R9551 Crashed Yoxall, Staffs 25.3.41.
6480 R9552, G-AKRO, F-OAOY Dbf on start up Colomb Bechar, Algeria 22.10.54.
6481 R9553 Crashed Rednal, Shropshire 27.4.43.
6482 R9554, G-AKTZ Crashed nr Benghazi, Libya 27.5.57. **Mk 4**
6483 R9555 Soc 13.3.46.
6484 R9556, G-ALAS [not taken up], G-ALEJ Crashed nr Newcastle under Lyme, Staffs 14.9.56.

6485 R9557 To spares Witney 1.1.45.
6486 R9558, G-AHJA Crashed Castle Donington, Leics 20.5.69.
6487 R9559, G-AKED, F-DABY, F-OBHH Wfu Algiers, Algeria 30.8.62. **Mk 4**
6488 R9560, G-AKUB, EP-AND. **Mk 4**
6489 R9561 Crashed Prestwick, Ayrshire 22.2.41
6490 R9562, G-AKSF Dbf Prestwick, Ayrshire 23.7.49.
6491 R9563 Crashed Kempstone Hill, nr Stonehaven, Aberdeenshire 7.7.41.
6492 R9564, G-AKOB, VP-KNS, 5H-AAM Dbf Dar-es-Salaam, Tanzania 13.9.66.
6493 E-0228, X7320 Soc Witney 30.10.45.
6494 X7321, G-AHLF Wfu Biggin Hill, Kent on CofA expiry 22.2.60 and scrapped Portsmouth, Hants.
6495 X7322 Damaged beyond repair in air raid St Athan, Glamorgan 29.4.41.
6496 X7323, G-AJFM, VP-KEE, Israeli AF 1310, 4X-AEH Crashed Lydda Airport, Israel 2.7.54.
6497 X7324, G-AIWG, VH-AIK Dbf on start-up Turkey Creek, WA 29.9.51.
6498 X7325, G-AIHN, ZS-DJT Ground-looped and badly damaged Ladysmith, South Africa 11.10.63. **Mk 4**
6499 X7326, G-AGJF Crashed Barra, Hebrides 6.8.47.
6500 X7327, G-AJSK, VP-KMD, VP-YOE Wfu Salisbury, S Rhodesia on CofA expiry 27.3.57.
6501 X7328 Crashed Abbotsinch, Glasgow 8.6.41.
6502 X7329 Soc 20.5.46.
6503 X7330, VT-ARR Wfu Calcutta, india 48/49.
6504 X7331, G-AKOY, AP-AGM, F-OAYN Destroyed in hangar fire El Aouina, Tunis 12.12.57.
6505 X7332 Scrapped Lossiemouth, Morayshire 8.60.
6506 X7333 Crashed Acklington, Northumberland 8.6.41.
6507 X7334, SAAF 1353, ZS-BEF, F-OBIO, 5R-MAO Regn cnx 7.67
6508 X7335, SAAF 1354, ZS-BCS, VP-YNU, OO-CJW, 9O-CJW,
9Q-CJW Wfu .68.
6509 X7336, G-AGIF To spares Newtownards, NI after CofA expired 24.1.50.
6510 X7337, SAAF 1356, ZS-BCI Dbf on start up Welkom Airfield, OFS, South Africa 6.9.52.
6511 X7338, G-AJMY, CR-GAK To spares pre.63.
6512 X7339, SAAF 1355 Crashed Bloemfontein, OFS, S Africa 23.10.41.
6513 X7340, G-AKRN Wfu Southend, Essex after CofA expired 27.6.60.
6514 X7341 Scrapped Lossiemouth, Morayshire 7.63.
6515 X7342, G-AKND, VP-KGE To spares .50.
6516 X7343, G-AJNA, F-BEDI Crashed Tamatave, Madagascar 30.5.48.
6517 X7344, G-AGJG Current with Mark & David Miller, Duxford, Cambs
6518 X7345, G-AKNF, EP-ADP Cnx before .60. **Mk 4**
6519 X7346, G-AIUM, SE BTA To spares Portsmouth, Hants 7.63.
6520 X7347, G-AJFN, OO-CDE [not used], G-AJFN Dbf Kosti Airfield, Sudan 3.11.47.
6521 X7348 Soc RN Stretton, Cheshire 12.6.58.
6522 X7349, G-AGIC, F-BEDZ, F-OADZ, F-BAHZ Crashed La Madeleine par Nonencourt, France 24.2.51.
6523 X7350 Soc 18.6.51.
6524 X7351 To spares Prestwick, Ayrshire 4.46.
6525 X7352, G-ALBI, LX-LAD, G-ALBI, F-OBRV Crashed Boghe, Mauritania 4.8.61.
6526 X7353, G-ALVU Not converted Squires Gate, Blackpool, and scrapped .62.
6527 X7354 Crashed/dbf Hordley, Shropshire 7.12.41.
6528 X7368 Collided with Beaufighter R2252 on approach Cranfield, Beds 11.11.43.
6529 X7369, G-AKZH, CR-GAJ Regn cnx 11.80.
6530 X7370, G-AJXB, SE-CBU, VH-CBU, VH-ECW Dbf on start-up Blackall, QLD, Australia 30.3.68.
6531 X7371 Crashed Old Sodbury, Glos 20.10.41.
6532 X7372 Damaged 8.11.45 and soc 5.4.46.
6533 X7373 To spares Witney 31.7.45.
6534 X7374 Dbf in hangar fire Hendon, London 21.4.42.
6535 X7375 Soc for spares Farnborough, Hants 28.8.48.
6536 X7376, G-AKZI, Israeli AF S-76 Forced down nr Wadi Rabin, Israel 21.10.48 and burnt by Egyptians.
6537 X7377 Soc 16.9.46.
6538 X7378, G-AKOF Crashed in River Mersey nr Liverpool 11.11.48.
6539 X7379, G-AJKW Crashed Halfpenny Green, Staffs 7.5.67.
6540 X7380 Soc 18 MU Dumfries, Scotland 29.3.46.
6541 X7381, G-ALZF, F-BGON, F-AZCA Current with Jean Salis at La Ferté Alais, France.
6542 X7382 To spares RAE Farnborough, Hants 12.2.50.
6543 X7383, VH-BKM Crashed Daly Waters, NT, Australia 6.5.48
6544 X7384, SU-ACS(2) Damaged beyond repair Zaafarane 27.7.48.
6545 X7385, G-AHFJ, VP-KFW [not used]. Crashed on landing Mauritius 8.8.48.
6546 X7386, G-AKOI, TJ AAQ Shot down Irbid, Jordan 23.9.48.
6547 X7387, G-AGDG, F-BEDX, F-OADX, F-BAHX Damaged beyond repair Nam-Dinh, Vietnam 15.3.53.
6548 X7388, G-AGDH Damaged beyond repair in gales Stornoway, Hebrides 25.11.41.
6549 X7389, G-AKZJ, 4X-ACU Wfu Lydda, Israel .54.
6550 X7390, G-AKNZ, LV-AGY, LV-FEP Crashed (smuggling) 3.11.52.
6551 X7391, SU-ACT(2) Dbf Almaza, Egypt 25.2.51.
6552 X7392, G-AJFK, AP-AFN Dbf Karachi, Pakistan 28.9.52.
6553 X7393, G-AJKY, F-OAQZ Wfu Sam Neua, Laos 17.4.55.
6554 X7394 Crashed into Broadcrag, Scafell Pike, Lake District 30.8.46.
6555 X7395, G-AJKE, F-BEFU Crashed M'laca 30.4.60.
6556 X7396, G-APSD Wfu Shoreham, W Sussex after CofA expired 10.7.64.
6557 X7397 Damaged beyond repair Yeovilton, Somerset 3.8.56.
6558 X7398, G-AJTU, VP-KGS To spares Mombasa, Kenya 10.52.
6559 X7399, G-ALGM, F-BGOL, OO-CRS Crashed Maimanimba, Belgian Congo 5.7.56.
6560 X7400 Crashed Dun Rig, Peebles, Peebleshire 28.2.49.
6561 X7401, G-AHPY, ZS-BCP To spares Durban, S Africa .67.
6562 X7402 Crashed into Derwent Water, Cumberland 28.11.41.
6563 X7403, G-AKTY, F-BFVR, 5R-MAM, F-OCBX, 5R-MAM Wfu Ivato, Madagascar 11.66.
6564 X7404, SAAF 1362, ZS-BCR, CR-ADT To spares 1.58.
6565 X7405, G-AKUC, EP-ADM. **Mk 4**
6566 X7406, G-AKOD, F-OAQY Crashed Sam Neua, Laos 17.4.57.
6567 X7407 Soc Prestwick, Ayrshire 29.1.46.
6568 X7408 Soc in India 16.12.44.
6569 X7409, VT-ARF Crashed .50.
6570 X7410 Soc 18 MU Dumfries, Scotland 18.10.45.
6571 X7411, G-AMAM Wfu Wymeswold, Leics after CofA expired 20.11.60.
6572 X7412, G-ALBC Crashed on Kinder Scout, nr Edale, Derbyshire 30.12.63.
6573 X7413, G-ALZJ, F-OAME, TS-BME [not used] Wfu El Aouina, Tunis 19.1.60.
6574 X7414 Crashed Donibristle, Fife 18.1.45.
6575 X7415, G-AKZO, F-BHFM Wfu Strasbourg, France 11.66.
6576 X7416, G-AHLL Crashed St Just, Cornwall 21.5.59.
6577 X7417, G-AKOR, VQ-FAN, F-OAZT Wfu Nouméa-Magenta, New Caledonia 11.3.58.
6578 X7437, G-APJW, F-BHOB Wfu St Nazaire-Montoir, France 17.2.70. **Mk 4**
6579 X7438 Soc during maintenance 18.2.46.
6580 X7439, G-AKOJ, TJ-AAJ, JY-AAJ, F-OARH Wfu Majunga, France 14.11.62.
6581 X7440, G-AKYW, LV-AGR Wfu after CofA expired 28.9.65.
6582 X7441, G-AKOH, F-BGXH Crashed Lyon-Bron, France 11.10.64.
6583 X7442, G-AHGC Wfu on CofA expiry 4.7.68 and to spares at Netheravon, Wilts.
6584 G-AGDM, F-OAXK Wfu Cayenne, French Guiana 17.12.65. **Mk 4**
6585 X7443, G-AKBW Not converted Croydon, Surrey 5.48.
6586 X7444 Collided with Proctor DX223 & crashed Langwardine, Hereford 12.4.43.
6587 X7445, G-AJFJ Wfu Croydon, Surrey after CofA expired

26.6.48.
6588 X7446, VT-ASA, N2290B On display, Historic Aircraft Restoration Museum, Creve Coeur Airport, Saint Louis, Mo, USA
6589 X7447, G-AJGV Sold Paraguay 5.55.
6590 X7448 Soc RN Stretton, Cheshire, 27.8.49.
6591 X7449, G-AKNE, F-OBDV, 5R-MAN Wfu Ivato, Madagascar 18.5.68.
6592 X7450 Dbf refuelling Vizagapatam, India 24.12.43.
6593 X7451 Damaged on landing Razmak, India 17.7.44.
6594 X7452 Crashed Donibristle, Fife 20.1.55.
6595 X7453 Collided with Seafire SW822 and crashed Wimboldsley, Cheshire 11.2.46.
6596 X7454, G-AHKB, F-BEKB Wfu Bergerac, France on CofA expiry 12.65.
6597 X7455 Soc 5 MU Kemble, Glos 30.5.47.
6598 X7456, G-AKNN Wfu Dunkeswell, Devon on CofA expiry 29.8.69 and scrapped East Midlands.
6599 X7482 Crashed Lee-on-Solent, Hants 3.3.53.
6600 X7483, G-AJVA, TJ-ABM Destroyed in hangar fire Amman Airport, Jordan 9.5.53.
6601 X7484, G-AKOE Wfu Chirk, Powys when CofA expired 25.7.82 and remains stored. Mk 4
6602 X7485, G-AIUN, Israeli AF S-75, 1305. Wfu .49.
6603 X7486, G-AOZG, VR-LAC Crashed Hastings, Sierra Leone 30.5.58. **Mk 4**
6604 X7487 Soc 12.8.48.
6605 X7488 Soc Lossiemouth, Morayshire 13.1.59.
6606 X7489, G-AKRE, F-OABH Destroyed in hangar fire Gia Lam, Hanoi, Vietnam 5.6.52.
6607 X7490, G-ALBH, LX-LAC [not used], G-ALBH, OO-CJD, 9O-CJD, 9Q-CJD Last known .69.
6608 X7491, G-AHTY, F-BGIS Wfu Benoud 1.11.60.
6609 X7492, G-ALAU, LV-AER Wfu Asuncion, Paraguay 30.9.66.
6610 X7493 Damaged beyond repair 3.9.45.
6611 X7494 Crashed Donibristle, Fife 8.42.
6612 X7495, G-AKOV, VP-KNC, F-OAUH Dbf Madagascar 14.11.56.
6613 X7496 Flew into hill 13.9.44.
6614 X7497 Soc RN Stretton, Cheshire, 12.6.58.
6615 X7498 To Vendair Ltd, Croydon, Surrey for spares .55.
6616 X7499 Soc RN Stretton, Cheshire, 12.6.58.
6617 X7500, G-AKMF, Israeli AF S-74, 1304 Fate unknown
6618 X7501, G-AKOA, EP-ADO. **Mk 4**
6619 X7502, SAAF 1357, ZS-BMV, VP-UBB, VP-KFI To spares Nairobi, Kenya 10.52.
6620 X7503, G-AKON, VP-KFX, F-OAOS, 5R-MAP Wfu Ivato, Madagascar 3.64.
6621 X7504, G-AGED Crashed Renfrew, Ayrshire 2.2.43.
6622 X7505, G-AGEE, TF-KAA Wfu when CofA expired 18.5.63.
6623 X7506 Soc for scrap Stretton, Cheshire, 21.2.55.
6624 X7507 Soc for scrap Lossiemouth 13.1.59.
6625 X7508 Crashed Tain, Highlands 2.8.56.
6626 X7509, SAAF 1358, ZS-BEA Dbf on start-up Otjiwarongo, SWA 22.2.55.
6627 X7510, SAAF 1359, ZS-BCT, VP-KHF Crashed nr Garissa Aerodrome, Kenya 23.1.55.
6628 X7511, SAAF 1361 Crashed Bloemfontein, OFS, S Africa 22.10.42.
6629 X7512, G-AKNX, F-OATD Destroyed Tchibanga, Gabon 8.11.60.
6630 X7513 Crashed Braehead, 2 mls SW of Barrhead, Renfrewshire 1.3.44.
6631 X7514, G-AJFL, VP-UAW Dbf on start-up Zanzibar 21.9.47.
6632 X7515 Soc Ikeja, Nigeria 22.11.44.
6633 X7516, G-AHLU, VH-AHI Wfu Alice Springs, NT, Australia 13.5.58.
6634 X7517 Soc 18 MU Dumfries, Scotland 3.9.45.
6635 X7518, G-AKMG, F-BGPI Wfu Sam Neua, Laos 22.5.58.
6636 X7519, G-AKOP, Israeli Air Force.
6637 X7520, SAAF 1360, ZS-BMW Not converted & to spares .47.
6638 X7521, G-ALOV, F-OAPS Dbf on start up Ekouata, French Equatorial Africa 16.3.55.
6639 X7522, G-AKTX, Israeli AF S-72, 1302.
6640 X7523, G-AIUK, VP-KND Regn cld .64.
6641 X7524, SU-ACS Lost at sea on delivery 11.42.
6642 X7525, SU-ACT Lost at sea on delivery 11.42.
6643 HG644, TC-LAV
6644 HG645, TC-MUT
6645 HG646, TC-NUR
6646 HG647, TC-ZOR
6647 HG648, NZ523, ZK-AKS Crashed on Mount Soho, nr Arrowtown, NZ, 15.6.65; Croydon Aircraft Co, Mandeville, NZ, for rebuild.
6648 HG649, NZ524, ZK-BCP, VH-BGP On rebuild for Bruce Ivers, Perth, WA, Australia
6649 HG650, VT-ARL, MA964 Soc 31.2.46 [sic].
6650 HG651, VT-ARM, MA965, VT-ARM Regn cnx [78/84].
6651 HG652, VT-ARN, MA966, VT-ARN
6652 HG653, VT-ARK, MA963, VT-ARK Regn cnx 24.2.48.
6653 HG654, NZ525, ZK-AKY Current with Croydon Aircraft Co Ltd, Mandeville, NZ.
6654 HG655, NZ526, ZK-BAU Crashed Milford Sound, NZ 22.4.64.
6655 HG656, NZ527, ZK-ALB, VH-IAN, VH-UTV. Current with Roy Fox, Sydney, NSW, Australia.
6656 HG657, VT-ART Crashed Pratapgarh, India 35 ml N of Allahabad 8.4.46
6657 HG658, VT-ARV, G-AMJK, F-OBVL Wfu Cayenne 16.12.65.
6658 HG659, VP-YCI, ZS-DDI, OO-CJX, 9O-CJX, 9Q-CJX
6659 HG660, VP-YCJ, VP-NAK, VP-RCP Crashed 100 mls from Landazi, Nyasaland 30.8.53.
6660 HG661, VP-YCK, VP-RCI, VP-YLV Damaged beyond repair in hangar collapse Victoria Falls, S Rhodesia 6.1.55.
6661 HG662, VT-ARW Regn cld 16.5.47.
6662 HG663, NZ528, ZK-AKU Current with NZ Historic Aircraft Trust, Papakura, NZ.
6663 HG664, Free French AF. Crashed Tananarive, Madagascar 11.6.47.
6664 HG665, NZ529, ZK-ALC Dbf Rotorua, NZ 15.1.50.
6665 HG666, VP-YCL, VP-RBT Crashed Fort Manning, Nyasaland 28.9.50.
6666 HG667, VP-YCM, SR57, RRAF-57, VP-YOL, 9Q CJD.
6667 HG668, VP-YCN, ZS-DFG, VP-YMW, 9Q-CJK.
6668 HG669, NZ531, ZK-BBP, VH-AAG Wfu Darwin .63 after collision with kangaroo at Wolner Airstrip, NT, Australia.
6669 HG670, Free French AF.
6670 HG671, TF-ISM Wfu Reykjavik, Iceland 49/50.
6671 HG672, French AF, F-OANU Wfu Tananarive, Madagascar 19.1.54.
6672 HG673, G-AKEU, OD-ABL Dbf whilst refuelling Baghdad, Iraq 26.7.55.
6673 HG674, NZ530, ZK-AKT Crashed in Shotover River, nr Queenstown, NZ 15.4.67.
6674 HG689, Free French AF.
6675 HG690, G-AIUI Crashed nr Dalby, IoM 10.6.48.
6676 HG691 G-AIYR Current with Classic Wings, Clacton/Duxford, Cambs.
6677 HG692 Sold 27.1.48 but not converted.
6678 HG693, G-AHPW, ZS-BCO, SR24, VP-YOY Dbf on start up Kariba, Zimbabwe 25.11.57.
6679 HG694, G-ASFC Wfu Weston-on-the-Green, Oxon after CofA expired 27.8.65.
6680 HG695, SAAF 1364, VP-YEZ Damaged beyond repair in hangar collapse Victoria Falls, S Rhodesia 6.1.55
6681 HG696, VT-ARY Crashed/dbf nr Mohanbari, Assam, India 9.2.59.
6682 HG697, G-ANZP To France .65 for parts to build Fokker D.VII replica.
6683 HG698 Soc Lossiemouth, Morayshire for scrap 22.6.63.
6684 HG699, French Air Force.
6685 HG700 Soc Donibristle, Fife 25.8.48.
6686 HG701, TC-AGA
6687 HG702, TC-HAD Wfu .59.
6688 HG703, TC-PER Wfu .59.
6689 HG704, TC-VUR
6690 HG705, G-ALXI, OE-FAA. To Technisches Museum, Vienna, Austria but scrapped early 70s.
6691 HG706 Soc RN Stretton, Cheshire, 17.7.54.
6692 HG707, EP-AAD Regn cnx pre .59.
6693 HG708 Soc Lossiemouth, Morayshire for scrap 13.1.59.
6694 HG709 Damaged Roborough, Devon 1.9.61, to

Fleetlands, Hants for scrap.
6695 HG710, EP-AAE Regn cnx pre .59.
6696 HG711, EP-AAT
6697 HG712 Crashed nr Eindhoven, Holland 14.5.45.
6698 HG713 Soc Lossiemouth, Morayshire for scrap 5.7.63.
6699 HG714 Soc Losseimouth, Morayshire for scrap 22.6.63.
6700 HG715, G-ANET, VR-AAL, ET-P-22 Wfu Addis Ababa, Ethiopia after CofA expired 26.6.60. **Mk 4**
6701 HG716 Scrapped Lossiemouth, Morayshire 30.8.54.
6702 HG717 Soc Lossiemouth, Morayshire for scrap 29.4.54.
6703 HG718, G-ALWI, F-BGPJ Wfu Vientiane, Laos 22.5.59.
6704 HG719, G-AKMH, Congo.
6705 HG720, French AF Scrapped Villacoublay, France 1.56.
6706 HG721, G-ALGB, F-BHCD On display at Musée de l'Air, Le Bourget, France.
6707 HG722, G-ALWP, VQ FAL Crashed Lambasa, Vanua Levu Island, Fiji 24.4.54.
6708 HG723, G-AHLM Crashed St Marys, Isles of Scilly 20.7.63.
6709 HG724, G-AKPA, EI-AML, F-BLHZ, N89DH Current with RC Hood, Carthage, Mo, USA
6710 HG725 Crashed Donibristle, Fife 6.3.45.
6711 HG726 Crashed St Merryn, Cornwall 15.8.46.
6712 HG727 Dbf during ground engine test 4.47.
6713 HG728, G-ALNT, VH-CFA Crashed off Hinchinbrook Island, QLD, Australia 26.10.53.
6714 HG729, G-AMCT, F-BHTH Wfu Algiers, Algeria 4.66.
6715 HG730, G-ALXS, TJ AAU [not taken up], F-OAIH, TR-LKQ Wfu Libreville, Gabon 14.11.66.
6716 HG731 Sold 29.5.47 and to spares.
6717 HG732, VT-ARZ Crashed and regn cnx 17.2.51.
6718 NF847, G-ASIA Not converted and to spares, Abingdon, Oxon 9.63.
6719 NF848 Soc Lossiemouth, Moayshire as scrap 13.1.59.
6720 NF849 Soc Lossiemouth, Morayshire as scrap 7.54.
6721 NF850 Soc Stretton, Cheshire, as scrap 1.4.58.
6722 NF851, G-AJCL Wfu Fairoaks after CofA expired 11.1.71; stored with J Pierce, Chirk, N Wales.
6723 NF852, G-AKGY, F-BFEH Wfu Algiers, Algeria 5.6.63.
6724 NF853, G-AIUJ, VT-CHZ, F-OAIL, F-LAAB Wfu Vientiane, Laos 27.3.61.
6725 NF854 Soc Lee-on-Solent, Hants 15.12.54.
6726 NF855 Soc Lossiemouth, Morayshire as scrap 5.7.63.
6727 NF856, G-ALXA Sold to Vietnam and destroyed in hangar fire Gia-Lam, Hanoi, Vietnam 5.6.52.
6728 NF857 Crashed N of Chipping Sodbury, Glos 18.1.49.
6729 NF858, G-ALWN, F-BGPG, F-LAAC Wfu Luang Prabang, Laos 15.10.58.
6730 NF859, TF-ISO Crashed Grimseyjarsund, Iceland 27.8.45.
6731 NF860, French AF Soc .51.
6732 NF861 Crashed in Glendun Mountains, nr Cushenden, Co Antrim 15.9.53.
6733 NF862 Sold 11.1.50 to Short Bros & Harland Ltd, Rochester, Kent for spares.
6734 NF863 Soc 13.4.48.
6735 NF864, G-ASKO, F-OCHF Wfu Cayenne Rochambeau, French Guiana 22.3.68. **Mk 4**
6736 NF865, G-ALXT,CY-AAI, 4R-AAI, G-ALXT On display at The Science Museum, Wroughton, Wilts.
6737 NF866 Crashed 15.11.45.
6738 NF867 Soc Lossiemouth, Morayshire for scrap 22.6.63.
6739 NF868, R Belg AF D3 Crashed 21.8.52.
6740 NF869, R Neth AF V 3, PH-RAE, V 3, PH-VNC, V 3, PH-TGC, PH-OTA On display Militaire Luchtmacht Museum, Soesterberg, Netherlands, as V 3.
6741 NF870, G-ALWY Crashed Port Ellen, Islay, Argyll 19.4.52.
6742 NF871 Soc Lossiemouth, Morayshire for scrap 22.6.63.
6743 NF872 Crashed West Raynham, Norfolk 1.9.54.
6744 NF873 Soc Lossiemouth, Morayshire for scrap 13.1.59.
6745 NF874, R Belg AF D2 Damaged 2.6.55.
6746 NF875, G-AGTM, OD-ABP, JY-ACL, G-AGTM Current with Air Atlantique Ltd, Baginton, Coventry
6747 NF876, G-AHXV Crashed Ronaldsway, IoM 15.1.49.
6748 NF877, R Neth AF V 1, PH-VNA, V 1, G-APBM, F-OBRU Crashed Podor, Senegal 8.6.62.
6749 NF878, G-AGTN, TJ ABJ Crashed Amman, Jordan 1.5.53.
6750 NF879 Soc Lossiemouth, Morayshire for scrap 13.1.59.
6751 NF880 Soc Lossiemouth, Morayshire for scrap 22.6.63.
6752 NF881 Soc Lossiemouth, Morayshire for scrap 22.6.63.
6753 NF882, G-AJVB, TJ-AAZ,JY-AAZ, F-BHDY Wfu Limoges, France 16.8.63.
6754 NF883, G-AHLN, F-BGOQ Crashed Toussus-le-Noble, France 6.7.53.
6755 NF884, G-ALWM, F-OAGP Crashed Melilla, Spanish Morocco 17.5.53.
6756 NF885, G-AJFO, OO-CDF [not used],G-AJFO Dbf Kosti Airfield, Sudan 3.11.47
6757 NF886, G-ALPK Wfu Blackbushe, Hants on CofA expiry 4.6.66 and to spares Netheravon, Wilts
6758 NF887, G-AKOM, OO-DCB, G-AKOM, F-OGAU W/o Inini, French Guiana 5.8.60. **Mk 4**
6759 NF888, G-AHPV, ZS-AYG Crashed El Adem, Libya 31.10.46.
6760 NF889 Collided with Spitfire AR395 & crashed Witham-on-the-Hill, Rutland 20.3.45.
6761 NF890, SAAF 1365, VP-YFA, ZS-BZU Crashed Mokhotlong, Basutoland 10.9.54.
6762 NF891, VT-ASC Crashed nr Somarampet, India 22.1.60.
6763 NF892, G-AJKH, EP-AAV
6764 NF893, G-AKLA Crashed 38 mls NW of Jodhpur, India 15.6.54.
6765 NF894, G-AJBJ On rebuild by John Pierce, Chirk, N Wales.
6766 NF895 Sold 29.5.47 and used for spares.
6767 NF896, G-AKME Dbf on start-up Lympne, Kent 30.6.50. .
6768 NR669 Soc Lossiemouth, Morayshire for scrap 13.1.59.
6769 NR670, French AF, F-BDJX Wfu 1.68, painted as 'F-BGXT' for film 10.68 and sunk off Deauville, France.
6770 NR671, G-AJHP, F-OBOI Wfu Algiers, Algeria 18.4.62.
6771 NR672 Soc for spares at Stretton, Cheshire, 29.11.54.
6772 NR673 Sold Uruguay 6.47.
6773 NR674, G-AGZU, ZS-DLS Wfu 4.71 but parts SAAF Museum, Lanseria, S Africa for possible rebuild.
6774 NR675, PP-OMD
6775 NR676, G-AIWY, OY-AAO On display Danmarks Tekniske Museum, Helsingor, Denmark.
6776 NR677 Soc Lossiemouth as scrap 13.1.59.
6777 NR678, G-ALWJ, VP-KLL, 5Y-KLL Wfu when CofA expired 31.7.65. **Mk 4**
6778 NR679, G-ALNS, 9Q-CJK. **Mk 4**
6779 NR680, G-AKSC, F-OATC Wfu Noumea, New Caledonia 8.66.
6780 NR681, G-AGLP To spares Croydon, Surrey after CofA expired 17.10.50.
6781 NR682, G-AGLR Crashed/dbf Berkswell nr Coventry 7.10.56.
6782 NR683, G-AHXW, N683DH On rebuild by Bud Field and John M Reed at Calaveras Co Airport, San Andreas, CA, USA, Mk4
6783 NR684, OB-RAH-197
6784 NR685, G-AGLE Crashed Morden, Surrey 17.3.49.
6785 NR686, Belg AF D4, OO-ARN Crashed Luozi, Congo 20.6.60.
6786 NR687, G-ANAH, CX-API
6787 NR688, Belg AF D5, OO-ARI, G-APBN, OO-ARI, F-OBIA Wfu Tunis El Aouina, Tunisia 28.11.62.
6788 NR689, SAAF 1366, ZS-CAC, ZS-BZC Seized in Jordan 11.51.
6789 NR690, G-AKYZ, LV-AEO Crashed General Palmelo Airport, Buenos Aires, Argentina 24.1.49.
6790 NR691, G-AKZB Crashed St Just, Cornwall 12.12.61.
6791 NR692, G-AKTD, F-BFVM Crashed In-Amenas, Algeria 9.10.61.
6792 NR693, G-AHKV Wfu Elmdon, Birmingham when CofA expired 3.12.68.
6793 NR694, VT-ASJ Regn cnx 29.4.47.
6794 NR695, VT-ASQ, N2290F On display USAF Museum, Wright Patterson AFB, OH, USA, as USAAF 8th AF 'X7454, *Wee Wullie*'
6795 NR696, G-AGLN Crashed Abadan, Iran 15.12.46.
6796 NR697, G-AKGV, F-BFPU, G-AKGV, C-GXFJ, C-FAYE On display Bushplane Heritage & Forest Fire Educational Centre, Sault Ste Marie, Ontario, Canada
6797 NR698, G-ALXU, TJ-AAV, JY-AAV, F-OASC Dbf Fort Dauphin, Madagascar 20.5.57.

6798 NR699, OB-RAG-196
6799 NR700 Soc Accra, Gold Coast 1.1.47.
6800 NR701, G-AHXX, VR-OAB Damaged Lahad Datu, Malaya 27.3.59.
6801 NR713, G-AJSL, VH-UXZ On rebuild by Maurice Rolfe, Moorabbin, VIC, Australia.
6802 NR714, G-AKMD, F-OAKD Dbf on start-up Bealanana, Madagascar 15.3.52.
6803 NR715, G-AGNH, VG764, VP-KCT, G-AGNH, VR-AAP To spares Salalah, Oman 11.59.
6804 NR716, OB-RAF-195
6805 NR717, G-AKUS, Israeli AF S-77, 1306.
6806 NR718, VQ PAR, Israeli AF S-71, 1301 Scrapped .57.
6807 NR719, PP-DPH Wfu on CofA expiry 9.9.57.
6808 NR720, G-AHXY Crashed Renfrew Golf Course, Glasgow 27.12.48.
6809 NR721 Soc Gosport, Hants for spares 19.5.53.
6810 NR722, G-AHKU Wfu St Just, Cornwall when CofA expired 12.8.70.
6811 NR723, G-AHKT, F-OAUG Damaged beyond repair Rochambeau, French Guiana 20.11.61. **Mk 4**
6812 NR724, G-AHKS, VR-OAC Crashed Jesselton, Borneo 21.12.60. **Mk 4**
6813 NR725, G-AIBB, F-OBVJ Wfu Senegal 8.62.
6814 NR726, G-AKOC, VH-CFA Crashed in sea 15 ml NW of Cairns, QLD, Australia 26.11.51.
6815 NR727, G-AIYE, F-OAYS Wfu Bone, Algeria 18.5.62. **Mk 4**
6816 NR728, G-ANJR, F-OAKX Destroyed 15.8.56.
6817 NR729 Sold 29.5.47 and used for spares.
6818 NR730, G-AMDG, F-OAIR Crashed South of Phu Nhac, nr Nam Dinh, Vietnam 2.4.54.
6819 NR731, R Neth AF V-4, PH-RAF, V-4, PH-VND, V-4 Soc for spares 23.1.52.
6820 NR732 Sold 1.48 to Linea Aereas del Pacifico, Chile.
6821 NR733, G-ALBA Wfu Baginton, Coventry after CofA expired 29.9.61.
6822 NR734, G-AKYY, LV-AES Wfu .64.
6823 NR735, G-AHRH, F-OBOH Wfu Laghouat, Algeria 20.5.60.
6824 NR736, G-AHKR Crashed Mt Slieu Ruy, IoM 15.4.47.
6825 NR737, G-AHXZ Dbf whilst under maintenance Renfrew, Glasgow 28.8.51.
6826 NR738, G-AJSJ Crashed in Tunisia 18.9.47.
6827 NR739, G-APKA, VR-LAE Wfu Hastings Airfield, Freetown, Sierra Leone. **Mk 4**
6828 NR740 Soc for spares Stretton, Cheshire, 19.9.49.
6829 NR741, G-ALBB Crashed Heathrow 1.8.52.
6830 NR742, G-ALGO Crashed/dbf Abadan, Iran 10.7.51.
6831 NR743, VP-KEF, 5H AAN, VQ SAD, ZS-JGV On rebuild by Donald Johnson, Port Elizabeth, S Africa
6832 NR744, G-ALET, F-OALD, XW TAB.
6833 NR745, VP-YCO, ZS-DDH Wfu Germiston, S Africa on CofA expiry 28.3.57.
6834 NR746, VP-YCP, ZS-BYT, Israeli Air Force [possibly S-73].
6835 NR747, G-AJHO Crashed/dbf Woodeaton, nr Oxford 5.2.89.
6836 NR748, G-ANEU, F-OAQU Crashed Ekouata, French Equatorial Africa 18.1.55.
6837 NR749, G-AIUL wfu Booker after CofA expired 29.9.67 and stored by John Pierce at Chirk, N Wales.
6838 NR750, G-AKIF, LN-BEZ, G-AKIF Current with Sir Adrian Swire/Classic Wings at Duxford, Cambs
6839 NR751, G-AHKA, F-OAQL Damaged beyond repair in ground accident Cayenne, French Guiana 30.10.57.
6840 NR752, G-ALWO, VP-YHE, CR-ADM Crashed Praia, Zululand 15.3.55.
6841 NR753 Collided with Anson NL248 & crashed Bulford, Wilts 31.5.48.
6842 NR754 Crashed/dbf after collision with Anson NK738 Lee-on-Solent, Hants 25.1.46.
6843 NR755, LR-AAD, G-AKZV, LV-AGW Wfu when CofA lapsed 11.4.65.
6844 NR756, G-AOAO, F-BHGR Stored by Geoff Thomas, t/a Vintage Wings at La Ferté Alais, France pending rebuild. Mk 4
6845 NR769, G-ALWL, F-BGPH, F-BEPE, F-LAAE Crashed Ban-Ban, Laos 23.12.60.
6846 NR770, CR-LBH Dbf on start up Ambriz, Angola 10.5.57.
6847 NR771, CR-LBG, CR-A.. (?). Wfu Angola 70.
6848 NR772, G-AGOX, VP-KCU Abandoned after forced landing in bush 130 ml N of Mombasa, Kenya 28.6.46.
6849 NR773, G-AGOW, VP-KCV, G-AGOW To spares at Croydon, Surrey 1956/57.
6850 NR774, G-AGOJ Crashed Lympne, Kent 1.5.61. **Mk 4**
6851 NR775, G-ALAT, F-BHCE Wfu Strasbourg, France 3.69.
6852 NR776, R Belg AF D6, OT-ZCJ. Wfu Evere, Belgium 27.2.54.
6853 NR777, R Belg AF D7, ZK-SWR On rebuild in New Zealand for the Rapide Group/Fliegermuseum Altenrhein, Switzerland.
6854 NR778, G-AIYY Wfu Rochester, Kent after CofA expired 30.4.64.
6855 NR779, G-AGUF Crashed Ramsgate, Kent 29.6.57.
6856 NR780, G-ALWK, F-OBAL Wfu Algiers, Algeria 28.7.62.
6857 NR781 Soc Stretton, Cheshire, for spares 12.6.58.
6858 NR782, G-ASKI, I-BOBJ Wfu Turin, Italy after CofA lapsed 28.4.67.
6859 NR783, G-AGUG, AP-AGL, G-AGUG, F-OCAG Wfu Ziguinchor, Senegal 27.3.63.
6860 NR784, G-AJDN, F-OBIV Wfu Bone, Algeria 18.5.62. **Mk 4**
6861 NR785, G-AIZI Crashed Wallington, Surrey 14.9.52.
6862 NR786, G-AHGD Crashed Audley End, Essex 30.6.91.
6863 NR787, G-ALXJ Crashed off Laxey Head, Isle of Man 10.7.51.
6864 NR788, G-AKYX, LV-AEN, LV-FFO Wfu Buenos Aires, Argentina .60.
6865 NR789, G-AKSL, F-BGPL Wfu Saigon, Vietnam 14.6.52.
6866 NR790 Crashed nr Manorbier, Pembrokeshire 14.1.46.
6867 NR791, G-AIWZ Crashed Brough, Yorks 30.7.49.
6868 NR792, G-AJKI, EP-AAY
6869 NR793, VT-CBY Damaged in gales Calcutta, India 14.6.60.
6870 NR794, G-AKSE, EI-AKH, G-AKSE, F-BLHE Crashed Ouessant, France 28.9.66.
6871 NR795 Crashed Millfield Camp, Orkneys 1.6.45.
6872 NR796, R Neth AF V-2, PH-VNB, V-2, G-APBJ, F-OBGE Wfu El Aouina, Tunisia 19.8.63.
6873 NR797, G-AGOP Crashed nr Mile Post 100, Syria 25.6.48.
6874 NR798, G-AGOV, VP-KCY Crashed on take-off Kaabong, Uganda 23.12.61.
6875 NR799, G-AGOU, VP-KCW, VP-YNN To spares Salisbury, S Rhodesia after CofA expired 24.11.56.
6876 NR800,G-AGOT, VP-KCX Wfu Mombasa, Kenya 31.10.50.
6877 NR801, G-AGOR, VP-KLB, 5Y-KLB Crashed Bukoba, Tanzania 7.8.68
6878 NR802, G-AKOG, VP-RCH, VP-YLF, F-OBMQ Wfu Libreville, Gabon 30.5.63.
6879 NR803, G-AMAI, EC-AGP, 'G-RCYR', D-ILIT, G-AMAI, D-ILIT Current with Josef Koch, Grossenhain, nr Dresden, Germany
6880 NR804, G-AKJZ Wfu Biggin Hill, Kent after CofA expired 13.7.59.
6881 NR805, Belg AF D1, OT-ZCH. Written off in accident 24.2.53.
6882 NR806, G-AKZP Crashed and dbf Nabuel Beach, nr Hammamet, Tunis 16.3.57. **Mk 4**
6883 NR807, G-AJGZ Dbf Agha Jari, Iran 16.7.49.
6884 NR808, G-AGSH, EI-AJO, G-AGSH Current with Philip Meeson, Hurn, Hants.
6885 NR809, G-AGPI Crashed Cowes, IoW 16.6.49.
6886 NR810, G-AGSI, VH-BFS, VQ FAZ Wfu Fiji 5.62. **Mk 4**
6887 NR811, G-AGSK, TJ-ABP, JY-ABP Wfu Amman, Jordan 2.56.
6888 NR812, G-AGSJ, OY-ACZ Crashed nr Lynge, Frederikssund, Denmark 3.3.54.
6889 NR813, G-AGPH Crashed Barra, Hebrides 6.12.51.
6890 NR814, PH-RAA, VP-KEA Crashed Butiaba, Lake Albert, Uganda 24.1.54.
6891 NR815, PH-RAB, VP-KEB Crashed Kasese, Uganda 15.10.51.
6892 NR828, G-AKZA, LV-AEP Wfu Comodoro Rivadavia, Argentina 3.63.
6893 NR829, PH-RAC, VP-KEC Crashed Maha Island, Tanganyika 12.5.50.
6894 NR830, LR-AAE, G-AKZT, CY-AAK, 4R-AAK.
6895 NR831, PH-RAD, VP-KED, Israeli AF 1306, 4X AEI,

G-ADYL Wfu Fairoaks after CofA expired 16.12.58.

6896 NR832, LR AAF, G-AKZW, CR-GAI.

6897 NR833, YI-ABD, G-AKDW, F-BCDB, G-AKDW On display, de Havilland Heritage Museum, Salisbury Hall, Herts.

6898 NR834, YI-ABE, G-AKDX, VP-KIO Scrapped Khartoum, Sudan 10.52.

6899 NR835, CS-ADI, FAP 2307 In store Sintra, Portugal for Museo do Ar

6900 NR836, CS-ADJ, CR-SAD, CR-LKR On display Museu Aeroespacial, Campo dos Afonsos, Rio de Janeiro, Brazil as 'PP-VAN'

6901 NR837, CS-ADK, CR-SAE, CR-LKS Wfu Luanda, Angola .70s.

6902 NR838, G-AHGG, EL-AAA, OO-CMS Crashed nr Kikwit, Belgian Congo 8.7.56.

6903 NR839, G-AHGF, ZK-BCP [not used], ZK-BFK, VH-AWG, VH-BIF Wfu Archerfield, QLD, Australia 10.65.

6904 NR840, CR-LBN

6905 NR841, CR-LBO, CR-CAA

6906 NR842, YI-ABF, G-ALGC wfu Shobdon, Herefordshire on CofA expiry 21.7.66.

6907 NR843, YI-ABG, G-ALGE, EI-AMN, F-BLXX, N8053 Impounded for drug smuggling Phillipsburg, St Maarten, Dutch Antilles .75 and later scrapped.

6908 NR844, G-AGUU, VR-OAA Regn cnx10.3.61.

6909 NR845, YI-ABH, G-ALGI, F-OAND Crashed 6.54.

6910 NR846, G-AGUR Crashed Rhein Main, Frankfurt, West Germany 2.8.54.

6911 NR847, G-AGUP, F-OBGY, F-BJUZ Wfu La Ferté-Gaucher, France 10.64.

6912 NR848, G-AGUV Crashed Tarif, nr Bahrain 26.4.54.

6913 NR849, G-AGZO, F-BGZJ, OO-ITI Destroyed by UN bombing Kolwezi Airfield, Belgian Congo 29.12.62.

6914 NR850, ZS-ATV Crashed Thysville, Belgian Congo 5.6.51.

6915 NR851, ZS-ATW Crashed/dbf Beitbridge, Zimbabwe 11.12.46.

6916 NR852, G-AGWC, AP-ADM Crashed Nawabshah Aerodrome, Sind, India 17.3.53.

6917 NR853, G-AGWR, OY-DYA, SE-CDI Crashed Jusdala, nr Vimmerby, Sweden 23.12.56.

6918 RL936, G-AGWP, OO-CJE, 9O-CJE, 9Q-CJE. Wfu after accident Mweka , Belgian Congo .62

6919 RL937, SE-APH Destroyed in hangar fire Bromma, Sweden 9.4.47.

6920 RL938, PP-AIA Crashed Coroata, Maranhao, Brazil 10.5.56.

6921 RL939, PP-AID Crashed Congonhas Airport, Sao Paulo, Brazil 11.12.46.

6922 RL940, PP-AIB Crashed Fartura, Sao Paulo, Brazil 24.12.46.

6923 RL941, PP-AIC Crashed .52.

6924 RL942, VP-YDF, VP-RBU, VP-YDF Wfu on CofA expiry 10.8.54.

6925 RL943, VP-YDE, ZS-BZV, OO-CJT, 9O-CJT Crashed nr Molegbe, nr Brazzaville, French Equatorial Africa 6.10.60.

6926 RL944, G-AHAG Wfu when CofA expired 15.7.73 and stored by Ralph Jones, Membury, Wilts pending rebuild.

6927 RL945, PP-OMB Crashed Sao Joao del Rei, Minas Gerais, Brazil 20.9.46.

6928 RL946, CF-DIM Dbf Matane, Quebec, Canada 19.6.53.

6929 RL947, VH-BKR, VH-CLH Wfu Alice Springs, NT, Australia 31.7.62.

6930 RL948, G-ALAX Wfu Luton after CofA expired 8.3.67. Stored by David Johnson, Andover, Hants

6931 RL949, G-AKSG, F-BHAF Wfu Bastia, Algeria 7.3.62. **Mk 4**

6932 RL950, G-ALAZ, OO-CFI, CR-LCK Wfu Luanda, Angola .75.

6933 RL951 Crashed Mount Farm Airfield, Oxford 11.11.46.

6934 RL952, G-AHGH, SE BXZ Wfu on CofA expiry 23.4.59.

6935 RL953, G-AHGI, F-OANF, F-LAAF Crashed Phong Savanh, Laos 2.5.58.

6936 RL954, G-AGZJ To spares Cardiff after CofA expired 30.6.50.

6937 RL955, G-AGZK Destroyed in hangar fire Amman, Jordan 9.5.53.

6938 RL956, CF-DIN, YV-P-BPE Crashed Tucacas, 100 ml W of Caracas, Venezuela 17.1.50.

6940 RL958, G-AKRP, F-DAFS [not used], CN-TTO, G-AKRP Current with Barry Pearson/Eaglescott Dominie Group, Devon. Mk4

6941 RL959, G-ALRW, F-BGXT Wfu Doncourt-les-Conflans, France 10.70.

6942 RL960, G-ALAY, LV-AGX, LV-FET Crashed 29.2.60.

6943 RL961, G-ALGN, F-OAKE Crashed Port Berge, Madagascar 17.2.53.

6944 RL962, G-AHED Wfu on CofA expiry 17.4.68. Stored at RAF Cosford for RAF Museum

6945 RL963, G-AHEB, EI-ADP, G-AHEB, F-BHVQ To spares Castelnaudry, France 30.6.65.

6946 RL964, G-AHEA, F-BHCF Wfu Castelnaudry, France 19.10.64.

6947 RL965, VT-AVW Regn cnx .47.

6948 RL966, G-AHIA Wrecked when fell into excavation whilst taxying Maritse, Rhodes 5.3.51.

6949 RL967, G-AKSD, F-OBVI Crashed Podor, Senegal 17.9.62.

6950 RL968, G-AKRR, SN-ABB, G-AKRR, SN-ABB, ET-P-16 Dbf whilst refuelling Dire Dawa, Ethiopa 3.9.53.

6951 RL980, G-AKSB, VP-AAA.

6952 RL981, G-AKRS, 4X-970 On display Israeli Air Force Museum, Hatzerim as 'VQ-PAR'.

6953 RL982, VT-AVX Destroyed in hangar collapse in cyclone Juhu Bay, India 11.48.

6954 RL983, TJ-AAA Destroyed in hangar fire Amman, Jordan 9.5.53.

6955 RL984, TJ-AAB, Israeli AF [1311 or 1313?] Crashed off Ashkelon, Gaza 18.12.50.

6956 RL985, OY-DZY Crashed Kastrup, Copenhagen, Denmark 16.7.60.

6957 RL986, VT-AXG, F-OAHL Crashed Quang Tri, Indo China 26.4.54.

6958 TX300, TJ-AAC, Arab Legion Air Force R 300 Crashed Jerusalem, israel

6959 TX301, TJ-AAD, TJ-ACE, JY-ACE, JY-ACG, G-ASRJ Wfu Netheravon, Wilts early .70.

6960 TX302, PP-OMC Crashed Araguari, Minas Gerais, Brazil 4.2.47.

6961 TX303, TJ-AAE, JY-AAE, G-ASRM, 9Q-CPF Crashed N'dola, Zambia 9.12.66.

6962 TX304, G-AHTS Crashed in Middle East 29.4.47.

6963 TX305, G-AHPU, VR LAD Wfu Hastings Airfield, Freetown, Sierra Leone. **Mk 4**

6964 TX306, G-AHTR Dbf Abadan, Iran 10.7.50.

6965 TX307, G-AHWF, EP-AAW

6966 TX308, G-AHTT, EP-AAX

6967 TX309, G-AHJS Wfu Lasham, Hants on CofA expiry 20.5.66.

6968 TX310, G-AIDL Current with Air Atlantique, Baginton, Coventry

6969 TX311, ZS-AXS, VP-YIU, CR-AEQ wfu Beira, Mozambique .59.

6970 TX312, PP-AIE Damaged Ararangua, Brazil 31.10.48.

6971 TX313, PP-AIF Crashed Malhada de Pedra-Baia, Brazil 26.4.52.

6972 TX314, PP-AIG Wfu Caxias do Sul, Brazil on CofA expiry 20.10.49.

6973 TX315, OB-RAA-156

6974 TX316, OB-RAB-157

6975 TX317, OB-RAC-158

6976 TX318, OB-RAD-159

6977 TX319, OB-RAE-160

89232 [Assembled Downsview, Toronto, ON, 11.41 from spare fuselage] CF-BNJ wfu Ottawa, Ontario, Canada .55.

W.1001 see G-ACZE [c/n 6264]

W.1002 G-AKJS To spares Dinard, France 6.65 to construct a Fokker D.VII replica for film 'The Blue Max'

DH 90 DRAGONFLY PRODUCTION

First prototype E.2/G-ADNA, cn 7500, first flight 12 August 1935. Production started at Hatfield in January 1936.

TOTAL built 67.

7500 E.2, G-ADNA, X9452 To Witney for spares 19.8.42.
7501 G-AEBU First production DH 90A, F-AQEU, Spanish Republicans, Spanish Air Force 40-3.
7502 YI-HMK, Iraqi Air Force.
7503 G-AEDW, VP-YBR Crashed Gwelo, S Rhodesia 5.10.38.
7504 G-AECW Wfu Hatfield on CofA expiry 10.10.44.
7505 G-AECX, VT-AKC, G-AECX, AX855 To spares Witney 29.1.42.
7506 CF-AYF Crashed Kimberley BC, Canada 12.10.46.
7507 G-AEFN, X9390 Crashed nr Cosford Waterworks, Staffs 10.9.41.
7508 G-AEDT, VH-AAD, G-AEDT, N2034, G-AEDT, ZK-AYR For sale by Colin Smith/Croydon Aircraft Co, Mandeville, NZ
7509 G-AEDU [not taken up], G-ADXM, X9327 Soc as scrap 22.7.44.
7510 G-AEDH, AV987 Soc 1.1.41.
7511 G-AEDI, VR-SAX, MVAF 17 Destroyed in air raid, Kallang, Singapore 20.1.42.
7512 VP-YAX Crashed near Gwelo, S Rhodesia 20.12.38.
7513 VH-UXB Wfu and regn cnx 17.9.51.
7514 G-AEHC Crashed Darnaw, Minnigaff Parish, Kircudbrightshire 2.2.37.
7515 G-AEDJ, AV992 Soc as scrap 12.2.45.
7516 G-AEDG, VH-ADG Crashed Guildford, WA, Australia 1.12.47.
7517 G-AEDK, AW164 Soc Eaglescliffe, Northumberland as scrap 17.12.43.
7518 G-AEEK Crashed Beeding, near Shoreham, Sussex 17.8.37.
7519 F-AOZC, G-AFRF, AV993 To Witney for spares 27.7.42.
7520 VP-YBB Crashed Donga, nr Selukwe, S Rhodesia 20.10.38.
7521 F-AOYK, G-AFVJ, X9337 Crashed Old Sarum 24.6.41.
7522 CF-BBD, CF-MPC, RCAF 7628, CF-MPC, CF-BXU Crashed Thorhild, Alberta, Canada 23.12.45.
7523 ZS-AHV, SAAF 1403 Crashed.
7524 G-AEDV, X9389 Crashed Chedzoy, near Weston Zoyland, Somerset 3.9.41.
7525 YI-OSD, Iraqi Air Force.
7526 CR-AAB, ZS-CTR, G-AEDU, N190DH, G-AEDU Current with Torquil Norman, Rendcomb, Glos.
7527 VT-AHW, AX797 Soc in Ceylon 31.12.43.
7528 VP-KCA, KAAU (K13 or K14).
7529 F-APDE, Spanish Republicans ('706' or '756'), Spanish AF 40-4, EC-BAA, EC-AAQ, OO-PET, F-OAMS, G-ANYK Crashed La Baule, Loire Inferieur, France 23.6.61.
7530 CF-MPA, RCAF 7626 Soc to spares 28.1.43.
7531 CF-MPB, RCAF 7627, CF-BZA Crashed Indian Lake, NWT, Canada 17.11.48.
7532 CX-AAR Dbf at Museo Aeronáutico, Montevideo, Uruguay 4.12.97.
7533 VH-UXA, G-AFTF, BD149 Crashed 16.5.42.
7534 CX-AAS Wfu .46 and scrapped .49.
7535 ZS-AIK, SAAF 1408, ZS-AIK Crashed Rustenburg, S Africa 31.5.51.
7536 F-APAX, G-AFRI, AV994 Wfu after struck by taxying Tiger Moth BB687 Peterborough, Northants 4.5.41.
7537 R326, LV RDA [not used] Destroyed in hangar fire San Fernando, Buenos Aires, Argentina 25.11.37.
7538 CF-MPD, CF-BPD Crashed Edmonton, AB, Canada 13.4.43.
7539 PH-KOK, PH-ATK, LVA 962. Destroyed Ypenburg, Holland 10.5.40.
7540 VT-AHY, V4734 Crashed into ditch Barrackpore, india 28.5.43.
7541 I-DRAG Fate unknown.
7542 F-APFK Regn cancelled post-.39.
7543 CF-BFF, RCAF 7623, CF-BFF Crashed landing Ottawa River, Ontario, Canada 20.12.49.
7544 G-AESW, AV976 To spares Ringway, Manchester and soc 11.11.40.
7545 VT-AIE, HX792, VT-AIE Regn cnx 4.1.46.
7546 VH-UXS, A43-1, VH-UXS Wfu Darwin and regn cld 17.7.68. Reportedly to Nowra, NT, Australia as a derelict airframe for rebuild.
7547 YR-FLY Scrapped 10.45.
7548 YR-FLO Wfu 9.44
7549 YR-FLU Wfu .40.
7550 Swedish AF 906 Wfu after heavy landing 8.6.42.
7551 Danish Army AF S-23 Seized by Germans .40.
7552 Danish Army AF S-24 Seized by Germans .40.
7553 SU-ABW, G-AIYJ Wfu Gatwick on CofA expiry 17.2.48.
7554 G-AEXI, VP-KCS, KAAU (either K13 or K14).
7555 G-AEWZ, DJ716, G-AEWZ Crashed Elmdon, Birmingham 3.3.61.
7556 G-AFAN, TC-IDE, Spanish Republicans (LY-001?).
7557 RCAF 7624, CF-BXV Crashed Winnipeg, MB, Canada 3.4.45.
7558 RCAF 7625 Crashed Claresholm, AB, Canada 6.5.42.
7559 G-AEXN Crashed Hampden, nr High Wycombe, Bucks 21.7.39.
7560 ZK-AFB Lost en route Christchurch Milford Sound, NZ 12.2.62.
7561 OO-JFN To Vichy Government, France 8.40.
7562 VH-UTJ Dbf refueling Tennant Creek, NT, Australia 9.8.55.
7563 LV KAB Destroyed in collision with Ju52/3m PP-SPF Botafogo Bay, Rio de Janeiro, Brazil 8.11.40.
7564 ZS-ANM, SAAF 1404, ZS-ANM Crashed Pietersburg, S Africa 18.8.49.
7565 VR NAA Crashed Abeche, Chad 25.9.38.

APPENDIX 3
DH Type Commercial Users

British Commercial Operators of DH 84, DH 86, DH 89 and DH 90

Aberdeen Airways Ltd
DH 84
Adie Aviation Ltd
DH 89
Advance Air Lines Ltd
DH 84
Aerial Enterprises Ltd
DH 89
Aerocontacts (Aircraft Distributors) Ltd
DH 84
Aero Enterprises (JHS) Ltd
DH 84
Aikman Airways Ltd
DH 89
Air Charter Ltd
DH 84
DH 89
Air Charter Experts Ltd
DH 89
Air Commerce Ltd
DH 84
DH 89
DH 90
Air Couriers (Transport) Ltd
DH 89
Air Cruises Ltd
(Unlikely to have undertaken commercial operations).
DH 84
Air Dispatch Ltd
DH 84
DH 89
DH 90
Air Enterprises Ltd
DH 89
Air Kruise (Kent) Ltd
DH 89
Airmotive (Liverpool) Ltd
DH 89
Air Navigation and Trading Co Ltd
DH 84
DH 86
Air Taxis (Cumberland) Ltd
DH 89
Air Taxis Ltd
DH 84
DH 90
Air Taxis (Croydon) Ltd
DH 84
DH 89
Air Transport Charter (Channel Islands) Ltd
DH 89
Airviews Ltd
DH 89
Airwork Limited
DH 84
DH 89
DH 90
Allflights Ltd
DH 90
Allied Airways (Gandar Dower) Ltd
DH 84
DH 86
DH 89
Anglo-European Airways Croydon Ltd
DH 84
DH 89
DH 90
Anglo Diesel Co Ltd, London
DH 89
Arab Contracting and Trading Co.
DH 89
Army Free Fall Association
DH 89
Arrow Air Services Ltd
DH 89
Asiatic Petroleum Co Ltd
DH 89
Associated Airways Joint Committee
DH 89
Astral Aviation Ltd
DH 89
Bahamas Helicopters (UK) Ltd
DH 89
Bardock Aviation Ltd
DH 89
Barnstaple & North Devon Air Services
DH 84
BCI Airways Ltd
DH 89
Beagle Aircraft Ltd
DH 84
Bees Flight Ltd
DH 89
Birkett Air Service Ltd
DH 89
DH 90
Blackburn Aircraft Ltd
DH 89
Blackpool and West Coast Air Services Ltd
DH 84
DH 86
DH 89
Bond Air Services Ltd
DH 86
DH 89
Bournair Ltd
DH 89
Brian Allen Aviation Ltd
DH 84
British Air Navigation Co Ltd
DH 84
British Airways Ltd.
DH 84
DH 86
DH 89
British-American Air Services Ltd
DH 84
DH 86
DH 89
British Continental Airways Ltd
DH 84
DH 86
DH 89
British Eagle International Airlines Ltd
DH 89
British European Airways Corporation
DH 84
DH 89
British Midland Airways Ltd
DH 89
British Overseas Airways Corporation
DH 86
DH 89
British Westpoint Airlines Ltd
DH 89
Brooklands Aviation Ltd
DH 89
Cambrian Air Services Ltd
DH 89
Cecil Kay Aircraft (1945) Ltd
DH 89
Channel Air Ferries
DH 84
DH 89
Channel Airways Ltd
DH 89
Channel Island Air Services Ltd
DH 89
Channel Islands Airways Ltd
DH 89
Chrisair Ltd
DH 84
Ciro's Aviation Ltd
DH 89
Classic Wings Ltd
DH 89
Commercial Air Hire Ltd
DH 84
Crilly Airways Ltd
DH 84
Croydon Airways Ltd
DH 89
DH 90
Cumberland Aviation Services Ltd
DH 89
Darlington and District Aero Club Ltd
DH 89
de Havilland Aircraft Co Ltd
DH 89
Denham Air Services Ltd
DH 89
Derby Aviation Ltd
DH 89
Devonair Ltd
DH 90
Dominie Airways Ltd
DH 98
Dommett GA
DH 89
Don Everall (Aviation) Ltd
DH 89
Dragon Airways Ltd
DH 89
D W Gray
DH 89
East Anglian Aviation Society
DH 89
East Anglian Flying Services Ltd
DH 89
Ethyl Export Corporation
DH 89
E L Gandar Dower (Aberdeen Airways) Ltd
DH 89
Fairey Surveys Ltd
DH 89
Federated Air Transport Ltd
DH 89
Field Consolidated Aircraft Services Ltd
DH 89
Flightways Ltd
DH 89
DH 90
Flower Air Services Ltd
DH 89
Goodhew Aviation Ltd
DH 89

Great Western & Southern Airlines Ltd
DH 84
DH 89
Guernsey Airways Ltd
DH 86
Gulf Aviation Ltd
DH 86
Hampshire Aero Club
DH 86
Hanson and Son Ltd
DH 89
Hants and Sussex Aviation Ltd
DH 89
Hawker Aircraft Co Ltd
DH 89
Herts and Essex Aero Club Ltd
DH 89
Highland Airways Ltd
DH 84
Hillman's Airways Ltd
DH 84
DH 86
DH 89
Hornton Airways Ltd
DH 89
Hunting Surveys Ltd
DH 89
Hunting Air Travel Ltd
DH 89
Imperial Airways Ltd
DH 86
Independent Air Travel Ltd
DH 89
Inter-City Air Services
DH 89
International Airways Ltd
DH 89
Island Air Charters Ltd
DH 89
Island Air Services (London) Ltd
DH 89
Isle of Man Air Services Ltd
DH 84
DH 86
DH 89
Jersey Airlines
DH 89
Jersey Airways Ltd
DH 84
DH 86
DH 89
Kenning Aviation Ltd
DH 89
Kentair (Charters) Ltd
DH 89
Lancashire Aircraft Corporation
DH 86
DH 89
Lees-Hill Aviation (Birmingham) Ltd
DH 89
Lockwoods Flying Services, Ltd
DH 89
Luton Airways Ltd
DH 89
Luxury Air Tours Ltd
DH 84
MacSmith Air Charter Ltd
DH 89
Mannin Airways Ltd
DH 89
Manx Airlines Ltd
DH 89
Marshall's Flying Services Ltd
DH 89
Martin School of Navigation
DH 89
Mayfair Air Services Ltd
DH 89
Mayflower Air Services, Ltd
DH 89
McAlpine Aviation Ltd
DH 89
Melba Airways, Ltd
DH 89
Metropolitan Air Movements Ltd
DH 90
Mid-Fly Ltd
DH 89
Midland and Scottish Air Ferries Ltd
DH 84
Midland Metal Spinning Co Ltd
DH 89
Modern Transport (Wolverhampton) Ltd
DH 89
Morton Air Services Ltd
DH 89
Murray Chown Aviation Ltd
DH 89
National Air Communications (under DCA control)
DH 84
DH 86
DH 89
DH 90
Neil Tool Co Ltd
DH 89
Newman Airways Ltd
DH 89
Norman Edgar (Western Airways) Ltd
DH 84
DH 86
DH 89
DH 90
North Devon Flying Club
DH 89
North Eastern Airways Ltd
DH 84
DH 89
Northern Airways Ltd
DH 84
Northern & Scottish Airways Ltd
DH 84
DH 89
North Sea Air Transport Ltd
DH 89
North-West Airlines (Isle of Man) Ltd
DH 89
Ocean Airways
DH 89
Oldstead Aircraft Ltd
DH 89
Olley Air Service Ltd
DH 84
DH 89
Parachute Regiment Free Fall Club
DH 89
Patrick Aviation Ltd
DH 89
Peacock Aviation Ltd
DH 86
Personal Airways Ltd
DH 89
DH 90
Peterborough and Spalding Aviation Ltd
DH 89
Peirce, John E
DH 89
Pine's Airways Ltd
DH 89
Portsmouth Aviation Ltd
DH 89
Portsmouth, Southsea & IoW Aviation Ltd
DH 84
Private Air Hire Service Ltd
DH 89
Proteus Petroleum Ltd
DH 89
Provincial Airways Ltd
DH 84
Qantas Empire Airways
DH 86
RAF Parachuting Club
DH 89
Railway Air Services Ltd
DH 84
DH 86
DH 89
Riddell, L H
DH 89
Ringway Air Charter Services Ltd
DH 89
Rochester Air Charter Service Ltd
DH 89
DH 90
Rothmans of Pall Mall
DH 89
Scillonia Airways Ltd
DH 89
Scottish Airlines Ltd
DH 86
DH 89
Scottish Airways Ltd
DH 84
DH 89
Scottish Aviation Ltd
DH 89
Scottish Motor Traction Ltd
DH 84
Sear, JK and Co Ltd
DH 89
Shackleton Aviation Ltd
DH 89
Shell Petroleum Ltd
DH 89
Shorts Air Charter Service Ltd
DH 89
Silver City Airways Ltd
DH 89
Sivewright Airways Ltd
DH 89
Skegness Air Taxi Services Ltd
DH 89
Skyflights Ltd
DH 89
Skytravel Ltd
DH 89
Skyways Ltd
DH 89
Solair Flying Services Ltd
DH 89
Solent Airways Ltd
DH 89
Somerton Airways (Cowes) Ltd
DH 89
South Coast Air Services Ltd
DH 89
Southampton Air Services Ltd
DH 89
Southern Aircraft (Gatwick) Ltd
DH 89
Southern Airways Ltd
DH 84
DH 90
Southern Counties Aerial Contracts Ltd
DH 89
Spalding Airways Ltd
DH 89
Spartan Air Lines Ltd
DH 84
St Christopher Travel-ways, Ltd
DH 89

Stanley Spencer's Tours Ltd
DH 89
Starways Ltd
DH 89
Steiner's Air and Travel Services Ltd
DH 86
DH 89
Stramsway Ltd
DH 89
Surrey Flying Services
DH 84
DH 89
Swansea Airways Ltd
DH 89
Thorne Aviation Ltd
DH 89
Tippers Air Transport Ltd
DH 89
Tompkins, Wm Ltd
DH 89
Trak-Air Ltd
DH 89
Trans European Aviation Ltd
DH 89
Transair Ltd
DH 89
Treffield Aviation Ltd
DH 89
Trent Valley Aviation Ltd
DH 89
Tulloch, GK
DH 89
Tyne Taxis Ltd
DH 89
Tyne Tees Airways Ltd
DH 89
Ulster Aviation Ltd
DH 89
Union Air Services
DH 86
Union Founders Trust
DH 84
United Airways
DH 84
DH 89
Universal Flying Services Ltd
DH 89
West Coast Air Services Ltd
DH 86
DH 89
West Cumberland Air Services Ltd
DH 89
Westair Flying Services Ltd
DH 89
Western Airways Ltd
DH 89
DH 90
Western Isles Airways Ltd
DH 89
Westland Aircraft Ltd
DH 89
Westward Airways (Land's End) Ltd
DH 89
Whoopee Sports
DH 84
Wings and Wheels Ltd
DH 89
William Dempster Ltd
DH 89
Windmill Theatre Transport Company Ltd
DH 89
Wolverhampton Aviation Ltd
DH 89
Wright Aviation Ltd
DH 89
Wrightways Limited
DH 84
DH 86
DH 89
Wrightson & Pearce Ltd
DH 84
Yeadon Airways Ltd
DH 89
Yellow Taxi Company Ltd
DH 89
Yorkshire Aeroplane Club Ltd
DH 89

Overseas Commercial Operators of DH 84, DH 86, DH 89 and DH 90

Aden
Aden Airways Ltd
DH 89: VR-AAL; AAP

Argentina
Aeroexpresso Barcella
DH 89: LV-AEP; AES
Aerotransportes Rosario SRL
DH 89: LV-AGW
Compania Transportes Aereos Mediterranea Argentina Centro [COTAMA], Cordoba
DH 89: LV-AEN; AEO; AEP; AER: AES; AGR; AGV; AGW; AGX; AGY
Shell Mex Argentina Ltda, Buenos Aires
DH 90: R326; LV-KAB
Taxis Aereos Argentinos SA [TAASA], Buenos Aires
DH 89: LV-AES; AGV
Zonas Oueste y Norte de Aerolineas Argentinas [ZONDA]
Operated by COTAMA

Australia
Adastra Airways Pty Ltd, Mascot
DH 84: VH-AGC
DH 90: VH-AAD
Adelaide Airways Ltd
DH 84: VH-URE
DH 89: VH-UVI; UVT; UUO
Aerial Work Co, Temora, NSW
DH 84: VH-AYZ
Air Charter Services, Townsville
DH 84: VH-ASL/SJW
Aircrafts Pty Ltd, Brisbane
DH 84: VH-AAC; AIA; BJH; URD; UXG; UZZ
Airlines of Australia Ltd, Sydney
DH 84: VH-URE; URG
DH 89: VH-UBN; UFF; UUO; UVS; UVT; UXT; UZY
Airlines (WA) Ltd, Perth
DH 84: VH-URY
DH 89: VH-UFF; UZY
DH 90: VH-ADG
Air Travel & Survey Pty
DH 84: VH-AAO
Airwork Co Pty Ltd, Archerfield
DH 89: VH-AWG
Alpine Airways Pty Ltd, Cooma
DH 89: VH-AAG
Australian Aerial Medical Service, Sydney
DH 84: VH-URD; URE; UVN
Australian National Airways Pty Ltd [ANA], Essendon/Parafield
DH 84: VH-URD; URE; URG
DH,86: VH-USW; UUB
DH 89; VH-ADE; UFF; UUO; UVI; UVT; UXT; UXZ
Bush Church Air Society for Australia & Tasmania, Sydney
DH 84: VH-AGI
Bush Pilots Airways Pty Ltd, Cairns
DH 90: VH-AAD
Butler Air Transport Co Pty Ltd, Mascot
DH 84: VH-AAO; AEF; AIA; AVU; URU; URV
DH 89: VH-UUO; UVT
Carsair Air Service Pty Ltd, Archerfield
DH 89: VH-AAG; BIF
Connellan Airways Ltd, Alice Springs
DH 89: VH-AHI; AIK; BKM; BKR/CLH; UVT; UZY
DH 90: VH-UTJ; UXB
East Coast Airways Pty Ltd, Coolangatta
DH 89: VH-ECW
Fawcett Aviation Pty Ltd, Bankstown
DH 84; VH-AEF
Fostars Shoes Air Transport Pty Ltd, Mascot
DH 90: VH-UXA
Guinea Air Traders, New Guinea
DH 84; VH-AAC; BMX
Guinea Airways Ltd, Adelaide/New Guinea
DH 89; VH-ADE; UBN; UFF; UUO; UVI
Holyman's Airways Pty Ltd, Launceston
DH 84: VH-URD; URG
DH 86: VH-URN; URT; USW; UUB
DH 89: VH-UFF
Intercontinental Airways Pty Ltd, Sydney
DH 86: G-ADYH
James Air Charter, Wollongong
DH 89: VH-UFF
KMH Airways
DH 84: VH-AOM
MacRobertson Miller Aviation Co Ltd, Perth
DH 84: VH-ABK; URF; URW; URX; URY; UVN
DH 86: VH-USC; USD; USF; USW
Madang Air Charters/Madang Air Services Ltd, Madang, New Guinea
DH 84: VH-AOE; AQW
Mandated Airlines Ltd, Salamaua, New Guinea
DH 84: VH-AAC; AKX; AOP; AOQ; AOS; APL; ARJ; BDB; BDC; URW; USA; UTX; UVB
Marshall Airways, Bankstown
DH 84: VH-AQU
Mitchell Aerial Services Ltd, Cairns
DH 84: VH-AIA
Muir Aviation, Darwin
DH 84: VH-DMA; DMB
New England Airways
DH 84: VH-APP
North Australian Aviation Services Pty Ltd, Darwin
DH 84: VH-AFH; BDS
North Australian Uranium Corporation, Darwin
DH 84: VH-AFH
Northern Territory Aerial Medical Service, Darwin
DH 84: VH-ASK; ASL
North Queensland Air Transport Co, Mareeba
DH 84: VH-AYZ
North Queensland Airways Pty Ltd, Cairns
DH 84: VH-UXK; UZG
DH 89: VH-UZY
North Western Airlines Ltd, Moree
DH 90: VH-UTJ
Parers Air Transport, Wewak, New Guinea

DH 84: VH-AEA
QANTAS/Qantas Empire Airways Ltd, Brisbane
DH 84: VH-AIA; ALL: AMN; AOK; AON; AOR; AOT; ASU; AXL; AYM; BAF; BAH; BDS; URD; URV; URY; UZF
DH 86: VH-USC; USD; USE; USF; USG; USW; UUA
DH 90: VH-UTJ; UXB
Queensland Airlines Pty Ltd
DH 89: VH-UUO
Queensland Airplanters Pty Ltd, Childers
DH 84: VH-AGC; AIA; APJ
Queensland Air Transport Brigade, Cairns
DH 84: VH-AMB
DH 89: VH-BFS; CFA
Queensland Flying Services, Brisbane
DH 84: VH-UXG
Rockhampton Aerial Services Ltd, Rockhampton
DH 89: VH-UBN
[Royal] Flying Doctor Service of Australia
[NSW] DH 84: VH-AGM; URE/FDB
[Queensland] DH 84: VH-ALL; AMN; ASU; BAH; URY
[W Australia] VH-AGJ; ASO/FDA
Schutt Airfarmers Pty Ltd, Moorabbin
DH 84: VH-AMN; ASU
Shell Co of Australia Ltd, Melbourne
DH 89: VH-UVS
South Australian Air Taxis Ltd, Adelaide
DH 84: VH-BDS
Southern Airlines & Freighters Ltd, Mascot
DH 90: VH-UXS
South Queensland Airways Ltd, Archerfield
DH 84: VH-ABK
DH 86: VH-ADN
Tasmanian Aerial Services Pty Ltd, Launceston
DH 84: VH-URD
Taylor's Air Transport, New Guinea
DH 84: VH-AAC; AFK
Territory Airlines Ltd, Goroka, New Guinea
DH 84: VH-AIA; AON; APL; ASX; BDC
Trans Australia Airlines
DH 84: VH-AEF
WA Airways Ltd [West Australian Airways], Perth
DH 84: VH-URE; URO
DH 89: VH-UUO
Wagga Flying School Pty Ltd, Wagga Wagga
DH 84: VH-BDS
Western Mining Corporation Ltd, Perth
DH 84: VH-URF; URG
Wewak Air Transport, Wewak, New Guinea
DH 84: VH-AAC; AEA
WR Carpenter & Co Ltd [WRC Airlines], Salamaua, New Guinea
DH 84: VH-AAC; AKX; AOR; ARI; ARJ; ASU; AYB; BDB; BDC; URO; USA; UTX; UVB
DH 86: VH-ADN; UYU; UYV; UYW; UZX
DH 89: VH-UZY
Zinc Corporation Ltd, Melbourne
DH 84: VH-AQW

Belgium
Air Affairs SPRL, Gosselies
DH 89: OO-AFG
Air Brousse SPRL, Leopoldville
DH 89: OO-ARN; CJD; CJE; CJS; CJT; CJU; CJW; CJX; CMS; CRS
AMAMZ, Ndola
DH 89: 9Q-CJD; CJE; CJU; CJW; CJX
Avions Fairey SA, Gosselies
DH 89: OO-AFG
Cie Generale Aerienne Africain [Cogeair], Ndola
DH 89: OO-CJD; CJE
COGEA Nouvelle SA, Keerbergen
DH 89: OO-ARI; ARN
SABENA, Leopoldville
DH 89: OO-CFI

Borneo
Malayan Airways Ltd/Borneo Airways Ltd
DH 89: VR-OAA; OAB; OAC

Brazil
Arco-Iris Viacao Aerea SA, Sao Paulo
DH 89: PP-AIA; AIB; AIC; AID; AIE; AIF; AIG
Organizacao Mineira de Transportes Aereos [OMTA], Belo Horizonte
DH 89: PP-OMA; OMB; OMC; OMD
Viacao Aerea Rio Grandense SA [VARIG], Porto Alegre
DH 89: PP-VAN
Viacao Aerea Sao Paulo SA [VASP], Sao Paulo
DH 84: PP-SPC

Canada
Associated Airways Ltd, Edmonton
DH 90 CF-BZA
British North American Airways Ltd, Toronto
DH 89: CF-AYE
Canadian Airways Ltd, Montreal/Winnipeg
DH 84: CF-AEO; APJ; AVD; AVJ; BBC; BBH; BFL
DH 90: CF-BFF
Canadian Pacific Air Lines Ltd
DH 84: CF-APJ; AVD; AYE; BNG
DH 90: CF-BPD
Central Northern Airways Ltd, Winnipeg
DH 89: CF-AYE; BND
Consolidated Mining & Smelting Co Ltd, Trail, BC
DH 84: CF-AVI; BBH
DH 90: CF-AYF; BFF
Ginger Coote Airways Ltd, Vancouver
DH 89: CF-BNG
DH 90: CF-BPD
Gold Belt Air Service Ltd, Rouyn
DH 90: CF-BFF
Johannesson Flying Service, Winnipeg
DH 90: CF-BXU; BXV
Leavens Bros Air Services Ltd, Toronto
DH 90: CF-BPD
Maritime Central Airways Ltd, Charlotteville
DH 89: CF-BNJ
Noorduyn Aviation Ltd, St Laurent
DH 90: CF-MPD/BPD
North Shore Airways Ltd, Toronto
DH 84: CF-AVI
Quebec Airways Ltd, Montreal
DH 84: CF-AEO; AVD; AVJ; AYE; BBC; BFL; BFP; BND; BNE
DH 90: CF-BFF
Queen Charlotte Airlines Ltd, Vancouver
DH 89: CF-AYE; BND
Spartan Air Services Ltd, Ottawa
DH 89: CF-BNJ

Ceylon
Ceylon Air Academy
DH 89: CY-AAI/4R-AAI; AAK/4R-AAK

Chile
Linea Aerea del Pacifico Sur Ltda [LIPA-SUR}
DH 89: [3 unidentified]

China
China National Aviation Corporation
DH 89: '38'

Czechoslovakia
The Bata Shoe Co, Zlin
DH 84: OK-ATO

Denmark
Falcks Redningskorpset, Copenhagen
DH 89: OY-AAO
Provins Luftfartsselskabet A/S, Copenhagen
DH 89: OY-DIN
Zone-Redningskorpset, Copenhagen
DH 89: OY-ACZ; DYA; DZY

Egypt
Misr-Airwork SAE
DH 84: SU-ABH; ABI; ABJ; ABZ
DH 86: SU-ABN; ABO; ABV; ACR
DH 89: SU-ABP; ABQ; ABR; ABS; ABU; ACS; ACT
DH 90: SU-ABW

Ethiopia
Meat Export & Supply Co, Dire Dawa
DH 89: ET-P-16

Fiji
Fiji Airways, Fiji
DH 89: VQ-FAL; FAM; FAN
New Hebrides Airways Ltd, Port Vila
DH 89: VQ-FAZ

Finland
Aero O/Y, Helsinki
DH 89: OH-BLA; BLB
Lentohuolto O/Y, Helsinki
DH 89: OH-DHA; DHB
Veljekset Karhumaki O/Y, Kuorevesi
DH 89: OH-BLA/VKH; VKI

France & Overseas Territories
AC du Rhône et du Sud Est, Lyon
DH 89
Aigle Azur Indochine, Hanoi
DH 89: F-BGPG; BGPH; BGPI; BGPJ; BGPK; BGPL; BGPM
Air France
DH 89: F-BEDX/OADX/BAHX; BEDY/OADY/BAHY; BEDZ/OADZ/BAHZ
Air Ivoire, Abidjan
DH 89: F-OATT; OAUE; OBGY
Air Ouest, Nantes
DH 89: F-BGXT; BHAF
Cie Aéronautique Jean-Claude Brouillet - see Transgabon
Cie Bretonne Aéronautique [COBRA], Brest
DH 89: F-BHDY
Cie des Transports Aériens Intercontinentaux [TAI]
DH 89: F-OAUE
Cie Générale de Transports en Algérie [CGTA], Algiers
DH 89: F-BFVM; OBHH; OBOI
Cie Laotienne de Commerce et Transport, Hanoi
DH 89: F-BEPE; BGPG; BGPK; OAIL; OAJI
Cie Veha-Akat, Vientiane
DH 89: F-LAAB; LAAC; LAAE; LAAF; XW-TBI
Etablissments Rousseau Aviation, Dinard
DH 89: F-BEKB; BGZJ; BLHE
Lignes Aériennes Nord-Africaines [LANA], Algiers

DH 84: F-AMTR; AMUZ; ANES
Maroc Air-Service, Rabat
DH 89: F-OAGP; OAIR
Régie Air Afrique, Algiers
DH 84: F-AMTR; AMUZ; ANES
Societé Aérienne de Transport Guyane-Antilles [SATGA]; Cayenne
DH 89: F-OAQL; OAUG; OAXK; OBVL; OCHF; OGAU
Societé Aéronautique Air-Caen SARL, Caen
DH 89: F-BFPU
Societé Aéro Sahara, Tunis
DH 89: F-OBGE; OBIA
Societé Aéro-Sud, Bone
DH 89: F-BCDB; BEFU; BHTH
Societé Aérotechnique, Algiers
DH 89: F-OAPT
Societé Air Djibouti, Djibouti
DH 89: F-OCBX
Societé Air Madagascar, Tamatave
DH 89: F-BEDI; BFVR/5R-MAM; OAKD; OAKE; OAKF; OAKX; OANU; OAOS/5R-MAP; OARH; OASC; OAUH; OBDV/5R-MAN; OBIO/5R-MAO
Societé Air Oasis, Laghouat
DH 89: F-BHAF; OBOH
Societé Air Saoura, Colomb-Béchar
DH 89: F-BGIS; BGXT
Societé Algérienne de Transports Tropicaux, Algiers
DH 84: F-ANES
Societé Autrex Lopez et Cie [& Cie de Transports Aériens Autrex], Hanoi
DH 89: F-BAHX; BAHY; BGPI; BGPJ; OABH; OAGP; OAHL; OAIR; OAQY; OAQZ
Societé Calédonienne de Transports Aériens [Transpac], Nouméa
DH 89: F-OATC; OAVG; OAZT
Societé des Caoutchoucs d'Extrême Orient [Far East Rubber Co], Saigon
DH 89: F-OALD
Societé de Transports du Proche-Orient, Tripoli, Syria
DH 89: F-AQOH; AQOI
Societé Eurafair [SA Ardic], Dakar, Senegal
DH 89: F-OBRU; OBRV; OBRX; OBVI; OBVJ; OCAG
Societé Générale d'Affrétements Aériens [Air Fret], Algiers
DH 89: F-BFEH; BFVM; BGXT; BHAF; BHTH; OAPT; OAUE; OBAL; OBHH; OBHI; OBOI
Societé Indochinoise des Plantations, Saigon
DH 89: F-OANF
Societé Laos Air-Service, Vientiane
DH 89: F-BGPJ; LAAL; OAQY
Societé Norafor, Casablanca
DH 89: F-DABY
Societé Nord-Africaine de Travaux Aériens, Bône
DH 89: F-OAYS; OBIV
Societé Transports Aériens du Gabon [Air Gabon/Transgabon], Libreville
DH 89: F-OAIH/TR-LKQ; OAND; OAPS; OAQU; OATD; OAVZ; OBAQ; OBKH; OBMQ; OBOD
Societé Tunisienne de Réparations Aéronautique et de Construction [STRAC], Tunis
DH 89: F-OAME; OAYN; OBGE
Societé Vignafibre France, Algiers
DH 89: F-BFEH
Transports Aériens Waldberg, Nice
DH 89: F-BGOL

Germany
Deutsche Luftwerbung, Dusseldorf
DH 89: G-AGOJ
Hamburger Aero-Lloyd GmbH, Hamburg
DH 89: D-IDAK
Hanseatische Flugdienste GmbH, Hamburg
DH 89: D-IDAK

Iceland
Flugfelag Islands HF [Iceland Airways], Reykjavik
DH 89: TF-ISM; ISO
Flugskolinn Thytur HF, Reykjavik
DH 89: TF-KAA

India
Air India, Bombay
DH 89: VT-ARK; ARL; ARM; ARN
Air Services of India Ltd, Bombay
DH 89: VT-AHB; ALO; ARF; ARL; AVW; AVX; AXG; CBY; CHZ
DH 90: VT-AKC
Indian Air Survey & Transport Co Ltd [later Air Survey Co of India Ltd], Calcutta
DH 89: VT-ARF; ARR; ART; ARV; ARY; ASA; ASC; ASQ
Indian National Airways Ltd, Calcutta
DH 84: VT-AEK; AEL; AES
DH 89: VT-ARF; ART; ARV; ARW; ARY
Madras Presidency Airways Ltd, Madras
DH 89: VT-ARL; CBY
Tata Sons Ltd, Bombay
DH 86: VT-AKM; AKZ
DH 89: VT-AIZ; AJA; AJB
Varadaraja Airways Ltd, Madras
DH 89: VT-ARL; CBY

Iran
Iranian Oil Exploration & Production Co
DH 89: EP-ADM; ADN; ADO; ADP
Iranian State Airlines
DH 89: EP-AAA; AAB; AAC; AAD; AAE; AAT
National Oil Co
DH 89: EP-AAV; AAW; AAX; AAY

Iraq
Iraqi Airways, Baghdad
DH 89: YI-ABD; ABE; ABF; ABG; ABH

Ireland
Aer Lingus Teoranta, Dublin
DH 84: EI-ABI; ABI(2)
DH 86: EI-ABK; ABT
DH 89: EI-ABP
Aer Turas Teoranta, Dublin
DH 89: EI-AML
Air Kruise [Ireland] Ltd
DH 89: EI-AJO
Republic Air Charters
DH 89: EI-AGK
Weston Ltd
DH 84: EI-AFK
DH 89: EI-ADP; AEA

Israel
Arkia-Israel Inland Airlines, Eilat
DH 89: 4X-ACN; ACU; AEH; AEI
Aviron, Lydda
DH 89: 4X-ACU

Italy
Ala Littoria SA, Rome
DH 89: I-DRAG

Jordan
Air Jordan Co, Amman
DH 89: TJ-ABJ; ABP/JY-ABP
Arab Airways Association Ltd, Amman
DH 89: TJ-AAA: AAB; AAC; AAD; AAE; AAJ; AAP; AAQ; AAV; AAZ/JY-AAZ; TJ-ABM
Arab Contracting & Trading Co Ltd, Amman
DH 89: TJ-ACE/JY-ACE; JY-AAE; JY-ACG; JY-ACL

Kenya
Airspray [East Africa] Ltd, Nairobi
DH 89: VP-KMD
Airwork [East Africa] Ltd, Nairobi
DH 89: VP-KCV
Caspar Air Charters & Agencies Ltd/ Caspair Ltd, Nairobi
DH 89: VP-KCJ; KCV; KCY; KHF; KLB/5Y-KLB; KLL/5Y-KLL; KMD; KND
East African Airways Corporation, Nairobi
DH 89: VP-KCJ; KCT; KCU; KCV; KCW; KCX; KCY; KEA; KEB; KEC; KED; KEF; KNS
Jivrajs Air Services Ltd
DH 89: VP-KCX
Missionary Aviation Fellowship, Khartoum
DH 89: VP-KLB
Noon & Pearce Air Charters Ltd
DH 89: VP-KCY; KFX; KLL; KNC
Seychelles-Kilimanjaro Air Transport Ltd, Nairobi
DH 89: VP-KEF/5H-AAN; KNS/5H-AAM
Wilson Airways Ltd, Nairobi
DH 84: VP-KAW; KBA; KBG
DH 89: VP-KCG; KCJ; KCK; KCL; KCR
DH 90: VP-KCA; KCS

Latvia
Valsts Gaisa Satiksme [Latvian Post Office], Riga
DH 89: YL-ABC; ABD

Lebanon
Arab Contracting & Trading Co/Saad Transport, Beirut
DH 89: LR-ABH;OD-ABH; OD-ABL; ABP
Middle East Air Line Co, Beirut
DH 89: LR-AAD; AAE; AAF

Liberia
Liberian National Airways
DH 89: EL-AAA

Luxembourg
Luxembourg Airlines
DH 89: LX-LAD

Morocco
SA Agricolavia, Rabat
DH 89: CN-TTO

Netherlands
Aero Ypenburg NV, Rotterdam
DH 89: PH-OTA
General Aviation NV, Rotterdam
DH 89: PH-OTA
KLM Aerocarto NV, Amsterdam
DH 89: PH-OTA
Koninklijke Luchtvaart Maatschappij [KLM], Amsterdam
DH 89: PH-RAA; RAB; RAC; RAD; RAE/TGC/OTA; RAF
Koninklijke Nederlandsch-Indische Luchtvaart Maatschappij [KNILM], Dutch New Guinea
DH 89: PH-AKU/PK-AKU; PH-AKV/

PK-AKV; PH-AKW/PK-AKW

New Zealand

Air Charter [NZ] Ltd, Christchurch
DH 89: ZK-BCP
DH 90: ZK-AFB
Air Travel [NZ] Ltd
DH 84: ZK-AHT
DH 89: ZK-AHS
DH 90: ZK-AFB; AGP
Airwork [NZ] Ltd, Christchurch
DH 89: ZK-BBP; BCP
Coastal Airways Ltd, Auckland
DH 89: ZK-BCP
Cook Strait Airways Ltd, Wellington
DH 89: ZK-AEC; AED; AEE; AEW; AGT
East Coast Airways Ltd, Gisborne
DH 84: ZK-ADR/AER; ADS
Mount Cook Airlines Ltd, Christchurch
DH 89: ZK-AHS; AKY; ALB; BCP
Nelson Aero Club, Nelson
DH 84
NZ National Airways Corporation [NZNAC]
DH 86: ZK-AHW
DH 89: ZK-AHS; AKS; AKT; AKU; AKY; ALB; ALC
Ritchie Air Services Ltd, Te Anau
DH 89: ZK-AKY; ALB
Rolvin Airways Ltd, Palmerston North
DH 84: ZK-AXI
Southern Scenic Air Services Ltd, Queenstown
DH 89: ZK-AKS; AKT; BAU; BCP
South Island Airways, Christchurch
DH 89: ZK-BBP; BCP
Tourist Air Travel Ltd, Queenstown
DH 89: ZK-AHS; AKY; ALB; BCP
Trans-Island Airways Ltd, Omaru
DH 89: ZK-ALB; BCP
Union Airways of NZ Ltd, Wellington
DH 84: ZK-ADS; AER
DH 86: ZK-AEF; AEG/AHW; AEH
West Coast Airways Ltd, Hokitika
DH 89: ZK-AHS; AKT

Nigeria

Shell Co of East Africa Ltd, Lagos
DH 90: VR-NAA

Northern Rhodesia

Lusaka Air Charter Ltd, Lusaka
DH 89: VP-RCH
Northern Rhodesia Aviation Services Ltd
DH 89: VP-RBT; RBU
Windsor Aviation Ltd, Lusaka
DH 89: VP-RCH

Norway

Nor Flyselskap A/S, Honefoss
DH 89: LN-BFB
Skogbruksfly A/S, Sokna
DH 89: LN-BFB

Pakistan

Crescent Air Transport Ltd, Karachi
DH 89: AP-ADM; AFN; AGI; AGL; AGM

Palestine

The Aviron Co
DH 89: VQ-PAR
Palestine Airways, Jerusalem
DH 89: VQ-PAC

Paraguay

Aero-Carga SRL, Asuncion
DH 89: ZP-TDH

Portugal

Companhia de Transportes Aéreos [CTA], Lisbon
DH 89: CS-ADI; ADJ; ADK
Direcçao de Exploraçao dos Transportes Aéreos [DTA], Luanda
DH 89: CR-LAT; LAU; LAV; LBG; LBH; LBN; LBO; LCK; LCO
Divisao de Explraçao dos Transportes Aéreos [DETA], Lourenco Marques
DH 89: CR-AAD; AAE; AAM; AAN; AAT; AAU
DH 90: CR-AAB
Servico de Transportes Aéreos [STA], São Tomé
DH 89: CR-SAD; SAE
Transportes Aéreos de Cabo Verde, Santiago
DH 89: CR-CAA
Transportes Aéreos de Guiné Portuguesa [TAGP], Bissau
DH 89: CR-GAI; GAJ; GAK
Transportes Aéreos de Timor
DH 89: [unidentified]

Romania

Liniile Aeriene Române Exploatate de Stat [LARES]
DH 89: YR-DNC; DRA; DRI; DRO
DH 90: YR-FLO; FLU; FLY

Senegal

Cie Sénégalaise de Transports Aériens [CSTA], Dakar
DH 89: 6V-AAC

Seychelles

Air Mahé, Seychelles
DH 89: 5H-AAN

Sierra Leone

Sierra Leone Airways, Freetown
DH 89: VR-LAC; LAD; LAE

Singapore

Asiatic Petroleum Co [SS] Ltd, Singapore
DH 9:0 VR-SAX
Wearne's Air Services Ltd, Singapore
DH 86: VR-SBC; SBD
DH 89: VR-SAV; SAW
DH 90: VR-SAX

South Africa

Africair Ltd, Germiston
DH 89: ZS-BCI; DDH
African Air Photo [Pty] Ltd, Germiston
DH 89: ZS-DJT
African Air Transport Ltd, Germiston
DH 84: ZS-AEG
DH 89: ZS-AES
African Flying Services, Grand Central
DH 89: ZS-AKT; BCS; BCT
The Aircraft Operating Co of South Africa Pty Ltd, Johannesburg
DH 84: ZS-AEF; AEG; AEI
DH 89: ZS-ATV; ATW; AYF; AYG; BEA; BMV
Anglo-American Trading Corporation of South Africa, Johannesburg
DH 89: ZS-AME
Anglo-Transvaal Consolidated Investment Co Ltd, Rand
DH 89: ZS-BCI; DFG
Associated Manganese Mines of South Africa Ltd, Postmasburg
DH 89: ZS-DDI
Commercial Air Services Ltd [Comair]
DH 89: ZS-BZU; BZV
Drakensberg Air Services {Pty] Ltd, Ladysmith
DH 89: ZS-AKT; BZU; BZV; DDX; DJT
Field Aircraft Services Ltd
DH 89: ZS-BCO
General Aircraft [Pty] Ltd, Durban
DH 89: ZS-DLS
General Mining & Finance Corporation, Rand
DH 89: ZS-DJT
Ladysmith Air Charter, Ladysmith
DH 89: ZS-DJT; DLS
OFS Air Services [Pty] Ltd, Bloemfonteln
DH 89: ZS-BEA
Owenair [Pty] Ltd, Youngsfield
DH 89: ZS-BCP
South West Air Transport [Pty] Ltd, Windhoek
DH 89: ZS-AXS; BEF
Stewart & Lloyds of South Africa Ltd
DH 84: ZS-AEH
DH 89: ZS-AOM
Trans Oranje Air Services [Pty] Ltd, Zastron
DH 89: ZS-AKT; BEA
Vacuum Oil Co of South Africa Ltd
DH 90: ZS-AHV

Southern Rhodesia

Air Carriers Ltd, Bulawayo
DH 89: VP-YCN
Central African Airways Corporation, Salisbury
DH 89: VP-YBK; YBU; YCI; YCJ; YCK; YCL; YCM; YCN; YCO; YCP; YDE; YDF; YEZ; YFA
Field Aircraft Services of Rhodesia Ltd, Salisbury
DH 89: VP-YDF
Fishair [Pvt] Ltd, Marandellas
DH 89: VP-YDF; YKJ; YLF; YNJ
London & Rhodesian Mining & Land Co Ltd, Salisbury
DH 90: VP-YBB
Rhodesia & Nyasaland Airways Ltd, Salisbury
DH 84: VP-YBY
DH 89: VP-YAU; YBJ; YBK; YBT; YBZ
DH 90: VP-YAX; YBR
Southern Rhodesia Air Services
DH 84: VP-YBY
DH 89: VP-YAU; YCI; YCJ; YCK; YCL; YCM; YCN; YCO; YCP
Trevor Construction Co Ltd
DH 89: VP-YCN
Victoria Falls Airways {Pvt} Ltd, Victoria Falls
DH 89: VP-YCK; YEZ; YMW; YNU; YOL
Zambesi Airways Ltd, Victoria Falls
DH 89: VP-RBU; VP-RCI/VP-YLV; VP-YMW

Spain

Aeromar
DH 89: EC-AKO
Comercial Exportadora de Articules Perecederos SA [CEAPSA], Madrid
DH 89: EC-AGP
Iberia Airlines
DH 89: EC-AAR; AAS; AAV; AAX; AAY; BAC/AAR; CAQ/ABG
DH 90: EC-BAA/AAQ
Lineas Aéreas Postales Españolas [LAPE]
DH 89: EC-AGO; AZZ

Metamar SA, Barcelona
DH 89: EC-AKO
Sociedad Aerotaxi SL, Palma
DH 84: EC-TAT

Sweden
AB Europa-Flyg, Bromma
DH 89: SE-CDI
Duells Aero, Göteborg
DH 89: SE-BTA
Svenska Aero Westlund & Co, Örebro
DH 89: SE-BXZ
Svensk Flygjanst AB, Bromma
DH 89: SE-APH

Switzerland
Alpar Schweizerische Luftverkehr AG, Berne
DH 89: HB-AME; AMU
Farner-Werke AG, Grenchen
DH 89: HB-APA; APU
Ostschweiz AG, Altenrhein
DH 89: CH-287/HB-ARA
Swissair AG, Zurich
DH 89: HB-APA; APE; APU

Turkey
Devlet Hava Yollari [DHY], Ankara
DH 86: TC-ERK; FER; GEN; HEP
DH 89: TC-AGA; ARI; BAY; CAN; DAG; HAD; LAV; MUT; NUR; PER; VUR; ZOR
DH 90: TC-IDE
Hurkus Airlines, Ankara
DH 89: TC-ALI; BAY; CAN; ERK; HAD; PER

Uganda
The Uganda Co Ltd
DH 89: VP-UAW

Uruguay
Cia Expreso del Plata, Montevideo
DH 89: CX-ABI
Cia Primeras Lineas Uruguayas de Navegación Aérea [PLUNA], Montevideo
DH 86: CX-AAH; ABG
DH 90: CX-AAR; AAS

Venezuela
Riego Oil Co
DH 89: YV-P-BPE

Yugoslavia
Aeroput
DH 89: YU-SAS

APPENDIX 4
Military users: DH 84, DH 86, DH 89 and DH 90

DH 84

Royal Air Force
No 24 Squadron, Hendon, France
No 6 AACU
No 7 AACU
No 8 AACU
SF Ringway
No 1 Camouflage Unit
School of GR
110 (AC) Wing

DH 86

Royal Air Force
24 Squadron, Hendon
No 117 Squadron, Bilbeis
No 1 E and W School, Cranwell
No 1AA Unit, Middle East

Royal Navy
No 782 Squadron
No 783 Squadron

DH 89, 89A and DH 89B

Royal Air Force
Named Dominie C Mk I and Dominie C Mk II by RAF in 1941
521 delivered including those for RN use.

Main Users
24 Sqn, Hendon, Norholt
271 Sqn, Inverness
272 Sqn
173 Sqn Heliopolis, Egypt
1316 (Allied) Flight, Hendon
510 Sqn ; became Metropolitan Comm Sqn, Hendon
No 1 Radio School,Cranwell; No 1 SS
No 2 Radio School, Yatesbury; No 2 SS
No 4 Radio School; No 4 SS, Swanton Morley
Bristol Wireless Flight, Yatesbury

Secondary Users
2 Sqn, Sawbridgeworth
4 Sqn, Linton-on-Ouse
26 Sqn, Gatwick; Detling
173 Sqn
225 Sqn, Odiham; Old Sarum
418 Sqn, Debden
526 Sqn, Inverness
527 Sqn, Castle Camps; Snailwell
614 Sqn, Odiham; Grangemouth
1680 Flt, Doncaster; Abbotsinch; later formed 271 Sqn
1832 Sqn
1844 Sqn
No 1 Signals School, Cranwell

Communications Flights
AHQ Bengal Comm Unit, Chittagong
AHQ India Comm Flt, New Delhi
Allied Command SEA, Karachi
Army Cooperation Cmd Comm Flt
Air Defence of GB Comm Flt
Berlin Air Cd Comm Flt
Coastal Cd Comm Flt
Fighter Cd Comm Flt
Iraq and Persia Comm Flt, Habbaniya
Malayan Volunteer Air Force, B Flt, Kallang
Metropolitan Comm Sqn
Middle East Comm Sqn
RAF Denmark Comm Flt
Reserve Cd Comm Flt
Technical Training Cd Comm Flt
SHAEF Comm Flt, Denmark
Staff College Comm Flt
West Africa Cd Comm Flt
No 3 Gp Comm Flt, Mildenhall
No 4 Gp Comm Flt, York
No 7 Gp Comm Flt
No 9 Gp Comm Flt, Barton Hall
No 10 Gp Comm Flt, Colerne
No 15 Gp Comm Flt, Hooton Park
No 19 Gp Comm Flt, Roborough
No 22 Gp Comm Flt, Market Drayton
No 25 Gp Comm Flt
No 27 Gp Comm Flt
No 61 Gp Comm Flt
No 64 Gp Comm Flt
No 66 Gp Comm Flt
No 81 Gp Comm Flt, Worcester
No 83 Gp Comm Flt, Redhill
No 85 Gp Comm Flt
No 87 Gp Comm Flt, Le Bourget
No 16 Wing Comm Flt
No 32 Wing Comm Flt
No 33 Wing Comm Flt
No 34 Wing Comm Flt

Other Users
8 (C) OTU, Dyce
13 OTU, Bicester
41 OTU, Old Sarum
51 OTU, Cranfield
52 OTU, Debden
53 OTU, Heston, Kirton Lindsey
54 OTU, Church Fenton
55 OTU; Usworth; No 4 TEU; No 3 TEU, Annan
56 OTU, Sutton Bridge; N0 1 TEU, Tealing
57 OTU
58 OTU
59 OTU
60 OTU
63 OTU
80 OTU
Empire Test Pilots' School, Farnborough; Cranfield
Airborne Forces Experimental Establishment, Ringway
No 1 Armament Practice Camp
No 1 Parachute Training School
No 1 Beam Approach School
Belgian Training School
Central Signals Establishment
Empire Radio School
Fighter Leaders School
National Gas Turbine Establishment
Royal Aircraft Establishment, Farnborough
Royal Radar Establishment, Pershore
Radar Warfare Establishment, Watton
School of Air Support, Old Sarum
School of Flying Control, Watchfield
School of Air Transport
School of Land/Air Warfare
No 1 S of TT, Halton; No 10 (O) AFU
No 21 Air Depot, Henlow; Bougenais, France
No 2 (P) AFU
No 12 (P) AFU; Grantham; 12 SFTS
No 1 AONS, Prestwick; No 1(O) AFU, Wigtown
No 2 AONS; No 2 (O) AFU, Millom
No 3 AONS, Bobbington; No 3(O) AFU
No 6 AONS, Staverton; No 6 AOS; 6 (O)AFU, Morton Valence
No 7 AONS, Prestwick; No 7 AOS
No 4 AOS, West Freugh; 4 (O) AFU
No 7 AGS, Stormy Down
No 10 B & GS, Dumfries
No 1 Camouflage Unit, Baginton
No 77 (S) Wing, Woolton
No 79 (S) Wing, Portadown
No 110 (AAC) Wing, Ringway
No 6 AACU, Ringway
No 7 AACU, Staverton
No 8 AACU, Filton
No 1 Delivery Unit
No 2 Delivery Unit
No 3 Delivery Unit
No 4 Delivery Unit
No 11 Service Ferry Flight, Dumfries
Stn Flt, Andover
Stn Flt, Old Sarum
Stn Flt, Skeabrae
Stn Flt, Halton
Stn Flt, Kinloss
Stn Flt, Wick
HQ ATA, White Waltham
Ferry Training Unit, Honeybourne
No 3 FPP, Hawarden
No 7 FPP, Sherburn-in-Elmet

Royal Navy Service
Total of 65 served with RN :
701 Sqn, Culham, Culdrose, Yeovilton
712 Sqn
736 Sqn
740 Sqn
781 Sqn, Lee on Solent, Toussus le Noble
782 Sqn
787 Sqn, Westhampnett
790 Sqn
RNAS Radio Sqn
RN R&DU, Culham
NARIU, Middle Wallop
Stn Flt, Brawdy

Air Transport Auxiliary units
Operations began at White Waltham in February 1940, and ceased in December 1945. The Headquarters was at White Waltham, basic flying training unit was at Barton in the Clay, and advanced conversions were completed at White Waltham. The units, including Ferry Pilot Pools, were situated as follows:
HQ: White Waltham
1 FPP, 40-44 White Waltham
2 FPP, 43-44 Whitchurch Bristol
3 FPP, 40-42 Hatfield
3 FPP, 42-45 Hawarden
4 FPP Prestwick
5 Training FPP Thame
6 FPP Ratcliffe
7 FPP Sherburn
8 FPP Belfast (Sydenham)
9 FPP, 43-44 Aston Down
10 FPP Lossiemouth
12 FPP Cosford
14 FPP Ringway
15 FPP Hamble
16 FPP Kirkbride
AFTS White Waltham
EFTS Thame, then Barton in the Clay
Air Movements Flight White Waltham

RAF Dominies loaned to aircraft manufacturers, 1940-1945
Armstrong Whitworth Aircraft, Baginton
Gloster Aircraft, Hucclecote
Hawker Aircraft, Langley
Shorts Brothers, Rochester
Fairey Aviation, White Waltham
Blackburn Aircraft, Brough
Westland Aircraft, Yeovil

DH 90

No 6 AACU
No 7 AACU
No 8 AACU
No 7 FPP
No 2 TAF Comm Flight
110 (AC) Wing
15 Group Comms Flight
No 11 AONS

Other Military Users of DH 84, DH 86, DH 89 and DH 90

Austrian Air Force
DH 84
DH 89, Retlungsflugwacht, Vienna
Belgian Air Force
DH 89, Brussels (Melsbroek), Smalldeel
Brazilian Navy
DH 84, Sao Paulo
Ceylon Air Academy
DH 89, Colombo
Danish Army Air Force
DH 84
DH 90
Free French Air Force
DH 89, Meknes; Madagascar
Indian Air Force
DH 86, No 2 Coastal Defence Flight, Juhu Bay
Iraq Ministry of Defence
DH 84
DH 90
Irish Army Air Corps
DH 84
Israeli Air Force
DH 89
Lithuanian Air Force
DH 89
Kenya AAU
DH 84
DH 90
Portuguese Air Force
DH 84
DH 89, Sintra
Royal Australian Air Force
DH 84, No 33 Sqn
DH 84, No 34 Sqn
DH 84, No 35 Sqn
DH 84, No 36 Sqn
DH 84, No 1AONS
DH 84, No 2 AONS
DH 84, No 3 EFTS
DH 84, No 1 ATS
DH 84, No 1 W/Ag S
DH 86, No 35 Squadron, Essendon
DH 86, No 36 squadron, Maylands
DH 86, No 1 AA Unit
DH 89, Mascot, Laverton
DH 90
Royal Canadian Air Force
DH 89
DH 90
Royal Netherlands Air Force and Army Air Corps
DH 89, Schiphol, Valkenburg, Leeuwarden.
DH 90
Royal New Zealand Air Force
DH 84
DH 86, Observer and Gunnery School, Ohakea
DH 89
South African Air Force
DH 84
DH 89, Tempe
DH 90
Southern Rhodesian Air Force
DH 84
DH 89
Spanish Nationalist Air Force
DH 89
Spanish Republican Air Force
DH 84
DH 89
Swedish Air Force
DH 90
Turkish Air Force
DH 84
DH 89
United States Army Air Force
DH 89

ACKNOWLEDGEMENTS

I would like to thank all the following for their help in the construction of this book:

A&AEE staff, Boscombe Down
BAE SYSTEMS Archive staff, Farnborough
Gordon Bain
Paul Beauchamp-Legg
Bill Bedford
Fred Bird
Herman Bolte
Bruce Bowsher
Air Cdre 'Cyclops' Brown
Richard Clarkson
Peter Clegg
Miss Lettice Curtis
Geoffrey de Havilland Jnr
Gordon Edmondson
Malcolm Fillmore
Eric Franklin
Ken Fuller
Philip Gordon-Marshall
Phil Hagger
John Hamlin
Peter Harrison
John Havers
John Holmwood
Geoff Lee
Torquil Norman
Stuart McKay
Ray Mackenzie-Blyth
Sir Charles Masefield
Howard Marks
Mark Miller
Jaap Moll
Michael Oakey and staff of *Aeroplane*
National Archive Canada
PRO staff, Kew
Richard Riding
Hugh Scanlon
Piet Schmidt-Crans
Mike Stroud
Nick Stroud
JJ Sullivan
Bill Teague
Lord David Trefgarne
Peter Vines
Jan Voeten
Les Vowles
Richard Waugh
Bruce Winley

BIBLIOGRAPHY

Geoffrey Alington — *A Sound in the Sky*
J L Arense — *Luchtfotografie in Nederland*
Captain Dave Baker — *Yellow Wings (SAAF)*
Arthur Bradshaw — *Flying by Bradshaw*
Mary Bruce — *Nine Lives Plus*
Peter Clegg — *A Flying Start to the Day*
Sir Geoffrey de Havilland — *Sky Fever*
Neville Doyle — *Sea Eagle to Flamingo*
Fred Hotson — *de Havilland in Canada*
Gerald Howson — *Aircraft of the Spanish Civil War*
A J Jackson — *De Havilland Aircraft since 1909*
Macarthur Job — *Air Crash 1*
A C Merton Jones — *British Independent Airlines since 1946*
Peter W Moss — *Impressments Log*
C Martin Sharp — *A History of de Havilland*
Brian Waugh — *Turbulent Years*
Richard Waugh — *Strait Across*
Taking Off

AIR-BRITAIN SALES

This publication and companion volumes are available by post-free mail order from

Air-Britain Sales Department (Dept SDT)
41 Penshurst Road, Leigh,
Tonbridge, Kent TN11 8HL

For a full list of current titles and details of how to order, visit our e-commerce site at www.air-britain.co.uk
Visa / Mastercard / Delta / Switch accepted - please give full details of card number and expiry date.

THE DE HAVILLAND DRAGON/RAPIDE FAMILY

By John F Hamlin £19.95 (Members) £29.95 (Non-members)
An introduction to the development of each of the de Havilland twin-engine biplane family, followed by the detailed history of every individual example built of the DH.84, DH.86, DH.89 and DH.90. Background histories and fleet lists of the UK operators of all these types are included, together with regn/serial to c/n index and other Appendices. Over 450 black & white photos, 29 colour photos and 45 colour side-views. Hardback A4, 256 pages, dustjacket.

THE TRIPLE ALLIANCE - The Predecessors of the first British Airways

By Neville Doyle £18.00 (Members) £22.50 (Non-members)
The story of Hillman's Airways Ltd, Spartan Air Lines and United Airways Ltd, and other operators involved through mergers and take-overs, who amalgamated on 1st October 1935 to form British Airways Ltd. Fully illustrated with contemporary photos, timetables and advertising, and describing the personalities, routes flown and aircraft used. Hardback A4, 128 pages with 8 in colour.

THOSE FABULOUS FLYING YEARS - Joy-Riding and Flying Circuses between the Wars

By Colin Cruddas £19.95 (Members) £29.95 (Non-members)
First tracing the history of 'barnstorming' in the United States, this book then covers the history of British companies that attempted to bring aviation to every corner of the country, either through pleasure flying or aerial displays. While Cobham's extensive tours at home and abroad are covered, so too are the smaller companies, their fleet lists and the personalities who provided the thrills for the public. Profusely illustrated. Hardback A4, 128 pages.

THE SOPWITH PUP

By J M Bruce, Gordon Page and Ray Sturtivant £24.00 (Members) £30.00 (Non-members)
The definite work on the Sopwith Pup, covering in detail the aircraft's development, service history and units in a narrative account supported by all known details of individual aircraft histories, survivors and replicas. Hardback A4, 320 pages containing over 400 photographs and numerous colour and black-and-white scale drawings.

THE DH.4/DH.9 FILE

By Ray Sturtivant and Gordon Page £24.00 (Members) £30.00 (Non-members)
The story of the development of these types built in large numbers for the RFS, RNAS, RAF and USAAC. Another definitive work which includes details of widespread use overseas. Hardback A4, 300 pages including 450 photos and 16 pages of colour drawings.

THE DH.106 COMET An Illustrated History

By Martin Painter £29.50 (Members) £37.00 (Non-members)
The story of the development of Britain's pioneering jet airliner, its operators, routes, detailed individual histories, fates and survivors. Contains over 600 illustrations, 242 in colour. Hardback A4, 368 pages.

For civil aircraft enthusiasts Air-Britain publishes annually a series of titles covering UK and European Registers, worldwide Airline Fleets, Business Jets and a series of low-priced "Quick Reference" books on these topics.
Air-Britain also publishes a comprehensive range of military titles, please check for latest details of RAF Serial Registers, detailed RAF aircraft type "Files", Squadron Histories and Royal Navy Aircraft Histories.

IMPORTANT NOTE – Members receive substantial discounts on prices of all the above Air-Britain publications.
For details of membership see the following page or visit our website at http://www.air-britain.co.uk